MILLER'S ANTIQUES PRICE GUIDE

ISBN 0 86134 026 4

While every care has been exercised in the compilation of this guide, neither the authors or publishers accept any liability for any financial or other loss incurred by reliance placed on the information contained in Millers Price Guide.

Made and Printed in Great Britain by
The Fakenham Press Ltd.,
Norfolk.

MILLER'S ANTIQUES PRICE GUIDE

Compiled and Edited by

Martin & Judith Miller

mJm
PUBLICATIONS
Pugin's Hall
Finchden Manor
Tenterden
Kent
telephone 058 06 2234

Acknowledgements

Editorial

Pamela Stewart
Caroline Rainer
Janie Stewart
Hisako Kawahara
Erica Pavord
Frances Page
Samantha Miller
Marianne Hamlin-Marques

Photographic

Peter Mould
Simon Sorsbie

Art Work

Elizabeth Fry-Stone
Rosemary Mackew

The publishers would also like to acknowledge the great assistance given by:

John S. Herbert, Public Relations Director, Christie's
Nick Y. Long, Studio Antiques Ltd., Bourton-on-the-Water, B.A.D.A.
Richard Davidson, Lombard Street, Petworth. B.A.D.A.
B. and M. Jacobs, The Antique Shop, Tenterden. L.A.P.A.D.A.

Introduction

When the original, pilot issue of Miller's was in the earliest planning stage, it was decided that the book should have three distinct functions. It should provide an accurate, year-by-year reference to the market values placed upon antiques; it should build up into a formidable pictorial library at the rate of six thousand or more illustrations per year; and it should offer a certain amount of additional information regarding the dating and authentication of the widest possible range of goods. At the same time, one fundamental editorial guideline was laid down. Response to the published volume has proved that guideline to have been sound. It was: 'keep in touch with the trade'.

We think this edition of Miller's will show that we have, indeed, kept in touch with a broad cross section of the country's professional dealers, many of whom have earned our sincerest thanks for their generous help, advice and co-operation. They have allowed us to photograph their stocks, they have discussed prices and trends, and they have offered many helpful criticisms — of antiques guides in general, and of Miller's in particular. We have taken careful note of their comments, and have acted upon many of them in compiling this edition.

It is inevitable that any book purporting to set cash values upon antiques will raise protest from someone. This is as it should be, for, apart from the fact that there are no points of reference (such as makers' list prices and depreciation), the market is in a constant state of flux, and subject too, to apparently disproportionate variations in different parts of the country. If, in the course of a few weeks, an item is sold at a provincial auction, passes through several dealers' hands on the road to London — each time making a reasonable profit for the seller — and finds its way into a high-priced West End Showroom, who would dare quote a single figure and state 'this is its value'? Obviously, in such circumstances, the best that can be done is to give a broad estimate of probable price variation and rely upon the buyer's own good sense, bargaining ability and knowledge of local trading conditions to prove (or apparently disprove) the accuracy of the printed figures in each individual case.

Almost all the objects illustrated in this edition of Miller's have been sold at least once during the past year at a figure within the price range given — either through the trade, or at auction, or both. In a few isolated cases, actual prices realised have been completely disregarded and more realistic estimates substituted, for there will always be freak prices which, uncompensated, could prove entirely misleading to the unwary. Nevertheless, there will always be bargains and, in this respect, it cannot be too strongly emphasised that Miller's is a price **guide** and not a price **list.** Used as a guide, it will prove to be a valuable tool; used as a price list, its value will be lessened.

While many dealers have told us that they use Miller's price estimates as a reliable second opinion, all have been unstinting in their praise of the book as a source of pictorial reference. This gave rise to a strong temptation to cram in even more than the seven thousand plus photographs used in this edition, but the temptation was resisted on the grounds that this would have meant reducing the size of each illustration — with consequent loss of detail and clarity. In a field as diverse as that of antiques, it is impossible to lay too much stress on the importance of accurate visual source material. Subtleties of detail and proportion can only be portrayed reliably by properly taken photographs — at least until the holographic process has been perfected for general use — and over-small, or sketchy, illustrations can only be a source of annoyance, and even costly confusion. Most of the photographs in this edition were taken by our own photographers, all of whom were carefully briefed to refrain from using 'arty' or misleading lighting and camera angles — and to obtain photographs of as representative a selection of stock as possible. This directive is responsible for the inclusion of a number of early twentieth century items which, although not strictly antiques to the purist, are appearing more and more among the trade goods of the majority of dealers. Out of a total of well over fifteen thousand photographs, the final selection was made to provide the most balanced picture possible of the state of the trade as it stood in the month before going to press.

In addition to the numbers of our own photographs included in the book, popular demand has persuaded us to expand certain sections, notably those dealing with the recognition and authentication of particular items. Accordingly, this edition contains many new and useful guides to styles and dates, and to individual makers and techniques. At a time when the reproduction market is growing as never before, information of this kind will prove invaluable to collectors and also to all dealers confronted with items which, although possibly fairly familiar, do not fall within the bounds of the individual's own speciality.

Another much requested addition to this year's publication is a simple, yet comprehensive index designed to facilitate the location of specific items, styles, manufacturers and techniques where these are not listed under their own category headings in the contents.

A glance through the book will show that our determination to keep in touch with the trade has had a considerable influence on this edition. It has been extremely gratifying to find that, as a result, the trade has been keeping in touch with Miller's.

Key to Illustrations

Each illustration and descriptive caption is accompanied by a letter-code. By reference to the following list of Auctioneers and Dealers, the source of any item may be immediately determined. In no way does this constitute or imply a contract or binding offer on the part of any of our contributors to supply or sell the goods illustrated, or similar articles, at the prices stated.

The publishers wish to acknowledge a special debt of gratitude to the Members of the Cotswold Antique Dealers' Association for their untiring help and hospitality during the compilation of this volume.

A	Aldridges, 130-132 Walcott St, Bath
ADH	Alonzo, Dawes & Hoddell, Six Ways, Clevedon, Avon
AG	Anderson & Garland, Market St, Newcastle-upon-Tyne
AL	Ann Lingard, The Rope Walk, Rye, Sussex
AM	Arthur Middleton Ltd, 12 New Row, Covent Garden, London WC2
AP	Antique Pussy, 965 Fulham Road, London SW6
As	Astleys, 109 Jermyn St, London SW1
B	Boardman Auctioneers, Station Road Corner, Haverhill, Suffolk
BA	Brookland Antiques, Brookland, Kent
BB	Brian Ball, 227 Ebury St, London SW1
Bon	Bonhams, Montpelier St, London SW7
Buc	Buckell & Ballard, 49 Parsons St, Banbury, Oxon
BW	Burtenshaw Walker, 66 High St, Lewes, Sussex
C	Christie Manson & Woods Ltd, 8 King St, London SW1
CA	Cornucopia Antiques, 57 St. Leonards Rd, Bexhill, Sussex
CC	Christopher Clarke Antiques, The Dower House, Maugersbury, Glos
CCL	Chelsea Clocks, Antiquarius, Kings Rd, London SW3
CD	Clifford Dann, 20/21 High St, Lewes, Sussex
CE	Clive Emson & Co, 16 High St, Hythe, Kent
CL	Country Life Antiques, Sheep St, Stow-on-the-Wold, Glos
CP	Charles van Praagh, 30 High St, Arundel, Sussex
CSG	Church Street Gallery, Church St, Tewkesbury, Glos
CSK	Christie's South Kensington, 85 Old Brompton Rd, London SW7
DB	David Bateson Antiques, Townland Farm, Biddenden, Kent
DH	Dacre Son & Hartley, 1-5 The Grove, Ilkley, Yorks
DM	Daniel Mankowitz (Antiques) Ltd, 49 Chiltern St, London W1
EBB	Edwards Bigwood & Bewlay, The Old School, Tiddington, Stratford-on-Avon, Glos
GC	Geering & Colyer, Hawkhurst, Kent
GE	Gordon Emerson Antiques, Antiquarius, Kings Road, London SW3
GW	Gina Wilmshurst, Sandhill Barn Antiques, Washington, Sussex
HD	Halcyon Days, 14 Brook St, London W1

HG	Honiton Galleries, High St, Honiton, Devon
IN	Imogen Nichols Antiques, The Farrier's Cottage, St. Nicholas-at-Wade, Kent
L	Lawrence, South St, Crewkerne, Somerset
Lan	Langlois, Don St, Jersey, Channel Islands
LM	Lilian Middleton's Antique Doll Shop, Tudor House, Stow-on-the-Wold, Glos
M	Morphetts, 4-6 Albert St, Harrogate, Yorks
MHA	Manor House Antiques, 3 High St, Old Town, Bexhill-on-Sea, Sussex
MJ	Mendl Jacobs, The Antique Shop, 11 Ashford Rd, Tenterden, Kent
MM	Mark Maynard
MN	Mrs. M.K. Nielsen, Seaford House, High St, Moreton-in-Marsh, Glos
N	Neales, Nottingham
NF	Neale Sons & Fletcher, 26 Church St, Woodbridge, Suffolk
NO	Nice & Old, 91 Church St, Tewkesbury, Glos
O	Olivers, 23/24 Market Hill, Sudbury, Suffolk
OB	The Old Bakery Antiques, St. Davids Bridge, Cranbrook, Kent
OF	The Old Forge, Pilgrims Way, Hollingbourne, Kent
OL	Outhwaite & Litherland, Fontenoy St, Liverpool
P	Phillips Son & Neale, Blenstock House, 7 Blenheim St, London W1
PC	The Porcelain Collector, The Old Pony Stable, Shoreham, Kent
PCF	Pine & Country Furniture, North St, Worthing, Sussex
P&D	Pine & Design Gallery, Balcombe, Sussex
PK	Phillips, Knowle, Solihull, West Midlands
PW	Peter Wilson, Market St, Nantwich, Cheshire
PWC	Parsons Welch & Cowell, 129 High St, Sevenoaks, Kent
RB	Robert Barley Antiques, 48 Fulham High St, London SW6
RD	Richard Davidson Antiques, Lombard St, Petworth, Sussex
RSA	Rodney Stone Antiques
S	Sotheby's, 34-35 New Bond St, London W1
SA	Studio Antiques, Bourton-on-the-Water, Glos
SAL	Salmagundi, 63 Charlton St, Maidstone, Kent
SB	Sotheby's Belgravia, 19 Motcomb St, London SW1
SBA	Sotheby Beresford Adams, Booth Mansions, Watergate St, Chester
SBe	Sotheby Bearne, Rainbow, Torquay, Devon
SH	Sotheby Humberts, Magdalene St, Taunton, Somerset
SHA	Saddlers House Antiques, Bloxham, Banbury, Oxon
SKC	Sotheby King & Chasemore, Station Rd, Pulborough, Sussex
SM	Mrs. Susan March, Swig's Hole Farm, Horsmonden, Kent
SQE	Septimus Quayle's Emporium, Cranbrook Rd, Hawkhurst, Kent
SSP	Stanley Stripped Pine, Hayne Barn, Saltwood, Nr Hythe, Kent
STR	Strawsons Antiques, The Pantiles, Tunbridge Wells, Kent
SV	Sutton Valence Antiques, Sutton Valence, Kent
TA	Touchwood Antiques, 9 Park St, Stow-on-the-Wold, Glos
TT	Traditional Timepieces, Church St, Old Town, Bexhill, Sussex
V	Vidler, Rye, Sussex
VA	Village Antiques, 2/4 Cooden Sea Rd, Little Common, Kent
WHL	WH Lane & Son, Penzance, Cornwall

The Period Home
For those who own and enjoy Listed Buildings
Vol. 1 No. 2
Clarence House — story of a royal residence
The Georgian dining-room
The Oast House — a great building tradition
Quilts and the history of patchwork
How hearths and cooking developed
The Period Home
For those who own and enjoy Listed Buildings
Vol. 1 No. 1
Grants policies — Canterbury leads the way
The medieval house — historical outline
Windows — how they evolved
Herbs — and the smells of old England
A great hall house is restored

CONTENTS

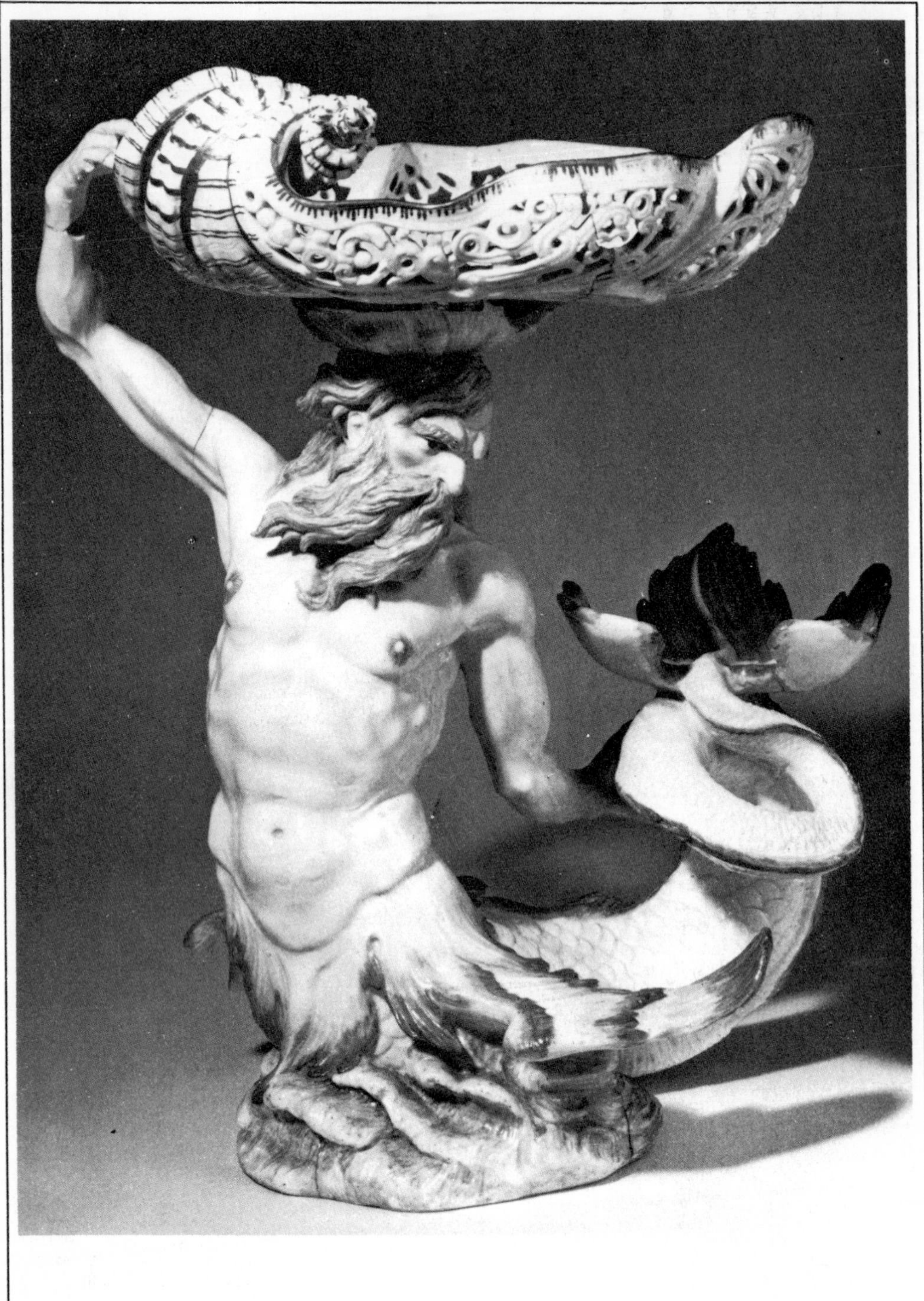

A large Meissen Triton Sweetmeat Dish by J. J. Kandler and J. F. Eberlein for Count Bruhl, enriched with gilding with sparse Kakiemon flowers, damage to arms, tail and the basket. c 1739. 45cm high. **£5,700–6,700** C

PORCELAIN & POTTERY

A Bow Figure of a New Dancer (firing crack to left foot) blue crescent mark, c. 1760, 19.5 cm. high. **£250-280** C

A Bow seated figure of a putto symbolic of Winter, 6¾ in., 17.1 cm., **£105-135** L

A Bow Figure of Bacchus, on high base with four scroll feet outlined in puce, 10½ in., 26.6 cm. (warped in the firing) **£210-250** L

A Set of Bow White Figures of the Seasons, (Spring and Summer with damage to hats, Winter lacks brazier) c. 1755 about 13 cm. high. **£550-600** set. C

A Pair of Bow Figures of the New Dancers (she with restoration to hands and neck) blue line marks, anchor and dagger marks in iron-red, c. 1758, 17.5 cm. high. **£750-900** C

A Pair of Bow Groups of Cupid kneeling, the tree supporting candle sconces, on scroll bases with four feet, outlined in green and gold, 10 in., 25.4 cm. **£450-530** L

BOW PORCELAIN

Bow porcelain is mostly unmarked.

- early incised marks. c1750.
- dagger and painted anchor mark. c1760 - 1776.

A Bow White Figure of an Itinerant Bagpiper (pieces missing from hat and instrument and fingers) c. 1755, 22.5 cm. high. **£400-500** C

A Bow Figure of a Shepherd playing the bagpipes (chips and crack to stump) c. 1755, 26 cm. high. **£600-650** C

A Bow Figure of Spring (minor chips to flowers) anchor and dagger-mark in iron-red, c. 1765, 28.5 cm. high. **£400-450** C

A Bow Figure of A Fish-Vendor (restoration to base, basket and left arm) c. 1752, 15.5 cm. high. **£330-350** C

A Bow Figure of Autumn from a Set of the Seasons, 7 in., anchor and dagger mark in red, c. 1765, chips to bocage. **£290-350** S

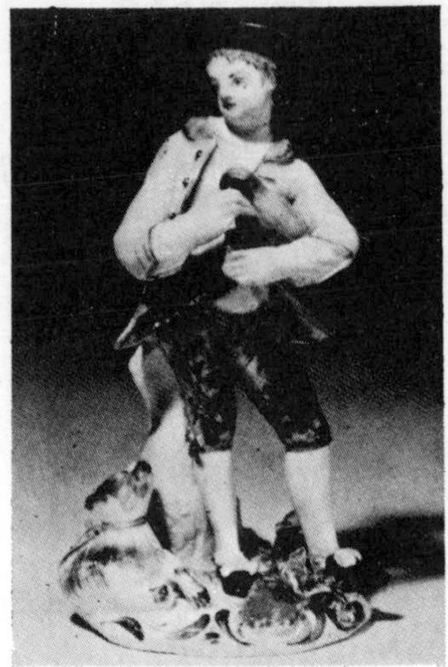

A Bow Figure of a Bagpiper with a dog (neck, fingers, jacket, one shoe and hat restored) c. 1758, 15 cm. high. **£275-300** C

A Bow Figure of Columbine (slight chips to hat and dress) c. 1755, 12 cm. high. **£600-700** C

A Bow Figure of a Sportsman, 6 in., anchor and dagger mark in red, cross in blue, c. 1765, some restoration and chips. **£290-360** S

A Pair of Bow Figures of 'New Dancers', 6 in., anchor and dagger marks in iron-red, c. 1755-60, some repair. **£890-990** S

A Bow Figure of a Turk's Companion after the model by J. F. Eberlein (minor chips to coat, finger and tree) c. 1755, 17 cm. high. **£600-800** C

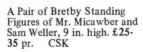

A Pair of Bow Figures of Dancers, (he with restoration to arms and left foot, she with restoration to skirt and left arm) both with anchor and dagger marks in iron-red, he with underglaze-blue M and she with A, c. 1765, 19.5 cm. high. **£500-600** pr. C

A Bow Figure of Winter (minor chips to flowers) c. 1765, 19 cm. high. **£300-350** C

A Pair of Bretby Standing Figures of Mr. Micawber and Sam Weller, 9 in. high. **£25-35** pr. CSK

A pair of Berlin figures of Malabar Musicians by F. E. Meyer, some damage, blue sceptre marks c. 1765-70, 23cm high. **£1,200–1,300** pr.

A Buen Retiro White Figure of Lucrezia (repair to left arm, minor chips firing crack to base) c. 1765 24 cm., high. **£320-380** C

A Pair of Bristol (Champion's) Figures of a Boy and Girl (his head repaired, lacks index finger, both dogs' hats with minor chips) c. 1775, 18 cm. high. **£1,000-1,200** pr. C

A Carl Thieme Potschappel Group of Count Bruhl's Tailor after the original Meissen model by J. J. Kaendler, printed F monogram and Dresden, late 19th C., 31 cm. **£380-440** SB

A Chelsea figure of the gold anchor period, not marked, 6¾ in. high. **£350-390** MJ

A Chelsea Figure of Winter (base restored) red anchor mark, c. 1755, 13 cm. high. **£500-600** C

A Chelsea figure of the gold anchor period, not marked, 6¾ in. high. **£350-390** MJ

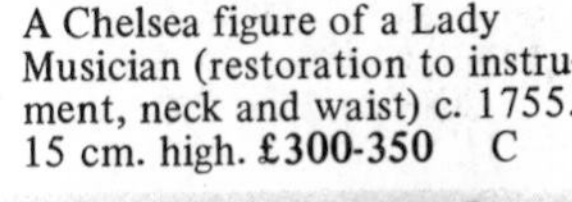

A Chelsea figure of a Lady Musician (restoration to instrument, neck and waist) c. 1755. 15 cm. high. **£300-350** C

A Pair of Chelsea sporting Figures, 9 in., anchor marks in gilding, c. 1765, restored. **£380-460** S

A Chelsea-Derby figure of a shepherdess, on scroll base outlined in turquoise and gold, 8½ in., 21.5 cm., patch marks (slight restoration) **£135-160** L

A Chelsea-Derby figure of a sportsman, on scroll base picked out in turquoise and gold, 8 in., 20.3 cm., patch marks (some restoration) **£110-140** L

A Pair of Continental China Figures, height 28 cm., late 19th C. **£150-180** S Be

A set of Continental figures of Actors & Actress, factory unknown c. 1880's. **£275-325** set. PC

Continental figure, 19th C, 3½" high. **£25-30** SQE

Continental Pin Cushion Head, c. 1890. **£18-20** CA

Continental Pin Cushion Head, c. 1890. **£8-10** CA

Continental Pin Cushion Head, c. 1890. **£12-15** CA

Continental Pin Cushion Head, c. 1890. **£22-25** unglazed bisque, CA

A Pair of Copenhagen Groups of a Sultan and his Sultana on circular marbled plinths (extensive repairs) blue wave marks c. 1787 18.5 cm., high. **£480-540** C

left

Copeland Parian Figure, height 54 cm., impressed P. MacDowell, R. A. Crystal Palace, Art Union, mid 19th C. **£75-95** S Be

A Copenhagen Group of Shepherd Lovers (chips to foliage and to ears of one sheep) blue wave mark c. 1775 22 cm., wide. **£420-490** C

POINTERS FOR CAUGHLEY 1772-1799
- continued by Coalport management

- Painted wares earlier than printed ones.
- Later printed wares with gilding, detracts from value.
- Main Marks, impressed Salopian S in underglaze blue and Capital C.
- Hatched crescents never occur on Caughley.
- Often shows orange tint by transmitted light.
- Glaze, good close fitting.
- Glaze when gathered in pools, may have greeny blue tint.
- Often confused with Worcester; have many patterns in common e.g. Fishermans and Fence.

A Pair of Copenhagen figures, circular grass-mound bases (extensively repaired), blue wave marks, c. 1786 19 cm., high. **£200-300** C

A Creamware Figure of a Lady (repair to plume, slight crack to base) c. 1785. **£250-300** C

A Set of Four Derby Figures of The Continents (Europe with extensive restoration to neck and arm, America with restoration to right arm and hand, all with minor chipping) c. 1770, 17 cm. to 18 cm. high. **£500-600** C

A Derby figure of a Young Man framed by finely decorated bocage c. 1850's. **£500-560** PC

A Derby Figure of St. Philip (firing cracks, minor chips) c. 1752, 24.5 cm. high. **£300-325** C

A Derby seated figure of a putto, symbolic of Summer, 6¾ in., 17.1 cm., patch marks. **£95-135** L

A Pair of Derby White Biscuit Groups of Earth and Air (minor chipping) incised no. 48, c. 1775, with wood stands and glass domes, 20.5 cm. high. **£450-500** C

A Derby Bust of George IV with the monogram GR IV (stem and base restored) Crown, crossed batons and D mark in iron-red, c. 1820, 11.5 cm. high. **£150-250** C

A Pair of Derby Figures of a Harvester and Companion (his left leg, her neck restored and some chipping) c. 1770, 18 cm. high. **£280-350** C

A Derby Bust of Voltaire, incised No. 159, c. 1780, 15 cm. high. **£140-180** C

A Derby Figure of Sir Charles Pratt as Lord Chancellor, c. 1765, 31.5 cm. high. **£450-500** C

A Pair of Bloor Derby Figures of Mansion House Dwarfs, with Crown and D mark in iron-red, with incised No. 227, c. 1825, about 17 cm. high. **£550-600** C

A Derby Figure of David Garrick as Richard III, c. 1770, 26.5 cm. high. **£300-350** C

right

A Derby Group of the Dancing Lesson, (heads restored) 28 cm. high. **£450-500** C

left

A Derby Figure of David Garrick as Richard III (arms and neck restored) c. 1770, 25.5 cm. high. **£240-280** C

A Pair of Derby Candlestick Figures of Mars and Venus, 8 in., c. 1765-70 some repair. **£290-350** S

A pair of Derby figures of autumn and winter, the girl 21 cm., the boy 20 cm., c. 1780. **£280-320** SKC

DOCCIA

- 1735 the Doccia factory founded by Marchese Carlo Ginori
- chief modeller Gaspare Bruschi
- 1757-91 the best period
- Doccia colouring inclined to be hard with a dry glazed appearance
- 1770 introduction of white tin glaze, liable to fire-cracks
- end of 18thC star from Ginori coat-of-arms used as factory mark

A Doccia Figure of a Youth, his flesh toned in typical dotted iron-red, 15.8 cm. c. 1760. **£410-450** S

A Doulton Figure 'The Land Of Nod', 24 cm., impressed and painted H. Tittensor. **£250-280** S Be

A Royal Doulton Figure 'The Coquette', signed and dated William White, 1913, 24.5 cm., No. 166 H.N.20. **£270-290** S Be

A Doulton Figure of 'Sweet Anne', 7 in. high (introduced 1932, discontinued 1967). **£55-60** CA

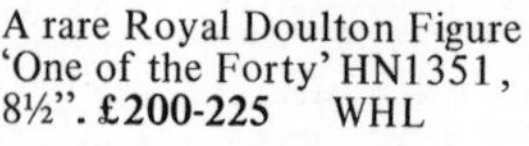

A rare Royal Doulton Figure 'One of the Forty' HN1351, 8½". **£200-225** WHL

A Royal Doulton figure 'The Parson's Daughter' hand-painted c. 1932 HN 564 10 in. high. **£190-210** PC

A Pair of "Dresden" Candlesticks, on four pink and gilt scroll feet, AR mark. 12¾ in., 32.4 cm. **£220-250** L

A Pair of Dresden figures, supporting candle sconces, decorated in blue and gold, crossed swords mark. 13¾ in., 35 cm. **£310-360** L

A Dresden group of Courtiers c. 1860. **£400-450** PC

A Royal Dux Group Depicting A Pair of Young Rustic Lovers, painted in green and brown, 53.5 cm., applied pink triangle, early 20th C. **£350-390** S Be

A Royal Dux Art Nouveau Group, 15½ in. high, pink triangle mark. **£210-240** CSK

One of a pair of Bock-Wallendorf Dresden 'Naughty Figures' c. 1900 (Companion piece-dog has pulled the skirt off). **£175-225** PC

ROYAL DUX. BOHEMIA

- 1860 founded by E. Eichler
- produced a wide range of ornamental ware
- wares extensively exported to America
- Dux not uncommon in England but of inferior artistic quality
- Marks:- Royal Dux, Bohemia
- Dux is now Duchov, Czechoslovakia

An English White China Figure of A Negro, height 40 cm., impressed numerals, late 19th C. **£120-150** S Be

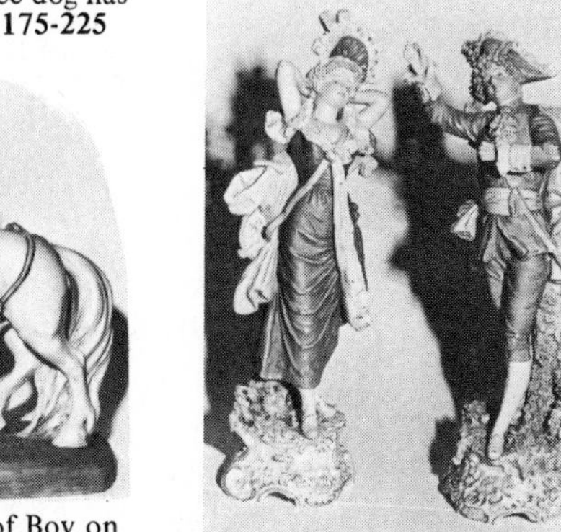

A Royal Dux Figure of Boy on Horseback, 14 in. high, 1920's. **£350-400** MN

A Pair of Royal Dux Musician figures c. 1900, 12 in. tall. **£275-300** pr. PC

A Pair of English Porcelain Busts of King William IV and Queen Adelaide, inscribed WR.IV, and Adelaide, c. 1830, perhaps Lloyd of Shelton, 19.5 cm. high. **£400-500** C

A Pair of Royal Dux Figures painted in green, pink and brown, 59 cm., applied pink triangle, early 20th C. **£620-690** S Be

A Dresden classical Figure c. 1880's 9 in. **£290-340** PC

A Frankenthal Group, on a gilt rococo scroll base, crowned C.T. cypher in underglaze blue. 7 in., 18.4 cm. **£420-530** L

A Furstenberg figure of a nymph modelled by A. Ch. Luplan, 18.5 cm. high, incised 214 and modeller's name, c. 1772. **£200-300** C

Early 20th C German Group, 5" high. **£25-30** SQE

A Frankenthal Group, the base outlined with rococo scrolls in relief in gold, crowned C.T. cypher in underglaze blue. 7½ in., 19 cm. **£520-600** L

A German Scent-Flask with gilt-metal foliage stopper and chain attachment, (chips to hat, base and goat's horns), probably Berlin, 18th C. 11 cm., high. **£480-520** C

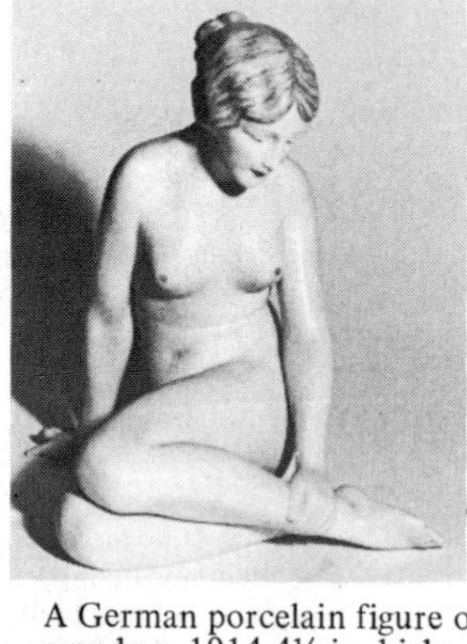

A German porcelain figure of a nude c. 1914 4½ in. high. **£100-140** PC

A German porcelain chinoiserie style Figure 6½ in. high, c. 1870-1880. **£40-50** PC

A Good Pair of French 'Bisque' Figures both picked out in gilding, 21 in., painted marks in blue, impressed numerals, broken forefinger, fingers on one hand missing, fan cracked, late 19th C. **£160-180** SBA

A German figure of Minerva (repair to her left arm) 20 cm. high, Wurzburg or Sulzbach, c. 1765. **£450-550** C

A Goldscheider Figure of an exotic young native dancer, 20 in. high, signed Podala, Goldscheider Wein. **£200-250** CSK

A German Art Deco figu
1920's 9 in. **£65-75** PC

left

A Pair of French Coloured Biscuit Figures, late 19th C., 28 and 29 cm. **£140-170** SB

A Herculaneum Pearlware Bust of Nelson (slight restoration to nose), impressed mark, c. 1805, 22 cm. high. **£250-300** C

A Japanese Porcelain Figure, 11 in. high, c. 1870. **£90-100** CA

A Japanese Porcelain Figure, 13½ in., high, c. 1870 (damaged). **£80-90** CA

A Japanese Porcelain Figure, 11 in. high, c. 1870. **£90-100** CA

A stylish Hutschenreuther porcelain Group, 43cms high, printed factory marks. **£680-720** P

A Hochst figure (repair to her right arm) 18 cm. high, blue crowned wheel mark, c. 1775. **£600-650** C

The Mackintosh Pair of Leeds Creamware Figures of Hamlet and Ophelia (he with minor damage to plume) c. 1775, 32 cm. high. **£1,500-2,500** C

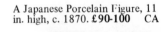

A Limbach figure, (minor chips) 14 cm. high, c. 1770. **£600-650** C

A Pair of Jacob Petit Figures, raised on gilt scroll bases and brightly coloured, underglaze blue J. P., late 19th C., 31 and 33.5 cm. **£210-260** SB

A London Tin-glazed Earthenware Group of a Court Lady and Gentleman covered in a rich blue glaze (she lacks part of right arm, part of base missing, glaze flaking) c. 1670, 12 cm. high. **£300-400** C

A Longton Hall White Figure of Harlequin (minor chips to foliage and hat) c. 1755, 12 cm. high. **£500-550** C

LONGTON HALL c1749 - 60
most pieces unmarked.
some marks in underglaze blue.

A Longton Hall Figure of Winter (slight chips), c. 1755, 12 cm. high. **£250-300** C

A Ludwigsburg figure of a sower (chips to his hat) 12.5 cm., high, blue crowned interlaced C mark, incised S.N.Z. c. 1765. **£800-900** C

A Meissen Figure of a Girl, underglaze blue crossed swords, incised and impressed numerals, late 19th C., 13 cm. **£210-240**

A Pair of Longton Hall Figures of a Sportsman and Companion (restoration to hands, his gun and her neck) c. 1775, 17.5 cm. high. **£900-1,000** C

Four Ludwigsburg figures of Putti musicians (minor chips) 13.5 cm. high, one with blue crowned interlaced C mark, two with impressed FI:3:M:50, one with C:C:Z:S, all with iron-red arrow mark, c. 1765. **£1,000-1,200** C

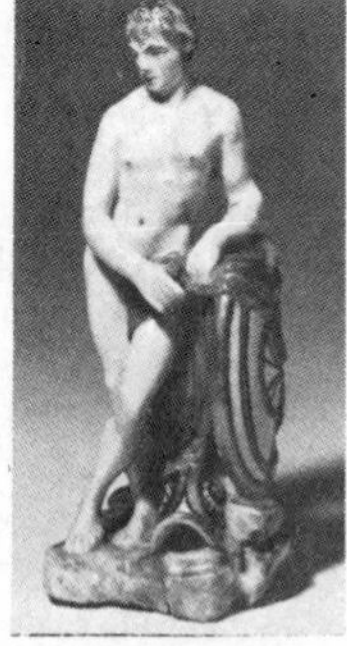

A Ludwigsburg Figure of a Warrior (firing crack to base) blue interlaced C mark, C. 1775 14 cm., high. **£240-270** C

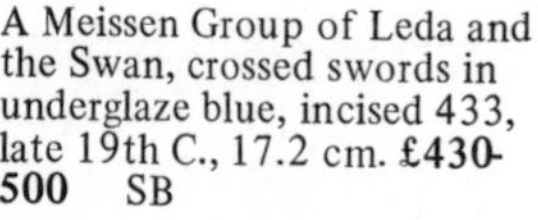

A Meissen Group of Leda and the Swan, crossed swords in underglaze blue, incised 433, late 19th C., 17.2 cm. **£430-500** SB

A good pair of late 19th C Meissen porcelain groups, 7" high, blue cross swords, incised and impressed numerals mark (small faults). **£750-800** PWC

A Pair of Meissen Figures of a shepherd and shepherdess, underglaze blue cross swords, incised 2784, mid 19th C., 14.8 cm. **£550-600** SB

A Large Meissen Style Group painted in enamel colours, 31 cm., late 19th C, some damage **£210-230** S Be

A Meissen Bacchic Group, height 20 cm., underglaze blue mark, incised numerals, late 19th C. **£300-340** S Be

A Meissen Group, underglaze blue crossed swords, incised D19, painted and impressed numerals, late 19th C., 16.5 cm. **£590-680** SB

A Meissen Figure brightly painted with floral sprigs, 19.2 cm., crossed swords in underglaze blue, late 19th C. some damage **£210-230** S Be

A Meissen Allegorical Group, height 18.5 cm., mark in underglaze blue, incised numerals, some damage **£185-200** S Be

A Meissen China Figure of Minerva in bright enamel colours, height 26.4 cm., late 19th C. some damage **£350-390** S Be

A Pair of Meissen Style Figures, 17.5 cm., late 19th C. **£65-75** S Be

A Pair of Meissen Figures of Beggar-Musicians modelled by J. J. Kandler, one with traces of blue crossed swords mark, c. 1748, 12 cm., high. **£1,500-1,700** C

A Meissen Group of Shepherd Lovers modelled by J. J. Kandler (repairs, firing crack to base, minor chips to flowers, c. 1740, 17 cm., wide. **£5,500-6,200** C

A Pair of Meissen Figures of a Shepherd and Shepherdess (chips to animals, his left hand repaired), blue crossed swords marks, c. 1755, 27.5 cm., high. **£1,800-2,000** C

A 19th C Meissen Biscuit Group of Two Naiads, 12" (32cms) high. **£180-220** SKC

A Meissen Italian Comedy Group of Pantaloon and Columbine modelled by J. J. Kandler (repair to her cloak and right arm) c. 1741, 16.5 cm., high. **£6,500-7,200** C

A Meissen figure of a mounted hussar (repairs to his right hand, gun and horse's legs) 8.5 cm. high, c. 1745. **£450-500** C

A Meissen figure of a naval gentleman 8½ in. high, c. 1810. **£350-380** PC

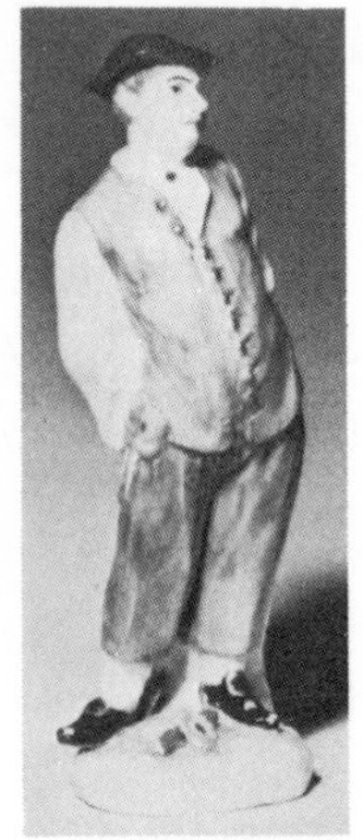

A Meissen Group of Shepherd Lovers, (chips to fingers, flowers and toes), blue crossed swords and dot mark, c. 1765, 19.5 cm., high. **£1,050-1,200**

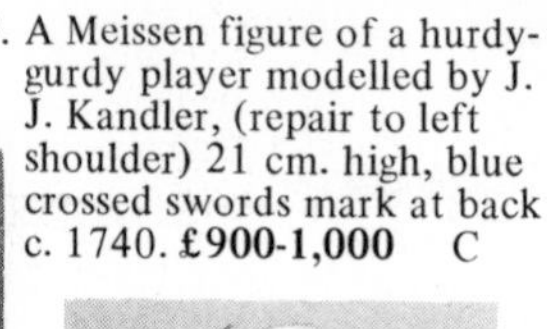

A Meissen figure of a hurdy-gurdy player modelled by J. J. Kandler, (repair to left shoulder) 21 cm. high, blue crossed swords mark at back c. 1740. **£900-1,000** C

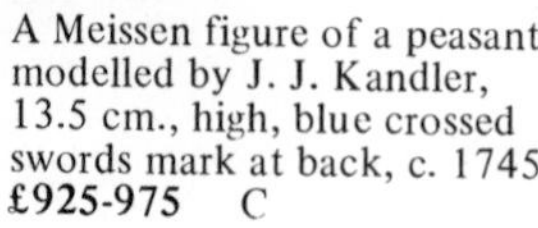

A Meissen figure of a peasant modelled by J. J. Kandler, 13.5 cm., high, blue crossed swords mark at back, c. 1745. **£925-975** C

right
A Naples (Ferdinand IV) Group of a Mother and Child, c. 1780 (right hand and tip of left foot of child repaired) 16 cm., high. **£3,500-3,900** C

A Meissen figure, modelled by P. Reinicke (chips) 14 cm. high, blue crossed swords mark at back, c. 1740. **£1,200-1,250** C

A Small Minton Parian Figure of a Girl, 4½ in. high, c. 1845. **£65-75** MN

A Nymphenburg figure of a shepherdess modelled by Dominicus Auliczek, (slight repairs to lamb) 17.5 cm. high, c. 1775. **£1,400-1,450** C

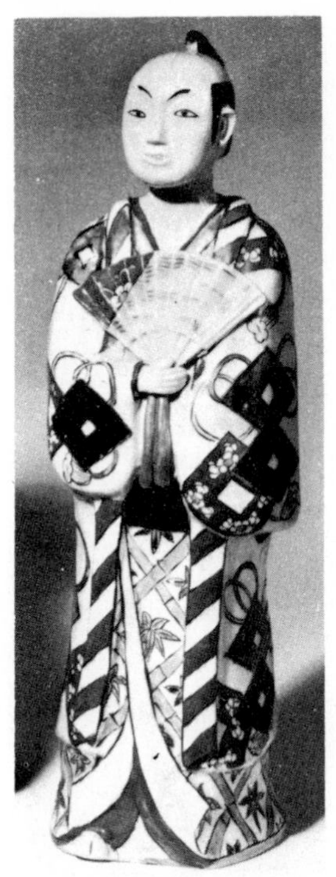

A rare Imari figure of an actor (neck restored), Genroku period, 39.8cms high. **£530-580** C

GLOSSARY OF MODERN CHINESE TERMS CONVERTED FROM THE WADE-GILES SYSTEM OF ROMANISATION TO THE PINYIN SYSTEM

PINYIN	WADE-GILES
Ming:	Ming:
Xuande	Hsuan Te
Zhengtong	Cheng T'ung
Jingtai	Ching T'ai
Chenghua	Ch'eng Hua
Jiajing	Chia Ching
Longqing	Lung Ch'ing
Wanli	Wan Li
Taichang	T'ai Ch'ang
Tianqi	T'ien Ch'i
Chongzheng	Ch'ung Cheng
Qing:	Ch'ing:
Shunzhi	Shun Chih
Kangxi	K'ang Hsi
Yongzheng	Yung Cheng
Qianlong	Ch'ien Lung
Jiaqing	Chia Ch'ing
Daoguang	Tao Kuang

Two famille verte figures of standing smiling boys (fritted, one base restored) Kangxi 27.5 cm. high. **£485-535** C

A Chinese Porcelain Figure of Shou Lao, painted in under-glaze blue, Wan Li period. 10 in., 25.4 cm. **£1,800-1,950** L

19th C Parian figure, 7" high. **£15-20** SQE

A Parian Standing Figure of W. G. Grace, 9¼ in. high. **£260-300** CSK

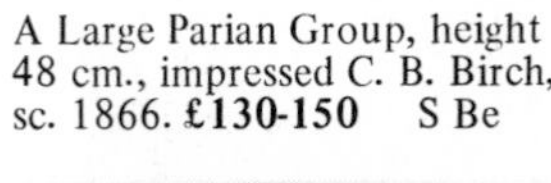

A Large Parian Group, height 48 cm., impressed C. B. Birch, sc. 1866. **£130-150** S Be

A Robinson & Leadbetter Parian Group with ivory finish, 1865-86. **£275-300** SQE

A Famille Verte Figure of a smiling boy, height 29 cm., Transitional. **£260-300** S Be

A Prattware Group of 'Babes in the Wood', 4" (10cms) high, late 18th C (chipped). **£80-100** SKC

A Pair of Staffordshire parian ware figures by Robinson & Leadbetter, late 19th C, 16½" high. **£160-190** SAL

A pair of traditional style English figures by Robinson and Leadbetter 10½ in. high, 1885. **£250-275** PC

A Rockingham White Biscuit Bust of The Duke of York, c. 1830, 18.5 cm. high. **£125-200** C

Robinson & Leadbetter Parian bust of Scott. **£35-40** NO

A Rockingham Figure of a Toper, (repaired at base) impressed Griffin mark and Rockingham Works Brameld and incised No. 29, 1826-1830, 10 cm. high. **£120-150** C

A Rockingham Group of The Whistling Cobbler, incised No. 39 and C3 in red, 1826-1830, 14 cm. high. **£450-500** C

Robinson & Leadbetter Parian bust of Rev. G. Dunnett. **£25-30** NO

A Rockingham White Biscuit Bust of William Wordsworth, c. 1828, 26 cm. high. **£350-400** C

A Rockingham Figure of John Liston as Madame Vestris, inscribed 'Buy a Broom' (neck repaired) red griffin mark and incised No. 6, 1826-1830, 16 cm. high. **£800-1,000** C

A Rockingham Figure of Paysanne De Sagran En Tirol, (minor chips) incised Rockingham Works Brameld and No. 22 and C1.2 in red, 1826-1830, 18 cm. high. **£500-600** C

A Rockingham Figure of a Toper modelled as a hunchback, inscribed 'St-eady L-ads' (repaired at base, pigment flaking) red griffin mark and incised No. 1, 1826-1830, 14 cm. high. **£150-180** C

A Pair of Samson 'Chelsea' Bocage Candlestick Groups, coloured in pastel shades and raised on gilt scroll bases, painted gilt anchor, late 19th C., 25 cm. **£240-280** SB

Two Samson 'Chelsea' Figures of Europa and Neptune, painted gilt anchor, late 19th C., 34.5 and 30.5 cm. **£160-190** SB

A Rosenthal portrait figure, by Ernst Wenck, green printed factory mark R, impressed Ernst Wenck 745, 12" high. **£210-240** CSK

A Samson Figure, copy of a Derby Boy, 7½ in. high, c. 1890 A.F. **£80-90** CA

A Samson copy of a Derby figure of a Cavalier with Derby marks 9 in. c. 1890. **£140-160** PC

A Samson Group of Cherry Pickers, 15 in., 38.1 cm. **£350-400** L

A Samson copy of a Derby figure c. 1890's 9 in. **£195-215** PC

A Sevres hardpaste white biscuit figure of Marechal de Turenne modelled by Pajou (sword missing, minor repairs) 47 cm. high. c. 1783. **£250-350** C

left

A Shelton (Lloyd) Porcelain Figure of Thomas Dartmouth-Rice as Jim Crow, impressed Lloyd Shelton, c. 1836, 16 cm. high. **£250-300** C

A Sevres 'semi-erotic' figure, stepping over a puddle which is a mirror, 'from naughty period' 1880's. **£240-270** PC

A Pair of Sitzendorf figures, Art Deco 7½ in. **£200-240** pr. PC

A pair of 'Sitzendorf Pirouette' figures c. 1920, signed by artist 7½ in. high. **£200-230** pr. PC

A Figure of the Empress Eugenie and the Prince Imperial, Untitled, 8" (23.3cms), c1856. **£90-110** S.B.

'Princess', a figure of the Princess Royal, 10" (26.8cms), c1853. **£50-70** S.B.

A Brightly Coloured Alliance Group, modelled as Albert and Napoleon III, untitled, minor restoration, 12" (31.2cms), c1854. **£110-150** S.B.

A Pair of Staffordshire figures of Tom Cribb and Tom Molineux (Cribb cracked) c. 1848, 19 cm. high. **£350-450** C

A Pair of Staffordshire Figures of sleeping cherubs, 5¼" (13cms) wide, early 19th C. **£95-110** SKC

A Staffordshire Coloured Salt-glaze figure of a Pastry Seller (hat damaged, chip to apron) c. 1750, 12.5 cm. high. **£800-1,000** C

A rare Staffordshire figure of Madame Vestris as "Paul" 16.5 cm., c. 1822. **£210-240** SKC

A Victorian Staffordshire Figure, c. 1880. **£33-36** AP

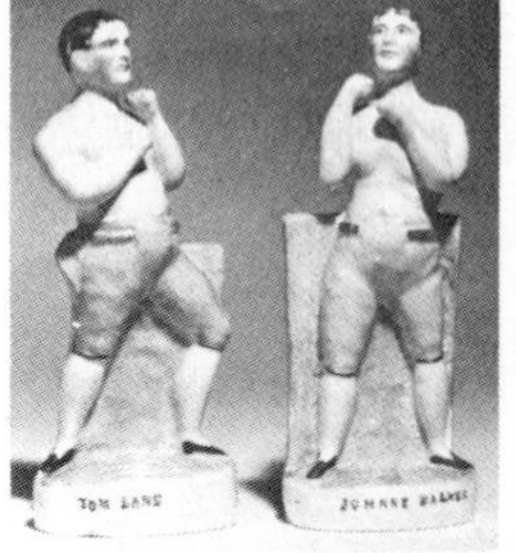

A Pair of Staffordshire figures of Johnny Walker and Tom Lane (restoration to Walker's left wrist and Lane's neck) c. 1848, 19 cm. high. **£650-800** C

A Staffordshire Porcelain Group of Mr. Van Amburgh, the American lion-tamer, inscribed in gilding, c. 1839, 16 cm. high. **£1,500-2,000** C

A Staffordshire figure of John Liston as Paul Try (hand restored) c. 1830, 15 cm. high. **£100-120** C

A Staffordshire Saltglaze figure of the Taoist Immortal, Chung-Li-Ch'uan, c. 1750, 18.5 cm. high. **£800-900** C

A Staffordshire Saltglaze Figure of a Court Lady (hat repaired) c. 1740, 9.5 cm. high. **£400-450** C

left

A 'Winter's Tale', a spill holder group of Jenny Marston as 'Perdita' and Frederick Robinson as 'Florizel', 11¾" (29.5cms), c1852. **£70-100** S.B.

A rare Staffordshire group, the Hairdresser, 18 cm. high. c. 1820 (restored). **£175-200** SKC

A Dixon, Austin & Co. Watch-case, 10" (25cms), impressed mark, c1820 (damaged). **£245-285** SKC

A Victorian Staffordshire Figure, 'Will Watch', 15½" high. **£50-75** OF

A Victorian Staffordshire Figure, 'The Scotsman', 15½" high. **£60-80** OF

A Staffordshire Figure of Napoleon, 8" high. **£90-100** OF

A Victorian Staffordshire Figure, 'The Prince & The Princess, 11" high. **£55-75** OF

The Allied Powers, with Queen Victoria standing between Napoleon III and Victoria Emmanuel II, 11¾" (29.8cms), c1854. **£350-450** S.B.

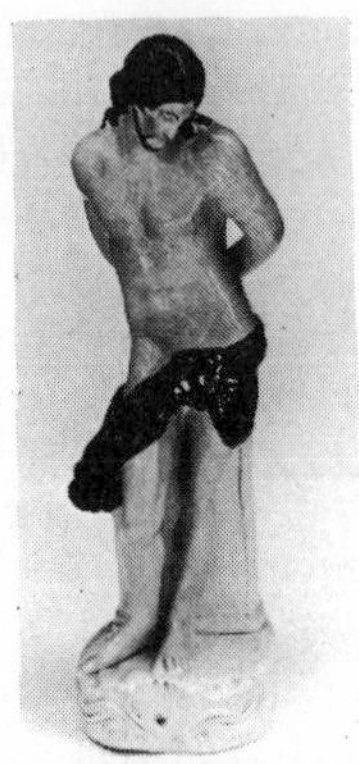

A Victorian Staffordshire Religious Figure, 16½" high. **£150-175** OF

A Victorian Staffordshire Group, 'Highland Jessie', 9" high. **£35-50** OF

Late 19th C Staffordshire Figure of Garibaldi, 9" high. **£125-145** OF

A Victorian Staffordshire Group, 'The Lion Tamer', 8½" high. **£50-70** OF

A Victorian Staffordshire Figure of 'A Prussian General', 12" high. **£55-75** OF

A Staffordshire Figure of Elijah by Sherratt, c1830-40, 10" high. **£145-165** OF

A Victorian Staffordshire Group, 'The Lovers', 9½" high. **£50-70** OF

A Staffordshire Figure, 19th C. **£55-75** OF

A Staffordshire Group, enamelled with a red-brown line and the title 'Friendship', 6¼" (16cms), early 19th C, possible Neale and Wilson (missing bocage). **£115-130** SKC

Group of 2 Turkish Soldiers, dating from Crimean War, 9½" high. **£55-70** OF

A Staffordshire Figure of 'The Huntswoman', by Neale, 7½" high, (repaired), 19th C. **£55-75**

A good Staffordshire 'Tithe-pig' group, 7½" (19cms), early 19th C (some damage). **£375-425** SKC

A Rare Staffordshire Pottery Bust of a man, possibly Cobbett, 7½" (19cms), early 19th C. **£170-200** SKC

A Staffordshire Saltglaze figure of a seated Pagoda figure c. 1730. 8 cm. high. **£400-500** C

A Staffordshire Group, 8 in. high, c. 1890. **£45-50** CA

A Staffordshire Watch Holder, 9 in. high, c. 1890. **£45-50** CA

A Staffordshire Highlander, 15 in. high, c. 1890. **£40-45** CA

A Staffordshire Pottery Bust of George Washington, 8¼" (21cms), early 19th C. **£290-320** SKC

A Staffordshire Group of Red Riding Hood, 10½ in. high, c. 1890. **£40-45** CA

A Staffordshire Group of Minstrels, 10 in. high, c. 1890. **£60-66** CA

A Staffordshire Figure 'Shepherd Boy'. 8 in. high, c. 1890. **£50-55** CA

A Staffordshire Quill Holder, 5½ in. c. 1890. **£27-30** CA

A Large Staffordshire Group, 14 in. high, c. 1890. **£47-50** CA

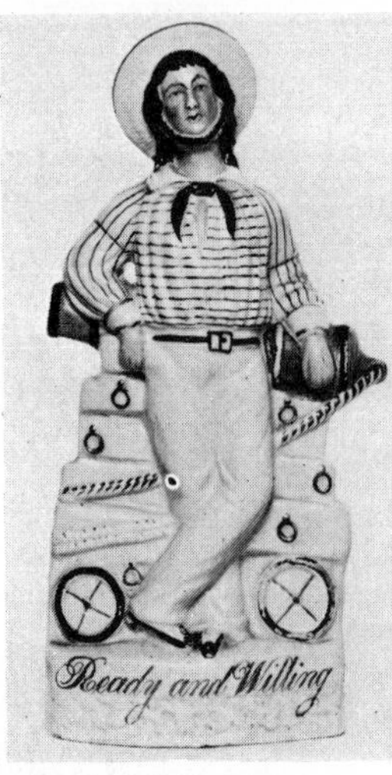

A Staffordshire Figure, 'Ready and Willing', 11¾in., 29.8cm., c1854 **£110-150** SB

A Rare and Finely Modelled Staffordshire Standing Figure of General Sir William Codrington, 13 in. high. **£650-700** CSK

A Rare Pair of Staffordshire Miniature Figures of Nelson and Napoleon 5¼ in. high. **£240-280** CSK

A Staffordshire Standing Figure of Nelson, 6¾ in. high (unrecorded). **£140-180** CSK

A Very Rare Staffordshire Standing Figure of Sir Henry Havelock, 12 in. high. **£260-290** CSK

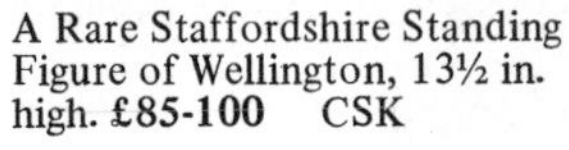

A Rare Staffordshire Standing Figure of Wellington, 13½ in. high. **£85-100** CSK

A Staffordshire Figure Group, entitled in raised capitals, 'The Soldier's Return', 12in high, **£180-220** CSK

A Staffordshire Group of a Sailor and a Young Lady, entitled in raised capitals 'Return', 12 in. high. **£240-290** CSK

A Staffordshire Group of a Soldier in Scottish Uniform and a Young Lady, entitled in raised capitals 'The Soldier's Farewell', 12½ in. high. **£190-220** CSK

A Rare Staffordshire Group of Prince Albert with Napoleon III, 7½ in. high. **£75-85** CSK

A pair of Crown Staffordshire figures 'Cinderella and Prince Charming'. **£50-60** pr. PC

A Staffordshire Group of 'Courting Under Difficulties', well modelled and coloured, 12¼ in. high. **£190-220** CSK

A Staffordshire Standing Figure of Gladstone, 15½ in. high. **£80-100** CSK

A Rare Pair of Small Staffordshire Figures, 4½ in. high. **£90-110** pr. CSK

A Rare Staffordshire Standing Figure of Thomas Sexton MP, 15¼ in. high. **£60-70** CSK

A Rare Staffordshire Standing Figure of Gladstone, 12 in. high. **£85-100** CSK

A Very Rare Staffordshire Figure of T. S. Duncomb, 9 in. high. **£120-150** CSK

right

A Rare Staffordshire Standing Figure of Edward VII, 9¼ in. high. **£65-75** CSK

A Rare Pair of Staffordshire Standing Figures of Queen Victoria and Prince Albert, 7¼ in. high. **£150-180** CSK

A Staffordshire Group of the Boxers Heenan and Sayers, 9¾ in. high. **£260-290** CSK

A Pair of Staffordshire Standing Figures of a Batsman and Bowler, 10½ in. high. **£400-450** CSK

A Staffordshire Group of an English Sailor standing back to back with a French Soldier, 9 in. high. **£85-95** CSK

A Ralph Wood Figure of the lost piece of silver modelled as a lady (handle to broom damaged) c. 1775, 22.5 cm. high. **£450-550** C

A Ralph Wood Figure of Charity holding a child, a naked child hiding in her robes. c. 1780, 24 cm. high. **£280-350** C

A Rare Staffordshire Group of Drummer Boys, 7 in. high. **£65-75** CSK

An Enoch Wood Bust of John Milton c. 1800, 29.5 cm. high. **£150-250** C

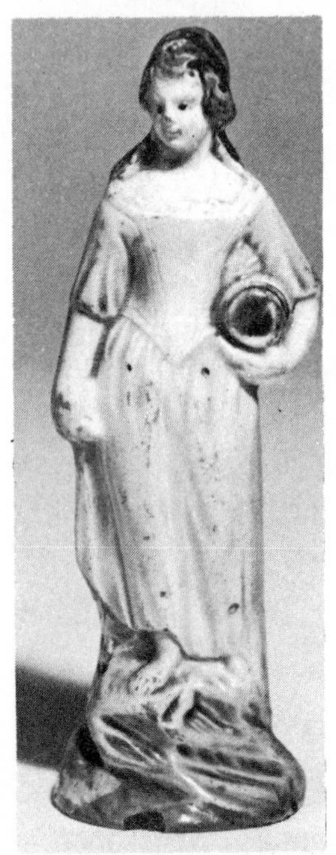

A Ralph Wood Figure of a Lady (base restored) c. 1775, 12 cm. high. **£200-250** C

An Enoch Wood Equestrian Group of William III in the guise of a Roman Emperor (base cracked, minor flaking and re-painting) c. 1790, 41.5 cm. high. **£800-1,000** C

A Ralph Wood Figure of a Seated Man with a Dog, c. 1780, 11.5 cm. high. **£150-200** C

A Ralph Wood Group of Cupid and a Quadruped (Cupid's wing restored) c. 1775, 21.5 cm. high. **£600-800** C

A Pair of Ralph Wood Figures of a Gardener and Companion (slight chips to base, his thigh restored) c. 1775, about 20 cm. high. **£800-1,200** C

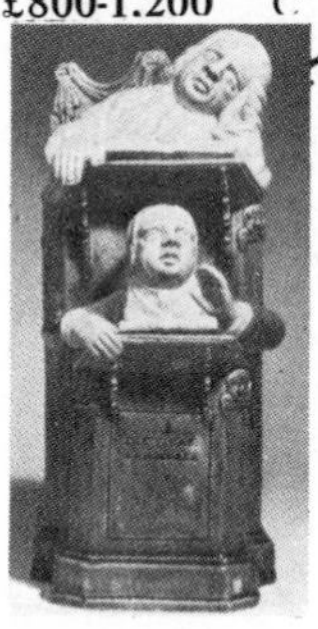

A Ralph Wood Vicar and Moses Group in a two-tier brown glazed pulpit (back repaired and minor restoration), c. 1775, 25 cm. high. **£320-350** C

A Rare Tittensor Group of a Fruit Vendor and Donkey, the reverse stamped 'Tittensor', the inside scored with a dash, 6¼" (16cms), c1815-25 (some damage). **£310-350** SKC

right

'Volkstedt' figure group 1860's (titled 'The Procurer') **£200-250** PC

A Tournai white group of a youth disturbing the slumbering girl (tree damaged) 16.5 cm. high, c. 1770. **£300-400** C

A Very Rare Biscuit Porcelain Turner Group, 10¾" (27cms), inscribed on the reverse 'Uncle Toby and Widow Wadman' and 'Turner & Co., Stoke', c1800. **£335-385** SKC

A Vienna figure of a skater (minor repairs to her right hand, brim of hat and coat) 19 cm. high, blue beehive mark, impressed P, c. 1770. **£540-600** C

A Volkstedt figure, 7 in. high, c. 1870. **£68-75** PC

A Wade Art Nouveau style figure c. 1930's 9 in. **£30-35** PC

A Whieldon Figure of Winter (cracked and restored) c. 1760, 11 cm. high. **£90-120** C

A Whieldon Figure of an Oriental Dignitary (neck and left hand restored) c. 1755, 14.5 cm. high. **£600-800** C

A Whieldon Figure of a Lady (hat damaged) c. 1740. 11 cm. high. **£500-600** C

A pair of Royal Worcester figures of 'Joy and Sorrow' 1870, 10 in. high **£375-400** pr.. PC (examples of this study made over many years and can vary in price **£200-500**) PC

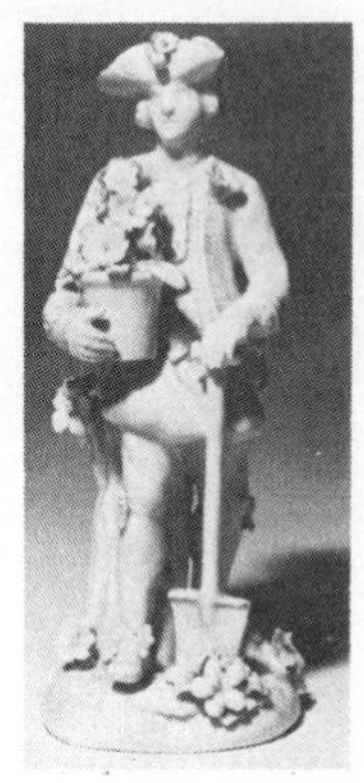

A Worcester White Figure of a Gardener (minor restoration to right hand, slight chips to flowers) c. 1770, 16.5 cm. high. **£850-950** C

A Royal Worcester Kate Greenaway Hadley figure group, undecorated piece c. 1875, 7½ in. **£250-275** PC

A pair of Royal Worcester figures, 'The Water Carriers', decorated in green and shades of gilt, 8". **£260-290** PWC

A Royal Worcester Hadley candle extinguisher, Rare c. 1875. **£140-180** PC

A Royal Worcester Crouching Figure of an Eastern Water Carrier, printed mark in puce, pattern No. 637,1877. 6 in., 16.2 cm. **£110-130** L

A Royal Worcester figure of 'the Blue Boy' by Hadley, shape No. 547 date 1900. **£140-160** PC

A Royal Worcester Hadley figure of a Monk c. 1875. Rare **£2,000+** PC

A Royal Worcester 'Bather Surprised' figure 1890-1915, 15½ in. **£700-750**; comes in many sizes value varies **£500-1,250,** some bear sculptors signature. PC

A Royal Worcester Hadley figure of John Bull c. 1875. **£175-195** PC

A Royal Worcester Crownware Art Deco figure, 11 in. tall, 1920's. **£95-105** PC

A pair of Royal Worcester figures c. 1875 11½ in. **£400-500** pr. PC

A Worcester Figure, 6¾ in. high, c. 1912. **£195-210** MN

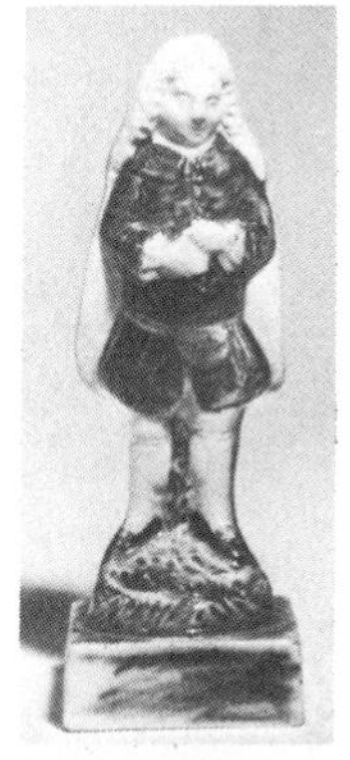

A Yorkshire Figure of a Gentleman in a long powdered wig, c. 1790, 14 cm. high. **£150-180** C

A Worcester Figure, one of Egyptian Female Musicians, shape 1084 c. 1896. **£265-290** MN

A Fine Porcellaneous Figure of Captain Cook, 7" (18cms), 1840-50. **£675-780** SKC

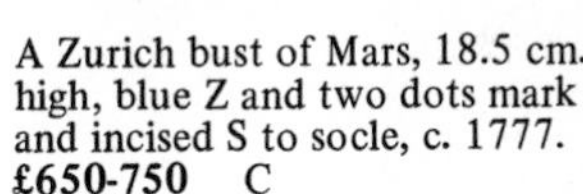

A Zurich bust of Mars, 18.5 cm. high, blue Z and two dots mark and incised S to socle, c. 1777. **£650-750** C

A privately sculptured porcelain figure, 1920's **£50-60** PC

Austrian Lady in pottery with large shell, 19 in. high. **£85-95** TT

Spillholder, with figure, 5" high. **£20-25** SQE

A Pair of modern Michael Sutty (limited edition 100) Masonic figures, after Meissen. In 1980 **£250-275** value orig. **£190** (in 1979) end of 1980. **£300+** PC

A turquoise and aubergine glaze tilemaker's pottery figure (chipped), late Ming/Qing Dynasty, 12¾" (32cms) high. **£120-150** C

A Pair of Bow Figures of a Cock and Hen, (their tails restored) c. 1760, 10.5 cm. and 10 cm. high. **£2,000-2,200** pr. C

A Pair of Bow Figures of a Cow and a Bull (restoration to horns, ears, tails and tree-stumps) c. 1755, 15 cm. wide. **£1,000-1,200** C

A Bow Figure of a Bird (slight chip to base) c. 1758, 5.5 cm. high. **£250-300** C

A Bow White Figure of a Lion, c. 1755, 10 cm. high. **£350-400** C

A Bow White Figure of a recumbent Pug (minute chip to ear) c. 1755, 11 cm. wide. **£200-250** C

A Documentary Creamware Figure of a Standing Lion by Benjamin Plant of Lane End, (restoration to tongue and tail) the base inscribed in incised script, B. Plant Lane End. c. 1815, 39 cm. wide. **£400-500** C

DERBY PORCELAIN

c1750 - 1848 and c1878

- most porcelain of 1750 - 85 unmarked.
- incised marks. c1750 - 5 – rare.

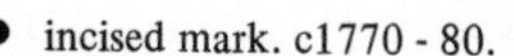

- incised mark. c1770 - 80.

Chelsea-Derby period. c1769'- 1755.

A Derby group of a sheep suckling a lamb, with gold foliage collars and gold hooves, the flowers edged with pink, the base with feathered brown border, 4 in., 10.2 cm. **£95-125** L

A Derby group of a cow suckling a calf, the green base with applied flowers, 5¼ in., 14 cm., small numerals 24 in red (slight restoration) **£110-130** L

A Derby group of a cow and reclining calf on green base with applied flowers, 6½ in., 16.5 cm, numerals 27 and 10 in red (slight restoration) **£85-125** L

A Pair of White Tin-Glazed Earthenware Seated Hounds with coloured glass eyes, 35 in. **£270-350** DH

A pair of attractive Imari models of carp (both restored), late 17th/ early 18th C, 24.5cms high. **£1,000-1,250** C

A Pair of English Porcelain Figures of Seated Pugs (both tails restored, one forepaw repaired and one with crack to neck) Longton Hall or Lowestoft, 18th C., 9 cm. high. **£500-550** C

A Meissen Figure of a Hen with her seven chicks, coloured in iron-red, brown and ochre, blue swords mark, c. 1755, 21.5 cm., wide. **£2,000-2,300** C

A Pair of Derby Figures of Red Squirrels, c. 1825, 16.5 cm. high. **£700-800** C

An English Delft Blue and white figure of a seated cat (back cracked, ears chipped) Mid 18th C. **£3,000-3,500** C

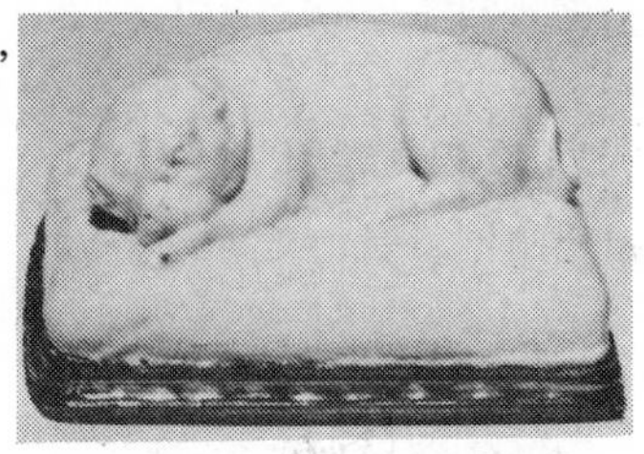

A Meissen White Recumbent Pug Dog (minor chip to rim), mounted as a snuff-box in gilt-metal, c. 1745, 8.5 cm., wide. **£450-550** C

One of a pair of Dresden Marly Horses 10 in. high, c. 1880. **£450-500** pr. PC

A Pair of small Ligurian tin-glazed figure of lions, 4¾" (12cms), 18th C. **£530-550** SKC

A 'Galle' Faience Cat with a Cheshire grin its pale green body brightly painted with flowers, painted E-Galle Nancy, c. 1890, 33 cm. **£1,100-1,300** SB

A Meissen Figure of a Starling modelled by J. J. Kandler, painted in black, brown and green, blue crossed swords mark, c. 1750, 15 cm., high. **£1,200-1,350** C

Two Meissen Figures of Guinea Fowl modelled by J. J. Kandler, painted in iron-red, pale-puce, black and blue (minor chips to foliage), c. 1741, 15 cm., high. **£2,400-2,600** C

A Rockingham White Figure of a Seated Hound, impressed Rockingham Works, Brameld, incised No. 101 and C1.1 in red, 1826-1830, 7.5 cm. high. **£200-250** C

A Pair of Portobello Figures of recumbent Cows (horns restored) c.1820, 10.5cm wide. **£200-250** C

A Rockingham Figure of a recumbent Ram with gilt horns, impressed Rockingham Works Brameld, incised No. 109 and C1.1 in red, 1826-1830, 7 cm. wide. **£360-400** C

A pair of Samson models of seated barking dogs, 19th C, 38.5cms high. **£825-900** C

A Portobello Cowcreamer and Cover, 5½ in., late 18th C., some restoration to tail and cover. **£220-280** S

A Rockingham Figure of a Seated Cat (ears chipped) impressed Rockingham Works Brameld, incised No. 77 and 1 size and C1.2 in red, 1826-1830, 6.5 cm. high. **£400-425** C

An attractive Satsuma model of a sleeping cat (small repair), signed Dai Nippon Satsuma Kizan zo, 19th C, 32cms long. **£700-750** C

A pair of small Qing mustard-yellow glazed figures of crouching tigers (chipped) 17th/18th C. 1¾ in., 4.5 cm. long. **£120-150** C

A Staffordshire Figure of a recumbent Leopard (base cracked), c. 1790, 9.5 cm. wide, **£180-220** C

A Staffordshire Napoleonic Bear-Jug and cover, inscribed 'Boney' c. 1815, 28 cm. high. **£300-350** C

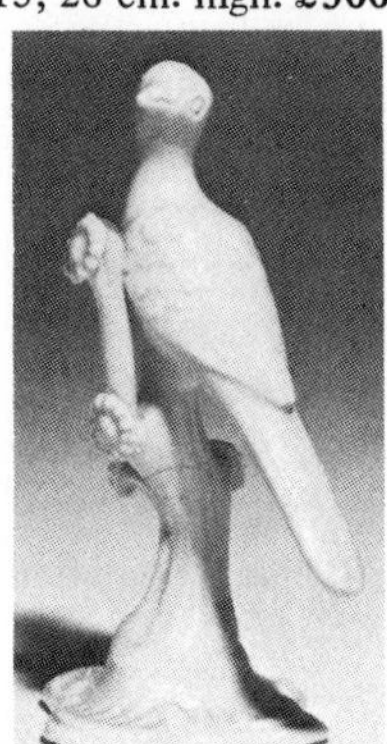

A Staffordshire Saltglaze figure of a Bird (tree cracked) c. 1745. 11.5 cm. high. **£400-450** C

A Staffordshire Saltglaze Figure of a seated Pug (crack to back and right paw, chips to base) 7 cm. high, c. 1740. **£250-300** C

A Staffordshire figure of a Norwich Cropper (minor restoration to tail) c. 1800, 10.5 cm. high. **£250-300** C

A Staffordshire Figure of a seated Spaniel c. 1825, 8 cm. high. **£100-120** C

A Pair of Staffordshire Figures of Crested Finches (one base cracked) c. 1800, 9 cm. high. **£500-600** C

A Staffordshire pen holder, surmounted by a greyhound c. 1860-1870 6½ in. long. **£35-38** PC

A Staffordshire Figure of a Brown-spotted Hound with a pantomime grin (enamels re-touched and crack to base) c. 1810, 13 cm. high. **£130-150** C

A Whieldon figure of a Seated Greyhound (slight chips to ear and base) c. 1770, 9.5 cm. high. **£350-400** C

A Whieldon Figure of a Hen (beak and tail restored) c. 1765, 9 cm. high. **£250-280** C

A Pair of Whieldon Figures of Buffaloes with a seated Oriental child (horns, ears, three legs and one muzzle restored). c. 1760. 25 cm. long. **£2,800-3,000** C

A Whieldon figure of a Cow (horns and base restored) c. 1770, 19.5 cm. wide. **£800-1,000** C

A Ralph Wood Figure of a recumbent Sheep, c. 1785, 15 cm. wide. **£150-200** C

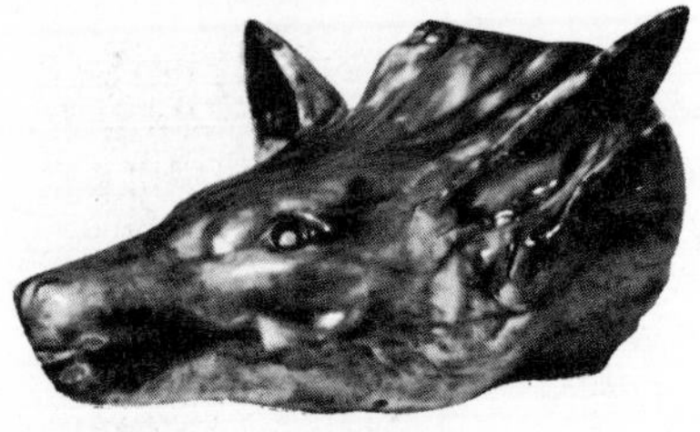

A Ralph Wood Fox Mask Stirrup-cup (ear restored) c. 1775, 11.5 cm. long. **£250-300** C

A Ralph Wood Figure of a Retriever, impressed R. Wood, c. 1775, 18 cm. wide. **£1,000-1,200** C

A Pair of Royal Worcester figures of elephants, registration and Worcester marks and name 'Hadleys' incised. 7¾ in., 19.7 cm. **£300-350** pr. L

A Ralph Wood Sphinx-Whistle c. 1785, 9.5 cm. high. **£170-200** C

A Pair of Ralph Wood Figures of standing Lions (one with tail restored and base riveted) c. 1775, 30.5 cm. wide. **£1,400-1,800** C

A Yorkshire Pearlware figure of a Stallion (restoration to tail and ears, hoofs and crack to body, base repaired) c. 1790, 36 cm. wide. **£2,200-2,500** C

A Ralph Wood Figure of a recumbent Lion, c. 1780, 11 cm. wide. **£120-150** C

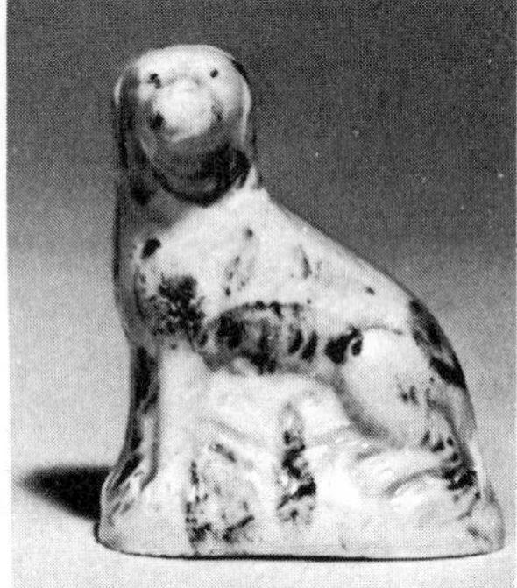

A Ralph Wood Figure of a seated Hound, c. 1775, 7.5 cm. high. **£100-120** C

A Yorkshire group of a horse trampling on a man (chips to ears) c. 1800, 18.5 cm. wide. **£1,100-1,300** C

A Ralph Wood Bull-Baiting Group, the fierce bull with his tail arched over his back scraping at a dog (tail, horns and ears restored, back leg cracked) c. 1785, 18.5 cm. wide. **£1,400-1,800** C

A Yorkshire Pearlware figure of a Lion, his left fore-paw resting on a yellow ball, c. 1800, 33 cm. wide. **£280-350** C

A Yorkshire figure of a Shire Horse (tail and one ear restored) c. 1785, 16 cm. wide. **£600-700** C

A Yorkshire Cow-group with a recumbent calf, c. 1800, 17 cm. wide. **£220-250** C

A pair of turquoise-glazed figures of Buddhistic Lions, (chipped) 18th/19th C., 4 in., 10.5 cm. wide. **£240-280** C

A large Arita blue and white slender oviform vase (rim chips), 19th C hexagonal wood stand, 81.4cms high. **£530-580** C

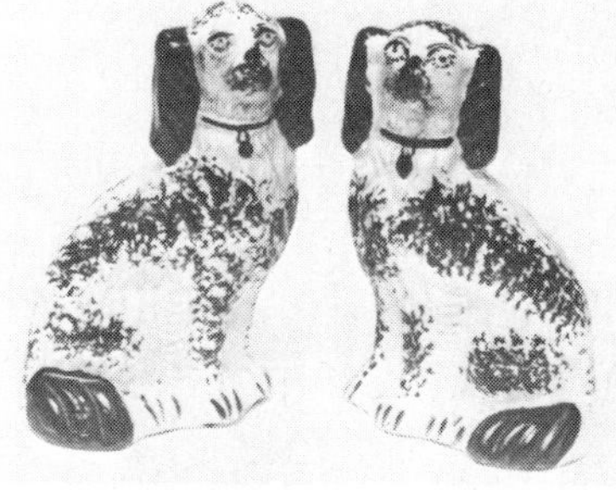

A Good Pair of South Wales Dogs, c. 1870, 7½ in. high. **£110-120** pr. SA

A pair of green-glazed tilemaker's pottery figures of Qilin (chipped), late Ming/Qing Dynasty, 9¾" (25cms) high. **£110-150** C

A fine Arita blue and white globular bottle vase painted with an overall takokarakusa design, 18th C. **£530-600** C

A tilemaker's pottery figure of a three-clawed dragon (some restoration), Qing Dynasty, 23" (58.5cms) long. **£110-150** C

A Pair of Late 19th C. Pottery Elephants. **£150-180** pr. RB

A pair of green glazed tilemaker's pottery figures of dragons (with some damage), late Ming/Qing Dynasty, 9¾" (25cms) wide. **£77-87** C

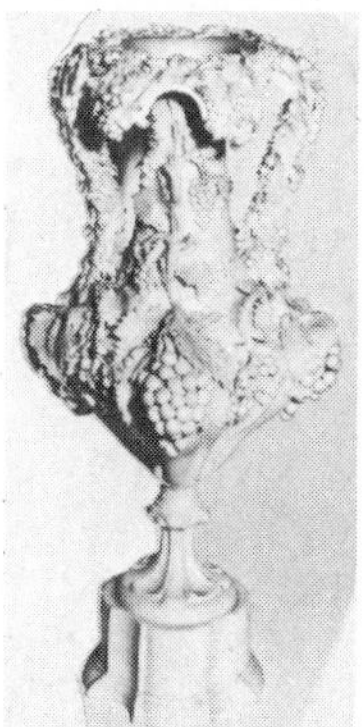

A Samuel Alcock Parian Vase, with encrusted grape vines 13 in. high. **£150-170** MN

An Interesting Awata Oviform Tokkuri with a finely crackled cream glaze decorated in underglaze-blue, and blue enamel (small chip on foot rim) impressed mark Taizan, probably 3rd or 4th generation, early 19th C. 13.2 cm. high. **£260-300** C

inscribed Kangxi renzi Zhonghe Tang zhi (made for the hall of Middle Harmony in the ren-zi year of Kangxi) date 1672. C

encircled Xuande six-character mark, early Qing Dynasty. C

encircled Kanxi six-character mark. C

A Pair of Cantonese large baluster Vases, 24" high. **£500-580** DH

A Pair of late 19th C. Cantonese Vases, 2 ft. ½ in. high. **£540-620** OL

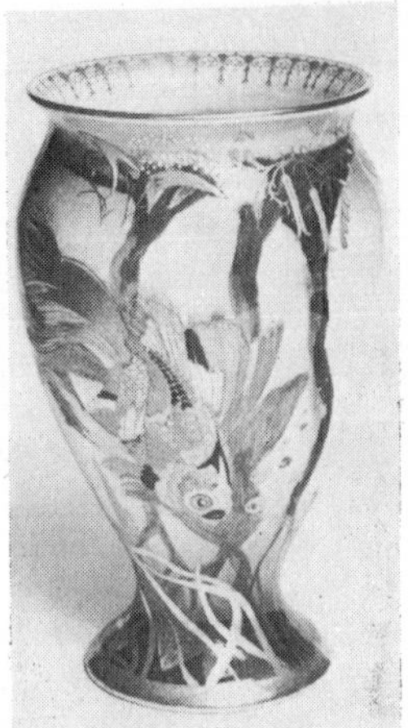

A Carlton-ware Vase with fish, c1920, 6¼" **£75-85**

A Pair of Cantonese Vases, late 19th C., 13 in. high. **£230-260** VA

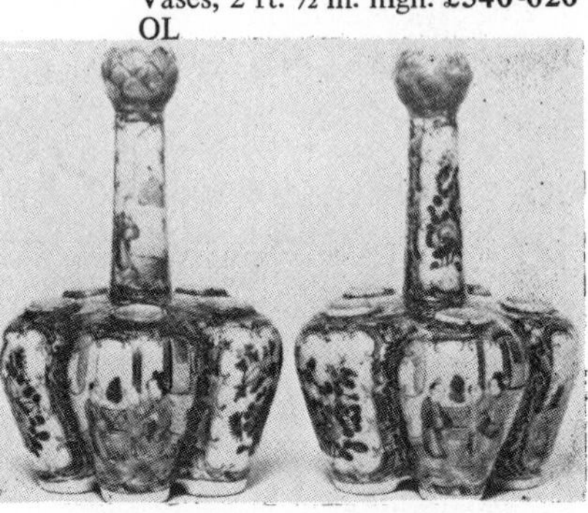

A Pair of Canton Quintal Vases, enamelled and gilt, 31 cm. painted four character mark of Qianlong (Ch'ien-lung), late 19th C. **£300-330** SB

A Carlton Ware Lustre Vase with dark blue ground, 10 in. high. **£70-80** CA

A Pair of Canton Vases, each with a simulated linen-fold neck and faintly ribbed body, 64.5 cm., c. 1900. **£1,250-1,300** SB SBe

A Pair of Carlton-ware Vases with butterflies, c1910, 6¾". **£90-100**

A Carlton Ware Lustre Vase with kingfisher on powder blue ground 10½ in., 1930's. **£70-80** CA

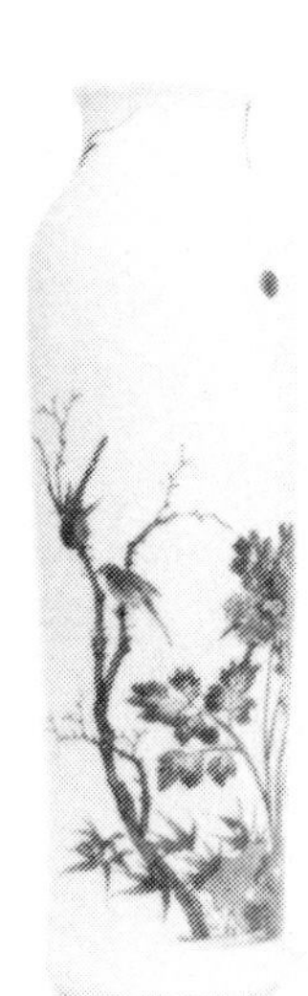

A transitional blue and white sleeve vase (cracked), c1640, 11" (28.5cms) high. **£130-150** C

A lavender-blue glazed rectangular vase (fritted, slightly chipped) unencircled Xuande six-character mark, 18th C., 13¼ in., 33.5 cm. high. **£700-750** C

A Ch'ing Blue and White baluster Vase (yen-yen), 18" (46cms), K'ang Hsi (small hair crack on neck). **£450-500** SKC

A Ch'ing Blue and White yen-yen vase, 17½" (44.5cms), K'ang Hsi (frit chips on rim). **£355-400** SKC

A late Ming blue and white hexagonal double-gourd vase (cracked and chipped, the waist repaired), late 16th C, 20" (51cms) high. **£600-650** C

A Qing pale celadon-ground baluster vase painted in underglaze-blue, copper-red and white slip (the base chipped), Kangxi, wood cover and stand. 9¾ in., 24.5 cm. **£400-450** C

Two Famille-Verte Vases, each of gu (ku) form with raised central panels of archaic vessels and characters, wavy scroll-decorated rim, 30.5 cm., mid 19th C. **£250-300** SB

A Ming Celadon Yanyan vase, with a widely crackled translucent olive glaze (cracked, the rim possibly reduced), 16th/17th C, wood stand, 16" (40cms) high. **£190-230** C

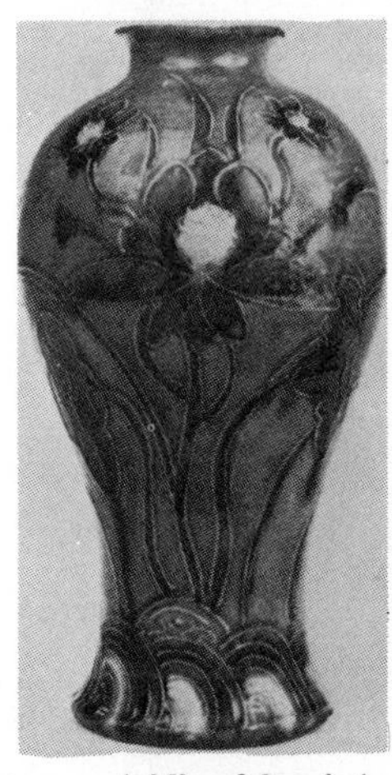

A Ming fahua baluster vase on a turquoise ground (restored, the handles removed) late 15th/16th C., 13¼ in., 33.5 cm. high. **£440-520** C

A Pair of Wucai (Wu-Ts'ai) Vases, 32 cm., early 19th C. **£530-600** SB SBe

A Pair of Famille-Verte Vases, lion mask and ring handles, 46.2 cm., late 19th C. **£700-750** SB SBe

A Famille-Rose Vase, 44.5 cm., fitted for electricity, c. 1880. **£170-200** SB SBe

A Chinese Pottery Vase, lacquered and gilt on a black ground, 32½ in., 82.5 cm. **£320-400** L

A Chinese Large Vase of cylindrical form decorated in 'famille verte' enamels. 34¾ in., 88.2 cm. **£600-700** L

A Tall Chinese Beaker Shape Vase, painted in underglaze blue, key fret and other borders, small rim crack, K'ang Hsi, 25¼ in., 64.5 cm., on wood stand **£280-340** L

A Pair of Powder-Blue-Ground Famille-Verte Vases, 45.5 cm., late 19th C. **£675-700** SB

A Chinese vase of compressed spherical form painted in underglaze blue, six character mark of Ch'eng Hua but K'ang Hsi, 15¼ in., 38.5 cm., **£210-250** L

A Pair of Chinese Famille Rose Vases, each ovoid body brightly painted, 46 cm., mid 19th C., damaged. **£540-600** S Be

A Pair of Large Blue and White Vases painted with dragons with 'Three Friends' borders, 53 cm. and 53.5 cm., mid 19th C. **£1,750-1,800** SB SBe

A Pair of Blue and White Vases, 35.5 cm. incised four character mark of Chenghua (Ch'eng-hua), late 19th C. **£280-340** SB

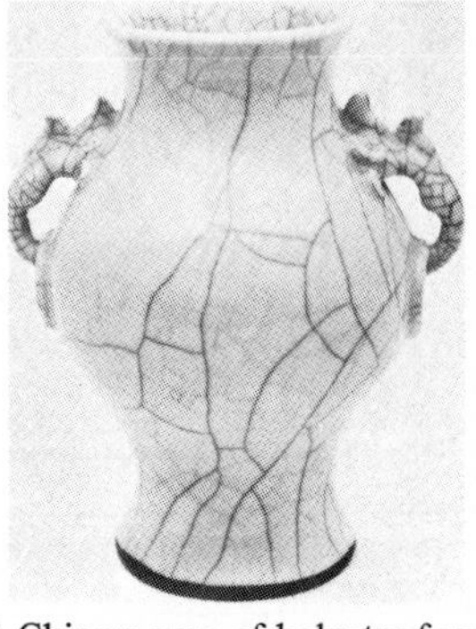

A Chinese vase of baluster form with moulded mask and ring handles, all covered in a pale celadon crackled glaze, 19th C. 10½ in., 25.5 cm. **£50-65** L

A Clarice Cliff Mask Hanging Vase. **£45-50** AP

A Coalport Campana Vase, c. 1870, 10 in. high. **£265-290** MJ

A Continental porcelain art Nouveau vase, 16". **£170-190** WHL

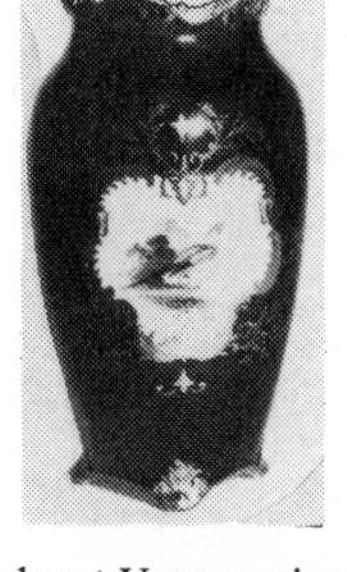

A Coalport Vase, unsigned, 6¼ in., c. 1910. **£95-100** MN

A 19th C. Delft Vase, 9½ in. high. **£160-180** SA

A Coalport Vase, signed Ball, 4½ in., c. 1910's. **£115-125** MN

A Coalport Trumpet-shape vase. 5 in., 13.6 cm. **£110-150** L

A Dutch Blue and White Delft baluster Vase, painted in Chinese Transitional style, 10¼" (26cms), leaf mark, late 17th C (chipped). **£300-350** SKC

A Coalport Spill Vase, painted with Dr. Syntax. 4 in., 10.4 cm. **£65-75** L

A Pair of Coalport Vases in naturalistic colours on a speckled ground, 26 cm., printed mark in green, late 19th C. some damage. **£260-290** S Be

A Pair of Dutch Delft small baluster vases, painted in blue with brass covers. 18th C., 6 in., 15.2 cm. **£70-80** pr. L

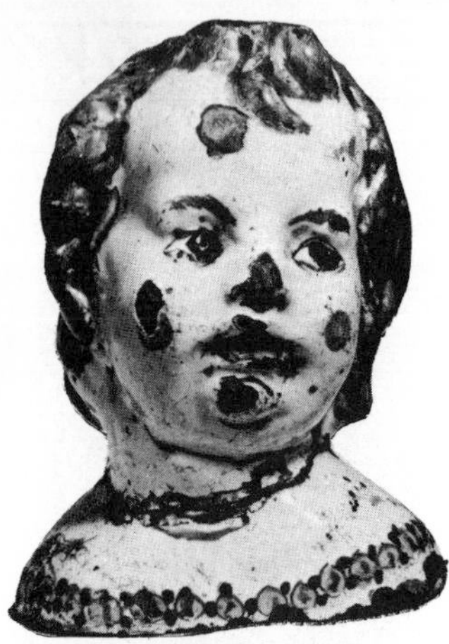
A London Delft Dated Polychrome Flower-Vase, the base inscribed TCE 1685 (neck cracked through and re-stuck, glaze flaking) 16.5 cm. high. **£850-950** C

A Crown Derby Miniature Vase, c. 1910, 3¼ in. **£75-83** MJ

A Crown Derby Miniature Vase, c. 1910, 3½ in. **£80-90** MJ

A Derby Campana Vase, c. 1910, 5½ in. **£310-350** MJ

A Pair of Derby Eel-Basket Vases, gold anchor marks, c. 1765, 24 cm. high. **£500-800** C

A Derby Campana with Stand, jewelled and gilded, 6 in., c. 1900. **£325-400** MN

A Crown Derby Miniature Vase, c. 1910, 3 in. **£65-70** MJ

A Bloor Derby Campana, 8 in., 1820-1840, rubbed. **£450-500** MN

One of a Pair of Art Nouveau Derby Vases. **£65-75** pr. AP

A Crown Derby Miniature Vase, c. 1910, 3 in. **£72-80** MJ

A Derby Vase with claret ground and raised gilding, 6¾ in., c. 1880. **£195-210** MN

A Set of Three Derby Vases, lobed panels on a dark blue ground gilt with foliage scrolls, with white and gilt swan's neck handles and square bases, 9¼ in., 23.5 cm., and 10¾ in., 27.3 cm. **£180-250** L

A Derby Campana, signed by Albert Gregory, 10 in., c. 1906. **£1,500-1,700** MN

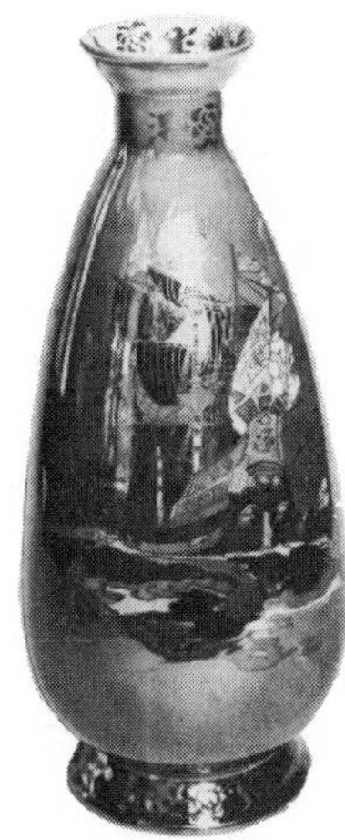

A Crown Devon Lustre Vase with petrol blue ground, 10 in. high. **£65-70** CA

A Crown Devon Lustre Spill Vase with petrol blue ground, slight crack, 9½ in. high. **£17-23** CA

A Devon Sylvan Lustre Vase, signed on mulberry ground with butterflies and gilt, 6½ in., 1930's. **£50-60** CA

A Bloor Derby Vase, painted perhaps by Daniel Lucas, in autumnal palette, 24½ in., printed circular mark in iron-red, c. 1830. **£300-400** S

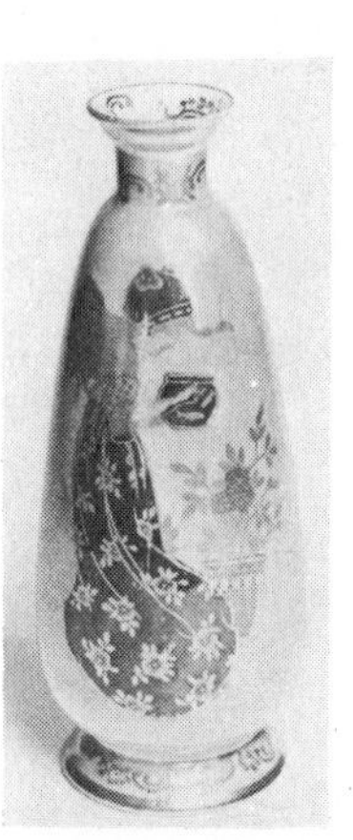

A Devon Lustrine Specimen Vase, with fairy looking into goldfish bowl, the reverse with elf, c1920's, 6". **£70-80**

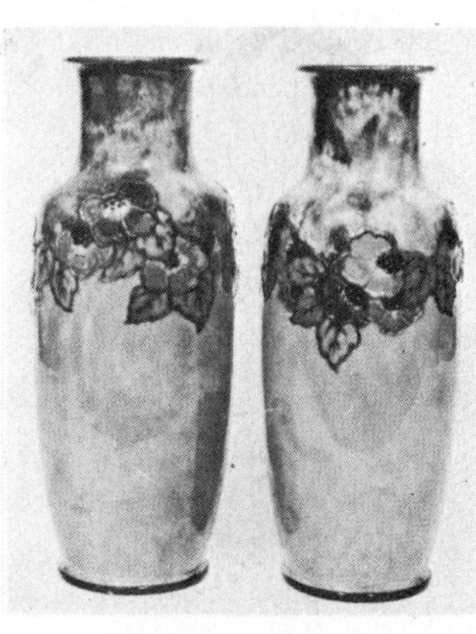

A pair of Royal Doulton Vases by Winnie Bowstead, with pastel blue and brown ground, 12". **£45-60** WHL

POINTERS FOR LUSTRE

- The technique of decorating pottery by depositing a thin metallic film on the surface of the glaze.
- Metals commonly used were gold, platinum, copper and silver.
- Fairyland Lustre - designed for Wedgwood by Daisy Makeig-Jones between 1914-1931, depicting fairies, goblins, and elves. The predominant features of the ware are an irregular blue ground and a markedly iridescent glaze.
- Dragon Lustre - designed for Wedgwood by Daisy Makeig-Jones.
- Carlton-Ware made by Wiltshaw & Robinson Ltd., Stoke on Trent.
- Moonlight Lustre - introduced by Wedgwood in early 19th C. also employed by Turners of Lane End. The gold, grey and pink marbled effect was difficult to produce, consequently examples are relatively rare.
- Sunderland Lustreware - decorated with marbled mauve pink lustre with black transfer prints of popular subjects and often doggerel verse. Made in several potteries.

A Doulton Lambeth Vase, 11 in. high (restored lip), c. 1915. **£30-35** CA

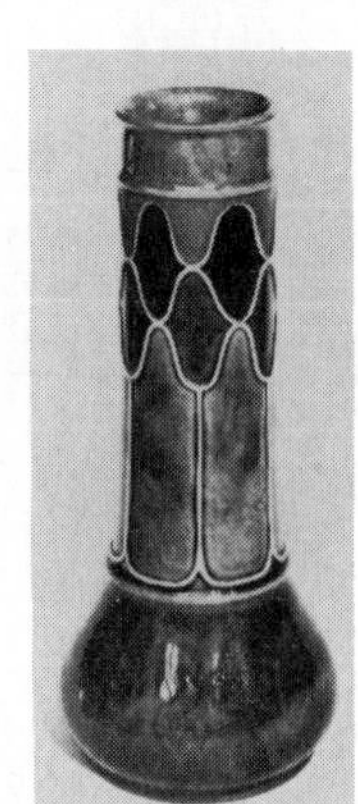

A Royal Doulton Vase, c. 1918. **£22-25** AP

A Doulton & Slater's patent vase decorated in brown, blue-glazed panels and beaded ornament on a patterned white ground, impressed mark. 7 in., 18.4 cm. **£40-50** L

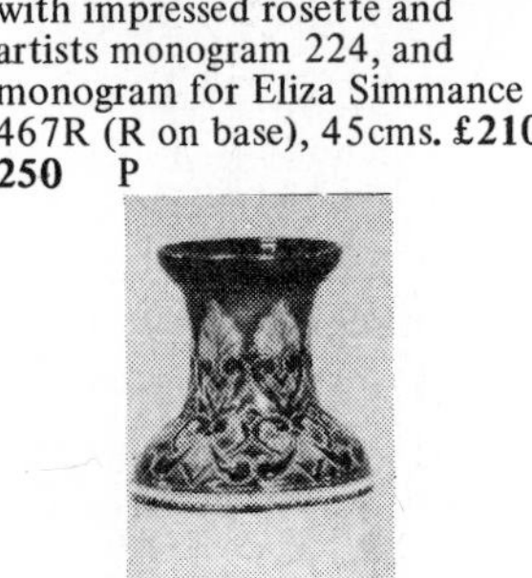

A Doulton Lambeth Baluster Vase, incised by Hannah Barlow, with impressed rosette and artists monogram 224, and monogram for Eliza Simmance 467R (R on base), 45cms. **£210-250** P

A Doulton Lambeth Stoneware Vase by Hannah Barlow, impressed mark Doulton Lambeth, 1886, NC inscribed H.B. **£110-130** PW

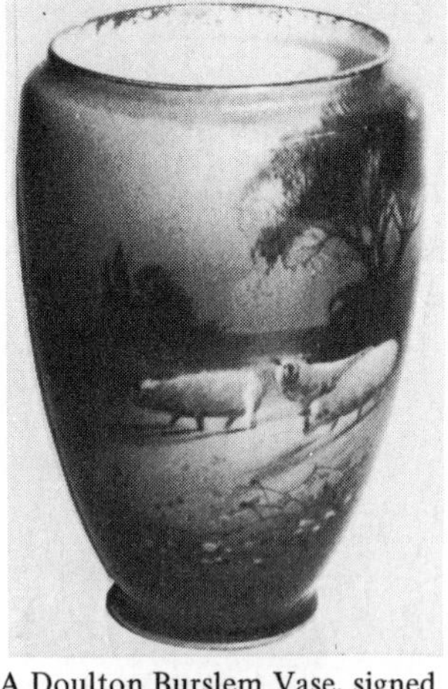

A Doulton Burslem Vase, signed H. Nixon, slight chip in rim. **£25-30** perfect **£40-45** CSG

POINTERS FOR DOULTON

- Doulton (Lambeth London)
- Stoneware Pottery founded by John Doulton (1793-1873)
- 1815 formed partnership with John Watts specializing in saltglaze stoneware and terracotta.
- 1854 Watts retired and the firm renamed Doulton & Company.
- 1860 Henry Doulton employed artists from the Lambeth School of Art who were permitted to sign or mark their work.
- 1872 Introduction of Lambeth Faience.
- 1880-1912 Silicon Ware was produced.
- The Doulton factory moved to Burslem Staffordshire in 1882.

- The most celebrated Doulton Artists:-
- Hannah Barlow 1872-1906 ( )
- George Tinworth 1867-1913 ( )
- Florence Barlow 1873-1909 ( )
- Arthur Barlow 1872-79 ( )

A Pair of Doulton Oviform Vases decorated by Hannah Barlow, incised artist's monogram and impressed marks, 17 cm. high. **£240-280** C

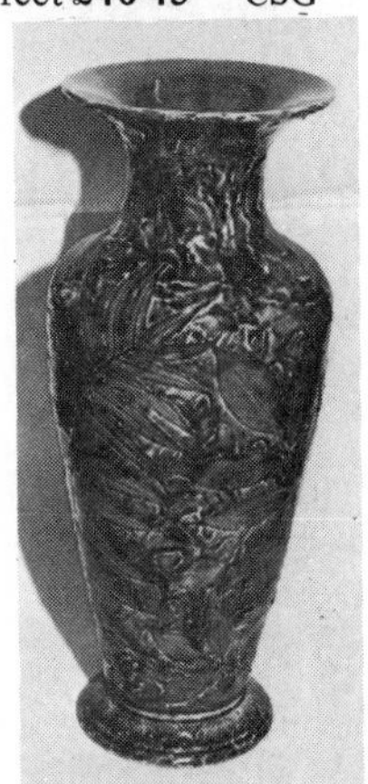

A Tall Vase, possibly Royal Doulton, 15½ in. high, c. 1930's. **£65-70** CA

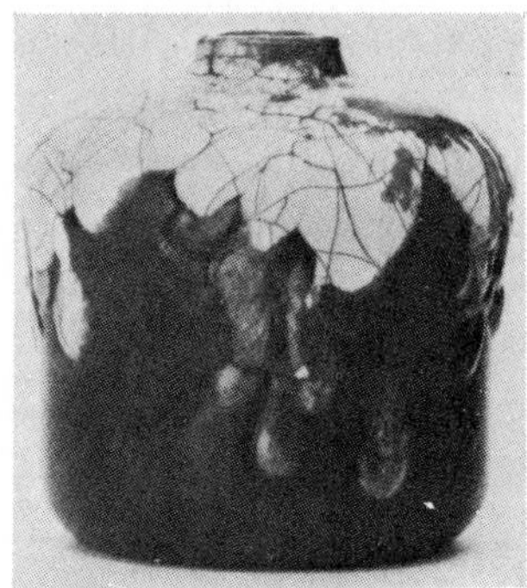

right

A Royal Doulton Chang Vase, by Charles Noke and Henry Nixon, in white, green and red on a mottled flambe ground, 14.6 cm. marked, impressed 7880, c. 1930. **£560-620** S Be

A Pair of Royal Doulton Vases, 14 in. high, c. 1930's. **£52-60** pr. CA

A Pair of Doulton Lambeth Stoneware Vases by George Tinworth and Eliza Hubert, 30.5 cm., impressed and incised marks, dated 1878. **£200-230** S Be

A Good Royal Doulton pear-shaped 'Chang' Vase, 41cms high, signed Noke, monogram for Harry Nixon and marked 'Sung'. **£500-550** P

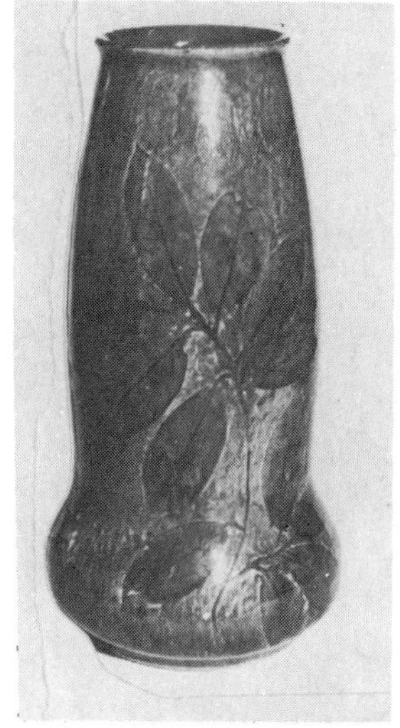

A Royal Doulton Vase with autumnal colours, 8 in. high, c. 1930's. **£25-30** CA

A Pair of Royal Doulton Vases by Emma Shute, incised and decorated in pale and dark blue glazes, artist's monogram, impressed marks and incised Art Union of London. 21 cm. high. **£140-160** C

A Doulton Lambeth Stoneware Vase with Arabic design, decorators mark Monogram LEW, assistants mark F, with lid, 13¼". **£120-140** WHL

A Royal Doulton stoneware vase by Eliza Simmance, painted in the art nouveau manner, green, blue and brown, 46 cm., impressed and incised marks, c. 1910. **£140-170** S Be

Hannah Barlow, A Royal Doulton Vase, with a mottled blue, grey and brown ground, incised BHB monogram and impressed mark. 11½ in., 28.8 cm. **£150-180** L

A pair of late Victorian German Vases with child artist figures, 7 in. high. **£25-30** pr. PC

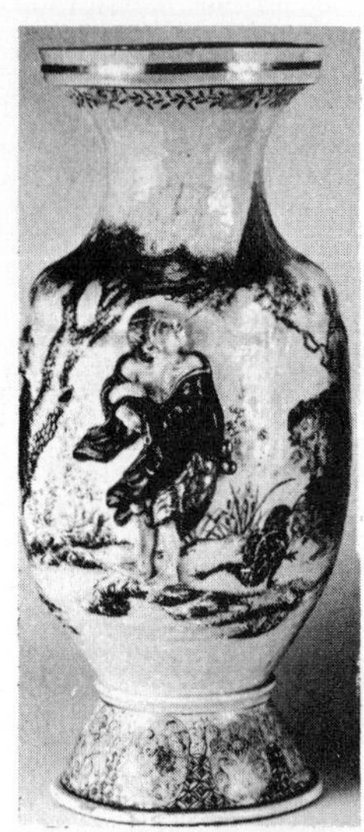

A pair of 19th C Japanese cream glazed vases, 56cms high. **£185-220** SH

A Japanese Imari Vase, the body lightly moulded with ribs, 16 in., c. 1900. **£90-110** SBA

A Pair of 19th C. Japanese Vases 10½ in. high. **£120-145** pr. CC

A fine Kaga globular bottle vase painted on a hatched-pattern ground, the base with a fuku mark, early 19th C, 36cms high. **£500-550** C

A Pair of Kyoto Slender Oviform Vases signed Choshuzan below a Shimazu mon. Meiji period, 36.4 cm. high. **£550-650** C

JAPANESE PORCELAIN

五良大甫
吳祥瑞造

ARITA (Hizen province) Gorodayu Go Shonzui. After 1510.

倣余祖先祥瑞
五良大甫所製

ARITA (Hizen province) Shonzui Gorodayu (imitation). 19th cent.

A pair of Imari bottle vases, early 18th C. 23.4cm high. **£1,400-1,600 pr.** C

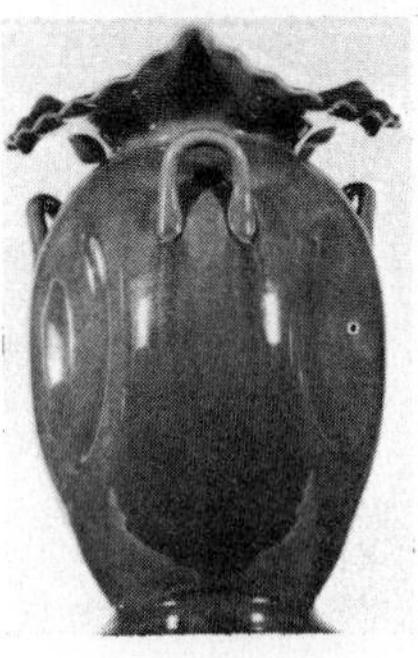

A Linthorpe Pottery Vase, the dimpled Oviform Body in a streaked ochre glaze with olive green rim and traces of dark brown, 9¾ in. high impressed Linthorpe 1677. **£30-35** CSK

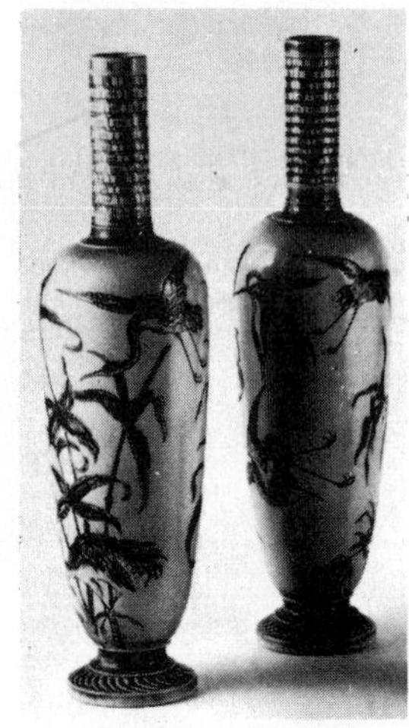

A pair of Martinware Vases, 36cms. **£490-530** SH

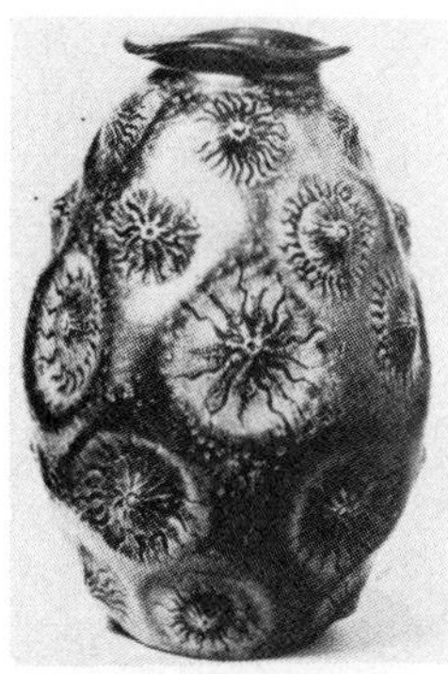
An unusual Martin Brothers oviform Vase, 23.5cms high, incised Martin Bros. London and Southall, 9-1894. **£250-300** P

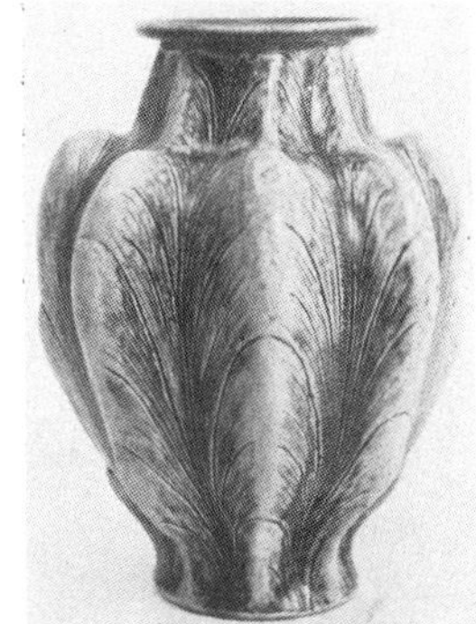
A Martin-Ware Vase, in brown on a light grey ground signed, 1906 10 in., 25.4 cm. **£200-280** L

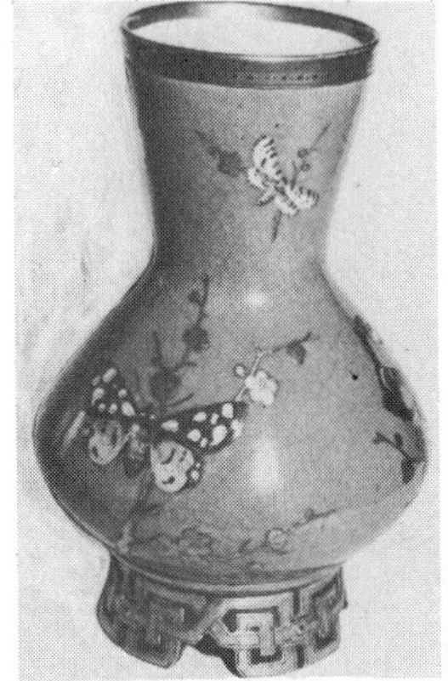
A Minton Vase in the Oriental Style with turquoise ground with butterflies and moths, 8 in. high, c. 1860, marked. **£85-95** CA

A Martin-Ware Vase, incised and decorated in cream and tones of brown. 9½ in., 14 cm. signed 1893. **£85-105** L

A pair of early ironstone campana shaped flower Vases and Ewers, decorated with tooled gilding on a deep cobalt blue ground, 10", 1815, probably Mason's factory. **£320-360** SH

An attractive Moorcroft 'Hazeldene' Vase of albarello form, with buttercup ground, 16cms high, signed W. Moorcroft des., on base. **£220-250** P

A Martin-ware small vase with mottled pinkish and greenish tones, signed 1904. 5½ in., 14 cm. **£85-100** L

A Mennecy Inverted-Baluster Pot-Pourri Vase painted in blue, manganese, yellow and green, on a pierced rockwood base (repaired chips), D.V. mark, 1755 14 cm., high **£300-350** C

A Moorcroft Two-Handled Bulbous Vase, painted in blue and light olive green, 7½ in. high, green painted signature W. Moorcroft Des, shape design No. 360576, Registered by Macintyre in July 1900. **£320-360** CSK

A Martinware Shaped Square Vase in pale brown and blue on a watery ground, enriched in green, incised Martin Bros., London & Southall, 11-1904, 12.5 cm. high. **£170-200** C

A Minton Spill Vase, oriental style, 9 in. high, c. 1860. **£85-95** CA

A De Morgan Copper-Lustre Vase (very small chip to rim) impressed flame mark, 10 cm. high. **£50-60** C

A De Morgan Lustre Vase decorated by Joe Juster, enriched in a golden lustre (slight rim chip) J. J. and W. De Morgan, Fulham printed marks, 27.5 cm. high. **£200-250** C

A Pair of Nantgarw Vases, painted with roses, c. 1815. **£550-600** pr. SA

A Nottingham Brown-Glazed Vase, thistle shape, incised, with a band of beading round the centre, 10½ in., 26.7 cm., 1791 **£185-250** L

A Pilkington Royal Lancastrian lustre oviform Vase, painted by William Salter Mycock, 28.5cms high, impressed marks and signed W.S.M. in monogram, 1927. **£240-280** P

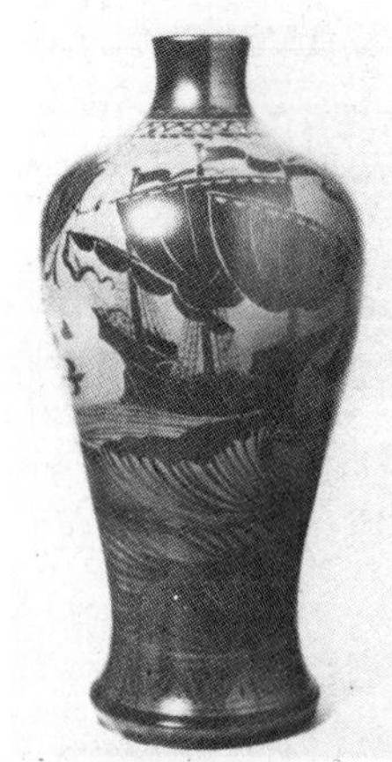

A Good Pilkington 'Royal Lançastrian' Baluster Vase, painted by W. S. Mycock in silver lustre and red. Impressed rosette mark and artists monogram, date code for 1913, 25cms high. **£290-360** P

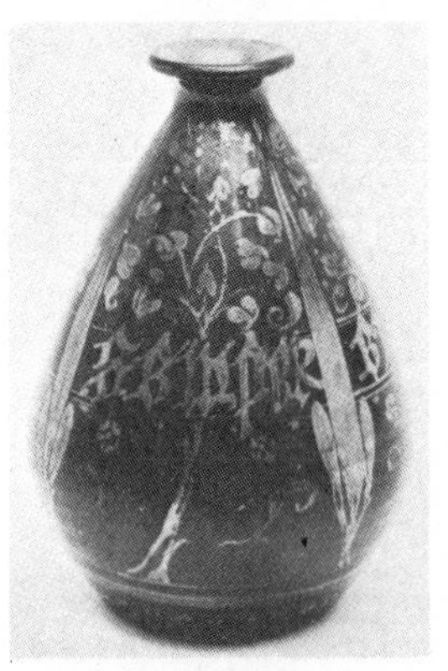

A Pilkington's Vase, decorated in gold lustre on a shaded dark blue ground, by Gordon M. Forsyth. 7 in., 17.7 cm. **£95-110** L

An attractive Rozenburg twin-handled pottery Vase, painted in violet, blues, greens, yellows and browns with a batik-style, 27.5cms high, painted factory marks and anchor date code for 1899. **£800-850** P

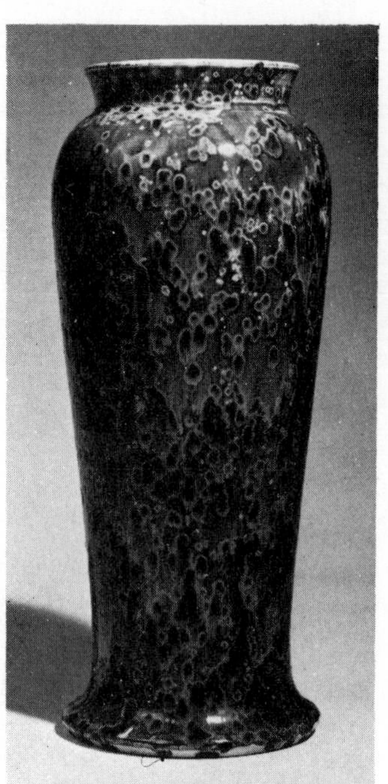

A Ruskin 'HIGHFIRED' Slender oviform Vase covered in a mottled green, blue and sang-de-boeuf glaze, impressed Ruskin, England, 31.5 cm. high. **£500-560** C

A Satsuma globular vase, late 19th C, 31.2cms high. **£440-500** C

A 19th C. Japanese Satsuma Vase, 1¾ in. high. **£24-28** SV

A 19th C. Japanese Satsuma Vase, 2½ in. high. **£20-23** SV

A pair of 19th C. Japanese Satsuma Vases, 2 in. high. **£60-65** pr. SV

A Satsuma Slender Oviform Vase, signed Satsuma yaki Genzan below a Shimazu mon. 19th C., 17.6 cm. high. **£280-360** C

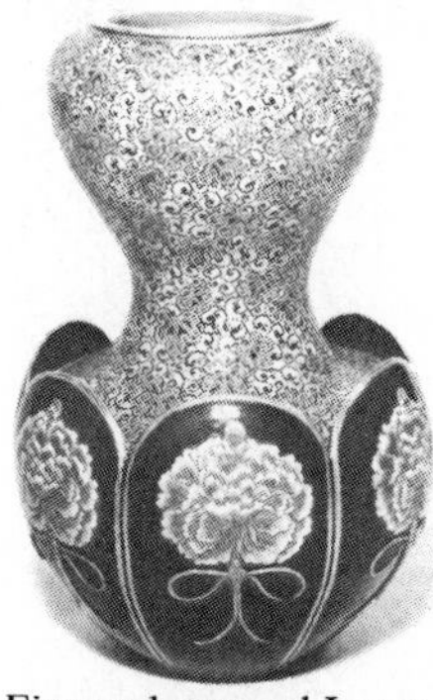

A Fine and unusual Large Satsuma Globular Vase painted in iron-red and gilt on a blue ground with tasselled peony (small crack) with an impressed signature. 19th C., 56.5 cm. high. **£1,800-2,000** C

A Fine Satsuma Oviform Vase, the neck with a row of Shimazu mon above a band of hanabishi design, signed on the base Satsuma yaki below a blue Shimazu mon. 19th C., 36 cm. high. **£820-950** C

A Pair of Satsuma Pottery Vases of hexagonal baluster form, enamelled and gilt on a deep blue ground heightened with a design in gold, 26.5 cm., mid 19th C. **£230-260** S Be

A Pair of Satsuma Vases, 36.8 cm., late 19th C., chip to rim. **£300-330** S Be

right

A Toshikata earthenware Vase, painted in heavy enamels and gilding 24 cm., signed Toshikata with red seals, 2nd half 19th C. **£240-280** SKC

A Satsuma Vase, the ovoid body enamelled and gilt, height 31 cm., late 19th C. **£350-450** S Be

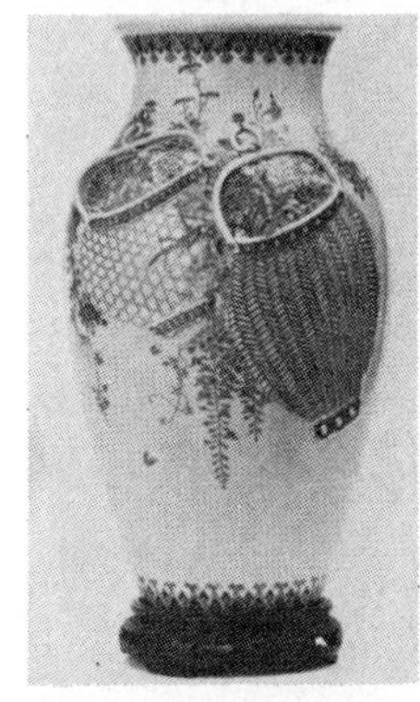

A Satsuma Vase, the ovoid body painted, the neck and base with blue and green bands, height 30.5 cm., painted marks, late 19th C., hair crack. **£260-290** S Be

A Pair of Vases, Torquay ware. **£19-22** NO

A Pair of 'Vienna' Vases, printed blue shield, painted Erbluth, Reflexion, Depose, late 19th C., 11.5 cm. **£360-400** SB

A Pair of Vienna Vases, painted with maroon and gilt borders and gilt scroll handles, shield mark. 22 in., 56 cm. **£370-430** pr. L

A Royal Vienna Shell Vase 7 in., c. 1900. **£175-200** PC

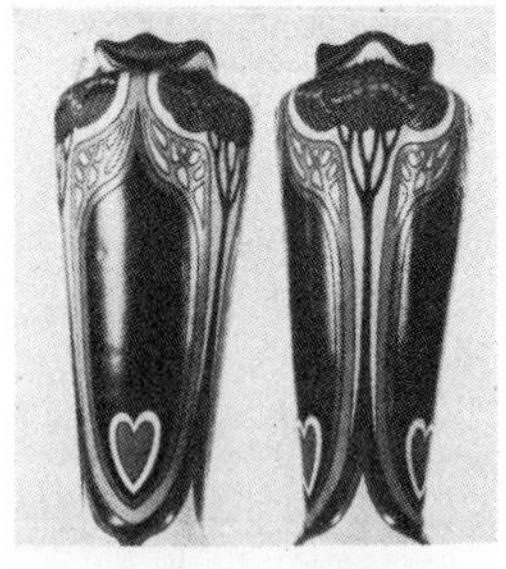

A Pair of Villeroy and Boch, Mettlach Vases, 14½ in. high, impressed Mettlach mark 2909. **£350-420** CSK

A Charles Vyse Stoneware Vase, with a rich celadon glaze, incised CV 1930, 27.50cms. **£180-210** P

A Pair of Watcombe Terracotta Two-Handled Vases, height 26.5 cm., late 19th C. **£160-190**S Be

A Wedgwood 'Dana' Fairyland Lustre Vase, printed urn mark, Z5125, 1920's, 19cms. **£360-400** SBe

left

A Wedgwood fairyland lustre beaker vase, printed mark. 11 in., 28.5 cm. **£480-560** L

A Wedgwood Portland Vase with black jasper dip body, impressed Wedgewood, late 19th C, 15.3cms. **£90-100** SBe

POINTERS FOR WEDGWOOD

- Josiah Wedgwood 1730-1795 gave a new direction to the potteries of England and of the civilised world.
- The factory employed the mark WEDGWOOD impressed since 18th C. together with large number of ancillary marks.
- Since 1878 bone china has been marked with a replica of the Portland Vase.
- The words Made in England added after 1891 to satisfy American Tariff regulations.
- Manufacturers of earthenware, basaltes, jaspers, porcelains, parian, majolica etc.

A Wedgwood Black Basalt copy of the Portland or Barberini Vase (slight chip to foot and cracks to relief) unmarked, early 19th C. 27 cm. high. **£420-500** C

A Wilton Ware Lustre Vase, on four gilt pad legs, 7½ in., 1930's. **£60-65** CA

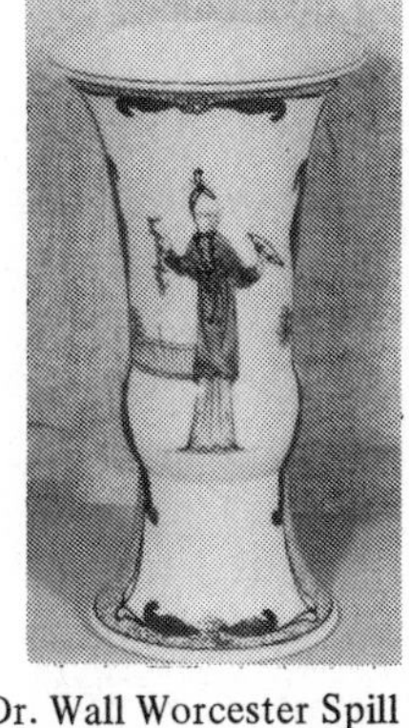

A Dr. Wall Worcester Spill Vase, painted in Chinoiserie, c. 1760. **£350-380** SA

A Royal Worcester Vase painted with a landscape, signed Harry Davis, 1900. **£600-660** SA

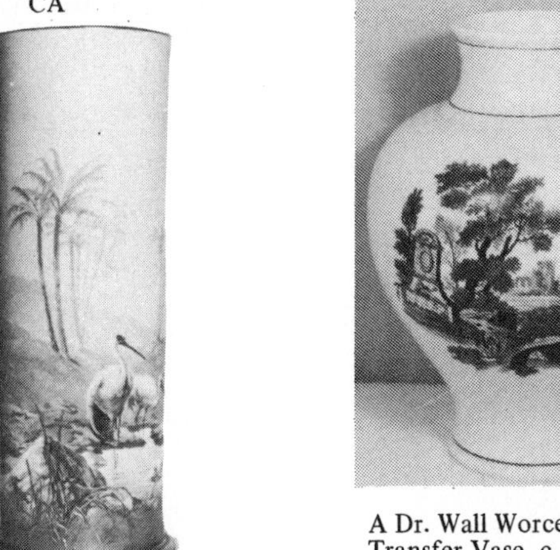

A Royal Worcester hand-painted Vase 10½ in. Reticulated base, 1912, **£500-600** PC

A Dr. Wall Worcester Colour Transfer Vase, c. 1760. **£400-440** SA

A Worcester Vase with lizard handle on gold and cream ground, 11 in. high, c. 1865. **£160-180** CA

A Dr. Wall Worcester Vase, painted with Japanese decoration, c. 1760. **£300-340** SA

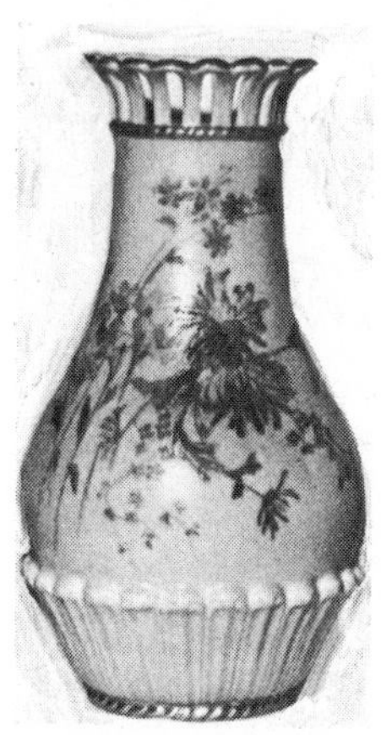

Royal Worcester Cabinet piece with satin finish with hand-painted floral design G. 1061 date 1901. **£65-70** PC

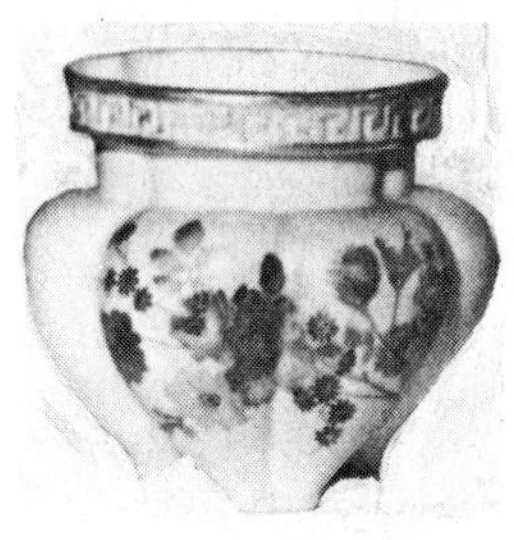

Royal Worcester cabinet piece with satin wear finish with painted floral design 1897 shape no. 1907. **£55-60** PC

left

Three Chamberlain Worcester Spill Vases. l) painted with a figure **£200-220** m) painted with feathers by Baxter **£500-560** r) painted with flowers on yellow ground **£200-220** SA

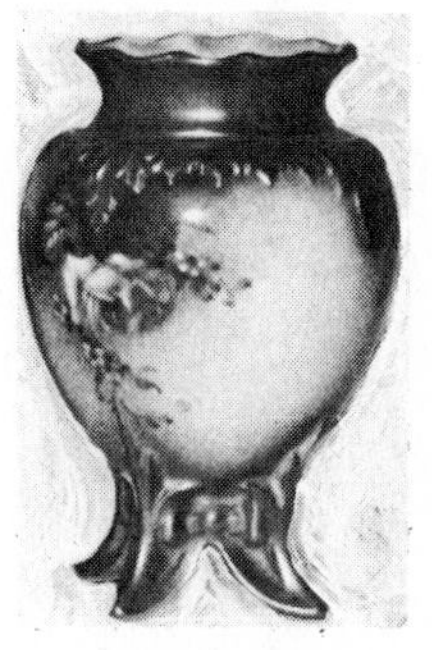

Hadleys Royal Worcester cabinet piece p. No. H230 1904. **£65-70** PC

Royal Worcester Cabinet piece with satin wear finish, with hand-painted floral design pattern No. G790 1905. **£50-55** PC

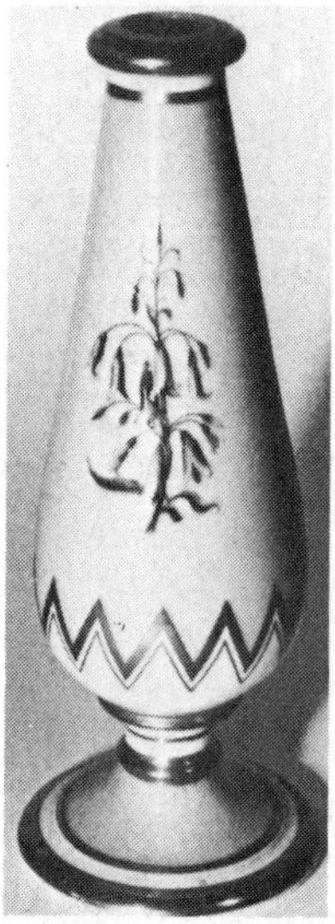

A Royal Worcester ivory ground Vase, 12½". **£160-190** PWC

A Royal Worcester ovoid vase, on three gilt mask and scroll feet, 5 in., 13 cm., unmarked. **£15-25** L

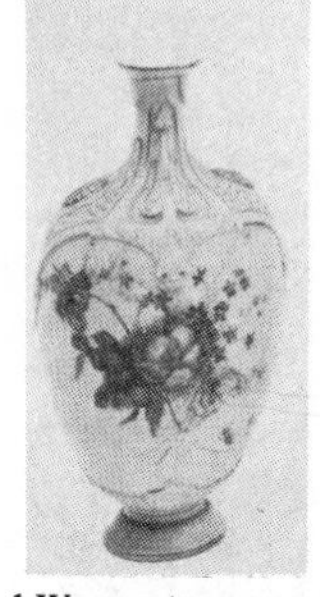

A Royal Worcester vase, on a shaded apricot ground, 8 in., 20.3 cm., printed mark in puce, no. 1625 **£60-80** L

A Flight, Barr & Barr Spill Vase with green ground, 6 in. high, c. 1800. **£125-150** SA

A Royal Worcester Two Handled Vase of Persian inspiration, height 40 cm., printed mark and date code 1890. **£360-400** S Be

A Royal Worcester vase, on a shaded apricot ground, on square base with re-entrant corners, 9 in., 22.8 cm., printed mark in green, 1903 **£120-140** L

A Pair of Worcester Vases, signed by James Stinton, with pheasants, 6 in. high, c. 1933. **£425-500** pr. MN

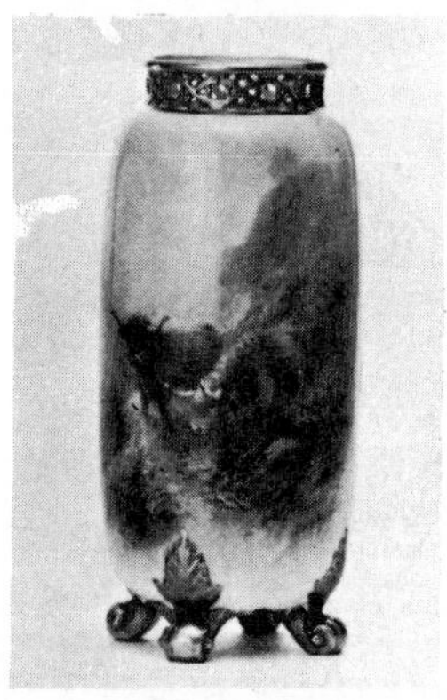

A Pair of Royal Worcester Vases, painted by Harry Stinton, height 15 cm., printed mark, 1926. **£480-520** S Be

A Large Zolnay Vase, marked, c1900, 19" high. **£120-140** SAL

An Art Deco Lustre Vase, c. 1920. **£33-36** AP

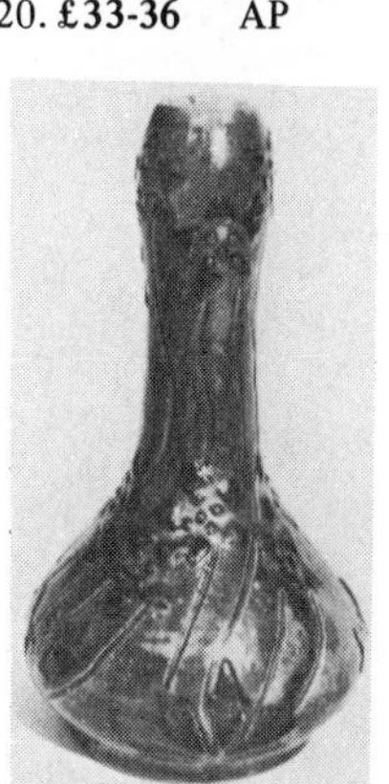
An Art Nouveau Vase, c. 1910. **£8-10** AP

A Pair of Art Nouveau 'Foley' Vases, c. 1895. **£55-60** pr. AP

An Art Nouveau Vase 'Torquay', c. 1910. **£33-36** AP

A Pair of Art Deco Vases on bright yellow ground with birds of paradise, 11 in. high. **£40-50** pr. SHA

A pair of pear-shaped bottle vases (chipped, one cracked) early 18th C., 9 in., 23 cm. high. **£200-225** C

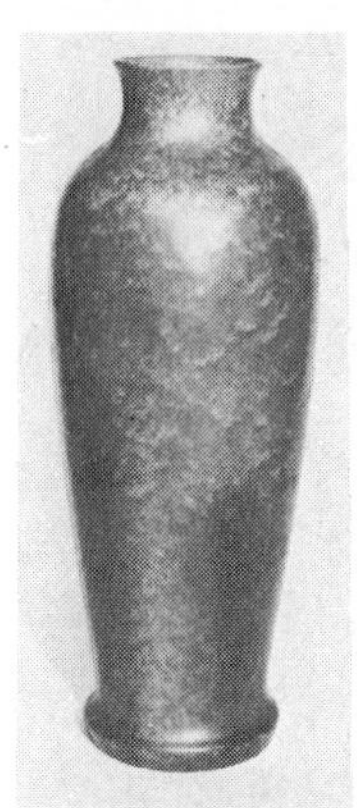
An Art Deco Lancaster Vase, 1920's. **£40-45** AP

A Pair of Adam Urns and Covers, signed George Jones, depicting the four seasons, (fine example), 11 in. high, Tunstall, 1847. **£350-375** pair MN

A Pair of Canton Vases and Covers, the handles in the form of Kuan Yin, 58 cm., c. 1820. **£1,430-1,540** SB SBe

A Pair of Large Canton Vases and Covers, the domed lids now applied with brass hinges, 63 cm., mid 19th C. **£1,650-1,750** SB SBe

A Large Canton Jar and Cover, on a gilt and green scroll ground, 66 cm., c. 1870. **£640-680** SB SBe

A Pair of Blue and White Vases and Covers, 38.5 cm., painted four character mark of Kangxi (K'ang-hsi), late 19th C. **£200-250** SB

A Pair of Coalport Vases and Covers, one cover restored, 13 in. high, c. 1910. **£650-730** pr. MN

A Derby Vase and Cover, pink ground, torquoise jewelling, raised gilding, 9½ in., c. 1888. **£650-700** MN

A good Meissen pot-pourri vase and cover, 18 cm., crossed swords marks in underglaze blue, c. 1755-60 **£450-500** SKC

A Coalport Vase with Cover, signed P. Simpson, 6½ in., c. 1910. **£195-220** MN

A Pair of Grainger Vases, 4¾ in. high, c. 1875. **£395-420** pr. MN

A Pair of Famille-Rose Vases and Covers, 48 cm., late 19th C. **£570-650** SB SBe

A Crown Derby two-handled Vase, c. 1910, 11 in. high. **£150-170** MJ

An Imari fluted baluster vase and domed cover with large knop finial, inscribed on the base Shogantei sei, 19th C, 54cms high. **£600-650** C

A Pair of Mintons Vases and Covers, with pate sur pate decoration, by A. Birks. Gilt crowned orb and Mintons mark England. 12 in., 30.5 cm. **£940-1,050** pr. L

A Derby Boat-Shaped Vase and Cover, signed Charles Harris, 6½ in. wide, c. 1896. **£750-820** MN

left

Two Japanese Imari Vases and Covers, each shouldered ovoid body moulded with ribs, decorated in iron-red and under-glaze-blue, 14 in., c. 1900, one cover chipped, other cover's knop been off. **£170-190** SBA

A Minton Vase and Cover, 7½ in., c. 1910. **£165-185** MN

A Pilkington's Royal Lancastrian Vase and Cover, by Gordon M. Forsyth, 9¼ in. high. **£140-160** CSK

A Good 19th C. Potschappel Marriage Vase lavishly decorated in polychrome enamels and gilding, underglaze blue Carl Thieme mark, impressed 787 3 ft. high. **£900-1,000** OL

A 19th C. Japanese Satsuma Vase, 6½ in. high, with cover, **£220-250** SV

A Small Satsuma Hexagonal Koro, the pierced shallow domed cover with karashishi finial, signed Satsuma yaki below a blue Shimazu mon, 19th C., 13.4 cm. high. **£520-600** C

A Pair of unusual Helena Wolfsohn Vases and covers, underglaze blue AR monogram, late 19th C., 38 cm. **£240-300** SB

A Royal Worcester Staff Commemorative Vase with Cover, in stipple red and gilt 6½ in. high, 1st World War. **£125** approx. PC

A Worcester Pair of Vases and Covers, green ground, signed by H. Chair, 9 in. high, c. 1902. **£695-750** pair MN

A Good Worcester Pot Pourri Vase, hand painted with roses and gold leaf, interior lid and crown openwork cover, 13 in. high. **£400-500** OL

A Large Arita Blue and White Mokko-shaped Bowl, 18th C. **£400-500** C

An Eastern Market Canton Bowl, the exterior with a gilt inscription, 40 cm., dated AH 1297 (A.D.1882) **£715-750** SB SBe

A blue and white armorial bowl (extensively repaired), encircled zhi seal mark, Kangxi 13 in., 33 cm. diam. **£110-150** C

A famille rose armorial hunting bowl (chipped), the porcelain and interior decoration Qianlong, the exterior decoration possibly European 10½ in., 26.5 cm. diam. **£420-450** C

A Bristol Blue and White Punch Bowl, the centre with three men working, 12 in., c. 1740, cracked, foot repaired. **£850-1,000** S

A Carlton Ware Lustre Bowl on dark blue ground, with death's head hawk moth, 5 in. high. **£70-80** CA

A pair of blue and white bowls (one damaged), encircled Chenghua six-character marks, Kangxi, 6" (15.5cms) diam. **£285-325** C

A Byzanta Ware Lustre Bowl, signed Ausin, with cuckaburras and humming birds (probably made for Australian market) 9 in., diam., c. 1930's. **£60-70** CA

A famille rose punch-bowl (restored) Qianlong, 15½ in., 39.5 cm. diam. **£175-220** C

An Ormolu-Mounted Canton Bowl of lozenge shape, the exterior brightly enamelled and gilt with bands, 44 cm., overall, mid 19th C. **£420-480** SB SBe

A pair of famille verte cafe-au-lait ground bowls (chipped, one cracked), encircled flower marks, Kangxi 6¼ in., 15.5 cm. diam. **£190-240** C

A late Ming blue and white bowl (chipped, minor foot crack) early 17th C. 4 in., 10 cm. wide. **£530-580** C

A Canton Bowl, enamelled and gilt, 40.3 cm. late 19th C. **£170-220** SB SBe

A Carlton-ware Powder Bowl, with "Egyptian" stamp and Stoke-on-Trent mark, c1910. **£75-85**

A Jun Yao shallow globular bowl under a widely crackled semi-translucent lavender glaze, Song Dynasty 4½ in., 11 cm. diam. **£550-600** C

A late Ming blue and white Kraak porcelain basin (crack restored in gold lacquer) Wanli, 14¼ in., 36 cm. diam. **£310-350** C

Two Famille verte "egg and spinach" bowls (cracked, chips restored), encircled square seal marks, Kangxi fitted box 7½ in., 19 cm. **£500-550** C

A fine Exportware Blue and White Punchbowl, 14¼" (36cms), Ch'ien Lung (chipped). **£355-400** SKC

A Flared Bowl, painted in inky underglaze cobalt-blue, 6¼" (16cms), six-character mark of Ch'eng Hua, K'ang Hsi. **£355-400** SKC

A rare Pair of Blue and White bowls, 8" (20cms), six-character mark shen te t'ang po ku chin (antique made at the shen te hall), K'ang Hsi period. **£365-400** SKC

A Ming Blue and White Bowl, painted in inky underglaze cobalt-blue, 12" (30.5cms), c1500 (with faults). **£100-120** SKC

An unusual Blue and White bowl, 5¾" (14.5cms), six-character mark of Chia Ching, K'ang Hsi. **£280-300** SKC

A Chinese Export Punch Bowl of large size, decorated in 'famille-rose' enamels. 15½ in., 39.4 cm. **£620-720** L

A Rose-Verte Fish Bowl with yellow ground, 22 cm., late 19th C. **£200-250** SB

A Mandarin Punch Bowl, decorated in 'famille-rose' enamels, on a rouge-de-fer and gilt Y pattern ground. Ch'ien lung. 11 in., 28.5 cm. **£200-250** L

A Dutch Polychrome Delft Punchbowl, 12" (30.5cms) c1720-30 (with faults). **£500-545** SKC

A Chinese Bowl painted with running horses, Chien Lung, 18th C. **£400-440** SA

A Chinese Famille Bowl, 9½ in. diam., chips to rim, c. 1760. **£125-150** CP

A Lambeth Delft Blue and White inscribed shallow bowl with the inscription 'Admiral Keppel for ever' (cracked and chipped) c. 1780., 18 cm. diam. **£350-400** C

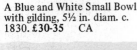

A Blue and White Small Bowl with gilding, 5½ in. diam. c. 1830. **£30-35** CA

A Blue and White Chinese Bowl, 7 in. diam. (A.F.) late 18th C. **£40-45** CA

A Devon Sylvan Lustre Small Bowl, 3½ in., 1930's. **£25-30** CA

A Blue and White Chinese Shallow Bowl, 8 in. diam. (A.F.), c. 1920. **£17-20** CA

A pair of blue and white colanders (fritted), Qianlong 8½" (21.5cms) diam. **£85-95** C

A Royal Doulton Bowl with a wide band of chine decoration in white and green on a gold ground. 4¾ in., 12 cm. **£42-52** L

A Blue and White Chinese Bowl, marked, 7 in. diam. (A.F.), c. 1920. **£17-20** CA

left

A Bristol Delft Blue and White Colander Bowl (rim chips) c. 1760, 22.5 cm. **£85-95** C

A Gombroon Bowl, in blue and black, covered with a thin glaze. Persian 17th-18th C. 8 in., 21 cm. **£65-75** L

An Imari Punch Bowl, painted in typical palette, 34.5 cm., late 19th C. **£300-340** S Be

A Large Imari Punchbowl, painted in underglaze blue, iron red, aubergine, yellow, turquoise and gilding, 14½" c1700 (cracked). **£450-500** SH

JAPANESE PORCELAIN

嘉永元年
南紀男山製

OTOKOYAMA (Kii province) produced in Otokoyama. 1848.

大日本
永樂造

KUTANI (Kaga province) produced in Kutani, in Great Japan. 19th cent.

An Imari Bowl, 7½ in. diam., cracked, c. 1880. **£15-20** CA

A fine Kakiemon deep bowl, late 17th C, 15.2cms diam. **£450-500** C

A Masons Ironstone Bowl on stand. **£245-285** MN

A Rare Imari Colander with foliate rim, painted in underglaze blue, iron red, colours and gilt, early 18th C., 24.2 cm. diam. **£500-600** C

A Rare Blue and White Christians Liverpool Bowl, c. 1765. **£195-215** CSG

A Fine Liverpool Creamware Punch Bowl, the interior printed with 'The Sailor's Return', 10½" (26.5cms), c1780-90. **£155-200** SKC

A Chaffer's Liverpool Bowl painted in clear 'famille-rose' enamels, 7½ in., c. 1758-62. **£200-300** S

A Pilkington's Royal Lancastrian Bowl decorated by Gwladys Rodgers, 12 in. diam., impressed rosette mark. **£80-100** CSK

A Ludwigsburg slop-bowl, 18 cm. diam., blue crowned interlaced C mark, Pressnummer 2DNM, c. 1770. **£450-500** C

A fine Satsuma Chawan, with a rich blue ground, 19th C, 11cms diam. **£925-1,000** C

A 19th C. Japanese Satsuma bowl, 42 cm., 16½ in., wide, together with stand, with some damage. **£250-280** O

A Meissen slop-bowl painted in the manner of B.C. Heuer, 17 cm. diam., blue crossed swords mark, Pressnummer 3, Giler's mark, c. 1740. **£1,700-1,850** C

An enamelled Satsuma earthenware bowl, 14.5 cm. diam. blue Shimazu mon, gilt mark, mid-19th C. **£375-400** SKC

A Satsuma Hexafoil Bowl, delicately painted and gilt with a millefleur pattern. 7½ in., 19 cm. **£130-160** L

A Newhall bowl c. 1800 7 in. diam. **£95-105** PC

A Samson Armorial Bowl, 10 in. diam. c. 1890. **£45-50** CA

A Seto Chawan, applied with an irregular mottled glaze, imitating a Chinese Sung original, 12 cm. Edo period. **£135-175** SKC

A Pair of Minton Bowls, with underglaze deep blue borders heightened with gold, diam. 28.5 cm., painted mark and pattern no. 499, c. 1810, some damage. **£165-195** S Be

A Samson Bowl, 8¼ in. diam. **£40-50** MJ

A Sevres two-handled seau a bouteille, 13 cm. high, blue FR and Sevres mark, c. 1795. **£200-250** C

A Sevres apple-green ground two-handled seau a bouteille, 11.5 cm. high, blue interlaced L mark, c. 1775. **£400-500** C

A fine Wedgwood fairyland lustre bowl decorated with sprites, goblins and winged fairies, 21 cm. printed mark and pattern no. Z 4968. **£290-320** SKC

A rare Dr. Wall Bowl of King of Prussia and winged figure of Fame, 5 in. wide, c. 1757. **£245-265** SA

A Spode Bowl, blue and white, 6¼ in. diam. c. 1820. **£50-60** CSG

A Worcester Pleated Bowl painted en camaieu rose, c. 1758, 12 cm. diam. **£320-350** C

A fine early Dr. Wall Bowl with decoration of Chinese ladies, and the fisherman known as Pu Tai, 6 in. **£365-400** SA

A Staffordshire Slipware inscribed and dated Bragget-Pot with the initials BB and RF, the border with the inscription "THE BEST IS NOT TOO GOOD FOR YOU, 1697" (restored) 32.5 cm. wide. **£2,200-2,500** C

A First Period Worcester bowl, c. 1790 4¾ in. **£110-130** MJ

A Dr. Wall Worcester Bowl, wet blue with reserves of fine exotic birds, 6½ in. **£400-430** SA

A First Period Worcester Bowl, c. 1790 5 in. wide. **£80-90** MJ

A Worcester Barr, Flight & Barr Bowl, on claret ground, 7 in. diam., c. 1810. **£180-190** SA

A late 18th C Sunderland Creamware Bowl, inscribed 'John Dawson, Success to she that carries me eather by Land or Sea'. 28cms diam. **£600-670** SH

A Fine Dr. Wall Period Bowl of the 'Red Bull and Sun pattern', 5 in. diam., c. 1770. **£365-380** SA

A Dr. Wall Worcester Bowl, with the pagoda island pattern painted, C mark, c. 1765. **£200-230** SA

An early Dr. Wall period moulded Bowl with interior decoration 4½ in. diam. **£185-215** SA

A First Period Worcester Blue and White Bowl, 7½ in., c. 1758. **£135-155** CSG

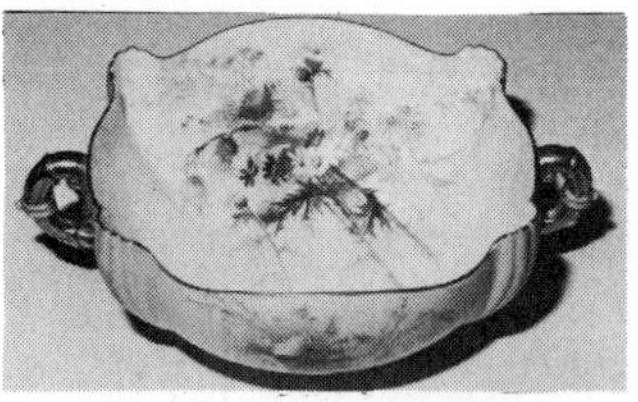

A Worcester Bowl with gilt handles, 11 in. across handles, c. 1900. **£275-300** MN

A Royal Worcester hand-painted pot pourri in Ivory and gilt finish, bird decoration, reticulated top and base, 7½ in., 1890 Rare. **£1,700-2,000** PC

A First Period Worcester Blue and White Potted Meat Dish, c. 1758. **£195-215** CSG

A Dr. Wall Period Worcester Bowl with Chinese Pagoda pattern, 9½ in. diam., slight chips to rim. **£135** perfect **£300-340** SA

An early pottery bowl, 5½" high. **£50-60** SAL

An Arras two-handled blue-ground jardiniere, the blue-ground enriched with gilt flower-sprays, the handles with foliage in gilt and blue, 12.5 cm. diam., blue AR mark, c. 1780. **£650-750** C

A Canton Jardiniere and Stand of hexagonal section, painted, on a gilt ground decorated with scrolling foliage, stand, 22.5 cm., c. 1880. **£285-325** SB

A Pair of Canton Hexagonal Jardinieres and Stands, 14.3 cm., mid 19th C. **£200-225** SB SBe

A Canton Jardiniere and Stand, painted in famille rose enamels on a turquoise ground, 12¾", mid 19th C (cracked). **£115-130** SH

A Jardiniere, highly decorative, Continental, 48 in. high. **£450-500** CA

A Famille-Rose Jardiniere, 26 cm., late 19th C. **£530-570** SB

A Massive Blue and White Jardiniere with a ruyi (ju-i) border, 67 cm., early 19th C. **£1,350-1,750** SB SBe

A Famille-Rose Jardiniere, 40 cm., late 19th C. **£500-550** SB SBe

A Royal Doulton Small Jardiniere with autumnal colours, 7 in. high. **£35-40** CA

A pair of Imari faceted jardinieres, late 19th C, 30.2cms wide. **£550-600** C

A Basalt Sugar Bowl, c. 1810. **£58-68** CP

A Doulton Lambeth Jardiniere, impressed mark Doulton, Lambeth, England, 7½". **£40-50**

A fine Kyoto compressed globular jardiniere, painted in colours and gilt, the base with impressed signature, Kinkozan zo, 19th C, 39cms diam. **£1,050-1,200** C

A Meissen K.P.M. oval sugar-basin and cover painted in the manner of B. G. Hauer, 12.5 cm. wide, blue K.P.M. and crossed swords mark, Gilder's mark 88, c. 1725. **£1,900-2,500** C

A Frankenthal small square jardiniere and stand, 10.5 cm., high, brown interlaced CT marks 71 and 72, 1771/1772. **£850-950**

A Royal Worcester Jardiniere painted with roses, details in gold, height 29.5 cm., printed mark, 1912, some damage. **£280-320** S Be

A Meissen Circular Sugar Bowl and Cover with flower-head finial (minor chip) blue crossed swords mark, c. 1745, 11.5 cm., diam. **£1,600-1,800** C

A French Soft Paste Jardiniere, painter and colour maker A. Fontelliau, 1747-80. **£600-700** SQE

A Minton Jardiniere, c1845, 8½" high. **£120-140** SAL

A Pair of Royal Worcester Jardinieres, in tones of pale green and apricot heightened with gold, height 22.5 cm., and 23.5 cm., printed mark, 1897, slight damage. **£360-400** S Be

A Ridgway Sucrier and Cover, 7 in. high, c. 1850. **£35-40** CSG

A Sevres bucket-shaped sugar-bowl and cover, 10.5 cm. high, blue interlaced L mark, date letter for 1790. **£300-350** C

A Sevres Apple-Green Ground Sugar-Bowl and Cover, puce interlaced L mark 1768 11.5 cm., high. **£220-260** C

A First Period Worcester blue and white sucrier and cover, 4½ in. high, c. 1790. **£110-115** MJ

A First Period Worcester 'Dry Blue' Sucrier and Cover, 5 in. high, c. 1790. **£400-450** MJ

An Art Deco 'Cottage' Sucrier. **£9-12** AP

A Berlin Circular Tureen and Cover, 12" diam., 19th C. **£420-450** SH

A Bow Faceted Pot-Pourri Bowl and Pierced Cover with scroll-moulded loop handles (cracks to rim of bowl) puce 5 mark, c. 1762, 23 cm. wide. **£1,000-1,200** C

A Canton Vegetable Dish and Cover with coats-of-arms, within borders of dragons, 28.5 cm. mid 19th C. **£175-200** SB SBe

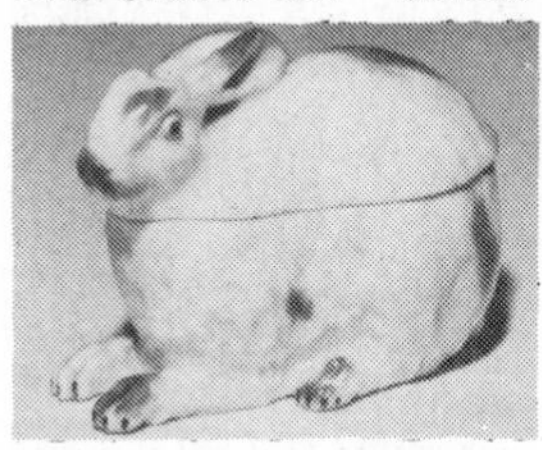

A Chelsea Leveret-Tureen and Cover, the cover with red anchor mark and 154, the base with 154, c. 1755, 9.5 cm. wide. **£1,000-1,050** C

A fine Pair of Enamelled Famille-rose circular Tureens of fluted European silver shape, 10¾" (27cms), Ch'ien Lung (one cracked, the other with repaired handle). **£830-880** SKC

A Famille-Rose Bowl and Cover, painted with mille-fleurs on a gilt ground, 26.5 cm., painted seal mark of Qianlong (Ch'ien-lung) c. 1880. **£275-325** SB

A shaped rectangular vegetable-tureen and domed cover with strawberry finial, late Qianlong, 10¾ in., 27.5 cm. wide. **£460-500** C

A Good Coalport Muffin Dish, c. 1818, 8½ in.diam. **£55-65** SA

A Copeland Sauce Tureen, Cover and Stand, c. 1860. **£125-140** CP

A Pair of Coalport (John Rose) Claret-ground Ice-Pails, covers and liners in the Chelsea style, edged with gilt scrolls. (one liner damaged, finials restored) c. 1810, 26 cm. high. **£650-800** pr. C

A Rare London Ointment Pot and Cover painted with trailing flower sprays in blue and 'trekked' in black, 3¼ in., late 17th C. cover restored, rim chipped. **£750-820** S

A Meissen Two-Handled Ecuelle, Cover and Stand painted in colours within a Dulong pattern border, blue crossed swords marks, Pressnummern 22, c. 1745 the stand 23 cm., diam. **£1,300-1,500** C

A pair of Imari deep bowls, covers and saucers (one cover restored), late 17th/early 18th C, the saucers about 19.2cms diam. **£900-1,000** C

A Longton Hall Dove Tureen and Cover (cover cracked across and restuck, one end of wing lacking) c. 1755, 21.5 cm. wide. **£500-550** C

A pair of Meissen (Marcolini) two-handled ecuelles, covers and stands, (one cover damaged) the stands 21.5 cm. diam. blue crossed swords and star marks, Pressnummer 20 to stands, 32 to ecuelles, c. 1775. **£500-600** C

An Imari circular shallow tureen and domed cover (cover with interior rim chips), early 18th C, 26.7cms diam. **£420-460** C

Mason's Ashworth's Pot and cover c. 1880. **£25-30** TT

An Attractive Minton 'Majolica' Game Pie Dish and Cover in brightly coloured translucent glazes, 14 in., impressed Minton and numerals, painter's mark T inside cover, mid 19th C. **£160-190** SBA

A Rice Serving Bowl and Cover (A.F.) 11 in. wide, 4 in. high, possibly Japanese, c. 1930. **£70-80** CA

A Meissen Two-Handled Tureen and Cover, height 17 cm., early 18th C. damaged **£1,300-1,450** S Be

A Samson 'Famille Rose' Cockerel Tureen and cover in green, yellow and aubergine glazes, blue glazed interior, late 19th C., 25 cm. **£180-220** SB

Blue and White Staffordshire Porringer. **£45-50** TT

A Vienna Two-Handled Ecuelle and Cover with strawberry finial (chip to finial), blue beehive mark, puce A.27 incised marks, c. 1775 19 cm., wide. **£180-220** C

A Flight, Barr and Barr Worcester Tureen and Cover, 9¼ in. long, c. 1810. **£195-220** MJ

A Worcester (Flight, Barr and Barr) Crested Oval Two-Handled Vegetable Dish, cover and liner, the liner with gilt gadrooned rim, impressed and printed marks. c. 1820, 32 cm. wide. **£460-500** C

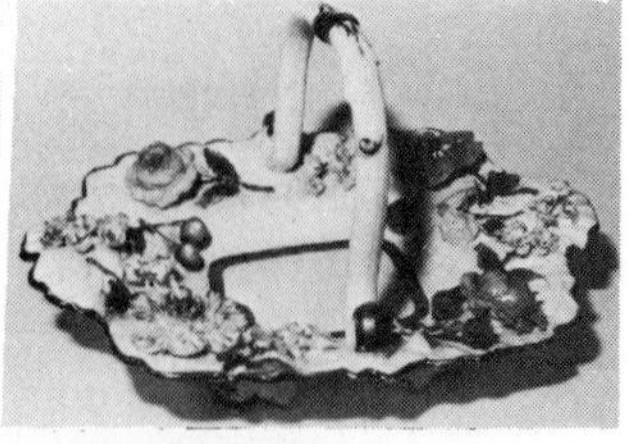

A Coalport Basket, c. 1835. **£450-500** MN

A Dresden Pierced Basket with painted enamel couple, c. 1880. **£275-295** MN

A Pair of Worcester Chestnut Baskets and Covers, in enamel colours, 17.8 cm., mid 18th C. (handle restored). **£280-320** S Be

A Pair of Lowestoft Baskets printed in under-glaze-blue with the 'Pinecone Pattern', 9¼ in., c. 1775-85. **£370-450** S

A Ridgway Small Basket, 6¼ in. wide. **£175-195** MN

A Chamberlain Worcester Large Basket, raised gilding restored **£150-170** perfect **£500-600** MN

A Pair of Worcester Baskets, in enamel colours, 16.5 cm., mid 18th C. hair crack to rim. **£500-600** S Be

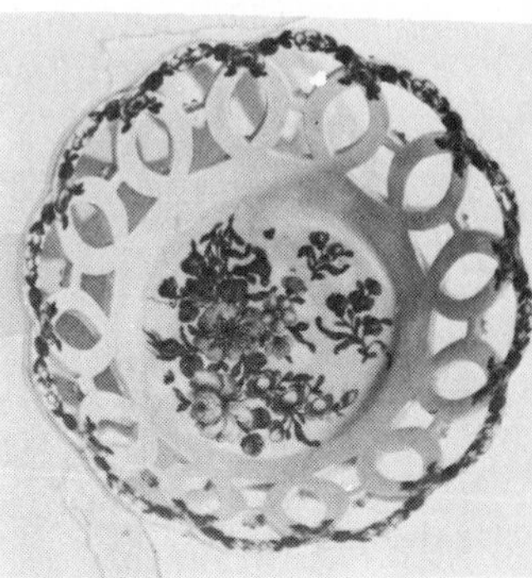

A Dr. Wall Worcester Basket with very good English flowers, possibly painted in London by Rodgers, 1760. **£750-850** SA

A Fine Oval Dr. Wall Chestnut Basket and Stand with applied flowers, c. 1770, base **£600-650** with basket **£1,600-1,800** SA

A Fine and Rare Dr. Wall Worcester Basket, Cover & Ladle with flower sprays in under-glaze blue, the lid with a flower finial and the ladle with a circular pierced bow, fine condition, c. 1770. **£1,950-2,100** SA

A First Period Worcester Blue and White Basket, pierced and flared, pine cone pattern, two very minor chips to florettes, c. 1770. **£265-300** CSG

An Arita Blue and White Dish late 17th C., 30.8 cm. diam. **£300-390** C

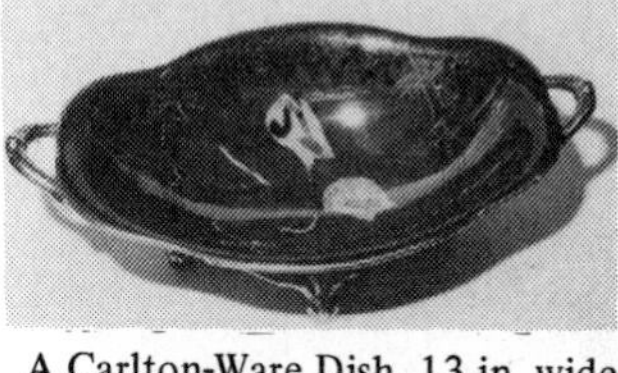

A Carlton-Ware Dish, 13 in. wide, 1930's. **£55-60** CA

A Caughley blue and white round dish, 8in. diam. c.1798 marked **£85-95** MJ

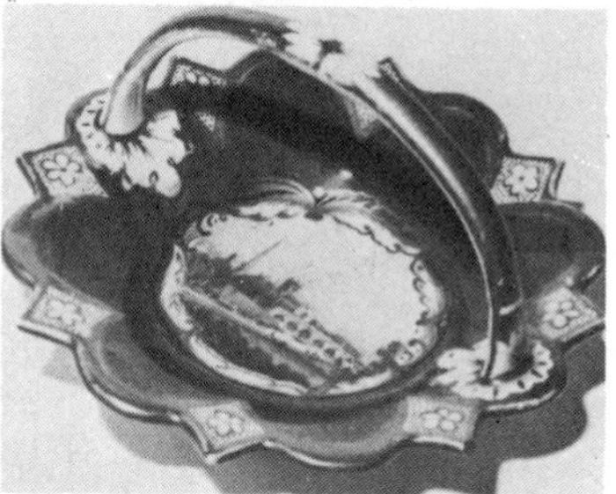

An Early Grainger Worcester Small Basket, 4 in. wide, c. 1840 cracked handle. **£85-95,** perfect **£145-165** MN

A pair of Berlin leaf-shaped dishes (one with minor rim chip) 23 cm. wide, blue sceptre marks, incised K and 13, c. 1770. **£1,200-1,300** C

A Caughley Temple Pattern blue and white oval dish, 10½ in. wide, c. 1800. **£50-60** MJ

A fine Arita fluted deep dish (rubbed), c1700, 20.5cms diam. **£350-400** C

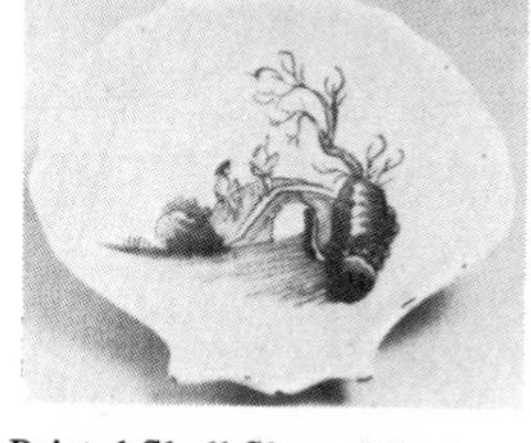

A Bristol Shell-Shaped Dish painted in blue, 3¾ in., c. 1760, very small chip. **£340-380** S

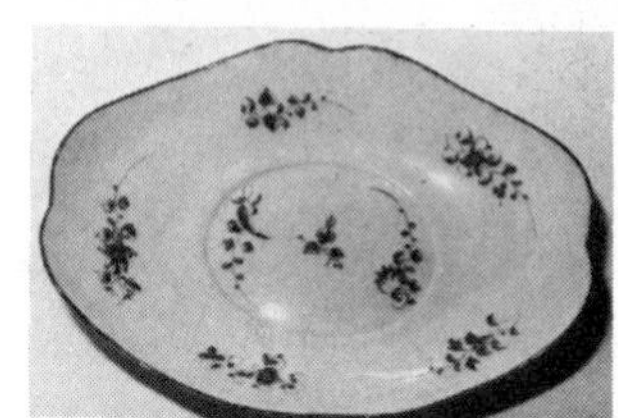

A Caughley oval-shaped dish 10 in. long, c. 1800. **£90-100** MJ

An Arita blue and white saucer dish, early 18th C, 37.9cms diam. **£825-900** C

A Caughley Shell shaped Dish, c. 1770, slight repair **£145-165** perfect **£265-285** SA

left

A Carlton-ware Dish with butterflies and nymphs, c1920, 10½". **£150-180**

A fine Caughley Dish, 10 in. wide, c. 1770 slight rim chip **£58-65** perfect **£150-170** SA

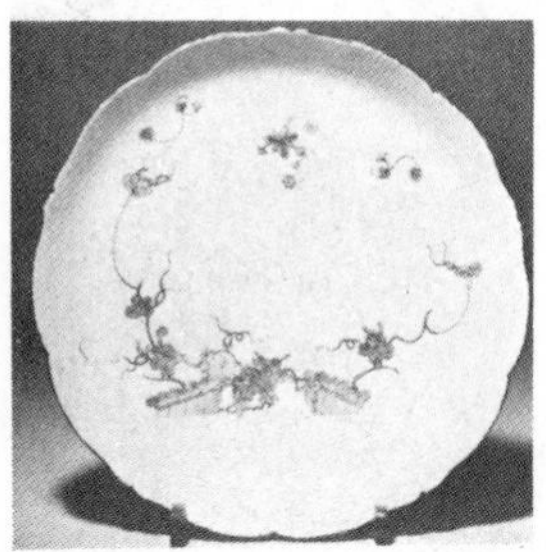

A Chantilly Saucer-Dish painted in the Kakiemon palette with a squirrel pattern, iron-red hunting horn mark, 1750 19.5 cm., diameter **£320-380** C

A Chelsea 'Japan pattern' Dish decorated in an Imari palette, 9¾ in., blue anchor period, c. 1752. **£400-450** S

A Chelsea 'Silver-shape' Dish, painted in a bold palette, 11½ in., red anchor period, c. 1752-54 **£230-260** S

A Chelsea Lobed Oval Dish, red anchor mark, c. 1755, 24.5 cm. wide, **£350-400** C

CHELSEA (soft paste porcelain) 1745-84

- the finest English 18thC porcelain
- earliest wares in milky white glassy porcelain
- Meissen inspired decorative style
- transfer prints are extremely rare and are thought to have been done at Battersea enamel factory
- from 1749 Chelsea managed by Nicholas Sprimont a silversmith from Liege so style remained the same during red anchor period
- three small projecting 'spur marks' within a ground-down foot rim found on useful wares
- Chelsea figures beautifully modelled and colour used sparingly

A Chelsea Hans Sloane Fluted Dish, red anchor mark, c. 1755, 27 cm. diam. **£650-700** C

A Chelsea Lobed Circular Dish painted in the Imari style, c. 1755, 28 cm. diam. **£450-500** C

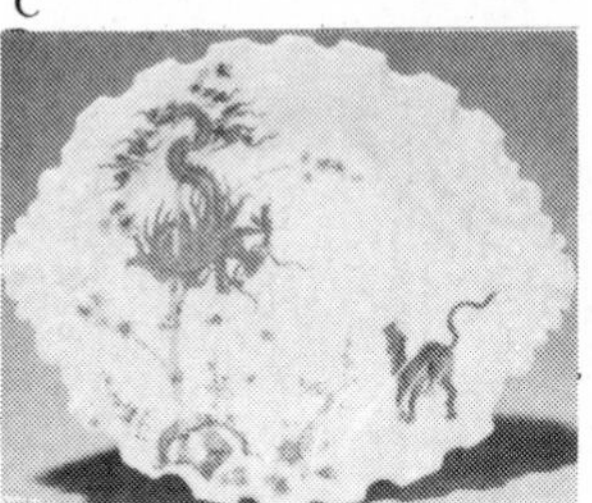

A Chelsea Silver-shaped Oval Dish, with shell-moulded thumbpieces painted in the Kakiemon style, raised anchor mark, 1749-1752, 24.5 cm. wide. **£1,200-1,500** C

A Chelsea Fluted Oval Dish painted in purple monochrome by Jeffereys Hamett O'Neale, red anchor mark, c. 1753, 16 cm. wide. **£900-1,000** C

A Chelsea Oval Basket-Work Dish with naturally coloured vinestock handles, c. 1755, 27.5 cm. wide. **£350-400** C

A Chelsea Leaf-dish with puce stalk handle and veins edged in tones of green and pale-yellow, c. 1755, 28 cm. wide. **£200-250** C

A Pair of Chelsea Peony-flower Dishes with green stalk handles (rims chipped, minor restoration, one leaf cracked) red anchor marks, c. 1765, 23.5 cm. wide. **£800-900** pr. C

A Chelsea Hexafoil Dish, (small restoration to rim) remains of raised anchor mark, c. 1752, 19 cm. wide. **£550-700** C

A late Ming blue and white deep dish painted with eight precious emblems (cracked) Wanli 17¾ in., 45 cm. diam. **£350-400** C

A late Ming Wucai octagonal dish, (fritted), square seal mark, Tianqi/Chongzheng 5¾ in., 14.5 cm. wide. **£165-200** C

A Chelsea Kidney-shaped Dish painted with fruit and moths, brown anchor mark, c. 1758, 27 cm. wide. **£300-350** C

A pair of pale lemon-yellow glazed saucer dishes, each incised with dragons, (cracked, one foot interior chipped) encircled Kangxi six-character marks 5½ in., 14 cm. diam. **£500-550** C

Six famille verte V-shaped sweetmeat dishes, (minor fritting, two chipped), Kangxi 5¼ in., 13.5 cm. long. **£285-320** C

A large Famille Rose oblong octagonal dish, Qianlong 18 in., 45.5 cm. wide. **£460-500** C

A large "famille rose" porcelain dish 38.5 cm., Qianlong (Ch'ien Lung) **£200-250** SKC

A pair of famille rose dishes (one minutely fritted), early Qianlong 12½ in., 31.5 cm. diam. **£900-1,000** C

A pair of Ming blue and white saucer dishes (slightly chipped, one minute rim crack) seal commendation marks in squares, late 16th C., 5¼ in., 13.5 cm. diam. **£310-350** C

A large "Famille rose" porcelain dish 48.5 cm. diam., mid-18th C. **£235-250** SKC

Three late Ming blue and white saucer-dishes (one chip reduced), four character marks, chang ming fu gul (long life, riches and honour), late 16th C, 5½" (14cms) diam. **£120-150** C

A Pair of Chinese Famille Verte Dishes, painted with the "Three Friends", pine, prunus and bamboo, K'ang Hsi, 13¾ in., 35.3 cm. **£1,100-1,250** L

A Pair of Chinese octagonal meat dishes, decorated in 'famille-rose' enamels with pink scale borders. Ch'ien Lung. 10 in., 25.4 cm. **£300-350** L

A Chinese circular dish decorated in "famille-rose" enamel, Ch'ien Lung. **£110-150** L

A Pair of Chinese circular dishes, painted in underglaze blue, the borders with flowers, fungus and bamboo. 18th C. 14 in., 35.5 cm. **£2,100-2,300** pr. L

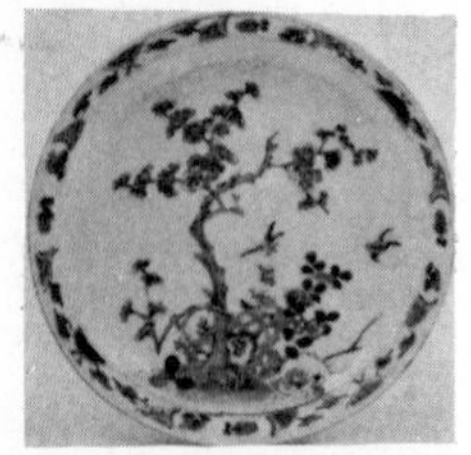
A Set of Twelve Chinese Saucer Dishes, decorated in 'famille-verte' enamels. 8½ in., 21.2 cm. late Ch'ien lung. **£490-580** L

A Set of Four Chinese Large Saucer Dishes decorated in 'famille-verte' enamels, late Ch'ien lung. **£320-400** L

A Pair of Famille Verte Shaped Oval Dishes with geometric patterns above a ju'i head border, 27.3 cm., K'ang-hsi. **£410-500** S Be

A Pair of Chinese Imari Fan-Shaped Dishes, finely painted, 26.1 cm. **£170-200** S Be

A pair of famille verte V-shaped sweetmeat dishes (chipped) iron-red marks, Kanxi 5 in., 12.5 cm. wide. **£90-125** C

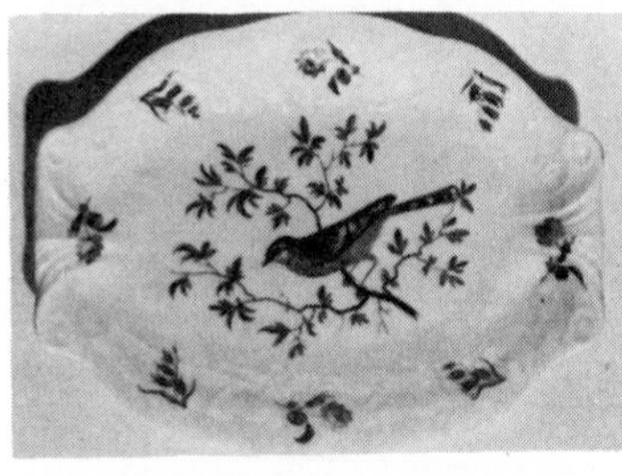
A Dish with Bird, possibly Coalport, 9 in. **£65-75** SA

A Coalport Dish, royal blue, with heavy embossed gilding, c. 1825. **£75-85** MN

An Early Coalport Dish, c. 1820's rubbed. **£75-85** perfect **£180-200** MN

A Rare Creamware Oval Dish, the centre finely painted in puce camaieu, 11½" (29cms), probably Neale and Wilson, c1785-90 (repaired). **£155-200** SKC

A Bristol polychrome Delft dish, naively painted in pillar-box red, green, cobalt blue and manganese, 8¾" (22cms), c1710-20. **£530-580** SKC

An Irish Delft Octagonal Dish, 6¾ in., numeral 12 in blue, mid 18th C., small chips. **£200-230** S

A Lambeth Delft Polychrome Dish painted in yellow, green, blue and iron-red c. 1760, 34 cm. diam. **£130-150** C

A Liverpool Delft Polychrome Dish painted in a Fazackerly palette of red, blue, green and yellow (minute rim chips) c. 1760, 34.5 cm. diam. **£460-500** C

A Bloor Derby Dish, c. 1850, 11½ in. **£200-230** MJ

A Derby Dish, hand painted, 1900. **£150-170** MN

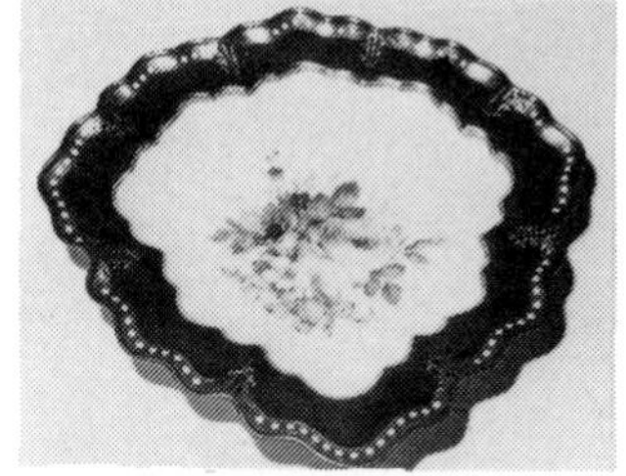
A Derby Dish painted by A. Gregory, not signed, made for Lord Rowe, jewelled gilt rim, pearl jewelling, c. 1912. **£250-300**, signed **£400-450** MN

A Derby Dish, 2451 pattern, c. 1925. **£125-145** MN

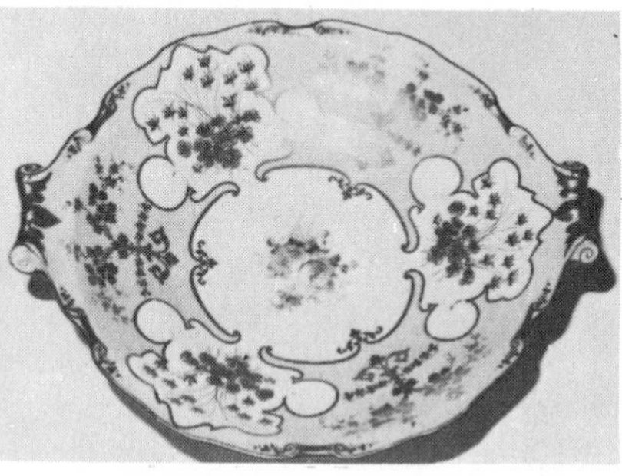
A Derby Dish, with yellow ground and raised gilding, c. 1903. **£75-85** MN

A Large Dublin Serving Dish 18¾ in., marked 6 or 9 in blue, Henry Dalamain's factory, c. 1755, chipped, short crack. **£600-700** S

An Armorial Dublin Serving Dish 20 in., c. 1740, chipped cracked. **£300-350** S

A German Faience Dish covered in a light blue glaze and painted in underglaze blue in Chinese style, 39.3 cm. probably Frankfurt, early 18th C. **£740-800** S

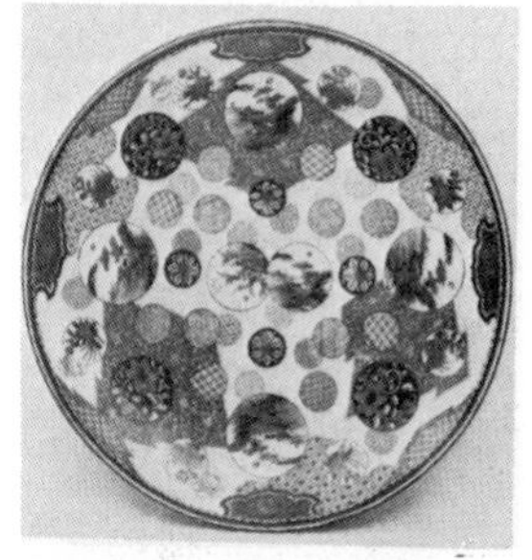
A Japanese Imari Circular Dish of large size, painted and enamelled with iron-red and gold on a ground of scattered mons, 24 in., 61 cm. **£550-650** L

A Large Imari Dish painted in underglaze-blue, iron-red, colours and gilt, 19th C., 61.3 cm. diam. **£1,400-1,800** C

An Imari Shaving Dish painted in typical colours, Genroku period, 26.1 cm. diam. **£660-760** C

A Small Imari Dish, 9 in. wide, c. 1880. **£60-70** CA

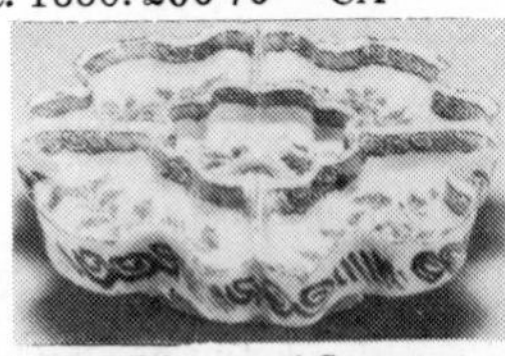
A Rare Liverpool Sweetmeat Dish painted in blue, 8¾ in., c. 1760, rim chips, hair crack. **£350-400** S

A Christian's Liverpool small Dish, small chip, c. 1765. **£40-45** perfect **£55-60** CSG

A Marseilles faience deep dish, painted in petit-feu enamels (chipped) 31 cm., c. 1770. **£380-400** SKC

A Masons Ironstone Leaf Dish, quite rare. **£75-85** MN

A Meissen large dish from the Grunes Watteau service painted in Kupfergrun within Gotzkowsky Ozier border (minor firing crack) 39.5 cm. diam., blue crossed swords mark, Pressnummer 21, c. 1742. **£1,000-1,200** C

A Meissen dish painted with the Gelber Loewe pattern in the Kakiemon palette 29.5 cm. diam. blue crossed swords mark, c. 1735. **£900-1,000** C

A Lowestoft Blue and White Fluted Oval Stand, painter's numeral 8, c. 1762, 18.5 cm. wide. **£260-300** C

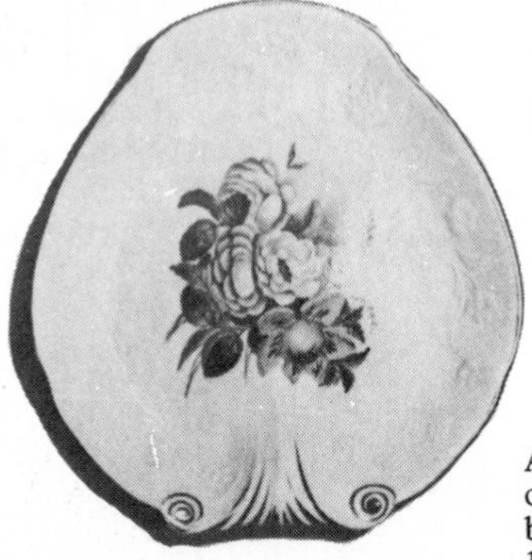
A Mayer and Newbold Dish, with gilt rim. **£42-50** CSG

A Meissen yellow-ground shaped oval spoon-tray, 17 cm. wide, blue crossed swords mark, c. 1745. **£275-350** C

A Ludwigsburg Saucer-Dish painted in colours and gilt, the Ozier border with gilt rim, blue crowned interlaced C mark, c. 1770 19 cm., diam. **£550-610** C

A Meissen fabeltiere dish with a yellow and lustre horned beast, 39 cm. diam, blue crossed swords mark and Pressnummer 26, c. 1740. **£2,850-3,250** C

A Meissen Shaped Quatrefoil Spoon-Tray painted en camaieu rose, blue crossed swords mark and gilt 6, c. 1735, 17.5 cm., wide. **£800-900** C

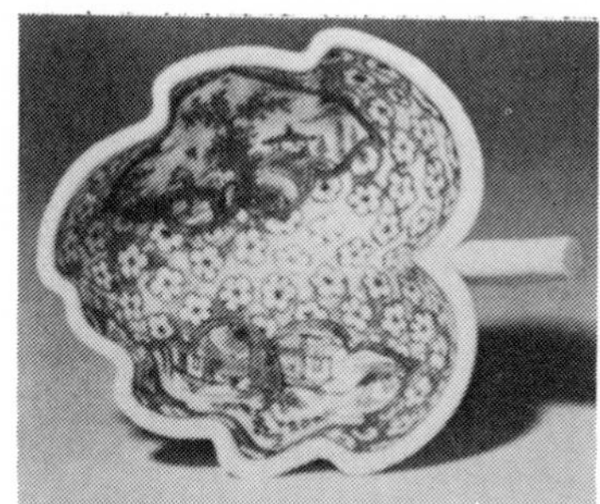

An Early Meissen Leaf-Shaped Pickle-Dish, decorated in Holland (handle with minor repair), c. 1725, 12.5 cm., **£550-610** C

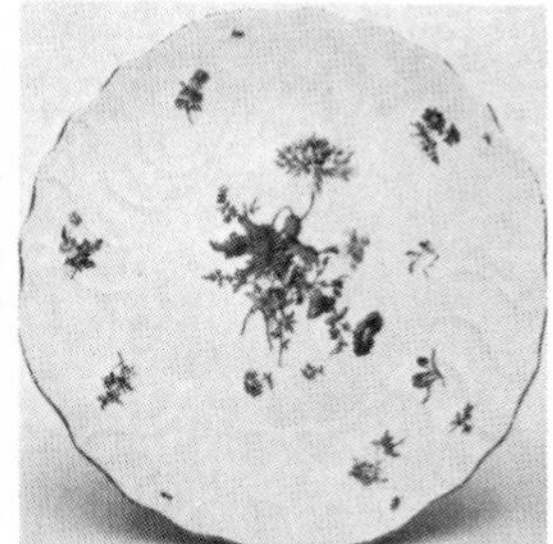

A Meissen Circular Dish, outlined with a band of osier pattern, gilt trim, crossed swords mark in underglaze blue, 9¾ in., 25.2 cm. **£200-280** L

An Impressed Nantgarw Dish, almost certainly by Billingsley with English flowers and butterflies, green spot border, c. 1815. **£850-930** SA

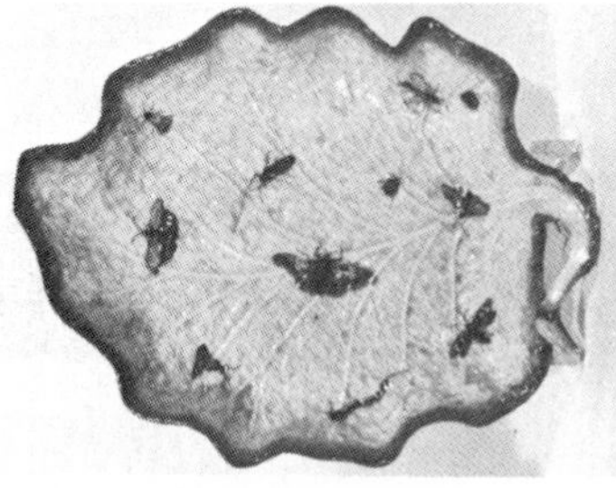

A Pair of Meissen Leaf-Dishes, blue crossed swords marks, c. 1755 26 cm., wide. **£600-680** C

A Meissen Pierced Dish painted in colour, the pierced Bruhlsches Allerlei-Dessin border with Gitterwerk, blue crossed swords mark, c. 1755. **£650-720** C

A Nantgarw Cushion-Shaped Dish, painted with view of Windsor Castle, impressed, **£1,100-1,250** SA

A Meissen Peony Flower-Dish with gilt rim, blue crossed swords mark, Former's mark of Rehschuh, c. 1745 19 cm., wide. **£400-450** C

A William de Morgan dish painted in ruby, ochre and mushroom lustre 36 cm., Fulham period. 1898-1907. **£420-450** SKC

A Spode Dish, 13½ in., c. 1825. **£165-190** CSG

A Meissen Leaf-Shaped Dish finely moulded with veins, the ground enriched in iron-red and gilt, blue crossed swords mark, c. 1745 25 cm., long. **£280-320** C

A Sevres Shaped Oblong Dish painted in colours with Wittelsbach pattern border, blue interlaced L marks, date letter K for 1763 29.5 cm., wide **£500-580** C

A William de Morgan saucer dish painted in ruby and ochre lustre 36 cm. Fulham period, 1888-1907. **£420-450** SKC

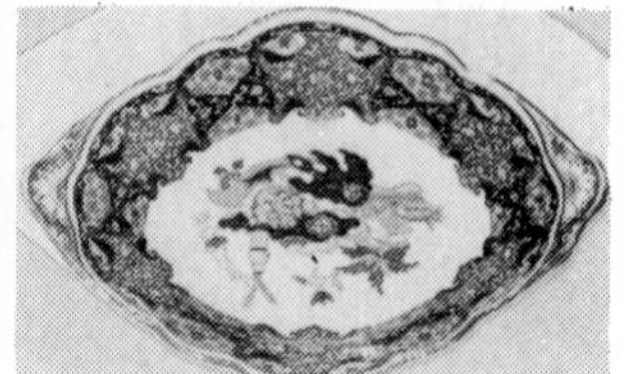

A Spode Dish, 10½ in. long, c. 1820. **£65-75** CP

A Pair of Strasbourg Fluted Saucer-Dishes painted in colours, the scalloped edges gilt (one with rim chip), underglaze blue and incised A14 marks, c. 1770 23 cm. **£400-450** C

A Pair of Tournai (The Hague decorated) spirally moulded large deep dishes, painted in colours, with shaped gilt rims, blue stork marks, c. 1775 39.5 cm., diam. **£900-1,000** C

A Vienna Dupaquier Schwarzlot Dish from a Jagd service (small chip restoration, minor foot rim chips) c. 1745 33.5 cm., diam. **£6,000-6,500** C

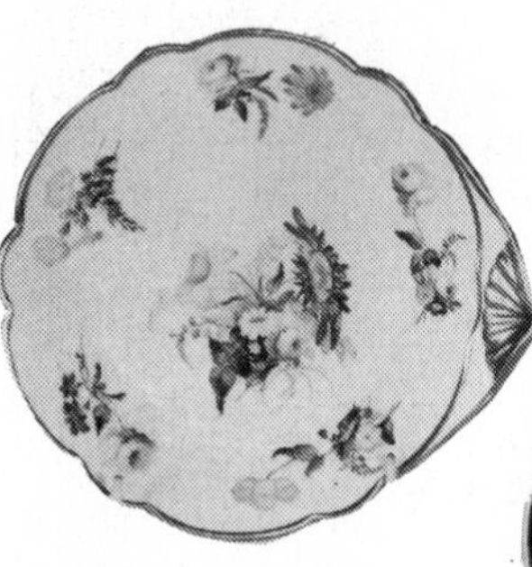

A Marked Swansea Dish, painted by Pollard, c. 1815. **£400-440** SA

A Pair of Tournai (The Hague decorated) spirally moulded shaped circular dishes, gilt scale-pattern on a blue ground, blue stork marks, c. 1775 31 cm., diam. **£800-900** C

A Vienna Dupaquier Schwarzlot Dish from a Jagd service painted perhaps by Jacobus Helchis, enriched in gilding, c. 1745 33.5 cm., **£7,000-7,900** C

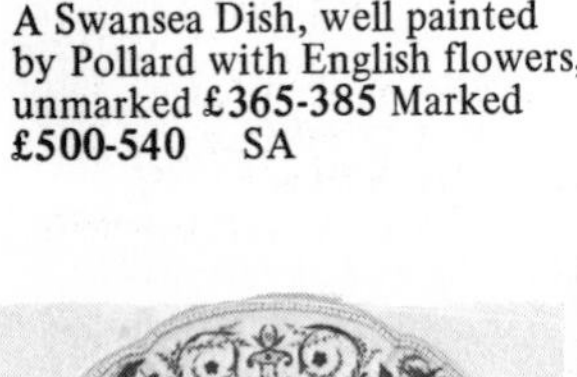

A Swansea Dish, well painted by Pollard with English flowers, unmarked **£365-385** Marked **£500-540** SA

A Wedgwood Lustre Tray, butterfly decoration, gilt rim, 4 in. **£50-55** CA

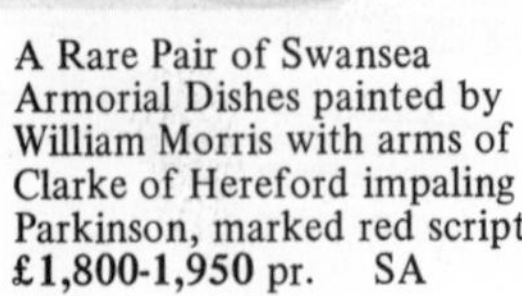

A Rare Pair of Swansea Armorial Dishes painted by William Morris with arms of Clarke of Hereford impaling Parkinson, marked red script **£1,800-1,950** pr. SA

A pair of Venice (Cozzi) cinquefoil saucer dishes, one with a lion, the other with a camel. 20 cm. diam. c. 1775. **£250-300** C

Pair of Wedgwood impressed Oval Dishes, early 19th C. **£75-85** pair.

A West Pans Leaf-Moulded Oval Dish the border modelled as overlapping leaves (minute rim chip) c. 1766, 18.5 cm. wide. **£360-400** C

A Dr. Wall Worcester Dish, pierced and painted with English flowers, dry blue border, c. 1765. **£950-1050** SA

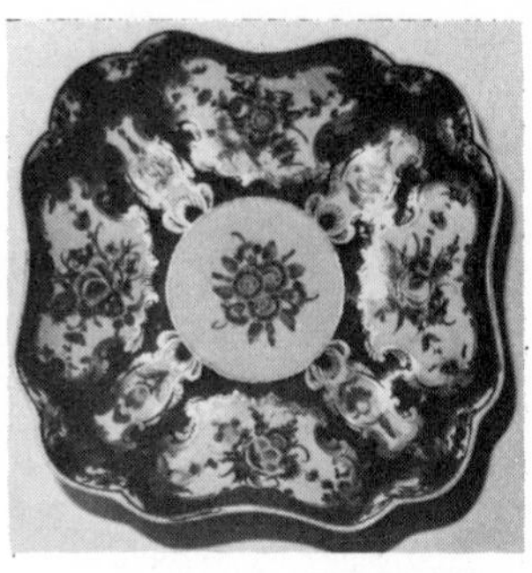

A First Period Worcester 'Scale Blue' cushion Dish, 8 in. wide, c. 1785. **£500-570** MJ

A fine Worcester Flight Period scalloped hexagonal teapot stand with radiating bands in underglaze blue and gilt, gilt dentil border, 6 in., diam., crescent mark in blue, c. 1785/90. **£75-90** NN

A Royal Worcester Oval Dish, painted by Po-Hing in enamel colours in Canton style, on a diaper ground in turquoise, dark blue, yellow and red, impressed mark c. 1870: and a pair of Canton plates with the same design. Dish 17 in., 43.2 cm., plates 8¼ in., 21.2 cm. **£100-150** L

A fine pair of Dr. Wall Period Dishes of lobed shape in strong Imari colours, 10 in. wide. **£685-700** pr. SA

A Worcester Octafoil Leaf-Moulded Dish, c. 1765, 28 cm. wide, perfect **£700-800** chip to rim **£600-700** C

A pair of First Period Worcester 'scale blue' Dishes, c. 1770, marked, 10 in. wide. **£1,250-1,400** MJ

A very good Dr. Wall Fluted Junket Dish, wet blue ground, in mint condition, c. 1765. **£795-850** slight rubbing **£400-440** SA

A Dr. Wall Worcester Kidney Shaped Dish, painted with flowers and butterflies, c. 1760. **£600-660** SA

A First Period Worcester Dish c. 1770 8¼ in. diam. **£320-360** MJ

A Worcester Saucer Dish, Sir Joshua Reynolds pattern, 10 in., c.1770 **£785-810,** rubbed **£400-430** SA

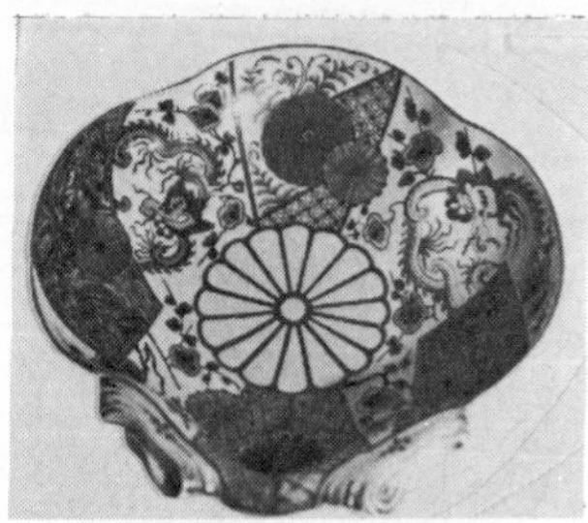

A very good pair of Dr. Wall Period Shell Shaped Dishes of the Brocage pattern, c. 1770 slight chip on back edge of one dish.
£850-930 SA

WORCESTER
c1751

FIRST PERIOD or DR WALL PERIOD
- crescent marks c1755 - 90 in underglaze blue.

FLIGHT PERIOD 1783 - 92
- small size crescent mark sometimes c1783 - 8

A Dr. Wall Leaf Shaped Dish painted by James Giles with aggressive birds, 10 in. wide, c. 1770. **£495-510** SA

A Pair of Dr. Wall Period Gros Bleu Kidney-shaped Dishes, crescent mark, 10½ in. wide.
£550-600 pr. SA

A Worcester Shell Dish, c. 1910.
£240-270 MN

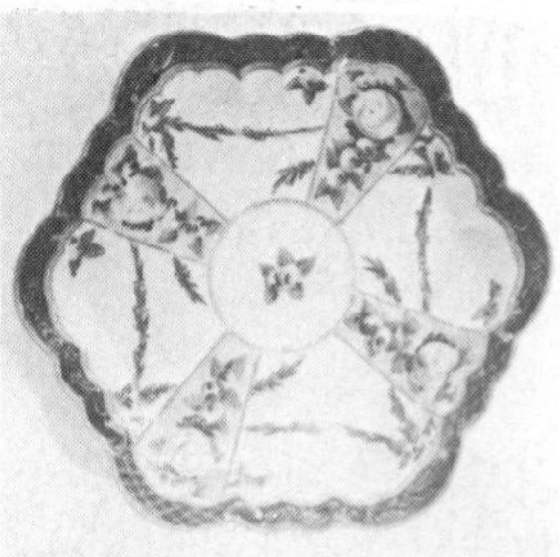

A Rare Dr. Wall Teapot Stand with fruit on turquoise border panels, painted by the spotted fruit painter, with blue border, c. 1765. **£800-870** SA

A Dr. Wall Teapot Stand with transfer 'L'Amour' by R. Hancock, c. 1765. **£200-230** SA

A pair of Worcester, Flight, Barr & Barr Cushion-shaped dishes, impressed marks, c 1820. 23.5cm wide
£200–250 pr. C

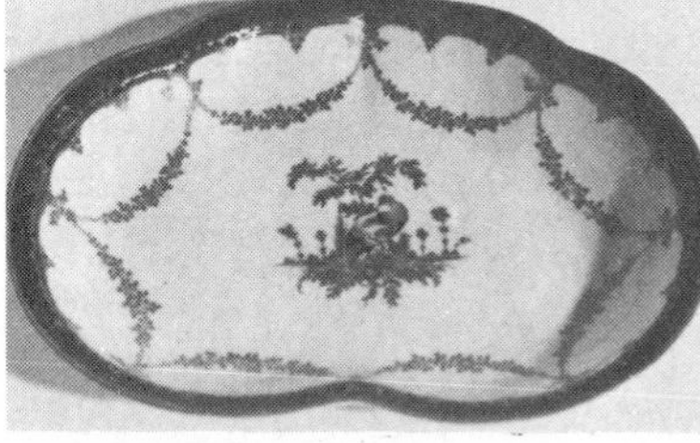

A Dr. Wall Worcester Heart Shaped Dish, 11 in., c. 1775.
£600-650 SA

A Worcester Barr, Flight & Barr Saucer Dish, interesting and unusual claret ground, 8 in. diam., rubbed border.
£100-120 perfect **£180-190** SA

A fine Pair of Dr. Wall Leaf Dishes. **£795-820** pr. SA

A round Dr. Wall Basket-Work Dish, 9 in. diam., c. 1765. **£420-460** SA

A Worcester Dr. Wall Blue and White Pickle Shell Dish with a bird on a rock, painter's mark, 1758. **£285-320** SA

A small Royal Worcester dish with hand-painted Chaffinch, signed by artist 4 in. diam. c. 1920. **£30-40** each. PC

A Royal Worcester Sebright Dish, 11 in. **£350-390** MN

A Worcester Dish by Freeman, c. 1948. **£95-105** MN

A Chamberlain Worcester Dish, green ground, 13 in. wide, c. 1840. **£150-170** MN

A Pair of Royal Worcester shell-shape dishes, painted and gilt, 5½ in., 14 cm., printed mark in puce. **£65-75** L

A Ding Yao saucer-dish, Song Dynasty, the rim mounted in copper, 4½ in., 11.5 cm. diam. **£750-800** C

A Polychrome Dish painted in bold tones of yellow, iron-red, green and blue, 13 in., numeral 5 in blue, probably Bristol, c. 1730, rim chips. **£200-300** S

A Large Faience Meat Dish, Rouen, 16 in. long, c. 1890's. **£45-50** CA

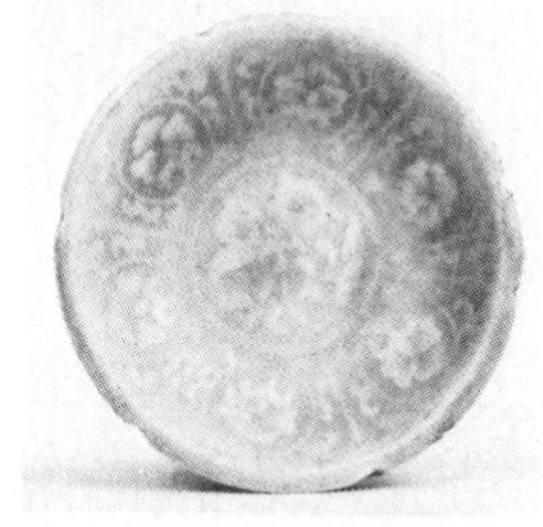

A northern Celadon hexafoil saucer-dish, a bubble-suffused rich pale olive glaze (chipped) Northern Song Dynasty, wood stand. 3½ in., 9 cm. diam. **£330-375** C

Blue and White pickle dishes, c. 1800. **£20-25** each

A Very Rare Blue and White Pickle Dish, in the form of a scallop-shell, 2½" (6.5cms), the base incised with the number 43, after 1750, perhaps William Reid's or Pomona Pottery (Newcastle-under-Lyme). **£500-550** SKC

Blue and White quartered dish c. 1830. **£25-30** TT

A Continental, 'French' Faience Comport Dish, 13 in. high, c. 1890. **£95-105** CA

A Crown Derby Imari Comport 1890, 12½ in. wide. **£275-310** PC

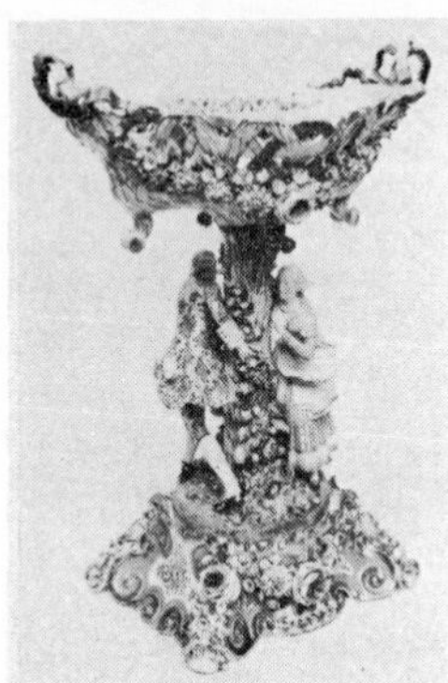

A Dresden Comport of Exceptional Size pierced and gilt with leaves, entwined with pink and blue ribbons, 25 in. high. **£550-650** N

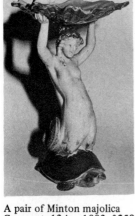

A pair of Minton majolica Comports 12 in., 1882. **£250-270** pr. PC

A Minton Lustre Comport Dish, 11 in. wide, 5 in. high, 1930's. **£160-180** CA

A Minton Comport, torquoise ground, with gilding, c. 1865. **£55-65** MN

A Royal Worcester Hadley Kate Greenaway Comport, in satin and green finish, 1907, 8½ in. high. **£250-280** PC

Ashworth's Plate with impressed mark, c. 1860 9 in. diam. **£15-20** TT

An Aynsley Plate, hand-painted and signed. **£35-40** PC

An Aynsley Plate signed by R. Keeling, fern jewelling, c. 1890. **£120-140** MN

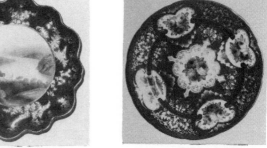

A Small Castelli Plate, 17 cm., early 18th C. **£300-340** S

A Small Castelli Plate painted in typical colours after Tempesta, 18.2 cm., early 18th C., slight restoration on rim. **£350-390** S

A Caughley Plate of the Weir pattern, 8½ in. wide, c. 1770. **£65-75** SA

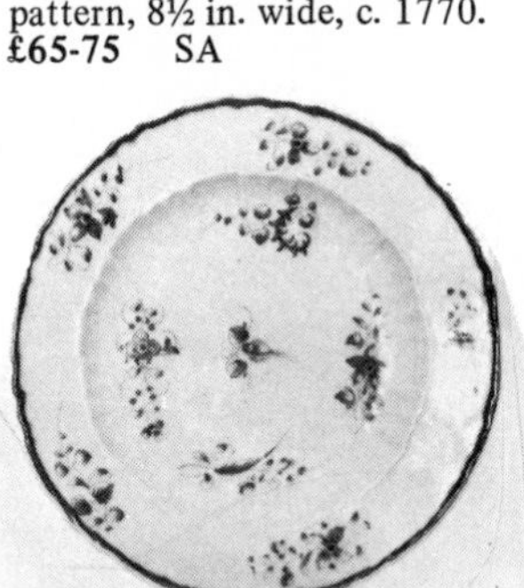

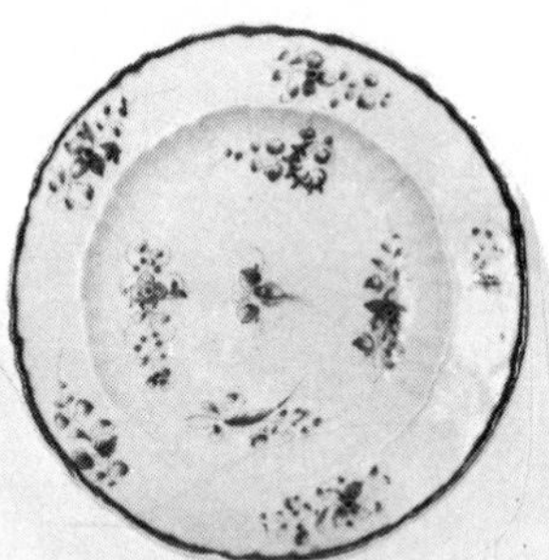

A Caughley Plate, blue and white, c. 1785. **£85-95** CSG

A Cauldon Plate with dark blue ground, c. 1890-1910. **£85-95** MN

A Pair of Chelsea Plates from the Duke of Cambridge Service painted with fruit and gilt scroll cartouches containing moths (one with minute rim chip) brown anchor marks, c. 1763, 23.5 cm. diam. **£900-1,000** pr. C

A Chelsea Plate with 'Gotszkowsky erhabene Blumen', and painted in the Kakiemon style, c. 1753, 24 cm. diam. **£200-250** C

A famille rose octagonal armorial plate, with helmet, crest and motto "Virtus radix honoris" (minutely fritted), c. 1765, 8½ in., 21.5 cm. wide. **£350-400** C

A famille rose armorial soup-plate, Qianlong 9 in., 23 cm. diam. **£170-200** C

A pair of indented-edge "famille verte" porcelain plates, shop marks, 26 cm. diam., Kangxi (K'ang Hsi) **£450-500** SKC

A 'Famille Verte' Plate, 8½ in. wide (damaged), c. 1790. **£65-75** CA

A Coalport Plate, slight hairline crack, c. 1830. **£20-25** perfect **£50-60** CSG

A Coalport Plate with landscape, c. 1860. **£145-165** MN

A Coalport Plate with rose, c. 1900. **£75-85** MN

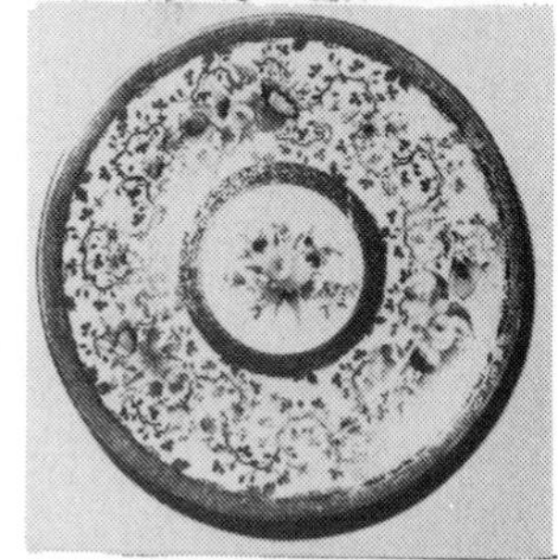

A Coalport Plate, c. 1820. **£85-100** MN

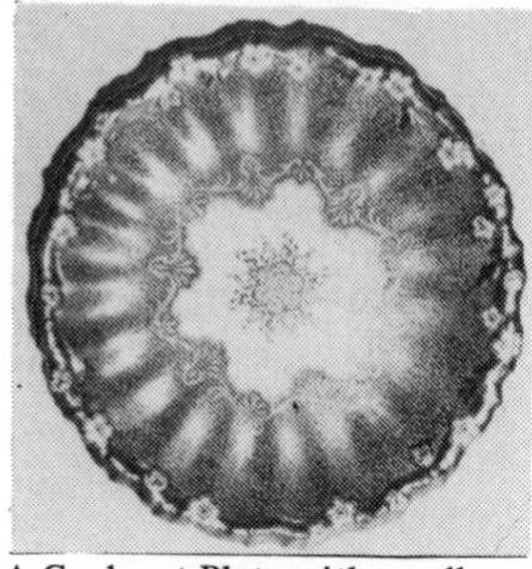

A Coalport Plate with small amount of jewelling and raised gilding c. 1890. **£95-105** MN

FAMILLE VERTE, ROSE, JAUNE AND NOIRE

- Albert Jaquemart classified the familles by choosing the predominant palette colour.
- all belong to Ch'ing dynasty and the best work was done between 1662-1760
- the verte is a brilliant transparent green enamel
- the highest quality rose is a beautiful rose pink
- on some 19thC export ware these two palettes are combined to produce rose-verte
- famille jaune (yellow) and famille noire (black) both rare; although latter has been forged

A Coalport Plate. **£30-40** MN

A Coalport Plate, signed Simpson, 9 in., c. 1900. **£220-250** MN

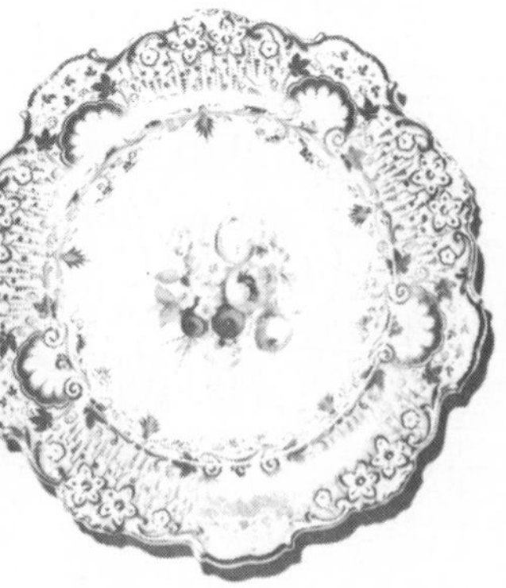
A Davenport Plate with raised gilding, c. 1830-45. **£95-105** MN

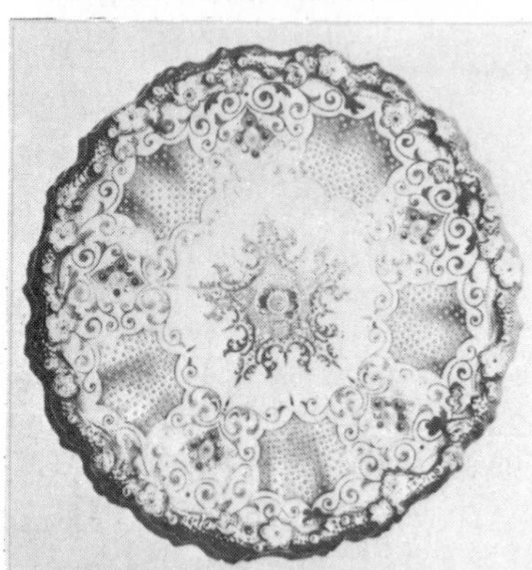
A Jewelled Coalport Plate with gilding, c. 1890. **£200-230** MN

A Coalport Plate, c. 1815-1830, in perfect condition. **£150-170** MN

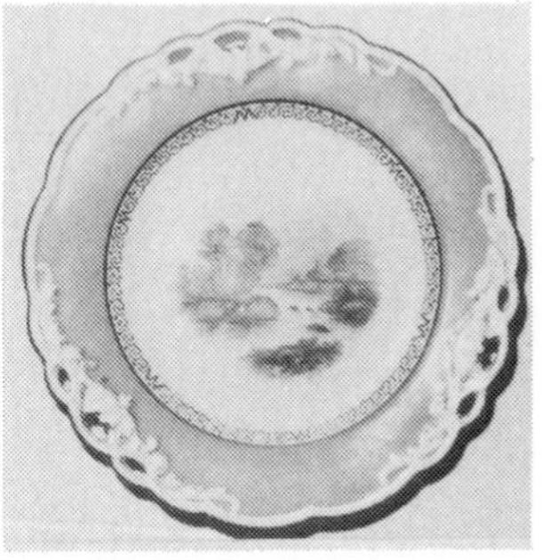
A Davenport Plate, blue anchor mark, c. 1860. **£65-67** MN

A Coalport Plate, with raised gilding, c. 1845. **£145-165** MN

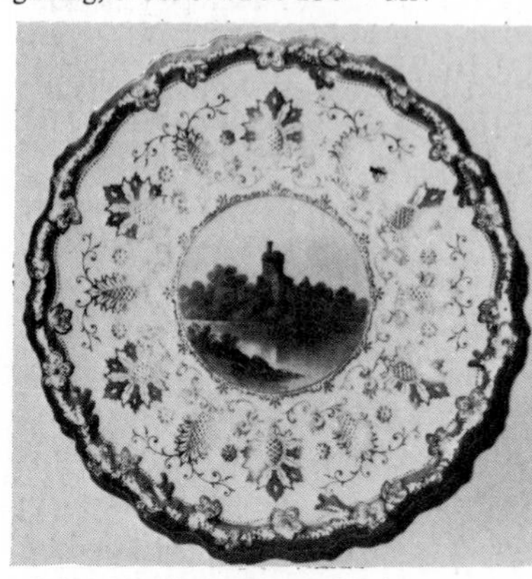
A Rare Coalport Plate of Caistor Castle, decorated and signed by Perry c. 1900. **£295-320** MN

A Copeland Plate, pierced rim with gilt, 9 in. c. 1890. **£150-190** MN

A Davenport Stoneware Small Plate, rare ochre ground with pierced border and puce decorations, 7¼ in. **£75-85** MN

A Coalport Plate, signed Simpson, 9 in., c. 1900. **£250-275** MN

A Davenport Plate, 6½ in. c. 1870. **£17-20** CSG

A Bristol Delft Polychrome Plate painted with a bird within a powdered manganese border (rim chips) c. 1750, 23 cm. diam. **£130-160** C

A Bristol Plate decorated in blue, 9 in., c. 1760, chips. **£160-180** S

A Bristol Plate painted in vivid tones of blue, 8¾ in., c. 1760, slight rim chips. **£100-120** S

A Bristol Plate with scalloped rim, all in shades of blue, 8¾ in., c. 1760, chip on rim. **£180-200** S

A Bristol Plate decorated in red, yellow and blue, 8½ in., early 18th C., rim rubbed. **£900-1,200** S

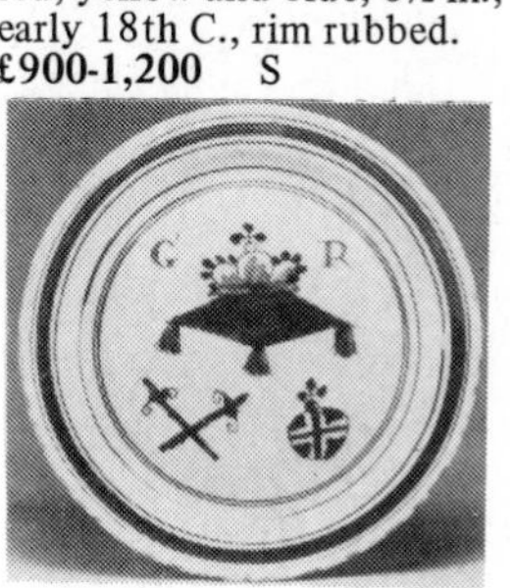

A Bristol Plate decorated in blue, 8½ in., c. 1714, rim rubbed. **£1,500-1,800** S

A Pair of Bristol Delft Polychrome Plates painted in blue, manganese and ochre (one with slight crack, minute chipping) c. 1760, 23 cm. diam. **£120-150** pr. C

A Pair of Bristol Delft Blue and White Plates (rim chips) c. 1760 22.5 cm. diam. **£150-200** C

A Bristol Delft Powdered-Manganese ground Plate (minute rim chip) c. 1760, 22.5 cm. diam. **£140-160** C

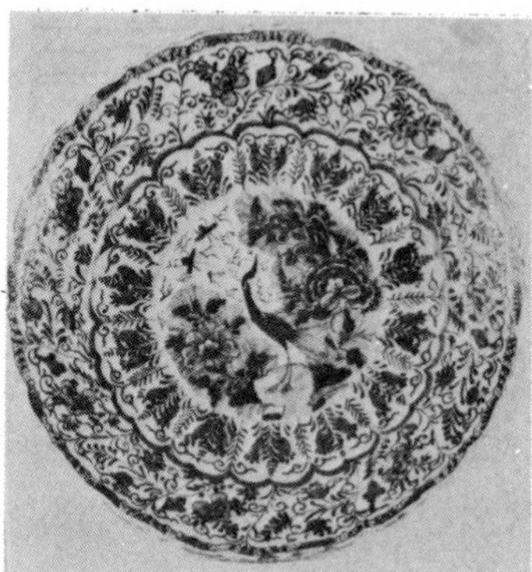

A pair of blue and white Delft Plates, painted in Kraak porcelain style, 12¾", De Claeuw factory, late 18th C. **£560-600** SH

A Dutch Delft Commemorative plate, painted in polychrome enamels with portraits of William V of Orange and his consort and inscription FSW-PWD5, 9" (23.5cms), c1787. **£310-350** SKC

A Plate in blue Chinese style, 9¼ in., possibly Glasgow, mid 18th C., rim chipped. **£140-160** S

A Lambeth Delft Polychrome Plate painted with a green and blue bird (minute rim chip) c. 1720, 22.5 cm. diam. **£290-350** C

A Lambeth Delft Blue and White Plate c. 1720, 19.5 cm. diam. **£260-300** C

A Rare London 'Pomegranate' Charger, in yellow-ochre, delineated in blue, 11 in., probably Southwark, mid-17th C., hair crack. **£2,600-2,800** S

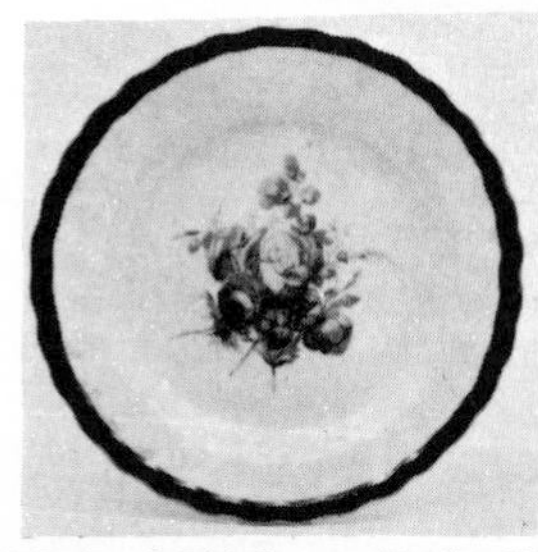
A Pair of Old Crown Derby Plates, painted by Billingsley, the borders outlined with bands of dark blue and gilt, pattern No. 100 crown, crossed batons and D mark and 100 in puce. 8½ in., 21.3 cm. **£330-390** pr. L

A Lambeth Delft Blue and White Armorial Plate (rim chip) c. 1740, 21.5 cm. diam. **£110-200** C

A London Plate in red, yellow, green and blue in Chinese style, 9 in., c. 1740, rim slightly chipped. **£200-230** S

A Derby Plate by Hancock of Chatsworth House, c. 1780, puce marked. **£400-450** MJ

A Liverpool Plate painted in Fazackerly palette, 8¾ in., c. 1760, chipped. **£200-250** S

A Delft Blue and White Charger, 13¼ in., c. 1750. **£125-150** CSG

A pair of Derby Plates by John Brewer, 8¾ in., c. 1810. **£625-700** pr. MJ

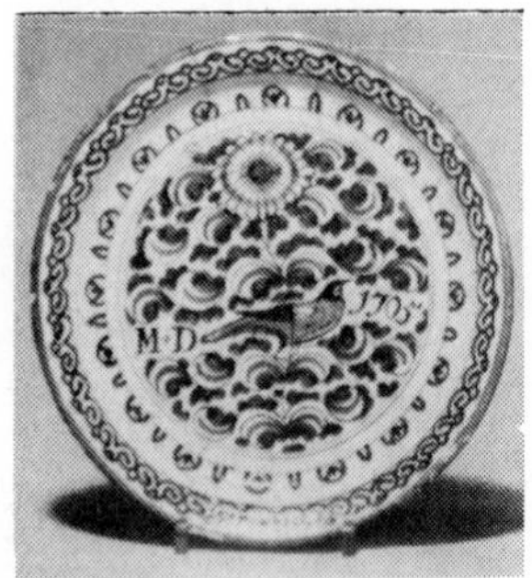

A London Delft Blue and White Dated Plate with the initials MD and the date 1705 (cracked and chipped) 22.5 cm. diam. **£110-150** C

A Fully Marked Derby Plate, painted by Quaker Peg, with blue mark. **£350-380** SA

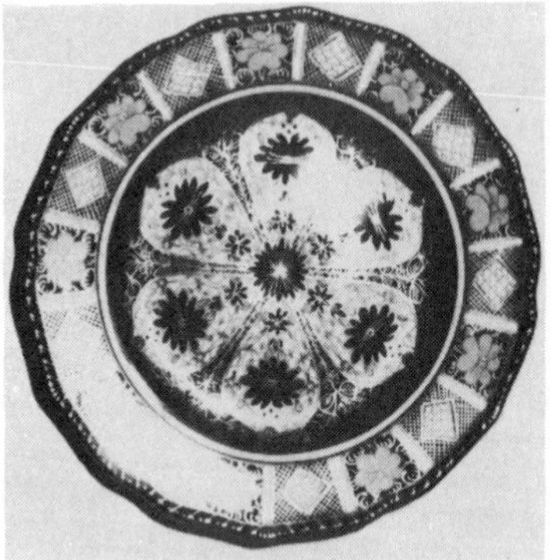
A Royal Crown Derby Plate marked, 1913. **£75-80** CSG

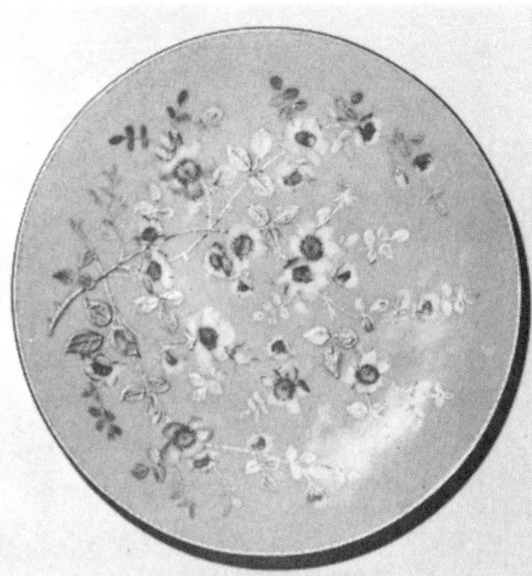

A Derby Plate on green ground, silver and gold 'resist' roses c. 1882. **£85-95** MN

A Derby Plate, rubbed, c. 1882. **£245-270** MN

A Derby Plate, claret ground, with raised gilding, c. 1906. **£65-75** MN

A Derby Plate with gilt rim, c. 1906. **£85-95** MN

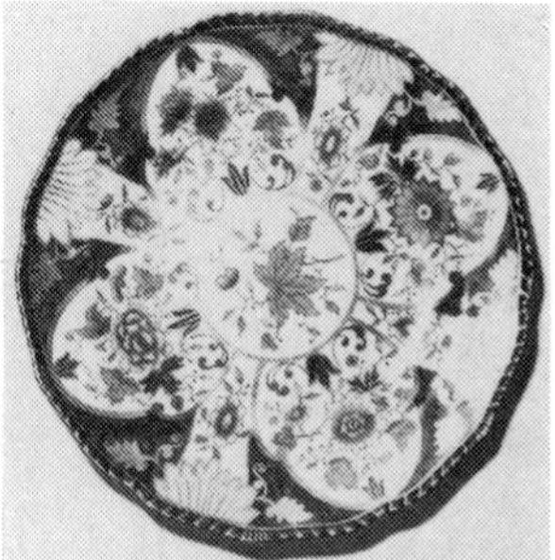

A Derby Plate. **£55-65** MN

A Derby Plate, signed Ruben Hague, rare coral ground, pierced border, blue enamelling, jewelling, yellow background with cherubs, 1904. **£600-700** MN

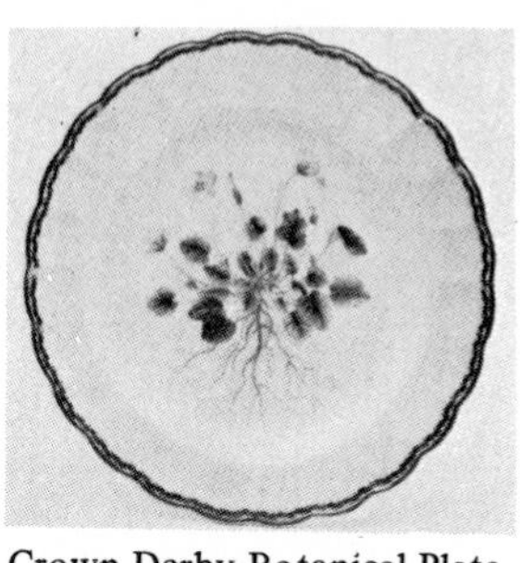

A Crown Derby Botanical Plate, painted with a flowering Dwarf Geranium plant, 8¾ in., 22.2 cm., named in blue script and with crown, crossed batons and D mark and pattern no. 141 in blue **£190-250** L

A Pair of Crown Derby Plates, surrounded by a dark blue band gilt with foliage, with scrolling foliage and white enamel flowers, 9½ in., 24.2 cm., named in script and with crown, crossed batons and D mark in red **£380-430** L

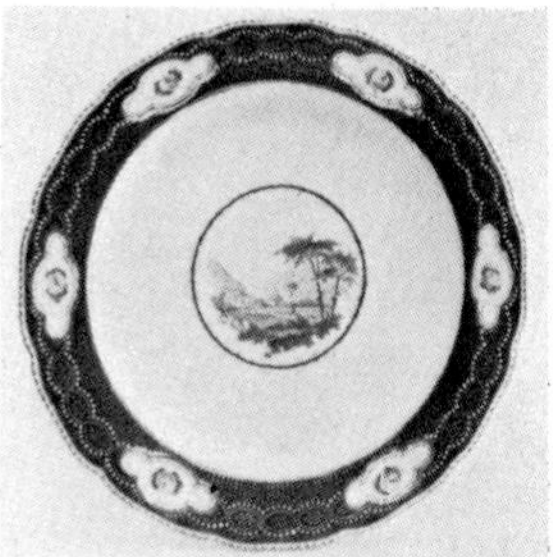

A Pair of Crown Derby Plates, painted by Zachariah Boreman 9½in., 23.8 cm., crown, crossed batons and D mark in puce **£330-380** L

A Doccia blue and white plate transfer-printed and stencilled, 22.5 cm. diam. c. 1765. **£350-450** C

Four Doulton Coronation Plates for Edward VII, each painted in underglaze blue, printed rosette mark. 9 in., 23.2 cm. **£110-150** set. L

An English Porcelain Turquoise-Ground Armorial Plate, perhaps Spode, c. 1840, 26.5 cm. diam. **£90-120** C

Blue and White Leeds impressed plate, c. 1800, 7 in. diam. **£28-34** TT

Mason Ironstone Plate c. 1820 with the Mason Black Mark, 9 in. diam. **£25-30** TT

A Meissen plate with a basket-work moulded border, 23.5 cm. diam. blue crossed swords mark, Pressnummer 15, c. 1745. **£200-225** C

Mason's Plate with Red mark very richly coloured on a yellow ground 10 in. diam. **£30-35** TT

A Set of Eight Meissen porcelain plates, with blue crossed swords and incised numeral marks, 9½" diam. **£750-800** P.W.C.

A Meissen plate, painted in the Kakiemon palette with the flying fox pattern, with a Sulkowski Ozier border, (minor rim chip repair) 25.5 cm. diam. blue crossed swords mark, c. 1740. **£450-500** C

A Meissen plate painted with the red dragon pattern, 23 cm. diam. blue crossed swords mark, puce K.H.C. mark, Pressnummer 10, c. 1740. **£550-600** C

Mason's Plate with impressed Miles Mason Mark. Unusual colour, c. 1800, 8 in. diam. **£30-35** TT

Mason's Plate with yellow ground 8 in. diam. **£20-25** TT

A pair of Meissen plates painted in the Kakiemon palette, 25.5 cm. diam. blue crossed swords marks, Pressnummer 52, c. 1740. **£1,350-1,500** C

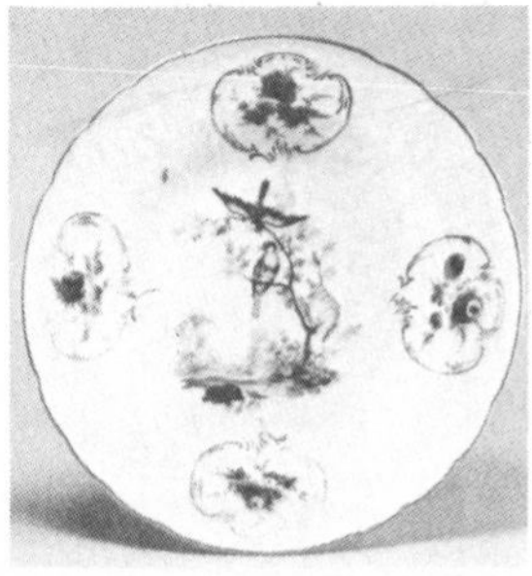

A Pair of Marcolini Meissen Soup Plates decorated with the 'Dulong' pattern, 23.7 cm., crossed swords and a star in underglaze blue, impressed numerals, c. 1770. **£550-600** S

A Porcelain Plate with superb gilding and English flowers, origin unknown, but English, c. 1820. **£45-55** CP

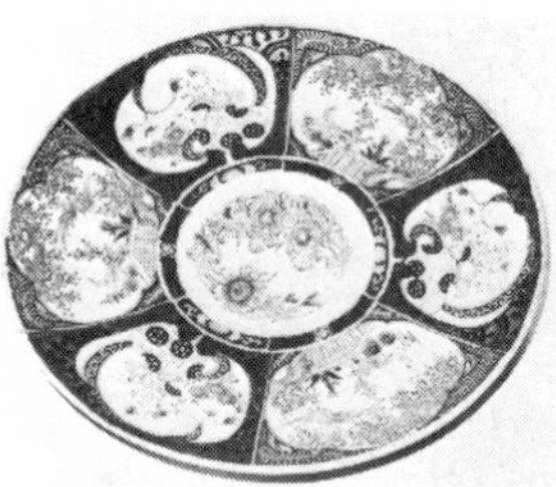

A 19th C. Imari Charger, 18 in. diam. **£220-265** SV

A Set of Three Imari Plates, painted in typical Imari colours, 27.3 cm. and 24.2 cm., late 18th C. **£390-430** S Be

A Set of Four Furstenberg Soup Plates, by Ahrend August Hartmann, 23.4 cm. script F mark in underglaze blue and incised W, c. 1775, three with chips to footrim and some gilding rubbed. **£600-650** S

A Small Imari Plate, 8½ in., c. 1880. **£30-35** CA

A Pair of North Italian Plates, decorated in blue and white, 24 cm., c. 1730 some chips on rims. **£260-290** S

A German foliate plate painted en camaeiu rose (minor foot rim chip) 22.5 cm. diam. brown NB mark, probably Hochst, c. 1765. **£250-350** C

A Pair of 'Kenjo Imari' Square Plates painted in underglaze blue, iron-red, colours and gilt, 18th C., Ch'eng Hua six-character marks, 17.8 cm. square. **£680-780** C

A Johnson Bros. 'Historic America' Plate, 1890-1910, 19½" wide. **£45-60** SQE

A pair of Famille Verte Imari soup plates (minor foot chips,) early 18th C., 8¾ in., 22.5 cm. diam. **£190-225** C

A Large Imari Plate, 13 in., c. 1880. **£95-105** CA

A Laterza Plate painted in blue by Angelo Antonio d'Alessandro, with a coat-of-arms in blue, green and yellow, 22.5 cm., late 17th C. cracked. **£600-670** S

A Meissen Plate, 24.7 cm. crossed swords in underglaze blue, impressed 22, c. 1740, footrim damaged. **£400-450** S

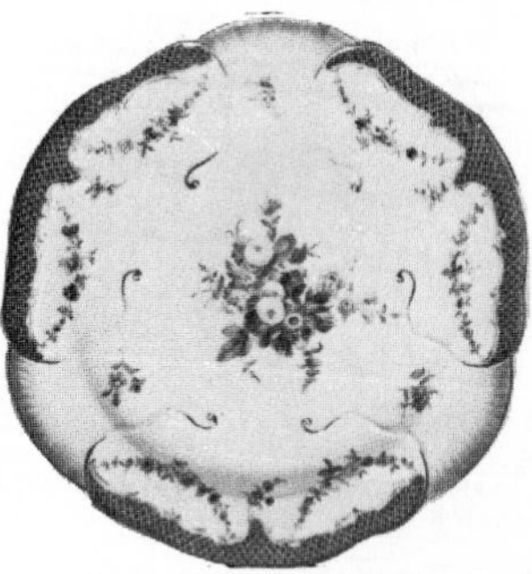
Four Meissen Pink Feuille-De-Choux Plates, the border with puce scale pattern divided by feuille-de-choux panels, with gilt rims, blue crossed swords and dot marks, c. 1755 24 cm., diam. **£850-950** C

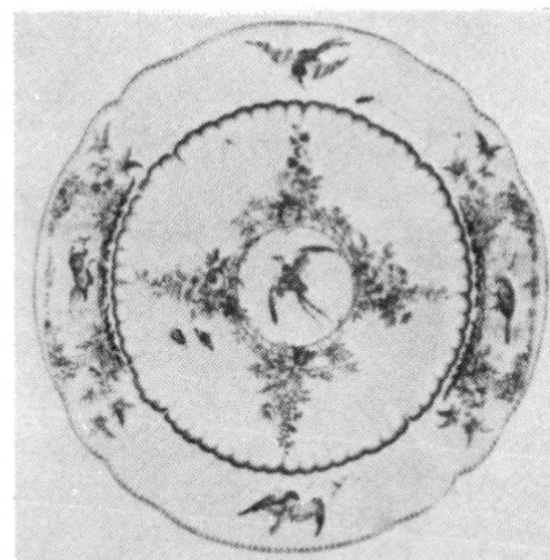
A Meissen Plate, diam. 24 cm., underglaze mark in blue, late 18th C. **£350-390** S Be

A Meissen Plate with a royal-blue border decorated with gilt, underglaze blue crossed swords, painted title, late 19th C., 20.8 cm. **£250-290** SB

Three Meissen (Marcolini) Plates painted in colours with shaped gilt rims, blue crossed swords and star marks, c. 1775. **£500-570** C

A Minton plate with landscape, c. 1850, 8¾ in. diam. **£90-100** MJ

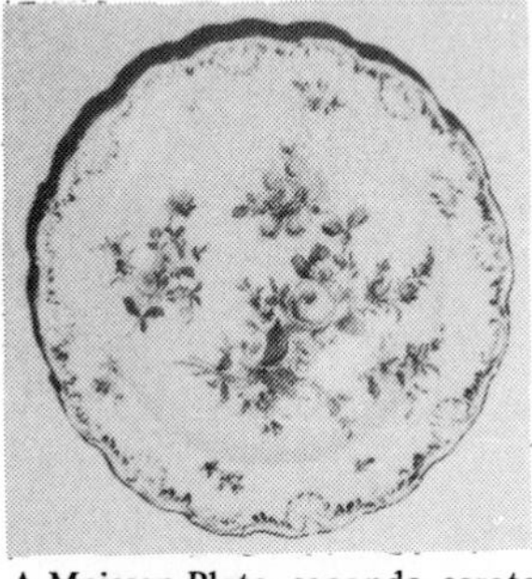
A Meissen Plate, seconds, scratch mark through crossed swords, c. 1880. **£65-75** MN

Twelve Meissen (Marcolini) Plates painted in colours within shaped gilt rims, blue crossed swords and star marks, c. 1775 24 cm., diam. **£1,100-1,300** C

A Minton Plate, turquoise with gilt rim, c. 1866. **£44-50** CSG

Six Meissen Plates painted in colours within shaped gilt rims (four with minor rim chips), blue crossed swords marks, Pressnummern 15 and 22, c. 1740 24.5 cm., diam. **£900-1,000** C

A Set of Seven Meissen Plates, width 24.6 cm., late 19th C. **£360-390** S Be

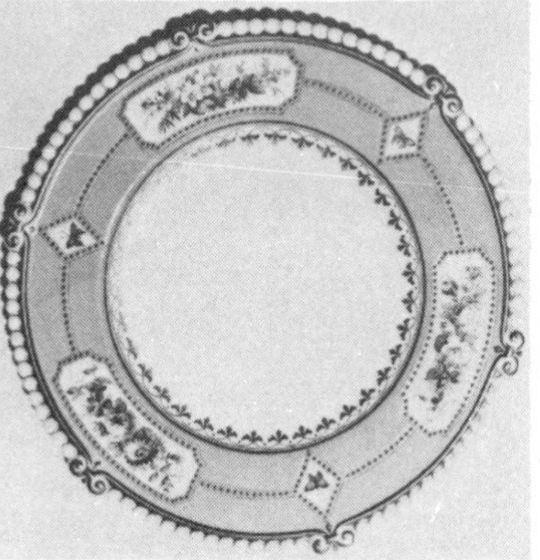
A Minton Plate, turquoise ground, beautifully jewelled, with gilding and with insect reserves. **£95-120** MN

A Minton Plate, made for American market, with cockerel **£300-350** MN

A De Morgan Lustre Charger, decorated in copper, pink and yellow lustres, Merton Abbey period. 36 cm., diam. **£530-600** C

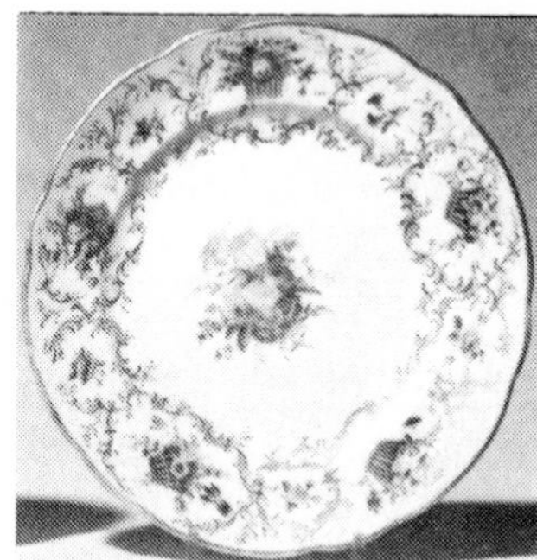
A Nantgarw Plate (some retouching to enamels and gilding) impressed mark, c. 1820, 24 cm. diam. **£360-400** C

A Minton Plate with typical Minton bright turquoise ground, jewelled gilding, c. 1860. **£220-240** MN

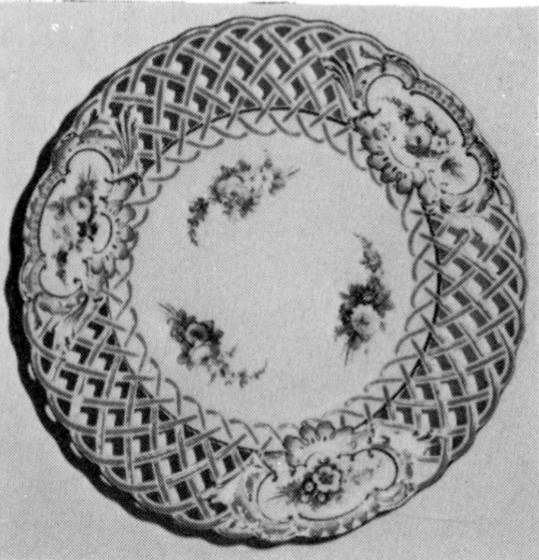
A Minton Plate with pierced border; impressed mark and small piece of enamelling missing, c. 1890. **£65-75** perfect **£100+** MN

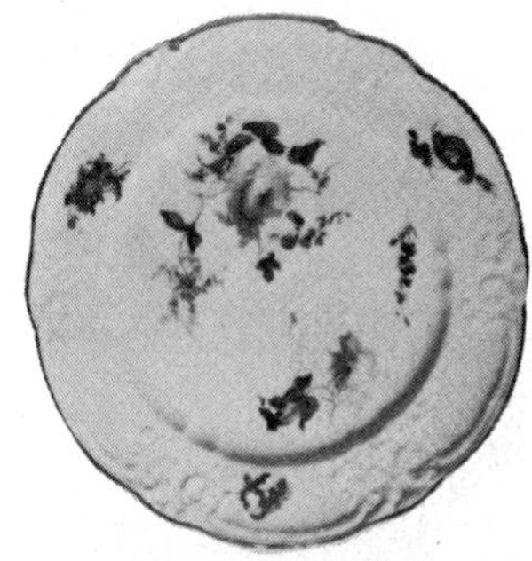
A Nantgarw Plate painted by Moses Webster, impressed mark, c. 1815, 25 cm. diam. **£600-700** C

A Minton Plate with torquoise border and gilt rim, 9 in., c. 1865. **£50-60** MN

A Naples saucer-dish, inscribed in iron-red Donna di Cascano casale di Sessa, (minor chip to rim) 19 cm. diam. iron-red crowned FR mark, c. 1775. **£250-300** C

A Nantgarw Plate from MacIntosh service, c. 1815. **£1,750-1,850** SA

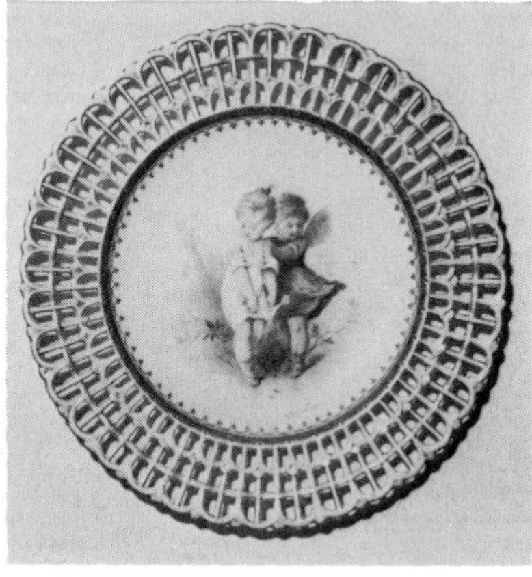
A Boullemier Minton Plate with pierced border and gilt jewelling, c. 1885. Restored **£300-340** Perfect **£500-550** MN

A fine Nantgarw plate 24 cm., impressed Nantgarw, "C.W." c. 1817-20. **£255-300** SKC

A Nantgarw Plate, outlined with scrolls in relief in white, with ribbon bows and flowers within a shaped dentil rim. 8½ in., 21.5 cm. **£350-400** L

NANTGARW (Glamorgan soft paste porcelain)

- 1813 started by W Billingsley at Nantgarw
- transferred to Swansea 1814-17
- the porcelain uneconomic to produce because it was unstable with nine tenths kiln wastage
- appearance white, glassy and translucent
- often simply decorated on site by Pardoe and Baxter
- eagerly sought after by London dealers and decorators who were responsible for elaborate decoration
- Marks:- NANTGARW NANT GARW or NANT GARW C.W.
- specimens are much sought after.

A Nymphenburg Plate painted in colours, blue hexagram mark, 1763/1767 25 cm., diam. **£280-320** C

Pratt Ware Plate, 'Cattle and Ruins', 7" diam. **£30-40** OF

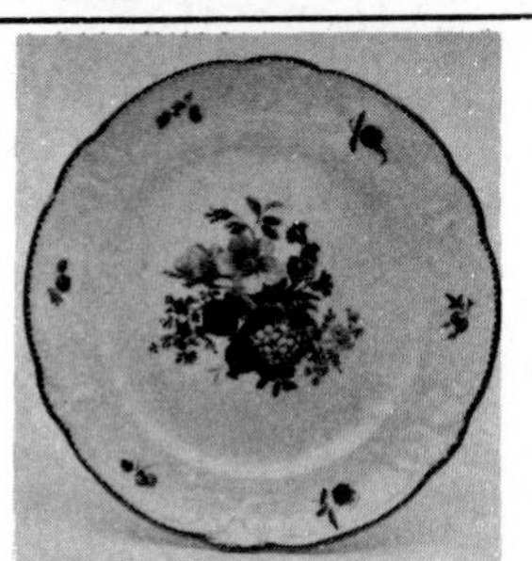

A Nantgarw Plate from the Brace service, with a shaped gilt dentil rim. 8¾ in., 22.2 cm., (impressed mark, Nantgarw c.w). **£725-825** L

A Pair of Paris Plates painted with a Dog and a Mongoose, 21.8 cm., early 19th C. light rubbing. **£440-500** S

Pratt Ware Plate, 'Shrimpers', c1860, 7" diam. **£30-40** OF

An Impressed Marked Nantgarw Plate with the Sevres green border and raised gilding, painted with English flowers and, unusually, with a pineapple, c. 1813-18. **£950-1,050** SA

Pratt Ware Plate, 'Kestrel', c1850-60, 9" diam. **£165-185** OF

Pratt Ware Plate, 'Roman Ruins', 9" diam. **£30-40** OF

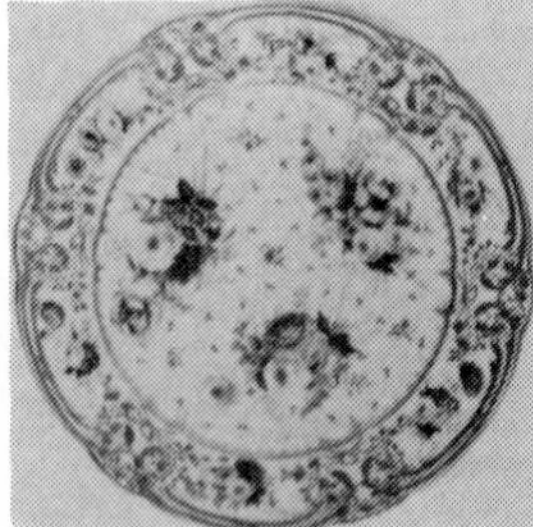

A Nantgarw Plate, the shaped rim moulded and accentuated with gilding, 24.4 cm., impressed NANTGARW.C.W., early 19th C. (two haircracks). **£200-230** S Be

Pratt Ware Plate, 'Bouquet', c1850-60. **£30-40** OF

Pratt Ware Plate, 'The Ruined Temple', 8½" diam. **£45-55** OF

A Ridgeway Plate, c. 1890.
£145-165 MN

A Sevres Plate, marked, c. 1830.
£280-350 MN

A Spode Plate, marked Spode 2214, c. 1815. **£45-55** CSG

A Rogers Plate, blue and white (firing flaw), c. 1825-36. **£17-22** CSG

Six Sevres Plates painted with rose-sprays, with gilt rims (two with minor repairs), blue and gray interlaced L marks c. 1770 24 cm., diam. **£280-340** C

A Spode Plate. **£85-95** MN

A pair of Sevres armorial ornithological bleu nouveau-ground plates painted after du Buffon, 24 cm. diam. blue interlaced L marks, 1793, Painter's mark of Vieillard, gilder's mark HP. **£1,600-1,700** pr. C

A Pair of Sevres Soup-Plates, the lobed borders with an acorn band, black interlaced L marks and DR, 1785 23.5 cm., diam. **£110-150** C

A Spode Felspar Plate, c. 1820. **£145-165** MN

A Pair of 'Sevres' Soft-Paste 'Jewelled' Plates, on a bleu-de-roi ground, painted interlaced L's and A, 18th C., 24 cm. **£250-290** SB

A Pair of Sevres Plates painted in colours, blue interlaced L marks, 1790 Painter's mark fx and sc 23.5 cm., diam. **£420-480** C

A Pair of Staffordshire Miniature Children's Plates printed and coloured, the borders with rare moulded and coloured busts commemorating the accession of King William and Queen Adelaide, 5 in. diam. **£50-60** pr. CSK

A Swansea Plate, painted probably by Henry Morris in soft colours, 8 in., c. 1813-22, slight rubbing. **£250-300** S

A Swansea Plate painted with flowers and insects, c. 1815. **£400-440** SA

A Fine Pair of marked Swansea Plates of the Mandarin pattern with panels of various perched birds, 8½ in., c. 1814. **£850-920** SA

A Swansea Plate of Burdett-Coutts type, impressed mark, c. 1815, 21.5 cm. diam. **£200-250** C

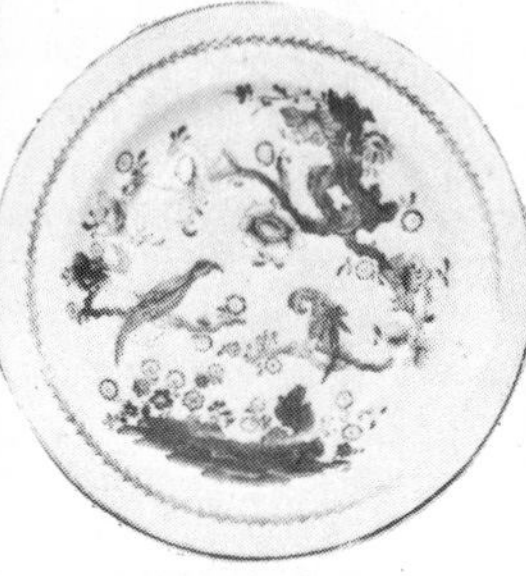

A Pair of Swansea Teaplates painted with 'Chained Parrot' pattern. **£350-400** pr. SA

A 'Vienna' Plate, the centre painted by H. Weigel, signed, on a bleu-de-roi ground, painted title 'Loreley', D110 and underglaze blue shield, late 19th C., 24 cm. **£460-500** SB

A Swansea Plate painted with scattered flower-sprays, red stencil mark, c. 1815, 21 cm. diam. **£100-120** C

A Swansea Plate, decorated in London by Bradley, of grey-headed green woodpecker, also with flowers and fruit. **£1,200-1,350** SA

A Vienna Beehive Plate. **£275-300** MN

A Swansea Plate with a spirally-painted blue and gilt border (gilding retouched) red stencil mark, pattern no. 470, c. 1815, 21 cm. diam. **£150-200** C

A Swansea Plate painted by Pollard with English flowers **£300-320** SA

A Vienna Plate, 11½ in., c. 1910. **£110-130** MN

A Pair of Vienna Plates painted in colours, (one with rim chip) blue beehive marks, incised marks, c. 1775 26 cm., diam. **£300-350** C

A Wedgwood Jorrocks hand-decorated Plate, pre-War. **£20-25** each PC

A Wedgwood Plate, signed Holland. **£85-95** MN

A Whieldon Commemorative Plate with the motto 'Success to the King of Prussia and his forces', 23 cm. diam. c. 1756. **£280-350** C

A Rare Armorial Wincanton Plate painted in blue, 8½ in., mid 18th C. **£140-160** S

A Barr, Flight & Barr Queen Charlotte Pattern Plate, 8 in. diam., c. 1810. **£100-120** SA

A Pair of Chamberlain Worcester Plates, with hand-painted roses. **£195-210** pr. MN

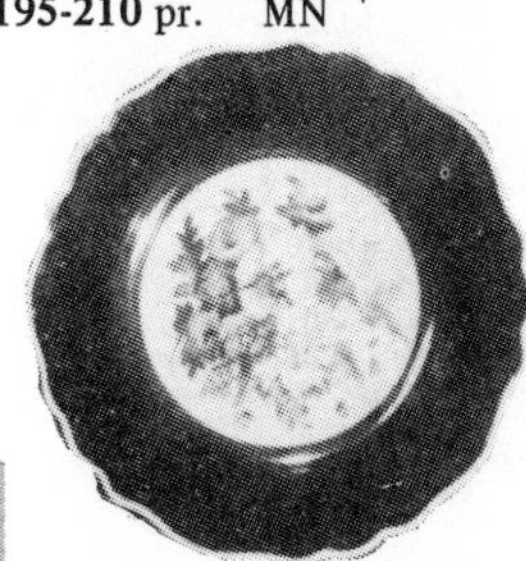

A fine Chamberlain's plate boldly painted with a display of summer flowers on a pale yellow ground, 9 in. diam., marked Chamberlain Worcester in red, c. 1825. **£100-120** NN

A Flight, Barr & Barr Worcester Plate with green rim, slightly rubbed, c. 1830-1840. **£75-85** MN

A Grainger Worcester Plate, 8½ in. **£95-105** MN

A Pair of Dr. Wall Small Plates, script W mark, 'Pine Cone' pattern 6 in. diam. **£250-275** pr. SA

left

A Davis, Flight Worcester Plate, painted with Prince of Wales plumes, from a service presented to George III on visiting factory, c. 1784. **£110-130** SA

A First Period Worcester Blue and White Plate, Crescent mark, c. 1770. **£95-105** CSG

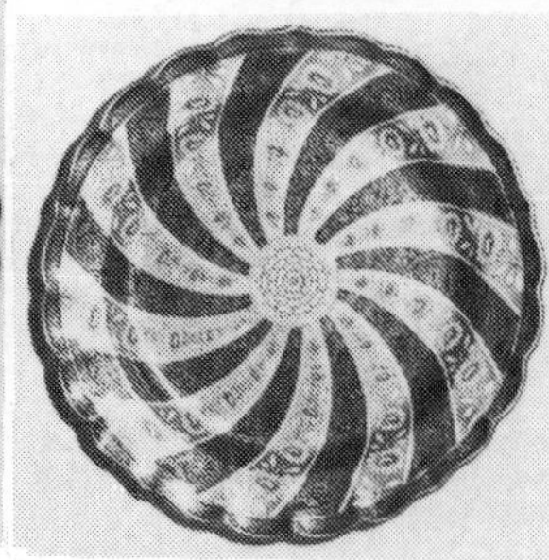

A Worcester Plate, c. 1888. **£65-75** MN

A Blue and White Plate, c. 1820. **£16-20** CSG

A Fine Dr. Wall Worcester Plate, painted by Giles, from the Lady Mary Montague Wortley Service. **£1,500-1,700** SA

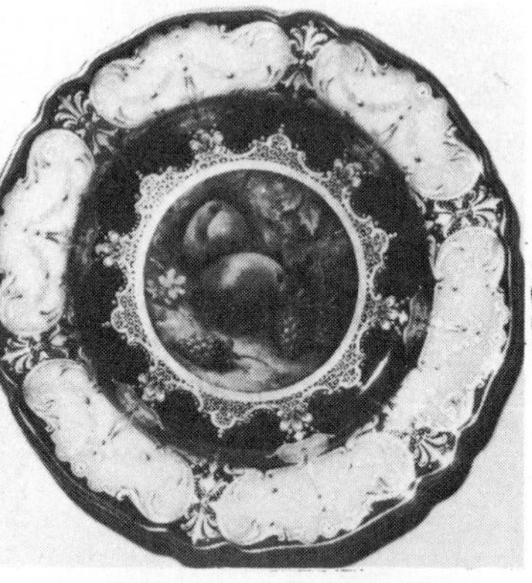

A Royal Worcester Sebright Plate. **£300-340** MN

An Early 19th C. Plate, J.B. impressed, raised gilt rim with flowers and insects, c. 1820. **£44-50** CSG

A Worcester Blue-Scale Plate painted in iron-red in the atelier of James Giles, blue crescent mark, c. 1770, 18.5 cm. diam. **£500-550** C

An Adam and Eve Charger showing Eve standing by an apple tree offering the fruit to Adam all in yellow and green with blue sponged foliage, and blue dash rim, diameter 35 cm., late 18th C. cracked. **£420-480** S Be

A Worcester Pierced Plate, possibly Owen piercing. **£500-600** MN

A Worcester Plate painted in the atelier of James Giles, c. 1770, 23 cm. diam. **£200-220** C

A rare set of four Regency copper lustre plates, c. 1810, one impressed "Wilson" 19.5 cm. diam. **£355-400** SKC

Pictorial Souvenirs of Britain (made in Germany for British market): Pink Pictorial plate. **£9-12** NO

A Part of an 18th C. Chi'en Lung Chinese Tea Service.
left to right:

A Teapot Stand	**£300-330**
A Teapoy	**£300-330**
A Teapot	**£500-550**
A Spoon Tray	**£300-330**

SA

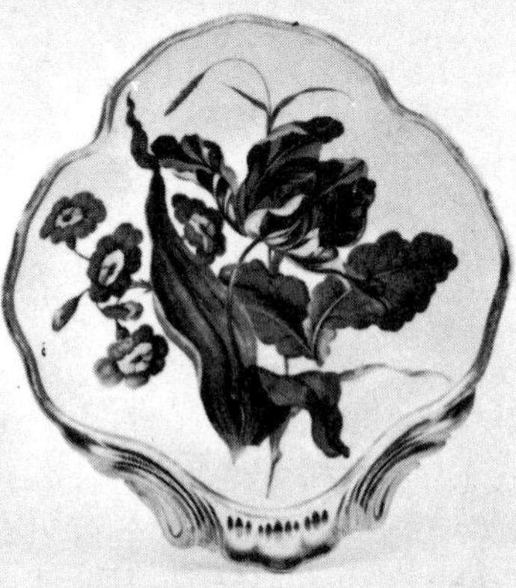

A Crown Derby Part Dessert Service, each piece superbly painted, comprising four shell-shape dishes, two lobed oval dishes and two lobed diamond-shape dishes, named in script and crown, crossed batons and D mark and nos. 3 to 12 in red **£520-600** L

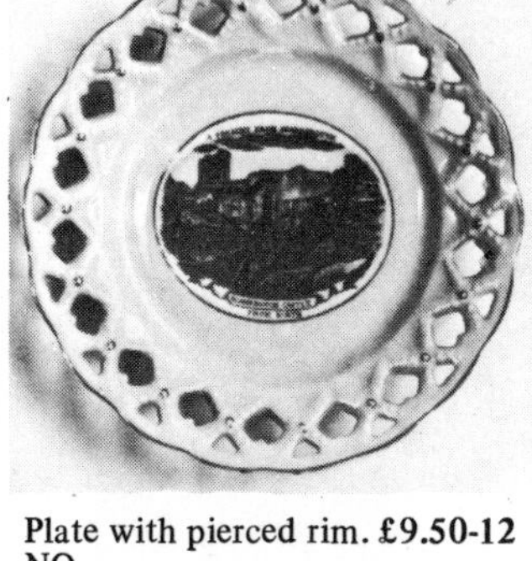

Plate with pierced rim. **£9.50-12** NO

A rare Meissen-decorated Chinese Batavian ware saucer, painted in the manner of Johann Gregor Herold, 12 cm., simulated crossed swords mark in underglaze blue, c. 1725. **£725-750** SKC

Ribbon plate, with peacock. **£9-11** NO

MEISSEN

- the most important 18th C. factory
- first porcelain made c.1709
- body was hard with slightly yellowish tinge
- displays a strong Chinese influence
- up to c.1720 influenced by J.F. Bottger
- Kaendler started in the Meissen factory in 1731 and began the period of the finest Meissen figures of the Baroque period
- 'Crinoline' groups painted in strong colours, were made from 1740-1745

A Dresden Dessert Service, ten plates, two oval dishes and two leaf-shaped dishes, painted mark and Dresden, c. 1900, plate 21.2 cm. **£250-290** SB

A Bayreuth Hausmaler Saucer decorated in the manner of J.P. Dannhofer, c. 1740. **£330-360** S

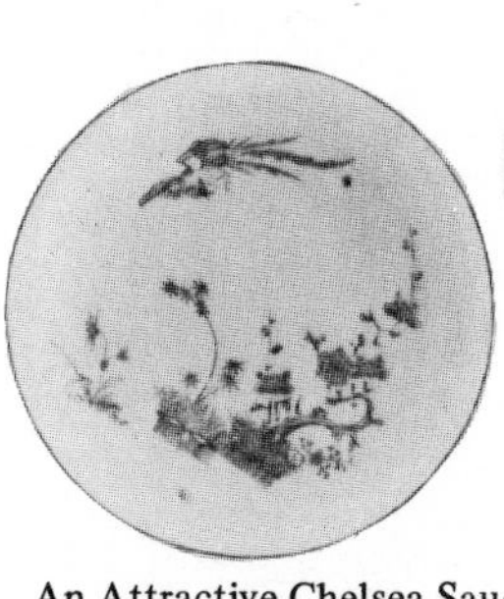

An Attractive Chelsea Saucer painted in a pale Kakiemon palette, raised anchor period, c. 1749-52. **£440-480** S

A Very Early Rare Coalport Breakfast Set, Teapot, Sucrier, 2 Cups and Saucers, Cream Jug, with dark blue ground, hand painted dogs, c. 1841. **£650-700** MN

A Wedgwood Tea Service, with 12 of everything, c. 1910-1920. **£175-195** MN

A Chelsea Fluted Teabowl and Saucer, red anchor marks, c. 1758. **£450-500** C

A Caughley teabowl and saucer, c. 1800. **£45-50** MJ

Three Dr. Wall Items from Kempthorne service.

Teapot Stand	**£250-280**	
Sucrier	**£350-380**	
Spoon Tray	**£300-330**	SA

A Caughley teabowl and saucer, c. 1800. **£55-60** MJ

A Chelsea Spirally moulded Teabowl, Coffee-cup and Saucer, painted with bouquets and scattered flowers (minute crack to cup) red anchor marks, c. 1755, **£400-450** C

A Caughley cup and saucer, marked c. 1800 **£150-180** MJ

A Royal Albert Cup and Saucer, 1950's. **£12-14** MN

A Champions Bristol Cup and Saucer, basket moulding and gilt rims, c. 1775. **£195-215** CSG

A Capodimonte (Carlo III) Teabowl and a Saucer painted by Guiseppe della Torre, with gilt rims, blue fleur-de-lys marks, c. 1750. **£2,000-2,300** C

A Caughley teabowl and saucer, c. 1800. **£55-60** MJ

A famille rose teabowl and saucer (chipped, the saucer cracked), Yongzheng/early Qianlong. **£65-75** C

A pair of Qing hexafoil semi-eggshell tea bowls and saucers painted en grisaille and gilt, 18th C. **£165-225** C

A pair of Tea Bowls and Saucers, pencilled in black in Chinese taste, Ch'ien Lung. **£120-160** L

A Coalport Teacup and Saucer, c. 1860. **£65-75** MJ

A Coalport Cup and Saucer, with hairline crack to saucer, **£25-30** perfect **£45-50** MN

A Coalport Chocolate Cup with Cover and Saucer, heavily embossed with flowers, c. 1830-1845. **£300-340** MN

A Coalport Cup and Saucer with green ground. **£30-40** MN

A Coalport Cup and Saucer, c. 1820. **£110-130** MN

A Coalport Teacup and Saucer, c. 1845. **£65-70** MN

A Copeland Jewelled Cup and Saucer, dark blue ground. **£35-40** MN

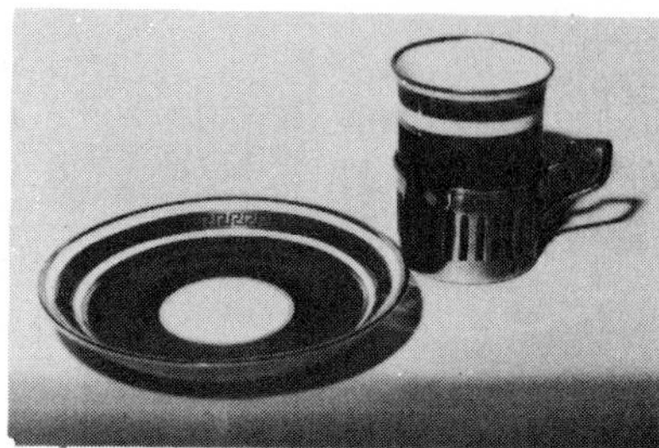

A Crescent China Cup and Saucer, with solid silver holder, c. 1910-1915. **£35-45** MN

An Unusual Davenport Cup and Saucer (in Minton style), blue marked, c. 1860. **£50-60** MN

A Davenport Cup and Saucer (in Persian style), puce mark c. 1870. **£50-60** MN

A Davenport Square Demi-Tasse Cup and Saucer, c. 1860. **£35-45** MN

A Bloor Derby cup and saucer, c. 1840. **£30-40** MJ

A Derby Can and Saucer, 2451 pattern, c. 1910. **£35-40** MN

A Derby Small Cup and Saucer, c. 1909. **£28-35** MN

An 'S & H' Derby Cup and Saucer, c. 1880. **£75-85** MN

A Derby Cup and Saucer, 1128 'In and Out' pattern, 1936. **£75-85** MN

A Derby Cup and Saucer, heavily gilded, c. 1878. **£65-70** MN

right
A Royal Crown Derby Cup and Saucer, 1128 pattern, c. 1930. **£50-60** MN

DERBY YEAR CYPHERS

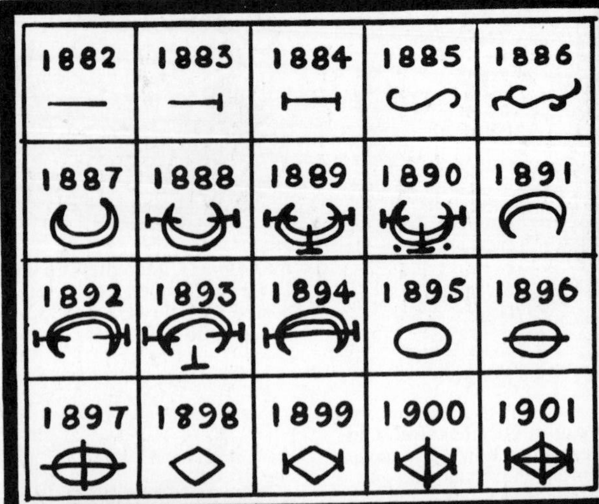

1882	1883	1884	1885	1886
1887	1888	1889	1890	1891
1892	1893	1894	1895	1896
1897	1898	1899	1900	1901

A Crown Derby Cup and Saucer on pink ground, c. 1910. **£110-130** MJ

A Derby Cup and Saucer, cream ground with silver and gold, slight rubbing, c. 1880. **£55-60** MN

A Derby Cup and Saucer, with claret ground, and jewelled gilding, c. 1899. **£135-145** MN

A Derby Teabowl and Saucer, c. 1875. **£75-85** MN

A Kloster Veilsdorf teacup and saucer, blue CV marks, c. 1775. **£400-450** C

A Limbach coffee-cup and saucer, painted en camaieu rose, with gilt rims, puce interlaced L marks, c. 1775. **£350-450** C

A Frankenthal tea cup and saucer, painted with figures within a gilt key pattern and green line border, crowned C.T. mark and B in underglaze blue. **£490-590** L

A Furstenberg teacup and saucer, blue F marks, c. 1775. **£200-250** C

A Loosdrecht teabowl and saucer painted in sepia monochrome, blue M.O.L. and star marks, incised marks, c. 1775. **£300-350** C

A Hague Cup and Saucer within purple striped yellow borders with blue and gilt edges, the saucer with stork mark in underglaze blue late 18th C. cracked. **£170-190** S

Mason's Cup and Saucer with gilt decoration on dark blue ground. **£30-35** TT

A Frankenthal teacup and saucer, painted by Jakob Osterspey, blue crowned interlaced CT mark and 76, incised marks, 1776. **£500-600** C

A Pair of Meissen Armorial Teabowls and Saucers painted by B. G. Hauer, blue crossed swords marks, Pressnummer 2, Gilder's mark 61, c.1743. **£2,600-2,900** C

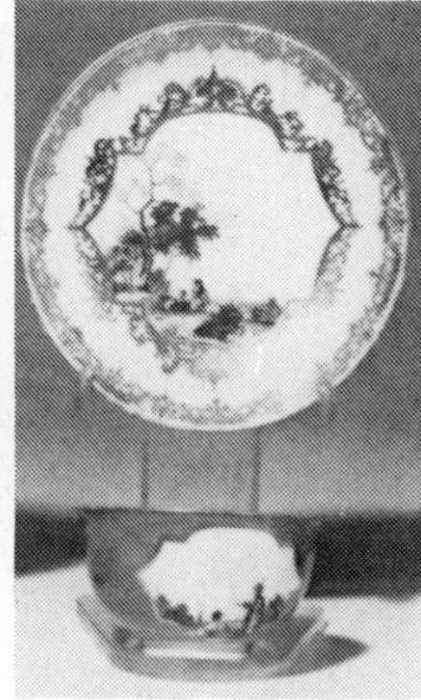

A Meissen Powdered-Purple Ground Teabowl and Saucer, blue crossed swords marks and gilt 35, c. 1740. **£1,300-1,400** C

A Meissen Teacup and Saucer (minute chip to cup), blue crossed swords marks, Pressnummern 66 and 64, c. 1745. **£550-600**

A Meissen Hausmalerei teacup and saucer, blue crossed swords marks, Gilder's mark 114 c. 1740. **£700-800** C

A pair of Meissen ornithological small teacups and saucers, blue crossed swords marks, the cups with Pressnummer 4, c. 1745. **£1,000-1,250** C

A Pair of Meissen Teacups and Saucers with gilt rims, blue crossed swords marks, Pressnummern 17 and 64, c. 1745. **£1,200-1,350** C

A Meissen chinoiserie beaker and saucer, painted in the manner of J. G. Herold, blue crossed swords marks, gilt H, c. 1750. **£1,100-1,250** C

A pair of Meissen ornithological coffee-cups and saucers, blue crossed swords marks, Pressnummer 52 to saucers, c. 1745. **£1,250-1,500** C

A Meissen Hausmalerei coffee-cup and saucer, blue crossed swords marks, Pressnummer 63, c. 1745. **£800-900** C

A Meissen fluted cup and saucer painted in the manner of C.F. Herold with chinoiserie figures (crack and chip to saucer) blue crossed swords marks, c. 1730. **£600-650** C

A pair of Meissen fabeltiere large quatrefoil teacups and saucers, blue crossed swords marks, the saucers with Pressnummer 23, c. 1740. **£4,250-5,000** C

A Marcolini Meissen Cup and Saucer, crossed swords and star in underglaze blue, c. 1770. **£340-400** S

A Meissen Tea Cup and Saucer, decorated in underglaze blue, iron-red, purple, green and gold, in Kakiemon style, crossed swords mark in underglaze blue and numeral 8 and cross in red. **£190-240** L

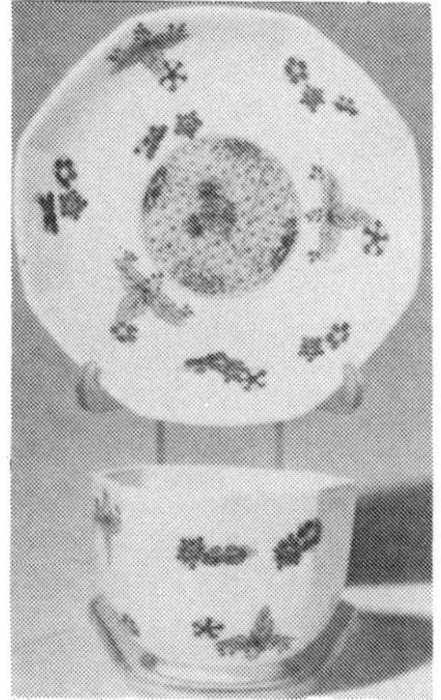

An Early Meissen Octagonal Beaker and Saucer painted in the Kakiemon palette, blue caduceus mark to beaker, Johaneum mark N351/W, c. 1725. **£1,700-1,900** C

A Meissen Powdered Lilac-Ground Coffee-Cup and Saucer painted by B. G. Hauer, blue crossed swords marks, Gilder's marks G, Pressnummer 6, c. 1740. **£1,200-1,300** C

A Pair of Meissen Blue and White Teabowls and Saucers painted en camaieu rose and gilt, blue crossed swords marks (one saucer with star crack to base and chip), Pressnummern 63, c. 1750. **£320-360** C

A Meissen (Marcolini) Cup, Cover and Saucer stippled en grisaille with a portrait of Frederick the Great, with gilt key-pattern borders, blue crossed swords and star marks, 1775-1814. **£900-1,000** C

A Meissen Hausmalerei Blue and White Teacup and Saucer painted in the Ferner workshop, the underglaze-blue ground enriched in gilding, within iron-red bands, blue crossed swords marks, c. 1735. **£450-510** C

MINTONS

- Thomas Minton (1765-1836)
- apprenticed at Caughley later worked for Josiah Spode
- 1796 open factory at Stoke making only pottery (great deal blue printed)
- made porcelain from 1798-1811 and again from 1821-5
- Marks:- M in Blue

right

A Minton Blue and White Coffee Can and Saucer, c. 1810. **£30-35** CSG

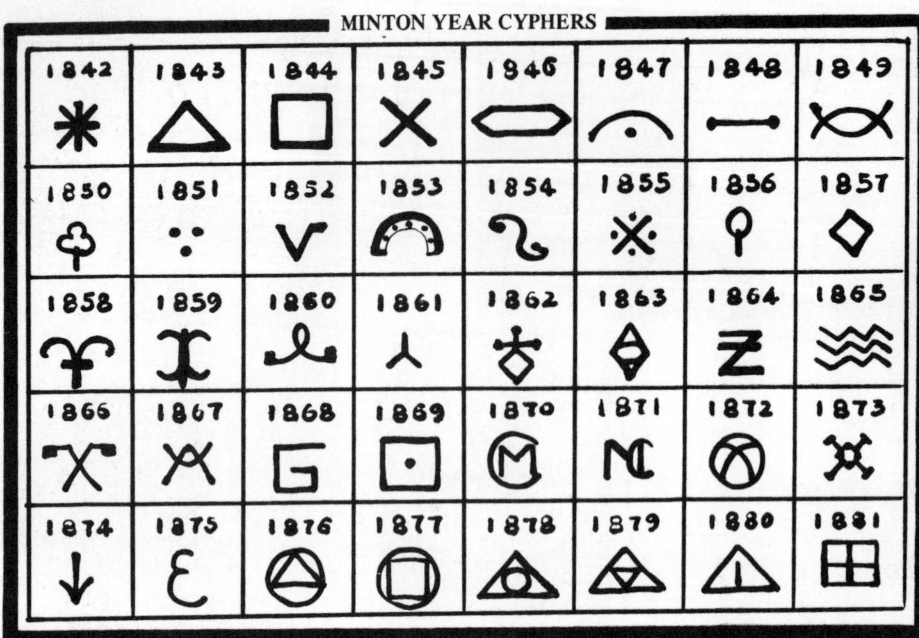

A Minton Cup and Saucer with pink ground, c. 1875. **£45-50** CSG

A Minton Cup and Saucer (in the Derby style), c. 1910. **£35-40** MN

A Nantgarw Coffee Cup and Saucer, the cup with high gilt scroll handle, painted by Billingsey inside and out with groups of pink roses and insects, the saucer also with pink roses, within gilt dentil rims. **£525-600** L

A Minton Cup and Saucer, green and gilt ground, c. 1845. **£45-55** CSG

A Minton Small Coffee Can and Saucer, c. 1910-20. **£35-40** CSG

A Minton Plain Cup and Saucer. **£8-10** MN

A Nantgarw Coffee Can and Saucer, painted with groups of flowers in panels bordered with gilt C scrolls. **£425-500** L

A pair of Nymphenberg cabinet cups and saucers, impressed shield mark, 9 cm., c. 1830-40. **£575-600** SKC

A Nantgarw Cup and Saucer, painted bouquet of flowers, with turquoise and raised gilt border, unmarked (as most tea wares were). **£400-440** SA

Four Satsuma Cups and Saucers finely painted with ho-ho birds, the insides of the cups with the 'thousand butterflies' pattern. **£150-170** L

A Nymphenburg teacup and saucer, impressed Bavarian shield mark, P and I, c. 1755. **£400-450** C

A pair of Sevres apple-green-ground coffee cups and saucers, blue interlaced L marks, 1768. **£650-700** pr. C

A Sevres Coffee-Cup and a Saucer painted in colours with Wittelsbach pattern border, blue interlaced L marks, 1759 **£320-370** C

A Paragon Cup and Saucer, c. 1925. **£13-15** MN

A Spode Cup and Saucer, c. 1815. **£95-105** MN

A Spode Cup and Saucer, with gilt rim, c. 1815. **£48-55** CSG

Pratt Ware Large Cup and Saucer. **£30-35** OF

A Sevres Cup and Saucer with cherub painting and pearl jewelling, c. 1805-1810. **£400-500** MN

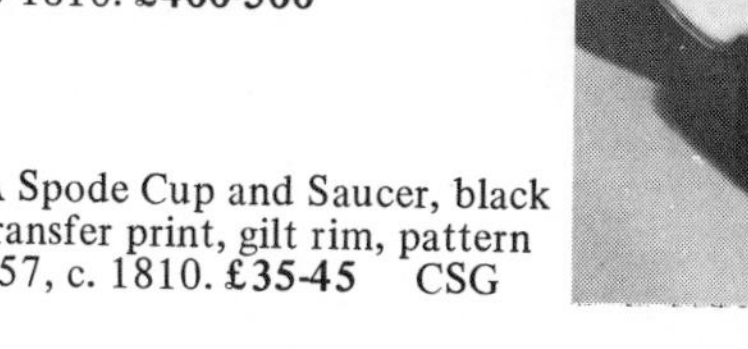

A Spode Cup and Saucer, black transfer print, gilt rim, pattern 557, c. 1810. **£35-45** CSG

A Swansea Tea Cup and Saucer, script Swansea mark in sepia. **£330-390** L

A Swansea Coffee Cup and Saucer, painted by William Pollard. **£525-600** L

A Swansea Teacup and Saucer, painted by William Pollard. **£425-500** L

A Tournai Coffee-Cup and Saucer painted en camaieu-rose, incised mark c. 1775. **£450-500** C

A Pair of Venice Tea Bowls and Saucers, with shaped green scale borders outlined with gilt scrolls, anchor mark in red, Cozzi factory. **£250-300** pr. L

A Pair of Venice (Cozzi) Coffee-Cups and Saucers, iron-red anchor marks c. 1765. **£400-460** C

A Venice (Cozzi) Teabowl and Saucer painted in iron-red, the saucer with gilt scroll and foliage borders, gold anchor mark, c. 1765. **£3,000-3,500** C

A Vienna cylindrical coffee-can and saucer, the interior to the cup entirely gilt, blue beehive marks, Pressnummer 809, 1809. **£550-650** C

A Vienna cup and saucer, blue beehive marks, c. 1785. **£300-350** C

A Vienna (du Paquier) Hausmalerei teabowl and later replacement saucer, (minor hairline crack to teabowl), the teabowl c. 1745. **£350-450** C

A Vienna (du Paquier) saucer and a Doccia tall beaker en suite, (rim chip repaired), the saucer c. 1730. **£1,000-1,200** C

A Vienna Dupaquier Two-handled Beaker and Saucer painted in Schwarzlot, enriched in gilding, c. 1750. **£2,200-2,500** C

A Wedgwood Cup and Saucer, c. 1910-1920. **£10-15** MN

A Wedgwood Cup and Saucer, dark blue, impressed, c. 1860. **£65-75** MN

A First Period Worcester fluted teacup and saucer of Lord Henry Thynne type c. 1770. **£400-450** MJ

A First period Worcester blue and white teabowl and saucer with the Mansfield pattern, c. 1790. **£50-60** MJ

A First period Worcester blue and white coffee cup and saucer, with the Fishermans pattern, c. 1790. **£95-105** MJ

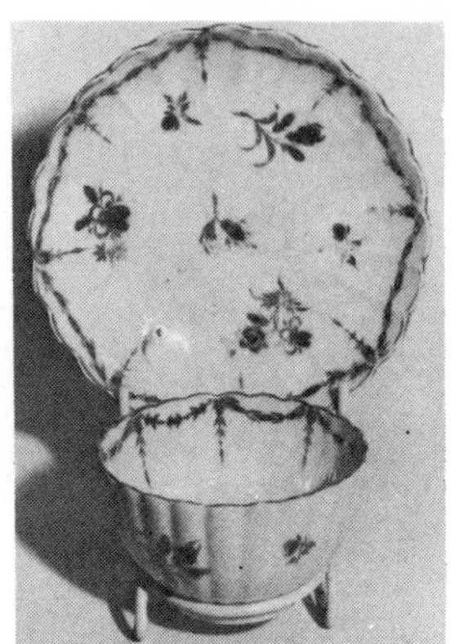

A First Period Worcester Tea-bowl and Saucer, c. 1790. **£70-80** MJ

A Dr. Wall Worcester Tea Bowl and Saucer with the oriental scene, c. 1770. **£150-175** SA

A Dr. Wall Blue and White Tea-bowl and Saucer, with the Prunus Root pattern, painted, c. 1760. **£220-40** SA

A Dr. Wall Scale Blue Tea Bowl and Saucer in the Kakiemon pattern, c. 1770. **£285-300** SA

A Dr. Wall Worcester Blue and White Coffee Cup and Saucer, painted with Chinese Figure, Long Eliza pattern, c. 1770. **£145-165** SA

A Chamberlain Worcester Cup and Saucer, 1845-1850. **£145-165** MN

A Worcester Barr, Flight & Barr Teacup and Saucer on claret ground, c. 1810., rubbed **£50-60** perfect **£125-150** SA

A Barr, Flight & Barr Cabinet, cup and saucer painted with view of Worcester, on blue ground, with butterfly handle, impressed mark. **£450-500** SA

A Chamberlain Worcester cup and saucer, c. 1830. **£65-75** MJ

A Dr. Wall Period Tea Bowl and Saucer, wet blue, with sprays of English flowers, c. 1770. **£325-375** SA

A Chamberlain Worcester Cup and Saucer, 'finger and thumb' pattern. **£95-105** MN

A Chamberlains Worcester Teacup and Saucer. **£70-80** MJ

Two Black Pencilled Dr. Wall Worcester Cups and Saucers with Chinoiserie decoration. **£400-460** each. SA

A Flight, Barr & Barr Teacup and Saucer, jabberwocky pattern. **£140-160** MJ

A Flight, Barr & Barr Cup and Saucer, c. 1820. **£45-55** CSG

A Worcester Cup and Saucer, jewelled, with Owen piercing, c. 1873. **£400-500** MN

A Worcester Teacup, Coffee-cup and Saucer painted in the Imari style with the 'Old Mossaik Pattern', mock Oriental marks, c. 1770. **£280-350** C

A Worcester Coffee-Cup and Saucer printed in black after Robert Hancock, the saucer with blue crossed swords and 9 mark., c. 1770. **£200-250** C

A Worcester Cup and Saucer, biscuit or peach ground, gold fern decoration, 1907. **£50-60** MN

A Worcester Fluted Coffee-Cup and Saucer, the border enriched with trellis-pattern and gilt herring-bone pattern, gilt crescent mark, c. 1775. **£500-550** C

A Worcester Miniature Teacup and Saucer, signed by James Stinton, with pheasants, gilt interior, 1924. **£145-165** MN

A Worcester Cup and Saucer, signed by Powell, with chaffinches, 1932. **£135-155** MN

A Worcester Teabowl, Coffee-Cup and Saucer, printed in black and coloured in over-glaze enamels with 'Les Garcons Chinois', c. 1760. **£500-600** C

A Worcester Miniature Teacup and Saucer, signed, c. 1912. **£95-105** MN

A very rare Coffee Cup and Saucer by the 'cut fruit painter', Dr. Wall Worcester, c. 1770, with gilding on saucer rubbed **£785-885** perfect **£2,500-2,800** SA

A Good Worcester Fluted Teacup and Saucer, painted with coloured garlands, early script mark, Dr. Wall 1st Period, 1770. **£550-590** SA

A pair of Royal Worcester floral decorated, hand-painted, cabinet cups and saucers, c. 1892. **£40-50** each. PC

A Worcester Fluted Teacup and Saucer, c. 1775. **£160-200** C

A Worcester 'Barker Sheep' Cup and Saucer, c. 1923. **£195-210** MN

A Worcester Small Cup and Saucer, cream ground, c. 1888. **£55-60** MN

A Worcester Cup and Saucer, c. 1903. **£55-60** MN

An Unusual Bristol Double-Handled Cup of silver shape, decorated in blue, in Chinese style, 5¼ in., early 18th C., damaged. **£280-320** S

CAUGHLEY PORCELAIN

- crescent or 'C' mark (to imitate Worcester). c1775 - 90.

C C

- printed marks. c1775 - 90. (in underglaze blue)

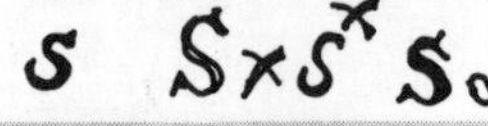

A Caughley Blue and White Coffee Cup, c. 1780. **£26-30** CSG

A Chelsea Fluted Teabowl, (two chips to rim) c. 1752. **£220-250** C

A Chinese Cup and Cover made for the Persian market, gilt with Islamic characters and the date 1230 (AD 1815) 5 in., 13.3 cm. **£120-160** L

A fine Pair of Imperial Yellow Beakers, 2½" (6.8cms), six-character mark and period of Yung-cheng. **£1,980-2,200** SKC

A famille verte hot-water cup (slightly chipped) encircled lingzhi mark, Kangxi with gilt bronze stand, 3¼ in., 8.5 cm. diam. **£175-225** C

A Coalport Two-Handled Loving Cup, c. 1840, 4 in. **£140-160** MJ

A Coalport Teacup, c. 1830. **£60-70** SA

A Worcester Miniature Cup and Saucer, fruit painting on green ground, raised gilding, signed by Ayrton, 1936. **£95-105** MN

A Royal Crown Derby Three-Handled Goblet, 7 in. high, c. 1920. damaged **£30-35** perfect **£180-210** CA

A Pair of Crown Derby Cups, with entwined Gilt handles terminating in foliage, on circular bases, with gilt borders, 5¼ in., 13.3 cm., crown, crossed batons and D mark and no. 19 in red **£330-380** L

An Artists piece: a two-handled loving cup by Doulton Lambeth in saltglaze, earthenware 6½ in., with silver rim, by Frank A. Butler numbered and dated 1881. **£175-200** PC

A Small Inuyama tea bowl, decorated in blue, green and red enamels on an uneven white glaze, character mark of Inuyama (also Kenzan) below. **£110-140** L

A Henan (Honan) teabowl, 11 cm., diam., Song (Sung) Dynasty. **£170-200** SKC

A Jianyao (Chien-Yao) Temmoku teabowl, 12.5 cm., diam., Song (Sung) Dynasty. **£170-200** SKC

A Liverpool Blue and White Coffee Can, c. 1780. **£65-75** CSG

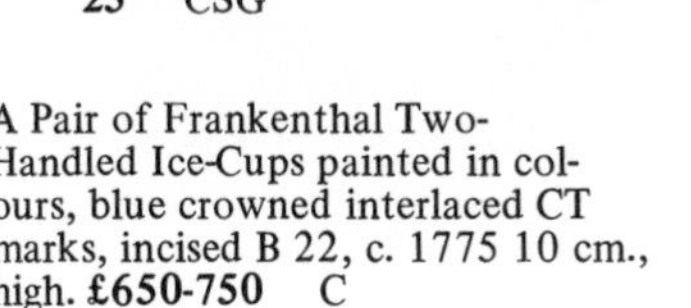
A Cup in the Chinese style, possibly Miles Mason, c. 1790. **£22-25** CSG

A Pair of Frankenthal Two-Handled Ice-Cups painted in colours, blue crowned interlaced CT marks, incised B 22, c. 1775 10 cm., high. **£650-750** C

A pair of Sevres ice-cups, 6.5 cm. high, c. 1795. **£200-250** C

A Fine Quality Tea Cup, possibly Spode, c. 1815. **£95-105** SA

A pair of Royal Worcester two-handled footed cups, signed William Chair, within orange grounds, 4". **£190-240** PWC

A Worcester Blue and White Tea Bowl, 3 in., c. 1770. **£35-40** CSG

A First Period Worcester Small Cup, c. 1765. **£35-40** CSG

A Dr. Wall Worcester Coffee Cup, painted with exotic bird in full landscape with pink sky – cup **£200-230** – cup and saucer **£900-980** SA

A First Period Worcester blue and white teabowl, c. 1790. **£25-30** MJ

A Caughley cylindrical Mug printed in blue with on one side 'La Peche' after Pillement, the reverse with 'La Promenade Chinoise', 6 in., S mark in blue, c. 1780. **£210-260** S

A Creamware Blue and White Cylindrical Mug inscribed (foot and rim chips) cracked. 11.5 cm. high. **£150-200** C

A Derby Cylindrical Mug with looped strap handle, c. 1760, 13 cm. high. **£550-600** C

A Derby Mug modelled as the head of Neptune (slight crack to rim), Crown, crossed batons and D mark in iron-red, c. 1810, 12 cm. wide. **£100-150** C

A Derby Mug modelled as the head of a Muse, (two chips to handle), Crown, crossed batons and D mark in puce, c. 1790, 12.5 cm. wide, **£200-250** C

A rare and early Hannah Barlow Doulton Tyg. 18.5 cm. high, undated, oval mark, c. 1871. **£170-200** SKC

A Plymouth Baluster Mug with an iron-red loop-and-dot-pattern rim, c. 1770 15.5 cm. high. **£1,600-1,650** C

Pratt Ware Mug, 3" high. **£35-45** OF

Pratt Ware Mug, 3½" high. **£50-60** OF

A Victorian Staffordshire Frog Mug, 4 in. high. **£45-55** SA

A Staffordshire Saltglaze Cylindrical Mug with reeded strap handle (slight crack to rim) c. 1750, 12.5 cm. high. **£600-650** C

A 19th C Staffordshire Floral Cup, handle restored. **£66-76** SAL

A Two-handled Mug, Watcomb, slight crack **£6-8** perfect **£8-10** NO

A Staffordshire Cylindrical Mug with the pugilists 'Cribb' and 'Molineux', c. 1811, 8.5 cm. high. **£150-200** C

A 19th C Staffordshire Loving Cup. **£48-55** SAL

A Worcester Baluster Mug with grooved loop handle gilt with the monogram GG and the motto 'Amity' c. 1770, 9 cm. high. **£400-450** C

A Sunderland Cylindrical Mug with theatrical scenes from the play 'Lord of the Manor' with John Liston in the role of Moll Flaggon (rim and base cracked) c. 1825, 13 cm. high. **£80-120** C

A First Period Worcester Mug, transfer printed. 4¾ in., 12 cm. **£420-500** L

A Staffordshire Creamware Cylindrical Electioneering Mug inscribed 'Pollington for ever' (cracked and chipped) c. 1790. 15.5 cm. high. **£130-150** C

A 19th C Sunderland pottery cup with 'Sailor's Farewell' inscription. **£48-58** SAL

A Very good and rare Mug of Small Size in the Fence pattern, 1st Period Worcester. **£95-105** SA

A First Period Worcester Cylindrical Mug, printed in underglaze blue. 5½ in., 14.3 cm., script W mark. **£160-190** L

Locke Worcester miniature mug, with hand-painted robin, c1900. **£20-25** NO

A Copeland Commemorative Tyg, made on the occasion of the conclusion of the Transvaal War. Hair crack in rim, printed mark including retailer's name and numbered 93 from an edition of 100, 1900, 6" (15.2cms). **£200-300** S.B.

A Chamberlain's Worcester Bell-Shaped Mug with gilt scroll handle and the monogram DS, c. 1825, 11.5 cm. high. **£160-200** C

A Yellow-glazed Cylindrical Mug with loop handle printed in black with a rhyme to health, wealth and friendship, (base cracked), c. 1790, 10 cm. high. **£70-90** C

George VI Coronation Mug. **£6.50-8** NO

Two Chamberlain Worcester Mugs, painted with views of Worcester. **£300-330** each. SA

(l) 1902 Mug. **£15-17** NO
(m) Victorian Beaker. **£24-26** NO
(r) 1911 Mug. **£11.50-13** NO

A fine and rare pair of Chamberlain Worcester Quart Mugs, painted with dead game birds, manufactured for their Royal Highnesses The Prince of Wales and The Duke of Cumberland, 6¾ in. high. **£1,850-2,000** pr. SA

1887 Queen Victoria Jubilee China Mug. **£30-34** NO

(m) Queen Victoria 1897 Diamond Jubilee China Mug. **£30-34** NO

(r) 1897 Queen Victoria Diamond Jubilee China Mug. **£30-35** NO

(l) 1902 Queen Alexandra and King Edward VII Mug. **£15-17** NO

(m) King George V & Queen Mary 1911 Mug. **£15-17** NO

(r) King George V Coronation 1911 Mug, with crest. **£15-17** NO

(l) King George V & Queen Mary Silver Jubilee, 1910-1935. **£12-14** NO

(r) Coronation of Edward VIII Mug, 1937. china **£12-14** earthenware **£9-11** NO

(m) Commemorative Piece 'Peace Mug', 1919. **£12-14** NO

A Rare Queen Victoria Child's Mug, probably made on the occasion of the proclamation or coronation of Queen Victoria, 3" (7.5cms) c1837-38. **£150-200** S.B.

A 'Caroline' Mug, 2¾" (6.8cms), c1820. **£125-175** S.B.

A 'Victoria Regina' Commemorative Mug, made on the occasion of the proclamation of Queen Victoria, Minor rim crack, 3" (7.5cms), c1837. **£150-200** S.B.

A Good Creamware Cylindrical Tankard, crisply printed in black, 6½" (16.5cms), c1790. **£245-285** SKC

A Cantonese Porcelain Tankard of large size, 6 in. **£365-385** SA

A rare Ming Blue and White covered Tankard of European silver-shape, 5¾" (14.5cms), Transitional. **£340-380** SKC

A Caughley Tankard with Zig-zag Fence pattern, 6 in. high. **£150-170** SA

A Pearlware Tankard, 5¼" c.1800. **£115-130** SKC

A very fine and rare Dr. Wall Tankard of 1st. Period Worcester with a portrait of the King of Prussia, fully signed and dated, 1757, 4½ in. high. **£585-650** SA

A Dr. Wall Lady's Tankard in scale blue with oriental flowers, 3½ in. high, c. 1765. **£325** with English flowers. **£600-660** SA

A fine Dr. Wall Period Tankard with the Fence pattern, 6 in. high, c. 1765. **£365-400** SA

A First Period Worcester Tankard, 4½ in. high, c. 1790. **£240-270** MJ

A Creamware Beaker transfer printed in black with a pastoral and farm-yard scene and a spray of lilies and other flowers, height 7.8 cm., late 18th C. probably Liverpool. **£105-130** S Be

A Hochst flaring beaker and trembleuse stand, painted en camaieu rose within an iron-red border, enriched in gilding, blue crowned wheel marks, impressed IN c. 1760. **£900-950** C

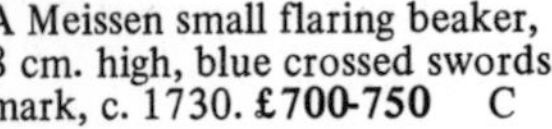

A Meissen small flaring beaker, 8 cm. high, blue crossed swords mark, c. 1730. **£700-750** C

A Pair of Worcester Flared Beakers, painted in the Kakiemon style with 'The Quail' pattern, gold crescent marks, c. 1770, 6 cm. high. **£350-400** C

An Arita Blue and White Broad Oviform Jar late 17th C., 16.3 cm. high. **£700-800** C

A Large Arita Oviform Jar and Domed Cover painted in underglaze blue, iron-red colours and gilt (cover damaged), 19th C., 66.7 cm. high. **£690-790** C

A Fine Pair of Arita Blue and White Oviform Jars, late 17th C., 20 cm. high. **£800-900** C

A Fine Arita Blue and White Oviform Jar painted with groups of Chinese scholars in garden landscapes, late 17th C., 26.9 cm. high. **£800-900** C

A Castel Durante Wet-drug Jar, 25 cm., mid 16th C., restored, cracked. **£700-790** S

A Ming Transitional Oviform Jar, the reverse with a twenty-character inscription, 10½" (27cms), late 17th C. **£830-880**

A large Arita octagonal baluster jar (slight glaze cracks around shoulder), early 18th C, carved wood cover, 51cms high. **£1,150-1.250** C

A Pair of Castelli Maiolica Albarelli, one inscribed SYR: CYDONIOR, the other SYR: CARDILL, 7½" (19cms), 18th C (cracked). **£540-600** SKC

A late Ming blue and white baluster jar (cracked), early 17th C, 16" (40.5cms) high. **£930-1,000** C

A Large Caltagirone Albarello, painted in polychrome enamels, 11½" (29cms), early 17th C. **£225-250** SKC

A famille verte oviform jar, Kangxi, wood cover 4½ in., 11.5 cm. high. **£190-230** C

A blue and white spherical condiment pot, Kangxi 4 in., 10.5 cm., wide. **£155-200** C

A Canton Globular Jar and Cover, painted in famille rose enamels, 9", late 19th C. **£135-165** SH

A Cylindrical Posset Pot in Chinese Transitional style, 5½ in., probably London, c. 1680-90, damaged. **£300-350** S

A Chinese Blue and White Ginger Jar, boldly painted with flowers and foliage, 22.8 cm., Ch'ien-Lung, carved wood cover and stand. **£125-150** S Be

A Pair of Imari Jars and Covers, height 57 cm., early 19th C. **£1,000-1,200** S Be

A Lambeth Delft Drug Jar, 11.5 cm., early 18th C. **£250-300** SKC

An Early London Drug Jar in Transitional style, 13 in., c. 1680-90, hair cracks and chips to base. **£500-600** S

A North Italian Double Handled Drug Jar, painted in blue on a berettino ground, 34.5 cm., late 16th C., damage to foot and terminals. **£330-370** S

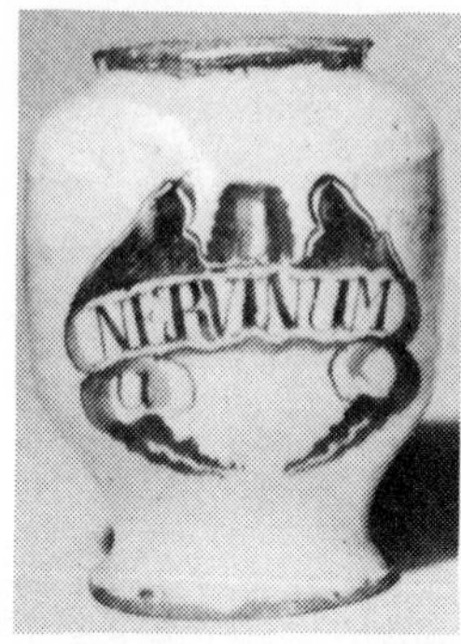

A London Delft Blue and White Oviform Drug-jar for 'Nervinum' (rim chip) c. 1690 17 cm. high. **£190-220** C

An Ointment Pot of albarello shape, 3 in., London or Netherlandish, late 16th/early 17th C. **£190-220** S

An Elton Oil Jar with six necks covered in a crackle gold ground, 9¾ in. high. **£45-55** CSK

A London 'Angel' Dry Drug Jar, with drug label 'E.SVCCO.ROS' 6¾ in., c. 1665-85, chips to rim and foot. **£270-300** S

A Martinware Tobacco-Jar and Cover incised R. W. Martin & Bros. London & Southall, 12.11.1903, 25 cm. high. **£900-1,000** C

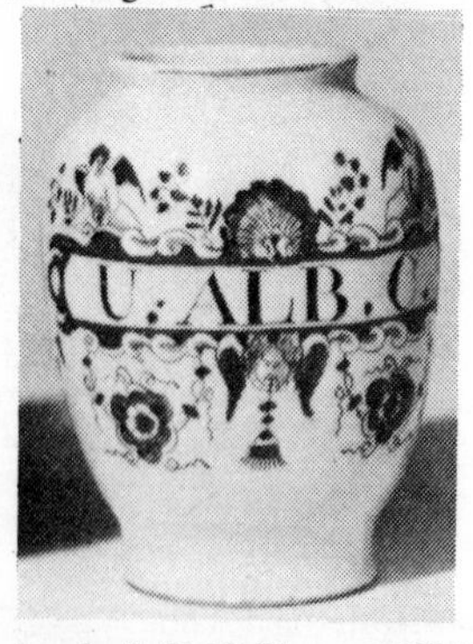

A Lambeth Delft Blue and White Oviform Drug-Jar for 'U.ALB.C' c. 1720, 18 cm. high. **£180-225** C

A London Wet Drug Jar painted in dark blue with a drug label inscribed 'OX:SCILLIT', 7½ in., early 18th C., repair to spout. **£160-190** S

A Samson 'Imari' Baluster Jar and domed cover with karashishi finial, painted in typical colours, 19th C. **£500-600** C

A Sicilian Drug Jar painted in blue and manganese, 60 cm., Trapani, 18th C., patches of glaze rubbed. **£450-490** S

A mounted transitional blue and white slender pear-shaped bottle (the neck reduced), c1640, mounted with gilt-bronze collar and cover overall height 7¾" (19.5cms). **£165-200** C

A Ming Blue and White Bottle, 15¼" (39cms), Transitional (cracked). **£340-380** SKC

An Attractive Sicilian Albarello, painted in green, manganese and ochre on a blue ground, 12½" (32cms), early 17th C Caltagirone. **£370-400** SKC

Two blue and white fluted pear-shaped bottles (the foot rims chipped), Kangxi, 5¼" (13.5cms) high. **£350-400** C

A Delft rose water bottle, damaged, 26 cm., c. 1750-60 Dublin or Liverpool. **£260-300** SKC

A Royal Worcester hand painted floral decorated pot pourri, Jar with inner lid and reticulated top, 1881, patt. no. 1314. **£195-225** missing inner lid **£145-165** PC

A pair of blue and white pear-shaped bottles under degraded glazes (fritted) early Ming Dynasty 6 in., 15 cm. high. **£330-375** C

A Royal Worcester Melon-Shaped Pot Pourri Jar and Cover, 21 cm., printed mark 1889. **£210-230** S Be

A Dutch Delft Water Bottle, the ovoid body painted in underglaze blue, 37.6 cm., A. K. monogram to base, late 17th C. some damage. **£480-540** S Be

A Crown Derby Pot and Cover c. 1910, 5 in high. **£120-150** MJ

A Crown Devon 'Metta Sung' Style Ginger Jar and Cover with turquoise ground 9 in. high, c. 1930. **£70-80** CA

An early 18th C Delft blue and white posset pot and cover, 6½" diam., 7" high. **£500-550** PWC

A Blue and White Dutch Delft 'Voc' Tobacco Jar, 10¼" (26cms) De Vergulde Bloempot factory mark, late 18th C brass stepped domed cover (damaged). **£490-520** SKC

A Fine Dutch Delft Tobacco Jar painted in cobalt-blue, 10½" (27cms), maker's mark for De Drye Flesschen, c1760-70. **£600-685** SKC

A Good Dutch Delft Tobacco Jar, painted in inky zaffre blue, with typical brass domed cover, 9½" (24cms), De Drye Clocken factory, late 18th C. **£575-600** SKC

A Faenza Albarello decorated in blue, 17 cm., 16th C. small crack on rim, chips on foot. **£480-520** S

A Pair of English China Jars and Covers with burnished gold borders on a powder blue ground, 10.8 cm., probably Minton, late 19th C. **£260-290**

A Frankfurt Faience Baluster Jar, painted in manganese, 8½ in., 21 cm., **£240-300** L

A Fine Imari Baluster Jar painted in underglaze blue, iron-red, colours and gilt, 18th C. 40.5 cm. high. **£1,100-1,200** C

A Fine Imari Baluster Jar painted in underglaze blue, iron-red, colours and gilt (some enamel chipped off around foot rim) late 17th/early 18th C. Wood stand. **£1,400-1,700** C

IMARI PATTERNS

- Decoration of Japanese Porcelain often based on brocade patterns
- made at Arita, Hizen Province from early 18thC until beginning 19thC
- Imari, name of port of shipment
- Imari patterns copied and adapted by Derby, Worcester, Spode, Minton, Mason etc.
- Imari patterns also made in China

A Sicilian Maiolica Bottle painted in manganese, ochre and green on a blue washed ground, 9½" (24cms), 17th/18th C. **£300-350** SKC

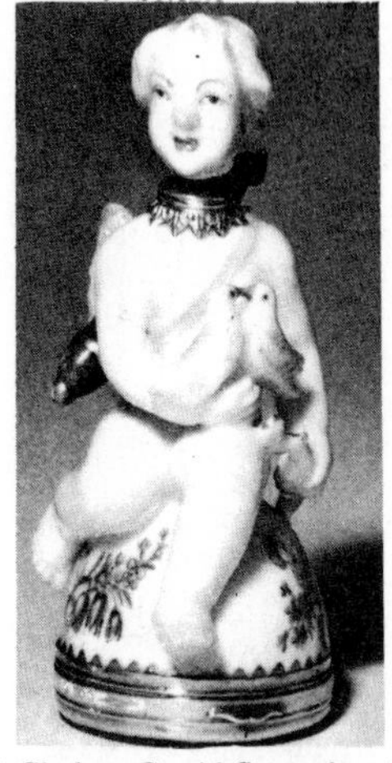

A Chelsea Cupid Scent-bottle and stopper, the base mounted in gold and set with a stone (restoration to quiver) c. 1755, 7.5 cm. high. **£1,000-1,200** C

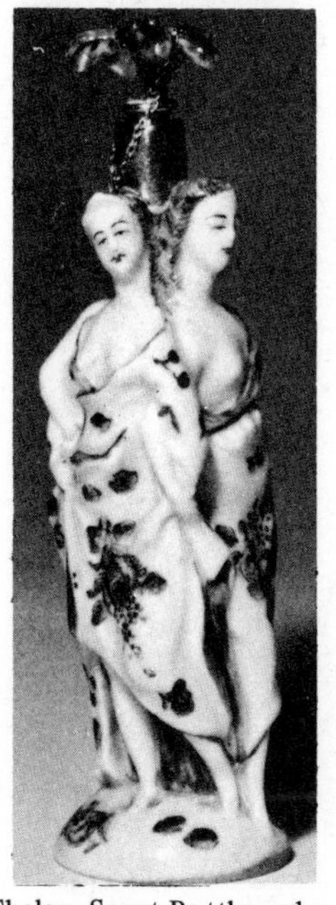

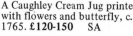

A Chelsea Scent Bottle and a Stopper of 'Girl in a Swing' type (base trimmed, neck damaged, stopper a replacement) c. 1753, 10.5 cm. high. **£160-250** C

A Very Rare Mid 19th C. Porcelain Scent Bottle in the form of a tulip, possibly Coalport, c. 1850. **£265-285** SA

An S. Mordan & Co., Silver-Mounted Porcelain Willow Pattern Scent Flask, maker's mark of Sampson Mordan, London, 1885. 5.5 cm. high. **£60-70** SB

A Barnstaple Slipware Oviform Jug with loop handle and scroll terminal, late 18th C., 22 cm. high. **£260-300** C

CHELSEA PORCELAIN

- triangle mark. c1745 - 50.

- raised anchor mark. c1749 - 52.

- painted in red, red anchor period. c1752 - 6.

- gold anchor mark. c1756 - 69.

A Fine Basalt Cream Jug, c. 1810. **£38-48** CP

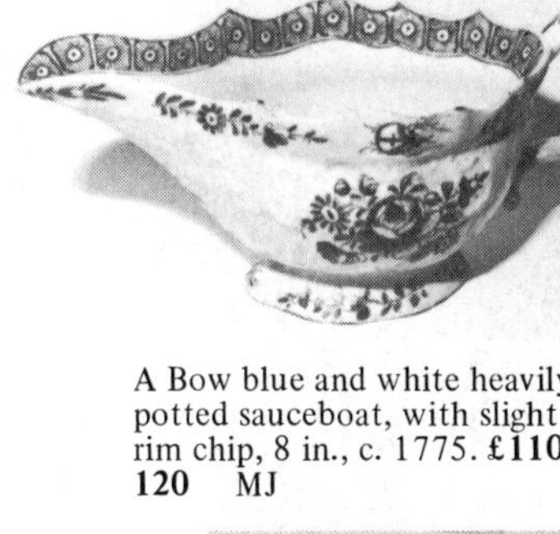

A Bow blue and white heavily potted sauceboat, with slight rim chip, 8 in., c. 1775. **£110-120** MJ

A Cambrian Yellow-ground Jug painted on an egg-yellow ground with red and white striped neck, 8¼ in., probably Haynes, Dillwyn & Co., c. 1802-10, restored lip. **£260-290** S

A Caughley blue and white Jug, 7 in. high, c. 1800. **£90-100** MJ

A Caughley Cream Jug printed with flowers and butterfly, c. 1765. **£120-150** SA

A Chelsea White Acanthus-Leaf Moulded Pear-Shaped Milk-Jug (minute chip and crack to lip) traces of an incised triangle mark, 1745-1747, 13.5 cm. high. **£3,500-4,000** C

A Crown Derby Miniature Jug, c. 1910, 2 in. **£50-60** MJ

A Crown Derby Miniature Jug, c. 1910, 3¼ in. **£75-85** MJ

A Doulton Lambeth Jug, one panel incised by Hannah Barlow, the other in pate-sur-pate technique by Florence Barlow, with impressed rosette mark and incised artists monograms, 23cms high. **£220-260** P

A Chinese Export Cream Jug, 5 in. high, **£25-30**. with lid and perfect **£100-120** CA

Hannah Barlow. A Doulton stoneware jug in blue on a brown reeded ground, silver mount, London 1872, incised BHB monogram and impressed Doulton Lambeth. **£220-260** L

A Royal Doulton Burslem masonic Commemorative Jug 8½ in. high. 1906. **£100-120** PC

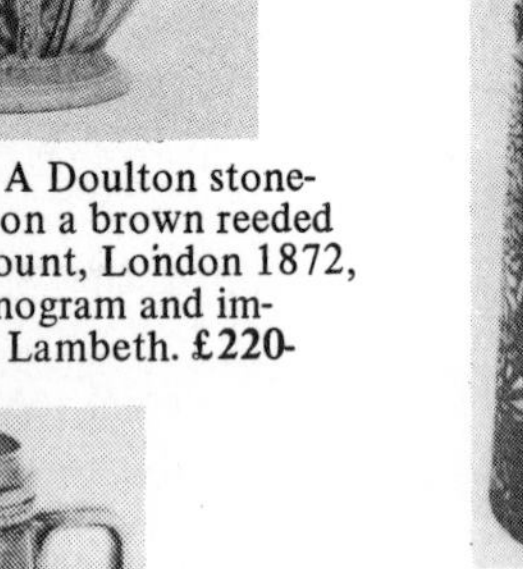

A Royal Doulton Milk Jug, c. 1910. **£45-50** AP

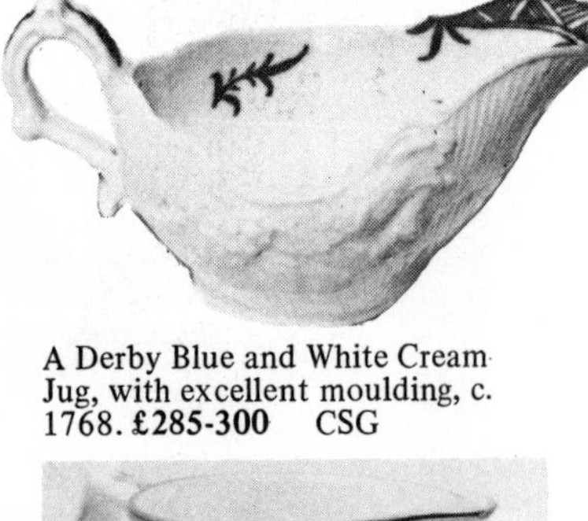

A Derby Blue and White Cream Jug, with excellent moulding, c. 1768. **£285-300** CSG

A Derby Jug with satyr mask picked out in gold, 7½ in., 19 cm. **£140-180** L

An Unusual Doulton Lambeth Rugby Football Jug, with impressed rosette mark dated 1881, and assistants mark for Annie Gentle, 23.50cms high. **£170-200** P

A Royal Doulton Harvest Jug and Beaker, silver rimmed. **£100-120** VA

A Rare Earthenware 'Reform' Jug, with base chip, hair crack. Printed lion and crown, GH, No. 1 and Staffordshire c1830, 5½" (13cms). **£150-200** S.B.

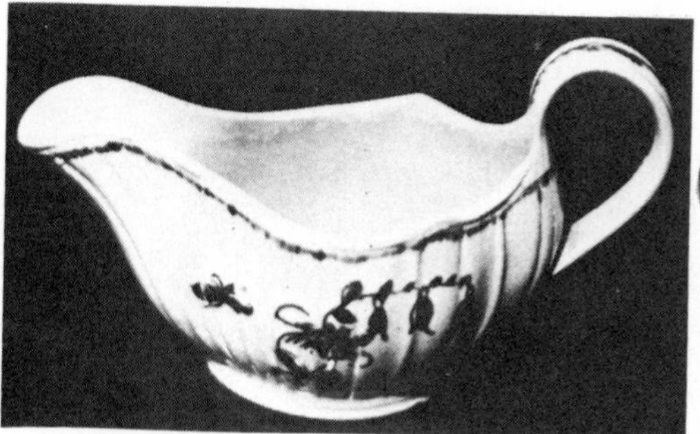

A Pair of late 18th C. Liverpool Pearl-Ware Sauceboats, **£80-90** each, **£140-160** pr. RD

A Lowestoft Sparrow Beak Jug, 3½ in., c. 1775. **£145-160** CSG

An English Porcelain Jug and Lid, hand-painted by A. Barclay, factory unknown 1886 10½ in. high. **£150-180** PC

A very fine Liverpool Sparrow Beak Jug painted with an exotic bird, Pennington, 1775. **£335-360** SA

A Liverpool Cream Jug, blue and white, 4½ in. high, c. 1790. **£52-60** CSG

A Liverpool large Jug, blue and white, 8½ in., c. 1780. **£70-80** CSG

A Liverpool Delft Puzzle Jug, with the inscription: 'Here Gentlemen Come try your skill, I'le hould (sic) a wager if you will . . . . , That you Dont Drink this liquor all, Without you Spill or let some fall', (with faults), 7¼" (18.5cms), c1750-70. **£420-500** SKC

A good Liverpool creamware jug, transfer printed in black, 23.5 cm., c. 1880. **£95-100** SKC

Liverpool Blue and White Chinese' Sparrow Beak Jug, c. 1780. **£115-125** CSG

A Liverpool Blue and White Sauce Boat or Cream Jug. **£195-210** SA

An Enamelled Longton Hall Jug, the glaze of pronounced greenish tint, 8" (20cms), c1755 (damaged). **£85-105** SKC

A Martinware Chocolate Brown Glazed 'Nottingham Jug', inscribed signature Martin, London, to base, 9cms high. **£120-150** SH

Mason's unmarked Jug, 3 in. high. **£25-30** TT

A Masons Ironstone Jug, chip to rim, c. 1850. **£22-30** SHA

A Pearlware Oviform Jug with the 'Liverpool Volunteers', c. 1800, 15.5 cm. high. **£150-180** C

A Pair of Rockingham Green-Ground Oviform Jugs, inscribed 'Beagle' and 'Vanish' (Vanish with crack to rim, Beagle with crack to body) raised 7 and puce griffin marks, c. 1835, 13 cm. high. **£380-400** pr. C

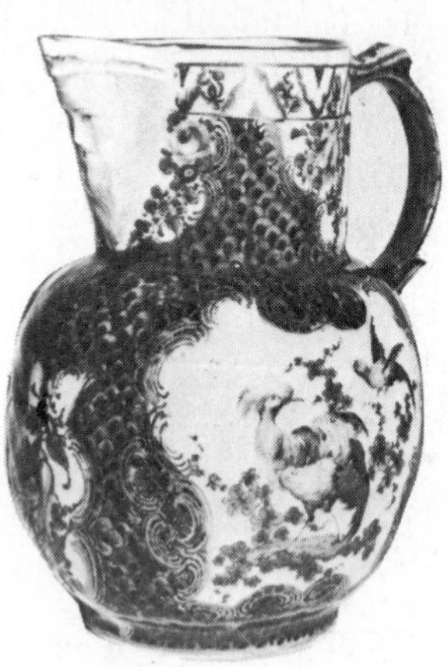

A Chamberlains Worcester Mask-head jug, copy by Samson, bearing Worcester marks, 7 in. high. **£140-160** PC

A Sevres small pear-shaped cream jug with trellis, hatched and oeil-de-perdrix panels, 8.5 cm. high, bearing blue interlaced L mark enclosing the date letter M, Painter's mark. **£250-350** C

left

Duke of York/Prince Cobourg (sic), a rare Prattware commemorative Jug, 7 in., late 18th C., spout chipped. **£180-210** S

A Sevres rose pompadour ground helmet-shaped cream jug, 11 cm. high, blue interlaced L mark 1770 **£250-350** C

A Sevres pear-shaped milk jug, 11 cm. high, puce interlaced L mark, 1786. **£250-300** C

A Sevres Apple-Green Ground Pear-Shaped Milk-Jug, enriched in gilding, blue interlaced L mark 1768 12.5 cm., high. **£250-290** C

A 19th C Staffordshire Commemorative Jug, marked 'Marquis Wellington' and 'General Hill', 6½" high. **£95-115** OF

A Staffordshire barrel-shape jug, painted with the Farmers Arms in a rococo scroll cartouche. 9 in., 22.8 cm. **£55-75** L

A Rare Stoneware Commemorative Jug, made to mark the death of George IV, c1830, 8⅞" (20.8cms). **£100-150** S.B.

A Stoneware Jug, 5½ in. high, c. 1840. **£65-75** CP

A Large Victorian Sunderland Lustre Masonic Jug, 8" high. **£65-90** OF

A Small Victorian Sunderland Lustre Cream Jug, 3" high. **£25-35** OF

A Very Good Sunderland Lustre Jug with ship and verse, (crack to lip) 5½ in. high. **£95-115** SA

Tewkesbury Commemorative Jug. **£6.50-8** NO

A Wedgwood Pearlware Oviform Jug painted in sepia, the neck and lip gilt with key-pattern, the lower part with fluting and gilding, impressed mark c. 1815, 16 cm. high. **£120-150** C

A Wedgwood Blue Jasper Dip Jug, impressed Wedgewood, late 19th C, 15.6cms. **£70-80** SBe

A Victorian Welsh Lustre Jug, 6½" high. **£38-45** SAL

A Ralph Wood Fair Hebe Jug inscribed 'Long Live the King' and 'GR III RESTOR'D' c. 1790, 21.5 cm. high. **£550-700** C

A Ralph Wood Jug with green twig handle c. 1790, 22.5 cm. high. **£150-250** C

A Ralph Wood Satyr's Milk-Jug with green-glazed dolphin spout and handle, c. 1775, 13 cm. high. **£175-200** C

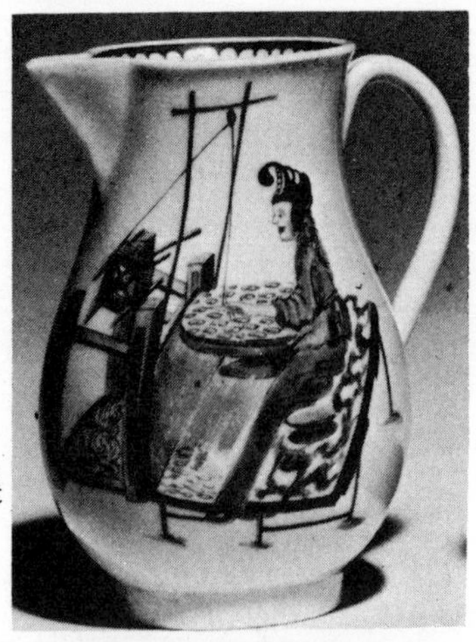

A Worcester Pear-Shaped Cream-Jug painted with 'The Spinning Maiden' pattern, c. 1770., 9 cm. high. **£350-400** C

A First period Worcester blue and white sauceboat, 7¼ in. wide, c. 1790. **£140-160** MJ

A First Period Worcester small Jug, 3¼ in. high, c. 1790. **£90-100** MJ

A Dr. Wall Worcester 'sparrow-beak' Jug, 5 in. high, c. 1760. **£100-115** MJ

A First Period Worcester Cream Jug (barrel shape), c. 1770. **£125-150** CSG

A Flight & Barr Worcester Jug, painted by Pennington, 7½ in., c. 1795. **£425-450** SA

An early Dr. Wall Moulded Butter Boat c. 1758 in white **£200-230** with any decoration **£600-650** SA

A Worcester Blue and White Jug, 5¾ in., c. 1775. **£280-320** CSG

A Worcester Sauce Boat, excellent blue-bell moulding, c. 1760. **£150-170** SA

A First Period Worcester blue and white 'sparrow beak' Jug, c. 1790 4½ in. **£100-120** MJ

A fine and rare Chamberlain Worcester 'Hunting Scene' Jug, fully marked in sepia, painted by H. Chamberlain, 7 in. high, c. 1810. **£2,000-2,150** SA

A Chamberlains Worcester Marriage Jug, 7 in., c. 1840. **£600-680** MJ

A Royal Worcester jug of cylindrical shape, painted and gilt 8¼ in., 21 cm., printed mark and pattern 1229 in puce, 1888. **£80-120** L

Queen Victoria Drum Jug. **£24-26** NO

A Worcester Wet Blue Star Pattern Milk Jug of poor shape. **£150-170** SA

A Quite Rare Collector's Jug by Jos. Twiggs of Swinton, Yorkshire, in polychrome colouring, 9 in., c. 1838-58. **£50-60** TA

A Pear-shaped Milk-Jug with trefoil-shaped lip c. 1775, 12 cm. high. **£70-100** C

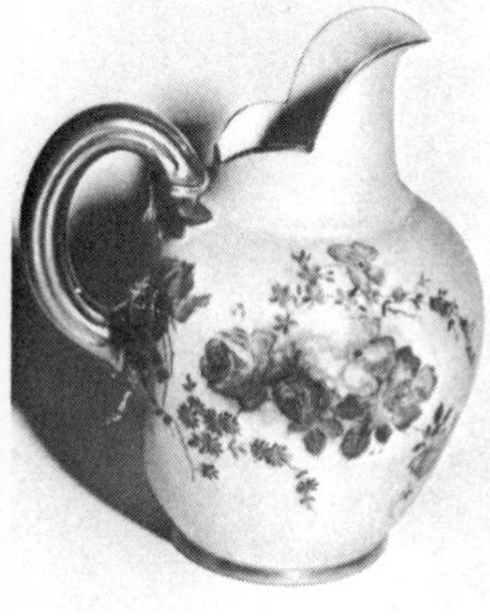

A Royal Worcester satin finish, hand-painted floral decorated gilt-handled flat-back Vase, Shape No. 1094. **£65-75.** This shape comes in nine sizes price ranging from **£45-165** PC

A 17th C. Bellarmine Jug. **£420-460** CC

A Silver Lustre Jug, (A.F.), 5 in. high, c. 1820. **£20-25** CA

Royal Worcester Jug, 1898. **£60-80** NO

A good Westerwald Salt-glaze Stoneware Krug, 7½" (19cms), c1714. **£310-350** SKC

A Blue and White Cream Jug, 4½ in., c. 1800. **£28-34** CSG

A Royal Worcester min. milk jug and basin with hand painted blue tits, signed by Powell, 1921. **£140-160** PC just painted with flowers **£70-80** not signed by artist **£70-90** PC

A Yorkshire Martha Gunn Toby Jug (minute chip to hat) c. 1800 16.5 cm. high. **£1,500-1,600**

A Rare 'Martha Gunn' Toby Jug, glazed in streaky manganese, 11½ in., c. 1780, small chip to rim. **£880-990** S

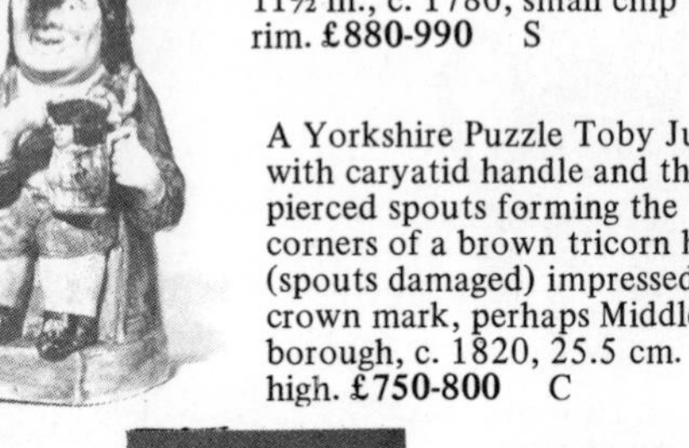

A Yorkshire Puzzle Toby Jug with caryatid handle and three pierced spouts forming the corners of a brown tricorn hat, (spouts damaged) impressed crown mark, perhaps Middlesborough, c. 1820, 25.5 cm. high. **£750-800** C

A Miniature Minton-van-Dyke pattern Jug and Basin in repaired condition, mid 19th C. **£55-65** TA

A Rare Pearlware Toby, the grooved strap handle charged with blue ropetwist motif, 9½ in., perhaps Yorkshire, c. 1780-90, small repair to mouth. **£880-980** S

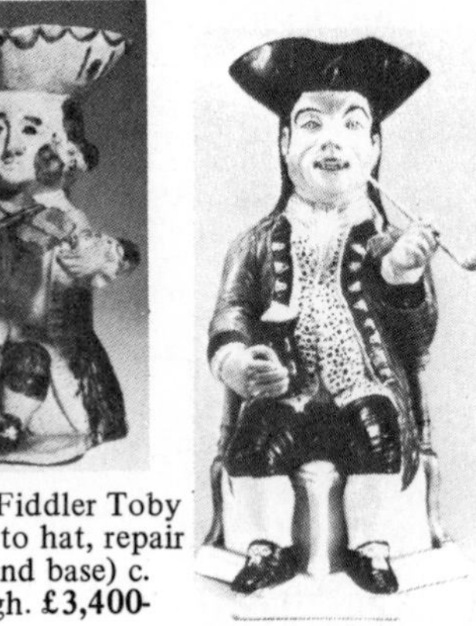

A Staffordshire Fiddler Toby Jug (restoration to hat, repair to fiddle, hand and base) c. 1750, 16 cm. high. **£3,400-3,500** C

A Staffordshire Toby Jug, 11 in., late 18th/early 19th C., pipe replaced. **£350-400** S

A Victorian Jug and Basin Set, 5 pieces. **£50-60** VA

A Yorkshire 'Squat' Toby Jug, the handle in the form of a caryatid, 7¾ in., late 18th C. **£480-580** S

A Rare Prattware Toby Jug, 10 in., c. 1780-90, some restoration to hat and pipe, slight flaking. **£260-290** S

A Yorkshire Martha Gunn Toby Jug holding a spotted jug and glass (hat restored) c. 1800, 26.5 cm. high. **£600-650** C

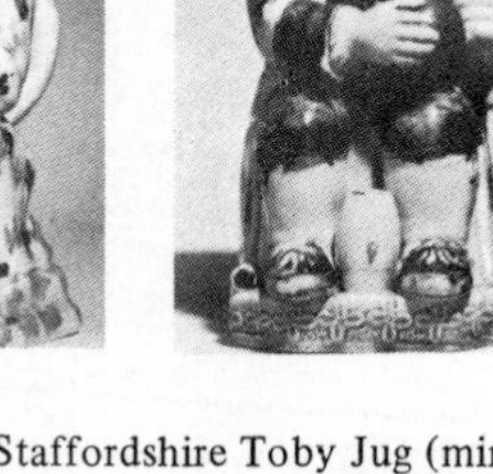

A Staffordshire Toby Jug (minute chips to hat) c. 1790, 25.5 cm. high. **£250-300** C

A Staffordshire Toby Jug, wearing green waistcoat, yellow breeches and pink coat. 10 in., 25.4 cm. **£60-80** L

An Enoch Wood Parson Toby Jug c. 1800, 21 cm. high. **£350-400** C

A Ralph Wood Toby Jug, his coat in a green translucent glaze, with dark brown details, height 23.5 cm., late 18th C. **£260-280** S Be

A Ralph Wood Toby Jug, a recumbent dog at his feet (some restoration to hat and hair) c. 1780, 25 cm. high. **£700-800** C

A Ralph Wood Jug, 11½ in., c. 1770, some restoration and repair. **£350-400** S

A Ralph Wood Thin Man Toby Jug (minor restoration to jug and base) c. 1775, 24.5 cm. high. **£750-800** C

A Dr. Johnson Toby Jug, height 24 cm., probably by Ralph Wood, c. 1780. **£260-290** S Be

A Black Basalt Coffee Pot, 10 in. high, c. 1800. **£75-85** CSG

A Furstenberg pear-shaped coffee-pot and domed cover by C. G. Albert, (minor chip to cover) 25 cm. high, blue script F mark and impressed 2, c. 1770. **£700-800** C

A Meissen ornithological pear-shaped hot-milk jug and a cover, 15 cm. high, blue crossed swords mark, c. 1745. **£600-650** C

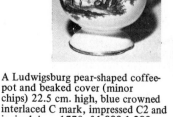

A Meissen Pear-Shaped Hot-Milk Jug and Cover, enriched in gilding (minor chip to spout and cover), blue crossed swords mark, c. 1745, 13.5 cm., high. **£500-600** C

A Booth fake of a First Period Worcester coffee pot with the pine cone pattern. The pot is of unusually light weight, 7½ in. **£25-30** MJ

A Ludwigsburg pear-shaped coffee-pot and beaked cover (minor chips) 22.5 cm. high, blue crowned interlaced C mark, impressed C2 and incised A, c. 1770. **£1,000-1,200** C

A Meissen pear-shaped coffee pot and cover, 25.6 cm. crossed swords mark and dot in underglaze blue, Academic period. **£860-900** SKC

A Meissen yellow-ground pear-shaped coffee-pot and domed cover painted in the manner of J. G. Herold (minor chips) 24.5 cm. high, blue crossed swords mark, gilt B., c. 1735. **£1,450-2,000** C

A Venice (Cozzi) Pear-Shaped Coffee-Pot and Domed Cover, the mask spout enriched in iron-red and brown, with gilt dentil rims, iron-red anchor mark c. 1765 21 cm., high. **£800-900** C

A First Period Worcester blue and white coffee pot and cover, 8¾ in. high, c. 1790 (repaired). **£175-200** MJ

A First period Worcester blue and white coffee pot and cover with the Mansfield pattern, 9 in. high, c. 1790. **£215-235** MJ

An Astbury Miniature Globular Teapot and cover, the rich brown ground moulded in cream slip (chip to base of handle) c. 1745, 12 cm. wide. **£650-750** C

A Chelsea Fable-decorated Teapot and Cover, painted by Jefferyes Hamett O'Neale., some damage, red anchor mark, c.1752, 18cm wide. **£5,500-6,000** C

An 18th C. Chinese Teapot and Cover, 5½ in. high. **£70-80** CA

A Continental Teapot, beautifully decorated, late 19th C. **£85-95** MN

A Cockpit Hill creamware Teapot and Cover, naively painted in rouge-de-fer, 4¾" (12cms), c1765-70. **£320-380** SKC

A green ground Imari wine ewe and cover painted in iron-red ar gilding 15.5 cm., fitted metal spout, (original spout apparentl intact) Arita in Hizen, late 17th C. **£1,150-1,250** SKC

A 1930 Japanese Small Teapot and Cover, 4½ in. high. **£47-50** CA

A Rockingham Miniature Teapot and Cover (minute chips to flowers) puce Griffin mark and C1. 2 in red, c. 1835, 10 cm. wide. **£350-400** C

A Sevres Apple-Green Ground Oviform Teapot and Cover, puce interlaced L marks 1768, painter's mark, incised mark 18.5 cm., wide **£350-400** C

A Meissen Hausmalerei teapot, painted by J. F. Mayer von Pressnitz, 15 cm. wide, blue crossed swords mark, c. 1735. **£650-750** C

An Attractive Staffordshire Saltglazed Stoneware Teapot and Cover, decorated in 'famille-rose' enamels with a conical 'Long Eliza', 3½ in., c. 1769, spout with small chip. **£330-360** S

A Meissen ornithological baluster teapot and cover (chip to finial) 16.5 cm. wide, blue crossed swords mark, c. 1745. **£825-900** C

A very rare Swansea Teapot, script mark, c. 1813. **£500-560** SA

A Rare Meissen Octagonal Globular Teapot and Cover, after a Yi Hsing original, blue crossed swords mark, c. 1728 16.5 cm., wide. **£850-950** C

A Staffordshire Monkey Teapot and a cover with a spout in the form of a serpent his tail forming the handle (cover cracked, handle restored) c. 1770 33.5 cm. high. **£175-250** C

A Torquay ware Teapot, Cottage pattern. **£6-8** NO

A Meissen Globular Teapot and Cover, painted in colours, blue crossed swords mark, c. 1745, 19.5 cm., wide. **£500-570** C

A Giant Staffordshire Teapot, 8½" high, 7" diam. **£25-30** SQE

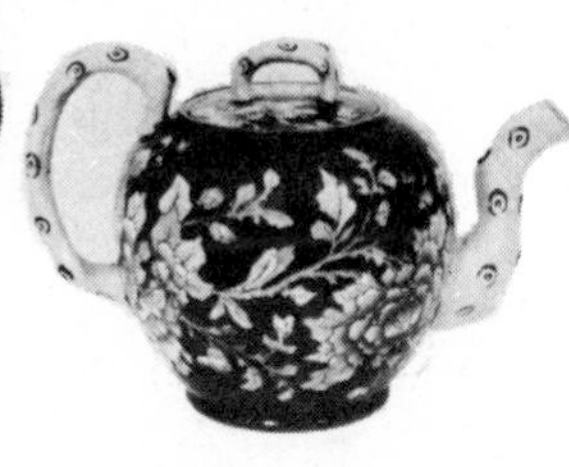
An early 19th C Wedgwood tea pot, Patent No. 2/5609X, impress Eturia, 4". **£70-90** WHL

A Wedgwood-Whieldon Teapot and Cover, picked out in coloured glazes, 5¼ in., c. 1760-65, spout chipped, cover damaged. **£170-190** S

A Dr. Wall Worcester Blue and White Teapot and Cover, Fence pattern, C. mark, in good condition, c. 1765. **£235-260** SA

A First Period Worcester blue and white teapot and cover, with the Fishermans pattern. **£240-260** MJ

A First Period Worcester Teapot and cover, 6½ in. high, c. 1785. **£250-280** MJ

A Grainger Worcester Pierced-Ware Teapot. **£450-500** MN

A Worcester Teapot by Barker with Sheep, 1919. **£350-400** MN

An Art Deco 'Cottage' Teapot. **£12.50-15** AP

A pair of famille rose gilt-ground globular ewers with dragon-masks serpentine spouts, gilt Qianlong six-character marks, late 18th/early 19th C. 7½ in., 19 cm. high. **£2,400-2,500** C

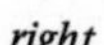

right

A late Ming blue and white broad oviform ewer (the handle cracked and chipped), early/mid-17th C, 9¾" (25cms) high. **£220-250** C

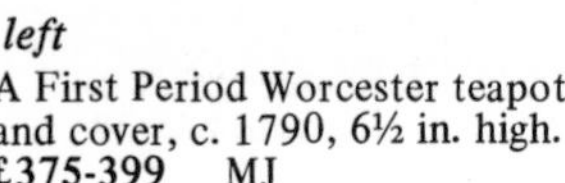

left

A First Period Worcester teapot and cover, c. 1790, 6½ in. high. **£375-399** MJ

An Arita Blue and White Ewer, the ovoid body painted, 10 in., 25.4 cm., late 17th C., handle cracked. **£310-350** S Be

A mounted blue and white pear-shaped ewer and related shallow domed cover (chipped), Kangxi, mounted with gilt-copper hinge and thumbpiece to cover 5¾" (14.5cms) high. **£285-325** C

A Samuel Alcock Parian Ewer, encrusted with grape vines, 10 in. high, c. 1850. **£120-140** MN

A Coalport Ewer, signed by Sutton, raised jewelling, masked handle, 11 in. high, c. 1910. **£595-650** MN

A Crown Derby Miniature Ewer Shaped Jug, c. 1910, 7 in. **£130-150** MJ

A Pair of Minton Ewers, finely painted in the style of Thomas Steel standing on pink and gilt circular pedestals and gilt square bases, 8½ in., 21.6 cm. **£350-450** L

A Royal Worcester ewer, on a shaded apricot ground, gilt scroll handle, 8 in., 20.3 cm., printed mark in puce **£45-60** L

A Bloor Derby Ewer, 13¾ in. damaged. **£200-220** perfect **£300-400** MN

A Fine Doulton Lambeth Ewer by A. Budden, 9½ in. **£105-115** CSG

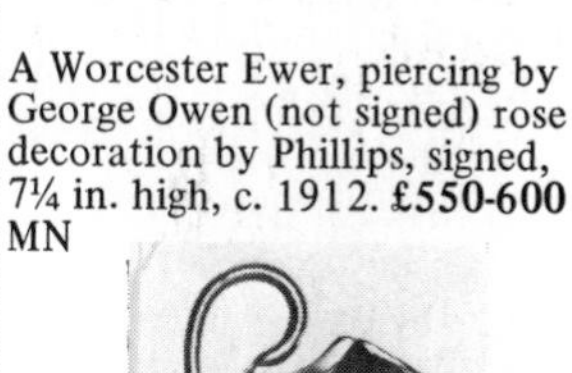

A Worcester Ewer, piercing by George Owen (not signed) rose decoration by Phillips, signed, 7¼ in. high, c. 1912. **£550-600** MN

A Royal Doulton Ewer, 11 in. high, c. 1930's. **£45-50** CA

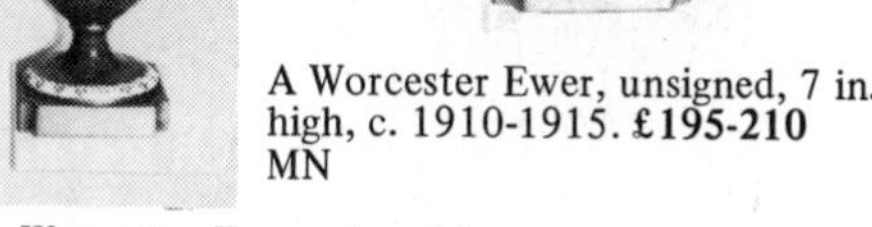

A Worcester Ewer, unsigned, 7 in. high, c. 1910-1915. **£195-210** MN

A Worcester Ewer, signed by Phillips, green ground, 7 in. high, c. 1912. **£350-400** MN

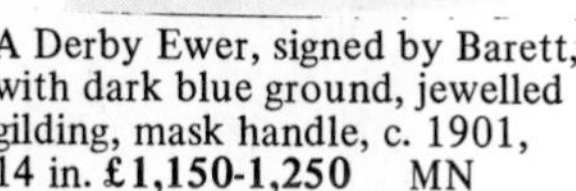

A Derby Ewer, signed by Barett, with dark blue ground, jewelled gilding, mask handle, c. 1901, 14 in. **£1,150-1,250** MN

A Yingqing pear-shaped ewer and cover with a pale bluish-white glaze, (slightly chipped) 13th/14th C. 4½ in., 11.5 cm. high. **£570-625** C

Two Ligurian Ewers, 9½" (24cms), one inscribed G.B. in manganese, 18th C (damaged). **£100-125** SKC

A Yingqing "ironspot" double-gourd ewer under a pale bluish-white glaze, (the handle and spout replaced in gilt-metal) 13th/14th C. 4½ in., 11.5 cm. high. **£150-200** C

A Meissen centre-dish modelled as Summer with Cupid, (some repairs) 48 cm. high, blue crossed swords mark, c. 1750. **£1,200-1,500** C

A Meissen Centre Piece, height 49.5 cm., mark in underglaze blue, late 19th C. some damage. **£780-850** S Be

A Derby Blue and White Centrepiece, surmounted by a shell containing a gherkin (minor chips to base) c. 1765, 21 cm. high. **£400-450** C

A Large Meissen Centre Piece representing the Fruits Of The Earth, height 43 cm., painted marks in underglaze blue, late 19th C. some damage. **£1,150-1,250** S Be

A Royal Vienna Table Centrepiece or Vase c. 1895, 19 in. wide. **£225-260** PC

A Royal Dux Centrepiece, coloured overall in green and pink tones with gilt details, applied pink triangle, c. 1900, 43 cm. **£260-290** SB

A Royal Worcester table centrepiece/flower holder 1875, came as a pair 18 in. long. **£650-700** pr. PC

A Meissen 'Onion pattern' Centrepiece, crossed swords in underglaze blue, incised C84, late 19th C., 43 cm. **£400-450** SB

A Royal Dux Centrepiece painted in green and pink with gilt detail, 39.5 cm., applied pink triangle, late 19th C. **£215-250** S Be

A Bow Candlestick-Group emblematic of Summer modelled as a nymph (minor chips) c. 1765, 27 cm. high. **£275-300** C

A Doulton Lambeth saltglaze earthenware candlestick with brass insets, in Art Nouveau style **£65-70** PC

A pair of Mennecy white candlestick groups, (both candle-nozzles reduced, one repaired) 19 cm. high, c. 1750. **£700-800** C

A Bottger White and Gold Baluster-Shaped Hexagonal Tea-Caddy and Cover (minor chips), c. 1720, 10 cm., high. **£1,000-1,100** C

A Pair of Doulton Gilt-Metal Mounted Candlesticks by Frank A. Butler, incised artist's monogram, impressed marks and dated 1886, 20.5 cm. high. **£140-160** C

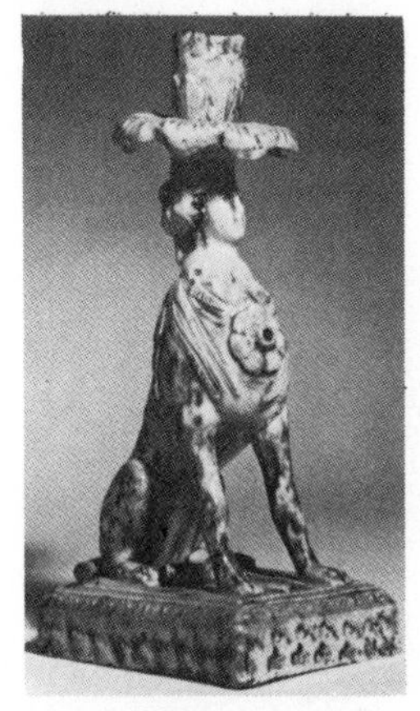

A Staffordshire Creamware Sphinx Candlestick (damage to tail and nozzle) c. 1775, 22.5 cm. high. **£200-300** C

A Caughley Fishermans pattern Teapoy and cover, 4½ in., c. 1800. **£100-115** MJ

A pair of Meissen chamber candlesticks, one with a gold-finch, the other with a deer, (minor repairs to foliage) 14.5 cm. high, blue crossed swords marks, c. 1755. **£1,500-2,000** C

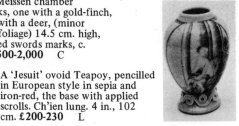

A pair of Kerr & Binns Worcester Candlesticks c. 1863. **£190-210** pr. PC

A 'Jesuit' ovoid Teapoy, pencilled in European style in sepia and iron-red, the base with applied scrolls. Ch'ien lung. 4 in., 102 cm. **£200-230** L

A Hochst rectangular arched tea-caddy and domed cover painted en camaieu rose (chip to cover, small firing crack to base) impressed 2, 11.5 cm. high, c. 1765. **£400-500** C

A Kloster Veilsdorf oblong octagonal teacaddy and cover, painted in sepia, 11 cm. high, traces of blue CV mark, c. 1775. **£550-600** C

A Liverpool Teapoy, blue and white, c. 1790 restored **£35-40** perfect **£58-65** CSG

An Early Meissen Hausmalerei Hexagonal Baluster Tea-Caddy painted by Ignaz Bottengruber, the shoulder and lower part with gilt gadroons (foot rim ground), c. 1724, 10 cm., high. **£880-980** C

A Dr. Wall wet blue Teapoy, with panels of English flowers, square seal mark without cover **£285-300** with cover **£600-650** SA

A Dr. Wall Fluted Tea Caddy with English flowers and turquoise reserves to top, and scrolled border, 7 in., with original top (rare), **£600-660** without top **£300-330** SA

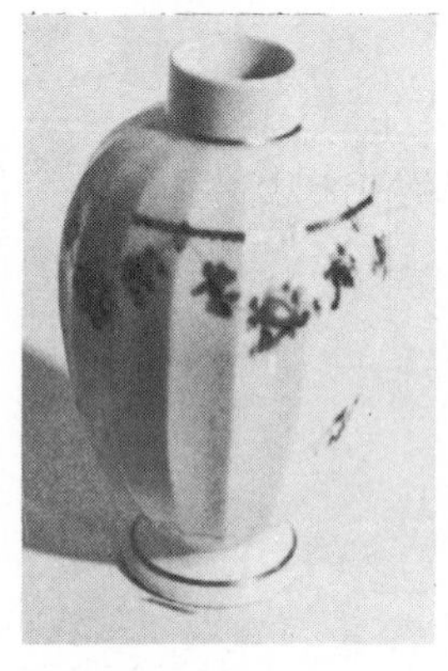

A Worcester Teapoy, with garlands and English flowers, without cover. **£265-280** SA

A Wedgwood Black Basalt Portrait Medallion, 2¾" (7cms), impressed SEL-NIC, wedgwood. **£36-40** SKC

A Wedgwood Portrait Medallion of Nelson, modelled after de Vaere, 4½" (11.5cms), impressed Wedgwood, early 19th C. **£85-95** SKC

JOSIAH WEDGWOOD (& SONS LTD.)

- impressed mark. c1759 - on. from 1891 'ENGLAND'

WEDGWOOD

- **impressed year letters** groups of 3 letters. 3rd denotes year.

O	1860	J	1881
P	1861	K	1882
Q	1862	L	1883
R	1863	M	1884
S	1864	N	1885
T	1865		
U	1866		
V	1867	O	1886
W	1868	P	1887
X	1869	Q	1888
Y	1870	R	1889
Z	1871	S	1890
A	1872	T	1891
B	1873	U	1892
C	1874	V	1893
D	1875	W	1894
E	1876	X	1895
F	1877	Y	1896
G	1878	Z	1897
H	1879		
I	1880		

A Wedgwood Fairyland Lustre Rectangular Plaque with pixies among toadstools and water weeds, unmarked, c. 1920, 40.5 cm. x 29.5 cm. **£600-1,000** C

An Art Nouveau Plaque, German, c. 1910. **£35-40** AP

A Vienna Wall Plaque painted with the three fates, with royal blue and burnished gold border, in a carved giltwood frame, width 56 cm., late 19th C. **£400-450** S Be

A West Pans Blue and White Rectangular Plaque, the ground in Littler's blue, pierced for hanging, c. 1766, 13.5 cm. x 9 cm. **£520-550** C

Art Nouveau pottery inkwell. **£45-55** TT

A Minton Pen Tray with Sevres mark, with applied flowers, 12 in. long. **£195-210** MN

A Rare Leeds Black Basaltes Oval Plaque of Albani, 1½" (4cms), impressed FRAN-ALBANI, and the reverse LEEDS POTTERY **£25-30** SKC

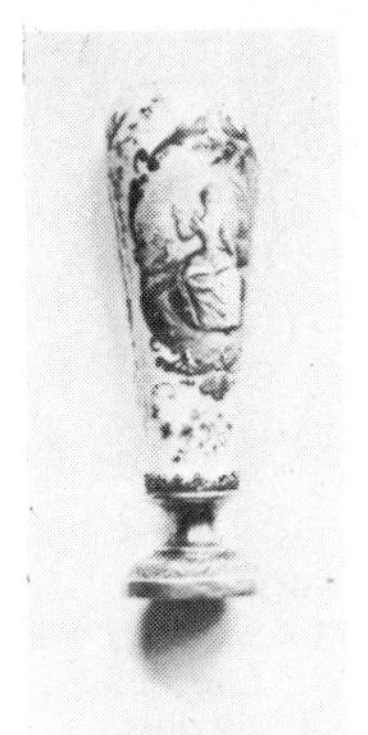
A Vienna Porcelain Seal with English Crest, c. 1840. **£225-250** SA

A Swansea Shell-Shape Inkstand, the outside marbled white and gilt, the top painted by William Pollard. 4 in., 9.8 cm. **£725-810** L

A very rare Flight, Barr & Barr Worcester Plaque 'The Bard' from 'The Tempest,' possibly painted by Joseph Flight, 5 in. x 7½ in., c. 1800. **£885-985** SA

A 19th C Staffordshire bird and lamb inkwell. **£40-50** SAL

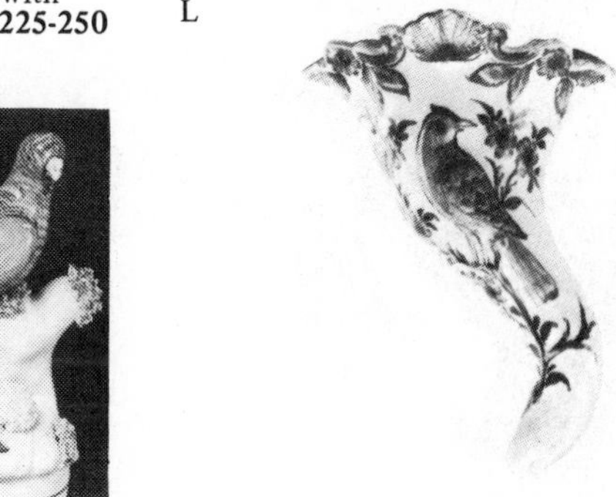
A Liverpool Cornucopia Wall Pocket, in blue, 8 in., mark in blue, c. 1760, some restoration to rim and foot, **£200-300** S

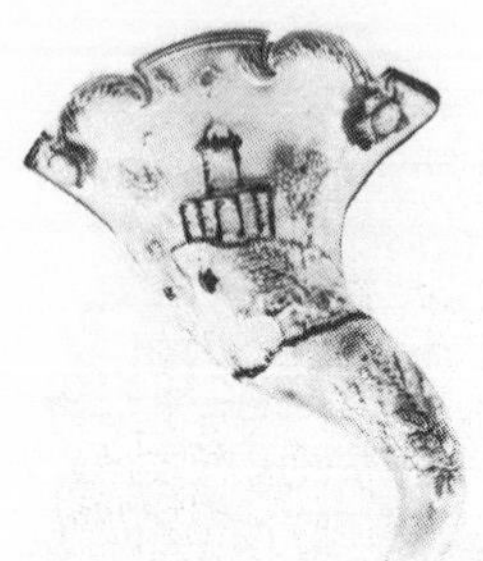

A Wedgwood-Whieldon Cornucopia Wall Pocket modelled probably by William Greatbatch, in washes of green, manganese and ochre, 8¼ in., c. 1760-65, some damage. **£120-140** S

A Pair of Meissen Porcelain Wall Scenes 10 in. wide, 9½ in. high, comprising a bracket shaped vase with 2 candleholders. **£200-290** DH

A Meissen cosmetic box and cover, with a view of Schloss Albrechtsburg at Meissen, 7.5 cm., crossed swords mark in underglaze blue, late 19th C. **£320-350** SKC

A Pair of Paris Cornucopiae, on matt turquoise ground gilt, 11½ in., 29.2 cm., **£380-480** L

An English 18th C. Delft Tile with manganese and blue decoration. **£25-30** RD

Royal Worcester Box, c1900. **£37-42** NO

Royal Worcester Box, c1900. **£35-40** NO

A Set of Four Royal Worcester Wall Brackets, modelled as the seasons in an irridescent pearl lustre glaze, height 24.5 cm., impressed mark, 1867. **£440-480** S Be

A Set of Twelve Burmantofts Faience Tiles, 22 in. long, 6 in. wide, made for pub interiors, c. 1880's. **£300-330** set **£45-50** single. CA

A Meissen Rectangular Gilt-Metal Mounted Snuff-Box and Hinged Cover painted in colours, c. 1745, 9.5 cm., long. **£1,300-1,500** C

A Royal Worcester Wall Bracket, one of 4 depicting the Seasons. **£250-280** each. PC

Victorian Tiles **£3-£5** CSG

A 19th C porcelain Snuff Pot, damaged. **£38-48** SAL

A Rare Butterpan and Stand decorated in Imari style and heightened in gilding, 8¼ in., SPODE and patt. no. 2283 in iron-red, c. 1815. **£220-260** S

A Staffordshire Lavender Ground Pastille-Burner, 5 in. high. **£50-60** CSK

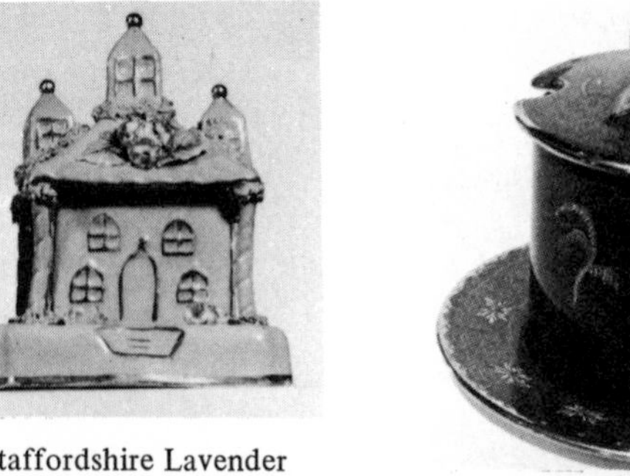

A Carlton-Ware Lustre Jam Pot and Stand, 1930's. **£17-20** CA

A Famille rose shaped oval butter tub, cover and stand. Qianlong, the stand 6¼ in., 16 cm. wide. **£410-450** C

A Pair of 'S & H' Derby Pastille Burners and Covers, 5½ in. high, c. 1880-1890. **£385-410** MN

A Rare Pair of Chamberlain Worcester Monogrammed Foxes Head Stirrup Cups, inscribed 'Tally Ho', c. 1830. **£650-750** pr. SA

A First Period Worcester sauce-boat, ladle and stand, stand 9½ in. wide, marked, c. 1780. **£800-890** MJ

left

A Fine Wet Blue Worcester Mustard Pot, Cover and Spoon, printed with flower sprays and a butterfly in the Mansfield pattern, c. 1770-75. **£765-800** SA

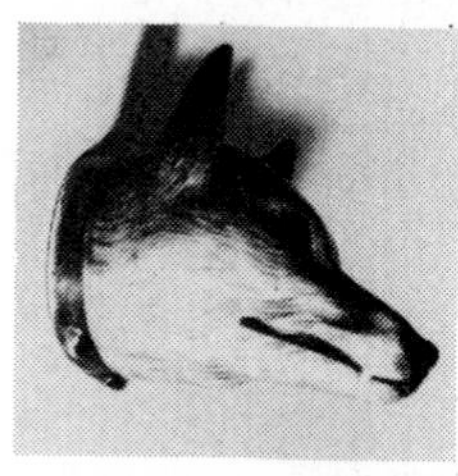

A Derby Stirrup Cup, by Rhyton, foxes head with gilt collar, 4 in. high, c. 1845. **£300-330** MN

A Rockingham Miniature Pastille-Burner and Pierced Cover (cover cracked) puce Griffin mark and C3 in gold, c. 1835, 13 cm. high. **£220-300** C

A Sevres Mustard Pot and Cover, bright turquoise ground, gilding, c. 1781. **£450-500** MN

A Lilac Ground Pastille Burner in the form of toll houses, encrusted with flowers, details in gold, height 14 cm., mid 19th C., slight damage. **£135-150** S Be

A Dr. Wall Worcester Blue and White Cupsidor with sprays of roses and butterflies, c. 1770. **£285-310** SA

A Rare Dr. Wall Worcester Blue and White Cupsidor with Handle. **£650-750** SA

A Pair of Plymouth Shell Salts in the white, on a bed of seaweed, in a smoky glaze, 5 in., c. 1768-70, some chips. **£190-250** S

A Meissen White and Gold Rococo Scroll-Moulded Clock Case, painted with scale-pattern panels (left arm of nymph missing, crack to base of case) blue crossed swords mark, c. 1755 40 cm., high. **£600-670** C

A Meissen spittoon painted en camaieu rose, with an elaborate gilt Laub-und-Bandelwerk cartouche repaired, 13 cm. high, blue crossed swords mark, c. 1750. **£350-400** C

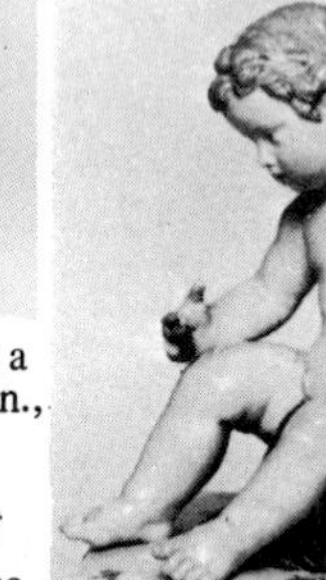

A Famille verte salt moulded as a flower-head (fritted) Kangxi 3 in., 7.5 cm. wide. **£165-185** C

right

A Meissen Clock Case underglaze blue crossed swords, incised model number D 78 late 19th C., 24.7 cm. long. **£390-450** SB

A Gilt-Metal and Porcelain Paper Knife, probably English, c. 1840, 22.2 cm. long. **£80-100** SB

A Chelsea Clock-Case, gold anchor mark at back, c. 1765 (she with restoration and with some minor chips and repairs) 38 cm. high. **£1,000-1,200** C

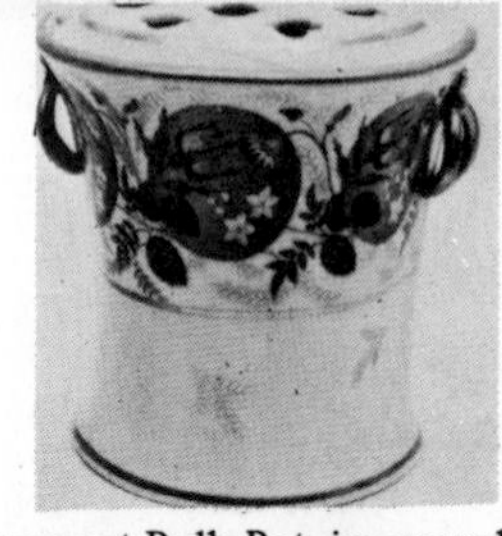

A Davenport Bulb Pot, impressed mark Davenport and an anchor, 6 in., 15.8 cm. **£125-145** L

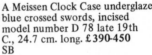

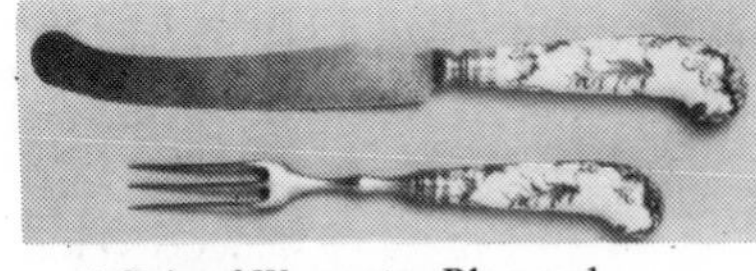

A Pair of Worcester Blue and White Knife and Fork Handles fitted with a steel three-pronged fork and curved blade, c. 1760, the handles 11.5 cm. and 10 cm. long. **£175-200** C

A Chamberlain's Worcester semi-circular bough pot, 22 cm. wide, c. 1805 (top riveted). **£200-250** SKC

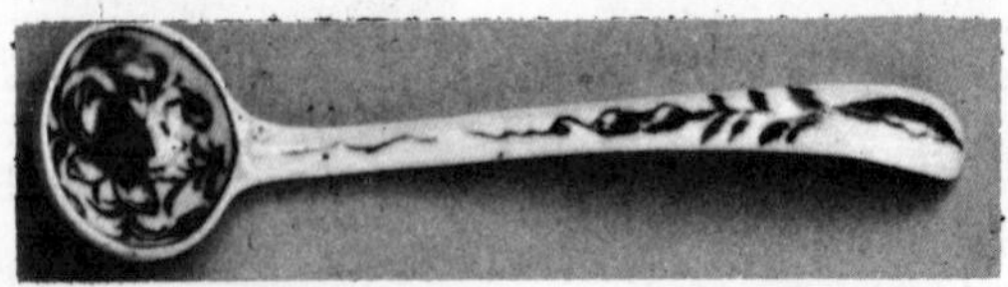

A Worcester Blue and White Mustard-Spoon (minute chip to bowl) c. 1770, 13 cm. long. **£200-225** C

right

A Bristol 'Flower' Brick painted in blue picked out in 'sponged' green, 5 in., mid 18th C. cracked. **£240-300** S

A Pair of London 'Flower' Bricks, decorated in blue, 7¾ in., mid 18th C., edges chipped, slight restoration. **£1,000-1,200** S

BRISTOL DELFT

A Rare Bristol Polychrome 'Flower' Brick painted with red and blue berries and pale green 'stencilled' leaves, 6 in., mid 18th C., slight chips. **£800-900** S

- English Delft manufactured from late 16th C until early 19th C.
- Bristol Delft has a distinctive pale lilac tinge
- red decoration often raised above the glaze
- earliest Bristol Delft made at Brislington

A Meissen Bourdalou (minor repair to tail of bird) 18 cm. long, blue crossed swords mark, c. 1735. **£1,000-1,250** C

A very rare pair of Minton wine coasters (one cracked) 23 cm., impressed Minton and date cypher for the year 1868. **£225-250** SKC

A Pair of Blue and White Moon Flasks, 30.5 cm., painted four character mark of Qianlong (Ch'ien-lung), late 19th C. **£200-250** SB

A Meissen Porcelain framed Mirror 33 in. high, 16 in. wide, highly decorated with applied flowers and leaves. **£390-450** DH

A Pair of Art Nouveau Fire Dogs, c. 1900. **£16-19** pr. AP

Art Deco Signed Denby Book-ends, 1930's. **£24-26** pr. AP

A Meissen Obelisk, painted in colours (chipped), blue crossed swords mark, c. 1750 22.5 cm., high. **£280-330** C

A Pair of Meissen Obelisks on ball feet and supported on square plinths moulded and painted in colours (one repaired) blue crossed swords marks. c. 1750 23 cm., **£550-620** C

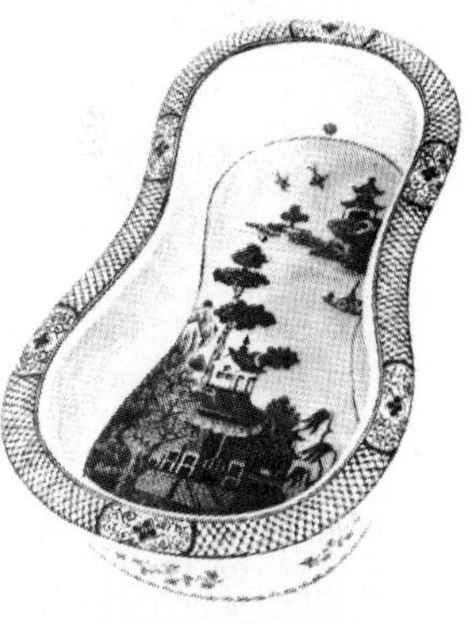

A blue and white violin-shaped bidet, Qinglong 24" (61cms) long. **£400-425** C

A blue and white barrel-shaped bird-feeder (minor wear on rim), Xuande four-character mark below the rim, late Ming/early Qing Dynasty wood stand, 3" (7.5cms) wide. **£240-280** C

A blue and white Kendi with knopped spout (rim reduced), Kangxi 8¼" (21,5cms) high. **£210-240** C

An Unusual Pair of Pounce Pots of capstan shape, 3" (7.5cms), K'ang Hsi (one chipped). **£170-200** SKC

A pair of blue and white bowls, chipped. one cracked, Kangxi, 6in, 15cm high **£170-240pr** C

A tilemaker's pottery hexagonal stand (chipped), 28¾" (73.5cms) high. **£165-200** C

A Ch'ing Blue and White Brushpot, 4¾" (12cms), K'ang Hsi. **£340-380** SKC

A Carlton Ware Lustre Biscuit Barrel, 5½ in., 1930's. **£27-30** CA

Two famille verte mustard-yellow and green-glazed models of walnut piles (chipped, one restored, the other base-cracked), 18th/19th C., 5 in., 13 cm. high. **£110-150** C

Two Paris night-light holders, with broad gilt borders. 6 in., 15.8 cm. **£200-250** L

A German Porcelain Pipe Bowl with Gilt-Metal Hinged Cover, painted with the head and shoulders of King George IV, 5½ in. long. **£110-140** CSK

A Victorian Cheese Dish. **£48-50** VA

'Greta Garbo' A Royal Doulton Face Mask, 20cms high, l.c.m., HN 1661 and date code for 1936. **£260-300** P

A Worcester Peach-Shaped Wine-Taster with entwined twig handle (one foot with slight restoration) c. 1765, 10 cm. wide. **£450-550** C

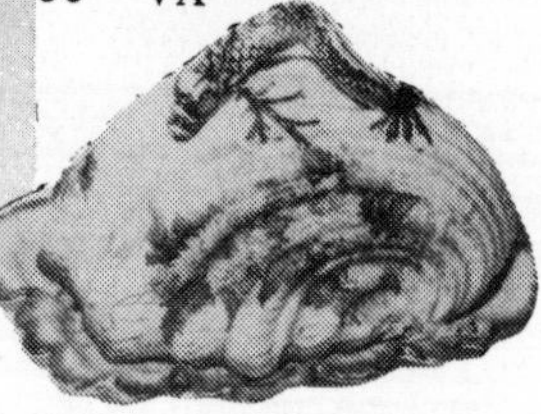

A Victorian Cheese Dish, 12 in. wide. **£50-60** VA

A white glazed globular vessel (with some damage), early/mid Qing Dynasty 5½ in., 14 cm. high. **£70-80** C

(l) Bears on Rocks (early bears grease lids), 3" diam. **£70-85** OF

(r) Bears at School, 3" diam. **£75-90** OF

A Seto chaire 5.5 cm., ivory cover, early/mid Edo. **£180-200** SKC

(l) Landing the Fare, Pegwell Bay, 3¾" diam. **£50-60** OF

(r) Alas Poor Bruin, 3" diam. **£75-90** OF

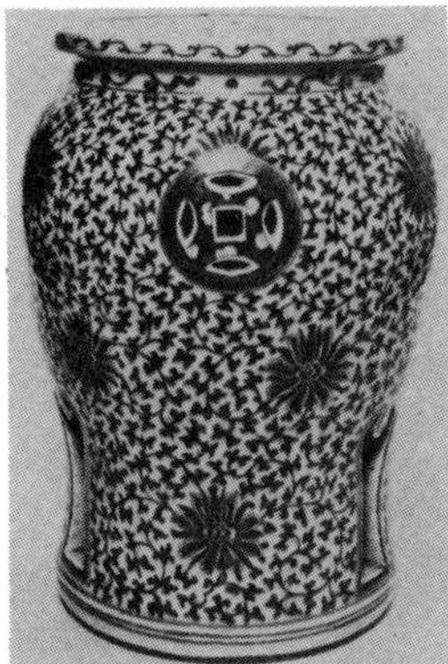

A Blue and White Garden Seat, the circular top pierced in the centre, 47 cm., late 19th C. **£220-300** SB SBe

(l) Bellevue, Pegwell Bay, 4¾" diam. **£50-65** OF

A Blue and White Garden Seat, pierced and moulded with studs, 47 cm., late 19th C. **£390-450** SB SBe

(l) Belle Vue Tavern (Kent series), 4¾" diam. **£60-75** OF

POINTERS FOR POT-LIDS

- Flat, circular lids used to cover low, cylindrical pots containing toilet preparations. Later contained ointments and meat pastes.
- Colour printing on ceramic ware perfected mid to late 1840's.
- Height of popularity 1850's to 1860's.
- Original lids were produced up to 1900 and were actually used for their original purpose.
- Very early - 1845 to 1860. (Flat top, usually Bear or Pegwell Bay subjects - good colours).
- Early - 1860 to 1875. (Convex top - good colours).
- Late - 1875 to 1900. (Heavier in texture - usually poor colours).
- Reissues - 1900 to the present. (Usually flat tops - no crazing).
- Best lids from Felix Pratt factory. Much of the engraving done by Jesse Austin whose name or initials can be found on some examples of his work.
- Over 300 patterns produced.
- 3 firms Pratt, Cauldon and Mayer produced the greater volume of underglazed colour printed wares.

Walmer Castle, 4" diam. **£50- 60** OF

Royal Harbour, Ramsgate, 4" diam. **£45-60** OF

Royal Harbour, Ramsgate, 5¼" diam. **£42-55** OF

Hauling in the Trawl. **£50-60** OF

The Shrimpers, 4" diam. **£30-40** OF

The Red Bull Inn, 4" diam. **£50-65** OF

Embarking for the East, 4¼" diam. **£55-65** OF

Albert Memorial, 4¼" diam. **£45-55** OF

Strasbourg, 4¾" diam. **£70-85** OF

Sandringham, the seat of H.R.H. The Prince of Wales, 4¼" diam. **£55-70** OF

L'Exposition Universelle de 1867, 4¾" diam. **£85-100** OF

Wimbledon, July 2nd, 1860, 4¼" diam. **£55-65** OF

Chapel Royal, Savoy, Destroyed by Fire, July 7, 1864. £55-70 OF

Philadelphia Exhibition, 1875, 4¼" diam. £55-65 OF

Napoleon & Empress Eugenie, 5" diam. £180-200 OF

The Late Duke of Wellington, 5" diam. £115-125 OF

Victor Emmanuel and Garibaldi. £65-75 OF

Garibaldi, 4" diam. £45-55 OF

War, 4¼" diam. £52-65 OF

Peace, 4¼" diam. £47-60 OF

The Ning Po River, 4" diam. £50-60 OF

Harbour of Hong Kong, 4" diam. £45-55 OF

The Room in which Shakespeare was born, 1564, 4" diam. £45-55 OF

Shakespeare's House, 4" diam. £45-55 OF

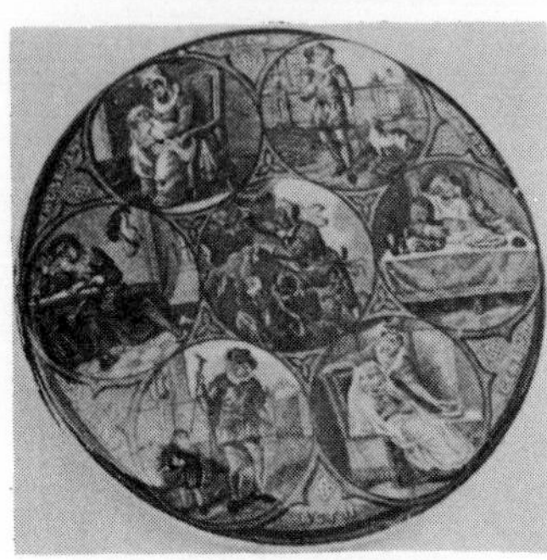

Seven Ages of Man, 4" diam. **£60-75** OF

Tam o'Shanter, 4" diam. **£65-75** OF

Hamlet and Father's Ghost. **£95-110** OF

The Village Wedding, 4" diam. **£45-55** OF

The Skaters, 3" diam. **£45-60** OF

The Skaters, 4" diam. **£75-90** OF

The Shepherd Boy, 4" diam. **£45-55** OF

Dr. Johnson, 4¼" diam. **£30-45** OF

Uncle Toby, 4¼" diam. **£35-50** OF

The Picnic, 5" diam. **£60-75** OF

The Return from Deer Hunting, 4¾" diam. **£85-100** OF

Persuasion, 4" diam. **£50-60** OF

The First Appeal, 4" diam. **£50-60** OF

The Poultry Woman, 4" diam. **£50-60** OF

The Lovers, 3¼" diam. **£100-110** OF

The Fair Sportswoman. **£60-70** OF

The Waterfall, 4¼" diam. **£50-65** OF

The Times, 4¼" diam. **£40-50** OF

I see you my boy, 4" diam. **£35-50** OF

Lend a Bite, 4" diam. **£45-60** OF

Hide and Seek, 4" diam. **£35-50** OF

French Street Scene, 5" diam. **£60-70** OF

The Race, 4¼" diam. **£45-60** OF

A Letter from the Diggings, 4" diam. **£50-60** OF

The Flute Player, 4" diam. **£50-60** OF

The Peasant Boys, 3½" diam. **£105-115** OF

The Children of Flora, 4¾" diam. **£76-90** OF

Summer, 4¼" diam. **£85-100** OF

Shells, 4¼" diam. **£40-50** OF

The Snow Drift, 4" diam. **£55-70** OF

Country Quarters, 5" diam. **£65-75** OF

Good Dog, 4¾" diam. **£55-70** OF

A Pretty Kettle of Fish, 4" diam. **£45-60** OF

The Wolf and the Lamb, 4" diam. **£40-55** OF

Rectangular Pot Lid, War. **£50-60** OF

Rectangular Pot Lid, Peace. **£50-60** OF

A Victorian Pot Lid. **£6.50-8** AP

POINTERS FOR GOSS CHINA

- W. H. Goss factory opened in 1858 and closed in 1944.
- 1872 W. H. Goss patented an improved method of manufacturing 'jewelled' porcelain. Moved to a larger factory, the Falcon Works in Stoke.
- Many pieces of Goss can still be bought for under £10.
- Condition is important, many damaged pieces are valueless.
- Pieces with masonic symbols, the crest of a warship or a military regiment are highly collectable.
- Believed to be over 7,000 different coats of arms on the heraldic ware.
- 1907 J. J. Jarvis founded the League of Goss Collectors.
- Usual marks are W. H. Goss, or a Falcon with W. H. Goss beneath.

A Victorian Pot Lid. **£7.50-9** AP

A Goss Beaker of Shakespeare's House, Stratford-on-Avon, 3 in. high. **£35-45** SA

A Goss Two-Handled Model of a Vase. **£7-9** SA

Pratt Ware Jar, 'Mending the Nets', 3" high. **£55-70** OF

£12.50-14.50 **£10.50-12.50** **£12-13**

Pratt Ware Jar, 'Continental Fish Market', 4" high. **£50-60** OF

Goss Parian bust of Mozart. **£100-120** NO

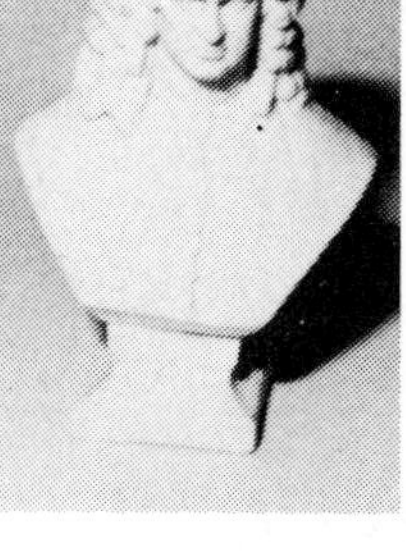

Goss Parian bust of Handel. **£100-120** NO

Goss Parian bust of Beethoven. **£95-105** NO

l - r: £5.50; £6.50; £4; £4.50
NO

l - r: £4.50; £5
NO

l - r: £3; £12.50
NO

Models of Vases, l - r: £3.50; £4.50; £5.50; £5 NO

l - r: £6.50; £4; £3.50; £7.50
NO

Crested ware, l - r: £4; £4.50;

£4.50; £2.50;

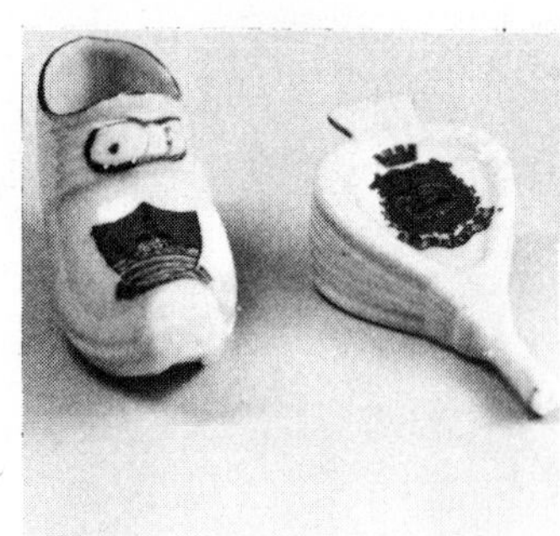

£5; £5

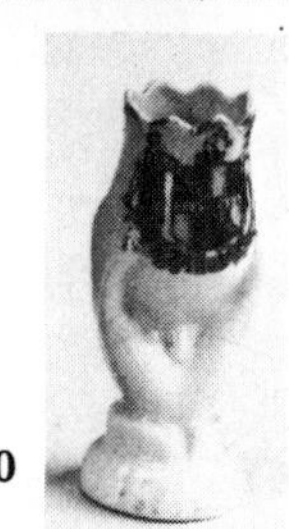

£3.50

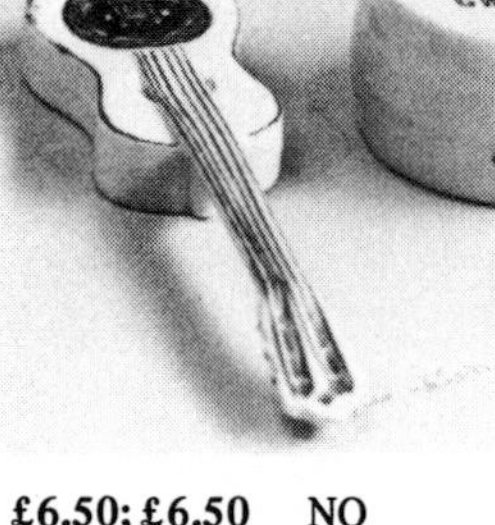

£6.50; £6.50 NO

£4; £4; £3;

£4.50; £3.50

£8.50

£8

Wartime Pieces. l - r: **£8.50; £12- 16; £10** NO

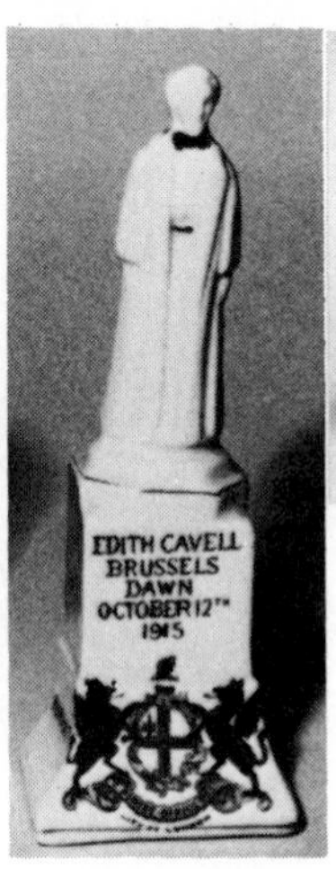

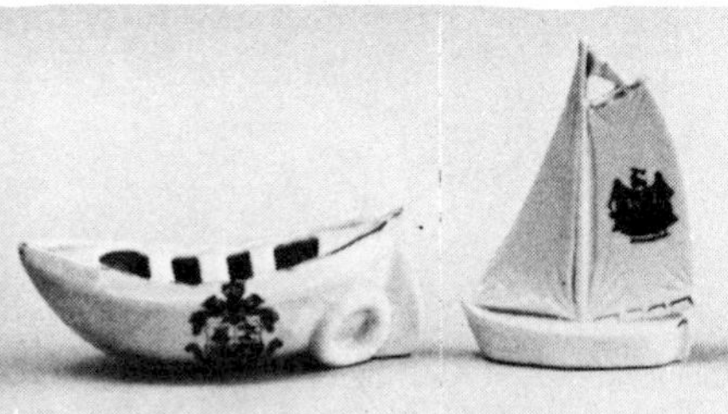

£6.50 **£6.50**

£6.50

(m) Shelley crested grandfather clock. **£12-14** NO

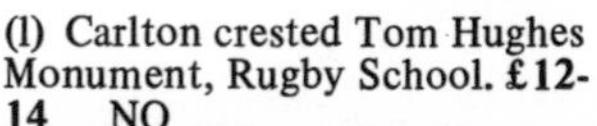

(l) Carlton crested Tom Hughes Monument, Rugby School. **£12-14** NO

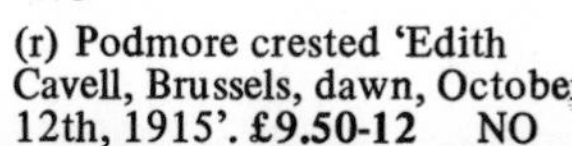

(r) Podmore crested 'Edith Cavell, Brussels, dawn, October 12th, 1915'. **£9.50-12** NO

Arcadian crested registered series, Comical Boy riding Pig. **£30-35** NO

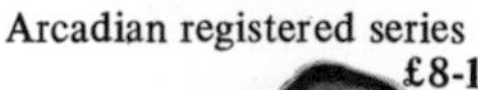

Arcadian registered series **£8-10**

Arcadian registered series **£30-35**

Shelley crested box of matches. **£6-8** NO

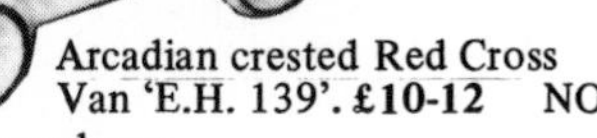

Arcadian crested Red Cross Van 'E.H. 139'. **£10-12** NO

Carlton crested Gramophone. **£14-16** NO

Grafton crested Yacht with billowing sail, named 'Polly'. **£15-17** NO

A Shelley China crested ware mug. **£5.50-7.50** NO

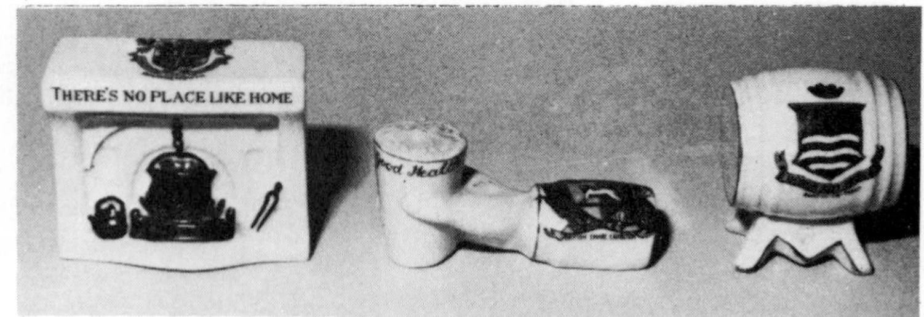

(m) Carlton Crested hand with glass. **£6-8** NO

(l) Arcadian crested Hearth, small. **£8-10** NO

(r) Willow Art crested barrel. **£6-8** NO

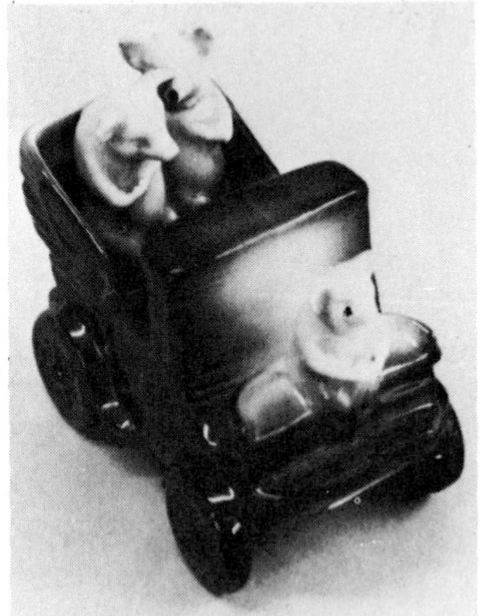

Piggies. **£28-30** NO

Arcadian crested bust of George V. **£25-30** NO

Arcadian crested bust of Alexandra. **£25-30** NO

Ashtray, not listed, Arcadian reg. series, bookie with greyhound and hare. **£18-22** NO

Robert Burns' Cottage, unmarked. **£30-35** NO

Piggies, made in Germany, 1902-11, (better, the more pigs). **£25-27** NO

Leicester Hospital, Warwick, by W. Smith & Sons, Warwick, Willow Art Cottage. **£30-35** NO

Gretna Green, Blacksmith's shop, Willow Art Cottage. **£25-30** NO

Willow Art Cottage, Bell Hotel. **£18-20** NO

Willow Art, Ann Hathaway's Cottage. **£18-20** NO

Willow Art Cottages:

Shakespeare's House. **£12-15** NO

Ann Hathaway's Cottage. **£12-15** NO

(l) Cat-and-Fiddle Inn, nr Buxton. **£165-185** NO

(l) Lloyd George's early home, Llanystymdwy, with annexe. **£95-105** NO

(r) First and Last House in England; Western Esplanade, Penzance, with grey roof. **£60-70** NO

(l) Old Maid's Cottage, Lee. **£90-100** NO

(r) Prince Llewelyn's House. **£80-90** NO

Model of Shakespeare's House. **£45-55** NO

(l) Gad's Hill, Rochester. **£95-105** NO

(r) Miss Ellen Terry's Farmhouse, nr Tenterden. **£325-400** NO

Ann Hathaway's Cottage. **£45-50** NO

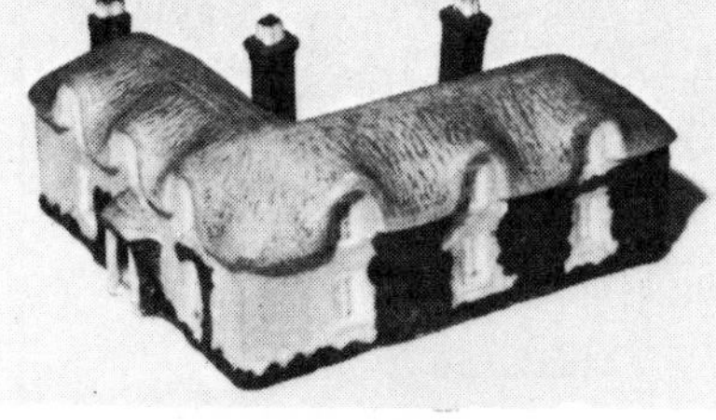

(l) Portman Lodge. **£345-400** NO

(r) Manx Cottage – glazed example. **£80-90** NO

Wordsworth's Birthplace, Cockermouth. **£190-220** NO

A Model of the Birthplace of Thomas Hardy, 'The Wessex Poet', Dorchester, with falcon mark, 103mm. **£250-300** L

A Model of Tudor House, Southampton, falcon mark, 75mm. **£90-100** L

A Model of Burns Cottage, with falcon mark, 60mm. **£60-70** L

Dove Cottage, Grasmere. **£350-450** NO

House at Lichfield in which Samuel Johnson was born. **£90-100** NO

A Model of Shakespeare's House, falcon mark, 78mm. **£35-40** L

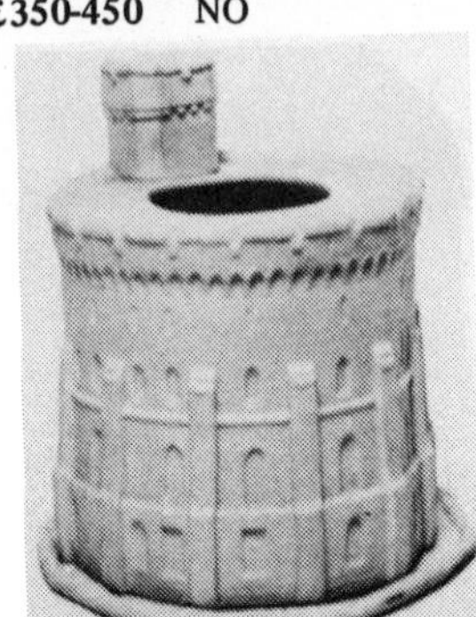

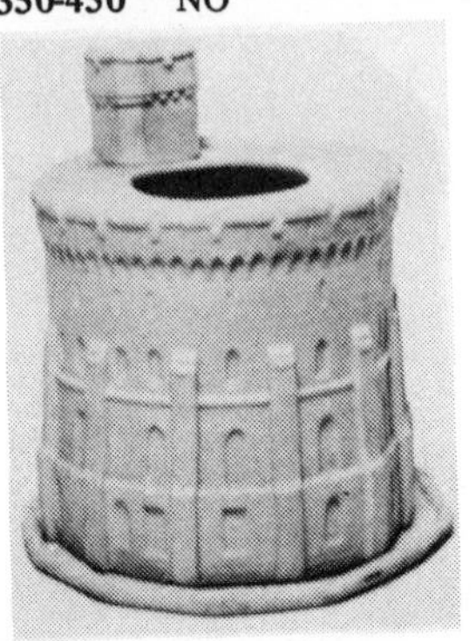

Round Tower, Windsor, a rare nightlight and base, -uncoloured base 5½" (14cms), printed goshawk, title and 'Pub. by Dyson & Sons, Windsor. C1900. **£180-260** S.B.

A Fairing, Welsh Tea Party. **£14-16** NO

A 19th C. Fairing 'Tug of War' **£49-53** SV

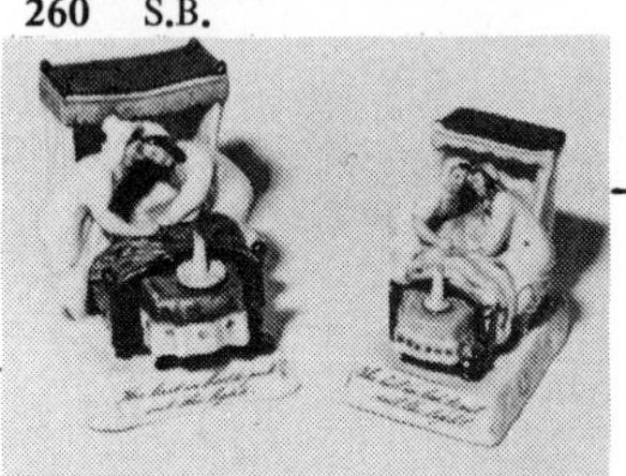

Two Victorian fairings 'Last into bed puts out the light'. **£35-45** PC

Early Bird Catches The Worm **£95-140**

Cousin And Cousine **£250-300**

By Golly I Am In Luck **£35-55**

Cabin Baggage **£20-40**

By Appointment The First Of April **£250-250**

Baby's First Step **£35-55**

Anxious To Study **£35-65**

An Awkward Interruption **£55-75**

After **£55-75**

Defeat **£65-85**

A Difficult Problem **£25-55**

The Decided Smash **£65-85**

Dick Whittington and His Cat **£25-55**

Come Along These Flowers Don't Smell Very Good **£65-85**

Can You Do This Grandma? **£95-155**

FAIRINGS

- Small cheaply made porcelain groups, originally bought or won as prizes at Fairground stalls.
- Usually bearing wry or slightly suggestive captions.
- Made in Germany mainly by Conta Boehme factory.
- Boxes, match-holders less highly prized than purely ornamental groups.
- Identical groups often bear different original captions.
- Captions removed or altered reduce value.
- Rare examples command disproportionately high prices.

Master's Winning Ways **£70-100**

Scratch your Match on my Patch **£15-25**

Favourable Opportunity **£30-50**

Now Marm Say When **£50-70**

Come Pussie Come **£30-50**

The Child's Prayer **£20-30**

Benoni And Leila **£30-45**

Baby- Rock Me To Sleep Mother **£20-40**

Attack **£50-70**

Five O'Clock Tea **£15-30**

First Temptation **£20-35**

A Funny Story **£55-75**

Gentlemen of the Jury **£30-45**

His First Pair **£20-35**

Hit Him Hard **£200-250**

Retour de Voyage **£400-450**

Fair Play Boys **£250-350**

FURNITURE

A Georgian serpentine front mahogany Bachelor's Chest of Chippendale design, 3'3" wide, 2'6½" high. **£2,400-2,600** Buc

A Mahogany Serpentine Chest of four graduated long drawers below a brushing slide with lobed top and scrolled angles, 48 in., 122 cm. wide, **£1,550-1,710** C

A Good Mahogany Chest of 4 Drawers with brushing slide, 37 in. wide, 20 in. deep, 34 in. high, English c. 1780. **£995-1,100** CP

A Hepplewhite-style figured mahogany serpentine-fronted Chest, 3' (92cms) high x 3'2" (97cms) wide, c1860. **£1,120-1,200** SKC

A George III Small Mahogany Serpentine Chest of Four Drawers, the top with boxwood edging, 38 in., 97 cm. **£2,600-2,900** L

A Victorian Bow-Fronted Mahogany Chest of Drawers, 41 in. wide by 20 in. deep by 40 in. high. **£130-150** VA

A George III Mahogany Rectangular Chest, the centre drawer with baize-lined writing surface and fitted drawer, 39½ in., 100 cm. wide. **£420-460** C

A Mid 18th C. Chippendale Period Mahogany Chest of Drawers, 31 in. wide, 19 in. deep, 31 in. high. **£880-980** SHA

An Early George III Mahogany Serpentine Chest with brushing-slide, 39½ in., 100 cm. wide. **£1,900-2,100** C

A Victorian Mahogany Chest of Drawers. **£160-185** SV

A George III Serpentine-fronted Mahogany Chest, 3'4", (102cms) wide. **£1,490-1,520** SKC

A 19th C Mahogany Military Chest in two parts, 39" (99cms) wide, c1880. **£290-330** SKC

A 'Chippendale' Period Mahogany Chest, 2 ft. 6½ in. carcass, 2 ft. 6½ in. high, 19 in. deep, c. 1765. **£900-1000** TA

A Jacobean Oak Chest, 3'6" (107cms) wide. **£1,500-1,600** SKC

An Oak Chest of small proportions, with later top, with fielded panel mouldings and brass loop handles, 17th C., 32 in., 81 cm. wide. **£360-400** L

A Georgian Mahogany Chest, 30½" (77cms) wide, 32in (81cms) high, 18½" (47cms) deep, c1750. **£820-920** L

A Charles II Oak Chest, each drawer concealing an arrangement of 'secret' drawers of later construction, with original escutcheons embossed with the lion and unicorn and with pear drop handles and original steel locks, c. 1680, 3 ft. 6¾ in., 109 cm. wide x 4 ft. 2 in., 127 cm. high. **£800-950** L

A Late 18th C. Oak Chest of Drawers, new handles and feet, secret drawer at back, c. 1780. **£250-280** SHA

A Dutch Mahogany Chest, 2 ft. 10 in. high x 3 ft. ½ in. wide, 87 cm. x 93 cm., c. 1780, floral inlay later. **£1,000-1,300** S

A Charles II Oak Chest fitted with three panelled and coffered drawers divided by split bobbins 38½ in., 98 cm. wide. **£700-770** C

A Nice Oak and Pine Chest of Drawers in two parts, 3 drawers with applied geometrical mouldings, original except handles, 38 in. wide, 21 in. deep, 36 in. high, c. 1660. **£620-680** DB

An Oak Chest in two parts, 3 ft. 6 in. high x 3 ft. 7½ in. wide, 107 cm. x 110 cm., c. 1660, probably Flemish. **£500-650** S

A late 17th C Flemish Parquetry Oak Chest, 105cms wide. **£450-500** SH

A Charles II Walnut Chest of Drawers, 2 ft. 11 in. high x 3 ft. 2 in. wide, 89 cm. x 96 cm., c. 1670. **£800-1,000** S

A George I Walnut Chest with panels outlined with feather-banding, the ogee moulded top quarter veneered with a wide mitred banding, on later bun feet, 39¾ in., 101cm. **£1,900-2,100** L

A William and Mary walnut and marquetry rectangular chest, inlaid throughout, on later bracket feet. 38 in., 97 cm. wide. **£1,600-1,900** C

A Queen Anne Chest of Drawers of good patina with walnut top and front and pine sides, original brass escutcheons, later replaced handles, 36 in. wide, c. 1700. **£1,475-1,650** RD

An 18th C Walnut Chest. **£200-240** L

DRAWERS – GUIDE TO DATING

- early 17th C. drawers were nailed together, with side runners which fitted into deep side grooves
- bottom runners, usually made of oak, appeared c.1680
- no 18th C. drawer completely fitted the space between front and back – a space left for ventilation
- good quality drawers had sides of oak, with rounded top edges
- up to 1770 grain in bottom boards of drawers ran from front to back, from 1770 the grain ran from side to side
- 18th C. cabinet makers made the bottom boards from 2 or 3 pieces of the same wood; the Victorians used one piece which was usually screwed
- corner mouldings were a Sheraton innovation, hence give a date of after 1799

A Good Queen Anne Walnut Chest, crossbanded and decorated with feather banding, bracket feet and handles not original, 39 in. wide, 22 in. deep, 36 in. high, c. 1710. **£1,525-1,750** CP

An Early Georgian Walnut Chest with cross-banded quartered top, 38 in., 96.5 cm. wide. **£800-880** C

An Early Georgian Walnut Chest, 3 ft. 1 in. high, c. 1740. **£760-830** OB

An Early George I Walnut Chest with crossbanded quartered top, on later bracket feet, 39½ in., 100 cm. wide. **£820-900** C

A Charles II Oak and Walnut Chest in two sections, later handles and some restoration 39 in., 99 cm. x 44 in., 112 cm. high. **£750-850** L

A Very Fine William and Mary Walnut Chest, veneered drawer fronts, panelled ends, 36 in. wide, 21 in. deep, 34 in. high, c. 1680. **£950-1050** SHA

An Antique Walnut Sectional Chest having crossbanded and parquetry top, with brass bale handles and escutcheons, 3 ft. 2 in. wide, 2 ft. deep, 38 in. high. **£650-750** V

A Commonwealth Walnut Chest, 100cms wide. **£650-700** SH

A Queen Anne walnut chest, 39" wide. **£430-480** SH

A Georgian Burr Walnut Chest raised on shaped bracket feet, 18th C., possibly from a larger piece, 38½ in., 98 cm. **£350-450** L

An 18th C. Dutch serpentine burrwood chest, 112 cm., 44 in. **£900-1,000** O

A William and Mary Oyster Laburnum Chest of Drawers, with brass handles and escutcheons, all with crossbanded decoration, 37 in. wide, 31 in. high, c. 1685-90 **£2,500-3,000** RD

A Walnut Chest of Drawers, the crossbanded top inlaid with brass drop handles and escutcheons, faults. 18th C., 38 in., 97 cm. wide x 37 in., 94 cm. high. **£470-570** L

A Late George III Satinwood Chest of Drawers with bowed top crossbanded with rosewood, 35½ in., 90 cm. wide. **£750-825** C

A William and Mary Marquetry Chest of Drawers on later bracket feet. 38 in., 96 cm. **£3,500-4,000** L

An Unusual Queen Anne Walnut and Fruitwood Chest, early 18th C, 30" x 32½" (76cms x 83cms). **£450-550** SBA

A late George III rosewood work-table, enclosing a leather-lined easel flanked by lidded compartments, inlaid with gothic-pattern boxwood. 36 in., 91.5 cm. wide. **£2,300-2,530** C

A William and Mary Oyster Walnut Chest, decorated with crossbanding and inlaid with sycamore stringing, 3'5" (104cms) wide. **£1,050-1,150** SKC

A Queen Anne Oyster-Veneered Walnut Chest inlaid in boxwood with concentric circles and scrolls with crossbanded drawers on bracket feet, 37¾ in., 96 cm. wide. **£3,400-3,740** C

A fine William & Mary period Walnut oyster veneered and seaweed marquetry Chest, 3'1". **£2,100-2,300** Buc

William & Mary Oyster Veneered Walnut & Laburnum Chest. **£1,050-1,200** EBB

A Good Oyster Pieces Chest, the top with geometric parquetry inlay and thumb moulded edge, 18th C. 37½ in., 95 cm. wide x 31½ in., 80 cm. high. **£2,100-2,400** L

A 17th C. English Chest, inlaid with various woods 24 in. deep x 33 in. high x 44 in. wide. **£1,400-1,500** RB

A Charles II Elm and Walnut Chest of Drawers, 3 ft. 5 in. high x 3 ft. 2 in. wide, 104 cm. x 97 cm. c. 1670. **£500-700** S

An elm Chest, the sides inset with arched panels painted with coats-of-arms, early 18th C. 33 in. (84 cm.). **£340-370** C

A Small Oak and Pine Chest, rebacked, 31 in., 79 cm. **£190-220** L

Pine chest of drawers with oak lined drawers 40 in. wide 41 in. high 19 in. deep. **£105-115** AL

Small chest of drawers with bun feet. 34 in. long 32 in. high 18 in. deep. **£90-100** AL

An Edwardian pine Chest of Drawers with galleried top and porcelain handles. 44 in. wide, 51 in. high, 21 in. deep. **£120–140** MM

A Victorian pine Chest with a flight of eight drawers, on shaped bracket feet, 38 in. high, 33 in. wide, 15 in. deep. **£110–130** GW

Victorian pine Chest of Drawers, recently painted with ship designs. 44 in. high, 48 in. wide. **£100-120** SSP

A small 19th C. pine Chest of Drawers with mahogany handles and gesso mouldings 36 in. wide, 30 in. high, 18 in. deep. **£90–100** MS

19th C. pine Chest of Drawers with attractively shaped back and deep golden colour. 45 in. wide, 22 in. high, 21 in. deep. **£90-100** AL

A small, 18th C., pine Scandinavian Chest of Drawers, with reeded columns, panelled centre drawer and shaped plinth. 36 in. wide, 30 in. high. **£160–180** SM

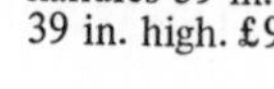

Chest of drawers with porcelain handles 39 in. wide, 20 in. deep, 39 in. high. **£95-110** AL

19th C. pine Double Chest of Drawers on turned feet. 60 in. wide, 32 in. high, 21 in. deep. **£150–200** AL

Plain pine Victorian Chest of Drawrs with new wooden handles. 42 in. high, 21 in. deep, 42 in. wide. **£75-80** SSP

18th C. pine Chest of Drawers in good condition, sides extended to form feet. 36 in. wide, 29 in. high. 19 in. deep. **£100–120** AL

A 19th C. pine Specimen Chest with a flight of ten drawers with mahogany handles. 28 in. high, 12 in. deep. **£95–120** AL

Edwardian satin walnut Chest of Drawers with original handles. **£50-55** SSP

19th C. pine Chest of Drawers with shaped base and mahogany handles. 36 in. wide, 29 in. high, 19 in. deep. **£95–110** AL

Victorian pine Chest of five Drawers with mahogany handles standing on high turned feet. 38 in. wide, 37 in. high, 18 in. deep. **£85–90** AL

A flight of specimen drawers 48 in. wide, 8 in. deep. **£150-180** SM

Edwardian pine Flight of Drawers with open pigeon holes in centre and original handles to drawers. 48 in. wide, 10 in. deep. **£85–95** AL

A Rosewood Wellington Chest with a bead and reel border, 39½ in. x 30½ in., 100 x 77.5 cm., c. 1840. **£500-600** SB

A French empire mahogany semainier with gilt brass mounts and drop-ring handles, height 61 in., 155 cm. width 45 in., 114 cm., c. 1810. **£600-680** SBe

Early Elm and pine chest of drawers 31 in. high 29 in. wide 17 in. deep. **£120-140** AL

An 18th C oak Dresser, with brass swan-neck handles, 54". **£690-790** BW

A Georgian Oak Dresser Base, with panelled sides, construction by quarter sawn oak with muntins and rails joined by single and double raised pegs, consistent restoration, 6 ft. 3 in., 190.5 cm., 18th C. **£1,500-1,700** L

A Charles II Oak Dresser Base, 2 ft. 11 in. high x 6 ft. 2 in. long, 89 cm. x 188 cm., c. 1670. **£1,400-1,800** S

An Oak Low Dresser. Late 17th/ 18th C, with restorations, 69" (175cms). **£940-1,000** L

A Rare Early 18th C. Yew Wood Dresser with fielded panels to the front, 68 in. wide. **£5,950-6,500** RD

A Georgian oak Low Dresser, the top crossbanded with mahogany and with later ledge back. 73 in. (187 cm.) wide. **£850-940** C

An oak Dresser, on baluster legs and block feet, 18th C. 84 in. (213 cm.) wide. **£1,100-1,250** C

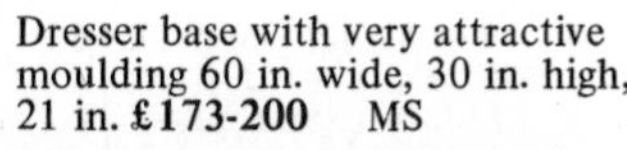
Dresser base with very attractive moulding 60 in. wide, 30 in. high, 21 in. **£173-200** MS

left
A Charles II Oak Dresser Base, brass ring handles and escutcheons with ogee mouldings, on baluster turned legs, late 17th C., 71½ in., 181 cm. **£2,150-2,550** L

A late 18th C. unstripped pine Irish Dresser Base with two cupboards and two drawers, a shaped plinth and moulded sides. 66 in. long, 18 in. wide. **£200–230** SM

right
A William and Mary Oak Dresser Base. **£500-600** B

An 18th C oak Welsh Dresser, 62". **£1,450-1,650** BW

A Late 17th C Oak High Dresser, 97" (247cms) wide, 23¼" (59cms) deep, 83" (212cms) high. **£1,900-2,100** L

An oak Dresser with moulded cornice and pierced frieze, 18th C. 80 in. (213 cm.) wide. **£2,800-3,000** C

A Georgian Oak High Dresser, 79" (200cms) wide, 21" (54cms) deep, 91½" (232cms) high, c1770. **£800-900** L

A George III oak dresser. 5 ft. 7 in., 170 cm. wide. **£1,150-1,200** SKC

A George II Oak Welsh Dresser, 168cms wide. **£450-500** SH

A fine late 17th C. oak dresser, with later plate racks. 5 ft. 3 in., 160 cm. wide. **£1,220-1,300** SKC

A George III Oak Welsh Dresser, width 178cms, height 184cms. **£580-620** SH

Small 18th C Oak Dresser. **£1,000-1,500** EBB

An Oak Welsh High Dresser possibly from South Wales, of good patina, the rack with moulded cornice and shaped sides, 17th/18th C., 4 ft. 10 in., 148 cm. x 6 ft. 2½ in., 189 cm. high. **£2,500-2,700** L

An Oak Dresser with later backed shelves with reeded edge and iron hooks, 18th C., 68½ in., 177 cm. **£1,200-1,400** L

An 18th C oak Yorkshire Dresser, with brass swan-neck handles, 72". **£700-800** BW

An 18th C French provincial oak dresser, brass barrel hinges, handles and key plates, 50" wide.
£700-750 PWC

Inlaid Oak Dresser. **£700-900**
A.D.H.

A Georgian inlaid Oak High Dresser of unusual design, the rack with moulded cornice on a shaped apron, 18th C. Possibly from Shropshire, 7 ft. 2 in., 218 cm. wide x 6 ft. 2 in., 188 cm. high. **£1,900-2,400** L

ENGLISH FURNITURE

Oak

- from the Middle Ages to the Restoration 1660, furniture almost entirely oak
- furniture in oak generally rectangular in construction put together with mortice and tenon held with wooden dowels
- styles are affiliated to architectural styles:- Gothic, Renaissance, Jacobean and Commonwealth

Walnut

- the great period of walnut covered the best part of a century beginning 1660
- advantages:- beautiful colour, suitable for veneer work, burr and curl particularly beautiful, easy to carve and not prone to movement
- disadvantages:- liable to worm
- cabinet makers replaced joiners as supreme craftsmen
- London became furniture making centre
- the first time one was able to distinguish between town and country pieces
- Charles II reign heralded return of exiled aristocracy plus continental fashions in furniture
- furniture influenced by architects Christopher Wren and Grinling Gibbons and later William Kent 1684-1748 who used gilt ornament and gesso decoration

Mahogany and Satinwood

- the use of Mahogany was encouraged by the shortage of European walnut after the Spanish succession War
- furniture styles of the 18thC take their names from leading designers and not reigning monarchs i.e. Chippendale, Hepplewhite and Sheraton etc.
- from 1750 the many virtues of mahogany made it the premier wood in cabinet making
- from 1770 Satinwood became popular for more delicate aspects of furniture also used for inlaying and veneering.

An Oak Dresser, 6 ft. 3½ in. high x 4 ft. 6½ in. wide, 192 cm. x 138.5 cm., c. 1700 the back replaced and the base with some restoration.
£900-1,200 S

A Georgian Oak High Dresser, with engraved brass plate handles and ebonised escutcheons,73" (186 (186cms) wide, 17" (44cms) deep, 86" (208cms) high, George III.
£890-990 L

A Georgian Oak Dresser, 6 ft. high, 53 in. wide, 19 in. deep.
£1,100-1,200 DB

An Early 18th C beech Dresser, 72" wide, 75" high. **£750-850** DH

18th Century Dresser in two pieces with three drawers and three cupboards 68 in. wide 85in. high 18in deep **£300-400**

English Dresser 76 in. wide 84 in. high 18 in. deep. **£190-220** MM

One piece narrow Irish dresser with two drawers and two cupboards 54 in. wide 78 in. high. **£260-300** SSP

A small, early 19th C. Pot Board Dresser with close-boarded back and two drawers, 82 in. high, 50 in. wide, 21 in. deep. **£230–250** PCF

Small narrow dresser 67 in. high 30 in. wide 11 in. deep. **£100-130** AL

Small Irish Dresser with restored cornice. **£325-350** SSP

19th C. pine Dresser with four drawers above fielded panel cupboard doors. 72 in. wide, 78 in. high. 22 in. deep. **£350–400** AL

A 19th C. pine Irish Dresser with reeded columns, two drawers and two cupboards, all in totally original condition. 96 in. high, 67 in. wide. **£250–300** SM

A small 19th C. pine Dresser with centre cupboard flanked by six drawers, standing on six turned feet. 53 in. wide, 81 in. high, 18 in. deep. **£320–350** MS

A good 19th C walnut and marquetry credenza, 5'1" wide. **£775-850** PWC

A Walnut Credenza, 42 by 66 in., 107 by 168 cm., c. 1870. **£800-930** SB

A Victorian large walnut and ormolu-mounted Credenza, with porcelain mounts and satinwood inlay, 3'11½" (121cms) high x 7'1½" (217cms) wide, c1855. **£1,675-1,750** SKC

A Regency Rosewood Chiffonier with galleried shelf on reeded gilt-metal supports 58 in., 147 cm. wide. **£1,450-1,600** C

A Victorian walnut and floral marquetry ormolu-mounted Credenza, 3'7½" (110.5cms) high x 6'8" (203cms) wide, c1855. **£3,100-3,250** SKC

A Victorian finely figured walnut Credenza, rosewood crossbanded and inlaid with satinwood and other veneers. 6ft wide. **£780-880** G&C

A 19th C. pine Lincolnshire Sideboard with panelled cupboard doors, on bun feet 48 in. long. **£120–130** P and D

A Victorian walnut and satinwood inlaid ormolu-mounted breakfront Credenza, 3'7" (110cms) high x 6'6" (196cms) wide, c1855. **£900-1,000** SKC

A 19th C. pine Lincolnshire Sideboard on bun feet with concave open pot board flanked by two cupboards. 42 in. long, 42 in. high, 19 in. deep. **£275–290** MS

A 19th C. pine Lincolnshire Sideboard with four drawers and side cupboard, with added bracket feet. 46 in. long, 33 in. high, 19 in. deep. **£140–150** PCF

A late 19th C. pitch pine Lincolnshire Sideboard. **£170–190** PCF

Sideboard with seven drawers and centre cupboard. **£220-270** MS

Lincolnshire sideboard 60in long, 54in high, **£240-260**

A Very Fine Old English Side Board with Spice Rack, 6 ft. long, c. 1740. **£2,950-3,100** CP

A Georgian Mahogany Breakfront Sideboard, 42½" (108cms) wide, 21½" (55cms) deep. **£650-750** L

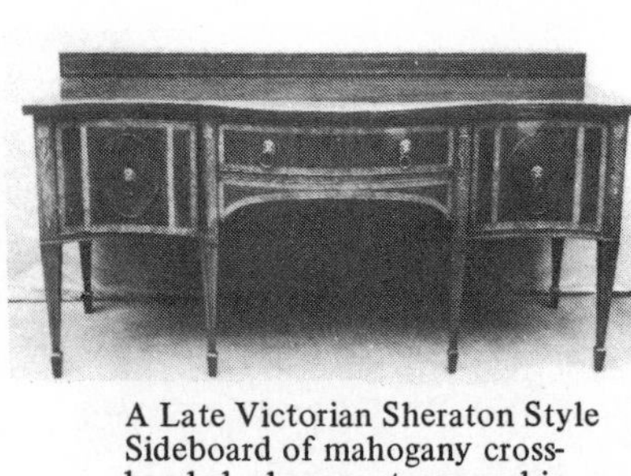

A Late Victorian Sheraton Style Sideboard of mahogany cross-banded, chequer-strung and inlaid, having a serpentine front, 6 ft. 6 in. long, 2 ft. 10 in. wide, 3 ft. 4¼ in. high. **£620-720** OL

A Late Georgian Large Mahogany Sideboard, inlaid with stringing and narrow bands, and panels, 68½ in., 174 cm: **£650-730** L

An Oak Buffet the frieze carved with entrelac the central door with canted sides. On later turned feet, 17th C. 51½ in., 131 cm. wide. **£780-850** C

A mid 17th C German oak Buffet, height 56", width 73½". **£1,720-1,900** SH

A George III Mahogany Serpentine Sideboard with a drawer above a tambour cupboard in the arched centre flanked by a zinc-lined drawer on the left, 64 in., 162 cm. wide. **£1,450-1,550** C

A George III Mahogany Sideboard inlaid with boxwood lines flanked by 2 lead-lined cellarette drawers mounted with blue and white enamel brass-framed ring handles, 80 in., 203 cm. wide. **£1,500-1,650** C

An oak buffet, the frieze carved with S-scrolls, 17th C. 49 in. (123 cm.) wide. **£2,000-2,200** C

A 'Sheraton' Mahogany Breakfront Sideboard, the top crossbanded in satinwood, 65" (165cms) wide, 25¾" (65cms) deep, 19th C. **£650-720** L

A Late Georgian Small Mahogany Bowfront Sideboard, inlaid with ebony stringing. **£650-750** L

A George III Bow-fronted Mahogany Side-board, 6' (183cms) wide. **£1,050-1,150** SKC

A late Georgian mahogany bow fronted tallboy, with oval brass drop handles, 3'6" wide. **£600-650** P.W.C.

A mid-19th C. mahogany tallboy in the Georgian style, 6 ft. 2 in. 189 cm. high x 3 ft. 6 in., 107 cm. wide, c. 1860. **£420-480** SKC

A carved and panelled old oak Buffet, fitted with two drawers and four cupboards, 5'7" high, 5'4" wide. **£460-530** AG

Dresser base with three drawers 72 in. wide 33 in. high 23 in. deep. **£160-180** AL

A Queen Anne Walnut Tallboy, decorated with crossbanding and featherbanding, 3'5" (104cms) wide. **£2,800-3,000** SKC

A Fine George I Walnut Tallboy the base with a later secretaire drawer above three drawers, bottom drawer inlaid with a compass medallion, 42½ in., 108 cm. wide. **£6,800-7,480** C

A George III-design mahogany and later satinwood inlaid Tallboy, 6'5" (196cms) high x 3'6" (106cms) wide, c1790. **£830-900** SKC

Wardrobe with bottom drawer and oval bevelled glass 76 in. high 33 in. wide 19 in. deep. **£130-150** AL

A Very Attractive George I Walnut Tallboy, the top with reeded, canted corners, the base with a brushing slide and original bracket feet, brass handles are later replacements, 41 in. wide, c. 1720. **£3,950-4,100**
with original handles. **£4,500+**
RD

An 18th C Chippendale style mahogany tall-boy, with brass swan-neck handles, 32". **£600-680** BW

A chestnut Armoire, 18th C., possibly German 69 in., 175 cm. wide. **£1,430-1,500** C

A Large 17th C. Flemish Walnut Armoire, 6 ft. wide, 183 cm. **£700-800** B

An Antique fine quality German mahogany armoire, 6' wide, 2'2" deep, 8'10" high. **£1,400-1,450** PWC

A Flemish Chestnut Armoire with heavy pierced brass escutcheons and cylinder hinges, 59 in. wide x 97 in. high, 150 cm x 247 cm. **£550-650** L

Inlaid satin walnut wardrobe 78 in. high, 48 in. wide. **£150-180** MS

A late 17th C Dutch oak and ebony Armoire, with fitted shelves, 4'10" high, 4'11" wide. **£660-760** AG

A large 19th C. pine Wardrobe assembled in seventeen pieces. 74 in. high, 60 in. wide, 25 in. deep. **£390–420** MS

An early 19th C. oak armoire. 4 ft. 4 in., 132 cm. wide. **£800-900** SKC

A small 18th C South German Walnut and marquetry Armoire, in two sections, the shaped cornice inlaid and crossbanded in geometric patterns, 78" high, 64" wide (198cms x 162cms). **£1,400-1,600** B

19th C. pitch pine Wardrobe, constructed in eighteen pieces, the central shelf and drawer portion flanked by hanging spaces. **£275–300** AL

An Edwardian pine Wardrobe with hat cupboard. 84 in. high, 33 in. wide. **£170–180** P and D

An Art Nouveau Marquetry Oak Wardrobe inlaid in coloured woods with bands of chequer-pattern, stamped R 1091/129., 137 cm. wide. **£300-350** C

19th C. satin walnut Wardrobe with narrow reeded cornice and panelled doors. 35 in. wide, 68. in. high, 16 in. deep. **£100–130** AL

A Fine Georgian Mahogany Gentleman's Wardrobe in original condition with original brass work, 49½ in. wide, 78 in. high. **£825-925** CP

An Early George III Mahogany Clothes-Press with moulded cornice, 49½ in., 126 cm. wide. **£500-600** C

A William IV Mahogany Linen Press, 122cms x 213cms. **£490-530** SH

Early 18th C. pine Joined Clothes Press, with panelled sides and 'H' hinges. 57 in. wide, 72 in. high, 20 in. deep. **£400–450** AL

Linen Press. **£300-350** AL

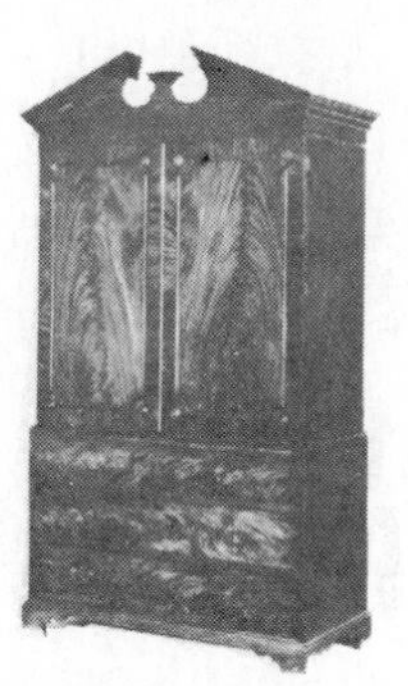

A George III Mahogany Clothes Press the frieze carved with blind fretwork. Enclosing slides and later drawers, 51 in., 129.5 cm. wide. **£1,400-1,550** C

An early 18th C Walnut Escritoire, decorated with crossbanding and featherbanding, 3'1½" (95cms) wide. **£3,300-3,500** SKC

A William & Mary Lacquered Chest-on-Chest with chinoiserie decoration, 36 in. wide, unrestored, c. 1690. **£1,400-1,600** restored **£3,000+** RD

An Early 18th C. Mahogany Chest-on-Chest with brushing slide, drawers oak lined, with replaced handles, 45 in. wide, 21¾ in. deep, 71¼ in. high, c. 1730-40. **£1,250-1,350** TA

An Antique Walnut Chest-Upon-Chest, the upper part having a plain moulded cornice, having brass bale handles and escutcheons, probably two top parts married up quite skillfully, 3 ft. 4 in. wide, 1 ft. 10 in. deep, 71 in high. **£700-850** V

An 18th C walnut Chest-on-Stand, 3'6" wide, 5'6" high. **£1,050-1,150** Buc

A William and Mary period walnut Chest On Stand, with featherbanding, 3'4" (102cms) wide. **£1,000-1,500** SKC

An Early 18th C Oak Chest on Stand, crossbanded in mahogany and with brass drop handles, 39½" wide. **£475-525** P.W.C.

A Queen Anne fruitwood miniature Chest-on-Stand, with original brass handles and escutcheons, height 43½", width 24". **£2,550-2,750** SH

An early 18th C. walnut chest on later stand, decorated with crossbanding and featherbanding, 3 ft. 2 in., 96.5 cm. wide. **£1,080-1,150** SKC

An Early 18th C. Oak Chest on Stand, 38 in. wide, 21 in. deep, 45 in. high. **£800-890** OB

A Good Oak Chest on Stand, the upper part in two sections, with moulded cornice above the drawer with quarter sawn oak linings, 17th/18th C., 3 ft. 6½ in., 108 cm. wide x 4 ft. 6 in., 137 cm. high. **£600-750** L

A George I Walnut Chest on Stand with cavetto cornice, on short cabriole legs, some later alterations., 38 in. x 52½ in., 96 cm. x 133 cm. high. **£900-1,000** L

An Elm chest-on-stand with moulded cornice and convex frieze, 40½ in., 103 cm. wide, mid-18th C.
£2,000-2,225 C

An Antique Walnut Cross-banded Chest-on-Stand having brass bale handles, 3 ft. 3 in. wide, 1 ft. 9 in. deep, 45 in. high. **£600-680** V

An Elm Hanging Cupboard, 21 in. wide, 10 in. deep, 24 in. high, c. 1780. **£115-145** CP

An 18th C crossbanded figured walnut Chest on stand, 40".
£1,450-1,650 BW

19th C. pine Hanging Cupboard with galleried upper shelf and original drop handle. 27 in. wide, 19 in. high, 6 in. deep.
£35–40 AL

A small Edwardian pine Hanging Cupboard with shaped back plate. 15 in. wide, 20 in. high. **£30–40** AL

Small, late 19th C., pine Hanging Cupboard decorated with poker work, having one internal, and one external, shelf. 24 in. high, 17 in. wide.
£35–40 AL

Small, late 19th C., pine Hanging Cupboard with new brass handle. 16 in. wide, 14 in. high.
£30–35 AL

Late 18th C. pine Hanging Wall Cabinet with central shelf support 46 in. wide, 35 in. high, 6 in. deep
£60–70 AL

An 18th C. French Plate Rack, oak with fruitwood turnings, 8 in. deep x 46 in. wide x 45 in. high. **£250-275** RB

Hanging cupboard with panelled doors. 21 in. wide, 19 in. high. **£45-55** AL

Hanging corner cupboard 17 in. wide, 14 in. high. **£31-41** AL

A Quite Rare Charles I Oak Spice Cupboard with original handles, breathing vents to drawers, 4 short, 4 long drawers, from S. Devon, or Cornwall, 19¼ in. high, 14¾ in. wide, 6½ in. deep, c. 1640. **£1,500-1,700** TA

Old Pine Spice Rack, 39 in. high. **£110-130** SHA

An Early 19th C. Oak Plate Rack. **£125-150** CSG

A Welsh Oak Corner Cupboard, 35 in. high, c. 1815. **£220-240** SHA

A Queen Anne Oak Corner Cupboard, 41½ in. high, c. 1710. **£170-190** SHA

A simple, 18th C., country made elm Corner Cupboard with good figuration. **£95–120** SM

An English Burr Walnut Corner Cabinet in the French Manner 41 in. high, c. 1850. **£360-400** SHA

Fruitwood corner cupboard, 31 in. wide, 44 in. high. **£172-120** MS

18th C. pine Corner Cupboard with two interior shelves. 43 in. high, 33in. wide. **£150-170** AL

An Edwardian Crossbanded Mahogany Corner Cupboard, 2 ft. wide, 1 ft. 1 in. deep, 60 in. high. **£320-370** V

A George II Virginia Walnut Bow Corner Cupboard 36 in. high. **£750-830** CC

18th Century Corner Cupboard probably French with grill front normally backed with material. **£350-400** SSP

Early 18th C Oak Bow-Fronted Corner Cupboard, with chinoiserie decoration and butterfly hinges, 36" high. **£350-450** STR

18th C Oak Corner Cupboard with brass H hinges, 37" high, 25" wide. **£150-200** STR

An 18th C. Oak Bow-Fronted Corner Cupboard on later stand 67 in. high, 22 in. deep. **£250-270** OB

A 19th C. Red Lacquer Corner Cupboard. **£170-195** SV

A Richly Coloured Cherry-Wood Corner-Cupboard with shaped interior, probably American, 30 in. wide, 3 ft. high, c. 1770. **£420-460** TA

A Lacquer Corner Cupboard in original condition, 36 in. high, English c. 1720-40. **£395-495** CP

A Late 18th C. Oak Corner Cupboard of mellow colour and small size, 34 in. wide, c. 1795. **£700-850** RD

A George III Oak Standing Corner Cupboard, 3'8" (112cms) wide. **£950-1.000** SKC

A fine Georgian mahogany inlaid standing corner cupboard, with painted classical shell and scrolling foliate designs, 4' wide, 7'4" high. **£1,100-1,250** PWC

A Georgian fruitwood standing Corner Cupboard, 44 in. (113 cm.). **£620-680** C

A George III Standing Oak Corner Cupboard, in two parts with a dentil cornice, later block feet. 48 in. x 86½ in. high, 122 cm. x 220 cm. **£1,150-1,300** L

Corner Cupboard 40 in. high 34 in. wide. **£82-92** AL

A George III Mahogany Standing Corner Cupboard with two geometrically glazed cupboard doors, 41½ in., 105.5 cm. wide. **£3,400-3,750** C

A 19th C. pine Corner Cupboard with diagonally boarded doors and one interior shelf. **£70–80** P and D

19th C.cupboard with two shelves and glazed top 45 in. wide, 56 in. high. **£110-160** MS

An oak Press with two small cupboard doors carved with roundels, 17th C. (some re-decoration) 76 in. (193 cm.) wide. **£900-990** C

A late 18th C. half-glazed Corner Cupboard with reeded cornice and columns, and panelled sides, 72 in. high, 57 in. wide. **£400–430** P and D

An Oak Hanging Cupboard with fielded and panelled doors inlaid with compass medallions, the drawers crossbanded with mahogany 63 in., 160 cm. wide. **£580-640** C

An Oak Court Cupboard, 18th C. 57 in. x 74 in., 146 cm. x 188 cm. **£1,600-1,800** L

A fine mid-17th C. oak court cupboard. 4 ft. 6 in., 137 cm. wide. **£1,150-1,200** SKC

Early 18th C. Duodarn with Arcaded Fielded Panels to Doors, probably Welsh. **£1,850-2,000** DB

Glazed, pitch pine corner cupboard 82 in. high. **£400-450** MS

An 18th C carved oak court cupboard, bearing the initials and date W.M.C., 1722, 52" wide. **£450-520** M

A fine 18th C. panelled pine Cupboard with four drawers in base, standing on bracket feet. 78 in. high, 60 in. long. **£400–430** P and D

A Commonwealth Oak Press the frieze carved with S-scrolls inlaid with date 1640 and initials WR with two panelled doors inlaid with chequered lines, 67 in., 170 cm. wide. **£1,300-1,450** C

A Commonwealth Oak Court Cupboard, with frieze drawer inlaid in bone and mother-of-pearl, 44 in. (113 cm.) wide, **£2,200-2,500** C

A small early 18th C Oak Duodarn, 48" wide (122cms). **£900-1,000** B

Cupboard with two shelves inside and two drawers, 57 in. long, 19 in. deep, 43 in. high. **£155-175** PCF

Narrow, late 19th C. pine Cupboard with panelled door. 25 in. wide, 59 in. high, 16 in. deep. **£85–95** AL

A small, late 19th C., pine Cupboard with one drawer and two interior shelves. 30 in. wide, 30 in. high, 18 in. deep. **£75–85** MS

An oak chest with dentilled frieze, with split bobbins above two arcaded panelled doors enclosing two drawers, 17th C. 49 in. (123 cm.) wide. **£1,150-1,260** C

A Charles II Oak and Walnut Veneered Chest with two panelled and coffered drawers, the lower inset with an arcaded niche inlaid with ebony and ivory 50 in. 127 cm. wide. **£1,300-1,450** C

A Jacobean oak chest. 3 ft. 3 in. 99 cm. wide. **£510-550** SKC

A Commonwealth oak Chest, with panelled frieze drawer inlaid with arabesque mother-of-pearl designs and dated 1654, 45 in. (114 cm.). **£1,300-1,450** C

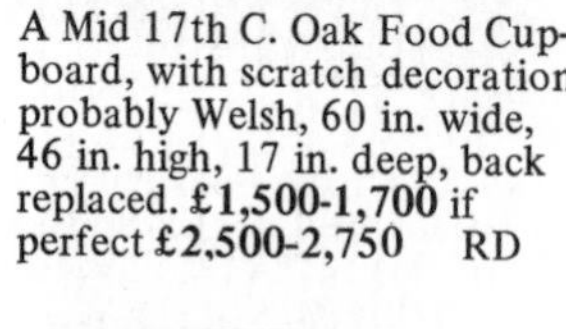

A Mid 17th C. Oak Food Cupboard, with scratch decoration, probably Welsh, 60 in. wide, 46 in. high, 17 in. deep, back replaced. **£1,500-1,700** if perfect **£2,500-2,750** RD

An Oak Food Cupboard with slatted frieze, 18th C. 44 in., 112 cm. wide. **£500-550** C

A Gothic Oak Food Cupboard with the front pierced and carved with Gothic tracery, 15th C. 49 in., 124.5 cm. wide. **£2,800-3,050** C

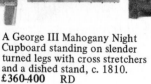

17th C Aumbry Food Cupboard, 48" wide, 17" deep, 31" high. **£700-1,000** STR

A George III Mahogany Night Cupboard standing on slender turned legs with cross stretchers and a dished stand, c. 1810. **£360-400** RD

A 17th C. German Oak Standing Cupboard, 79 in. long, 300 cm. **£3,400-3,800** B

A small 19th C. oak Cupboard, 18 in. high. **£35-38** SV

A Fine Regency Pedestal Cupboard, c. 1815. **£395-425** CSG

An early 19th C. barred and padlocked pine Cupboard, probably used for carrying silver, with original baize lining and brass carrying handles. 28 in. wide, 18 in. high, 9 in. deep. **£45–55** AL

Bedside cupboard 29 in. high 25 in. wide. **£35-40** SSP

A 19th C. Pot Cupboard. **£100-125** SV

An 18th C Venetian painted and gilded bombe cupboard, with serpentine simulated marble top. **£2,000-2,200** B

North Country Cupboard on double chest base c. 1840 88 in. high 60 in. wide 24 in. deep. **£350-400** MHA

An early 19th C. pine Warming Cupboard with tin lining, on castors. 41 in. wide, 40 in. high, 13 in. deep. **£120–140** AL

An 18th C. French Cupboard, 53 in. high, 33 in. wide, c. 1730. **£325-400** SHA

An Oak Hutch with triple-plank top and a single panelled cupboard door 17th C. 45 in., 117 cm. wide. **£2,400-2,650** C

An Edwardian pine Bedside Cupboard on turned legs. **£45–55**

Plain cupboard with two shelves. 40 in. high 36 in. wide 16 in. deep. **£70-80** AL

18th Century French Pine Cupboard with original hinges and two bottom drawers 72 in. high 52 in. wide. **£500-550** DM

A Continental Walnut Cupboard in two parts, 17th C, with later cornice and turned feet, 5'2" (132cms) x 64" (163cms) high. **£1,900-2,000** L

Pitch Pine bookcase 58 in. wide 56 in. high. **£75-85** SSP

A 17th C Oak Cupboard, inscribed with the date 1635, 4'7" (140cms) wide. **£1,270-1,300** SKC

An Antique Oak Cupboard with moulded cornice, the double panelled doors having brass acorn handles, 4 ft. 3 in. wide, 1 ft. 6 in. deep, 71 in. high. **£420-500** V

An early George III Mahogany Linen Cupboard in Chippendale style, the back of the lower part fitted with two secret drawers, on bracket feet with original brass castors, 49 in., 125 cm. x 76 in., 194 cm. high. **£1,100-1,300** L

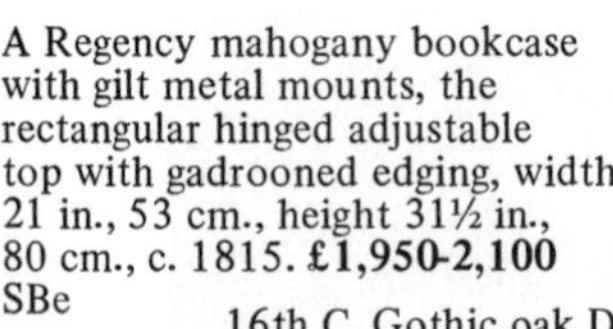

A Regency mahogany bookcase with gilt metal mounts, the rectangular hinged adjustable top with gadrooned edging, width 21 in., 53 cm., height 31½ in., 80 cm., c. 1815. **£1,950-2,100** SBe

Cupboard on Chest with three shelves 75 in. high, 22 in. deep, 54 in. wide. **£160-180** PCF

Cupboard in two pieces, top with shelves, base with sliding doors. 86 in. high 62 in. wide. **£350-380** AL

19th C. mahogany open Bookshelves, 20 in. high. **£40-45** SV

16th C. Gothic oak Double Cupboard. Upper cupboard of two panelled doors with linenfold carved centres with Iron strap hinges, 51", 130 cm. high x 22", 56 cm. deep x 51", 130 cm. wide. **£1,500-1,800** L

A George III Mahogany breakfront bookcase with moulded cornice, 90 in., 228.5 cm. wide (adapted). **£4,000-4,400** C

A fine George III Mahogany Secretaire Bookcase, 4' (122cms) wide. **£3,100-3,300** SKC

An attractive Edwardian mahogany breakfront bookcase with geometric satinwood stringing and rosewood banding. 182 cm. 71¾ in. **£1,700-1,900** O

A Mahogany Bookcase with moulded recess-centred cornice, c. 1830, 83¾ in., 213 cm. wide. **£1,300-1,450** C

Irish Bookcase 102 in. high. **£400-430** P&D

A George III mahogany bookcase with a dentil cornice, fluted frieze applied with roundels, height 89 in., 226 cm., width 54 in., 137 cm., c. 1780, doors possibly glazed at later date. **£1,200-1,350** SBe

A Georgian Mahogany secretaire bookcase, 44" wide. **£700-800** P.W.C.

A 'Chippendale' Period Secretaire Bookcase with later Edwardian carving. **£1,450-1,650** without later carving. **£5,000+** CP

A George III mahogany secretaire bookcase, height 95 in., 242 cm., width 43 in., 109 cm., the top c. 1810., the base c. 1780, feet restored. **£830-910** SBe

A Continental large carved oak bookcase, 9'1" wide, 8'8" high. **£820-900** P.W.C.

A late 18th C mahogany satinwood crossbanded and ebony inlaid Secretaire Bookcase, 43" wide. **£1,650-1,850** NF

A Fine Late 18th C. Mahogany Secretaire Bookcase, the interior with satinwood drawers, 43 in. wide, c. 1795-1800. **£3,000-3,500** RD

A 19th C Dutch oak Bookcase, with six drawers and secret recess under, enclosed by two panel doors, 7'2" high, 3'9" wide. **£1,250-1,450** AG

A mid 19th C mahogany breakfront Library Bookcase, 88" high, 59' wide. **£1,700-1,900** DH

A 19th C. Secretaire Bookcase delineated with selected mahogany veneers and crossbanding, 4 ft. 4 in. long, 1 ft. 10 in. wide, 8 ft. high. **£1,250-1,450** OL

A Regency Rosewood Secretaire Bookcase inlaid with satinwood, the fall front revealing a fitted interior of small drawers and pigeon holes, 3 ft. 7 in. wide. **£1,950-2,100** M

A George III Mahogany Secretaire Bookcase, 47 in., 119 cm. wide. **£2,500-2,700** C

A Victorian figured mahogany Secretaire Bookcase, 3'8" wide, 8'2" high. **£900-1,000** PW

An Antique Satinwood and rosewood crossbanded Secretaire Bookcase, the lower part with fall front drawer enclosing stationery drawers and compartments, 2 ft. 9 in. wide, 1 ft. 6 in. deep, 84 in. high. **£1,300-1,600** V

An 18th C Dutch Marquetry Cabinet On Chest, 7'7" (232cms) high x 5'9" (176cms) wide, c1770 with later decoration.
£2,550-3,000 SKC

A Fine Small William and Mary Burr Walnut Cabinet Upon Chest, enclosing fitted interior of pigeon holes with pull-out slides to secret compartments beneath, an unusual feature of this cabinet is the secret guinea slides within the half-round moulding of two of the bottom small drawers, 42 in. wide, 107 cm. **£2,900-3,800** B

An Oriental lacquered cabinet on stand, 31" wide. **£320-360** DH

A Late George III Mahogany Breakfront Bookcase, 101 in. x 97 in. high, 287 cm. x 246 cm. high.
£6,000-7,000 L

A 17th C Oak Chest/Cabinet, 43" (110cms) wide, 23" (58.5cms) deep, 45" (115cms) high, c1690.
£770-870 L

A Mother O' Pearl inlaid black lacquer Domed Casket on stand with engraved brass clasps and corners, and original brass hasp and lock, original handles and on later stand, 18th C., 25½ in., 65 cm., long, 13 in., 33 cm. wide, 41½ in., 106 cm. high overall.
£680-780 L

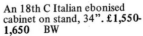

An 18th C Italian ebonised cabinet on stand, 34". **£1,550-1,650** BW

19th C. pine Lancashire Bookcase on Chest with five drawers in unusual arrangement. 76 in. high, 62 in. wide, 15 in. deep.
£450-500 SSP

A George I Walnut Cabinet-On-Chest enclosing shelves with two candle-slides above four long drawers, 38 in., 96.5 cm. wide. **£2,400-2,650** C

A Charles II Black and Gold Lacquer cabinet-on-stand with two cupboard doors enclosing eleven various-sized drawers decorated with chinoiserie scenes, (the giltwood stand adapted and restored) 50 in., 127 cm. wide. **£1,500-1,650** C

A Fine Early 18th C. Dutch Walnut and Marquetry Cabinet on Stand, the two panelled doors to the upper part profusely decorated in marquetry, 46 in. wide x 69 in. high, 117 x 175 cm. **£2,000-2,300** B

A 19th C Japanese Lacquer Cabinet on a parcel gilt walnut stand, of George I design, height 48" (123cms), width 27" (68cms). **£880-950** SH

A walnut Cabinet in the style of Androuet du Cerceau 16th C. and later, 51 in. (131 cm.) wide; 21 in. (54 cm.) deep; 60 in. (154 cm.) high. **£550-600** C

A 19th C. Lacquer Cabinet on Stand, 23 in. high. **£125-155** SV

A pair of North German oak Cabinets-on-Stand of 17th C. design, 36 in. (93 cm.) wide. **£550-600** pr. C

A William and Mary Walnut and Floral Marquetry Cabinet-On-Stand with convex frieze drawer above two cupboard doors inlaid with shaped panels enclosing eleven drawers. The stand on later spirally-turned legs, 36½ in., 93 cm. wide. **£2,800-3,080** C

An Oriental Lacquer cabinet on stand, decorated in gilt and inlaid with Mother-of-Pearl, 18" wide. **£475-525** P.W.C.

A 19th C Flemish ebony Cabinet, with 11 drawers and centre cupboard painted in the manner of Philip P. Roos, 23" wide, 57½" high. **£3,200-3,500** Buc

An 18th C Chinese double-doored Cabinet on Stand, with red lacquer, hardstone and ivory decoration. 37in wide. **£2,000-2,200.** Lan

A Dutch Oak Cupboard on Stand, the sides panelled and the front carved with foliate scrolls. 35 in. x 81 in., 90 cm. x 206 cm. **£1,400-1,600** L

A Georgian walnut and oak Cabinet, 5'3" wide, 6'7" high. **£1,700-1,800** Buc

An Edwardian Satinwood Display Cabinet, the upper part with arched pediment, painted throughout with female masks, drapes, trophies and foliage, 63 by 27½ in., early 20th C. **£550-600** SBA

Edwards and Roberts – a Fine Sheraton Revival Mahogany Serpentine Salon Display Cabinet with engraved harewood and stained inlays of ribband-tied swags, urns and pendants, gilt-brass loop handles, square tapered supports, with spade feet, stamped, 62 in. wide. **£4,500-5,200** N

An 18th C walnut Cabinet, inlaid with herringbone stringing, and fitted with three shallow specimen or medal drawers, 3'7" wide, 7'3" high. **£1,600-1,800** Buc

A Chippendale Style Breakfront Mahogany China Cabinet, the base carved with acanthus and Grecian key motif, 48½ in., 143 cm. **£700-800** L

A Mahogany display cabinet in the Chippendale manner with fitted adjustable shelves enclosed by a pair of astragal glazed doors, 4'6" wide. £900-1,100 G & C

A pair of late Victorian painted satinwood display cabinets with rosewood, boxwood and ebony bandings, height 68 in., 173 cm., width 45 in., 115 cm., c. 1900., now fitted for electricity. **£2,300-2,600**

A Regency period Amboyna & Ebony chiffonier. **£1,100-1,350** EBB

An Edwardian Crossbanded Mahogany Display Cabinet, 1 ft. 9 in. wide, 1 ft. 3 in. deep, 45 in. high. **£140-180** V

A Boulle Display Cabinet, 44 in. x 29¼ in., 112 cm. x 74 cm. **£420-500** SB

A 19th C Chinese Carved Padoukwood Display Cabinet, 6'8" (203cms) high x 3'3" (99cms) wide, c1880. **£390-430** SKC

An Art Nouveau mahogany mirrored and glazed display cabinet inlaid with metals, 83 in. high. **£250-300** CSK

An Attractive Regency Rosewood Display Cabinet of arched design with carved cornice, 44 in. wide, c. 1815. **£1,950-2,100** RD

A Victorian Walnut Display Cabinet of serpentine shape, inlaid with satinwood arabesque marquetry, flanked by pillars with ormolu mounts on shaped apron base, c. 1860., 32 in., 81 cm. **£860-960** L

A 19th C kingwood Vitrine with ormolu mounting and Vernis-Martin panels, 34". **£1,250-1,450** BW

A Cloisonne and Hardwood Small Side Cabinet, on a pale-blue ground, 117 cm. x 79 cm. c. 1900. **£500-550** SB

A Mahogany Display Cabinet, 72 by 40 in., 183 by 101.5 cm., made up from a George III cabinet, 1880-1900. **£300-340** SB

A Dutch Marquetry Display Cabinet, 19th C., 36 in., 92 cm. wide x 56 in., 142 cm. high. **£500-600** L

A Victorian walnut and cross-banded ormolu-mounted display cabinet, 3 ft. 6 in., 108 cm. wide x 4 ft. 8½ in., 144 cm. high, c. 1860. **£500-550** SKC

A George III Mahogany Side Cabinet inlaid with ebonised ovals on square tapering feet, 55½ in., 154 cm. wide. **£1,500-1,650** C

A Victorian Burr Walnut ormolu-mounted display Cabinet, inlaid with boxwood lines, 2' 10½" (118cms) high x 2'5½" (75cms) wide, c1855. **£620-660** SKC

A late George III pollard elm side cabinet, 56½ in., 144 cm. wide. **£2,860-3,000** C

A 19th C. walnut and tulipwood side cabinet, the door stiles and frieze inlaid in satinwood with foliate scrolls, 84 cm., 33 in., **£640-740** O

A Pair of 19th C French Ebonised Side Cabinets, with Wedgwood-type blue jasper plaques, 47" (119cms) wide, c1880. **£800-900** SKC

An attractive and good quality Victorian walnut breakfront side cabinet, the frieze inlaid in various woods with floral sprays, 183 cm., 72 in. wide. **£1,650-1,850** O

A fine quality Victorian burr walnut breakfront side cabinet, applied with gilt brass mounts throughout, outlined with box-wood, tulipwood, satinwood and burr yew crossbandings, width 73 in., 185.5 cm., c. 1865. **£3,200-3,700** SBe

A fine quality Victorian walnut serpentine side cabinet, the top with wide banding between satinwood stringing above frieze with ribbon-tied floral sprays in various woods. 198 cm., 78 in. wide. **£3,800-4,800** O

A Good Burr-Walnut Jasper-Mounted Side Cabinet, with a gilt-brass leaf-cast border, in-laid with stringing, 42½ by 32½ in., 108 by 82.5 cm., late 1850's. **£640-720** SB

An Ebonised Wood and Thuya-wood Side Cabinet, 40 by 70½ in., 101.5 by 179 cm., c. 1870. **£540-620** SB

A Hardwood Cabinet, the brass straps and mounts with stylised foliate engraving, the interior fitted with one long and five short drawers, probably Korean, 19th C., 71 cm. **£300-350** SBe

A late 17th C. Italian marquetry cabinet, inlaid with ebony and ivory panels, width 23 in., 58 cm. **£500-600** SBe

left
A Satinwood pedestal vitrine cabinet with chamfered glazed lid and glazed sides, 20 in., 51 cm., square, 19th C. **£580-640** C

A 19th C. Oriental Lacquer Cabinet. **£90-110** SV

A Victorian Walnut Marquetry Pier Cabinet, the cavetto moulded top crossbanded in kingwood, c. 1850, 31 in., 79 cm. wide, 43½ in., 110 cm. high. **£680-780** L

A George III Mahogany Toilet Cabinet enclosing an adjustable mirror, 2' (61cms) wide. **£720-780** SKC

A fine late 18th C Indian carved ivory and tortoiseshell Miniature Cabinet, 9¾" x 7¾". **£1,000-1,100** Buc

A Regency Bird's-Eye Maple Folio Cabinet with mottled grey marble top inlaid with a mirror figured fossil lozenge, 53 in., 135 cm. wide. **£3,200-3,500** C

A George IV Pollard Elm Dwarf Cabinet with white marble top, doors edged with foliate gilt-metal borders decorated with later book-spines 72½ in., 184 cm. wide. **£1,100-1,250** C

A Regency ebony dwarf cabinet 50 in., 127 cm. wide. **£800-900** C

A Fine Regency Rosewood Cabinet, the front inlaid with brass in the French Boulle manner (the stand modern), 32 in. wide, 13½ in. deep, c. 1810-15. **£975-1,100** RD

A Regency Mahogany Cabinet, brass-grilled sides and back, cupboard doors backed by pleated silk, 23 in., 58.5 cm. wide. **£1,000-1,100** C

An Unusual French Walnut Surgeon's Cabinet, 19th C. 32 in., 82 cm. wide x 61 in., 155 cm. high. **£620-720** L

A Fine and Rare William & Mary/ Queen Anne Double-Domed Walnut Bureau Cabinet with fitted interior, bracket feet not original, 40½ in. wide. **£8,000-10,000** RD

A Mahogany Bureau-Cabinet of Chippendale style. Sloping flap enclosing a fitted interior on ogee bracket feet, 53 in., 135 cm. wide, 98 in., 249 cm. high. **£2,600-2,850** C

A 'married' George II Period Mahogany Bureau Cabinet with replaced bracket feet fitted interior, marriage **£1,750** not marriage **£3,000+** RD

A Queen Anne Walnut Bureau-Cabinet, the base in two parts with sloping crossbanded burr flap enclosing a fitted interior, 41 in., 105 cm. wide, 90½ in., 230 cm. high. **£6,000-6,600** C

A George I Walnut Bureau Cabinet with inlaid feather banding, moulded cornice and gilt bordered panel doors with vauxhall glass, c. 1725 40 in. wide, 84 in. high. **£7,500-8,500** CP

A Mahogany Bureau-Cabinet with two panelled and fielded cupboard doors enclosing a red walnut fitted interior with pigeon-holes, racks and drawers, basically 18th C., 39 in., 99 cm. wide. **£2,000-2,200** C

A Fine Burr Walnut Bureau Cabinet, with pigeon holes over drawers, with sunken well and 'secret' front letter compartments, 24" (61cms) deep, 40" (102cms) wide, 84" (213cms) high, early 18th C. **£6,600-7,600** L

A transitional piece showing the Georgian taste superimposed upon the original William & Mary concept of a bureau on chest.

An unusual rare early 18th C. mahogany bureau cabinet 76 cm. 30 in., wide, (two panes missing). **£2,000-2,400** O

A George II mahogany bureau-cabinet with a dentil cornice, two fielded panelled doors, height 87½ in., 222 cm., width 45 in., 114 cm., c. 1755. **£2,300-2,600** SBe

A Mid-Georgian mahogany bureau-cabinet with triangular broken pediment 45 in., 114 cm. wide. **£2,400-2,640**

A South German walnut bureau bookcase. **£5,500-6,000** Bon.

A George III mahogany bureau bookcase with a beaded moulded inlaid cornice, height 93½ in., 237 cm., width 51 in., 130 cm., c. 1780. **£1,450-1,600** SBe

A mid-Victorian mahogany Bureau Bookcase, 97" high, 43" wide. **£600-700** DH

A Georgian Oak, Stained Mahogany Bureau Bookcase, the lower part with a writing flap enclosing a well fitted interior of pigeon holes and drawers, c. 1780, 3 ft. 9¾ in., 116 cm. wide x 7 ft. 6 in., 228 cm. high. **£850-950** L

A William and Mary Walnut Double Dome Bureau/Bookcase of Very Fine Quality, an interior with four small drawers to the bottom, and with bevel-edged mirrored doors above candle slides. Upon a bureau with a concave and stepped interior of eight small drawers with feather edged banding flanking a central door above a well, 38 in. wide x 87 in. high x 23 in. deep; 97 x 221 x 58 cm. **£6,000-7,500** B

An 18th C. Figured Walnut Bureau Bookcase, the top with two mirrored doors, the shaped interior with drawers and a well with secret compartment, with brass handles, on shaped bracket feet, 38 in. wide, c. 1710-20. **£7,000-8,500** RD

A Georgian mahogany Bureau/Bookcase, with fall-flap revealing fitted interior, drawers and pigeon holes, 38" wide. **£2,100-2,300** NF

A George III mahogany Bureau Bookcase, with well-fitted interior, 37". **£1,050-1,150** BW

A George III mahogany bureau bookcase, crossbanded with satinwood, height 97 in., 247 cm., width 43 in., 110 cm., c. 1770. **£2,500-2,800** SBe

A Late Victorian mahogany cylinder Bureau Bookcase in the Chippendale style, 7'10" (239cms) high x 3'6" (107cms) wide, c1880. **£1,325-1,400** SKC

A George III mahogany secretaire, with later inlay. **£4,300-4,700** Bon.

An early 19th C mahogany secretaire of German or Scandinavian origin, 43" wide. **£550-600** P.W.C.

A George III Mahogany Bureau with bookcase. **£1,000-1,250** EBB

A Korean brass mounted elm secretaire, 38" wide. **£350-400** PWC

An Anglo-Dutch Walnut and Marquetry Secretaire with convex frieze drawer above the crossbanded fall-flap. The base with a drawer on cabriole legs headed by later C-scroll brackets, late 17th C. (restorations) 45½ in., 116 cm. wide. **£1,050-1,200** C

A Camphorwood Campaign Secretaire, 36" (92cms) wide, 18" (46cms) deep, 38" (97cms) high. c1850. **£560-620** L

A North Italian Walnut Bureau Bookcase, with engraved bone, copper and pewter marquetry and brass lines, some imperfections, early 19th C., 37 in., 94 cm. **£580-680** L

A William and Mary Walnut Secretaire, the writing fall crossbanded and feather-banded, enclosing an arrangement of pigeon holes and fitted drawers, later brass handles, on later shaped bracket feet, c. 1700., 44½ in., 113 cm. wide. **£1,700-1,900** L

A Georgian Secretaire Chest, and a bookcase top with dentil moulded pediment over a pair of astragal glazed doors, of different style, base 36 in., 92 cm. wide. **£800-900** L

A Coromandel Secretaire Chest with solid silver handles and escutcheons, probably made on East Coast of India, c1800-1820, 43" wide, 45" high. **£800-1,000** STR

A Good Old Fake Secretaire Chest made from old wood. **£1,700-1,900** if original. **£5,000**

An Elegant Victorian Rosewood Secretaire Cabinet decorated with swags, urns and floral scrolls and with ormolu mounts, the fall front revealing a fitted interior with three drawers and a sunken well, 3 ft. 4 in. wide, by Hampton & Sons, London. **£1,400-1,600** M

A mid-Georgian oak Bureau-Chest, 24 in. (60 cm.). **£1,000-1,100** C

A mid-18th C Dutch Walnut Bombe Bureau, 3'6" (107cms) wide. **£3,100-3,300** SKC

In Italian walnut bureau cross-banded with stained wood, width 40 in., 102 cm., c. 1760. **£840-920** SBe

A Queen Anne walnut bureau. **£2,700-2,900** Bon.

A Queen Anne walnut bureau, all feather banded, 3' wide. **£1,850-1,900** PWC

A George II Small Oak Bureau, on bracket feet. 30 in., 76 cm. **£1,600-1,800** L

A Fine Very Small Mahogany Inlaid Bureau with fitted interior, inlaid with floral swags, paterae and stringing, 2 ft. 3 in. wide, 1 ft. 6 in. deep, 3 ft. 2 in. high, 19th C. **£525-600** TA

A George II Oak Bureau, the shaped interior with pigeon holes, drawers, a narrow drawer and a well, on later bracket feet, 34½ in., 88 cm. **£800-900** L

An early 18th C. oak bureau, the interior with pigeon holes, drawers, cupboard and well with secret drawer 99 cm., 39 in. **£800-980** O

A Dutch Satinwood Bureau, 19th C, 41" x 37" (104cms x 94cms). **£600-800** SBA

A George II Walnut Bureau of dark colour with a sparsely fitted interior, on bracket feet. 38 in., 97 cm. **£1,200-1,400** L

A Rare and Small William & Mary Bureau in oak, feet and handles restored, 35 in. wide, 38 in. high, 17 in. deep, c. 1690. **£1,525-1,750** CP

Small George III Mahogany Bureau. **£675-750** EBB

A Small George II Walnut Bureau with some reveneering to top, new handles, 27 in. wide, 17 in. deep, 34 in. high. **£3,250-4,000** in perfect condition. **£10,000+** CP

A Marquetry Bureau of bombe shape, the fall front enclosing a shaped and stepped interior, crossbanded and inlaid with geometric lines, inlaid with intricate foliate scroll design with urns of flowers and birds on a walnut ground, 38 in., 97 cm. **£1,850-2,000** L

An Exceptionally Fine Mid-Georgian Bureau, 49 in. wide, 41 in. high, c. 1770. **£880-980** SHA

A Georgian Flame Mahogany Bureau, 40" (102cms) wide, 19¾" (50cms) deep, 43" (109cms) high, 19th C. **£580-675** L

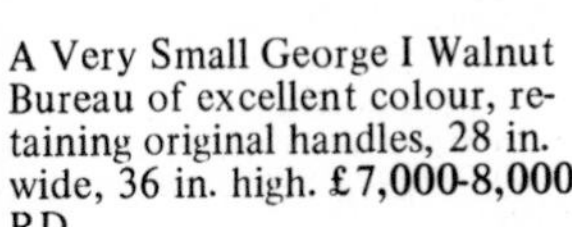
A George I walnut bureau fitted interior, width 33 in., 84 cm., c. 1725, damaged and with some restoration. **£950-1,050** SBe

A Very Small George I Walnut Bureau of excellent colour, retaining original handles, 28 in. wide, 36 in. high. **£7,000-8,000** RD

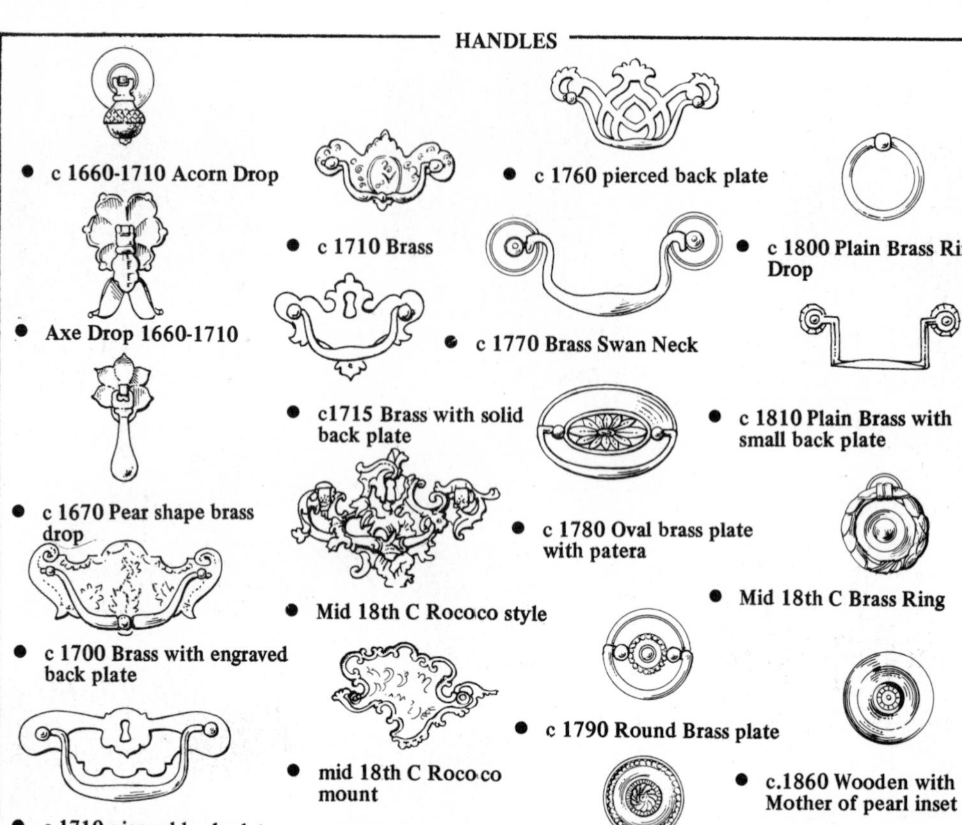

A fine small early 18th C walnut Bureau inlaid with double herringbone stringing, only 2'2" wide. **£1,100-1,200** Buc

A Georgian fruitwood Bureau on bracket feet, 37". **£900-1,000** BW

A George I walnut bureau, with feather crossbanding, 36" wide. **£1,230-1,300** SH

A Queen Anne Walnut Bureau cross-banded and inlaid with a herringbone line, with fitted interior cupboard, drawers, pigeon holes and a well, restored, 37½ in., 95 cm. **£1,950-2,150** L

A Georgian mahogany Bureau on bracket feet, with well-fitted interior, 42". **£800-900** BW

A George II Walnut Bureau, crossbanded and feather-banded, the interior with pigeon holes and drawers, somewhat distressed and later feet and handles, 33½ in., 85 cm. **£500-600** L

A Georgian teak Bureau on bracket feet, with ornate brass loop handles and well-fitted interior, 38". **£800-900** BW

Late 18th/Early 19th C Oak Bureau, crossbanded and inlaid, 40" wide. **£550-750** STR

An Antique Mahogany Bureau with fall flap enclosing stationery drawers and compartments, 3 ft. wide, 1 ft. 8 in. deep, 39 in. high. **£420-500** V

A Georgian Oak Bureau, crossbanded in mahogany, 39½" (100cms) wide, 29" (53cms) deep, 43" (109cms) high. **£570-650** L

A George III mahogany Bureau, 3'3" wide. **£500-600** PW

An 18th C mahogany, crossbanded and inlaid Bureau, 38" wide. **£870-960** NF

A Continental Oak Bureau Cabinet of small proportions, the moulded cornice above two fielded panel doors. 18th C. 36" (92cms). **£1,450-1,600** L

A Georgian Walnut Bureau, with crossbanded top, raised on later bun feet, restorations, 29½" (75cms) wide, 19" (48cms) deep, 37½" (95cms) high, 18th C. **£1,800-2,000** L

An Oak Fold-Front Bureau with bun feet, stepped interior with wells and brass handles, 36 in. high, c. 1699. **£1,300-1,400** OB

An Edwardian Crossbanded Bureau, the fall flap with shell decoration, 2 ft. 6 in. wide, 1 ft. 5 in. deep, 38 in. high. **£280-340** V

A George I walnut bureau with sloping flap inlaid with burr-walnut panels and borders and herring-bone bands, on later bracket feet. 37 in., 94 cm. wide. **£1,800-2,000** C

An Early 18th C. Oak Fall-Front Bureau, 35 in. high. **£800-890** OB

A George III style Miniature oak bureau, 49cms. **£140-180** SH

A Georgian oak Bureau, with brass loop handles, fitted interior and well, 36". **£600-680** BW

A Dutch Marquetry Cylinder Bureau inlaid overall on a mahogany ground, late 19th C., 36½ in. x 51 in. high, 93 cm. x 130 cm. **£1,200-1,350** L

A George III Burr-Yew Cylinder Bureau crossbanded with satinwood enclosing a well-fitted interior with leather-lined reading flap, 36 in., 91.5 cm. wide. **£7,000-7,800** C

A Good George III Rosewood Cylinder Bureau, inlaid with boxwood strings, late 18th/early 19th C, 41" x 30" (104cms x 76cms). **£1,300-1,500** SBA

A Charles X mahogany cartonnier with eight leather-covered filing boxes 25½ in., 65 cm. wide. **£1,200-1,350** C

A late 19th C Walnut veneered and Marquetry inlaid slope front bureau, 2'7½". **£1,025-1,100** WHL

A Late 19th C. French Mahoga[ny] and Brass-Mounted Writing Des[k] the cylinder front opens to reveal 3 small drawers and pull-out writing slide, 35 in. wide. **£1,050-1,200** M

A Mid-19th C kingwood and floral marquetry Bureau de Dame, with ormolu and pierced gallery, 2'2" (66cms) wide, c1850. **£830-900** SKC

An attractive 19th C. Dutch marquetry bureau, raised on slender cabriole legs, the sides, drawer front, and top similarly inlaid. 84 cm., 33 in. **£2,700-3,000** O

A William IV rosewood Davenport, 1'7" (48cms) wide, c1835. **£685-760** SKC

A 19th C. Mahogany Davenport, with some damage. **£200-225** SV

A Victorian Mahogany Writing Desk having a tambour front revealing small drawers, pigeon holes and pull-out writing slide, 33 in. wide. **£350-400** M

DAVENPORTS

- First made in late 18th C by Gillows for a Captain Davenport.
- Earliest style had a sliding or swivelling top
- Finest quality pieces generally of mid 19th C manufacture, veneered in burr walnut
- Often have secret drawers

A Victorian walnut piano-top Davenport, the fitted interior with lined writing slide, 2'11½" (90cms) high x 1'10½" (57cms) wide, c1855. **£780-860** SKC

A 19th C Walnut Davenport, the burr maple interior with three fitted drawers, c1860, 24" (61cms). **£500-600** L

A Queen Anne Black and Gold Lacquer Union Suite the bureau base enclosing drawers and pigeon holes, (restorations) 21½ in., 54.5 cm. **£1,300-1,450** C

A Victorian Burr Walnut Davenport, height 32" (681cms), width 21" (53cms). **£440-500** SH

A Victorian walnut-veneered Davenport Desk, 20". **£400-450** WHL

An Inlaid Walnut Davenport, late Victorian. **£550-600** VA

A Victorian carved oak Davenport. **£540-595** SV

A Victorian Walnut Davenport, the serpentine fronted hinged top enclosing a satinwood interior, 1 ft. 10 in. wide, 1 ft. 10 in. deep, 35 in. high. **£500-600** V

A Good Victorian Burr Walnut Davenport, bears penwork presentation label and date 1853, considered contemporary, c. 1850., 1 ft. 8 in., 56 cm. **£775-850** L

A Good Rosewood Harlequin Davenport, 22½ in., 57 cm. wide closed, late 1830's. **£900-1,000** SB

A Good Victorian Walnut Davenport with a hinged cylinder front enclosing a sliding writing compartment and drawers, 22½ in., 57 cm. **£660-760** L

A George III Mahogany and Inlaid Bonheur-du-Jour, the D-shaped raised back with galleried top and taper stand, 34 in. wide, 41½ in. high. **£1,750-1,850** DH

A Louis XV Style Walnut and Ormolu Mounted Bonheur Du Jour, the frieze drawer inset with Sevres style porcelain plaque, crossbanded overall with kingwood and ormolu mounts, and borders. 19th C., 44½ in. x 39½ in. high., 108 cm. x 100 cm. high. **£1,300-1,450** L

A Good Mahogany and Satinwood Bonheur du Jour in the Sheraton Manner, the upper bookcase section inlaid with figured satinwood ovals, 19th C., 51½ in., 131 cm. high x 30½ in., 77.5 cm. wide, 20½ in., 52 cm. deep. **£720-800** L

A Well-Figured Walnut Bonheur-du-Jour on cabriole legs applied at the knees with gilt-bronze foliage mounts, crossbanded throughout in tulipwood, 39½ by 43½ in., 100 by 110 cm., 1860's. **£1,550-1,700** SB

A Mahogany Serpentine Desk/ Dressing Table, inlaid with kingwood and satinwood geometric patterns, 46" (117cms) wide, 27" (69cms) deep. **£550-620** L

A 19th C. Continental 'Table a Ecrire', the top crossbanded in mahogany, c. 1850, top 24 in., 61 cm. x 20 in., 51 cm. **£370-420** L

19th C. pine Kneehole Desk with five drawers. On turned legs with castors. 49 in. long, 23 in. deep. **£175–200**

A Dutch Mahogany Cylinder Bureau, with a 'sans traverse' marquetry interior, 42" (108cms) wide, 20½" (52cms) deep, 45" (114cms) high. **£1,100-1,300** L

A Bamboo Writing Desk, with Chinese black and cinnamon lacquer panels, 20¼in (51.5cm) wide, c. 1900, **£200-250** C

A Regency rosewood Work and Writing Table, 24in (61cm) wide, **£2,000-2,300** C

An Italian walnut kneehole desk, mid-18th C., 59½ in., 151 cm. wide. **£1,540-1,650** C

A Continental early 19th C mahogany and Marquetry cylinder desk, 42" wide. **£625-700** P.W.C.

An Edwardian richly inlaid mahogany kidney shaped Writing Desk with inset leather top, 4'4½" wide. **£1,200-1,400** AG

Bow fronted desk with gesso decoration 53 in. wide, 27 in. deep. **£575-610** MS

A mid 19th C Satinwood Carlton House Desk, 106cms wide. **£900-1,000** SH

A Charles II Oak Desk, 79cms wide. **£320-380** SH

A Mahogany Library Table, the crossbanded and boxwood inlaid top inset with tan leather, the stampedbrass oval handles with medalions of Nelson, Duke of Bronte in relief, 19th C., 4 ft. 122 cm. **£330-410** L

A George III mahogany partners' desk. 54½ in., 138.5 cm. wide. **£3,200-3,500** C

A satinwood pedestal desk with six short drawers crossbanded with rosewood 64 in., 138 cm. wide, late 19th C, stamped Gillows. **£1,450-1,650** C

A Fine George II mahogany kneehole desk with serpentine top enclosing a divided and fitted interior and an easel mirror, on ogee bracket feet, 44½ in., 114.5 cm. wide. **£4,500-4,950** C

An early George III kneehole desk. 46½ in., 119 cm. **£1,900-2,100** C

An Early Victorian Lady's Pedestal Desk in original condition except for new green leather inset, 36 in. wide, 24 in. deep, 29 in. high, c. 1850. **£885-1,000** CP

A good late Victorian Partners' Desk, 56" x 45" x 32". **£400-500** PW

A George III Mahogany Kneehole Desk with cloth-lined top and two cupboard doors fronted with dummy drawers, 47½ in., 121 cm. wide. **£1,100-1,250** C

A mid-18th C. style mahogany kneehole desk crossbanded and inlaid, width 35 in., 89 cm. **£750-830** SBe

A fine George III mahogany partners' desk, with leather-line top. 42 in., 107 cm. wide. **£4,200-4,800** C

An Oak Partners' Desk, 60 by 41 in., 152.5 by 104 cm., wide and deep, c. 1880. **£300-500** SB

A fine quality 18th C. walnut kneehole desk in the Queen Anne manner decorated with crossbanding and featherbanding. 2 ft. 8 in., 81 cm. wide. **£2,000-2,300** SKC

A Victorian pine Pedestal Desk with nine drawers, all with original handles. **£300–350** SM

A Georgian Mahogany Kneehole Desk/Secretaire, 33" (84cms) wide, 21¼" (54cms) deep, c1760. **£1,600-1,800** L

A Victorian Mahogany Flat Top Kneehole Writing Desk, 4 ft. wide, 2 ft. deep, 30 in. high. **£400-500** V

A Rosewood Marquetry Inlaid Desk, 45" (115cms) wide, 24" (61cms) deep, late 19th C. **£640-700** L

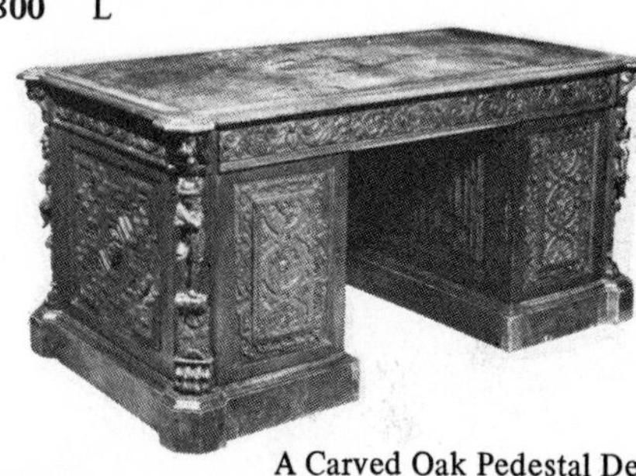
A Carved Oak Pedestal Desk, 62 in. x 34 in., 157.5 cm. x 86.5 cm., mid 19th C. **£530-600** SB

A George III mahogany dressing-table with double-flap top, the interior with hinged flaps. 26 in., 66 cm. wide. **£1,250-1,500** C

An Edwardian rosewood inlaid writing desk, leather writing surface, 36 in., 91 cm. **£400-500** L

Dressing table with gesso decoration and cabriole legs, 68 in. high, 48 in. wide, 24 in. deep. **£260-300** MS

A Kingwood Parquetry Dressing Table with serpentine hinged top with gilt-metal mounts throughout, the lock stamped L. Grade Paris, 27½ in. x 20½ in., 70 cm. x 52 cm., mid 19th C. **£320-380** SB

Dressing Chest 57 in. high, 33 in. long, 17 in. deep. £75-90

A George III satinwood dressing-table with divided twin-flap, top inlaid with amboyna ovals enclosing a leather-lined easel and pop-up sections. 25 in., 63.5 cm. wide. **£1,600-1,800** C

A Good 19th C English Walnut Bureau Plat of Louis XV style, top inlaid with rosewood within kingwood and walnut crossbanding, 63" (160cms) wide. **£1,490-1,550** SKC

An 18th C. Dutch oak lowboy, width 33 in., 84 cm. c. 1750. **£740-840** SBe

A Mahogany Georgian Lowboy, oaklined drawers, (had been painted all over, needs more polishing), 34 in. wide, 20 in. deep, 28 in. high, c. 1780. **£325-400** SHA

A Queen Anne Oak Lowboy, 32 in. wide. **£450-520** M

An Early Georgian Lowboy, 28 in. high, 33 in. wide, c. 1760. **£465-500** OB

A mid-18th C. oak lowboy. 80 cm. wide. **£560-600** SKC

A Queen Anne crossbanded walnut Lowboy on cabriole legs (not original), 30" x 19". **£1,025-1,150** BW

An Oak Lowboy, the top with moulded edge, on four cabriole legs with pad feet, 18th C. restored., 31½ in., 80 cm. **£450-550** L

A George I Oak Lowboy, the deep top with an ogee moulded edge and with fruitwood crossbanding. 31½ in., 80 cm. **£700-£800** L

A Victorian Mahogany Supper Table, in need of some repair, 36 in. wide, extended. **£200-245** SV

A Regency Supper Table, with two drawers, 36" wide. **£340-420** STR

A Fine Pale Mahogany George III Period Tip-Top Supper Table, 37 in. wide, 27 in. deep, 29 in. high, c. 1790. **£390-440** TA

A Georgian Mahogany Circular Supper Table, 31½" (80cms) diam., c1760. **£350-420** L

A George II Drop Leaf Dining Table with cabriole legs, carved decoration, 57 in. x 45 in. claw and ball feet, unrestored **£1,200-1,400**, restored **£1,600-1,800** RD

A George IV mahogany rectangular extending Dining Table, with concertina action, 4'6" (137cms) x 4'8" (142cms) extending with five additional leaves to 15' (460cms), c1825. **£1,675-1,750** SKC

An Oak Dining Table Attributed to Ernest Gimson, 75" (190cms) long, 37" (94cms) wide. **£1,300-1,450** L

A Georgian Style Mahogany Pillar Dining Table, **£370-420** L

A Georgian Oval Mahogany Dining Table, 56½" (144cms) long extended, 44" (112cms) wide, c1750. **£330-395** L

A George IV Mahogany Two Pillar Dining Table, with three extra leaves and pine box container, one side faded, 53 in., 135 cm. x 47 in., 120 cm. x 118 300 cm. extended. **£2,900-3,200** L

A Mahogany Drop-Leaf Table, c. 1780. **£295-315** CSG

A George II Mahogany Drop Leaf Dining Table on cabriole legs, 57½ in. wide, 54 in. deep, c. 1740. **£1,450-1,600** RD

A William IV Mahogany Extending Table (Dining), four extra leaves and raised on turned and reeded supports, the leaves not the originals, 55 in., 140 cm. x 164½ in., 417 cm. extended. **£1,200-1,400** L

A Victorian Oval Burr Walnut Dining Table, with tilting action, 59" (150cms) long, c1860. **£480-560** L

A Mid-Georgian Red Walnut Gateleg Dining-Table on cabriole legs and hoof feet of square section, 57½ in., 147 cm. wide, open. **£1,800-1,980** C

right

A George III Oak Dining Table, 50 x 44 x 29 in. high, c. 1770. **£375-425** OB

An 18th C mahogany marquetry oval drop-leaf Dining Table, with satinwood inlay, 3'½"(92cms) wide, c1760, later marquetry. **£500-580** SKC

A Victorian Pollarded Oak Circular Dining Table, with one insertion extending to 83" (211cms) diam. **£450-500** SKC

A Large William IV Rosewood Dining Table, 52 in. diam., c. 1830. **£650-700** SHA

A George I Oak Gateleg Dining Table, width 42" (107cms). **£150-200** SH

A George IV mahogany rectangular drop-leaf Breakfast Table, crossbanded in padoukwood, 3'1½" (95cms) wide, c1825. **£580-680** SKC

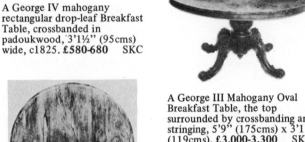

A George III Mahogany Oval Breakfast Table, the top surrounded by crossbanding and stringing, 5'9" (175cms) x 3'11" (119cms). **£3,000-3,300** SKC

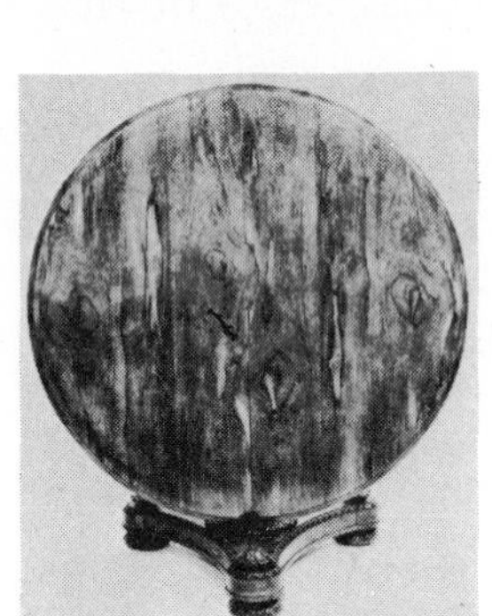

A 19th C rosewood circular Dining Table by C. Hindley & Sons, London, 52" diam. **£420-490** WHL

A George III Mahogany Breakfast Table, the two flap top over single frieze drawer the underframe with pierced fret food cage in the Chinese Chippendale manner, c. 1760, 40 in., 102 cm. extended. **£500-600** I

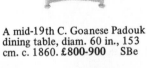

A mid-19th C. Goanese Padouk dining table, diam. 60 in., 153 cm. c. 1860. **£800-900** SBe

A Victorian burr walnut oval loo table with quartered veneered top 4 ft. 3 in., 130 cm. wide, c. 1850. **£400-450** SKC

A George III Mahogany Breakfast Table with tip-up top, 60 in., 152.5 cm. wide. **£2,700-3,000** C

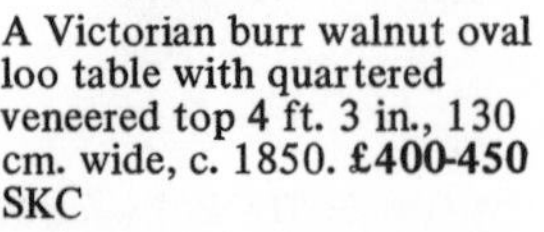

A Regency Rosewood and Amboyna Breakfast Table, the top of segmented rosewood panels flanked and centred by amboyna inlay 4 ft. 6 in., 137 cm. diam. **£900-1,000** B

A Regency Mahogany Breakfast Table, inlaid with a broad ebonised band, height 28" (72cms) diam. 42" (107cms). **£760-820** SH

A Regency Rosewood Drum Table with circular leather-lined top on ebonised baluster shaft and arched quadripartite base, 36 in., 91.5 cm. diam. **£2,300-2,550** C

Drop leaf Pine table with one drawer 18 in. wide 35 in. long extended 38 in. **£50-55** SSP

A Regency Rosewood Centre Table tip-up top inlaid with a band of cut-brass, turned simulated rosewood shaft, 42 in., 107 cm. diam. **£1,800-2,000** C

A Rosewood and Marquetry Inlaid Breakfast Table, 49 by 32 in., 124.5 by 81.5 cm., c. 1860 **£520-630** SB

A 19th C. Coromandel Breakfast Table, 4 ft. diam. **£800-950** V

A Regency Mahogany Drum Table, four drawers inlaid with key-pattern lines divided by false drawers, 46 in., 115 cm. wide. **£1,300-1,430** C

A George III Mahogany Drum Table 50 in., 127 cm. diam. **£1,300-1,450** C

A Walnut Centre Table in well-figured wood, 30 by 48 in., 76 by 122 cm., c. 1870. **£400-470** SB

A Mahogany Breakfast Table crossbanded in satinwood with rosewood edging on a gun barrel turned column. Basically Georgian origin with later top, 55" (140cms). **£460-520** L

A Regency rosewood and brass line inlaid Pedestal Table, 3'9½" (116cms) diam, c1810. **£1,270-1,300** SKC

A chunky, Victorian Drop Leaf Table with one end drawer and turned legs. 30 in. wide, 17 in. closed and 34 in. extended. Pine **£40–50** MM

A Regency Amboyna centre table with tip-up top with a broad rosewood band inlaid with cut-brass, 42 in., 107 cm. diam., stamped MCA below a coronet. **£1,550-1,710** C

A Regency rosewood centre table with crossbanded circular tip-up top carved with parcel-gilt foliage and giltwood paw feet. 54 in., 137 cm. diam. **£1,100-1,400** C

An Edwardian Oval Marquetry Table, with one drawer and overall inlay, 41" 104cms. **£350-400** L

A Black and Gilt Japanned Circular Table, the tip-up top on bird cage and baluster support. Early 19th C, 38½" (98cms) diam. **£460-500** L

A Mid-Victorian Rosewood Centre Table of serpentine design, with moulded edged top, carved and scrolled end supports, 60 in. long. **£480-560** DH

A 17th C. Milanese walnut centre table, the top crossbanded and inlaid with burr yew, width 43 in., 109 cm., c. 1685, restored. **£800-900** SBe

An Oak and Fruitwood (plum-tree) Centre Table with drawer, 30 in. wide, 20½ in. deep, 25 in. high, c. 1655. **£875-925** TA

A Mid-Georgian Walnut Centre Table with mottled grey marble top, 48 in., 122 cm. wide. **£600-660** C

A Chinese Export Black Lacquer Centre Table, the top decorated, early 19th C., 38½ in., 98 cm. wide. **£1,200-1,380** C

A Rosewood Centre Table, 80 cm. x 183 cm. x 87.5 cm., late 19th C. **£600-650** SB SBe

A French Walnut Centre Table with gilt metal mounts and borders, 19th C., 45 in., 114 cm. x 24½ in., 62 cm. **£620-720** L

An unusual early Georgian mahogany centre table (two legs replaced, adapted) 24 in. 61 cm. wide, 27½ in., 70 cm. high, 16¼ in., 41 cm. deep. **£1,250-1,350** C

An 18th C style Ornate Ebonised and Floral Marquetry Centre Table, 2'7" (79cms) high x 4'2" (127cms) wide, c1850, now with a plate-glass top. **£900-1,000** SKC

A Louis Quinze-style small kingwood and floral marquetry ormolu-mounted centre table, 3'3½" (100cms) wide, c1920. **£720-780** SKC

An Antique Walnut, Ebony and Boxwood Strung Rosewood Centre Table, the top with brass bordered edge, 3 ft. 6 in. wide, 2 ft. deep, 30 in. high. **£490-580** V

A Continental Oval Centre Table, with bands of satinwood, kingwood and ebony, 37¼" (95cms) long, 27¼" (69cms) wide, 19th C. **£570-650** L

A Victorian Drop-Leaf Table with drawer. **£200-235** SV

A 19th C Louis XV-style floral marquetry inlaid, banded, and ormolu mounted rosewood centre table. **£800-900** CD

A Walnut Gateleg Dining-Table of fine colour with two drawers, late 17th/early 18th C. 60½ in., 154 cm. wide, open. **£1,750-1,900** C

A 17th Oval Pearwood Gateleg Table, 4' (122cms) wide. **£1,490-1,520** SKC

A 17th C Oak Table on barley twist legs, 150cms x 115cms. **£1,220-1,300** SH

A George II Oak Gateleg Dining Table, mid 18th C, with restorations, 56" (142cms) extended. **£450-550** SBA

A mid-17th C. oval oak gate-ieg table with two drop leaves and drawer, 36 in., 91.5 cm. wide. **£380-400** SKC

An oak Gateleg Table, on baluster supports and bar feet, 17th C. 35 in. (90 cm.) wide open. **£820-900** C

An Oak Gateleg Table, 32 in. wide, 26 in. deep, 29 in. high, c. 1700. **£290-320** OB

A fine late 17th C Oval Oak Gateleg Table, 3'5" (104cms) wide. **£1,150-1,200** SKC

An Oak Gateleg Table with turned stretchers and legs, 64 in. x 54 in , c. 1680. **£1,300-1,500** DB

An Oak Gateleg Table, 18th C. 50 in. x 62 inx., 127 cm., x 157 cm. extended. **£1,300-1,500** L

A late 17th C Oak Gateleg Table, 108 x 103cms. **£480-520** SH

A Charles II Oak Gateleg Table, 2 ft. 7½ in. high x 3 ft. 11½ in. wide by 4 ft. 11 in. open, c. 1670. **£700-900** S

A Charles II Oak Games Table 31 in. wide, 79 cm. **£750-850** B

An 18th C Oak Gateleg Dining Table, (restored), 161cms wide. **£800-850** SH

A James II Oak Gateleg Table, 51 by 38 in., late 17th C . with restorations. **£320-370** SBA

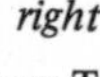

right

A 17th C. Oak Refectory Table, the three plank top with cleated ends, frieze rail with gouge decoration to one side and ends only, 86 in. long x 32 in. wide; 218 x 81 cms. **£1,700-2,000** B

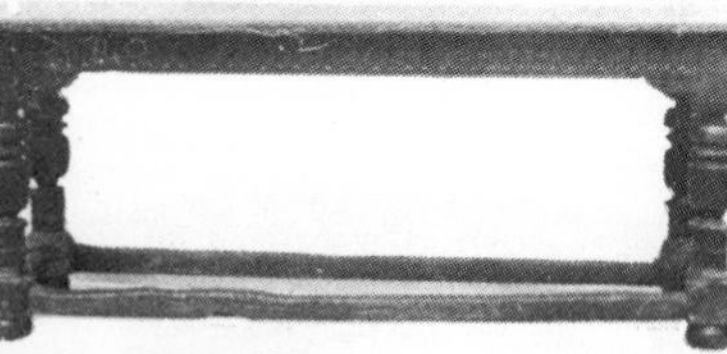

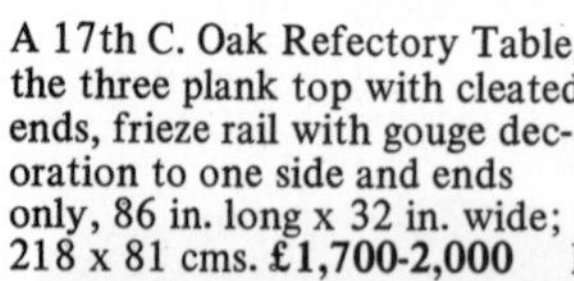

A Late 17th C oak gate-leg dining table, 4'7" by 5'5" opened. **£2,000-2,300** G & C

A Large Louis XV Period French Oak Refectory Table, the wide two plank top with cleated ends, 9 ft. 2 in. long x 3 ft. wide, 223 x 91 cms., 18th C. with restorations. **£890-1,000** B

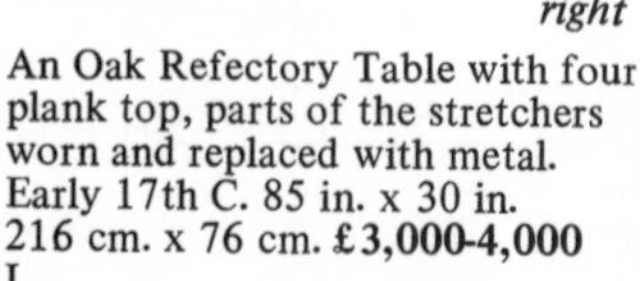

right

An Oak Refectory Table with four plank top, parts of the stretchers worn and replaced with metal. Early 17th C. 85 in. x 30 in. 216 cm. x 76 cm. **£3,000-4,000** L

A 19th C. Oak Refectory Table with plain top, vine carved frieze, 104 x 30 in. **£825-925** DH

A Mid 18th C. Oak Offertory Table, 31 in. high, 72 in. long, 26 in. deep. **£950-1,050** DB

A late 17th C-style Oak Refectory Table, length 73", width 29", reconstructed from a larger table. **£1,600-1,700** SH

An oak Refectory Table, 17th C. 76 in. (194 cm.) wide, **£1,850-2,050** C

19th C. pine Refectory Table with sturdy centre stretchers and supports, and shaped top rails. 60 in. long, 33 in. wide. **£130–150** MM

A Large Charles II Oak Drop leaf Dining Table, 176cms wide, 163cms long. **£1,450-1,500** SH

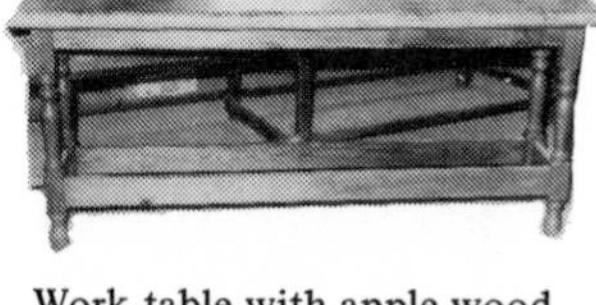
Work table with apple wood top 78 in. long, 14 in. wide. **£130-160** AL

An Edwardian pine Wind-Out Table on heavily turned legs with castors. Closed, 42 in, opened 59 in, 39 in wide. **£120–140** AL

A Good Oval 19th C Mahogany Pembroke Table, the top crossbanded in kingwood, and inlaid with stringing and a green stained chequered line, 39¼" (100cms). **£620-690** L

A George IV Rosewood veneered Bedside Pembroke Table with satinwood stringing, 1'7¾". **£310-350** WHL

A Regency Rosewood Pembroke Table with the reversible central panel inlaid with chess squares and enclosing a leather-lined backgammon well, 42 in., 107 cm. wide, open. **£2,000-2,200** C

A George III Mahogany Butterfly Shape Pembroke Table, 31 in., 79 cm. **£350-450** L

A Georgian Pembroke Table of good size and colour, note feet 42 in. long, 25 in. wide. **£395-495** CP

A Sheraton period satinwood Pembroke Table, having ebony inlay decoration, 36" x 32". **£450-500** A

Late 18th C Pembroke Table with boxwood and ebony inlay. **£240-300** STR

A Good 19th C Pembroke Table, crossbanded with satinwood and rosewood and inlaid with stringing, 39" (99cms). **£600-680** L

A Regency mahogany and rosewood banded Sofa Table, 59" x 26". **£360-420** A

A George III Mahogany Pembroke Table with pierced cross-stretchers, 37¾ in., 96 cm. wide, open. **£360-395** C

An 18th C mahogany Pembroke Table, the top of butterfly form with satinwood crossbanding, line inlay, and shell inlaid central panel, 36" x 35". **£520-580** NF

A Regency Rosewood Sofa-Table, inlaid with brass lines and foliage, 57½ in., 147 cm. wide, open. **£1,200-1,350** C

A William IV Walnut Sofa Table, the top with wide crossbanding, 57½ in., 146 cm. extended. **£500-600** L

A Regency Rosewood Sofa Table on four in-curved supports joined by a circular platform, 59 in., 150 cm. wide, open. **£900-1,000** C

A Regency mahogany Pembroke Table, inlaid with ebonised stringing, 2'9" (84cms) wide, c1810. **£355-400** SKC

A Regency banded mahogany Sofa Table, 4'9" extended. **£570-670** HG

A Georgian inlaid mahogany Sofa Table, 36" x 24". **£1,250-1,400** BW

A George IV Rosewood Sofa-Table, crossbanded top inlaid with brass lines, 64½ in., 164 cm. wide, open. **£900-1,000** C

A Regency Rosewood Sofa Table, crossbanded and inlaid with stringing, 59¾ in., 152 cm. **£1,100-1,250** L

A Regency rosewood sofa-table with brass-inlaid two-flap top 56 in., 142 cm. wide, open. **£1,750-1,950** C

A Regency rosewood sofa table with rounded rectangular top and two drawers, 61 in., 155 cm. wide,open. **£1,500-1,700** C

A Rosewood Library Table on a self-tapering column with outset and turned feet, 45 in., 114 cm., wide, c. 1840. **£580-680** SB

A George III Mahogany Sofa Table cross-banded with rosewood, on solid trestle ends joined by flying brackets, 59½ in., 151 cm. wide, open. **£3,400-3,750** C

A William IV Rosewood Library Table, c. 1840, 48 in., 122 cm. **£500-600** L

A Regency mahogany rosewood cross-banded and line inlaid sofa table, 60½" wide (some pieces of veneer loose). **£650-750** G & C

A Regency Simulated Rosewood Sofa Table with giltmetal guilloche border 65½ in., 156 cm. wide, open. **£1,000-1,500** C

A Late Regency Rosewood Library Table, faults, 62" (158cms) wide, 27" (68cms) deep. **£500-580** L

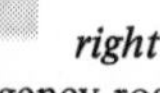

right

A Regency rosewood sofa table with rounded rectangular twin-flap top inlaid with a satinwood line, 59 in., 150 cm. wide, open. **£1,850-2,035** C

A Georgian rectangular mahogany reading or writing table, 33" wide. **£450-500** PWC

A Walnut Inlaid Card Table, mid-Victorian, baize lined. **£550-620** VA

A Walnut Card Table with a moulded serpentine swivelling top, 34 in., 86.5 cm., wide, late 1850's. **£360-410** SB

A William IV Mahogany Fold Top Card Table, 2'11½". **£225-275** WHL

An Early Victorian rosewood Card Table, 3'1" (94cms) wide, c1845. **£270-300** SKC

A George III Satinwood Card-Table with baize-lined top decorated with peacock feathers and summer flower swags crossbanded with rosewood, 41½ in., 105 cm. wide. **£950-1,045** C

A Regency Calamanderwood Card-Table with baize-lined top inlaid with boxwood lines, 36 in., 91.5 cm. wide. **£1,500-1,750** C

A Sheraton Mahogany Semi Lunar Card Table, 39" (99cms) wide, George III. **£390-450** L

A Queen Anne black and gold lacquer Card-table with lobed top enclosing counter-wells and candle-stands on plain frieze, 32 in., 81 cm. wide, labelled 'Cowdray 1919 35'. **£360-400** C

A George III Mahogany Card-Table with serpentine cross-banded baize-lined top with later concealed drawer, 38 in., 96.5 cm. wide. **£800-880** C

A George III mahogany card table having a folding baize lined elliptical top crossbanded with satinwood and inlaid, width 36 in., 91 cm., c. 1800. **£410-490** SBe

A Walnut Card Table with shaped swivel fold-over top with baize lining, two counter wells and two plated screw-on candlesticks, and brass studded leather edging, 19th C., possibly North American. 39 in., 99 cm. **£450-550** L

A Dutch Marquetry Serpentine Card Table inlaid on mahogany, 2 ft. 5½ in. high x 2 ft. 6 in. wide, 75 cm. x 76 cm., c. 1750, inlay 19th C. **£1,100-1,300** S

A George I Mahogany card-table with lobed baize-lined top with candle recesses and counter-wells, 32 in., 82 cm. wide. **£1,150-1,265** C

A 19th C. walnut marquetry card table with gilt brass mounts, width 36 in., 92 cm., c. 1890. **£900-1,000** SBe

A Satinwood Envelope Card Table, 22 in., 56 cm., square, c. 1910. **£300-360** SB

A Parcel-Gilt Ebonised Card Table, the concave-fronted hinged top enclosing dice wells, 29½ by 36½ in., 75 by 93 cm., c. 1870. **£150-190** SB

A George II mahogany card-table with lobed folding baize-lined top edged with ribbon-and-rosette ornament, (the legs with restorations) 33¾ in., 85 cm. wide, 28½ in., 72.5 cm. high, 16½ in., 2 cm. deep. **£2,530-2,600** C

A Pair of 19th C Marquetry Card Tables, with folding top and baized interior and crossbanded in kingwood, 35" (89cms) wide, late 19th C. **£720-790** L

A Rosewood Envelope Card Table, containing a baize-lined playing surface, 29 by 22 in., 73.7 by 56 cm., c. 1900. **£290-340** SB

A Pair of Mid-Georgian Mahogany Card-Tables with baize-lined tops, concertina actions, 36 in., 91 cm. wide. **£1,000-1,200** C

A George III Mahogany card table. **£570-670** EBB

A George III mahogany and satinwood banded 'D' -shaped Card Table, 3' (91cms) wide, c1800. **£500-550** SKC

Chippendale period fold-over top Card Table. **£600-1,000** STR

An important George II Mahogany Concertina table, 2'11". **£970-1,000** WHL

A Burr-Walnut Combined Games and Work Table on leaf-carved turned trestle supports, 29½ by 27 in., 75 by 68.5 cm., c. 1860. **£650-720** SB

A George III mahogany card table, 36" wide. **£725-800** SH

A 19th C Oriental-style lacquer work table with Chinoiserie decoration, some damage. **£246-280** SAL

A Regency rosewood and brass-mounted Games Table, the reversible top revealing chess board inlay and backgammon inset, 2'4½" (73cms) high x 2'1½" (65cms) wide, c1810. **£1,485-1,520** SKC

A Late Victorian Barley-Twist Rosewood Sewing Table, fitted interior, 22 in. wide, 16 in. deep, 30 in. high. **£400-460** VA

A Victorian walnut veneered worktable with crossbanded top, the top drawer with satinwood lidded compartment inscribed "Maria" and dated 1889, 55 cm., 22¾ in. wide. **£240-320** O

An Early Victorian Walnut Work Box, 24 in. wide, 27 in. high, c. 1850. **£240-260** SHA

A Fine Regency Rosewood Work Table, c. 1820-30. **£575-615** CSG

A Mid-Victorian Figured Walnut Writing-Table, the quartered serpentine top inlaid with ribbon-tied rushes, 39½ in., 100 cm. wide. **£1,050-1,200** C

A Regency rosewood Games-Table, 28½in (72cm) wide, **£1,000-1,200** C

An unusual George III Mahogany Writing Table having two fold-over flaps to the top, 2'8" (81cms) wide. **£1,900-2,000** SKC

A 19th C Dutch marquetry and mahogany serpentine-fronted Card Table, 2'4" (71cms) wide, c1880. **£470-500** SKC

A George III Mahogany Writing-Table with crossbanded top, 58 in., 147.5 cm. wide. **£950-1,050** C

A Rare and Fine Queen Anne Period Walnut Fold-Over Games Table with candle and games wells and fitted drawer, shallow ball and claw foot, acanthus knee carving, reproduction handles, 33 in. wide, 16½ in. deep, 28 in. high, c. 1710-15. **£6,500-7,000** TA

A George III Mahogany Writing-table with baize-lined top and three drawers inlaid with boxwood and ebonised lines, 60 in., 152.5 cm. wide. **£1,600-1,750** C

A George III Mahogany Serpentine Tea or Games Table, late 18th C, 35" (89cms) wide. **£350-450** SBA

A Fine and Rare Old English 'Chippendale' Design Games Table in original condition, 28 in. wide, 22 in. deep, 30 in. high. c. 1775. **£1,800-2,000** CP

A Late Regency Mahogany work Table, 18" (46cms). **£330-380** L

A Fine Sheraton Parquetry Rosewood Work Table, the top with a cube design of various exotic woods, having a pull out slide for a work bag, 28¾ in. high, top 15 x 12 in. c. 1800. **£1,950-2,100** RD

A Regency small mahogany Work Table, inlaid with ebony stringing, 2'2½" (67cms) high x 1'9" (53cms) wide, c1810. **£530-580** SKC

left

A 19th C shaped rectangular satinwood needlework table, the rising top painted, 23" wide. **£320-360** PWC

right

A Regency Rosewood Games Table, inlaid with broad and narrow cut-brass strings and paterae, early 19th C, 28" x 34" (71cms x 86cms). **£700-900** SBA

A Rosewood Games and Work Table, the folding top inlaid for chess, cribbage and backgammon, fitted with sliding work box, c. 1850., 20 in., 51 cm. wide. **£250-350** L

A Regency ebony and penwork games-table, with ivory-inlaid three-cornered base. 24 in., 61 cm. wide. **£620-700** C

A Mahogany Work Table, the top enclosing a well fitted interior with ten lidded compartments, c. 1850, 19½ in., 50 cm. wide. **£310-400** L

A Mahogany Work-Table with eight lidded compartments and a tray revealing a work bag, 31 in., 79 cm. high, 1830's. **£300-360** SB

A late Victorian rosewood and satinwood inlaid lady's combined Writing and Work Table, 3'8" (112cms) high x 2' (61cms) wide, c1890. **£485-525** SKC

A Victorian walnut and floral marquetry lady's Work Table, the interior with well and compartments, 2'4" (71cms) high x 1'6" (46cms) wide, c1855. **£350-400** SKC

A Rosewood Teapoy containing two fitted caddies, 30 in., 76 cm., c. 1840. **£250-320** SB

A Regency Simulated Rosewood Teapoy densely inlaid with cut-brass, enclosing a divided and lidded interior including two cut-glass jars, 15 in., 38 cm. wide. **£900-1,000** C

A George IV Mahogany Teapoy of sarcophagus shape, 19" (49cms) wide. **£225-300** SKC

A Georgian Rosewood Fitted Teapoy, with heavily carved base and paw feet, 33" high, 19" wide, 16" deep. **£300-400** SQE

An oak Side Table, 17th C, 25in (63.5cm) wide. **£800-1,000** C

A 19th C serpentine fronted mahogany sidetable, with broad satinwood bands, 42" wide. **£420-480** PWC

An Edwardian satinwood side table in the Adam manner, the top centred with a burr walnut medallion and inlaid with a radiating fan design, width 58½ in., 148 cm., c. 1900. **£450-550** SBe

An Unusual George IV Yew-Wood Teapoy, the top opening to reveal four fitted tea canisters and recesses for two mixing bowls, 29 in., high, mid 19th C. **£325-370** SBA

A Regency rosewood and satinwood band inlaid side-table, 4'10½" wide (top split). **£1,000-1,200** G & C

A good Sheraton period 'D' shaped mahogany fold over top card table with satinwood crossband & decoration, 3' wide. **£500-550** PWC

A Painted Satinwood Side Table with chamfered bowed top, the frieze and sectional tapering legs decorated, 58½ in., 148.5 cm. wide. **£600-660** C

A Regency Rosewood Teapoy, c. 1830. **£290-320** OB

A George III Mahogany Side Table of break-front outline, 36 in., 91 cm. **£650-730** L

An early Victorian rosewood side table, 132 cm., 52 in. **£400-500** O

A George III Satinwood Side Table with D-shaped top cross-banded with rosewood, (adapted) 46½ in., 118 cm. wide. **£450-500** C

A Fine Satinwood Demi-Lune Side Table with original painting, English, 30 in. high, c. 1790. **£1,295-1,450** CP

An Oak Side Table (replaced top) 32 in. wide, 19 in. deep, 28 in. high, c. 1790. **£145-165** SHA

A Victorian side table, 29" high. **£175-200** SAL

A Georgian Mahogany Side Table with chamfered legs (inside) 32½ in. wide, 21 in. deep, 28½ in. high, c. 1770. **£395-480** CP

Small, 19th C. pine Side Table with one drawer and turned legs. 17 in. wide 28in. long. **£32-40** SSP

A simple, early 19th C. country made Side Table with one drawer and sturdy, tapered legs. 38 in. wide, 19 in. deep, 29 in. high. **£40–50** MM

A Very Fine Oak and Yew Tree Side Table of the Sheraton Period, of West Country origin, with period reproduction handle, 28½ in wide, 17¼ in. deep, 28½ in. high, c. 1770. **£395-450** TA

A Queen Anne Burr-Walnut Side Table crossbanded and inlaid with feather bands, 30 in., 76 cm. wide. **£1,300-1,450** C

A mid-18th C Mahogany Side Table, 2'1½" (65cms) wide. **£900-1,000** SKC

A Pair of George I Walnut side tables, one with moulded grey fossil marble rectangular top, the other lacking top, with cavetto friezes, 48 in., 122 cm. and 45 in., 144 cm. wide (cut down). **£3,400-3,750** C

A Late Georgian Oak Side Table, top and drawer crossbanded in mahogany, (one new leg) 31 in. wide, 17 in. deep, 29 in. high, c. 1800. **£105-125** SHA

A George I walnut side table with rectangular verde antico marble top and cavetto frieze on lappeted club legs. 38½ in., 98 cm. wide. **£950-1,100** C

A Gilt-Gesso Side Table with re-entrant corners incised and decorated, the frame early 18th C. 34 in., 86 cm. wide. **£680-750** C

An Elm Side Table with baluster turned legs, handles replaced, 30 in. x 26 in. high, c. 1700.
£330-360 DB

A late 17th C Oak Side Table.
£405-445 SH

A Good 17th C French Provincial Side Table, 39" (99cms) wide, c1680. **£690-830** SKC

A Walnut and Chestnut Side Table, with rare reversed baluster turning, 32 in. top, 23 in. wide, 21 in. deep, 28½ in. high, c. 1670-90.
£1,200-1,400 TA

A William and Mary Marquetry Side Table, 37½ in., 95 cm., restored, on later feet. **£4,000-5,000** L

A James II Oak Side Table, all original except for feet and drawer, front mouldings, top with some restoration, 37 in. wide, 26 in. deep, 28 in. high, c. 1670. **£320-360** SHA

A Black Cipollino marble and polished steel console Table and Wall Mirror in the Art Deco style, table 37" high x 60" wide, mirror 29½" x 39½".
£700-800 CSK

A pair of 19th C. stripped oak Wall Consoles. 28 in. wide, 34 in. high. **£250–270**

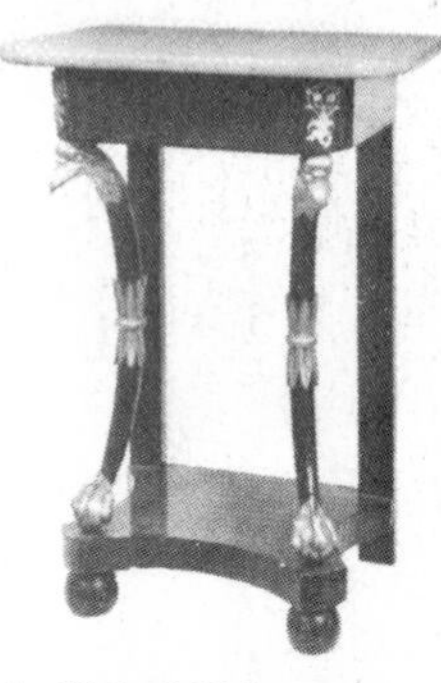

An Early 19th C Mahogany Console Table, with a later white marble slab, 17" (44cms) wide.
£530-600 SKC

A George III mahogany serving-table 54 in., 138 cm. wide.
£1,900-2,700 C

A George III mahogany serving table, the serpentine top cross-banded with rosewood and inlaid with chequered lines. 56¼ in., 143 cm. wide. **£1,100-1,300** C

A pair of early 18th C French console tables in stained pine.
£480-550 B

A Flemish 17th C-Style Trestle Table, length 63". **£340-380** SH

A Chippendale period Cuban mahogany, single plank, snap-top Table, c1750, 33" diam. **£400-600** STR

An 18th C mahogany Tripod Table, with tip-up top, 24" diam. **£700-800** NF

A Yew Tree and Oak Candle-Table with Tripod base, 16¾ in. diam., 28¾ in. high, c. 1780. **£240-260** TA

A George III mahogany tripod table, baluster stem and cabriole base with claw-and-ball feet, 27 in., 69 cm. diam. **£1,750-2,000** C

A Mid-Georgian mahogany gaming-table with tip-up top on baluster stem, cabriole base and pad feet, 46½ in., 118 cm. diam. **£550-605** C

A Fine 18th C. Mahogany Tripod Table with a dished top, English, 25 in. diam., 28 in. high, c. 1770. **£550-630** RD

An Oak Rent Table with holly inlay, 40 in. wide, 28 in. deep, 29 in. high, c. 1620. **£4,000-5,000** OB

A Victorian Mahogany Tripod Table. **£110-135** SV

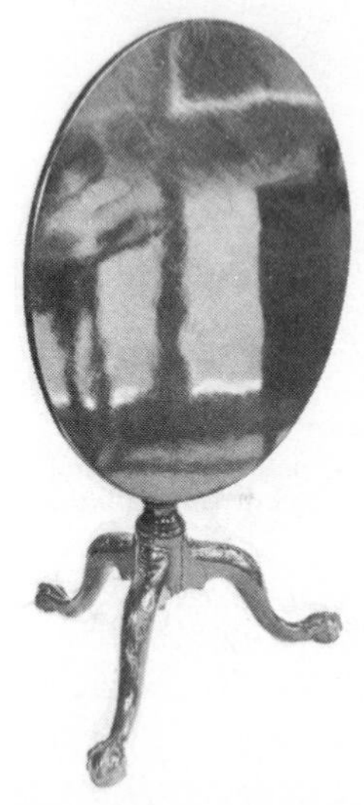

A Fine Quality 'Chippendale' tilt-top mahogany Tripod Table, 30" diam. **£675-775** SAL

left
A George III fiddle-back mahogany tripod table with tip-up top crossbanded with satinwood and mahogany bordered with rosewood 45 in. 145 cm. wide. **£1,650-1,750** C

A Victorian walnut tripod Table, top inlaid with parquetry star and cube design, top 24 in. diam. **£350-425** SV

A Regency polychrome lacquer tripod table, decorated with chinoiserie figures and pavilions heightened with mother-of-pearl. 33 in., 84 cm. wide. **£560-700** C

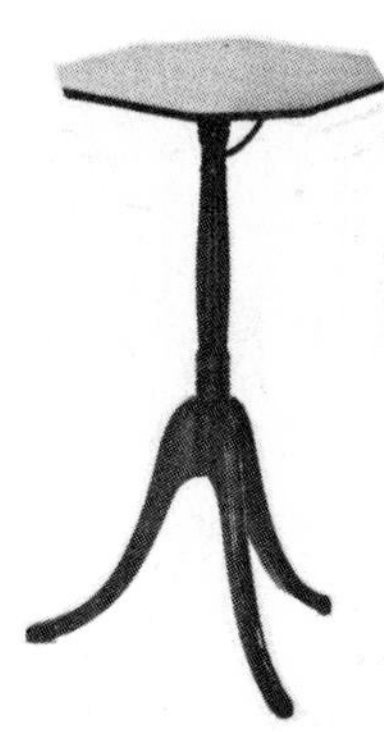

A Regency mahogany reading table, height 46 in., 117 cm., c. 1820. **£160-190** SBe

A Good George III tip-top Occasional Table. **£220-240** SAL

A fine Chippendale period mahogany circular tilt-top occasional table, 2'5" diam. **£700-900** G & C

A George III mahogany tilt-top Occasional Table, 2'5" (73cms) high, x 3'1" (94cms) diam., c1770 **£270-300** SKC

An Early Victorian Mahogany Occasional Table, 23½" (60cms) wide, c1840. **£290-330** SKC

A Galle Beechwood and Marquetry Occasional-table inlaid with a flower-spray and the inscription 'Souci de plaire', signed. 71 cm. wide. **£460-500** C

An early George III period mahogany piecrust edge circular tilt-top occasional table, 2'7½" diam. **£430-470** G & C

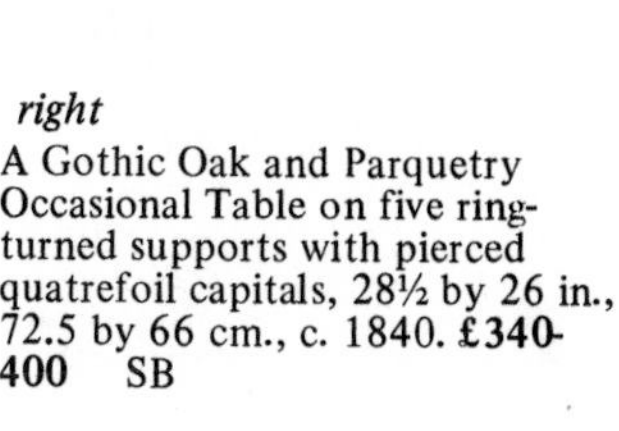

A Second Empire ormolu-mounted mahogany occasional table with leather-lined top 24 in., 61 cm. wide. **£600-700** C

right
A Gothic Oak and Parquetry Occasional Table on five ring-turned supports with pierced quatrefoil capitals, 28½ by 26 in., 72.5 by 66 cm., c. 1840. **£340-400** SB

A 19th C Walnut Sutherland Table, 29" high, 38" wide. **£275-300** SAL

A Regency rosewood writing table, the crossbanded top with a tooled leather writing surface, width 39 in., 99 cm., c. 1820. **£420-520** SBe

A 19th C. inlaid Sutherland Table. **£100-115** SV

A Papier Mache Occasional Table, the oval top inlaid and painted with roses and leaves above a double baluster stem and lobed base, 26½ in. x 26½ in., 67 cm. x 67 cm., mid 19th C. **£90-110** SB

A Rare George II Corner Table, c1725. **£525-600** SAL

A Victorian, figured walnut and shaped-top, Sutherland Table, 42" x 36". **£240-290** A

A French Art Nouveau marquetry Table in the manner of Emile Galle, the top in various fruitwoods, 92cms diam. **£475-525** P

A 19th C. French rosewood table a rognon in the Louis XV style, pierced gallery to the veined rouge marble top, width 20½ in., 52 cm., c. 1880. **£180-280** SBe

An Edwardian mahogany Bijouterie Table, inlaid with chequer stringing, 2'6" (76cms) x 2'3" (68cms) wide, c1910. **£320-350** SKC

A Portuguese Jacaranda Tip-up Table, on bobbin-turned legs with gateleg action, 18th C. 24 in., 61 cm. diam. **£400-440** C

A Charles I Oak drop leaf table, 46cms x 61cms. **£1,150-1,200** SH

A Set of Four Regency Satinwood Quartetto Tables, the rosewood tops crossbanded with burr-yew, 19 in., 48 cm., to 12½ in., 32 cm. wide. **£2,800-3,000** set. C

A Satinwood Circular Table, with glass top, 32¾ in., 83 cm. diam., c. 1900. **£560-630** SB

A 17th C Spanish Walnut Table (some restoration), 113cms wide. **£350-400** SH

A Victorian Mahogany Table, 28 in. high, 39 in. wide, open. **£200-245** SV

A small, early 19th C. Spanish fruitwood Table with one drawer. 24 in. high, 24 in. wide, 18 in. deep. **£150–180** SM

A George II red walnut tea table, width 26½ in., 67.5 cm., c. 1730. **£850-930** SBe

An Irish mid-Georgian mahogany tea-table with lobed folding top. 33¾ in., 86 cm. wide. 29½ in., 75 cm. high. **£1,450-1,500** C

A Regency mahogany 'fold over top' Tea Table, 3'1" wide. **£450-500** P.W.C.

A Regency and Rosewood and brass inlaid Tea Table, with swivel fold over top, 36" (92cms). **£680-780** L

An Early George III Padoukwood Tea-Table with tapering legs and block feet (restorations) 35 in., 89 cm. wide. **£300-400** C

A Regency Rosewood Tea Table, inlaid with stringing and headed by inlaid Maltese crosses, 36 in., 92 cm. **£650-750** L

A Victorian mahogany manx man tray top table, 18" high, 22" wide. **£75-95** SAL

A 19th C. Brass Galleried Table, 29 in. high. **£90-115** SV

A Galle Oak and Marquetry Etagere, inlaid in various fruitwoods, inlaid signature 79 cm. wide. **£310-350** C

An Ormolu Mounted Mahogany 2-Tier Table with variegated marble top, 1 ft. 11 in. wide, 1 ft. 4 in. deep, 29 in. high. **£140-190** V

A Late Victorian/Edwardian Mahogany Etagere, c1900. **£195-215** SAL

Round Table 36 in. diam. **£58-68** AL

A pair of giltmetal-framed mahogany two-tier etageres 15 in., 38 cm. wide **£550-650** C

An early 19th C. Welsh pine Cricket Table, 28 in. high, 17 in. diam. **£65–75** . GW

A Victorian Mahogany Reading Table. **£425-485** SV

A Fine Fruitwood 'Cricket' Table with chamfer and shaped rails, possible timber apple and cherry tree, 36½ in. wide, 25½ in. high, c. 1800. **£210-230** TA

A George III Mahogany Architect's Table, 35 in., 89 cm. **£700-950** B

A 19th C French Small mahogany and Gilt Metal Vitrine, 17" (43cms) x 43½" (110cms). **£340-400** L

A 19th C. Coaching Table. **£100-125** SV

A walnut Sofa with waved padded back, out-scrolled arms and cushion seat, 90in (299cm) wide, **£1,100-2,000** C

A walnut Sofa of early Georgian design, on cabriole legs headed by C-scrolls and bellflowers, 26in (113cm) wide, **£800-1,000** C

A fine George III giltwood Sofa, 69in (175cm) wide, **£1,100-1,500** C

A giltwood Settee of early Georgian design, 52in (133.5cm) wide, **£975-1,250** C

A George III giltwood Sofa, 72in (183cm) wide, **£1,250-1,550** C

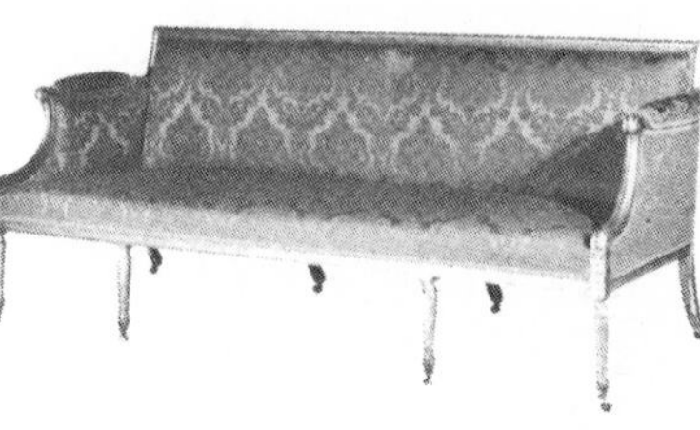

A pair of George III giltwood Settees, 86¼in (219cm) wide, **£1,200-1,400** C

A George III white-painted and gilded Sofa, 69½in (177cm) wide, **£1,600-1,800** C

A walnut button-upholstered Chair-Back Settee, 72in (183cm) wide, restored, c. 1860, **£500-600** C

A George II walnut Settee, some restoration, 61in (155cm) wide, **£800-1,000** C

A pair of Louis XV white-painted and gilded Canapes, probably Italian, 57in (145cm) wide. **£1,500-1,600** C

A Victorian Walnut Frame Settee, with serpentine seat and the acanthus leaf hand-grips continuing to short cabriole legs. 79 in., 201 cm. **£720-820** L

A Dutch Marquetry Two Seat Settee, on cabriole legs with carved claw feet. **£600-700** L

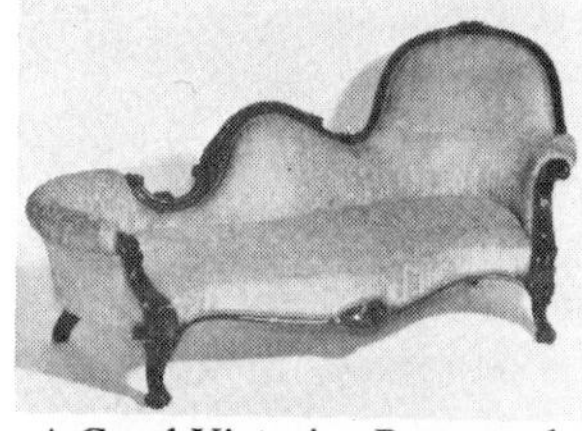

A Good Victorian Rosewood Settee, the scroll shaped back with moulded rail carved with flowerheads and foliage, on cabriole legs, 75 in., long, mid 19th C. **£510-570** SBA

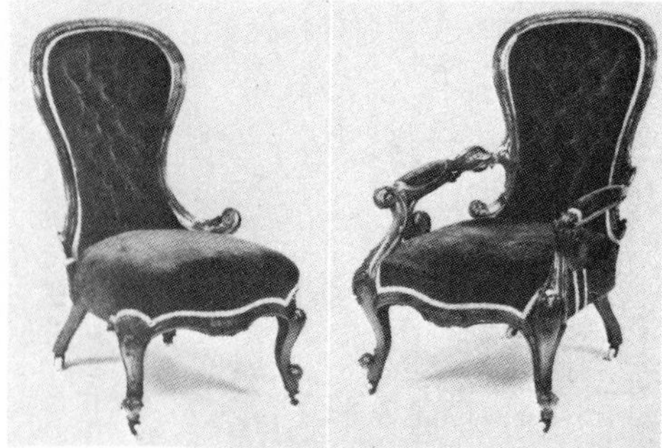

A Suite of Walnut Drawing Room Furniture, comprising a set of 6 balloon-back dining chairs, an armchair, and a nursing chair and a settee, c. 1860, **£2,500-3,000** C

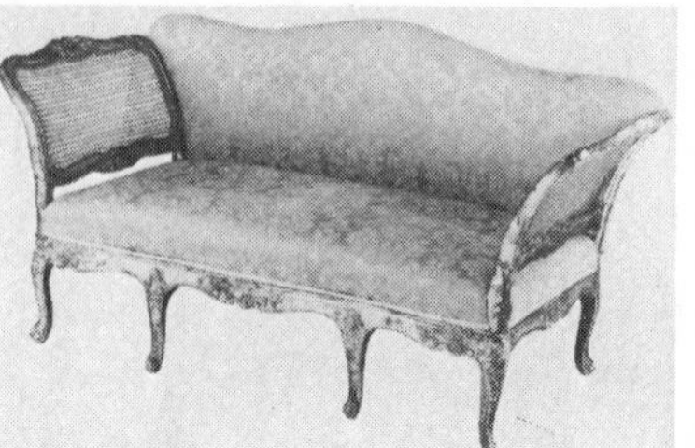

A Regency rosewood and cut brass inlaid Settee in the Grecian style, 6'8" (203cms) wide, c1815. **£720-795** SKC

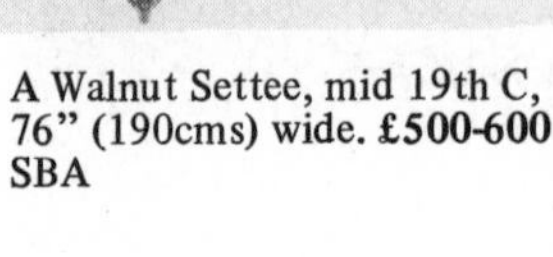

A Giltwood Bench 6 ft. 1 in., 185 cm. long, c. 1750, North Italian or South German, the serpentine stuffed back added at a later date. **£440-500** S

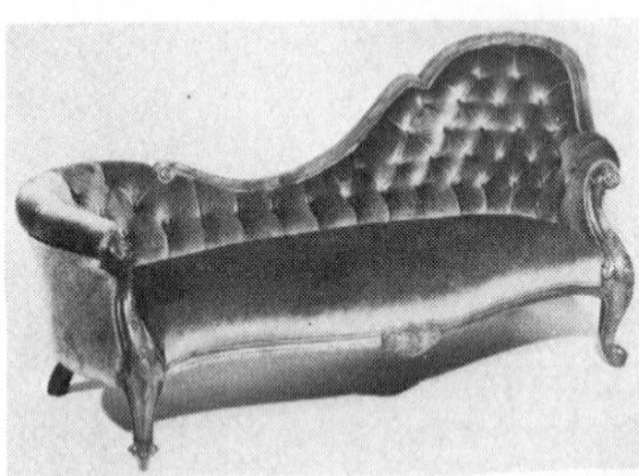

An early George III mahogany settee. Width of seat 53 in., 135 cm., height of back 36 in., 91.5 cm. **£1,200-1,500** C

A Walnut Settee, mid 19th C, 76" (190cms) wide. **£500-600** SBA

A Good Walnut Settee, mid 19th C, 73" (85cms). **£1,000-1,200** SBA

An early 'George II' walnut and burr-walnut Chair-Back Settee, 56in (142.3cm) wide, 1900-1920 **£300-400** C

A Burmese Carved Hardwood Settle, 173 cm. x 140 cm. late 19th C. **£170-200** SB SBe

A George II mahogany Settee, 55in (140cm) wide, **£2,250-3,000** C

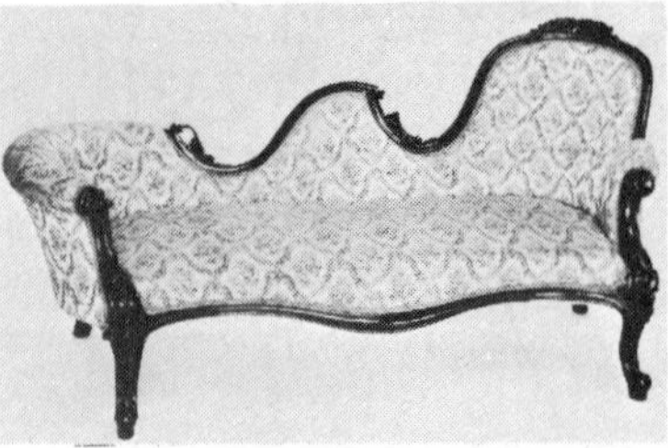

A Victorian Rosewood Frame Sofa, 77" (196cms). **£700-780** L

A Polished Pine Settle, 49 in. wide, 42 in. high. **£260-340** CP

A walnut-framed settee in the Chippendale manner, width 58 in., 147 cm. **£730-830** SBe

An Oak Settle with open arms and chest base having a panelled back carved with five Kings beneath a rail dated 1713, 5 ft. long, 3 ft. 8½ in. high. **£680-780** OL

A Mid-Welsh Oak Child's Settle, 46 in. wide, 43 in. high, 20 in. deep mid 17th C. **£850-1,000** TA

A fine mid-17th C. oak box-seat settle. **£575-650** SKC

A fine mid-17th C. box-seat settle. 4 ft. 6 in., 137 cm., wide. **£750-800** SKC

An early 18th C Oak and Elm Settle, height 65", width 79". **£470-520** SH

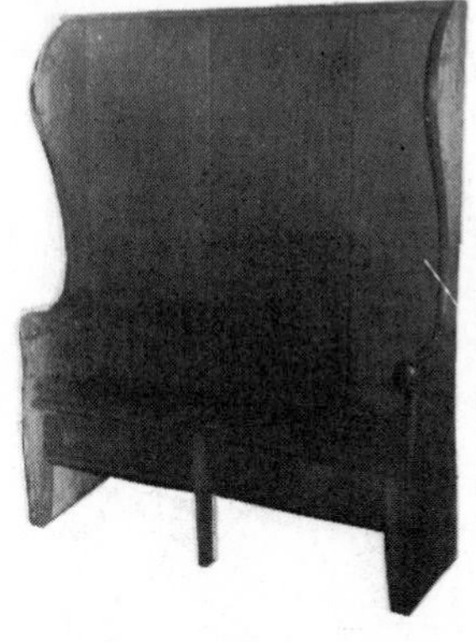

A late 18th C. pine Settle with two drawers under seat. 57 in. long, 66 in. high, 16 in. wide. **£350–400** GW

Irish Settle 72 in. long, 24 in. deep. **£189-210** P&D

18th Century Settle with fielded panels. **£240-260** SSP

A Late 19th C panelled oak Settle, decorated in William Morris style, 82" high, 78" wide. **£4,700-5,000** DH

A pair of giltwood-framed fauteuil in the Louis XIV manner, upholstered in Aubusson tapestry. **£470-550** SBe

A Good Set of Rosewood Chairs comprising:- four dining chairs, two open armchairs, and a settee, late 19th C., settee 124 cm. **£700-800** SBe

A Set of Three Yew and Elm Windsor Armchairs and another of similar form, late 18th/early 19th C. **£650-750** S

A Broad Arm Windsor Chair. **£230-260** SHA

A Very Fine and Rare Windsor Yew Wood Chair, c. 1740. **£625-700** CP

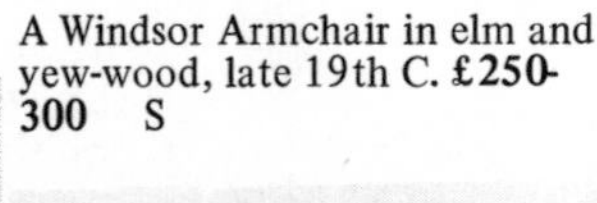

A Windsor Armchair in elm and yew-wood, late 19th C. **£250-300** S

A Good Yew and Elm Windsor Arm-Chair, early 19th C. **£250-350** SBA

A Windsor Armchair, in elm and ash, original patina, 33 in. high, c. 1800. **£175-195** SHA

Two High Back Yew-Wood Windsor Elbow Chairs, one with a plume of feathers in a pierced splat, the other with a pierced scroll shape splat, early 19th C. **£500-600** K

A 19th C Yew and Elm Windsor Rocking Chair. **£520-550** SH

An early 19th C yew wood high hoop back Windsor elbow with elm seat. **£275-300** PWC

A Victorian Elm Rocking Chair. **£220-250** SH

An early 19th C yew wood high hoop back Windsor elbow chair with elm seat. **£300-340** PWC

A 19th C Windsor Chair. **£150-180** SAL

A Set of four Elm and Yew Windsor Armchairs. **£3,000-3,300** C

An Elm Windsor Elbow Chair with wheelback and wood seat. **£90-110** V

A Late 18th C/early 19th C Windsor elm and yew armchair. **£320-360** SH

An Antique Elm Windsor Elbow Chair with comb back and wood seat. **£110-130** V

A Windsor Elm Armchair. **£175-200** SH

A Windsor Elm and Yew Armchair. **£250-300** SH

A set of six early 19th C Windsor Elm and Yew Chairs. **£1,500-1,600** SH

A panelled oak Chair, the back dated 1675 **£540-600** NF

A Charles II Walnut Armchair, c. 1680. **£400-500** S

A late 18th C Yew and Elm Windsor Armchair. **£265-300** SH

A William and Mary beech and walnut armchair. **£220-260** B

A Georgian Ash Wheel Back Arm Chair, cane seat req. some repair 44 in. high, c. 1800. **£100-120** SHA

A Composite Set of Four Yew-Wood Windsor Elbow Chairs, almost matching, the turned supports joined by crinoline stretchers, late 18th/ early 19th C. **£1,250-1,450** L

A Carolean Oak Chair, English, c. 1680. **£595-690** CP

A Chippendale Period Elm, Merchants Elbow Chair. **£200-260** SAL

An early 17th C oak elbow chair. **£480-520** PWC

A Charles II Oak Derbyshire Chair. **£430-480** SH

An 18th C. Fruitwood Arm Chair (commode chair originally), c. 1760. **£185-200** SHA

A 19th C. Mahogany Child's Chair, front missing. **£200-225** SV

A 19th C. ebonised Armchair. **£70-75** SV

A Queen Anne walnut elbow chair. **£480-520** PWC

One of a Pair of Chippendale Carver Chairs, of highest quality. **£2,000-2,200** SA

A Pair of George III Mahogany Open Arm Chairs, late 18th C. **£300-400** SBA

A 19th C. Painted Rocking Chair, replaced seat. **£49-54** SV

A Pair of Sheraton satinwood and painted Armchairs, c1790. **£1,220-1,300** SKC

left

A Set of Three Regency Ebonised and Gilded Open Armchairs, one stamped W.P. and another G.D., the back of one inscribed Blackmore Park, (one partly rerailed) and another en suite of a later date. **£2,100-2,300** C

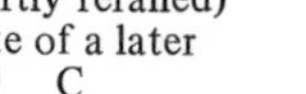

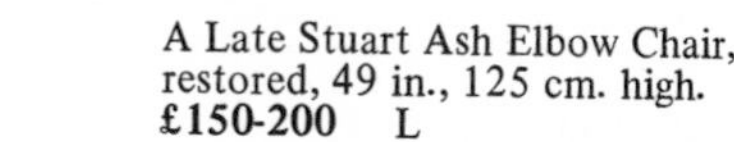

A Late Stuart Ash Elbow Chair, restored, 49 in., 125 cm. high. **£150-200** L

A George III Mahogany Elbow Chair, c. 1770. **£245-300** CSG

An antique Chinese Chippendale Elbow Chair in mahogany. **£640-700** NF

A George III Mahogany Library Armchair of Chippendale style. **£2,000-2,200** C

A 19th C. Beech Elbow Chair with original painted decoration. **£195-210** RD

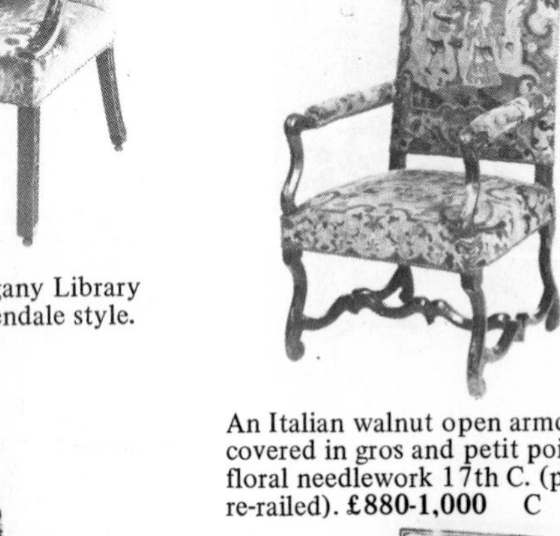

An Italian walnut open armchair covered in gros and petit point floral needlework 17th C. (partly re-railed). **£880-1,000** C

A Dutch Marquetry Elbow Chair, raised on cabriole legs inlaid overall with masks, shells and floral marquetry. **£220-260** L

A Charles II Walnut-frame Scroll Arm-chair. **£530-580** SKC

An Unusual Dutch Marquetry Armchair, early 19th C. **£700-800** S

A pair of George III giltwood open armchairs. **£1,300-1,500** C

A Cow Horn Arm Chair, c. 1900, **£150-200** C

A pair of Walnut Open Armchairs of 17th C. style, on faceted legs and stretchers, **£520-570** pr. C

A pair of 16th C walnut armchairs. **£440-500** B

One of a pair of Victorian Elbow Chairs. **£625-725** pr. SV

A Victorian Rosewood Frame Easy Chair, the spoon shape back carved, with scrolling leafage. **£400-450** L

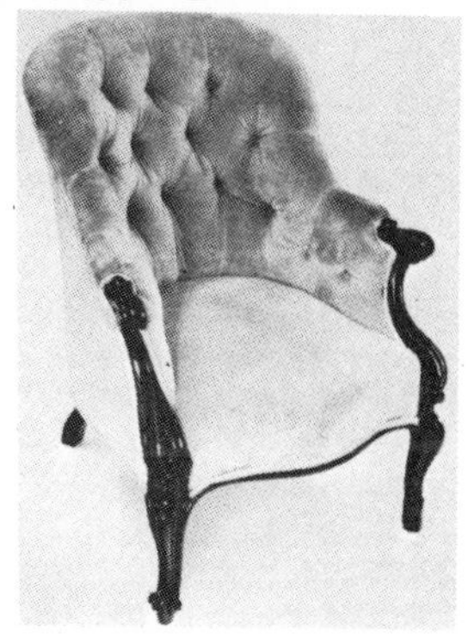

An Early Victorian Rosewood Scoop Back Armchair, c1850. **£280-340** L

A Pair of Spanish Walnut Open Armchairs with backs and seats upholstered in Turkey-work surmounted by gilded finials 17th C. **£550-600** pr. C

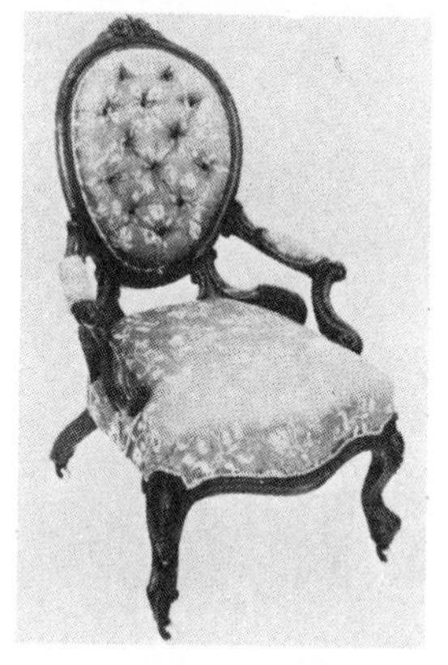

A Victorian Carved Walnut Lady's Armchair, c1860. **£410-450** L

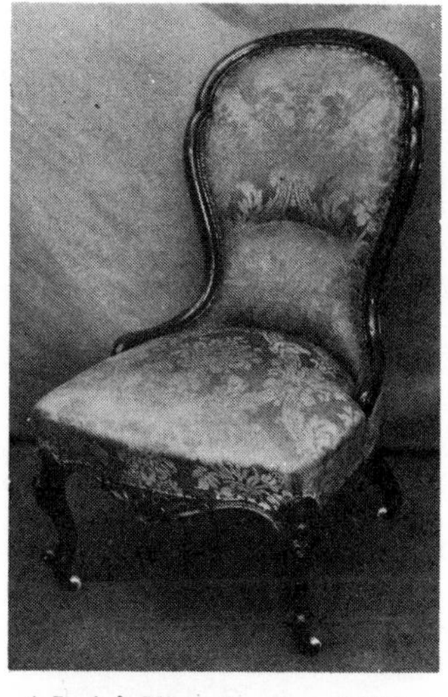

A Lady's Victorian Carved Walnut Spoonback Fireside Chair, c. 1850-60, 2 ft. 11½ in. high. **£400-500** OL

A Victorian Mahogany Chair, 43 in. high, c. 1870. **£175-200** SHA

A Rosewood Low Armchair, pierced vase splat flanked by double baluster spindles on twist-turned legs, 1840's. **£250-320** SB

A Victorian Carved Rosewood Frame Buttoned Back Easy Chair. **£290-310** A

A Victorian Rosewood Salon Chair, mid 19th C. **£250-350** SBA

A Pair of Regency mahogany bergeres. **£2,500-2,750** C

A Queen Anne period walnut-frame wing arm easy chair. **£900-990** SKC

A George I Small Arm Chair, extensively restored. **£300-380** L

A beechwood wing Armchair with arched eared padded back, on scroll feet, late 17th C. (restorations). **£680-750** C

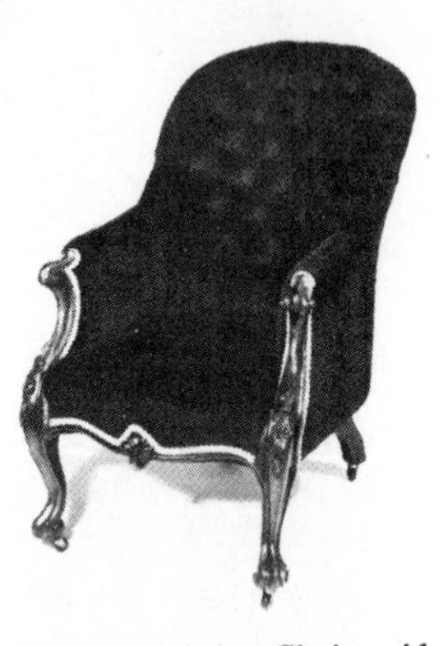

A Mahogany Salon Chair, mid 19th C. **£300-400** SBA

A fine pair of early George III mahogany window seats 40¾ in., 103.5 cm. wide, 31½ in., 80 cm. high. **£2,860-3,000** C

GUIDE TO STYLES

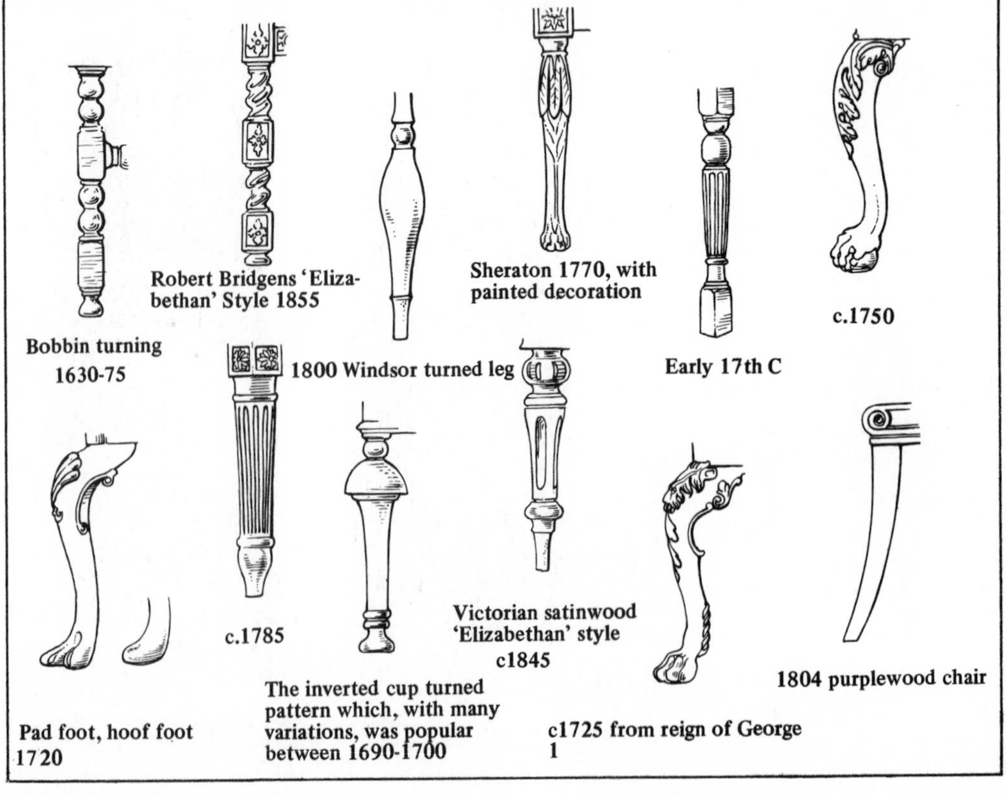

Bobbin turning 1630-75

Robert Bridgens 'Elizabethan' Style 1855

1800 Windsor turned leg

Sheraton 1770, with painted decoration

Early 17th C

c.1750

Pad foot, hoof foot 1720

c.1785

The inverted cup turned pattern which, with many variations, was popular between 1690-1700

Victorian satinwood 'Elizabethan' style c1845

c1725 from reign of George 1

1804 purplewood chair

A Set of Six Victorian Rosewood Salon Chairs, on serpentine shaped stuff over seats, cabriole legs, carved at the knees and terminating in carved scroll toes, some non-matching upholstery, c. 1860. **£820-920** L

A Set of Seven Victorian Walnut Dining Chairs, carved with leaves at the knees and scroll toes, one leg broken, c. 1850. **£750-850** L

A Pair of George II Mahogany Side Chairs. **£520-620** L

A Victorian Rosewood Salon Chair, mid 19th C. **£220-300** SBA

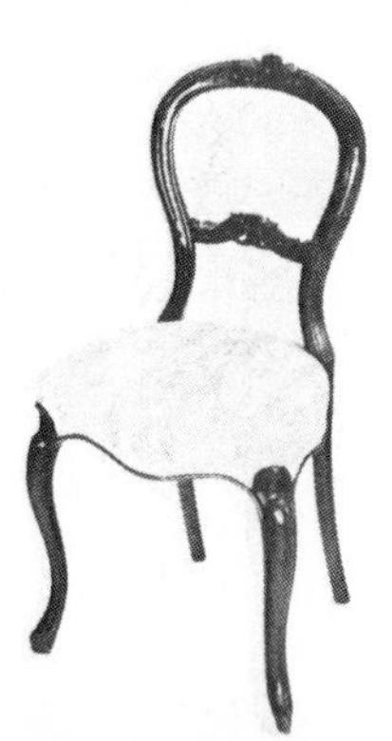

A Set of Six Victorian Walnut Drawing room Chairs. **£700-780** L

A Set of Four Georgian Oak Country Chairs, c1750. **£420-470 470** L

A Set of Four Mahogany Side Chairs on moulded cabriole legs, c. 1860. **£420-490** SB

A Victorian Rosewood Frame drawing room chair. **£250-300** L

A Set of Six Late Georgian Mahogany Side Chairs, c1830. **£620-700** L

A Fine 'Chippendale' Provincial Side Chair, seat in cherrytree, 21¼ wide, 17 in. deep, 37 in. high, c. 1760. **£185-200** TA

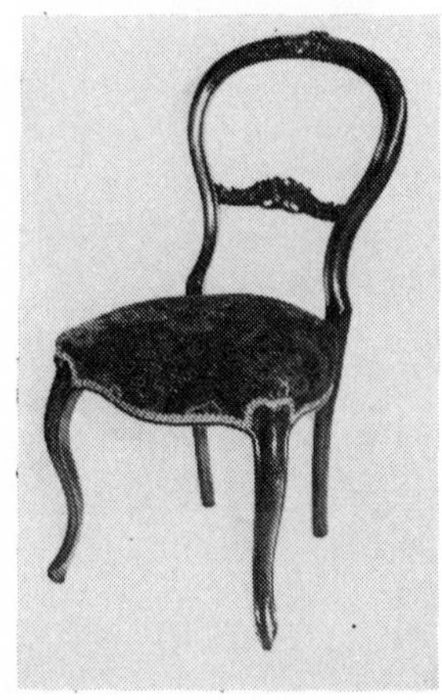

A Set of six Victorian walnut balloon-back Chairs. **£900-1,075** set SV

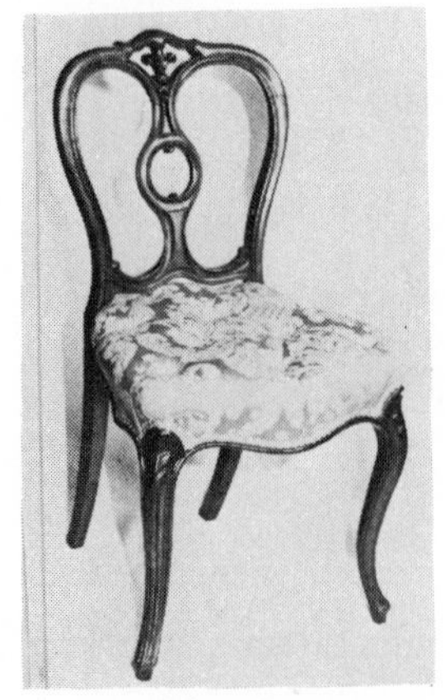

A set of four mid-Victorian balloon back walnut Chairs, stamped by Gillow. **£700-785** set SV

A Pair of Oak Chairs, c. 1720. **£780-880** pr CP

A Set of Six Victorian Mahogany Chairs with waisted balloon backs. **£600-700** L

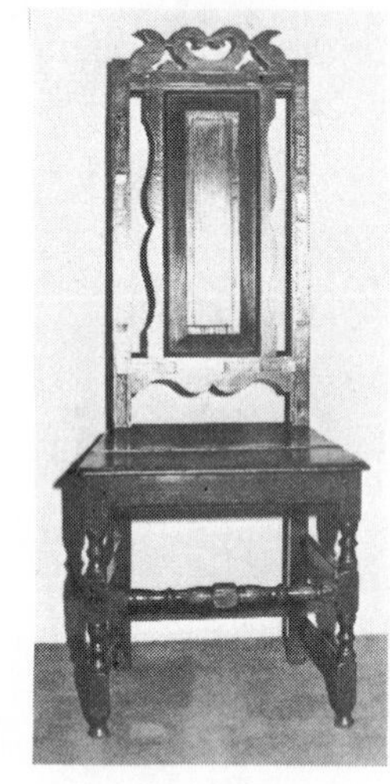

A Pair of Late 17th C. Oak High Back Chairs of good colour, c. 1685-1700. **£495-560** pr. RD

A Fine Oak Charles II Period "Fire of London" design Chair with cane panels, Spanish scroll feet with blue-bell carving to top rail, 19 in. wide, 15 in. deep, 42 in. high, c. 1670-80. **£340-380** TA

A Charles II Oak Slat Back Chair, with heart motif and unusual double ball turning and reverse baluster rail, 46 in. high. **£400-440** TA

Oak Country Chairs, c. 1820 single **£45-55+**, pair **£120-140**, set of 4 **£400-500** set of 6 **£700-800** CP

A Set of Six Mahogany Balloon Back Chairs, c. 1840. **£500-600** SB

A Set of Five Victorian Walnut Drawing Room Chairs, in Louis XV style. **£465-525** SH

A Pair of late 17th C oak solid seat hall chairs. **£500-550** SKC

A William and Mary Walnut Hall Chair. **£600-650** SKC

19th C Ebonised Hall Chair, possibly Dutch. **£50-70** STR

One of a pair of 19th C. Hall Chairs. **£100-115** pr. SV

One of a set of four Victorian Hall Chairs with painted emblem. **£360-390** SV

A Set of 8 Victorian mahogany balloon-back Chairs, c1855. **£800-900** SKC

Six fine quality Victorian mahogany dining chairs, the balloon backs with pierced foliate scroll clasps. **£620-700** O

A Set of six Victorian beech balloon-back Chairs. **£100-120** set SV

Victorian carved oak Folding Chair. **£45-60** STR

A Pair of Oak Splat-Back Country Chairs, c. 1720. **£150-180** pr., single **£60-70** DB

An Early 18th C. Oak Standard Chair. **£110-130** OB

An Oak Carolean 17th C. Chair with turned stretchers. **£110-130**, pair **£250-300** DB

An Oak Country Chippendale Chair, c. 1770. **£55-60** pair. A set of 6 **£500-560** (rare) OB

A Set of Six Georgian Oak Rush Seated Chairs, c. 1790. **£590-640** set SHA

Two Queen Anne Oak Chairs. **£130-150** SH

A pair of George I Oak Chairs. **£400-450** SH

A Pair of George I Oak Chairs. **£130-150** SH

A Mid 17th C. Oak Chair with carved back and turned legs, English. **£160-180** DB

An Early Georgian Corner Chair in elm, c. 1740. **£240-270** SHA

A George II Walnut Desk Chair, with horseshoe top rail. **£270-320** SH

One of four Art Nouveau inlaid oak Dining Chairs. **£440-480** A.D.H.

A pair of Louis XVI beechwood bergeres en encoignure, with detached baluster arm-supports, possibly Low Countries. **£770-900** C

A Pair of Regency Mahogany Chairs 'Thomas Hope' **£320-340** CSG

A Set of 6 Victorian carved oak Jacobean style Dining Chairs, some dissimilarities. **£400-450** PW

A George II Walnut Waiting Chair, c. 1750. **£395-420** OB

A Set of Eight Mahogany Dining Chairs with a dipped top-rail and waisted pierced splat on square tapering legs, inlaid with boxwood stringing, c. 1910. **£450-520** SB

A Set of 8 late 19th C mahogany chairs in the Chippendale style, comprising six standard and two carvers, c1890. **£1,080-1,150** SKC

A 19th C. inlaid Corner Chair, in need of re-upholstering. **£60-68** SV

A Set of 6 mahogany framed baloon-backed Dining Chairs. **£350-400** CE

GUIDE TO STYLES

Dates	Monarch	Period
1603-1625	James I	Jacobean
1625-1649	Charles I	Carolean
1649-1660	Commonwealth	Cromwellian
1660-1685	Charles II	Restoration
1685-1689	James II	Restoration
1689-1694	William & Mary	William & Mary
1694-1702	William III	William III or more often William & Mary
1702-1714	Anne	Queen Anne
1714-1727	George I	Early Georgian
1727-1760	George II	Georgian
1760-1812	George III	Late Georgian
1812-1820	George III	Regency
1820-1830	George IV	Regency
1830-1837	William IV	William IV
1837-1860	Victoria	Early Victorian
1860-1901	Victoria	Late Victorian

A Matched Set of Elm Chairs. Six. **£580-620** SH

A set of four late George III mahogany dining-chairs in the Louis XVI style. **£1,050-1,255** C

An unusual set of ten mahogany dining-chairs, 18th/19th C. possibly Anglo-Chinese. **£500-550** C

A Set of Six Sheraton Period Mahogany Dining Chairs, c. 1790. **£590-650** L

A Matched set of eight 18th C North Country Dining Chairs, including two armchairs (some restoration). **£1,070-1,150** SH

A Set of Four George III Mahogany Dining Chairs in the Sheraton style, one slightly damaged. **£400-500** L

A Harlequin set of six Elm Ladderback Chairs. **£240-280** SH

A Set of Eight George III Mahogany Dining-Chairs including a pair of armchairs with comb splats. **£2,600-2,850** C

A set of four walnut Dining-Chairs in the style of Daniel Marot, on cabriole legs, joined by waved stretchers, c. 1700 (restorations). **£2,500-2,750** C

A Set of Six Mahogany Veneered Dining Chairs, German, 1840's. **£600-700** SB

A set of 8 early Victorian walnut single Dining Chairs. **£740-800** NF

One of a Set of 6 early Victorian Mahogany Dining Chairs with Trafalgar seats, c1840. **£550-650** STR

A Set of 4 mid-Victorian carved rosewood Occasional Chairs. **£360-400** PW

A Set of Six Victorian Mahogany Dining Chairs. **£520-600** L

One of a Set of 6 Victorian Mahogany Dining Chairs, with turned legs and over-stuffed seats, c1870. **£380-480** STR

A Set of Six William IV Campaign Dining Chairs, the front legs unscrew, the rear legs are removable. **£550-650** L

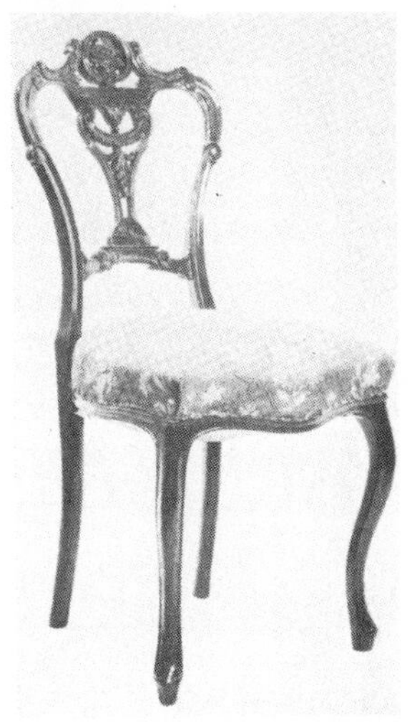

A Set of 4 mahogany Occasional Chairs. **£290-350** PW

One of a set of six Victorian Chairs. **£600-650** set. SV

A Set of Six Early Victorian Mahogany Dining Chairs. **£300-380** L

Seven William IV Dining Chairs (carver and 6 single chairs). **£600-680** BW

Six Late Regency Mahogany Dining Chairs, c1830. **£780-880** L

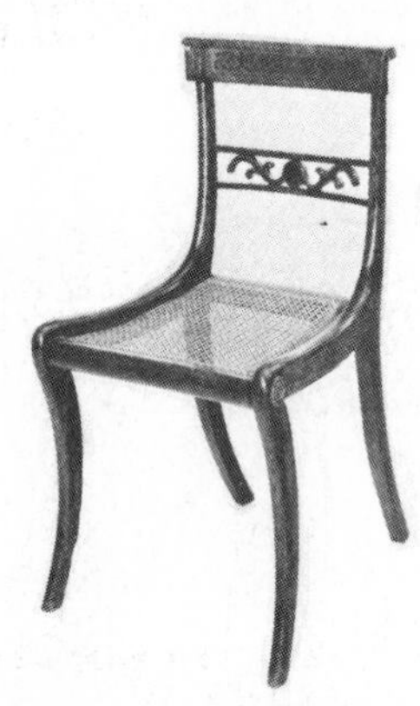

A Set of Six Regency Simulated Rosewood Dining Chairs, the curved top rail inlaid with cut brass scrollwork, some faults. **£1,000-1,200** L

A Set of six Regency mahogany rail-back Chairs, four standards and two carvers, c1810. **£1,450-1,500** SKC

A Set of Eight Late Regency Rosewood Dining Chairs with curved cresting rails. **£900-1,000** L

A Set of Eight William IV Rosewood Dining Chairs with solid curved cresting rails, stylised horizontal splats. **£1,100-1,300** L

A good set of 8 early 19th C mahogany Dining Chairs, string inlaid and with satinwood panel (the 2 elbow chairs, 4 standard chairs matched and 2 side chairs very closely match). **£850-950** P.W.C.

A Set of six William IV mahogany Chairs. **£580-640** set SV

A Set of 6 Regency Mahogany Dining Chairs. **£1,000-1,200** M

A Set of Nine Late Regency Mahogany Dining Chairs including two armchairs, all with lift out seats and sabre supports. **£1,850-2,030** L

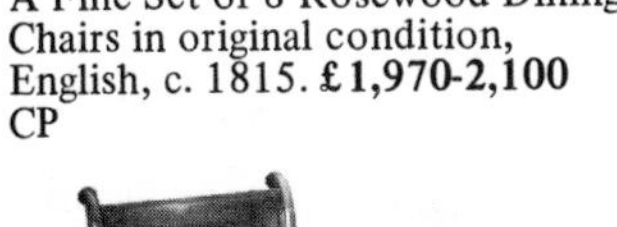

A Fine Set of 8 Rosewood Dining Chairs in original condition, English, c. 1815. **£1,970-2,100** CP

A Set of Four Regency Mahogany Dining Chairs including one arm chair, with rope twist horizontal bars, fluted curved cresting rails. **£500-600** L

A set of eight Regency-style mahogany framed dining chairs, brass inlaid reeded horizontal splats. **£1,000-1,200** SBe

Three Regency Mahogany Dining Chairs. **£200-250** L

Seven Regency mahogany dining chairs (1 elbow, 6 single). **£810-900** O

A set of 8 William IV mahogany dining chairs (including 2 elbow chairs). **£1,550-1,700** PWC

A Set of Eight late Regency Mahogany Dining Chairs including two arm chairs, restored. **£2,000-2,500** L

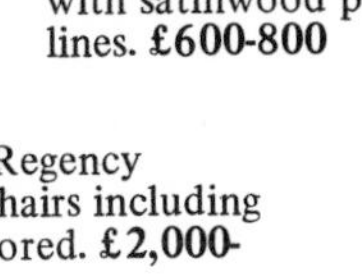

A Set of Six Regency Mahogany Dining-Chairs the top-rails inlaid with satinwood panels and brass lines. **£600-800** C

Set of six Regency period mahogany Dining Chairs. **£1,150-1,300** EBB

One Carver and 5 Elm Dining Chairs, c. 1800. **£390-420** OB

One of a set of six Regency Style Chairs, 2 carvers, 4 single. **£290-325** set SV

A Set of 6 Harlequin Suffolk Chairs, in oak and sycamore, c. 1830. **£290-330** SHA

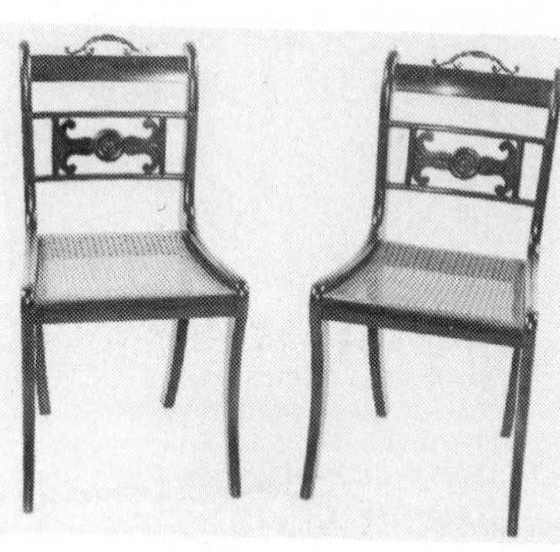

Seven Regency simulated rosewood Dining Chairs. **£800-900** BW

A Set of four Regency ebonised and gilded dining-chairs painted en grisaille with dolphins and trellis-pattern splats, on turned tapering legs (re-decorated); a pair of dining-chairs and a pair of armchairs en suite of later date. **£3,000-3,300** C

A Good set of 6 Rope Back, Sabre Legged, Mahogany Dining Chairs, grained to simulate rosewood having an applied brass motif, c. 1815-25, 2 ft. 10 in. high. **£1,750-1,950** OL

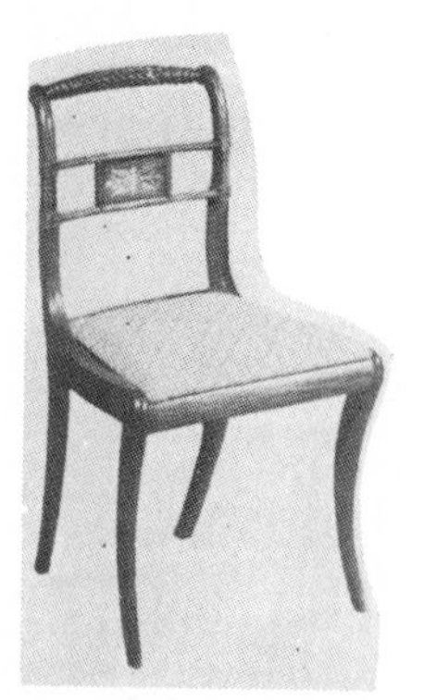

A Set of 6 Regency mahogany Dining Chairs, c1820. **£1,600-1,800** AG

A set of eight Regency ebonized and gilded dining-chairs including a pair of armchairs. **£3,200-3,600** C

A Pair of George III Mahogany Single Chairs with shaped C-scroll decorated cresting rails, pierced and carved splats. **£180-240** pr. DH

A Set of 6 19th C. Elm Lancashire Ladder Back Single Chairs. **£850-950** DH

A Set of 4 Single and 2 Carver Mahogany Dining Chairs with square reeded backs. **£900-1,000** DH

One of a set of six 19th C. Chairs. **£340-375** Set SV

A Set of 6 Ash and Elm Ladder Back Chairs, all in good order, (one new seat), c. 1800. **£520-620** set. SHA

A Pair of Early 19th C. Fruitwood Chairs. **£275-300** CSG

One of a set of eight 19th C. Ladder-back Chairs. **£750-825** set. SV

A set of six 17th C oak dining chairs. **£1,050-1,150** PWC

A Late 17th C. James II Chair with slat back, probably from S. Yorkshire. **£320-350** TA

A Set of Three Georgian Mahogany Dining Chairs, with pierced centre splats. **£900-1,000** L

A Set of Six Mahogany Dining Chairs in the Heppelwhite manner, 19th C. **£770-850** L

A Set of Six Regency Ebonised Dining-Chairs bobbin-turned top-rails and bar splats mounted with gilt-metal roundels on sabre legs, Scottish. **£520-570** C

A Set of 6 George III 'Hepplewhite' Mahogany Dining Chairs, the frames stamped with maker's name R.C. **£750-850** B

A Set of Six Late Georgian Mahogany Dining Chairs, with pierced vase splats, carved with leafage. **£750-900** L

A fine set of fourteen George III mahogany dining-chairs. **£8,200-9,000** C

One of pair of George II walnut chairs c1740. **£2,000-2,500** Bon.

A Set of 6 19th C Chippendale-style carved mahogany chairs, c1870. **£860-960** SKC

A Set of 6 George III Oak Dining Chairs, late 18th C. **£350-450** SBA

A Set of Six 'George III' Mahogany Dining Chairs, each with a yoke-shaped top-rail, 1920's. **£220-400** SB

A Set of Seven Sheraton Mahogany Dining Chairs, including one elbow chair, restorations, George III. **£660-740** L

DETAILS OF CHAIR BACKS

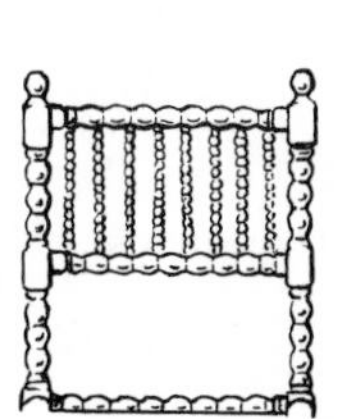

- 1670 Walnut chair, with scrolled front legs and stretcher caned seat & splat panels.

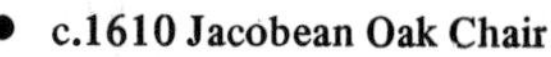

- c.1610 Jacobean Oak Chair

- 1660 fruitwood joined chair, with ball turning

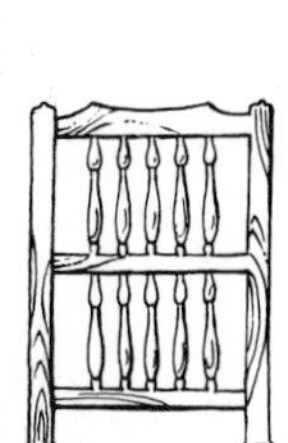

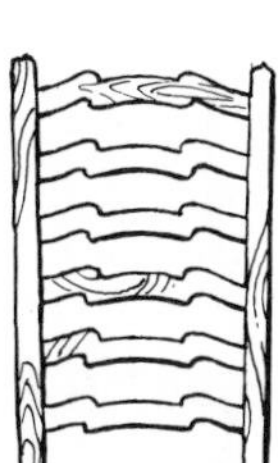

- c.1725 carved & gilt Walnut chair with caning

- 18th C Country spindle back.

- c.1785 Ladderback chair

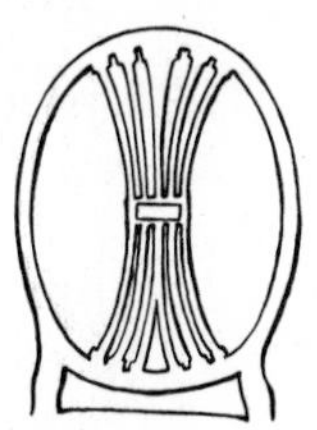

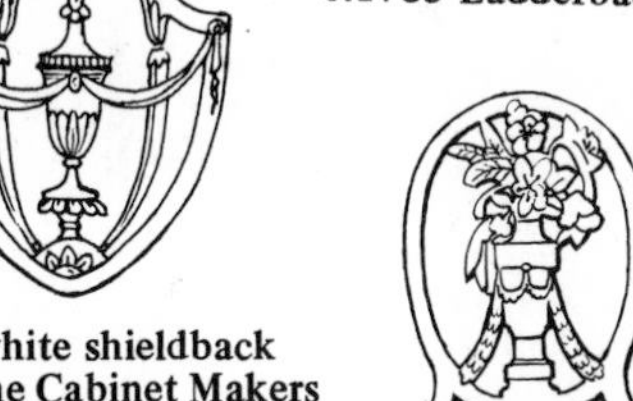

- Hepplewhite shieldback from 'The Cabinet Makers Upholsterers Guide' published 1788

- Resembling chairs made by John Linnell (1720-63) often veneered in satinwood & Kingwood. Neo-Classic.

- Hepplewhite 'Wheatsheaf' pattern c.1786

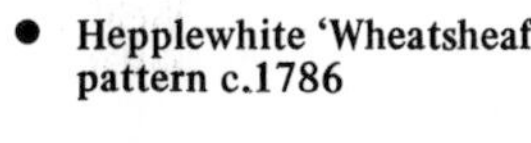

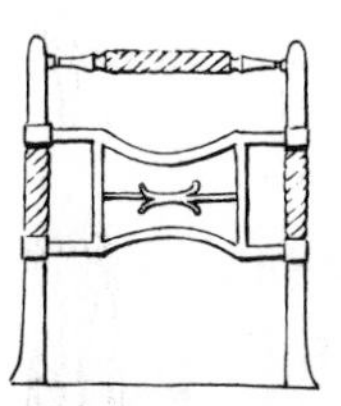

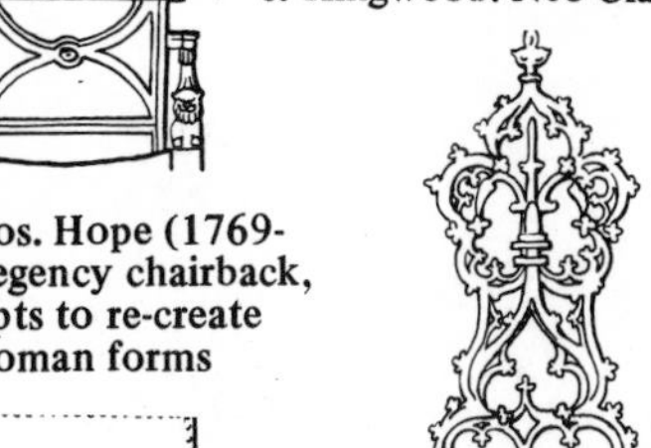

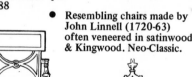

- 1807 Thos. Hope (1769-1831) Regency chairback, in attempts to re-create Greek/Roman forms

- 1805 Regency 'Trafalgar' Chair the gilt cable moulding of the back is a nautical emblem

- 1826 chair from A.C. Pugin's 'Gothic Furniture'

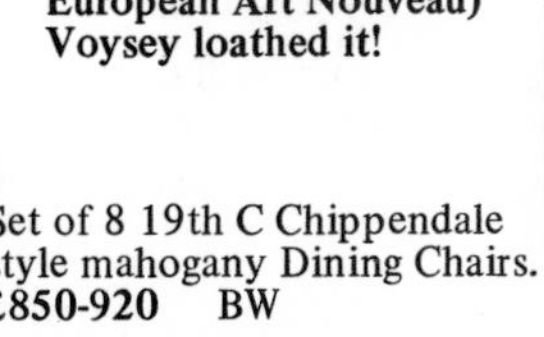

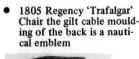

- 1899 Commercial adaptation of C.F.A. Voysey design. (Acknowledged by certain designers of European Art Nouveau) Voysey loathed it!

Set of 8 19th C Chippendale style mahogany Dining Chairs. **£850-920** BW

A Set of Six George III Mahogany Dining Chairs in the Chippendale style. **£1,200-1,400** L

A Set of Six Mahogany Dining Chairs, including one armchair, in the Chippendale manner. **£500-600** L

A Mid-Georgian Mahogany Dining-Chair, **£700-750** C

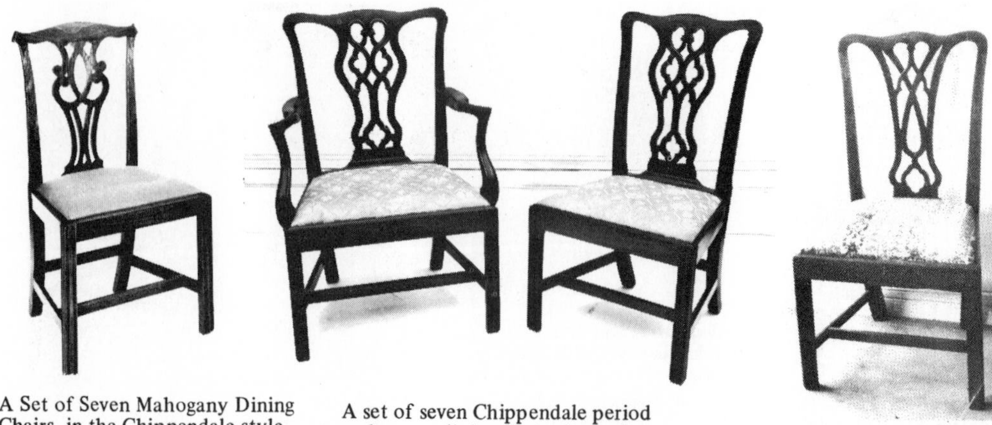

A Set of Seven Mahogany Dining Chairs, in the Chippendale style, including one armchair, with pierced case splats. **£1,300-1,450** L

A set of seven Chippendale period mahogany dining chairs (including one elbow chair). **£2,450-2,500** PWC

A Set of 6 Georgian single Dining Chairs. **£870-970** HG

A Pair of Country 'Chippendale' Elm and Fruitwood Dining Chairs, c. 1760-70. **£350 -380** pr, single **£120-150** RD

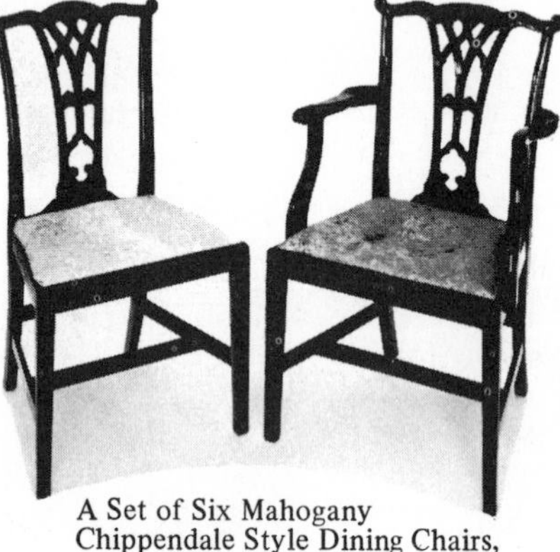

A Set of Six Mahogany Chippendale Style Dining Chairs, including two armchairs, with centre pierced Gothic style splats. **£430-500** L

A Set of six early George III mahogany dining-chairs, H-shaped stretchers (one back rail replaced, the others re-supported). **£1,500-1,650** C

A Queen Anne Elm Cabriole Leg Chair, bold splat with heart motif, c. 1700-10. **£420-440** if walnut **£1,000+** TA

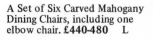

A Set of 10 late Victorian carved mahogany chairs in the Chippendale style, c1900. **£1,550-1,600** SKC

A Set of Six Carved Mahogany Dining Chairs, including one elbow chair. **£440-480** L

A Set of Eight 'George II' Mahogany Dining Chairs, with arched top-rail and waisted pierced splat, on scroll feet, c. 1880. **£1,800-2,050** SB

A Good Set of 4 George III Style Dining Chairs, late 19th C. **£700-800** SBA

A Set of Six 19th C Hepplewhite-style mahogany dining chairs. **£1,150-1,200** SKC

A Good Set of Six Hepplewhite Mahogany Dining Chairs. **£1,400-1,500** L

A Good Set of Six Hepplewhite Mahogany Dining Chairs. **£3,800-4,000** L

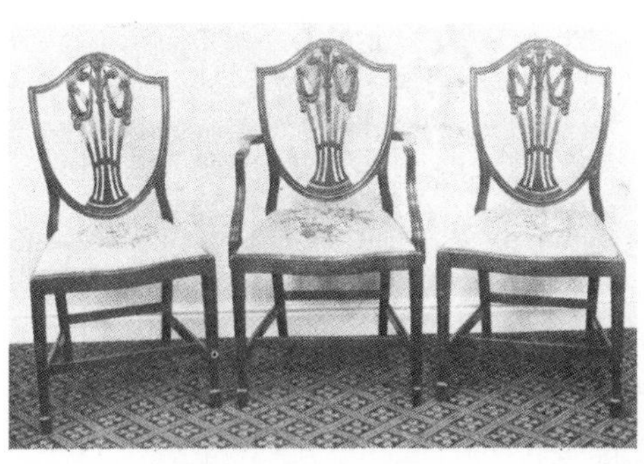

A Choice Set of 6 Hepplewhite Design Mahogany Dining Chairs, comprising 4 singles and 2 carvers, having shield-shaped backs, carved with Prince of Wales feathers and drapes. **£1,200-1,400** M

A Set of Three Chippendale Mahogany Dining Chairs, c1760. **£280-360** L

A Pair of George I Walnut Dining-Chairs. **£1,250-1,325** pr. C

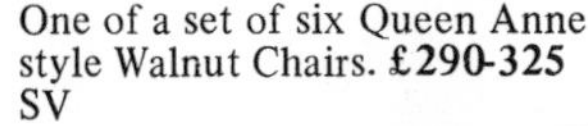

One of a set of six Queen Anne style Walnut Chairs. **£290-325** SV

One of a set of six 19th C. walnut Chairs. **£500-575** set SV

A Pair of late 18th C marquetry inlaid mahogany standard chairs. **£180-200** CD

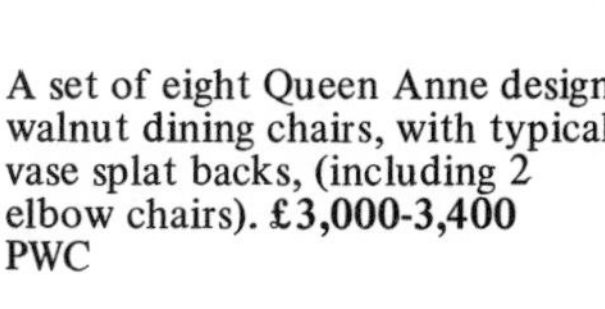

A set of eight Queen Anne design walnut dining chairs, with typical vase splat backs, (including 2 elbow chairs). **£3,000-3,400** PWC

A Pair of George I walnut dining-chairs with arched backs and solid urn-shaped splats. **£700-775** C

A Set of Six George II Mahogany Dining-Chairs on cabriole legs edged with C-scrolls and pad feet, possibly American. **£5,400-5,950** C

A Set of 6 early 18th C walnut Dining Chairs, c1710. **£1,350-1,500** AG

A pair of Louis XV provincial beechwood chairs. **£330-400** C

A Set of 8 Victorian Walnut Dining Chairs. **£305-350** SKC

A set of six George III mahogany dining-chairs on square legs and H-shaped stretchers. **£2,600-2,900** C

19th C. pine kitchen carver chair with turned legs and splats. **£50-60** SSP

Kitchen Chair from Midlands. **£18** each SSP

A Set of four George III mahogany dining-chairs with moulded cabriole legs headed by shells. **£800-880** C

18th C. pine Fool's chair from Yorkshire. **£24-30** SSP

A set of six 19th C. pine Kitchen Chairs with turned legs and splats **£140–170** MS

A set of four 19th C. pine Kitchen Chairs with pierced centre splats flanked by turned splats and on turned legs. **£95–110** MS

A set of six 19th C. pine bar-back Kitchen Chairs. **£140–170** MS

A Childrens 'Barber's' High Chair in ash and fruitwood, 15 in. wide, 16 in. deep, 37 in. high, c. 1830. **£295-340** TA

A 19th C. Child's Commode Chair in beech. **£55–65** MS

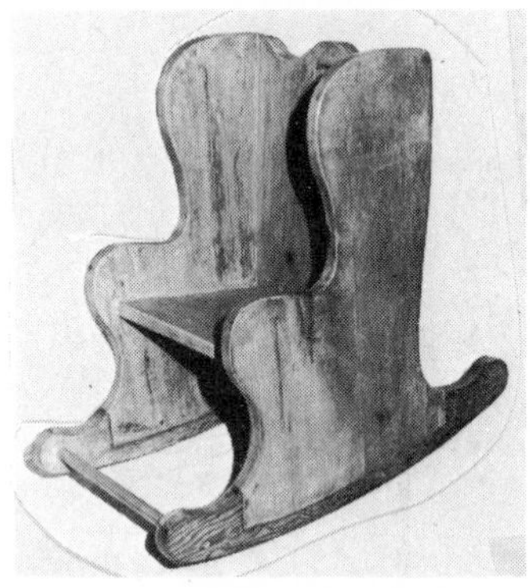
A 19th C. Child's pine Rocking Chair with pitch pine rockers. **£55–65** MS

A 19th C Walnut Country-made Child's Chair. **£50-80** STR

A Child's Oak High Chair, 17th/18th C. **£105-140** C

A Superb Small Charles II Period Child's Chair in Oak with roundal carved top rail signed L.W., top centre restored, 18 in. wide, 14 in. deep, 40½ in. high, c. 1660. **£255-275** TA

A 19th C. elm Child's Chair with turned side rails and legs. **£55–65** MS

Childs Chair with rush seat. **£40-45** SSP

An Antique oak Cock-Fighting Chair. **£165-200** SAL

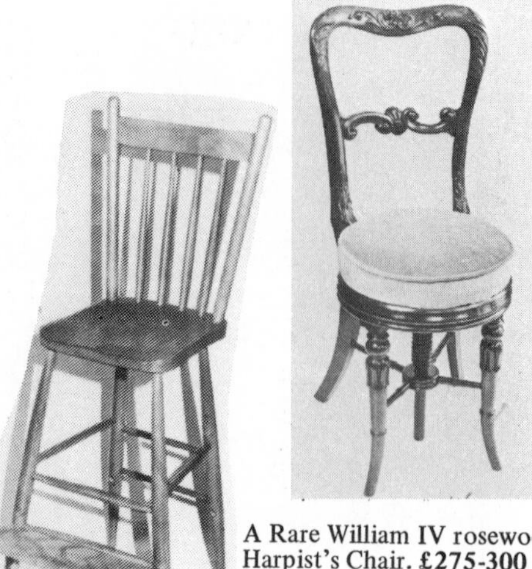

19th C. Child's High Chair in beech, with plain turned splats, legs and stretchers. **£30–40** AL

A Rare William IV rosewood Harpist's Chair. **£275-300** SAL

A Victorian Nursing Chair, the ebonised beech frame with gilt mounts. **£55-65** PW

An interesting country night commode chair, the back panel painted with name 'James Slade. Maker, Febry 5th. 1837 in the 88th year of his age.' 42 in., 107 cm. high. **£250-300** L

A Pair of Early Victorian Rosewood Prie-Dieu Chairs, c1850 **£100-120** L

A Carved Walnut Chair, c1860. **£165-185** SAL

A Bugatti Chair, impressed with B.C. initials, 35" high. **£1,100-1,300** CSK

A pair of Italian Limewood Throne Chairs with carved top-rails centred by a mask. **£900-1,000** pr. C

A Very Fine 18th C. Hall Porter's Chair in mahogany. **£2,000-2,200** SA

JOINED STOOLS

A 17th C Oak Joined Stool, 45cms. **£430-450** SH

A James I Joyned Stool, of North Devon origin, with lunette rail carving, c. 1630. **£800-870** TA

A 17th C Oak Joined Stool, 52cms. **£650-700** SH

An oak Joint Stool on turned legs with understretchers, 16¼" high. **£600-700** AG

A 17th C Oak Joined Stool, width 18". **£380-420** SH

A mid 17th C Oak Joined Stool, 46cms. **£450-500** SH

An Early 18th C. Child's Joint Stool, 18 in. high, 14 in. wide, wrong top **£180-210** with right top **£300-350** DB

An Important Oak Joint Stool with carved frieze and gun barrel turned legs, 27 in. wide, 24 in. high, late 17th C. **£500-560** DB

A Late 17th C. Oak Joint Stool, with boxwood and ebony inlaid frieze, 21 in. high, a bit battered. **£320-350** perfect **£450-500** DB

18th C. pine joint stool with restored top. **£30-40** SSP

A 19th C. Joint Stool in 17th C. Style. **£125-150** RD

A Finely Carved 19th C. Mahogany Stool in the George II style, the cabriole legs boldly carved, 24 in. high, 19 in. top, c. 1860. **£375-450** Original George II **£1,500+** RD

A George I red walnut close stool, width 21 in., 53 cm., c. 1720. **£420-500** SBe

A pair of early George III mahogany Stools, 21½in (55.5cm) wide, **£6,000-7,000** C

A George I walnut and elm stool (re-supported and restoration) 21½ in., 54.5 cm. wide., 16½ in. 42 cm. high. **£460-500** C

A Mahogany Stool in original condition, 21 in. long, 17 in. deep, 17 in. high, c. 1780. **£225-300** CP

A pair of George III cream and grey-painted Window-Seats, cut down, 44in (112cm) wide, **£600-700** C

A George III cream-painted Window-Seat, 37½in (95cm) wide, **£300-350** C

A 'Thebes' stool by Liberty & Co. Ltd., ivory retailer's label, design registered 1884, 14½" high. **£110-140** CSK

A 19th C. pitch pine Footstool. 12 in. wide, 6 in. deep. **£8–10** MS

Small, early 19th C., pine stool. **£10–12** AL

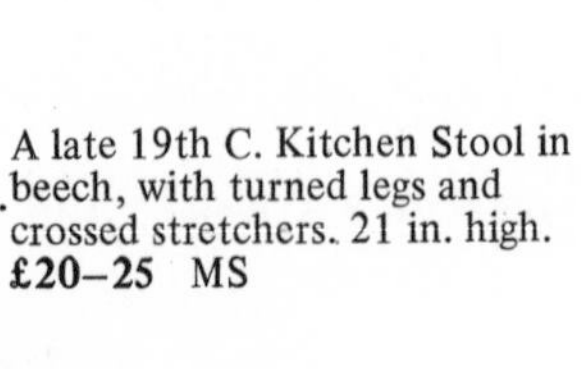

A late 19th C. Kitchen Stool in beech, with turned legs and crossed stretchers. 21 in. high. **£20–25** MS

A set of three George III mahogany window seats 30 in., 76 cm. wide. **£2,600-2,700** C

Early 19th C Milking Stool in elm. **£15-25** STR

Small 19th C. stool with turned pine legs and oak top. 10 in. wide, 7 in. deep. **£8–10** AL

An early 19th C. pitch pine Foot-stool. 12 in. x 6 in. **£8–10** MS

An 18th C. fruitwood Milking Stool. **£40–50** SM

A small 19th C. elm Stool on close-turned legs. **£25–30** MS

Late 19th C. beech Kitchen Stool, the oval seat with mainetrou. **£18–22** MM

MINIATURE FURNITURE

A Miniature Japanese black lacquer Cabinet-on-Stand with inset ivory panels with gold on lacquer scrolls, 19th C., 1 ft. 4¾ in., long, 2 ft. ¾ in. high, **£220-280** OL

An Apprentice Chair, c. 1840, 12 in. high. **£220-246** HD

A miniature Chest of Drawers, made up from old pine. 22 in. high, 24 in. long. **£70–80** P and D

An Early George III Style Mahogany Bureau Cabinet, 4 in. **£100-150** CSK

A George I Style Mahogany Tallboy, 3¼ in. **£100-150** CSK

A George II walnut small cabinet-on-stand, bearing a label inscribed Colonel M. Beevor 17 in., 43 cm. wide. **£660-760** C

A Mid-Georgian Style Mahogany Low Dresser, 6½ in. **£50-80** CSK

An Early 18th C Solid Walnut Miniature Chest 9½ in. wide, 11 in. high. **£290-310** CC

Miniature chest of drawers, 10½ in. wide, 11½ in. high, 5 in. deep. **£32-42** AL

A Georgian Mahogany Miniature Chest of Drawers, c. 1800, 7 in. high, 6 in. deep. **£165-185** SA

Regency Pine Shelves with simulated bamboo, c. 1810. **£125-150** CP

Late 18th C. Mahogany Shelves. **£190-210** CC

An early 19th C. pine Gun Rack, unpolished. 54 in. high, 60 in. wide. **£250–300** SM

19th C. pine Hanging Bookshelves with shaped sides and divided lower shelf. 26 in. wide, 39 in. high, 8 in. deep. **£45–50** AL

19th C. pine Hanging Shelves with shaped sides, of deep golden colour. 18 in. wide, 16 in. high, 5 in. deep. **£20–25** AL

18th C. pine hanging Bookshelves with shaped sides and narrow, reeded cornice. 35 in. wide, 31 in. high, 7 in. deep. **£70–75** AL

Late 19th C. pine set of Pigeon Holes, used as display unit. 51 in. wide, 25 in. high, 12½ in. deep. **£100–125** AL

19th C. pine Hanging Shelves with support rails and shaped sides. 26½ in. wide, 21 in. high, 6 in. deep. **£36-42** AL

A 19th C. mahogany Bracket, 11 in. high. **£35-39** SV

A pair of Italian stripped pine Wall Brackets **£150–200** SM

Pair of matching, 19th C., pine Hanging Shelves with attractively shaped sides and deep golden colour. 26 in. high, 25 in. wide, **£70–80** AL

A 19th C. pine wall hanging Kitchen Plate Rack. **£5–8** MM

A set of late 19th C. pine Wall hanging Corner Shelves with shaped sides and front. 30 in. high. **£45–60** SM

WASHSTANDS

Corner cupboard washstand with plug and chain 42 in. high 27 in. deep. **£90-100** AL

19th C. pine Washstand with high back, two drawers, shaped frieze and turned legs with side stretchers. 36 in. wide, 39 in. high, 20 in. deep. **£60–65** AL

Small 19th C. pine Washstand with scalloped back and sides, turned legs and drawer to base. 24 in. wide, 34 in. high, 15 in. deep. **£35–40** AL

Washstand with cupboard. 30 in. wide 29 in. high 16 in. deep. **£65-70** AL

An Edwardian pine Marble Topped Washstand with two drawers, fretwork sides and shaped centre stretcher. **£50–60** MM

Small 19th C. pine Washstand with high shaped back and one drawer in base. 38 in. high, 29 in. wide, 16 in. deep. **£40-45** (exclusive of Jug and Basin) AL

Late Victorian Adjustable Shaving Mirror, (with counter-balance). **£120-150** STR

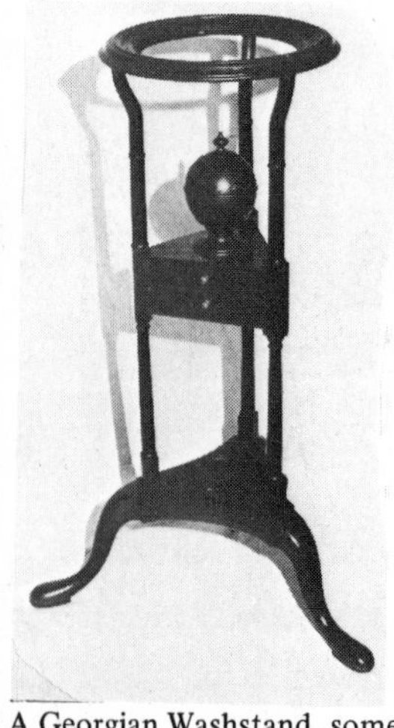

A Georgian Washstand, some restoration, 30 in. high, c. 1750. **£340-380** SHA

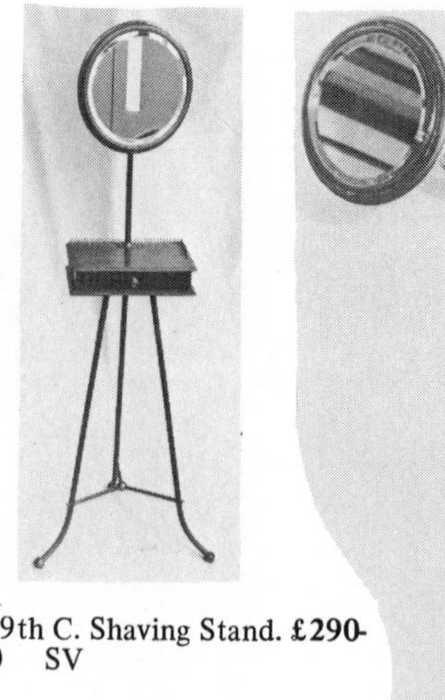

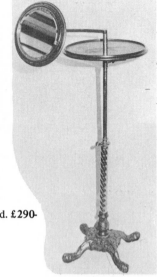

A 19th C. Shaving Stand. **£290-320** SV

Victorian Adjustable Shaving Stand and Mirror, with cast-iron base and brass column. **£90-120** STR

BEDS

An Italian walnut Four-Poster Bedstead with partly fluted Corinthian capital up-supports partly 17th C, 70in (178cm) wide; 108in (274cm) high. **£3,500-4,500** C

An oak Four-Post Bed of Gothic style with moulded cornice, 73in (185.5cm) wide **£1,000-1,200** C

A mahogany Four-Poster Bedstead with moulded cornice and reeded posts, partly 18th C, 54in (137cm) wide; 88in (223.5cm) high. **£2,000-2,500** C

A Good Victorian mahogany half tester bed, 5' wide. **£880-1,100** P.W.C.

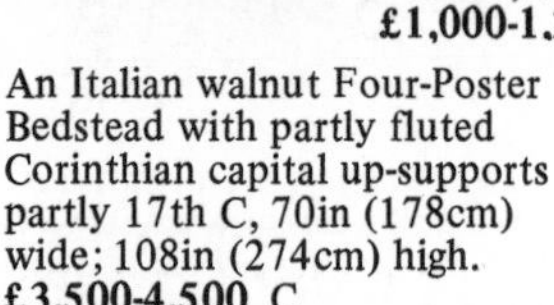

A Georgian mahogany half-tester Bed, 70in (178cm) wide, **£500-600** C

A Massive Carved Oak Four Poster Bedstead in 16th C. style, fitted with box base and spring mattress, a reconstruction using various timbers from 17th and 19th centuries, overall 88 in., 224 cm. long x 64 in., 163 cm. wide x 94 in., 239 cm. high. **£2,000-2,300** L

Large Scandinavian Double Bed. 72 in. wide. **£885-895** P&D

A 19th C. pine Rocking Cradle. **£115–125** MS

A 19th C. pine Folding Bed with turned legs and reeded rails. 72 in. long, 24 in. wide. **£95–110** MS

A large Victorian Mahogany Sarcophagus Cellarette, 33" x 25". **£370-420** A

A George III Mahogany Octagonal Wine Cooler, late 18th C, 27" x 18½" (69cms x 47cms). **£700-800** SBA

WINE COOLERS

A Fine Chippendale Mahogany Cushioned Top Cellaret with fitted interior and brass carrying handles. **£480-570** M

A Regency mahogany wine-cooler, with a zinc-lined interior later liner. 27 in., 68.5 cm. wide. **£3,400-3,900** C

A George III Mahogany Wine Cooler, crossbanded and inlaid with stringing, 18½ in., 46 cm. **£550-625** L

A 19th C Mahogany Urn Stand, in the Chippendale manner, with sliding drip tray, c 1860, 13½" (34cms). **£200-230** L

An 18th C. pine Rocking Cradle. **£180–200** GW

A George III brass-bound mahogany wine-cooler, the hinged lid with circular opening and japanned liner, 11 in., 28 cm. wide. **£1,050-1,150** C

A George III Octagonal Mahogany Wine Cooler, the top decorated with featherbanding. **£1,600-1,800** SKC

A Circular Hardwood Urn Stand with an inset marble top, 67.5 cm. x 58.5 cm., c. 1900. **£200-250** SB SBe

A Rosewood Double Urn Stand, 74 cm. x 70 cm., c. 1900. **£170-200** SB SBe

A 19th C. Hardwood Stand, inlaid with mother-of-pearl, 31½ in. high. **£200-230** SV

A Victorian Stand, with faults, 14 in. high. **£60-68** SV

A Large Stained Rosewood Urn Stand, 112 cm. x 63 cm., mid 19th C. **£225-250** SB SBe

A Georgian Mahogany Commode, 30 in. high, 21 in. wide, c. 1780. **£340-380** SHA

A Good 18th C. German Walnut Commode, with original brass fretted handles, 48 in. wide x 32 in. high, 122 x 81 cms. **£780-880** B

A 19th C. Boxwood strung, floral marquetry inlaid and ormolu mounted serpentine front kingwood Commode, 2 ft. 2 in. wide, 1 ft. 3 in. deep, 32 in. high. **£420-500** V

A 19th C Louis XV-style ormolu mounted and floral marquetry inlaid kingwood Bombe Commode, 3'6". £1,100-1,300 CD

A Louis XV Oak Commode, 122cms. **£470-530** SH

A late 18th C. Dutch mahogany bombe commode, width 33 in., 85 cm., c. 1780. **£1,050-1,150** SBe

A 19th C Continental Mahogany Commode, 82.5cms wide. **£550-600** SH

A Georgian Mahogany Tray Top Commode, 21½" (54cms) wide, 19" (48cms) deep, 30½" (77cms) high. **£240-290** L

A 19th C. French kingwood and marquetry commode in the Louis XV style, veined rouge marble serpentine top, width 27½ in., 70 cm., marble top damaged. **£410-500** SBe

A Georgian Mahogany Commode (converted). **£98-108** CSG

A Kingwood 19th C French petite commode, 18" wide. **£470-500** SH

19th C. pitch pine Commode with diagonal-planked front panel. **£40–45 (plants extra!)** AL

COFFERS

A 16th C Spanish walnut cassone, 54" wide. **£800-900** PWC

A late 16th/early 17th C Italian walnut cassone, 5' wide. **£950-1,050** PWC

A late 17th C polarwood Italian Casonne, 5'2" x 1'10". **£590-690** Buc

An oak Coffer with parquetry panels of holly and ebony, mid-17th C, 53½in (136cm) wide. **£1,000-1,200** C

A 17th C. Italian Walnut Cassonne with carved decoration and marquetry, on lions' paw feet, 63 in. wide, 20 in. deep, 22 in. high, c. 1650. **£1,425-1,625** RD

A fine Charles I small oak Coffer with moulded hinged lid enclosing a small drawer, hinge replaced, 27 in (68.5cm) wide. **£800-1,000**

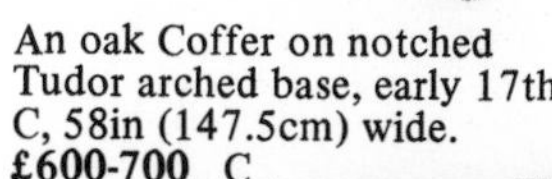
An oak Coffer on notched Tudor arched base, early 17th C, 58in (147.5cm) wide. **£600-700** C

A Continental antique oak Chest, with iron side handles, 4'7¼". **£380-400** GC

A 17th C Oak Coffer, carved to the front and sides, 5'2" (158cms) wide. **£610-680** SKC

A 17th C Coffer, 48" x 18".
£190-210 A

POINTERS FOR COFFERS

- Until the end of 18th C. the most usual form of storage.
- Earliest form, scooped out tree trunk with crude lid.
- 13th C. crude carving and hinged lids with locks.
- 16th C. joined frames with panels and possibly with carving and inlays.
- 17th C. introduction of the mule chest, a coffer with two drawers in base.
- 18th C. use of Walnut and lighter wood often mounted on stands.
- 19th C. often over-carved to appear Gothic.

A 16th C German Chest with marquetry inlay, 67" wide (170cms). **£440-500** B

An Early 17th C. Coffer with linen-fold carving, original lock plate, 40 in. x 18 in. x 28 in. high. **£750-830** DB

An oak Coffer, with lunette frieze, 17th C. 51 in. (131 cm.). **£520-570** C

A Particularly Rare Elizabethan 10-Panel Centre-of-the-Room Chest, with unrecorded top rail carving, with fruitwood and bog-wood geometric inlay, in original condition, except for lock plate 62 in. long, 24 in. wide, 30 in. high. **£2,000+** TA

A 17th C Panelled Oak Coffer, width 55" **£200-250** SH

A 16th C Oak Coffer, 3'10" (117cms) wide. **£1,720-1,850** SKC

An early 17th C Oak Coffer, fitted with iron-handles, 4'2" (127cms) wide. **£900-990** SKC

A Good 17th C. Oak Coffer, 23 in. high, 41 in. wide, 15 in. deep. **£545-620** CP

A 16th C panelled oak Coffer with linenfold panels to front, some damage, 48" x 23". **£900-1,000** BW

A Late 17th C. Panelled Oak Coffer, 50 in. long, 26 in. high, 22 in. deep, c. 1690. **£330-360** OB

Late 17th C Oak Coffer, 40" x 19" x 25" high. **£400-500** STR

An Oak Coffer with plank top and triple-panelled front on moulded block feet, 17th C. 62¼ in., 158 cm. wide. **£500-550** C

A Georgian Black and Gold Lacquer Coffer on stand decorated 50 in., 127 cm. wide. **£1,000-1,100** C

An Oak and Yew small Coffer with cupboard door pierced with a lozenge and roundel, 17th C. 30 in , 76 cm. wide. **£900-990** C

A 19th C. pitch pine panelled Coffer, the interior fitted with one deep drawer and candle box. 22 in. wide, 12 in. high, 11 in. deep. **£45–55** MS

Early coffer with planked top and three panels. **£200-230** AL

Planked coffer with drop front. 37 in. wide 22 in. high 20 in. deep. **£52-62** AL

19th C. pine Coffer with iron handles. 16 in. high, 37 in. wide. **£35-40** SSP

Early 18th C. pine Coffer with lock missing. 47 in. wide, 26 in. high, 18 in. deep. **£130–140** AL

19th C. pine Coffer in exceptionally good condition, with original hinges. 38 in. wide. 19 in. deep, 19 in. high. **£50-60** SSP

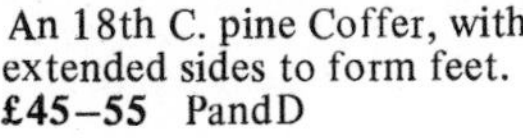

An 18th C. pine Coffer, with extended sides to form feet. **£45–55** PandD

Early 19th C. pine Blanket Chest with two small drawers to base, and internal candle box. Original iron handles and strap hinges. 45 in. wide, 22 in. high, 21 in. deep. **£78-88** AL

Early 19th C. domed Pine Coffer, with interior candle box, on bracket feet. 43 in. long, 29 in. high. **£130–150** AL

A Georgian Oak Dower Chest, the rail inscribed with 'A Fool's Bolt is soon Shot', the frieze with date '1764' and initials 'h' and 'N', 59" (150cms) wide, 22½" (57cms) deep, 37" (94cms) high, 18th C. **£280-360** L

A George III Oak Chest, crossbanded with mahogany, width 51". **£210-250** SH

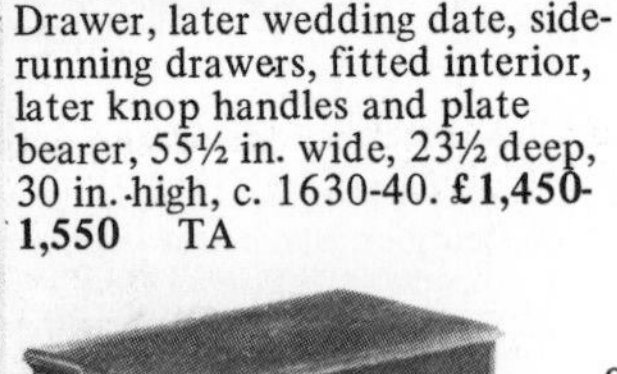

A Carved Oak Chest with Drawer, later wedding date, side-running drawers, fitted interior, later knop handles and plate bearer, 55½ in. wide, 23½ deep, 30 in. high, c. 1630-40. **£1,450-1,550** TA

A George I Oak Mule Chest with a rectangular hinged top above a four-panelled front fitted with two drawers below on stump feet, 28 by 51 in., early 18th C. **£280-310** SBA

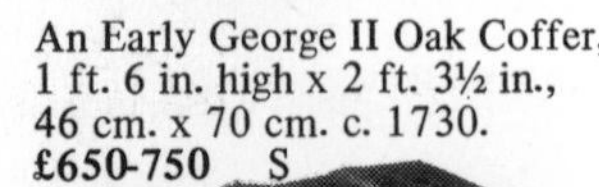

An Early George II Oak Coffer, 1 ft. 6 in. high x 2 ft. 3½ in., 46 cm. x 70 cm. c. 1730. **£650-750** S

Small Chest with two drawers, 27 in. wide, 20 in. high. **£80-90** MS

An 18th C. pine Mule Chest with two drawers in base and on bracket feet, 24 in. high, 38 in. long, 20 in. wide. **£120–140** GW

A Rare 17th C. Small Iron Bound Chest with original large lock and carrying handles, 22 in. wide, 13 in. high. **£1,200-1,400** RD

Large mule chest with long drawer in base interior fitted with candlebox and two small drawers. 49 in. wide 27 in. high 25 in. deep. **£135-145** AL

Mid 19th C. pine Coffer with two drawers in base and shaped plinth. 44 in. wide, 29 in. high, 20 in. deep. **£120-130** SSP

A Rectangular Black Lacquered Church-Style Chest decorated in gold and silver hiramakie (old damage) Momoyama period. 44.4 cm. x 32 cm. x 29.1 cm. **£1,350-1,550** C

A Rectangular Hasamibako decorated in gold hiramakie on a nashiji ground with large kiku mon among scrolling karakusa, engraved gilt kanagu (some damage) 18/19th C., 64 cm. x 42.7 cm. x 41.5 cm. **£2,800-3,500** C

A brass-mounted oyster-veneered walnut coffre fort mounted with scrolled and shaped gilt-brass bands, angles, lock-plate and hasp, late 17th C. (restorations) 15½ in., 39.5 cm. wide. **£460-520** C

A Late 17th C Dutch Marquetry and Ebonised Coffer, 1'6½" (47cms) high x 2'2" (66.5cms) wide, c1680. **£1,380-1,450** SKC

A German painted iron Strong-Box, with nine-tongued central lock, 17th C, 32in (81cm) wide, **£1,200-1,300** C

A George III mahogany dumb waiter, height 36½ in., 93 cm., diam., 22½ in., 57 cm., c. 1780. **£750-830** SBe

A late George II Mahogany Three-Tier Dumb Waiter, mid 18th C, 43" x 24" (109cms x 61cms). **£750-850** SBA

A Late Georgian Mahogany Whatnot, the four tiers separated by ring and tulip turned uprights, some faults, c. 1830, 1 ft. 7 in., 48 cm. **£470-570** L

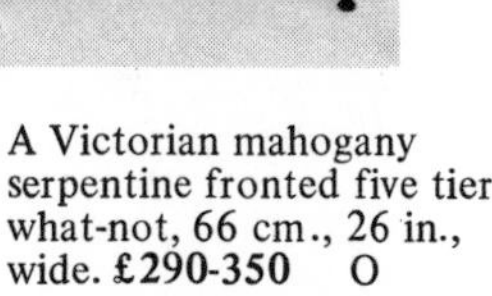

A Victorian mahogany serpentine fronted five tier what-not, 66 cm., 26 in., wide. **£290-350** O

An 18th C. Mahogany Dumb Waiter with gun barrel stem on a tripod base, originally 3-tier, c. 1770. **£600-650**
with 3-tier. **£800+** RD

A George III Mahogany Three Tier Dumb Waiter, 23 in., diam. x 44 in., 59 cm. x 112 cm. high. **£1,500-1,700** L

A Regency Mahogany three-tier Dumb Waiter with turned brass supports, 19½ in., 50 cm. diam. **£1,100-1,215** C

A Late Georgian Music Canterbury with drawer edged in ebony, on turned baluster supports terminating in brass bucket castors, some restorations c. 1820. **£400-500** L

A Regency simulated rosewood Canterbury, 18in (46cm) wide, with trade label of 'J. Wilmott Upholder Cabinet Maker . . . ' **£350-500** C

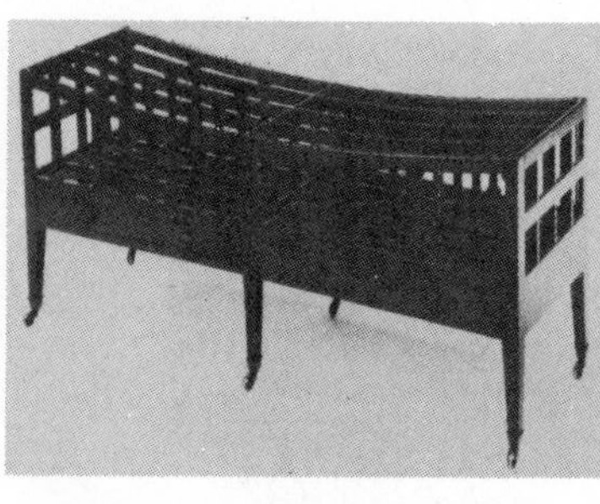

An Unusual Regency Mahogany Canterbury with eight concave divisions 43 in., 109 cm. wide. **£1,000-1,450** C

A Walnut Canterbury, late 19th C, 37½" x 22" (95cms x 56cms). **£200-250** SBA

A Victorian Walnut Whatnot/ Canterbury, 40 in. high. **£480-550** SV

A 19th C rosewood Canterbury, 19". **£375-420** WHL

A George IV Rosewood Canterbury, mid 19th C, 20½" x 18" (52cms x 46cms). **£250-350** SBA

A Victorian walnut music cabinet 38 in. high. **£350-450** BA

A Regency rosewood Music Canterbury on turned supports, headed by finials and terminating in brass bucket castors, c. 1820, 20 in., 51 cm. **£400-500** L

A Victorian Mahogany Music Cabinet with galleried top. **£125-145** SV

A Late 18th C. Convex Wall Mirror with two candle sconces, rococo, 38 in. high. **£550-600** OB

A Regency Mahogany Mirror with drawers (mirror needs some work) c. 1810. **£100-120** SHA

A George III satinwood toilet-mirror crossbanded with mahogany and inlaid with lozenge-pattern parquetry, 17½ in., 44 cm. wide. **£930-1,000** C

A fine George III giltwood mirror with later plate. 43½ in. x 35 in., 110 cm. x 89 cm. **£680-750** C

An 18th C. Italian Mirror, 12 in. high, c. 1750. **£48-58** OB

A 19th C. Mahogany Toilet Mirror, 21½ in. high. **£140-165** SV

An Unusual George I Walnut Veneered Toilet Mirror (replaced glass) 26 in. high, c. 1720. **£275-300** SHA

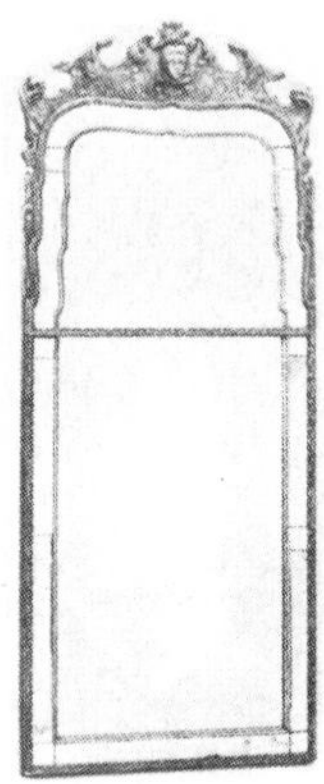

A pair of George II style giltwood and composition-framed pier glasses, height 78 in., 198 cm., width 33 in. 84 cm. **£710-810** SBe

A George II Walnut Wall Mirror, mid 18th C, possibly re-veneered, 37½" x 22" (95cms x 56cms). **£350-450** SBA

A late 19th C/early 20th C. Mahogany swing mirror. **£12-15** SV

A George III giltwood mirror, 63 in. x 30 in., 160 cm. x 77 cm., (re-gilded). **£2,900-3,200** C

A Mid 18th C Italian Carved Giltwood Wall Mirror, height 38" (97cms). **£130-170** SH

A Mahogany and Parcel Gilt Pier Glass, in the Georgian manner, 58" (148cms) high, 29" (74cms) wide. **£220-245** L

Small dressing mirror with drawer, 15 in. wide, 19 in. high, 8 in. deep. **£52-60** MS

A George III giltwood overmantel, with fluted pilaster angles, the frame carved with rocaille, C- and S- scrolls. 56 in. x 67 in., 142 cm. x 170 cm. **£2,300-2,600** C

A 17th C. Spanish Gilt Mirror 19 in. high. **£430-460** CC

A Mid 19th C. Gilt Wood Mirror, 41 in. high. **£240-260** RB

A Girandole **£45-50** TT

A Queen Anne Walnut Mirror with original bevel pier glass, 22½ in. high x 12 in. wide, c. 1710. **£285-310** TA

An Early 19th C. Continental Mirror, inlaid with bloodstone and lapis, 14 in. high. **£150-175** RB

A 19th C pine framed mirror 30in x 30in. **£60-65** S.M.

An Early 19th C. Rosewood Dressing Table Mirror, 18 in. high. **£175-200** SA

A Victorian Mahogany Mirror, 25 in. high. **£65-75** SV

An Edwardian Dressing Table Mirror. **£300-350** SV

A 'Chippendale' Mahogany Mirror, c. 1745-55. **£350-400** TA

A Queen Anne Walnut Dressing Table Mirror, c. 1810. **£400-440** SA

A Victorian pine Dressing Table Mirror with finely carved mirror supports and carved feet. **£55–65** MS

Small, 19th C., pine dressing Table Mirror on ball feet. 21 in. wide, 14 in. high. **£40–45** AL

A Late Victorian Dressing Table Mirror 36 in. high. **£60-70** VA

A Cheval Glass on trestle supports and paw castors, inlaid with harewood leaves on a satinwood and mahogany ground, 79 by 30½ in., 200 by 77.5 cm., 1880's. **£280-360** SB

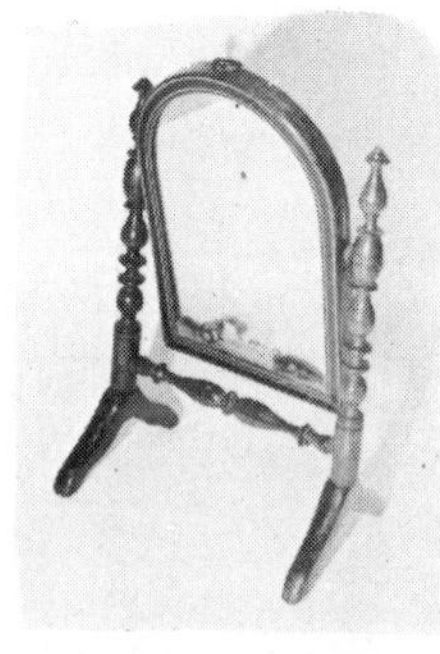

An 18th C. Apprentice Cheval Mirror, 9½ in. high. **£170-190** HD

A 19th C. Tray on Stand.
£40-45 SV

A Mahogany Butler's Tray with carrying handles, unrestored, **£120-140** restored, **£180-200** RD

19th C Mahogany Tray with boxwood string inlay and brass handles, 23" wide. **£40-50** STR

A Superb Sheraton Satinwood Tray, 27 in. wide, c. 1795.
£285-350 CP

An Edwardian mahogany and satinwood inlaid oval tray, 2'2¾" (68cms) wide, c1910.
£225-250 SKC

Kitchen Chest 34 in. high, 48 in. wide, 18 in. deep. **£100-130** GW

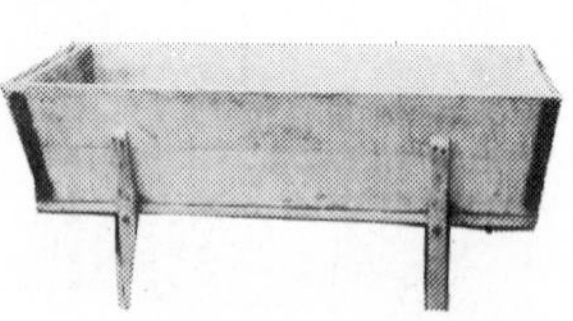

Dough Bin without cover 65 in. long 31 in. deep. **£45-55** MM

Baker's Bin with front opening, top drop 60 in. long. **£250-270** P&D

Early 19th C. pine Kitchen Table, the two drawers with cup handles. 60 in. long, 30 in. wide.
£90-100 SSP

19th C. pine Vegetable Rack with four compartments of varying depths. Sturdy construction. 36 in. high, 15 in. wide.
£35–40 MM

Chunky Kitchen Table 43 in. wide 32 in. long, 32 in. high. **£120-140** GW

Pine Edwardian folding Library Steps, 28 in. high. **£30–40** GW

Late 18th C. Elm Dough Bin.
£235-265 SHA

A mid-Georgian walnut Exercising Chair with leather-upholstered concertina seat, solid base and retractable step, 29in (74cm) wide, **£450-500** C

An oak Table Chair, late 17th C, Gloucestershire, 27¾in (70.5cm) wide, **£1,000-1,300** C

A Regency mahogany Duet Table with quadruple flap, the top on flying bracket supports, 23½in (60cm) diam, **£625-675** C

Regency mahogany metamorphic Library Steps formed as an open armchair, **£550-600** C

A William IV rosewood Book Rack, 16in (40.5cm), c. 1835, **£150-250** C

18th C. cane Library Steps. **£750-830** CC

A set of George III mahogany metamorphic library steps in the form of a side table, 29½in (75cm) wide, **£1,100-1,250** C

19th C. pine kitchen Plate Rack. **£35–40** AL

Hanging plate rack 22 in. high, 14 in. wide. **£19-25** AL

A 19th C. pitch pine, Baby's Bath. 29 in. long, 19 in. wide. **£35–45** MS

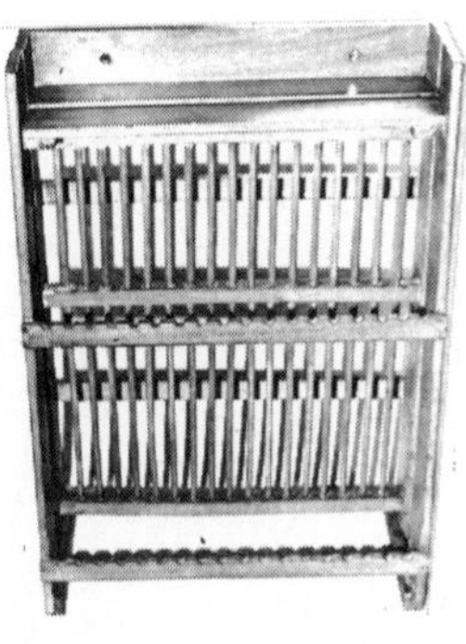

Pine plate rack. **£36-40** A.L.

18th C. pine 'winter hedge' Towel Rail. **£16–18** AL

19th C. pine Towel Rail with turned end supports and feet. **£15–20** AL

A 19th C. Hallstand, 30 in. high. **£40-45** SV

19th C. pine Towel Rail with double bars. **£20–25.** AL

19th C. Pine bath rack. **£7-9** A.L.

An Elephant's Foot. **£60-70** VA

An Antique Brass Bound Jardiniere in Oak. **£125-150** RD

A Fine George III Stripped Pine Chimney-Piece with later eared top, 88½ in., 225 cm. wide, 62 in., 158 cm. high. **£1,000-1,200** C'

A Miniature Dutch Press, 3¼ in., 8.7 cm., by Paulus de Soomer, Amsterdam, 1756. **£320-350** S

Late 19th C. pine Shop Counter with inset panel front. 60 in long, 32 in. high. **£70–80** MM

An Oak Brass Bound Bucket, 16 in. high, c. 1860. **£75-85** CP

A 19th C. pine Harvest Barrel with iron carrying handle. 10 in. high. **£35–45** AL

A William IV Rosewood Polescreen, with needlework panel. **£100-120** WHL

A Good Mahogany Music Stand, the music rest with fine pierced and interlacing floral and leaf scrolls, terminating in pad feet. **£560-660** L

A Chinese black and gold four-leaf Screen decorated and encrusted with hard-stones, 19th C, each leaf 18½in (47cm) wide: 75½in (192cm) high, **£650-700** C

A black and gold lacquer six-leaf Screen inset with Japanese paper panels laid on canvas, 19th C, 26½in (57cm) wide; 95¾in (243cm) high, **£1,200-1,300** C

A 1930's three-fold zebra skin screen, designed by Oliver Hill, length 90 in. **£50-60** CSK

A South German Walnut Prie-Dieu, with an ogee front, the moulded base with hinged kneeler, 3 ft. 2½ in. high x 2 ft. ½ in. wide, 97 cm. x 62 cm., c. 1740. **£1,500-1,700** S

A Chinese Export Black and Gold Lacquer Toilet-Mirror Base with four drawers, early 19th C. (lacking mirror) 19½ in., 49.5 cm. wide. **£200-220** C

A Late 19th C Swiss 'Recharge Mandolin', with 36 airs, 6 cylinder musical box by F. Conchon, in a lady's writing desk with walnut veneer, restored, 44" high. **£4,000-4,500** SAL

A 19th C Spinning Wheel. **£195-215** SAL

Mid 18th C Spinning Wheel in fruitwood with turned bone decoration, 47" high. **£250-300** STR

A Painted Wooden Spinning Wheel, c. 1880 3 ft. 3 in. by 3 ft. 6 in., 90 by 107 cm. **£150-230** SB

A 19th C. painted Coal Box, 12 in. high. **£80-86** SV

A Harvest Barrel of Unusual Shape, 10 in. long (one iron band missing) c. 1800. **£30-40** SHA

A Georgian mahogany Coal Box with string inlay and marquetry motif, with brass handle and shovel, 13½" wide x 14" high. **£80-95** SOE

A pair of Spanish softwood Panelled Doors with two opening inner sections. 69 in. high, 45 in. wide. **£200–250** SM

A 19th C. Coal Box. **£30-32** SV

A 19th C. Coromandel Jewel Box. **£95-105** CSG

A Victorian Walnut Jewel Box, brass carrying handle (modern converted interior) c 1870. **£48-58** CSG

A Victorian Walnut Jewel Box, with mother-of-pearl nameplate 'Annie' c. 1870. **£60-68** CSG

An Anglo-Indian Ivory-Inlaid Hardwood Toilet-Box enclosing an easel mirror and lidded compartments with a drawer below, late 18th C. Vizagapatam 17¼ in., 44 cm. wide. **£650-720** C

A Regency Jewel Box, heavily decorated in worked brass, c. 1810. **£145-165** CP

A Victorian Inlaid Walnut Veneered Vanity Box, with complete fitted interior, with silver-topped bottles and drawer, 12 in. wide. **£120-140** VA

A fine Victorian rectangular coromandel wood travelling dressing case, fitted with bottles and boxes with silver covers hallmarked London 1861, maker's mark JV, secret drawers with panel inscribed 'Toulmin & Gale, Makers, London, 15½" wide. **£750-800** PWC

An Asprey & Co. Brass-Mounted Rosewood Dressing Case, with fifteen various silver mounted cut glass and leather containers, the front fitted with mother-of-pearl and steel needlework and manicure items, the case with drawers and secret compartments, silver makers mark J.V., London, 1853, 15¼ in., 39 cm. wide, some damage. **£440-510** SBe

A Late 19th C Coromandelwood Dressing Case, inlaid with brass, the lower drawer being fitted with various implements of work, the cabinet having a 'secret' drawer, the silver-gilt London 1870, 13" (33cms). **£750-800** SKC

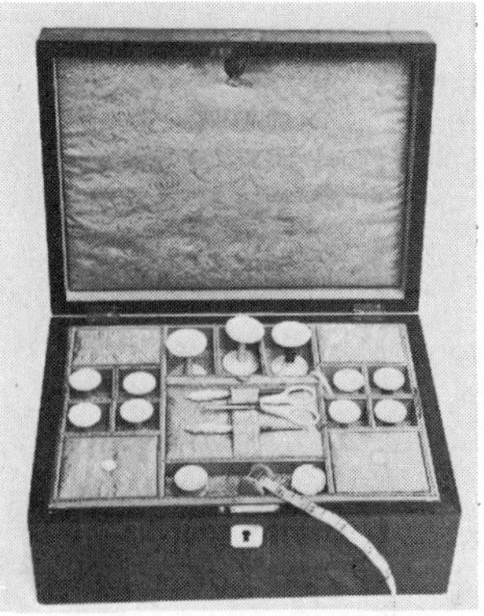

Early 19th C rosewood Workbox, with mother-of-pearl fittings. **£135-150** IN

Early Victorian Work Box, with mother-of-pearl fittings, c1840. **£125-150** IN

A Good Late Georgian Burr Yew Wood Work Box with central hinged cover revealing a fitted interior with removable compartments and two further compartments with hinged side opening covers, 14 in., 36 cm. **£90-110** L

A 19th C. Yew Wood and Rosewood Sewing Box. **£65-75** CSG

An Indo-Portuguese Coromandel Wood Box, inlaid with ivory, with two trays, 18 in. wide. **£220-250** RB

Pretty Edwardian Satinwood Sewing Box with painted floral decoration in unused condition. **£95-105** RD

A Victorian Compendium comprising chess, backgammon, dominoes, draughts, cribbage, roulette and four decks of playing cards, contained in a fitted coromandel wood case, 32 cm. **£300-360** SBe

A 19th C. Coromandel Sewing/Writing Box with key. **£105-125** CSG

An Anglo-Indian Ivory-Veneered Work-Box on silvered-metal paw feet 11¾ in., 30 cm. wide. **£300-330** C

An Anglo-Indian Ivory and Ebony-Veneered Games-Box the interior with a backgammon board and three boxes containing counters, shakers and dice, early 19th C., 18 in., 46 cm. wide. **£400-450**

An Anglo-Indian Ivory-Veneered Work-Box on silvered-metal ball feet, late 18th C., 12 in., 30 cm. wide. **£180-200** C

A Good Apothecary's Chest, the mahogany case which opens to a fully fitted interior with twelve medicine bottles, and drawer with five small bottles. English, c. 1850 8¾ by 9 by 7 in., 22 by 23 by 18 cm. **£350-400** SB

An Apothecary's Chest, the mahogany case opening to a fitted interior with twelve medicine bottles and with drawer in the base containing six small bottles, English, c. 1830 10½ in., 26.5 cm. wide. **£380-410** SB

An Early 19th C. Mahogany Apothecary's Cabinet, with fitted interior, with sixteen bottles all having original labels, drawer below, with various contents including scales, bottles etc., height 8½ in., 21.5 cm. **£270-340** SBe

A Victorian burr walnut Stationery Cabinet, with fitted interior including perpetual calendar, inkwells, blotter, small drawers, writing slope, etc., 1'6", (46cms) wide, c1870, writing inset stamped Cole Bros., Sheffield. **£190-220** SKC

An 18th C. Boxed Set of Perfume Flasks. **£75-85** RB

A William IV rosewood Letter Casket, the borders with mother-of-pearl, inlaid titles 'Answered' and 'Unanswered', 8½" (21.5cms) wide, c1835. **£200-225** SKC

A Late Victorian Marquetry and Inlaid Writing Slope with key, 18 in. long by 12 in. wide. **£150-160** VA

Brass bound Rosewood Writing Box. **£60-70** TT

A Rosewood Inkstand complete with glass inkwells with original pressed brass tops, c. 1840, 10 in. long. **£210-230** HD

Regency rosewood Writing Box, with inlaid mother-of-pearl (one inkwell missing). **£65-75** IN

An Anglo-Indian ivory inlaid ebony writing-box enclosing pigeon-holes and drawers, 13 in., 34 cm. wide. Late 18th C. **£320-355** C

Brass Inlaid Rosewood Writing Box with well fitted interior and brass handle. **£80-90** TT

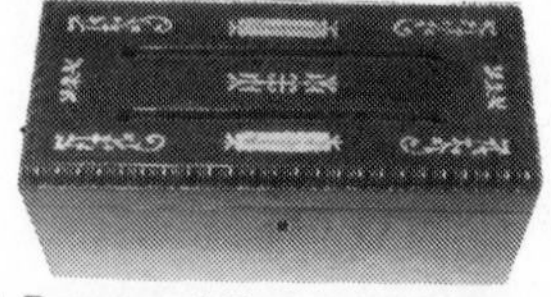

A Rosewood Correspondence Box, c. 1830, 9 in. long. **£165-185** HD

A Victorian Letter Rack and Ink Tray, 13 in. high. **£90-100** VA

A Fine 19th C. Mahogany Writing Slope, with brass inlaid corner decoration, complete with ink bottles, keys and secret drawers, original leather. **£175-195** CSG

19th C Pine Inkwell **£5-8** A.L.

A William IV satinwood and rosewood crossbanded Writing Box, inlaid with pewter stringing and mother-of-pearl, 1'1¾" (35cms) wide. **£70-100** SKC

A 19th C. pine Writing Slope with hinged lid. Interior not fitted. 19 in. wide, 15 in. deep. **£25–30** MS

A French iron-bound and tooled leather oak Document Chest, with hinged domed lid, 16th C. 16 in. (41 cm). **£400-440** C

A Victorian Writing Slope with Drawer, 22 in. by 16 in. deep. **£70-80** VA

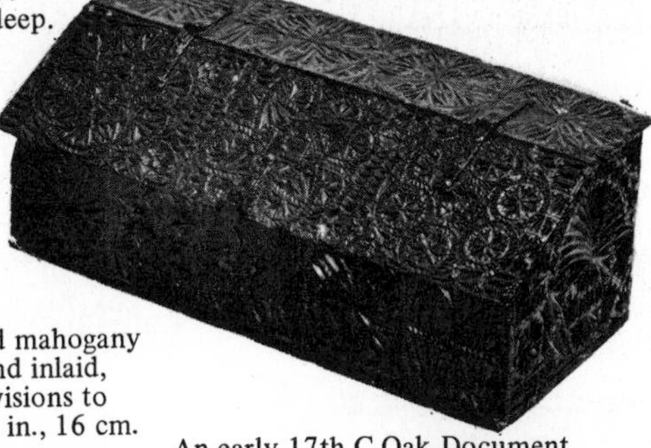
A George III figured mahogany box, crossbanded and inlaid, the interior with divisions to hold six bottles, 6¼ in., 16 cm. **£40-50** L

An early 17th C Oak Document Box, width 20". **£380-400** SH

A Mother-of-Pearl Casket, mid 19th C., 7 in. long. **£95-105** RB

A Regency Box, 13 in. long. **£65-75** CP

A Fine Regency Cross-Banded Silk Box, c. 1820. **£110-130** CSG

A Silver-Mounted Ebony Box, Indo-Portuguese, c. 1700, 15 in. long. **£260-290** RB

A Pair of Indo-Portuguese Boxes in rosewood and ivory, 5 in. x 3 in. **£140-160** pr. RB

A Rectangular Black Lacquer Casket and Hinged Domed Cover, decorated in gold and brown hiramakie and inlaid in mother-of-pearl, interior fitted as a tea-poy (old damage) Momoyama period. 22.4 cm. wide. **£890-990** C

Regency painted box. **£85-95** IN

An Anglo-Indian tortoiseshell casket with ripple-moulded sides, 8¼ in., 21 cm. wide, late 18th C. **£75-85** C

An Artists' Colorman wooden box, G. Rowney & Co. **£5-7** A.L.

An 18th C. Dome-Top Box, 17 in. long, c. 1720. **£44-50** OB

A fine miniature rectangular cabinet, encrusted with Shibayama style flowers signed Masahisa, late 19th C, 10.8 x 9.9 x 7.7cms. **£1,650-1,750** C

Early 19th C French Glove Box, with spring opening. **£45-55** IN

Early 18th C. pine Box with oak lid and original clasp, 15in wide, 10in high, **£40-50** A.L.

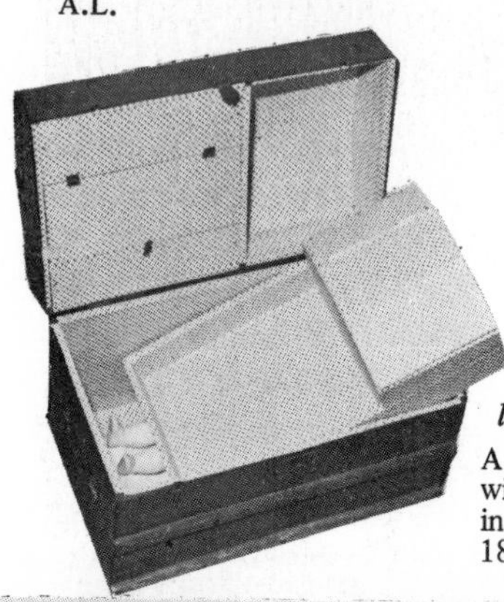

left

A Metal French Doll's Trunk with Accessories Trays, box in lid for hats and boots, c. 1880. **£80-120** LM

A Victorian Elm Glove Box, with brass plate engraved 'Gloves', c. 1870. **£20-25** CSG

A Pair of Mid-Georgian Mahogany Cutlery-Boxes enclosing fitted interiors, one with sixteen bone-handled forks and six similar smaller, 9¾ in., 25 cm. wide. **£550-600** C

National Provincial Bank money box, 3" high. **£7-10** SQE

Victorian oak liqueur tantalus with original bottles, and spring-loaded lock, 8" high. **£85-100** STR

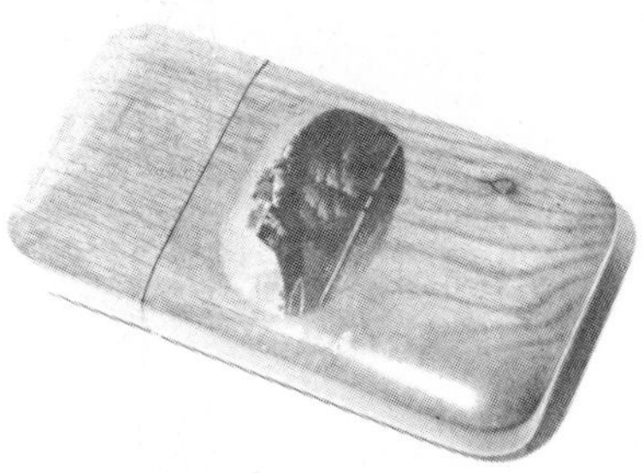

A Scottish Wooden Cigar Case, c. 1860. **£123-143** HD

A Fine Tortoiseshell Tea Caddy in original condition, English, 6 in. wide, 4 in. high, c. 1780. **£265-280** CP

A 19th C. Tortoiseshell Caddy inlaid with mother-of-pearl 7 in. wide. **£280-310** CC

A George III partridgewood single-division tea caddy, inlaid with ebonised and satinwood stringing, 4½" (11.5cms) wide, c1800. **£225-275** SKC

A Huntley & Palmer's 'book' Biscuit Tin, early 20th C. **£42-46** RB

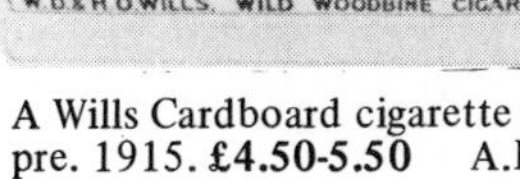

A Wills Cardboard cigarette box, pre. 1915. **£4.50-5.50** A.L.

TEA CADDY

- **In use from 1680**
- **Closely lidded box for storing dry tea leaves**
- **Two compartments for green and bohea tea with glass bowl in centre for mixing and blending**
- **Boxes kept locked because tea was very expensive**
- **Made in various materials and highly decorative**
- **Boxes with interior lids intact and original glass bowl are few and consequently more expensive**

A Georgian Burr Elm Tea Caddy, c. 1800, 7½ in. wide. **£155-165** SA

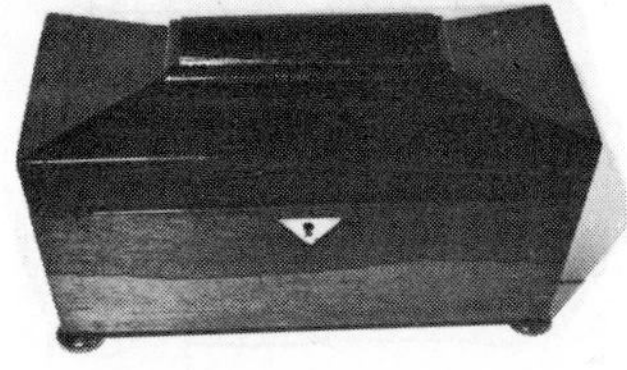

A Rosewood Tea Caddy, c. 1850. **£50-60** CSG

An Oak Cigarette Case. **£5-6** SQE

A George III pale tortoiseshell-veneered tea-caddy, 4 in., 10 cm. wide. **£90-110** C

A Silver Inlaid Tortoiseshell Caddy. **£220-250** CC

A George III Tea Caddy, inlaid in ivory and various woods, c. 1770, 11 in., 29 cm. **£110-170** L

An 18th C. Harewood caddy inlaid with shells. **£120-140** CC

A Large George III satinwood tea-caddy, with lidded interior, inlaid with vases of flowers, 12 in., 30.5 cm. wide. **£140-155** C

A Superb Quality 18th C. Satinwood Tea Caddy in fine original condition, 5 in. high. **£415-435** SA

An early Victorian Sheraton-design satinwood and cross-banded Tea Caddy, bearing monogram, 11½" (29.5cms) wide, c1845. **£110-150** SKC

A George III satinwood tea-caddy, inlaid in stained woods with flower-sprays, the green-stained chamfered angles with urns and foliage, 7½ in., 19 cm. wide. **£160-180** C

A Fine Rosewood Tea Caddy, inlaid, 9 in. wide, 7 in. high. **£125-150** CP

A George III satinwood tea-caddy, inlaid with foliage ovals and chequered line borders, 9½ in., 24 cm. wide. **£90-100** C

A George III satinwood tea-caddy inlaid with shells and chamfered fluted angles, 7½ in., 19 cm. wide. **£310-350** C

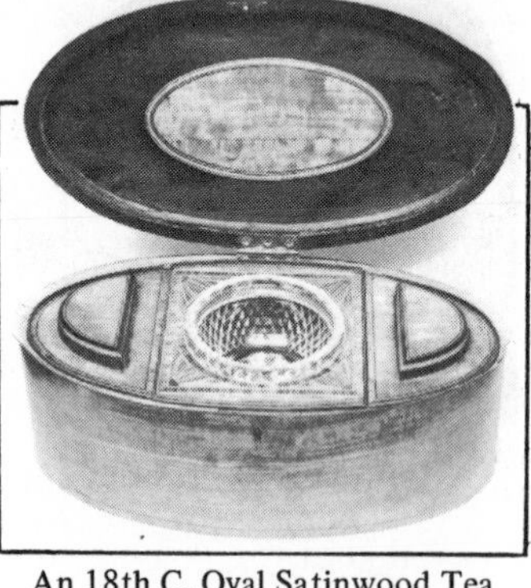
An 18th C. Oval Satinwood Tea Caddy, inlaid with various woods, including yew wood, excellent condition, 12½ in. wide. **£520-560** SA

A George III satinwood tea-caddy inlaid with shells and scorched lines, the angles with fluting, 7½ in., 19 cm. wide. **£280-320** C

A George III Mahogany Tea Caddy of Chippendale style, the interior with divisions and the right-hand side rising to reveal a spring operated secret drawer, 9½ in., 25 cm. **£40-55** L

A George III satinwood tea-caddy, crossbanded with rose-wood and inlaid with foliate ovals, 8½ in., 22 cm. wide. **£170-195** C

A George III satinwood tea-caddy, crossbanded and inlaid with shell and foliage ovals, 8 in., 20 cm. wide. **£205-235** C

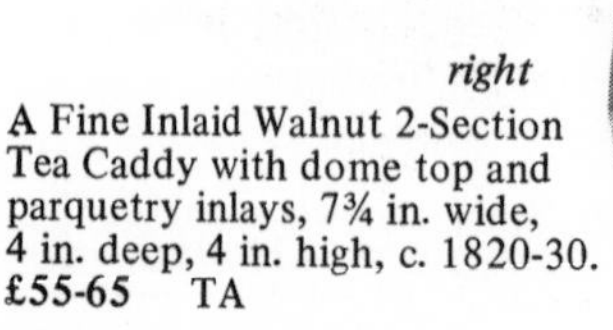
A George III satinwood tea-caddy inlaid with shell ovals, cross-banded with rosewood, 6¼ in., 16 cm. wide. **£250-280** C

right
A Fine Inlaid Walnut 2-Section Tea Caddy with dome top and parquetry inlays, 7¾ in. wide, 4 in. deep, 4 in. high, c. 1820-30. **£55-65** TA

A Fine 18th C. Rolled Paper-work Tea Caddy, 5 in. high. **£295-320** HD

A Late Regency Mahogany Tea Caddy, the interior with moulded glass bowl and two lidded re-movable compartments, 12 in., 31 cm. **£80-160** L

A Mahogany Tea Caddy, original throughout, including interior 8 in. wide, 5 in. high. **£100-120** CP

Inlaid Walnut Tea Caddy with original glass liner. **£85-95** TT

A Good George III Bow Front Mahogany Tea Caddy, with brass ring handles and original satin-wood feet, the interior with three lidded compartments, 11½ in., 29 cm. **£100-150** L

A George III mahogany Tea Caddy, 7½" (19cms) wide, c1790. **£85-100** SKC

A Georgian Mahogany Tea Caddy, 7 in. wide. **£215-230** HD

Mahogany Tea Caddy inlaid with mother of pearl. **£50-60** TT

Selection of small boxes. **£3-12** IN

Tool box with leather top and brass plaque. Unstripped (collectors prefer them with original paint. **£20-25** A.L.

A Dutch Marquetry Musical Instrument Chest, the top, sides and front inlaid, on bun feet, 19th C., 44 in. x 27 in. x 29 in. high, 112 cm. x 69 cm. x 74 cm. high. **£750-850** L

Strong Box with compartments. **£24-30** GW

A Chinese red leather trunk 19th C., 33 in.; 84 cm. wide. **£1,100-1,250** C

19th C., dovetailed pine Ammunition Box. 31 in. wide, 12 in. deep. **£20–30** MM

A small early 19th C. domed pine box with iron handles and clasp. 20 in. long, 12 in. deep, 10 in. high. **£35–45** MS

A fine mid 19th C carved wood post box, inscribed 'The Lord Foley, Worksop Manor', inscribed underneath 'W. Perry, London 1859'. 13" x 8" x 6". **£390-480** PWC

Early 18th C Bible Box, with original lock, 28" x 16" x 11" high. **£100-140** STR

Early 18th C Oak Bible Box, hinges not original, 25" x 17" x 8½" high. **£110-140** STR

A Louis Philippe ormolu-mounted faded tulipwood Casket, mounted with a Sevres pattern plaque. 16½in (42cm) wide. **£620-680** C

A Flemish silver-mounted ebonised Table Cabinet, early 18th C. 11½in (29cm) wide, **£350-385** C

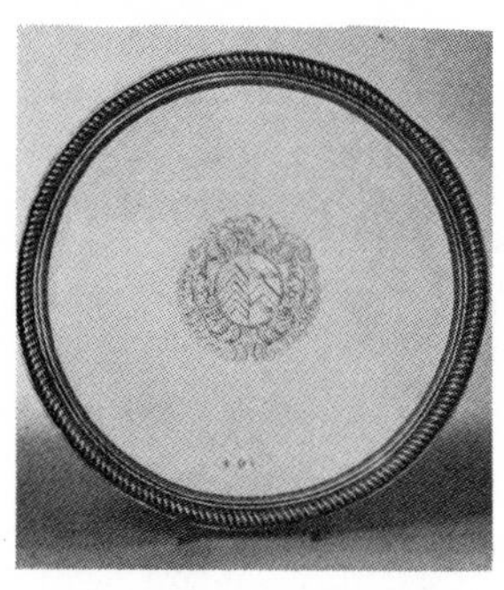

A Queen Anne circular salver on central trumpet-shaped foot, 1705 maker's mark illegible, 22 ozs., 11 in., 27.8 cm. diam. **£1,500-1,650** C

A George II Shaped Circular Waiter, 7¼ in., 18.5 cm., by John Robinson, London 1740, 8 oz. **£240-320** SBe

A George II plain shaped circular salver on three hoof feet by John Swift, 1739, 21 ozs., 10½ in., 26.5 cm. diam. **£1,600-1,750** C

A pair of George III oval salvers, each on four fluted feet by D. Smith and R. Sharp, 1783, 9¼ in., 23.5 cm., long 25 ozs. **£1,550-1,750** C

SILVER

Some dates of importance in study of silver:-

- 1660 restoration of Charles II – beginning of great era of domestic English silver
- c.1670 influence of acanthus leafage and fluted baroque
- 1685 The Revocation of the Edict of Nantes – brought Huguenot silversmiths to England
- 1697 introduction of Britannia standard. Lasted until 1720
- 1740's early signs of rococo
- 1750's revival of chinoiserie
- 1760's influence of neoclassicism.
- 1800-1820 tendency to add decoration to plainer style
- 1820's revival of rococo style
- By 1830's machines much in use
- 1880's Arts and Crafts movement – influence of Art Nouveau

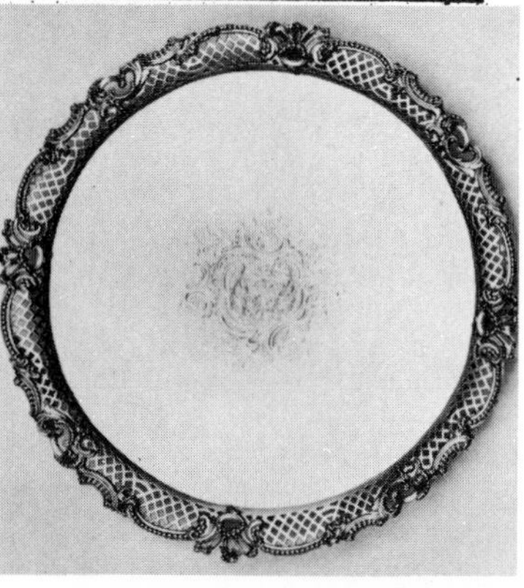

A George II Silver Salver, 1759 by Samuel Courtauld 1.13 in. 13 cm. diam. **£900-1,000** L

An Early George III Salver, 1762 by Ebenezer Coker, 12½in (31.8cm) 30oz. **£460-530** L

A George I square Salver, 6 in. square, by Abraham Buteux, London 1723, 7 oz. 12 dwt. **£550-610** S

A George II shaped circular Salver, 12½ in. diam., by William Peaston, London, 1756, 32 oz. 11 dwt. **£800-900** S

A Pair of George III Circular Salvers by John Carter, London, 1775, repaired. 7 in., 18.5 cm. 20½ oz. **£440-520** SBe

A George III plain oval Salver by William Bennett, 1807 16½in (41.9cm) long, (44ozs) **£1,100-1,250** C

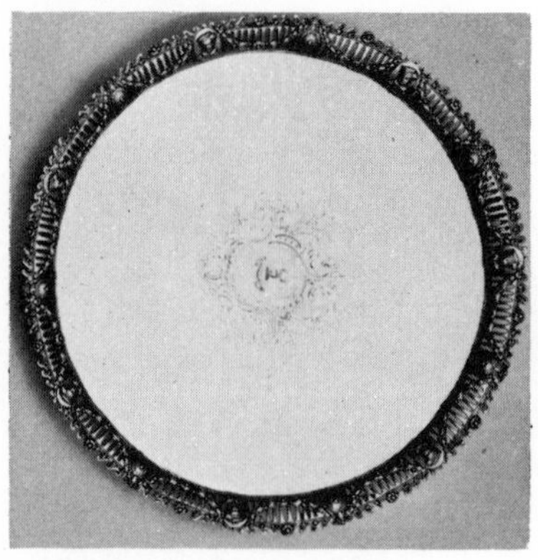

An Early Georgian Circular Salver, 1761 by Alexander Johnson, 13½in (34.5cm) diam., 41oz. **£520-600** L

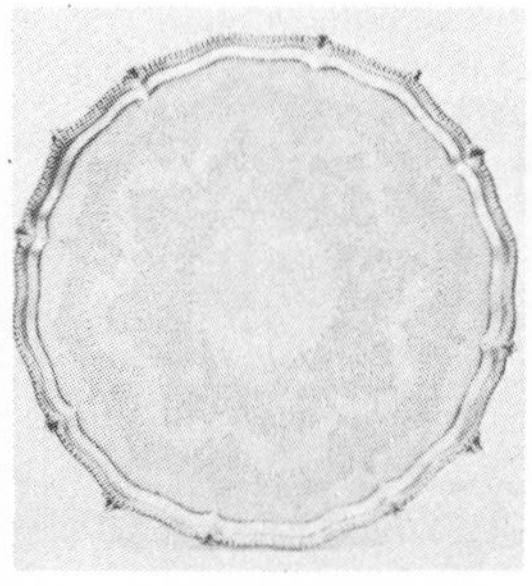

A Victorian Shaped Circular Salver, the centre bright cut with scrolling strapwork, 12 in., 30.5 cm., diam. by Thomas Bradbury and Sons, London 1888, 27 oz. **£300-340** SBe

A George III Silver Salver, the pie crust rim chased with scrolls and raised on three hoof and scroll feet, 1767 by John Carter II., 28 oz., 13 in., 33 cm. diam. **£200-300** L

A Victorian Large Silver Salver, 1848 by Edward Barnard & Son., 16 in., 14.4 cm. diam., 48 oz. **£780-860** L

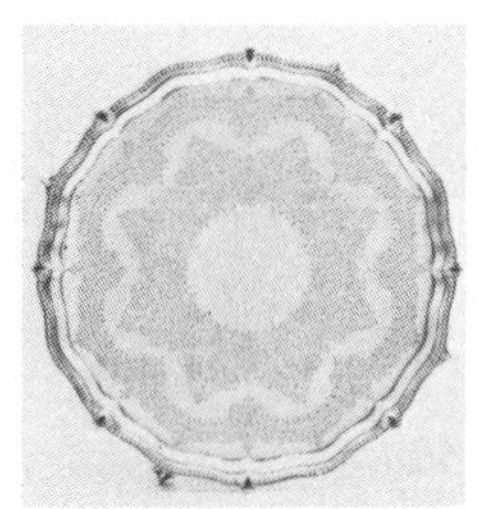

A Victorian Shaped Circular Salver, 10¼ in., 26 cm. diam. by Thomas Bradbury & Sons, London, 1885, 18½ oz. **£200-230** SBe

A Victorian-Shaped Circular Salver by E & J Barnard, London, 1865. 10¾ in., 27.3 cm., diam., 18 oz. **£300-380** SBe

A George III two-handled oval tray by J. Wakelin and R. Garrard, 1795, 80 ozs., 20 in., 51 cm. long. **£2,500-2,750** C

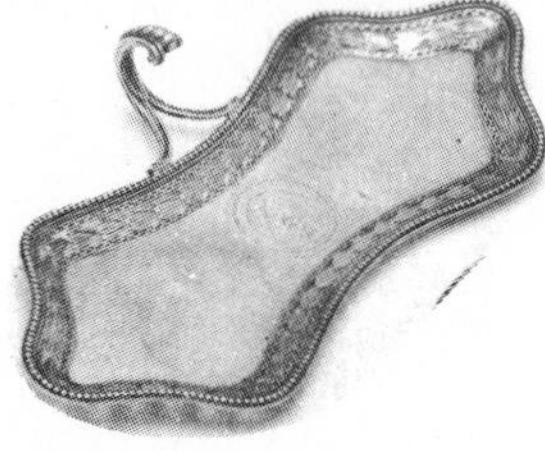

A George III Silver shaped oblong Snuffer Tray, hallmarked London 1778, maker William Plummer, 22cms wide, 3ozs., 8dwt. **£200-250** SKC

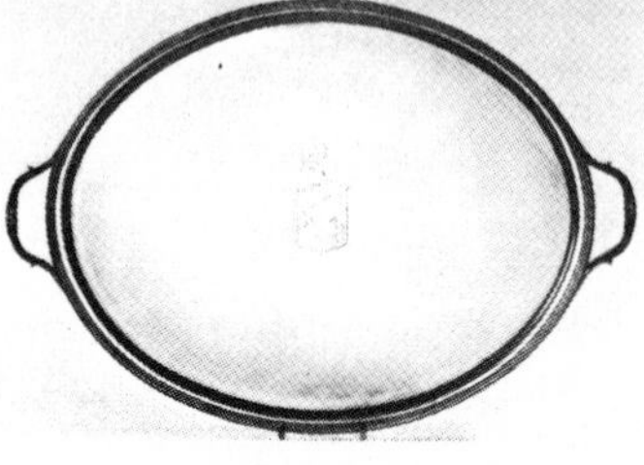

A George III plain oval two-handled tray by William Bennett, 1801, 20½ in., 52 cm., long, 84 ozs. **£3,000-3,250** C

A Victorian oval two-handled tray 1892, maker's mark JWFCW 20 in., 50.8 cm. long., 101 ozs. **£800-850** C

An Edwardian rectangular silver tray, maker's mark A. & J. Z., Birmingham 1902, 13½ oz., 33 cm., 12 in. wide. **£140-170** O

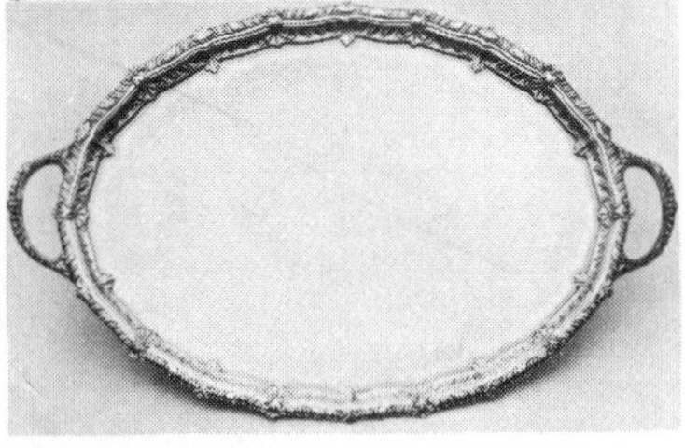

A Fine Victorian Silver Oval Two Handled Tea Tray, Sheffield 1889 by Francis Elkington, 28 in. 71 cm. across handles., 126 oz. **£1,400-1,600** L

A Joseph Rodgers & Sons Shaped Oval Two-Handled Tea Tray, 72.5 cm., over handles, makers' mark and Trade mark, Sheffield, 1903, 4.258 gm.
£1,750-1,950 SB

A Silver Salver by Stephen Smith of London, 1873. **£425-500** SA

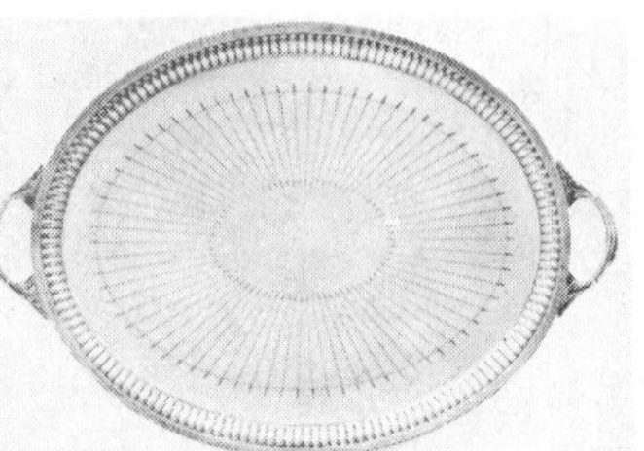

An Edward VII Oval Two-Handled Tea Tray by the Goldsmiths & Silversmiths Co. Ltd., London, 1902. 25¾ in., 65.5 cm., 104 oz.
£1,100-1,250 SBe

A late Sheffield Silver Tray, by Walker and Hall, dated Sheffield 1902, 65cms diam., 100ozs.
£560-600 SKC

An early 19th C. continental alms dish in the 16th C. style by continental silversmith, single Dutch punch mark "Z. I." (alloy 925) on underside of rim, 42.5 cm., 16¾ in. diam.
£560-620 O

A George III Irish Circular Wine Funnel Stand, by James Scott, Dublin, 1813., 4 in., 11 cm., 4¼ oz. **£210-250** SBe

A Pair of Early George III Irish Waiters, maker's mark indistinct, probably for Robert Glanville, Dublin, c1760, 7" (18cms) diam., 15ozs. **£355-400** SKC

A Pair of Silver Pierced Coasters, by Edward Lowe of London, 1771 with exceptional marks.
£825-925 pr. SA

A William IV oval silver gilt dish, London 1837, maker Robert Hennell, 12¾ozs. **£275-325** P.W.C.

An Early 18th C Italian Silver Tazza, 10¼" (26.5cms) diam., 2½" (6.5cms) high, Padua c1730.
£500-550 SKC

A pair of Regency Circular Wine Coasters, 14.5cms diam., by John Roberts & Co. Sheffield, 1813. **£640-680** SH

A Fine Sheffield Coaster, c. 1830. **£75-85** CSG

A German two-handled circular ecuelle and cover, by Abraham Drentwet, Augsburg, 1769/71 15 ozs. 4 dwts., 5½ in., 14.3 cm. diam. **£4,400-4,800** C

A pair of George III oval sauce-tureens, supported by four hoof feet, by Robert Hennell, 1777, 48 ozs. **£2,250-2,500** C

A Good Victorian Silver Plate Soup Tureen and Cover by William Hutton & Sons with an Old English pattern soup ladle, 16 in., 40.5 cm. **£200-230** L

A Victorian silver plated Entree Dish, E.P.N.S., 11" long. **£40-48** SQE

DECORATIVE BORDERS ON SILVER

- **Shell and Scroll 18th C to present day**

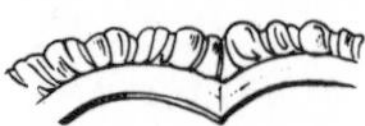

- **Gadroon 18th C to present day**

- **Ovolu Border Early 19th C**

A Pair of George IV Circular Wine Coasters, the sides chased, 6½ in., 16.5 cm., by S. C. Younge & Co., Sheffield, 1824. **£570-630** SBe

A Pair of Hawksworth, Eyre & Co. Ltd. Shaped Oval Entree Dishes, covers and handles, maker's mark, London 1911, 33.5 cm. long, 2,824 gm. **£1,000-1,200** SB

A French Shaped Circular Two-handled Bowl, cover and stand, maker's mark PA/T a star above, a rampant lion, c. 1870, 21.2 cm. wide. 729 gm. **£320-380** SB

A good pair of old Sheffield plate sauce tureens with part ivory handles and feet. **£240-285** W.C.

A Fine Pair of Silver Plated Coasters. **£100-120** CSG

A George III Circular Dish-Ring by Richard Williams, Dublin, c. 1770, (11ozs 15dwts) **£870-980** C

A pair of George IV two-handled sauce-tureens and covers by T and J Settle, Sheffield 1821, 86 ozs., 8¾ in., 22.2 cm. long. **£3,000-3,200** C

A Pair of Early Victorian Sheffield Plate Two-Handled Shaped Oval Sauce Tureens and Covers, detachable loop handles, beaded edging, 7¾ in., 20 cm., by Walker Knowles and Co., 1840 a.f. **£370-410** SBe

A set of four early 19th C silver plate Entree Dishes, probably by Smith & Co. each with draining plate, liner & lid. **£1,000-1,100** WHL

A Hukin and Heath Electroplate Soup Tureen and Ladle, 12¼" (31cms) maker's mark, stamped Designed by Dr. C. Dresser, Numbered 2123, c1885. **£250-300** SBe

A Pair of Plated Entree Dishes, Covers and Heater Bases, 14 in. c. 1825. **£500-560** S

A Victorian Plated Four Piece Tea Service, makers marks T.H&S. **£160-185** L

An Old Sheffield Plate Dinner Service. **£5,200-5,600** Bon.

A George III Silver Three Piece Tea Service 1798/9 by John Emes., 32 oz. **£750-850** L

A Three Piece Tea Service in the style of the 1830's, 1931 by Messrs. Barnard, 35oz. **£280-310** L

POINTERS FOR OLD SHEFFIELD PLATE

- Old Sheffield plate made from 1740's - 1840's when it was replaced by electro-plating.
- A problem arises over all electro-plating being called Sheffield Plate and hence the original plate should be notated OLD Sheffield Plate although frequently this title is omitted.
- Aid to dating Old Sheffield Plate by edge identification.
- Until 1785 edges merely turned over or with simple punched-in beading.
- By 1789 beading, reeding or gadrooning.
- 1800 shells, dolphins, oak leaves.
- 1815 vine leaves and flowers, altogether much more elaborate.
- Check for a seam on hollow ware as electroplate completely covers the piece.

A Silver Plated Muffin Dish, late 19th C., 9 in. wide. **£60-70** VA

A Victorian Five-Piece Tea Service, 1878 by Francis Elkington, 68oz, **£690-750** L

A Victorian melon shaped silver four piece tea and coffee service, London 1840, maker J.W. Figg, 70¼ozs. **£1,175-1,250** PWC

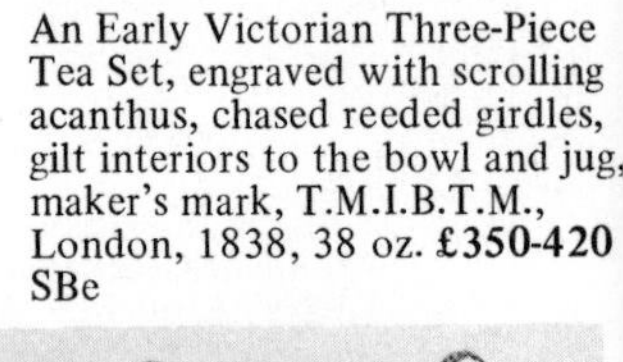

An Early Victorian Three-Piece Tea Set, engraved with scrolling acanthus, chased reeded girdles, gilt interiors to the bowl and jug, maker's mark, T.M.I.B.T.M., London, 1838, 38 oz. **£350-420** SBe

A Lee and Wigfull Five-Piece Tea Set, gadroon rims and collars, maker's mark, Sheffield, 1903/04/12, 89 oz. **£650-720** SBe

A George III Silver Three Piece Tea Service, 1821 by Joseph Angell, 50 oz. **£800-880** L

A Victorian Electroplated Four Piece Tea Service, the tea pot with a flower finial (perhaps a replacement) by Elkington & Co. **£180-220** L

A Victorian 4-piece Tea and Coffee Service, London marks 1847, maker E.J. & W. Barnard, 6702, 15dwts. **£1,500-1,700** AG

A Victorian Three-Piece Tea Set, of tapered cylindrical form, by William Smiley, London, 1857, 42 oz. **£500-600** SBe

A Victorian Four-Piece Tea and Coffee Set, of pear shape, engraved with crests, by Hands & Son, London, 1860, 71 oz. **£1,100-1,250** SBe

A Bachelors' Tea Set painted in aesthetic taste by Barnards of London, 1884 (with tray). **£700-770** SA

An oval fluted four piece silver teaset, Birmingham 1904 and 1905, 53¼ozs. **£700-800** P.W.C.

A Three Piece Silver Tea Service (the tea pot with hinge pin missing.) Chester 1908 by Henry Barraclough & Son, 38 oz. all in. **£330-400** L

A William IV Three-piece Silver Tea Set, by William Esterbrook, London 1833, 44ozs. **£1,380-1,400** SKC

A Four piece silver tea set, Sheffield 1908/9/10, maker GB & S, 64ozs., including wooden handles. **£900-1,000** SH

A Victorian Three-Piece Tea Service and matching plated Hot Water Jug by Elkington & Co., London, 1893, fitted oak case, 41 oz. all in. **£670-770** SBe

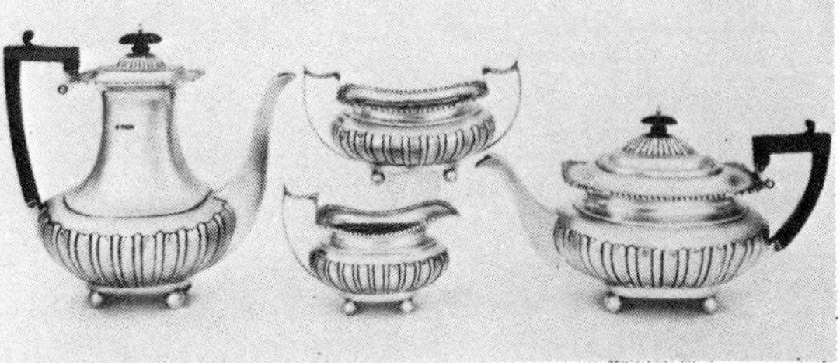

A Good Silver Four Piece Tea and Coffee Service, Sheffield 1917 by James Deakin & Son., 70 oz. all in. **£500-600** L

A 3 piece Georgian style Teaset, Birmingham mark 1902, 33ozs., 12dwts. **£300-350** PW

A George V Four-Piece Tea Set of shaped oval form with everted rims and double reed to each corner, maker's mark T.W. and Co. Ltd., Sheffield, 1923/4, 52 oz. **£500-600** SBe

A Composite Silver four piece tea service, Birmingham 1911 etc. makers mark W.A. **£360-400** 58 oz. all in. L

A Good Three Piece Silver Tea Service, Sheffield 1919 by Martin Hall & Co. Ltd., 40 oz. all in. **£440-480** L

A George VI Five-Piece Tea Set of octagonal vase-shape, maker's mark, B.B.S. Ltd., Birmingham, 1939, 84 oz. **£750-850** SBe

A Blackensee & Son Ltd., Four-Piece Tea Service in the George III style, maker's mark Chester 1924/27, 68 oz. all in. **£800-950** SBe

A Three Piece Silver Plate Tea Service by Elkington & Co., No. 16644. **£70-90** L

A Regency Sheffield Plate Three-Piece Tea Set with lobes and flutes to lower bodies, gadroon and foliate rims, bun feet, birds mask spout to teapot, probably by Gainsford & Nicholson, c. 1815. **£230-260** SBe

Silver Plate on Britannia Metal, Tea and Coffee Set, Teapot, Coffee Pot, Cream Jug, Sugar Bowl, c. 1920's. **£80-95** VA

A George III Silver Neo-Classical Style Teapot, by John Parker I and Edward Wakelin, hallmarked London 1775, 23ozs., 21cms high. **£510-600** SKC

A Foreign Silver Teapot, 15cms high, the hallmark indicates Dutch silver, town mark Haarlem, c1770. **£1,000-1,150** SKC

A Small Dutch Bullet Teapot, with ivory handle and finial, by Retners Elgrsna Leeuwarden, c1755, 10ozs. 4½" (11.5cms). **£1,330-1,400** SKC

A George III Silver Shaped Oval Tea Pot on Stand, the handle and finial Victorian replacements, 1789 by John Denziloe, the Tea Pot 5 in., 13.5 cm. high, the stand 7 in., 17.8 cm. across, 22 oz. all in. **£660-720** L

A George III Rounded Rectangular Tea Pot by Thomas Wallis and Jonathan Hayne, London, 1810. 5½ in., 14 cm. high, 18 oz. **£400-490** SBe

A George II Bullet-Shaped Teapot, moulded foot, straight tapering spout, by Chas. Gibbons. 1732. **£1,950-2,050** SA

A Late George III Silver Teapot, maker's mark rubbed, possible William Fountain, London 1815, 26ozs. **£345-385** SKC

A George IV silver Teapot, by Robert Garrard, London 1822, 16ozs. **£370-400** SKC

A Fine George IV Silver Teapot, by Paul Storr, 15cms high, 29ozs. **£390-430** SKC

A George IV silver Teapot, 11½" (29cms), possibly by Thomas James, London 1824, 20ozs, 6dwt. **£225-275** SKC

A Hunt and Roskell Melon-Shaped Teapot, 6½ in., 16.5 cm. high, maker's mark of John S. Hunt, London, 1846, impressed marks: Hunt & Roskell/late/Storr Mortimer & Hunt, 22½ oz. **£410-450** SBe

A George IV Compressed Circular Teapot, crested below a chased collar of reeds, 5 in., 13 cm., marked by Charles Fox, London, 1826, 18 oz. **£220-250** SBe

A Silver Tea Pot and Milk Jug, 1850 by Robert Garrard, 30 oz. all in. **£380-460** L

A Victorian Silver Tea Pot, 1868 maker's mark A. N. overstriking another, 5¾ in., 14.5 cm. high, 21 oz. **£420-490** L

A Victorian silver Bachelor's Teapot, Dublin 1879-80, maker's mark possibly J. Scriber, weight 9ozs. 6dwt, 11cms high. **£95-105** SKC

A circular silver teapot, China trade, c. 1850 marked KHC (Khecheong) (gross 50 ozs.) **£880-940** C

A Plated Edwardian 'picnic' teapot, with internal compartments for tea & sugar. **£45-50** BA

A George III Oval Teapot, marked on base and cover by Richard Cooke, London, 1805. 5¾ in., 14.5 cm. high, 19 oz. all in. **£520-600** SBe

A George III Shaped Oblong Teapot on four ball feet, the bulbous body chased with a band of reeding, domed cover with gadrooned finial, 6 in., high, by C. Fox or Fuller, London, 1810, 18 oz. **£200-230** SBA

A Victorian Teapot and matching Two-Handled Sugar Bowl, bright-cut with foliate drapery between bands of wrigglework and paterae, maker's mark H. H., London, 1868, 35 oz. **£350-450** SBe

A George II plain tapering cylindrical coffee-pot engraved with a coronet and initial, by Edward Feline, 1728, 9 in., 24.1 cm. high, gross 26 ozs. **£2,250-2,750** C

A George III baluster silver coffee pot, 10½" high, London 1765, 23ozs. **£800-900** PWC

A George II coffee-pot by Isaac Cookson, Newcastle, 1750, 9 in., 22.8 cm. high., gross 26 ozs. **£1,430-1,500** C

A very fine George III Coffee Pot of plain baluster form, 32cms high, diam. of base 11cms, 27ozs, maker Thomas Ollivant. **£1,100-1,250** SKC

A William IV Coffee Pot, 1832 by George Burrows II and Richard Pierce, 8¾in (22.2cm), 29oz. **£400-450** L

A George II Coffee Pot, with tuck under base, later ebonisec double scroll handle, 8¾ in., 22.5 cm., by Richard Bayley, London, 1750, 22 oz., repairec **£700-800** SBe

A George III plain pear-shaped coffee-pot, 1768, maker's mark obliterated 10 in., 25.5 cm. high, gross 21 ozs. **£990-1,050** C

A George II Coffee Pot, 7 in., 17.5 cm., marked by Edward Feline, London, date letter worn, c. 1745, 13½ oz., repaired. **£600-700** SBe

A George III Baluster Coffee Pot, 11" (28cms) high, marked, by Charles Wright, London, 1770, 29ozs. **£560-620** SBe

An Early George III Baluster Coffee Pot, engraved with a griffon crest with acorn finial, shell moulded swan neck spout, spreading gadroon base, 10 in., 25.5 cm. high, marked, by Francis Crump, London, 1762, 24 oz. **£2,000-2,200** SBe

A Fine George III Chinoiserie Coffee Pot, pear-shaped and chased 11¼ in., 29 cm., marked, by William Fountain, London, 1814, 49 oz. **£1,650-1,850** SBe

A George III Baluster Coffee Pot, wooden handle (repaired), 11 in., 28 cm., marked by Charles Wright, London, 1770, 29 oz. **£700-800** SBe

A George III Baluster Hot Water Jug, 9 in., 23 cm., marked, by John Scofield, London, 1798, 20½ oz., repaired. **£300-400** SBe

A Goldsmiths & Silversmiths Co. Ltd., Baluster Coffee Pot in mid 18th C., taste, with domed cover, wood handle, 22 cm. high, makers' mark, London, 1911, 704 gm. **£350-400** SB

A George II-Style Baluster Hot Water Jug, 8¼ in., 21 cm., by Elkington & Co., Ltd., Birmingham, 1936, 18 oz. **£200-250** SBe

A George III Vase-Shaped Coffee Pot, 12 in., 30.5 cm. high, marked, by John Robins, London, 1797, 28 oz. **£1,200-1,400** SBe

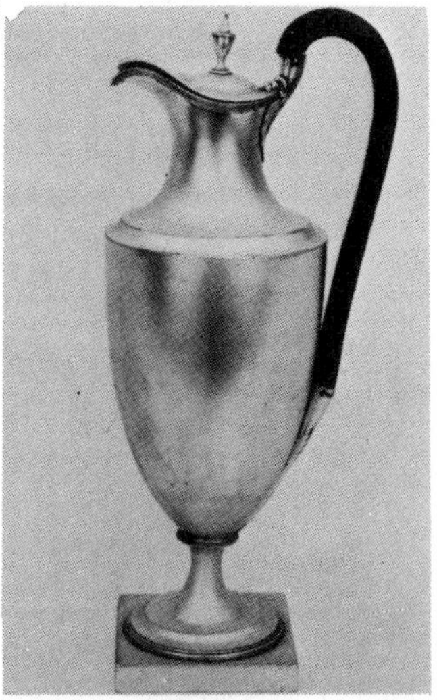

A George III Silver Vase-shaped claret or hot water pot, the handle a replacement. 1791 by Henry Chawner, 12¼ in., 31.2 cm., 24 oz. all in. **£420-480** L

A Fine Regency Silver Coffee Pot, by William Eley II, 21cms high, 23ozs. (engraved crest), London 1828. **£560-600** SKC

A Victorian Pear-Shaped Hot Water Jug with wrythen finial, reeded cover and lower body, moulded acanthus spout, beaded edging, 9¼ in., 23.5 cm., by Mappin & Webb, London, 1879, 13½ oz. **£200-230** SBe

A Victorian Large Baluster Jug, 8¼ in., 21 cm., maker's mark J.A.T.S., London, 1889 33½ oz. **£390-450** SBe

A Victorian Electroplate Large Covered Jug, 10½" (26.5cms) high, by Martin Hall & Co., c1865. **£200-250** SBe

A Fine Victorian Claret or Hot Water Pot, Sheffield 1867 makers mark S.R. & C.B., probably for Roberts and Briggs, 14in (35.5cm) high, 35oz. **£730-800** L

A good Victorian silver coffee pot, 11" high, London 1826, maker's mark WS, 28¾ozs. **£400-450** PWC

A French plain pear-shaped chocolate-pot with wood handle, Paris, 1783, maker's mark apparently FCR, 8¾ in., 22.3 cm., high, gross 23 ozs. **£1,045-1,150** C

A George II Silver Gravy Argyll by Charles Kandler, c. 1750. **£950-1,050** SA

A Thomas Bradbury & Sons Ltd., Tapering Cylindrical Coffee Jug, 23.2 cm. high, makers' mark, London, 1906, 403 gm. **£250-300** SB

An Early Victorian Silver Coffee Pot, by the Barnard family, hallmarked London 1838, 26ozs., 24cms high. **£490-540** SKC

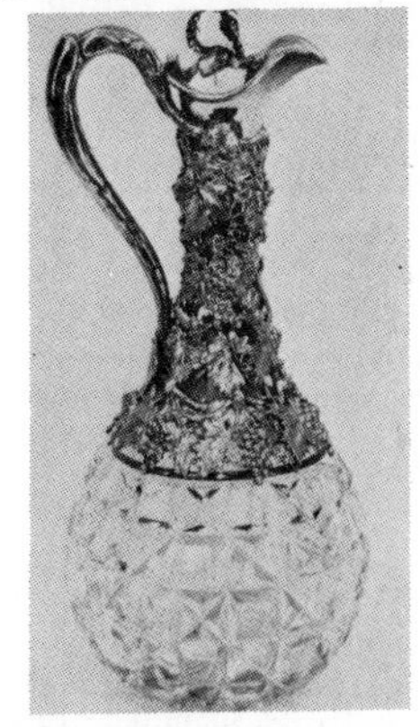

A Victorian Claret Jug, the neck and shoulders applied with a matted cagework of fruiting vines. 11¼ in., 28.5 cm. **£160-190** L

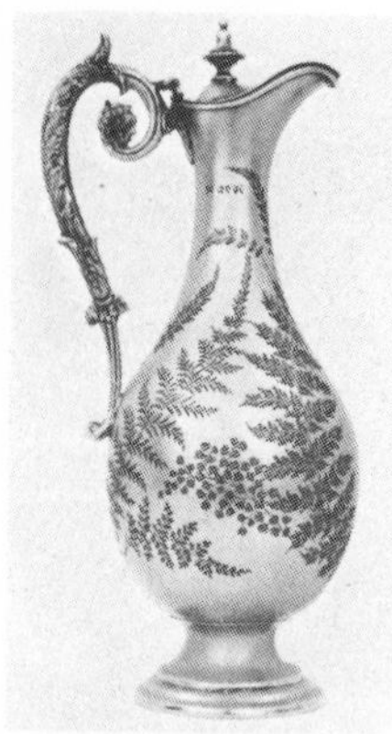

A Victorian Silver Gilt Claret Jug 1886 by Charles Boyton, 11¾ in., 29.5 cm., 19.8 oz. **£420-480** L

An Indian Silver Ewer, 31.5 cm., late 19th C., 1,362 gm. **£600-650** SB

An Unusual Australian Electroplate-Mounted Ostrich Egg Ewer, 34.4 cm. high, unmarked, c. 1880 **£450-530** SB

A good quality Tiffany & Co., silver tea kettle on spirit stand, stamped Tiffany & Co., 550 Broadway, English Sterling 925-1,000, No. 7758, 67 oz., 42 cm., 16½ in. high. **£630-700** O

A Good Silver Replica of a George I Octagonal Tea Kettle, 1921 by The Goldsmiths and Silversmiths Company Ltd., 15 in., 38 cm. high., 92 oz. **£700-800** L

A Thomas Bradbury & Sons Ltd., Tea Kettle On Lampstand, 31.5 cm., high, makers' mark, London, 1913, 1,565 gm. **£700-780** SB

A George III two-handled vase-shaped tea-urn by Edward Fernell, 1787, gross 100 ozs., 23 in., 58.5 cm. high. **£2,400-2,800** gross 47 ozs., 15 in., 38 cm. high. **£1,750-2,000** C

Silver Plate Kettle with Spirit Burner and Raffia Handle, c. 1920's 11½ in. high. **£30-35**

A Silver Plate Kettle on Spirit Burner, 12 in. high, c. 1840. **£150-160** VA

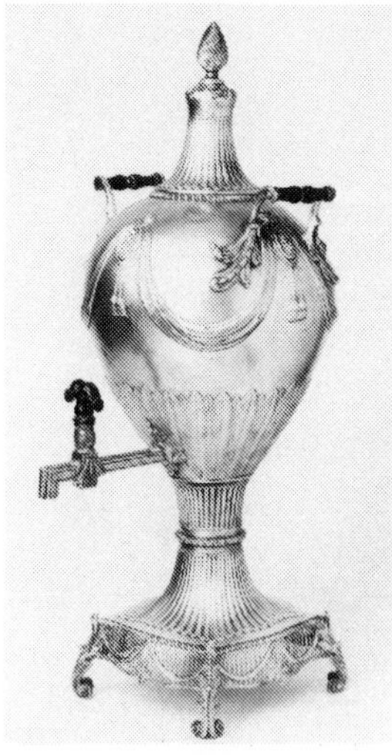

A Fine George III Tea Urn by W.T., London 1774, 92ozs., 21" high. **£1,400-1,600** Bon.

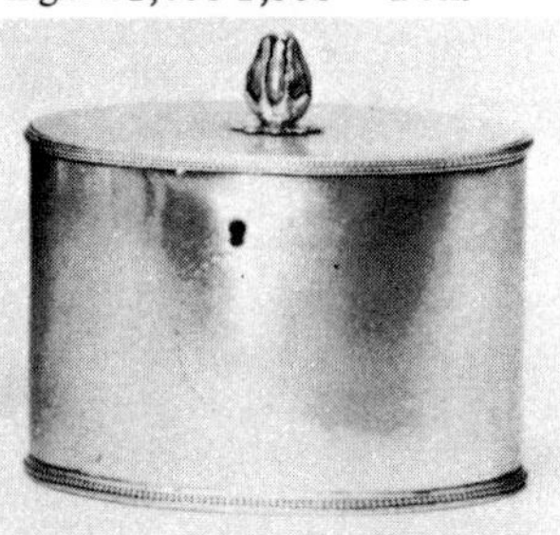

A George III Straight-Sided Oval Tea-Caddy, hinged flat lid with border of bright-cut wrigglework and patterae, 4¼ in., 11 cm., marked by Samuel Wood, London, 1778, 12 oz., key wanting. **£700-800** SBe

A George III oval tea-caddy, the domed cover with stained green ivory pine-apple finial, by Henry Chawner, 1794, 12 ozs. 7 dwts. **£1,480-1,580** C

A George III Plain Oval Tea Caddy with ivory finial, 5¼ in., 13.5 cm. high, marked by Thomas Howell, London 1791, 12½ oz., key wanting. **£400-480** SBe

A Sheffield Tea Urn, 19¼in (49cm) high, **£200-230** L

A Continental Silver Tea Caddy, marks poorly struck, probably Dutch, 4½in (11.5cm) high, **£100-120** L

A George III oval Tea Caddy, 4½ in. maker's mark W.C. struck over that of William Vincent, London, 1780, 14 oz. 19 dwt. **£1,250-1,350** S

A George III oval Tea Caddy, 5¾ in, marked by Hester Bateman, London, 1784, 10 oz. 18 dwt. **£1,900-2,100** S

Edwardian Plate Samovar, 16 in. high. **£140-160** VA

A Regency Sheffield Plate Two Handled Tea Urn with detachable cover, plume headed tapered supports. 16½ in., 42 cm. high. **£210-260** SBe

An Oval George III Tea Caddy with key, 11ozs., 13cms x 8.5cms, by Robert Hennell, London 1788. **£1,150-1,250** SKC

A pair of George III square tea caddies by R and S Hennell, 1803 and 1804, on wood plinths 26 ozs. **£2,300-2,500** C

A George I plain octagonal caster, by Thomas Bamford, 1726, 6½ in., 16.2 cm., high., 6 ozs. 10 dwts. **£770-850** C

A George I plain octagonal pear-shaped caster, by Thomas Bamford, 1719, 7½ in., 19 cm., high, 9 ozs. 11 dwts. **£1,100-1,250** C

A George II octagonal Caster, 6 ¾ in., maker's mark of Gabriel Sleath struck over that of Benjamin Pyne, London, 1727, 9 oz. 9 dwt. **£2,000-2,200** S

A George II vase-shaped Caster, 6 in. high, marked on base and lid, by Thomas Bamford, London, 1729, 5 oz. 15 dwt. **£800-900** S

A George II Baluster Caster, 7¼" (18cms) high, by Samuel Wood, London 1743, 7ozs. **£530-590** SKC

A George II Provincial Baluster Sugar Castor, no maker's mark. Newcastle, 1743. 7¾ in., 20 cm., high, 10 oz. **£400-490** SBe

A Fine George III Silver Castor by Robert Peaston, dated 1770. **£265-285** SA

A George II Caster, by Samuel Wood, London 1745, 4ozs., 5" (13cms). **£290-320** SKC

A George III Caster, 3ozs., by Hester Bateman, London 1781, 5½" (14cms). **£360-400** SKC

A George V silver muffineer, London 1915, height 20cms, 12ozs. **£160-200** SH

A George III Caster, by Samuel Wood, London 1763, 3ozs., 5¼" (13.5cms). **£265-285** SKC

A George III Caster, 3½ozs., London 1783, by Thomas Shepherd, 6¼" (16cms). **£180-200** SKC

A George III Caster, London 1795, by John Moore, 3½ozs., 6" (15.5cms). **£145-175** SKC

A Good George III Plain Silver Castor by Duncan Urquhart and Naphtal Hart, dated 1802. **£235-255** SA

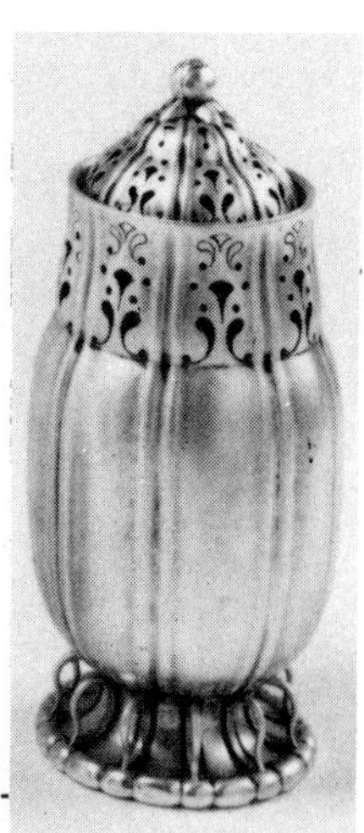

A Georg Jensen oviform Sugar Caster, 16.5cms high, silver-coloured metal stamped with Danish makers' marks, GI 8305 and 'Copenhagen'. **£275-300** P

An Octagonal Victorian Sugar Caster, 8½ozs., London 1897, 6¾" (17.5cms). **£225-250** SKC

A fine quality Victorian large silver castor, 10" high, London 1894, makers Carrington, 16½ozs. **£225-275** PWC

A George II cruet-frame, by Jabez Daniell, 1749, 55 ozs. **£2,750-3,000** C

A good Victorian circular silver cruet stand, with seven cut glass bottles, three with silver covers, London 1838, maker Charles Fox. **£400-450** PWC

A George II Silver Oil & Vinegar Cruet Stand by Samuel Wood, 1757. **£675-775** SA

A Dutch Silver cruet frame, Amsterdam, 1772 maker's mark GA 16 ozs. 19 dwts. **£500-550** C

A Victorian Novelty Cruet Set in form of a bath chair. **£250-280** SA

Edwardian Six-Piece Silver Plated Cruet Set. **£45-55** VA

An early George IV Regency Silver Seven-bottle Cruet Stand, by William Barrett, hallmarked London 1823 (one bottle not matching). **£400-450** SKC

Edwardian Four-Piece Silver Plated Cruet Set. **£40-50** VA

A William IV Parcel-Gilt Salt, 5" (13cms) wide, by Paul Storr, London 1833, 4ozs. **£355-385** SKC

A George III Shell-shaped Salt Cellar, by George Andrews, 10cms max. diam., 6cms high, 4ozs., hallmarked London 1801. **£160-200** SKC

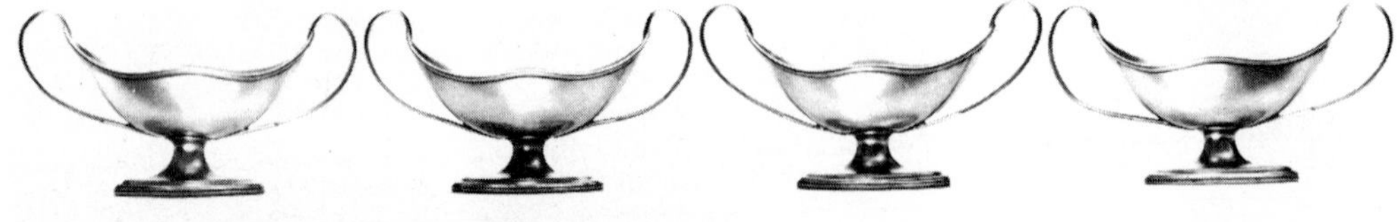

A set of Four George III salts., 5¾" (14.5cms) over handles, by Henry Chawner, London, 1787, 10½ozs. **£370-420** SBe

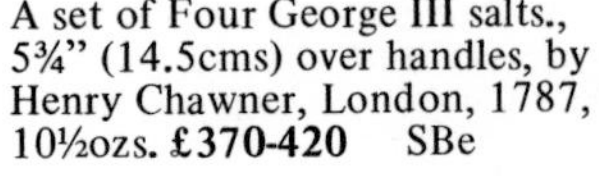

A set of George III silver salt cellars, London 1775, maker Thomas Hemming, 18½ozs., blue glass liners. **£400-450** PWC

A Set of Four George III Pierced Silver Salts by Joseph Bell, 1792, London. **£575-625** set. SA

A Set of four Regency silver Salts, 4" (10cms) by Abstainando King, London 1817, 14ozs. **£320-350** SH

Four George III circular vase-shaped salt-cellars, by Paul Storr, 1804, 21 ozs. **£2,300-2,500** C

A 17th C. German Sweetmeat Dish, 5¼ in., 13.5 cm. wide, maker's mark H.B. conjoined, Augsburg, c. 1675, 2 oz. 9 dwt. **£680-780** S

A George III shaped oval cake-basket with pierced swing handle, engraved with a coat-of-arms by Emick Romer, 1767 26 ozs., 14 in., 36.2 cm. long. **£1,450-1,750** C

Four George III boat-shaped sweetmeat-baskets by Henry Chawner, 1794 with blue glass liners, 5½ in., 13.9 cm. long, 16 ozs. 19 dwts. **£2,300-2,500** C

An early Victorian Silver Cake Dish, Sheffield 1841 by Howard & Hawksworth, 12¾ in., 32.6 cm. diam., 34 oz. **£380-480** L

A Victorian Dessert-Stand by Robert Garrard, 1855, 9½in (24.1cm) high, (33ozs) **£750-850** C

A Victorian shaped circular Dessert Stand, maker's mark JF over EH, London, 1872, 9" diam., 27ozs., 15dwt. **£250-350** SBA

A Silver Plate Bon-bon Dish, late 19th C., 12 in. wide. **£30-35** VA

A Victorian Silver Pierced Fruit Basket, marked, London 1875, 24ozs. **£400-480**

A Silver Basket by John Edward Terry, London, 1823. **£1,350-1,550** SA

A George V Boat-Shaped Dessert Basket and Smaller Pair, En Suite, 10½ in., 27 cm. and 6½ in., 16 cm., Birmingham, 1914, 30½ oz. **£350-400** SBe

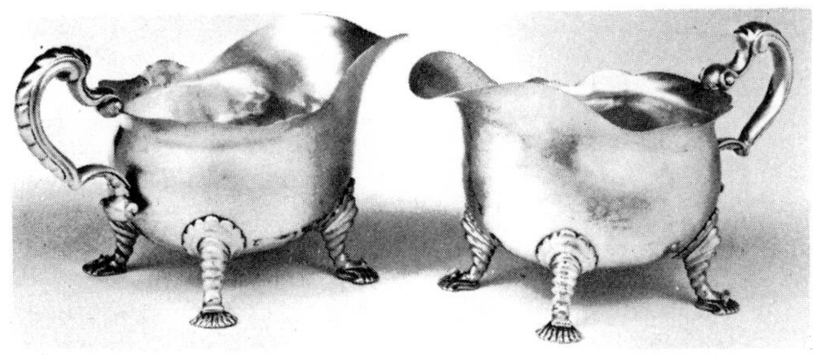

A pair of George II plain oval sauceboats on knurled scroll and shell feet, by Thomas Heming 1756, 23 ozs. **£825-900** C

A pair of Victorian Oval Sauceboats in the George II style, 7¼" (18cms) long, by Charles Fox, London 1838, 20ozs. **£760-840** SBe

A Matching Pair of George II Oval Sauce Boats by Joseph Sanders, London, 1741-1742. 7 in., 18 cm., long, 19¾ oz. **£1,200-1,400** pr SBe

A George IV oval Sauce Boat, 7 in., by E.E.J. and W. Barnard, London, 1829, 17 oz. 1 dwt. **£980-1,100** S

A pair of George II plain sauce-boats, engraved with a later crest, 1747, maker's mark probably that of Peter Archambo, 23 ozs. **£1,100-1,250** C

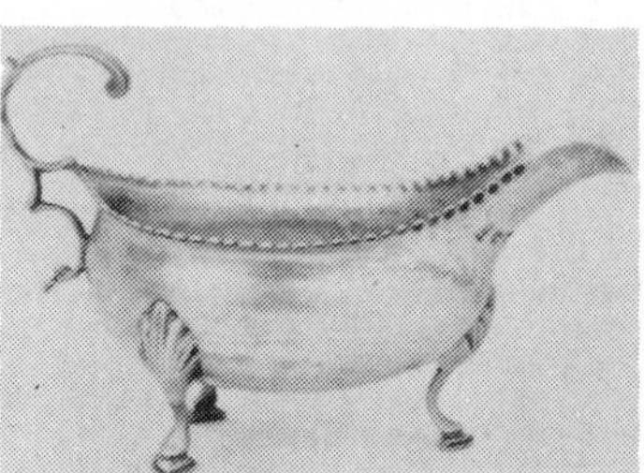

Hester Bateman, A Good George III Cream or Butter Boat, 1789, 5½ in., 13.8 cm. across. **£300-350** L

A pair of William IV shell-shaped sauceboats, by Charles Fox, 1836, 34 ozs. **£2,500-2,750** C

A pair of George II oval sauce-boats by John Pollock, 1745, 18 ozs. 14 dwts. **£715-775** C

A George III Cream Jug of vase-shape, engraved with a later monogram, 5¾ in., 14.5 cm., by Samuel Hennell, London, 1795, 5¾ oz. **£320-350** SBe

A George III Silver Cream Jug 1796 by John Robins, 4¼ in., 11 cm. high, 5.4 oz. **£260-290** L

A George III Silver Sauce Boat by W. Stephenson, dated 1760. **£750-850** SA

An Early Georgian Silver Embossed Cream Jug, 4½ in. high, c. 1780, London, marked. **£160-180** CA

A Silver Cream Jug by Peter & Ann Bateman, 1791-1802.
£275-310 SA

A Good Quality Silver Cream Jug and Basin, dated 1908, by Carrington & Co. of London.
£220-240 SA

A George III Scottish Helmet-Shaped Cream Jug, crested and monogrammed, 6¾ in., 17 cm., by W & P Cunningham, Edinburgh, 1795, 5½ oz. **£300-350** SBe

A good quality pair of William IV silver gilt oil and vinegar ewers, London 1837, maker Robert Hennell, 7½ozs. **£385-425** P.W.C.

A George III large helmet-shaped Milk Jug, 5 in. high, by Robert Sharp, London, 1793, 7 oz. 8 dwt. **£380-450** S

A Silver George II Baluster Cream Jug, hallmarked London 1739, maker Thomas Stackhouse, 2ozs., 8dwt., 11cms high (a). **£90-100** SKC

A George III Helmet-shaped Cream Jug, by Peter and Ann Bateman, 15cms high, 3ozs., 7dwt (b). **£170-200** SKC

An Early George III Cream Jug of baluster form, hallmarked London 1768, maker Edward Read, 2ozs., 8dwt, 10cms high (c). **£95-105** SKC

An Early George III Silver Cream Jug, 3ozs., 6dwt, hallmarked London 1771, maker Charles Clark, 12cms high (d). **£100-110** SKC

A Helmet-shaped Cream Jug, punch mark to base for George Gray, London 1789, 3ozs., 6dwt, 15cms high (e). **£135-150** SKC

An Early George III inverted pear-shaped Cream Jug, hallmarked London 1761, maker David Mowden, 2ozs., 27dw, 10cms high (f). **£100-110** SKC

An Early George II Cream Jug, hallmarked London 1765, maker probably Jacob Marsh, 2ozs., 12dwt, 10cms high.(g)..**£135-150** SKC

A very fine Helmet-shaped Cream Jug, by Peter and Ann Bateman, hallmarked London 1795, 4ozs., 10dwt, 14cms high (h). **£190-220** SKC

A George II plain circular sugar bowl and cover, 1742, probably by William Williams, I., 9 ozs. **£860-950** C

A Silver Basket by Peter & Ann Bateman, 1791-1802. **£475-525** SA

A George III Rectangular Boat-Shaped Sugar Basket with canted corners, 5¾ in., 15 cm., marked, by Robert Sharp, London, 1793, 9½ oz. **£380-420** SBe

A George III Boat-Shaped Sugar Basket, bright cut with wriggle-work and paterae, 5¾ in., 15 cm. wide, by Thomas Daniell, London, 1783, 8¾ oz. **£280-360** SBe

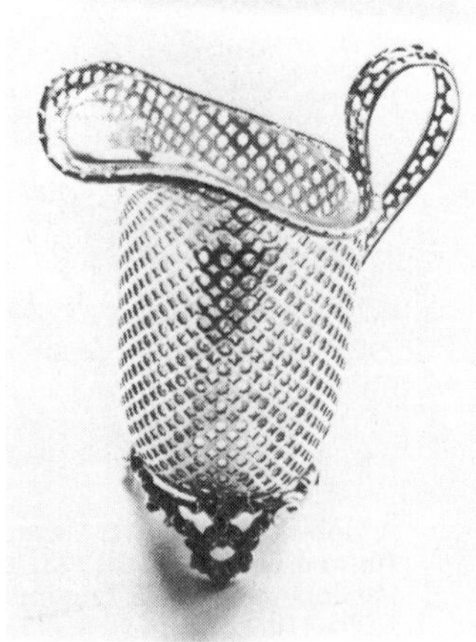
A Silver Cream Jug with glass liner. **£68-78** SA

A George III Silver Sugar Vase, 1796 by Henry Chawner and John Emes. 5¼ in., 13.7 cm., 6.7 oz. **£330-390** L

A George III Boat-Shaped Sugar Basket, engraved with open drapery cartouches, 5¼ in., 13.5 cm. wide, marked by Andrew Fogelberg, London, 1799, 7½ oz. **£290-350** SBe

A Good Pair of George III Silver Sugar and Cream Pails 1794 by John Denziloe, 6 in., 15.6 cm. and 5 in., 12.9 cm., 14.9 oz. **£700-800** L

A George III Boat-shaped Sugar Basket, 5½" (14cms) wide, marked, by Robert and David Hennell, London 1797, 6ozs. **£280-300** SBe

A George III Boat-Shaped Sugar Basket, thread swing handle, gilt interior, 5 in., 13 cm. wide, marked, by William Abdy II London, 1796, 5½ oz. **£440-500** SBe

A George III Boat-Shaped Sugar Basket, 6 in., 16 cm. long, by Robert Hennell, London, 1787, 6½ oz. **£350-410** SBe

A Good George III Silver Cream Pail 1796 by John Robins, 6½ in., 16.2 cm. across, 10.4 oz. **£600-680** L

A Victorian Circular Sugar Vase and Cover, pierced and engraved, 7½ in., 19.5 cm. high, by J. and J. Angel, London, 1840, 16 oz., with blue glass liner. **£340-380** SBe

A George III Irish boat-shaped Dish, 6" (16cms) wide, possibly by Richard Williams, Dublin 1876, 6ozs. **£230-270** SKC

A Victorian E.P.B.M. Sugar Bucket, 4½" high. **£20-25** SQE

An Edwardian Sugar-Bowl, with lazy-tongs in lid, 4½" high. **£24-30** SQE

A Good Queen Anne Two Handled Cup, 1706 by Joshua Field, 6¾ in., 17 cm. across, 9.1 oz. **£380-420** L

A Charles II plain silver-gilt porringer engraved under the foot with initials EM, 1676, maker's mark TC, a fish above. 7 ozs. 7 dwts., 3½ in., 8.9 cm. high. **£900-1,000** C

A George II Porringer, 5½ozs., London 1757 (maker's mark rubbed) 4" (10cms) diam. **£355-400** SKC

A Large Brittania-silver Queen Anne Porringer, 5½" (14cms) diam., 4¾" (12cms) high, 14½ozs., by John Wisdome, London 1709. **£775-825** SKC

An Early George I Two-Handled Cup, 5¼ in., 13.5 cm., by Seth Lofthouse, London, 1715, 13½ oz. **£340-420** SBe

A George III Porringer, by John Langlands, Newcastle 1770, 4" (10cms) high, 4ozs. **£210-250** SKC

An early George III silver porringer, 4½" diam., 4½" high, London 1766, 10½ozs. **£325-375** PWC

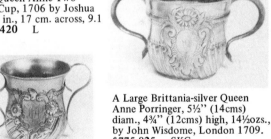

A William and Mary Two-Handled Porringer, 2¾ in. high, maker's mark T.K., a fish above and a tre-foil below, London, 1693, 4 oz. 3 dwt. **£600-670** S

A George II silver porringer, London 1731, by Sarah Parr, 10ozs. **£270-300** SH

A Commonwealth beaker, York, 1660, maker's mark IG 3 ozs. 3 dwts., 3½ in., 8.5 cm. high. **£450-500** C

A Victorian Silver Two Handled Sugar Bowl, 1848 John and Joseph Angell, 8¼ in., 21 cm. across handles, 13.1 oz. **£200-250** L

A William IV silver-gilt cylindrical Beaker, 3¾ in. high, by Charles Rawlings and William Summers, London, 1834, 6 oz. 19 dwt. **£460-520** S

A Rare William III provincial Tumbler Cup, 2¼ in., by Elizabeth Haslewood, Norwich, 1697, 3 oz. 19 dwt. **£2,400-2,600** S

A German silver-gilt Beaker, 3in., 8 cm high, by Rheinhold Riel, Nuremberg c.1685, 20oz 8dwt. **£700-780** S

A Swedish parcel-gilt beaker, with wrigglework rim, by Didrik Heitmuller, Nykoping, 1777, 16 ozs. 9 dwts., 8½ in. 21 cm. high. **£1,250-1,300** C

A Pair of George III Wine Goblets, gilt interiors, 5½ in., high, apparently no maker's mark, London, 1813, 16 oz. 18 dwt. **£1,100-1,300** S

A George III Goblet with gilt interior, by Peter, Anne and William Bateman, London, 1800., 6 in., 15.5 cm. high, 7 oz. **£330-400** SBe

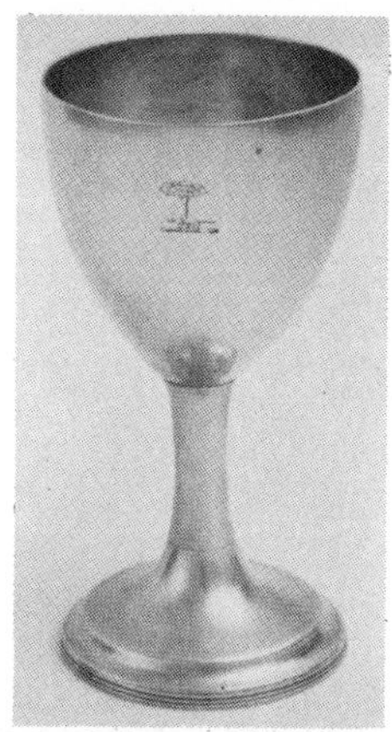

A Pair of George III Irish Goblets, by Joseph Jackson, Dublin, 1788, 6½" (17cms) high, 12ozs. **£690-840** SKC

A George II Bell-shaped Mug with a leaf-capped double scroll handle, 5" (13cms) high, by William Shaw and William Priest, London 1751, 12ozs. **£450-500** SKC

A Parallel-sided small Victorian Beer Can, parcel-gilt, 6ozs., 3½" (9cms) high, London 1862. **£170-200** SKC

A Queen Anne large plain cylindrical tankard on rim foot, cover with corkscrew thumbpiece, by Samuel Wastell, 1702, 7¼ in., 18.4 cm., high, 39 ozs. **£3,300-3,500** C

A George II Mug of baluster form, 12½ozs., by Francis Pages, London 1731, 4¼" (11cms). **£600-650** SKC

A Victorian Silver Goblet, by Martin Hall and Co., Sheffield 1865, 12cms high, 6ozs. **£145-175** SKC

A George V Campana-Shaped Christening Mug, 4¾ in., 12.5 cm., by Rebecca Emes and Edward Barnard, London, 1827, 8½ oz. **£200-240** SBe

A Late 18th C. American Baluster Mug with leaf capped double scroll handle, spreading base initialled 'I.K.', by Joseph & Nathaniel Richardson, Philadelphia, 5 in., 13.5 cm., high, 5½ oz. **£800-900** SBe

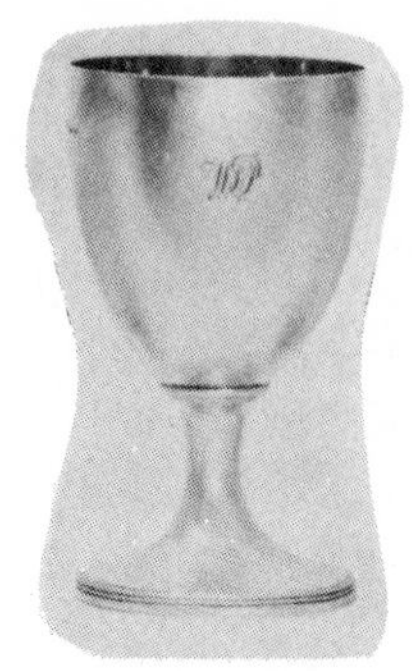

A George III Wine Goblet by William Barratt, London, 1814, 5 in., 13.5 cm., 5½ oz. **£270-350** SBe

A George III Mug, London 1764, by Thomas Whipham and Charles Wright, 14ozs., 5" (12.5cms). **£500-550** SKC

A William IV Campana-Shaped Christening Mug with chased leaves, foliate scroll handle, gilt interior, 5¼ in., 13.5 cm. high, by James Hobbs, London, 1834, 5¾ oz. **£140-160** SBe

A Good George III Tankard, by John Bailey London, 1751, 31ozs., 8" high. **£1,600-1,800** Bon.

A George II Baluster Tankard, 7¾ in., marked, by William Soame, London, 1748, 24 oz. 13 dwt. **£1,350-1,500** S

A Parallel-sided Victorian small beer Mug, parcel-gilt, 5½ozs., London 1871, 3½" (8.7cms). **£145-175** SKC

A George II Baluster Tankard, later monogrammed J.R.M., initialled I.M., 7¾" (19.5cms) high, marked, by Langlands an Goodrich, Newcastle, 1755, 24 24½ozs. **£920-1,100** SBe

A George III Tapered Cylindrical Tankard, 7¾ in. high, marked by Langlands & Robertson, Newcastle, 1785, 27 oz. 15 dwt. **£1,200-1,500** S

A Peter and Anne Batema Tankard, with engraved in London 1795, 28.5ozs., 9' **£850-950** Bon.

A Victorian cylindrical flagon dated 1880, by Robert Hennell III, 1840, 11 in., 28 cm., high, 65 ozs. **£2,000-2,200** C

A Silver Replica of a Stuart Tankard, 1909 maker's mark H. S. Ltd., and stamped Collingwood & Co., 6½ in., 16.5 cm. high., 20 oz. **£200-300** L

A George II Two-Handled Cup and Cover, leaf capped double scroll handles and on spreading foot, the domed cover similarly chased below the baluster finial, 11 in. high, marked on base and cover, by Thomas Wallis, London 1755, 38 oz. 13 dwt. **£1,250-1,400** S

A 20th C. Swedish Peg Tankard in the Late 17th C. Style, the hinged cover inscribed 'AKTIE-BOLAGET MOLNBACKA TRYSIL', 8¼ in., 21 cm., maker's mark C.G.H., silver coloured metal, 32 oz. **£300-350** SBe

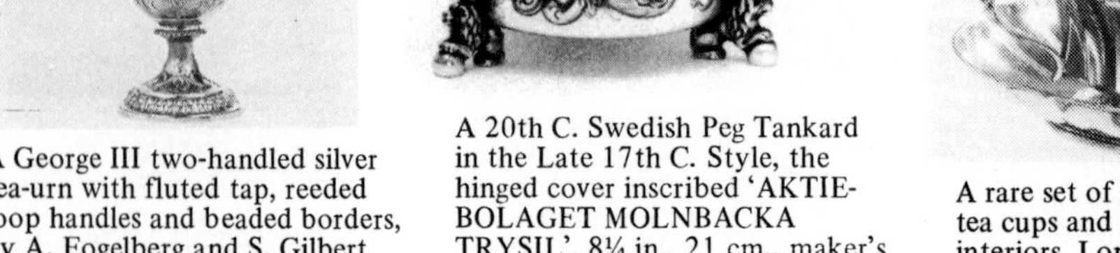

A George III two-handled silver tea-urn with fluted tap, reeded loop handles and beaded borders, by A. Fogelberg and S. Gilbert, 1780, 21¾ in., 55.2 cm., high, gross 122 ozs. **£3,100-3,400** C

A rare set of six William IV silver tea cups and saucers, with gilt interiors, London 1833, makers mark S & S, 47¼ozs. **£1,600-1,700** P.W.C.

A George III octagonal Mustard Pot, 1791 by Peter and Ann Bateman, with a spoon 1887 by Aldwincle and Slater, 3½ in., 9 cm. high. **£360-390** L

A George II two-handled Cup and Cover, 10" (26cms) high, by John Swift, London 1755, 34ozs. **£775-880** SKC

A German beaker and cover, Augsburg, c. 1690, maker's mark illegible 4½ in., 11.5 cm., high, 4 ozs. 15 dwts. **£935-1,000** C

An Early 19th C. Peruvian Chamber Pot, apparently unmarked. 7 in., 18 cm. diam., 27½ oz. **£400-480** SBe

A Charles II Bleeding Bowl, marks worn, apparently 1663, maker's mark conjoined, two pellets above. 7½ in., 18.8 cm. across, 6.4 oz. **£300-350** L

A Guild of Handicrafts Ltd. Mustard Pot and Cover with matching Spoon, designed by Charles Robert Ashbee, (finial missing), blue glass liner, 7cms high, 3ozs., stamped with maker's marks for London, 1903. **£200-225** P

A Dutch oval Brandy Bowl, 9¾ in., 25 cm. wide, by Ate Scheverstein, Leeuwarden, 1723, 7 oz. 18 dwt. **£1,900-2,100** S

A Victorian Presentation Punchbowl, 1891 makers mark FS & JH, 12¼in (31cm) diam, 67 oz. **£520-600** L

A Dutch Silver Vegetable Dish, 8" (20cms) diam., by Frans Simons, The Hague, 1799. **£1,220-1,250** SKC

By Hester Bateman, A George III Oval Straight Sided Mustard Pot with matching mustard spoon, makers mark London, 1787, with blue glass liner repaired. 4½ in., 11.5 cm. wide, 3½ oz. **£420-500** SBe

An Edward VII Circular Punch Bowl, presentation inscription dated 1904, 12" (30cms) by Mappin & Webb, London 1903. 53½ozs. **£440-480** SBe

A Circular Rose Bowl, chased with flowers and foliate scrolls, 11½ in., diam. by Messrs. Barnard, London, 1888, 47 oz. **£520-580** SBA

A Victorian silver-gilt punchbowl in George III taste, engraved with a presentation inscription dated 1906, by Elkington & Co., Birmingham, 1900, 12 in., 30.5 cm. diam., 89 ozs. **£1,375-1,500** C

An Interesting Silver Replica of The Glastonbury Bowl, Sheffield, 1923 by Thomas Bradbury & Son., 4½ in., 11.4 cm. diam., 12 oz. **£120-150** L

A Late Victorian Punchbowl of monteith form, 1895 makers mark WW & BT, 11½in (29cm) diam, 53oz. **£460-500** L

A Silver Rose Bowl, Birmingham 1938, 20ozs. **£250-300** HG

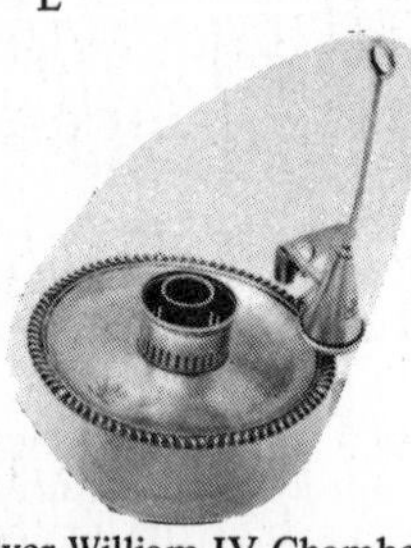
A Silver William IV Chamber Stick, hallmarked London 1833, maker 'E.E.J.W. Barnard', 5ozs., 6dwt. **£255-300** SKC

A William IV Chamber Candlestick, marked on base and extinguisher, by James Charles Edington, London, 1836, 5 in., 13 cm. diam., 13 oz. **£560-620** SBe

A George IV Chamber Candlestick, 5½" (14.5cms) diam. fully marked, by Richard Sibley London 1827, stamped Makepeace, London, 11½ozs. **£420-460** SBe

A Fine Victorian Silver Plated Chamberstick and Snuffer. **£55-60** CSG

A Sheffield Plate Chamberstick and Snuffer. **£28-35** SQE

A pair of George II candlesticks, 1735, maker's mark indistinct, 6¾ in., 17.5 cm. high, 24 ozs. **£2,400-2,600** C

A Good Victorian Silver Chamber Candlestick, 1852 by Robert Garrard, 6¼ in., 15.8 cm. across, 15 oz. **£440-500** L

A Pair of George II Table Candlesticks, 9¼ in., marked by Edward Wakelin, London, 1753, 54 oz. 7 dwt. **£3,200-3,400** S

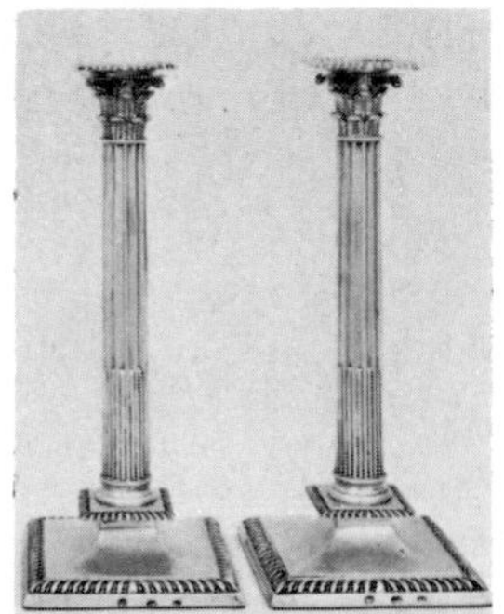

A Good Set of Four George III Candlesticks, Dublin, no date letter c. 1765 maker's mark RW probably for Richard Williams, 11 in., 27.8 cm. **£2,600-2,800** L

A Pair of Large Silver Candlesticks, of unusual Continental shape, by James Walker of Dublin, 1770. **£2,200-2,400** pr. SA

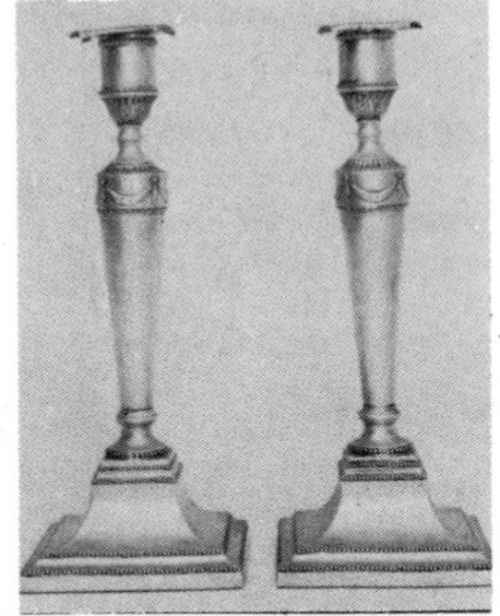

A Pair of George III Silver Candlesticks, Sheffield 1781 by Nathan Smith & Co., 11½ in., 29.3 cm. loaded. **£800-890** L

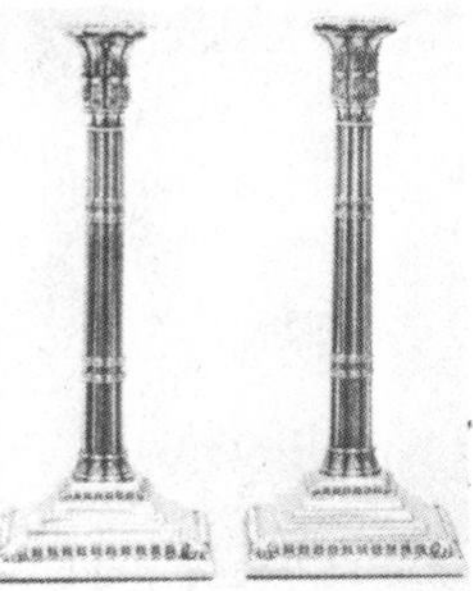

A Set of Four George III Cluster Column Candlesticks marked on bases and nozzles, by Ebeneezer Coker, London, 1769, loaded, 12½ in., 32 cm. high. **£2,000-2,200** SBe

A pair of Ebenezer Coker Candlesticks, London 1765, 37.5ozs., 10¼" high. **£1,850-2,000** Bon.

A Set of 4 silver Candlesticks, Sheffield 1902, 10¾" high. **£550-600** DH

A Pair of George III Table Candlesticks by John Carter, London, 1767., 10 in., 26.5 cm. high, one with repair to the stem, 40 oz. **£1,600-1,800** SBe

A Pair of Cast George II Silver Candlesticks by Ebenezer Coker, London 1753, 10 in. high. **£1,950-2,050** pr. SA

A Pair of George III Silver Candlesticks, by John Carter, London, c. 1780, of very good quality. **£1,950-2,050** pr. SA

A pair of George III candlesticks with detachable nozzles by D. Smith and R. Sharp, 1787, one nozzle 1802, maker's mark WS 10 in., 25.4 cm. high, 34 ozs. **£2,250-2,750** C

A Set of Four Hamilton & Inches Table Candlesticks, 24.5 cm., high, makers' mark, Edinburgh, 1904, stamped: 10976/K, loaded, worn. **£540-600** SB

A Pair of Edward VII Table Candlesticks in the mid 18th C., style, by the Goldsmiths and Silversmiths Co. Ltd., London, 1909, loaded, 10 in. 25 cm., high. **£500-600** SBe

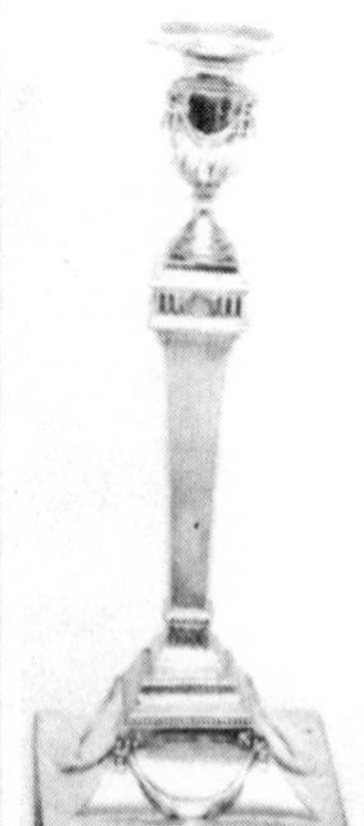

A Pair of Old Sheffield plate extending Candlesticks, 8½" (21.5cms) high (closed) and 10¾" (27.5cms) high (exten by Blagden, Hodgson and C c1820. **£170-200** SKC

A set of four George III Adam design Candlesticks 12½" high, Sheffield 1778, by John Smith, with separate sconces. **£1,160-1,200** A

A Pair of Sheffield Plated Telescopic Candlesticks, fitted with cranberry oil lamps, 19½" high, 21½" extended. **£200-230** pair SQE

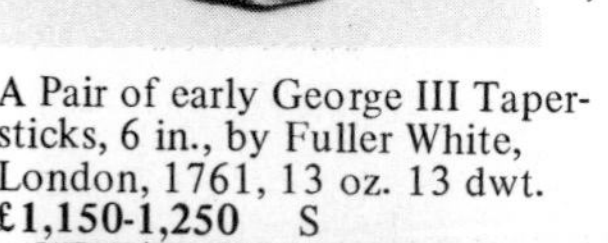

A Pair of early George III Taper-sticks, 6 in., by Fuller White, London, 1761, 13 oz. 13 dwt. **£1,150-1,250** S

A Set of Four Silver Plated Victorian Candlesticks, 9½ in., 24 cm. high. **£230-280** L

A Pair of James Dixon & Sons Arts and Crafts style silver Candlesticks, makers mark Sheffield 1905, 15¾" high. **£140-180** CSK

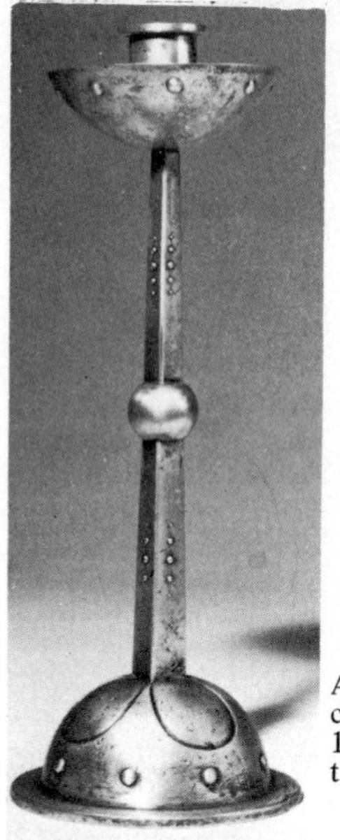

A set of four plated table candlesticks in George II-style 11½" (29.5cms) high, mark of the Cross Keys. **£250-300** SBe

A Pair of W. M. F. Plated Candlesticks, WMF marks, 27.5 cm., high. **£100-130** C

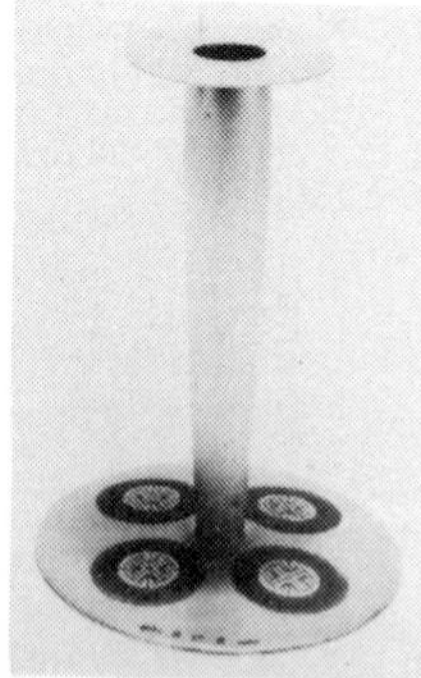

A Pair of Liberty & Co 'Cymric' silver and enamelled Candlesticks, embellished with four green-blue enamelled roundels stamped L & Co. 'Cymric', Birmingham hallmarks for 1901, 15.50cms high. **£240-280** P

A Set of Four Hawksworth, Eyre & Co., Electroplated table Candlesticks, maker's mark, late 19th C., 30.8 cm. high. **£360-400** SB

A Pair of Hawksworth, Eyre & Co., Ltd., Table candlesticks, maker's mark, Sheffield apparently 1895, loaded. 21 cm. high. **£560-620** SB

A Pair of Old Sheffield Plate Telescopic Candlesticks, c. 1815. **£85-95** CSG

A Large Victorian Centrepiece in the Form of Seven-Light Candelabrum, with crest and presentation inscription, central detachable foliate branch, 32½ in., 82.5 cm. high, fully marked, by Smith & Nicholson, London, 1854, 275 oz. **£3,500-4,500** SBe

A shaped circular Austrian Table Centrepiece in Art Nouveau style, in silver-coloured metal, c1900, 12" (33cms), 37ozs., 8dwt. **£250-350** SBA

A Three-Branch Sheffield Plate Candelabra (single), late Victorian, 17 in. high. **£110-130** VA

One of a Pair of Silver-Plated Candlesticks, 10 in. high. **£65-75** RB

A Victorian Electroplate Centre-Piece, 27" (69cms) high, c1860. **£400-550** SBe

A Large Victorian Electroplate Seven Light Candelabrum and Mirror Plateau. 29 in., 73 cm. high to centre. **£550-650** SBe

A Sheffield Table Centrepiece in the Regency style, c. 1820, no maker's mark, the original glass dishes missing, 17½in (44.5cm) high, **£470-560** L

An English Electroplated Table Centrepiece, fitted with dish holders (no dishes), 56 cm. high, apparently unmarked, c. 1861. **£390-460** SB

A Victorian Electroplate Centre-Piece and Mirror Plateau, three branches terminating in candle holders, 29¼ in., 74.5 cm. high, dish missing. **£300-340** SBe

A Victorian Centrepiece, engraved with presentation inscription dated 1853, by J.S. Hunt, 1854, 25¾in (65.4cm) high, (180 ozs), **£1,300-1,450** C

A Joseph Rodgers & Sons Ltd., Epergne, 61 cm. overall width, makers' mark, Sheffield, 1904, stamped: 10674, 1,352 gm. **£620-700** SB

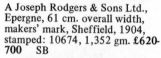

A George III Inkwell, 6¼ in. high, marked, by Benjamin Smith II and III, London, 1817, 32 oz. 10 dwt. **£1,900-2,050** S

A good George III silver inkstand, the three diamond cut receivers with silver covers, hallmarked London 1819, maket John Angell, 13¼ozs. **£375-425** P.W.C.

A George III Four-Branch Epergne, 8½ in., fully marked by Matthew Boulton, Birmingham, 1811, 64 oz. 2 dwt. (excluding five glass dishes). **£1,600-1,800** S

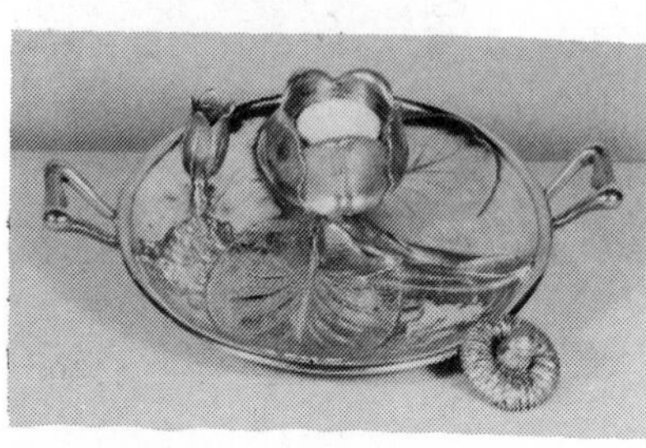

A Silver Inkwell in the form of a Waterlily by C. Jordan of London, 1836. **£500-550** SA

A William IV Unusual Inkstand in the form of a clam shell, 5¼ in., 13 cm. high, fully marked, by Thomas Dexter, London, 1833. **£190-240** SBe

A French silver-gilt two-handled Pot-Pourri Stand Paris, 1819-38, makers mark indistinct 5¼in (13.3cm) high, (gross 9ozs) **£870-970** C

A Victorian large silver vase, chased and applied with three putti by Messrs. Hancock, 1866, 20¾ in., 52.7 cm. high, 203 ozs. **£3,000-3,250** C

A Silver Filigree, Lacquer and Shibyama Dish, the shaped filigree border enclosing a gold lacquer panel decorated in shibyama, signed. 11½ in., 280 cm. across. **£850-950** L

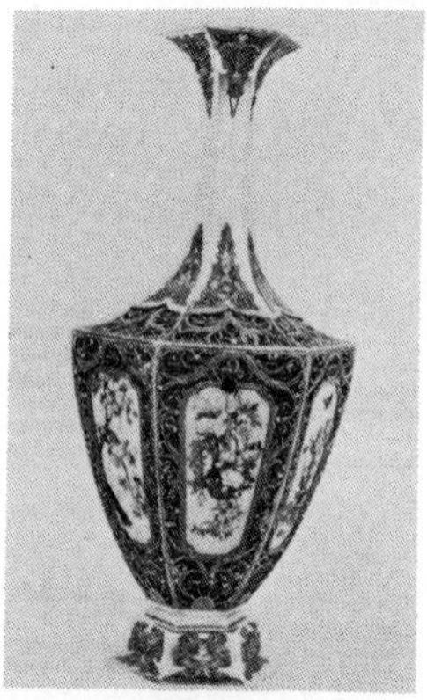

A Fine Silver Filigree Shibyama and coloured enamel vase, one panel signed Yasu. 10½ in., 26.7 cm. high. **£1,250-1,350** L

A fine Victorian silver Standish by the Barnard family –'E.E.J. and W.' with two cut-glass bottles, and a chamber-style taper stick and wax holder, London 1838, 14ozs. **£375-400** SKC

An Old Sheffield Plate Standish, 7¼" x 5½". **£155-200** SKC

A Late Victorian Rectangular Inkstand with pierced foliate three-quarter gallery, gadroon edging, flanked by two square cut glass bottles with silver mounts, makers mark J. G. & S. London, 1898, 12 in., 31 cm., 36 oz. weight of stand. **£450-520** SBe

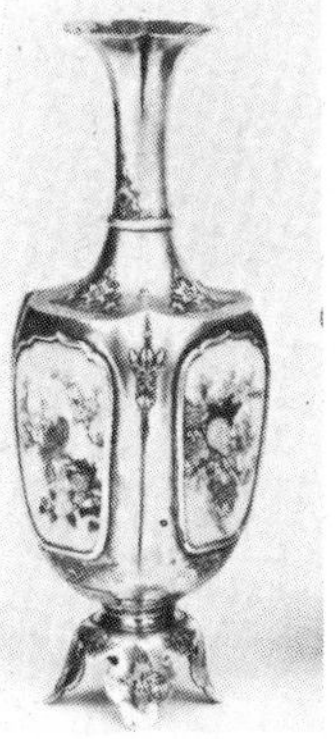

A fine pair of Shibayama-style silver quatrefoil vases decorated in coloured enamels signed on the bases Kazunori, late 19th C, 19.3cms high. **£1,200-1,400** C

A Pair of George IV oblong seven-bar Toastracks, 6¼ in. wide, by Robert Hennell, London, 1824, 30 oz. 18 dwt. **£1,200-1,350** S

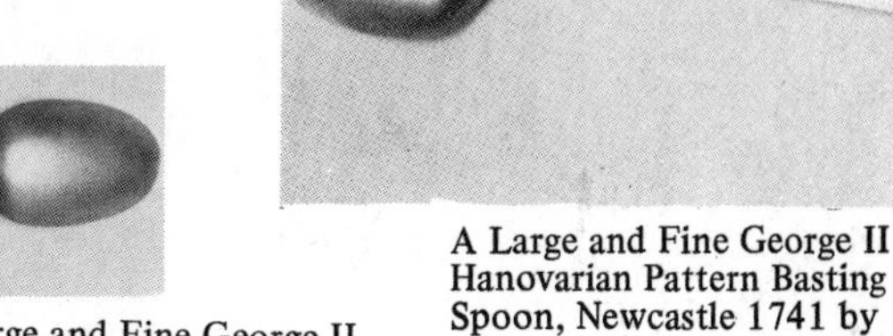

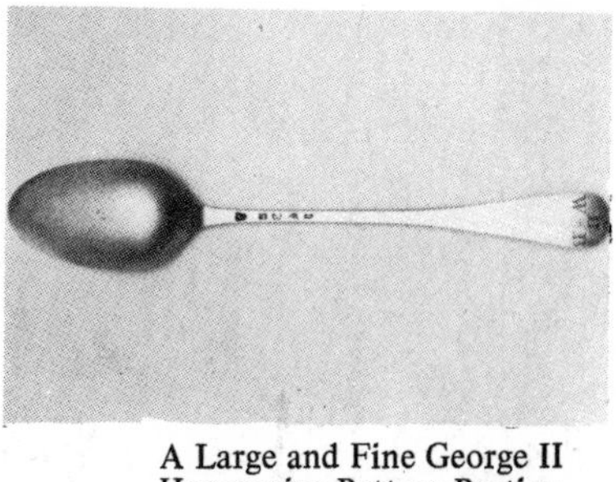

A Large and Fine George II Hanovarian Pattern Basting Spoon, Newcastle 1741 by Isaac Cookson, 7.5oz. **£330-400** L

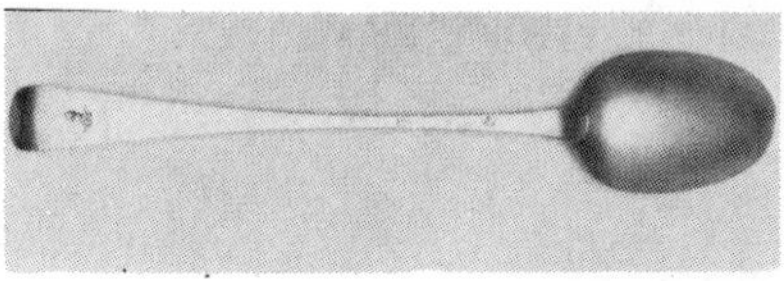

A Large and Fine George II Hanovarian Pattern Basting Spoon, Dublin 1743 by Christopher Skinner, 8.2 oz. **£430-470** L

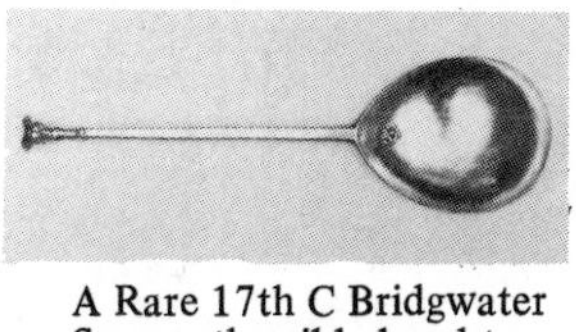

A Rare 17th C Bridgwater Spoon, the gilded seal top terminal priced ID 1660 ID, **£450-500** L

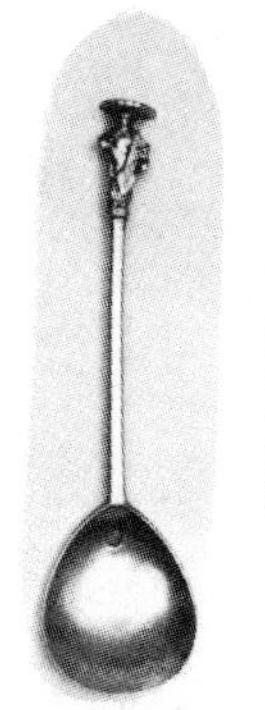

A Provincial Seal Top Spoon, marked with a cinquefoil in the bowl, probably Leicester, c. 1630, **£230-260** L

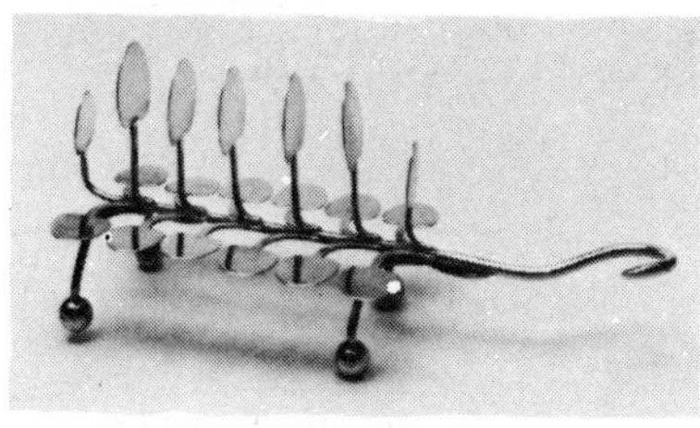

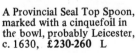

An Unusual Silver Toast Rack, dated 1858. **£215-235** SA

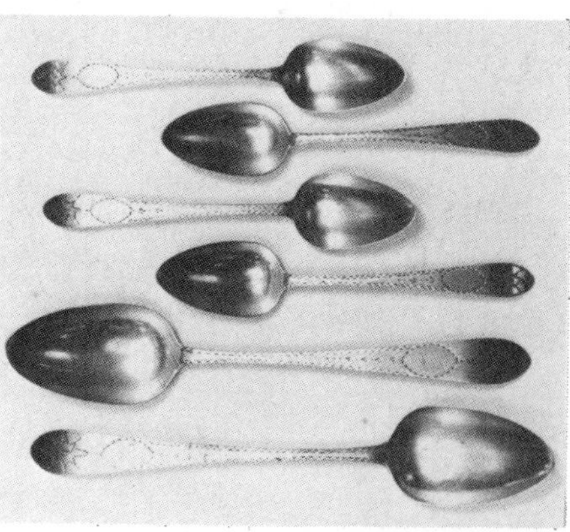

A Collection of six George III Irish silver Spoons, four desserts and two serving spoons, Dublin 1795, 7ozs. **£145-175** SKC

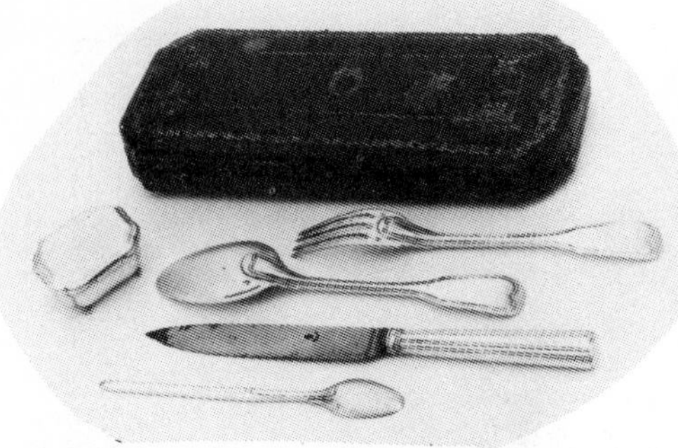

An Augsburg mid- 18th C silver travelling set. **£1,000-1,200** Bon.

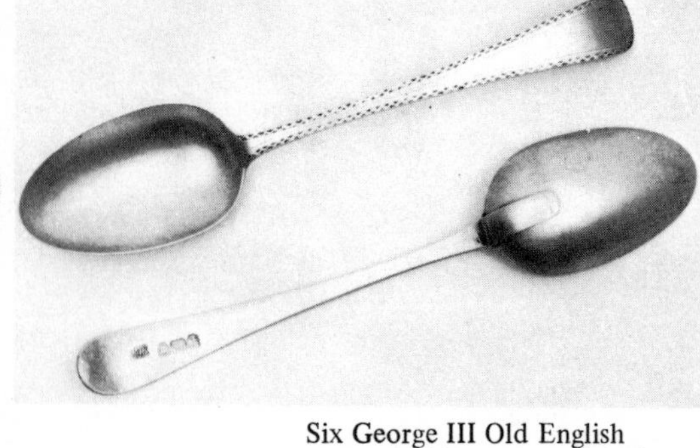

Six George III Old English pattern table spoons, the grips with chevron and wrigglework edges, 1781 by Hester Bateman, 12.1 oz. (6) **£300-340** L

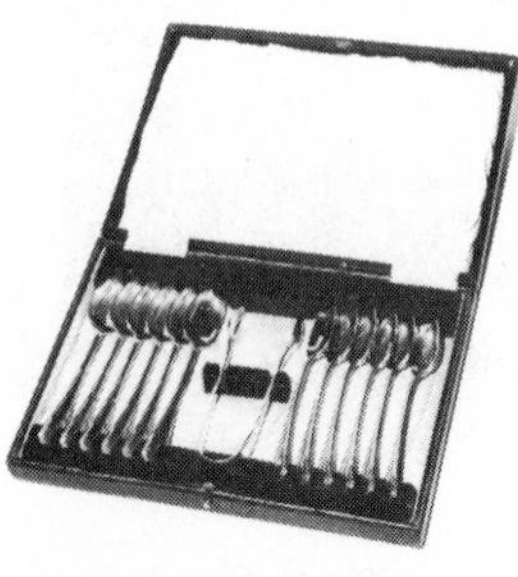

A Set of Twelve Silver Plate Teaspoons and sugar tongs, 20th C. **£20-25** VA

An Edwardian rectangular silver photo frame, in the Art Nouveau style, maker's mark A. & J. Z., Birmingham 1904, 27 cm., 10½ in. high. **£100-120** O

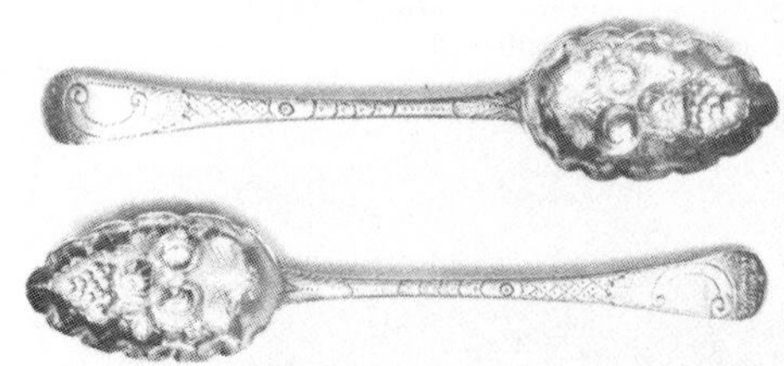

A Pair of George III Silver Berry Spoons, by William Eley, William Fearn and William Chawner, the bowls gilded, London 1811. **£65-75** SKC

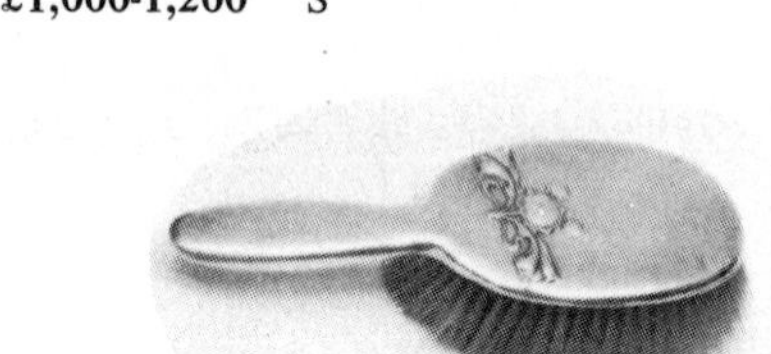

An 18th C. Dutch Fish Slice, 15 in., 38 cm., long, by Jan Diederik Pont of Bremen, Amsterdam, 1760, 6 oz. 15 dwt. **£1,000-1,200** S

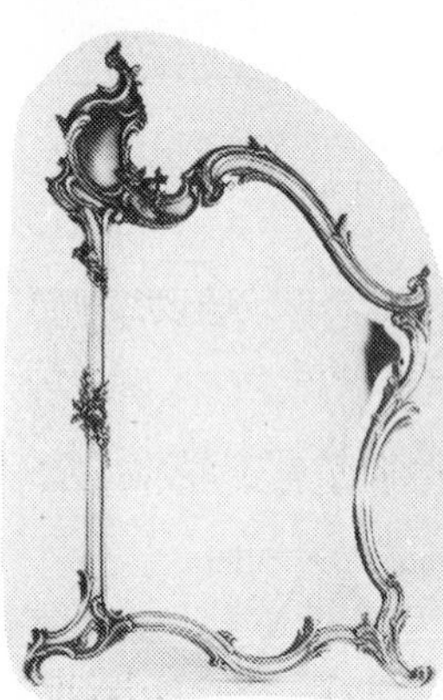

A large Russian silver-mounted dressing-table mirror in the art nouveau style, by Carl Faberge, Moscow with Imperial Warrant Mark, overall height 27¼ in., 69.5 cm. **£2,000-2,250** C

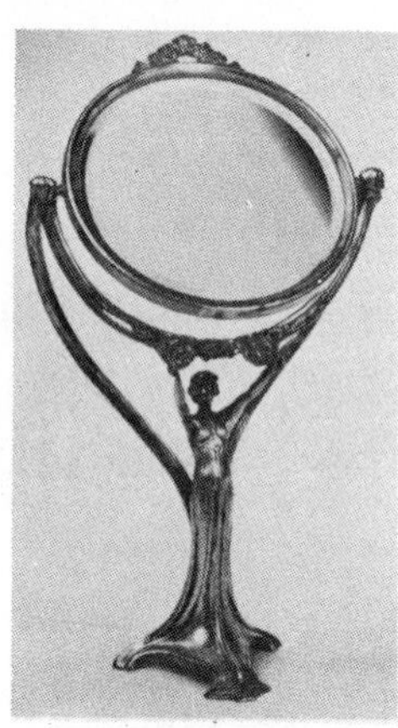

A W. M. F. Plated Toilet-Mirror, impressed marks, 51 cm. high. **£450-500** C

A George V oval silver photo frame London 1910, 26.5 cm. 10½ in., high. **£80-100** O

A George II Silver Ladle with shell bowl and Onslow handle, by Elizabeth Eaton, c. 1753. **£275-300** SA

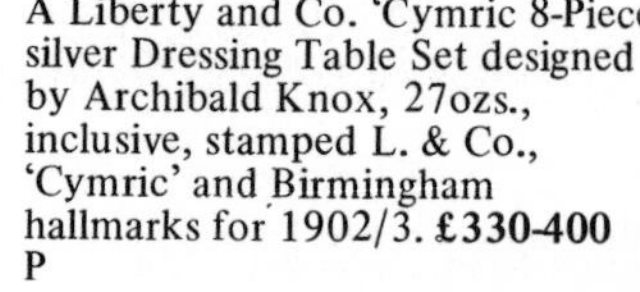

A Liberty and Co. 'Cymric 8-Piece silver Dressing Table Set designed by Archibald Knox, 27ozs., inclusive, stamped L. & Co., 'Cymric' and Birmingham hallmarks for 1902/3. **£330-400** P

A Pierced Horse-Shoe-Bowl Caddy Spoon by John Betteridge, Birmingham, 1804. **£95-105** SA

A Rare Sunflower Caddy Spoon, Hilliard & Thomason, Birmingham, 1852. **£140-160** SA

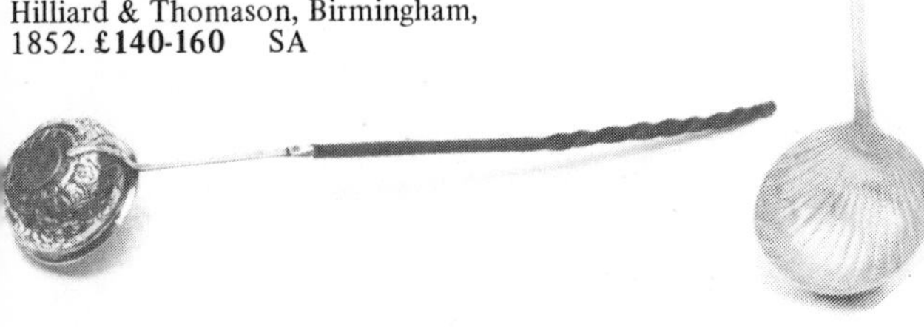

A Silver Punch Ladle with coin at bottom, late 18th C. **£95-105** SA

A George II Irish Soup Ladle, by James Douglas, Dublin 1736, 6ozs. **£255-300** SKC

A Gorham Manufacturing Co., Rectangular Easel Mirror, 43.2 cm., high, makers' mark, Birmingham 1912. **£400-450** SB

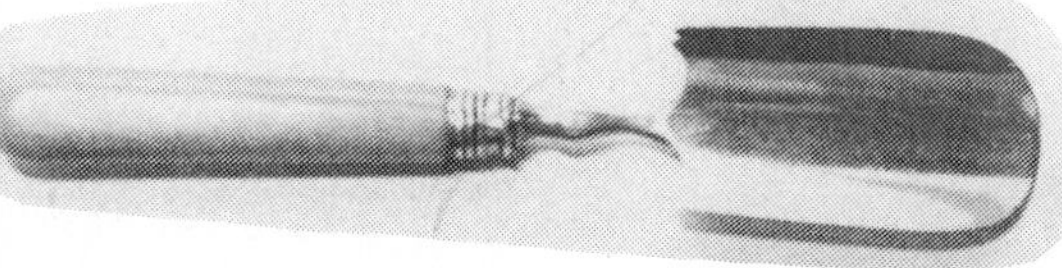

A Silver Cheese Scoop with bone handle, Birmingham, 1803, 6" long. **£65-75** SQE

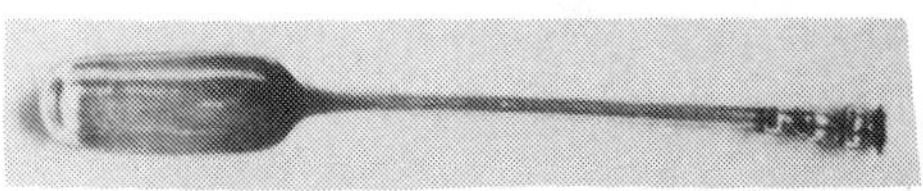

A Rare Marrow Scoop with a seal at top end, G. Angell, 1859. **£85-95** SA

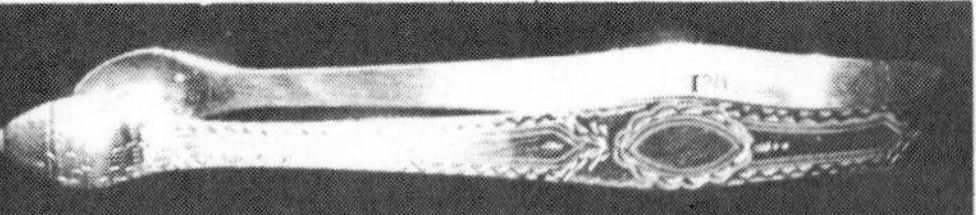

Silver Sugar Tongs, London c. 1780, Hester Bateman. **£55-60** CSG

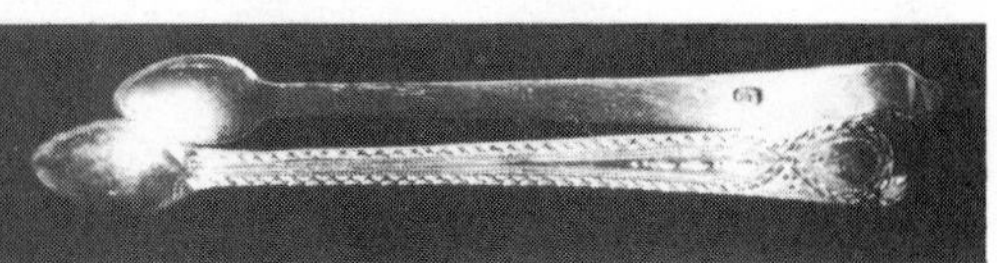

Silver Sugar Tongs, London, c. 1790, maker I.L., bright cut. **£24-30** CSG

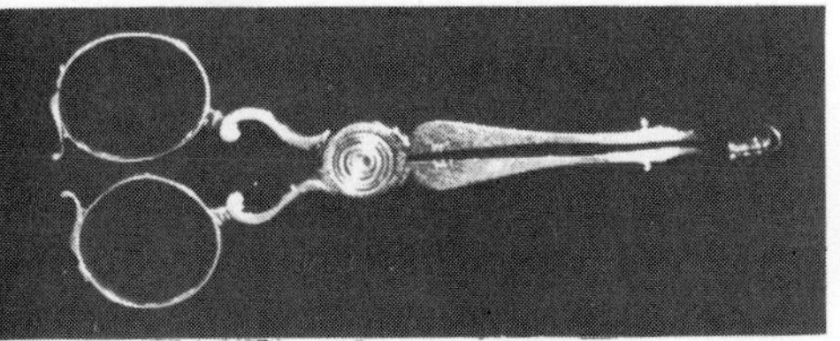

Early Georgian Sugar Nips, c. 1750, John Andrews. **£55-65** CSG

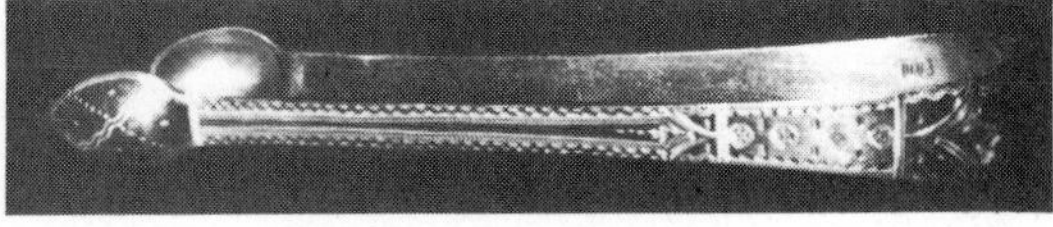

Silver Sugar Tongs, London 1825, Wm. Elliot, thread and shell. **£27-32** CSG

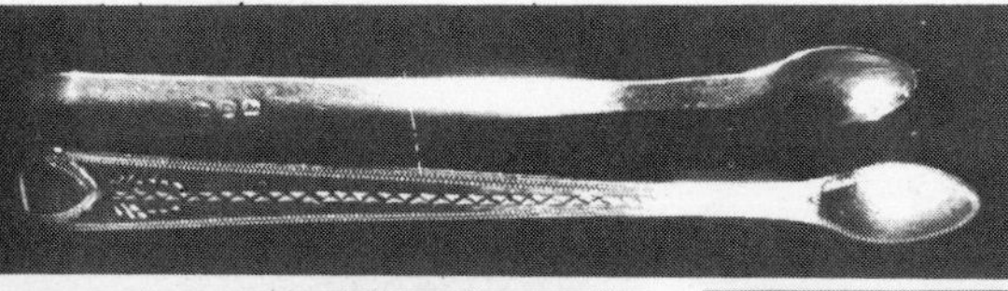

Silver Sugar Tongs, London 1811, A & G Burrows, bright cut. **£25-30** CSG

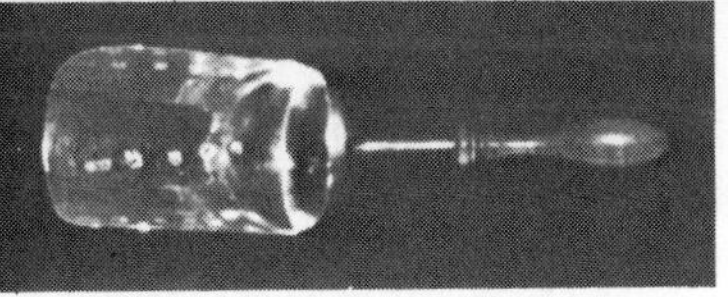

A Silver Caddy Spoon, Birmingham 1801, Cocks & Betteridge bone handle. **£44-50** CSG

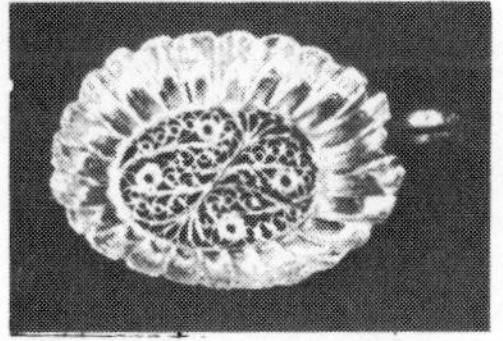

A Silver Caddy Spoon, Birmingham 1806. **£95-105** CSG

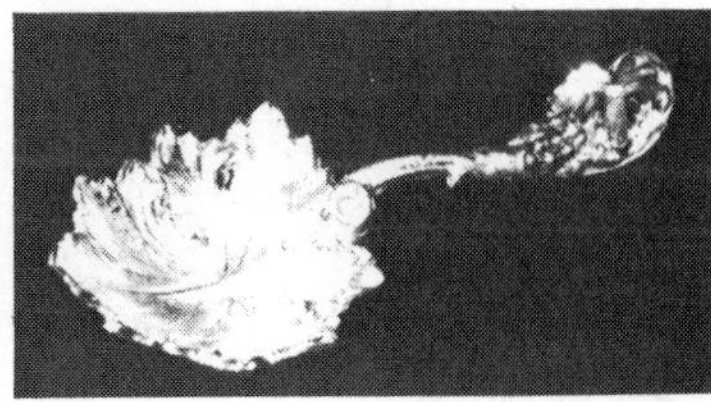

A Silver Caddy Spoon, London 1851, Edward Carrell. **£98-105** CSG

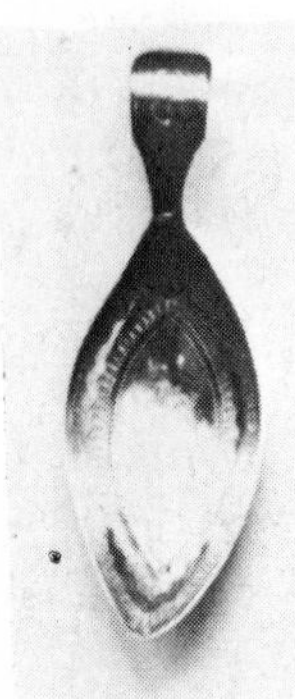

A Silver Flame-Bowl Caddy Spoon, William Pugh, 1810. **£85-95** SA

A Silver Pierced Caddy Spoon, George Baskerville, Birmingham, 1799. **£95-110** SA

A Silver Caddy Spoon, Joseph Taylor, 1827. **£95-110** SA

A Silver Wine Label by James Phipps, c. 1780. **£75-85** SA

Three Hester Bateman Wine Labels, with pierced dome tops, c. 1780. **£350-400** set. SA

A Set of Five George III Irish Wine Labels, by Benjamin Tait, Dublin, c1790. **£310-350** SKC

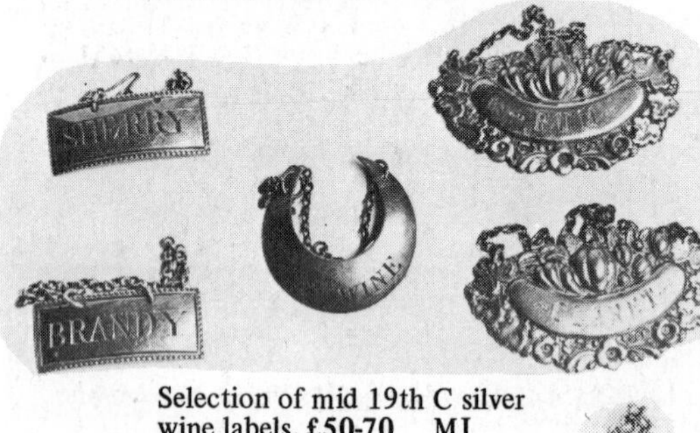

Selection of mid 19th C silver wine labels. **£50-70** MJ

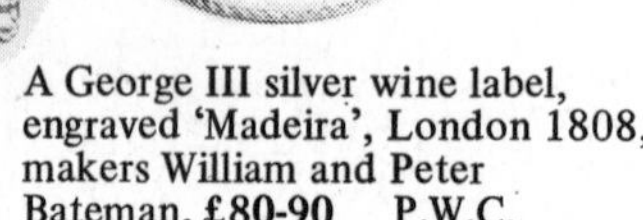

A George III silver wine label, engraved 'Madeira', London 1808, makers William and Peter Bateman. **£80-90** P.W.C.

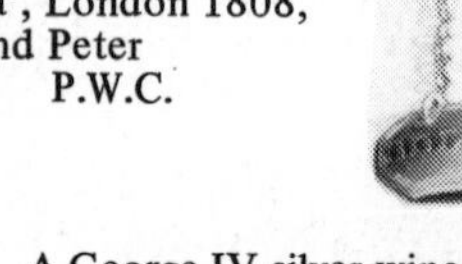

A George IV silver wine label pierced 'Hollands', Edinburgh hallmarks, makers mark A.W. **£40-45** P.W.C.

A George IV silver wine label, pierced 'Madeira', London 1824, maker's mark R.C. **£45-55** P.W.C.

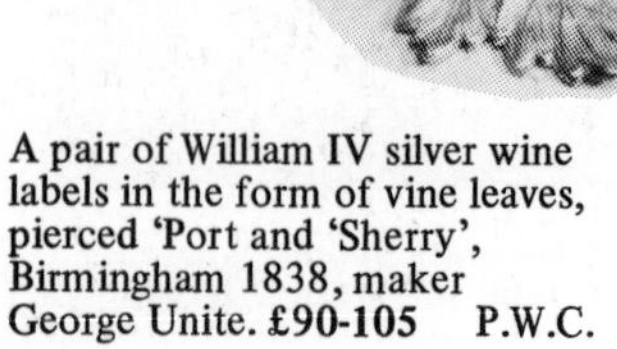

A pair of William IV silver wine labels in the form of vine leaves, pierced 'Port and 'Sherry', Birmingham 1838, maker George Unite. **£90-105** P.W.C.

A Victorian silver wine label, pierced 'Brandy', London 1853, makers Edward and John Barnard. **£45-55** P.W.C.

A George IV silver wine label, pierced 'Madeira', London 1830, makers Rawlings and Sumner. **£55-65** P.W.C.

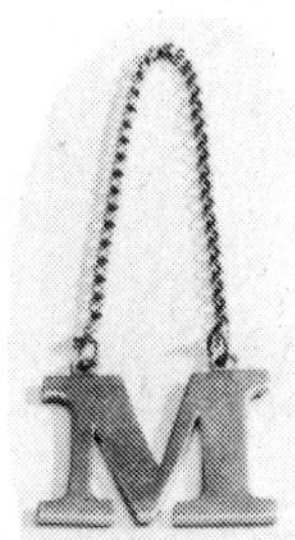

A William IV silver wine label, in the form of the initials 'M' (Madeira), Birmingham 1838, Makers mark R.F.A. **£40-45** P.W.C.

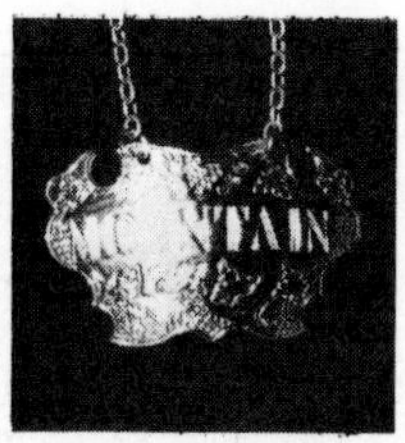

A Silver Wine Label, London 1824, John Reily (Madiera). **£50-60** CSG

A Silver Wine Label (Mountain), London, c. 1750 Sandilands Drinkwater. **£60-70** CSG

A Victorian silver wine label, engraved 'Whiskey', Birmingham 1867, maker George Unite. **£30-40** P.W.C.

A Silver Wine Label, Birmingham 1831, Taylor & Perry (Madiera). **£42-50** CSG

A French Art Deco Rectangular Casket, Silver coloured metal, 9 in., 23 cm., 42 oz. **£400-450** L

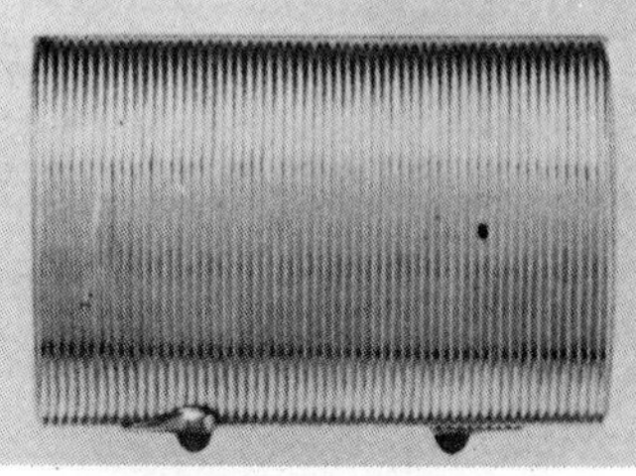

A Faberge reeded gold cigarette-case, the covers each with cabochon sapphire push-piece, 19th C. Imperial Warrant mark of Faberge, Moscow, 3½ in., 90 mm. long. **£2,600-2,850** C

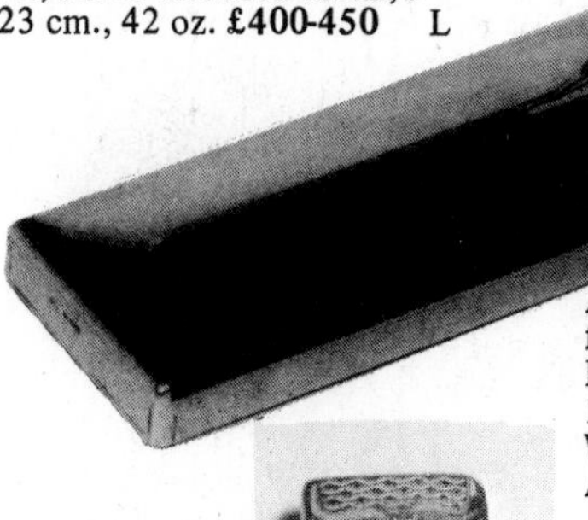

A Faberge Silver Gilt Box, the fastener set with blue gemstone, Bears import mark 925, London 1911, Bears mark of Henrik Wigstrom, 6½" x 1¾". **£720-780** A

Silver vinaigrette, c1820. **£200-225** MJ

Silver vinaigrette, c1820. **£120-150** MJ

Silver gilt vinaigrette by Edward Jones, Birmingham 1858. **£300-350** MJ

Silver gilt vinaigrette by Joseph Willmore, Birmingham 1820. **£200-250** MJ

A George III oblong silver-gilt Vinaigrette, 1¾ in. wide, by Phipps, Robinson and Phipps, London, 1813. **£600-670** S

Silver vinaigrette and pill box by William Pugh, Birmingham 1808. **£200-250** MJ

POINTERS FOR VINAIGRETTES

- Popular in the 1770's.
- Made in large numbers from 1800 until 1850's mainly in Birmingham.
- Most Vinaigrettes are rectangular, more rarely square, usually of silver.
- Later, embossed lids, were mechanically pressed.
- Some of the best work was done by Nathaniel Mills 1830's to 1840's.
- Made until the end of the 19th C.

A George III Vinaigrette, gilt interior, 1¼" (3cms), maker's mark I.B., Birm., 1818. **£80-110** SBe

Nathaniel Mills, A Victorian shaped rectangular Vinaigrette, Birmingham 1842, 1½ in., 4.2 cm. **£320-350** L

A George III Satchel Vinaigrette with gilt interior, by Samuel Pemberton, Birmingham, 1818, slight damage to hinge, 1¼ in., 3.5 cm. **£125-145** SBe

Silver vinaigrette by Joseph Willmore, Birmingham 1819. **£250-275** MJ

Silver vinaigrette by Thomas Shaw, Birmingham 1826. **£250-275** MJ

Silver vinaigrette, mark worn. **£200-225** MJ

A George III Vinaigrette, gilt interior, 1¾" (4.5cms) by Thomas Phipps and Edward Robinson 11, London, 1796. **£180-240** SBe

A George III Vinaigrette, with gilt interior, 1½" (4cms) by Nathaniel Mills, Birm., 1829. **£140-190** SBe

Silver vinaigrette by Thomas Pemberton, Birmingham 1825. **£300-350** MJ

A George III Rectangular Vinaigrette, gilt interior, chased and pierced acorn grill (hinge damaged) by Joseph Taylor, Birmingham 1807, 1¼ in., 3.3 cm. **£100-120** SBe

Silver vinaigrette by Gervase Wheeler, Birmingham 1835. **£200-250** MJ

A Good William IV Silver Gilt Vinaigrette, Birmingham 1836 by William Phillips, 1½ in., 3.6 cm. **£340-370** L

A George IV Rectangular Vinaigrette with engine-turned decoration, gilt interior, by Ledsam, Vale and Wheeler, Birmingham 1826, 1¼ in., 3.4 cm. **£180-210** SBe

Gold and moss agate vinaigrette, c1840. **£250-300** MJ

A Silver Purse Vinaigrette by Joseph Willmore, Birmingham, 1799. **£295-300** SA

A George III Shaped Rectangular Vinaigrette, with gilt interior, by Samuel Pemberton, Birmingham. 1816. **£80-95** SBe

Silver vinaigrette, indistinctly marked C.S., c1820. **£100-150** MJ

ilver vinaigrette by Thomas haw, Birmingham 1825. **£100-25** MJ

Silver vinaigrette, unmarked, c1820. **£250-275** MJ

Silver vinaigrette, mark worn. **£150-175** MJ

Silver vinaigrette by Matthew Linwood, Birmingham 1820. **£250-300** MJ

ilver vinaigrette marked J.L., irmingham 1815. **£200-250** J

Silver vinaigrette by Edward Smith, Birmingham 1833. **£200-250** MJ

Silver vinaigrette with repousse top, by Nathaniel Mills, Birmingham 1850. **£450-500** MJ

Silver vinaigrette by T. Pemberton & Sons, Birmingham 1825. **£300-325** MJ

ilver vinaigrette by Thomas haw, Birmingham 1825. **£150-75** MJ

Silver vinaigrette, Birmingham c1820. **£200-225** MJ

Silver vinaigrette by Francis Clark, Birmingham 1838, (damaged). **£100-125** MJ

Silver vinaigrette by Edward Thomason and William Fowke, Birmingham 1828. **£250-275** MJ

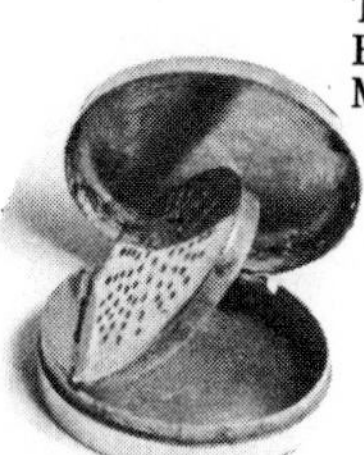

ilver vinaigrette by Edward ones, Birmingham 1858. **£250-75** MJ

Gold vinaigrette, mid 19th C. **£400-450** MJ

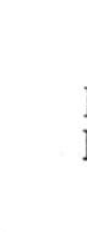

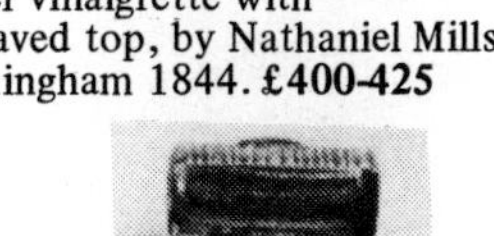

Silver vinaigrette by L & Co., Birmingham 1904. **£250-300** MJ

Silver vinaigrette with engraved top, by Nathaniel Mills, Birmingham 1844. **£400-425** MJ

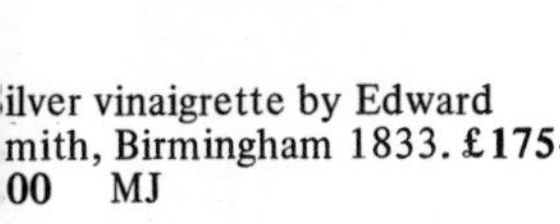

ilver vinaigrette by Edward mith, Birmingham 1833. **£175-00** MJ

Silver vinaigrette by Thomas Shaw, Birmingham c1820. **£200-225** MJ

Silver vinaigrette, Birmingham c1820. **£150-175** MJ

ilver snuff box by Nathaniel ills, Birmingham 1844. **£350-75** MJ

A Rectangular Vinaigrette, decorated with a view of Westminster Abbey 1½ in. wide, marked, by Frederick Marson, Birmingham, 1845. **£580-630** S

Silver vinaigrette by Joseph Willmore, Birmingham 1820. **£300-350** MJ

A Rectangular silver-gilt Vinaigrette, decorated with a view of Windsor Castle, 1½ in. wide, marked, by Nathaniel Mills, Birmingham, 1837. **£580-640** S

A Rectangular Vinaigrette, with a view of Windsor Castle, 1½ in. wide, marked by Nathaniel Mills, Birmingham, 1845. **£520-580** S

A Rectangular silver-gilt Vinaigrette, decorated with a view of Windsor Castle, 1½ in. wide, marked, by Nathaniel Mills, Birmingham, 1837. **£440-480** S

A William IV rectangular Vinaigrette, 1½ in. wide, marked by J. Willmore, Birmingham, 1832. **£260-290** S

A William IV oblong silver-gilt Vinaigrette, engine turned, 1¼ in. wide, maker's mark JB, Birmingham, 1830. **£190-240** S

A rectangular silver-gilt Vinaigrette, 1½ in. wide, fully marked, by Gervase Wheeler, Birmingham, 1838. **£580-650** S

A William IV oblong silver-gilt Vinaigrette, 1½ in. wide, fully marked, by Thomas Newbold, Birmingham, 1827. **£130-150** S

Gold vinaigrette with carved citrine top, mid 19th C. **£450-500** MJ

Russian silver snuff box with engraved top, c1850, (repaired). **£150-175** MJ

A George IV rectangular silve gilt Vinaigrette, engine turnec with a vacant cartouche and floral borders in relief, foliate grille, 1¼ in. wide, marked by J. Bettridge, Birmingham, 18 **£170-190** S

A Rare and Unusual Victorian Vinaigrette, with detachable gilt grille 1¼ in. wide, by Henry Wilkinson & Co., 1843. **£290-320** S

An Early Victorian Snuff Box, the lid dated 1842, gilt interior, 3½" (9cms), by Edward Smith, Birmingham, 1841, 4½oz. **£140-190** SBe

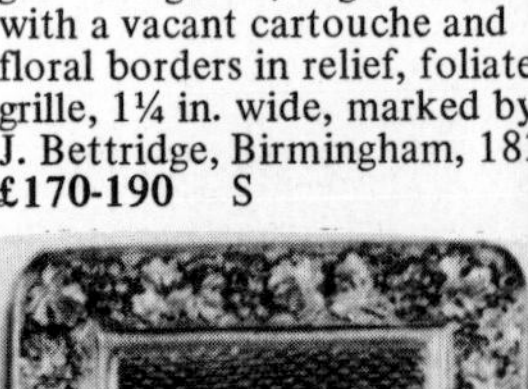

A George III oblong silver-gil Vinaigrette, 1½ in. wide, fully marked, by S. Pemberton, Birmingham, 1813 (fitted cas **£340-380** S

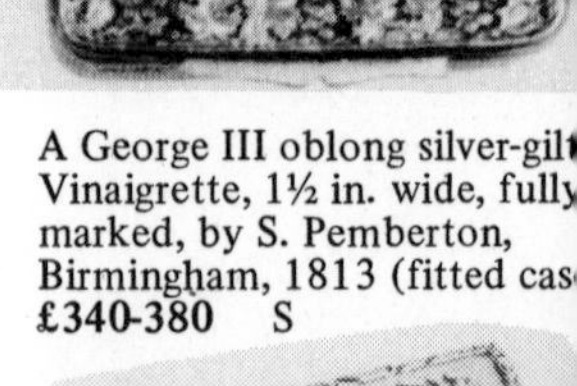

A George IV Heavy oblong Snuff Box, 3½" x 2½", parcel gilt interior, Birmingham 1826 by John Bettridge, 9ozs. **£500-520** A

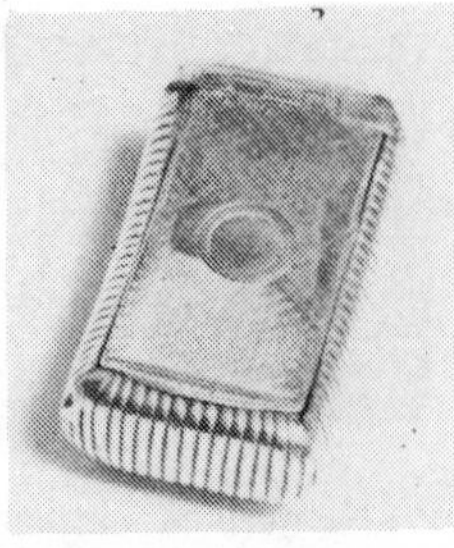

Small Silver Snuff Box, indistinctly marked WE, Birmingham c1835. **£150-175** MJ

Silver snuff box by Thomas Shaw, Birmingham, 1825. **£250-275** MJ

An Early Victorian Rectangular Snuff-Box with gilt interior, by Nathaniel Mills, Birmingham, 1837, 2¼ in., 6 cm., 1¾ oz. **£410-480** SBe

Silver Snuff Box by Nathaniel Mills, Birmingham 1850. **£400-450** MJ

Silver Snuff Box by Samuel Pemberton, Birmingham 1817, (damaged). **£120-150** MJ

A 19th C French Silver and Niello Snuff Box, 3¼" (8.5cms) wide, maker's mark worn c1830, 2¾oz. **£180-280** SBe

English Silver Snuff Box, unmarked, c1830. **£150-175** MJ

Silver Snuff Box, indistinctly marked F.E., Birmingham c1820-30. **£200-225** MJ

A Fine George III Gold Snuff Box, 1807 by Alexander James Strachan, 75 mm. **£1,350-1,450**

A Good Quality Early 18th C. Pique Snuff Box, c. 1720. **£275-320** SA

A Silver Snuff Box, John Jones, London, 1824. **£750-850** SA

A Nathaniel Mills Rectangular Snuff Box, the hinged lid engraved, maker's mark, Birmingham, 1839, 8.4 cm. long, 157 gm. **£300-350** SB

Nathaniel Mills, A William IV snuff box, Birmingham 1833, 2¾ in., 6.9 cm. **£150-180** L

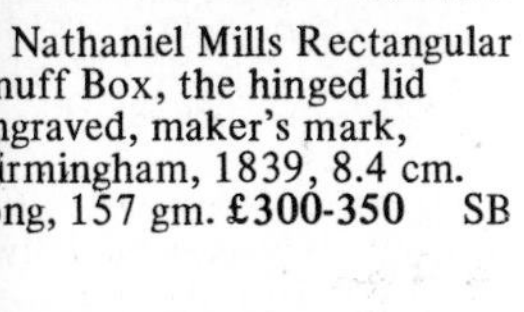

A Mid-19th C Russian Silver and Niello Snuff Box, 3¼" (8.5cms) wide, Moscow, date mark worn, possible 1859, 3½oz. **£190-290** SBe

A William IV Snuff Box, Birmingham 1836 by Edward Smith, 2¾ in., 7.3 cm. **£175-225** L

A George III Silver Navette Shaped Snuffbox, 1787 by James Hyde, 4 in., 10 cm., 5.1 oz. **£500-550** L

Silver snuff box, indistinctly marked WD, Birmingham c1830. **£220-225** MJ

Silver Snuff Box by Edward Smith, Birmingham 1844. **£250-300** MJ

George III Silver Table Snuff Box by John Crouch, Birmingham 1808. **£175-225** MJ

Silver Snuff Box by Francis Clark, Birmingham 1836. **£200-250** MJ

Russian Silver Snuff Box with engraved top, c1850, (repaired). **£150-175** MJ

Late 18th C silver nutmeg grater, Birmingham c1830-40. **£250-300** MJ

A Silver Card Case by Nathaniel Mills, 1852. **£185-195** SA

Silver Snuff Box by Thomas Shaw, Birmingham 1825. **£200-250** MJ

Silver Snuff Box by Thomas Shaw, Birmingham 1826. **£200-250** MJ

Silver Snuff Box, Birmingham c1830. **£150-200** MJ

A George III Nutmeg Grater, 1½" (4cms) by Thomas Willmore, Birm., 1802. **£150-200** SBe

A Good Quality Silver Nutmeg Grater, c. 1820. **£130-160** SA

A Good Silver Morden Card Case, well engraved with Kate Greenaway Scenes, 1889. **£185-200** SA

Silver Snuff Box, indistinctly marked W.A., Birmingham c1820-30. **£150-200** MJ

Silver Snuff Box, indistinctly marked W.S., Birmingham c183 **£200-225** MJ

A Very Rare Silver Canadian Posy Holder, c. 1800. **£225-275** SA

A Scandinavian silver nutmeg-grater with threaded cover, 18th C. 1¾ in., 45 mm. high. **£110-150** C

An Embossed Card Case, unknown scene, c. 1860
poor marks **£75-85**
good marks **£275-350** S

A Victorian Card Case, by Nathanial Mills, Birmingham 1846, 3¼" (8.5cms) high. **£225-300** SKC

A George V Large Rectangular Cigar Box, 12¼ in., 31 cm. wide, by Walker and Hall, London, 1925, wood lined. **£300-350** SBe

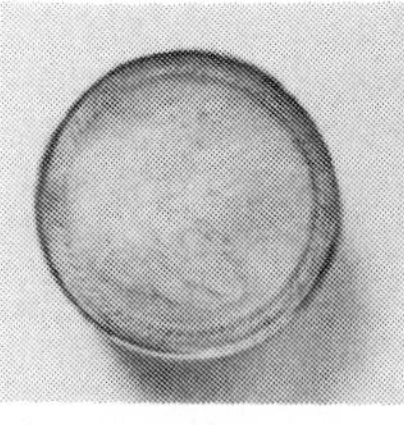
A Patch Box, Engraved with Portrait of Charles II, in mother-of-pearl and silver, 1685. **£275-325** SA

A Victorian silver Cheroot Case, by Nathaniel Mills, Birmingham 1847. **£265-285** SKC

An 18th century Dutch oblong Tobacco Box, 5 in., 13 cm. wide, by Evert Bot, Amsterdam, 1758. **£950-1,050** S

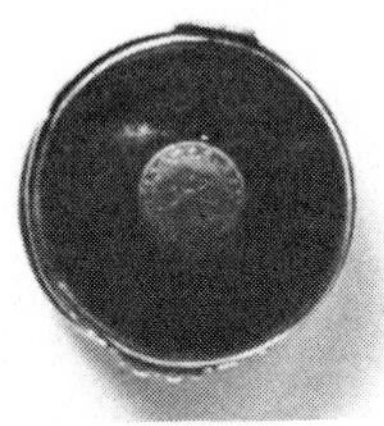
A 'Royal Oak' Patchbox, Charles II, in silver and oak, rare. **£375-400** SA

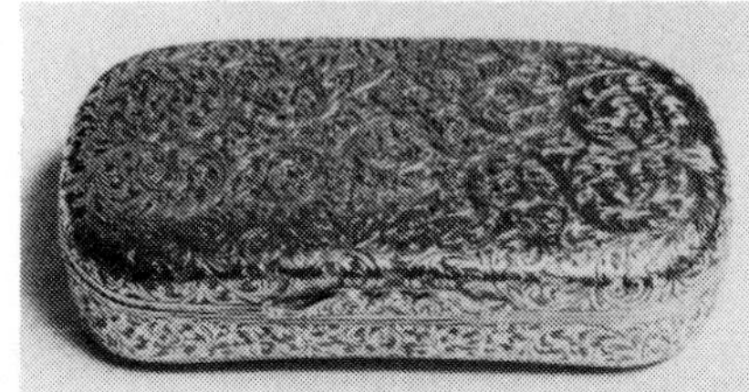
Victorian gold box. **£500-550** MJ

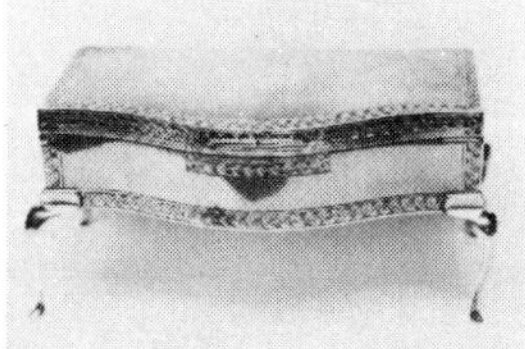
An Unusual and Very Good Quality Silver Jewel Case, 1903, by Goldsmiths & Silversmiths Co. **£330-360** SA

Mid 19th C enamel and silver box. **£60-70** MJ

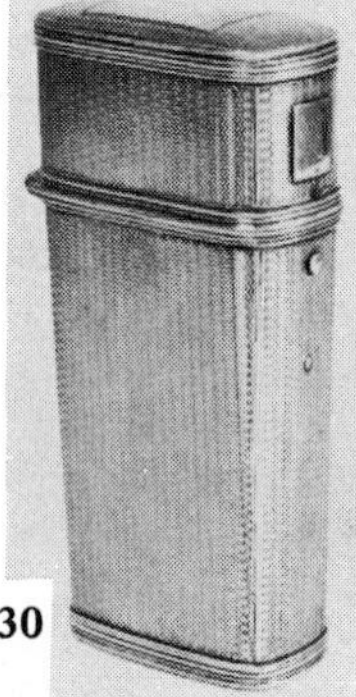
A Georgian silver case. **£200-230** SAL

A George III ovoid gold-mounted bloodstone bonbonniere with enamelled inscription "Contentment est un tresor" c. 1770 fitted shagreen case 1¾ in., 75 mm. high. **£1,980-2,225** C

A William III oval tobacco box, the base with initials RF, by Nathaniel Locke 1701, 3 ozs. 12 dwts., 3½ in., 8.5 cm. long. **£1,375-1,500** C

A Silver Birmingham Trinket Box, 4 in. long, 1914. **£70-80** VA

A George II Silver Tobacco Box, by Paul Crespin, maker's mark to cover and foot, London 1749, weight 14ozs., diam. 11.5cms. **£375-440** SKC

An 18th C. Dutch oblong Tobacco Box, 6¼ in., 15.8 cm. wide, by Christoffel Woortman, Amsterdam, 1797, 6 oz. 5 dwt. **£780-880** S

A Silver Filigree Card Case, 3½" long. **£70-85** SQE

A French shaped rectangular silver-gilt singing-bird box, with enamel flap 19th C., the French movement unsigned, fitted leather case 4 in., 100 mm. long. **£680-700** C

An Asprey & Co. Ltd., Rectangular Three-Section Box, for cigars, cigarettes and matches, 16.4 cm. long, makers' mark, London, 1912, stamped: 'Asprey/London' **£290-350** SB

A Mid-European Rectangular Cigarette Case, Birmingham import mark, 1913, 3½ in., 9 cm. **£250-290** SBe

An oval box, the cover 1807, maker's mark PC, the box and lining to the cover by Lambert & Co., 1871, 7½ in., 18.3 cm. long, 28 ozs. **£680-950** C

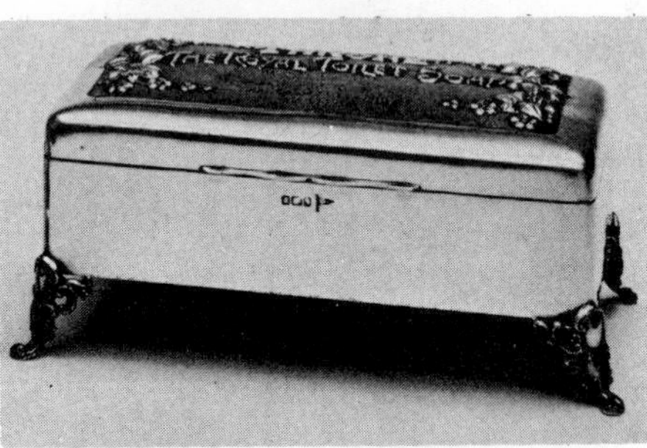

A Walker & Hall Oblong Soap Box, the interior plushly lined with velvet, 19.3 cm., long, makers' mark, Sheffield, 1901. **£170-200** SB

A pair of Victorian pepper-pots, 1872, maker's mark EC, 3½ in., 8.9 cm. high, gross 5 ozs. 8 dwts. **£880-950** C

A George V silver model of a golfer, London 1931, maker's mark G & S Co. Ltd., 6" high. **£200-230** GC

A Victorian Novelty silver Inkwell in the form of a tortoise, by Charles Rawlins and William Sumner, London 1847, 5" (12.5cms). **£325-350** SH

An Unusual E. H. Stockwell Model of a Water Cart, maker's mark, London, 1885, P.O.D.R. 7.5 cm. high., 176 gm. (all in) **£340-390** SB

A Dutch oblong tobacco box, the cover engraved with a battle scene, 1782, maker's mark illegible, 6 ozs. 7 dwts., 5½ in., 13.6 cm. long. **£2,200-2,500** C

A Rare Silver Child's Rattle and Whistle by Hester Bateman, c. 1779. **£675-700** SA

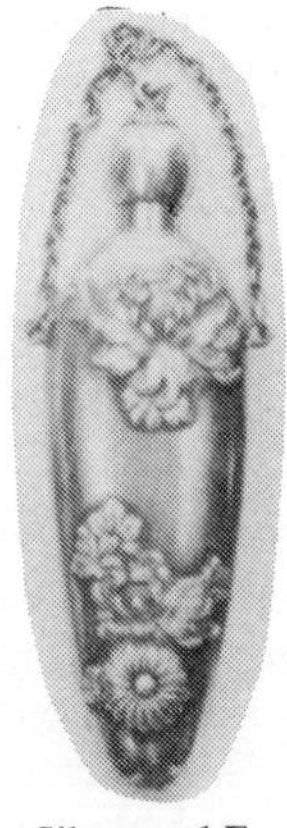

A Japanese Silver and Enamelled Perfume Bottle, with applied chased and enamel flowers, 2½". **£100-120** WHL

A Saunders & Shepherd Silver-Mounted Earthenware Scent Flask, maker's mark, Birmingham 1886, 5.4 cm. high. **£65-75** SB

Two Victorian small statuettes of jockeys, on marble plinths, by Barnard & Co., c. 1840., 6¾ in., 14.6 cm. high, 11 ozs. 11 dwts. **£420-500** C

An S. Mordan & Co., Silver-Mounted Earthenware Scent Flask, marks rubbed, maker's mark Sampson Mordan, London, 1885. 5.7 cm. high. **£65-75** SB

A Silver-Mounted Earthenware Scent Flask, unmarked, c. 1885, 7 cm. long. **£140-160** SB

A small silver filigree aeroplane, depicts a bi-plane of 1910, to contain a salt cellar. **£50-60** PC

A Good Quality Metal Gilt Writing Stand by Elkington & Co., with two glass bottles with similar mounts (one glass body damaged). 13½ in., 34.3 cm. across. **£200-230** L

SILVER MAKERS' MARKS

William Abdy, London	WA	1784
Robert Abercromby, London	RA	1739 1740
Stephen Adams, London	SA	1813
George Angel, London	GA	1850, 1861, 1875
John Angel & George Angel, London	J & A / G A	1840
Joseph Angel & John Angel, London	J A / I A	1831
Hester Bateman, London	HB	1761, 1774, 1776, 1778, 1789
Peter, Anne and William Bateman, London	PB / AB / WB	1800, 1800
Peter & Jonathon Bateman, London	PB / IB	1790, 1790
Ebenezer Coker, London	EC	1739, 1745, 1751
Thomas, James & Nathaniel Creswick, Sheffield	TJ&NC	1862, 1862
William Davie, Edinburgh	WD	1740, 1740
John Denziloe, London	ID	1774
William Frisby & Paul Storr, London	WF / PS	1792
Paul de Lamerie, London	LA	1712
Nathaniel Mills, Birmingham	NM	1826
Walker Knowles & Co Sheffield		1836
Paul Storr, London	PS	1807, 1808, 1817, 1834

Antique Silver-Plated Travelling Inkwell. **£10-12** SQE

A Pair of Silver William IV Reading Glasses with extending side pieces, Birmingham, 1830. **£75-85** SQE

A Boxed Set of Silver-Backed Brushes, 20th C. **£40-50** VA

A Silver Plate Entree Dish Cover, late 19th C., 16 in. wide. **£30-35** VA

A Victorian Six Division Egg Cruet, six cups chased in arabesque-style, 9¼ in., 23.5 cm. high, by Robert Hennell, London, 1852/55/59, 25 oz. **£290-320** SBe

A Silver Crumb Brush, late Victorian. **£30-40** VA

A Dutch Silver Corkscrew dated 1788, with portrait, maker's mark A.G. **£300-340** SA

A Very Rare Silver Egg Boiler, by Paul Storr, dated 1801. **£1,500+** SA

A Fine George III Taper Box with sides pierced, and with fretwork, by Edward Aldridge, 1767. **£265-300** SA

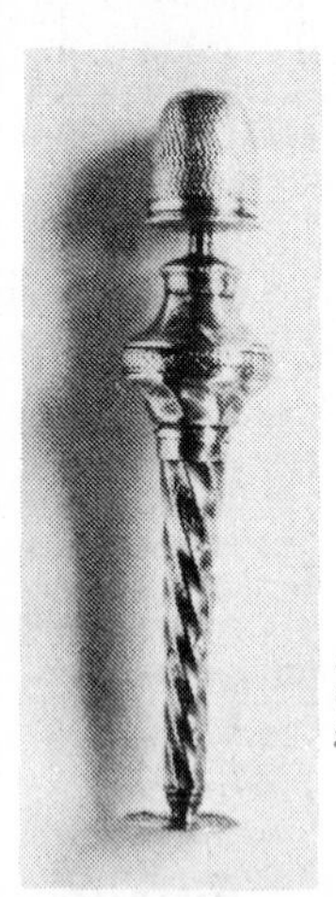

A Dutch Silver Thimble Etui, Amsterdam mark, c. 1790. **£300-340** SA

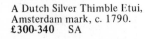

A French Walking Cane, early 20th C., 93.5 cm. long. **£330-390** SB

A Rare Silver Medical Implement, c. 1800. **£275-300** SA

A Mid 19th C. Piece for Waxing Cockspurs, well engraved. **£42-52** SA

A Silver Nurse's Buckle, London, 1897. **£40-50** SQE

A Japanese lemonade set, marked Arthur & Bond Yokohama Sterling, silver coloured metal, 40¼ozs. **£275-325** PWC

A Taper Holder, 4½ in., 11.3 cm. high, maker's mark G.V. probably German, c. 1800, 2 oz. 11 dwt. **£240-280** S

A George IV Scottish Wine Funnel, marked on funnel and strainer, makers mark G.M.H. Edinburgh, 1823, 5 in., 12.5 cm., 3½ oz. **£280-360** SBe

A George III Cream Pail, 3¾ in. high, by William Vincent, London, 1774, 1 oz. 16 dwt. (excluding a blue glass liner). **£340-400** S

A Pair of Late 19th C Dutch Silver Shoes, 8¼" (21cms) long, London import mark, 1892, 14¼ozs. in fitted case. **£450-500** SBe

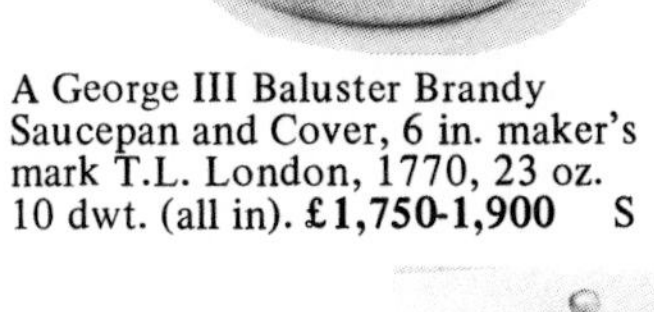

A George III Baluster Brandy Saucepan and Cover, 6 in. maker's mark T.L. London, 1770, 23 oz. 10 dwt. (all in). **£1,750-1,900** S

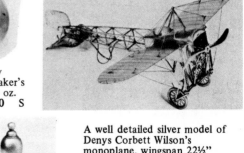

A George III Silver Wig Powder Pot, by William Kingdom, 1821, London. **£375-400** SA

A well detailed silver model of Denys Corbett Wilson's monoplane, wingspan 22½" (57cms), 46ozs., December 1912. **£1,200-1,500** CSK

Articulated silver fish marked T.H., Birmingham 1895. **£200-250** MJ

A George I plain table-bell by Edmund Holaday, 1716, 6 ozs. 19 dwts. **£2,200-2,500** C

Former Assay Office Marks. Several of the larger provincial cities had Assay Offices which are now closed. Each had its distinctive mark, some of the more important of which are shown below. There is also an Assay Office in Dublin and marks struck there before 1st April 1923 are recognised as approved British hallmarks. The Dublin mark is a figure of Hibernia.

gold & Sterling silver — Britannia silver

Exeter

Glasgow

Newcastle

Chester

Dublin

London

Year	Letter
1678	a
1679	b
1680	c
1681	d
1682	e
1683	f
1684	g
1685	h
1686	i
1687	k
1688	l
1689	m
1690	n
1691	o
1692	p
1693	q
1694	r
1695	s
1696	t
1697	a b
1698	c
1699	d
1700	e
1701	f
1702	g
1703	h
1704	i
1705	k
1706	l
1707	m
1708	n
1709	o
1710	p
1711	q

Year	Letter
1712	r
1713	s
1714	t
1715	v
1716	A
1717	B
1718	C
1719	D
1720	E
1721	F
1722	G
1723	H
1724	I
1725	K
1726	L
1727	M
1728	N
1729	O
1730	P
1731	Q
1732	R
1733	S
1734	T
1735	V
1736	a
1737	b
1738	c
1739	d
1739	d
1740	e
1741	f
1742	g
1743	h

Year	Letter
1744	i
1745	k
1746	l
1747	m
1748	n
1749	o
1750	p
1751	q
1752	r
1753	s
1754	t
1755	u
1756	A
1757	B
1758	C
1759	D
1760	E
1761	F
1762	G
1763	H
1764	I
1765	K
1766	L
1767	M
1768	N
1769	O
1770	P
1771	Q
1772	R
1773	S
1774	T
1775	U
1776	a
1777	b
1778	c
1779	d

Year	Letter
1780	e
1781	f
1782	g
1783	h
1784	i
1785	k
1786	l
1787	m
1788	n
1789	o
1790	p
1791	q
1792	r
1793	s
1794	t
1795	u
1796	A
1797	B
1798	C
1799	D
1800	E
1801	F
1802	G
1803	H
1804	I
1805	K
1806	L
1807	M
1808	N
1809	O
1810	P
1811	Q
1812	R
1813	S
1814	T

Year	Letter
1815	U
1816	a
1817	b
1818	c
1819	d
1820	e
1821	f
1822	g
1823	h
1824	i
1825	k
1826	l
1827	m
1828	n
1829	o
1830	p
1831	q
1832	r
1833	s
1834	t
1835	u
1836	A
1837	B
1838	C
1839	D
1840	E
1841	F
1842	G
1843	H
1844	I
1845	K
1846	L
1847	M
1848	N
1849	O

Year	Letter
1850	P
1851	Q
1852	R
1853	S
1854	T
1855	U
1856	a
1857	b
1858	c
1859	d
1860	e
1861	f
1862	g
1863	h
1864	i
1865	k
1866	l
1867	m
1868	n
1869	o
1870	p
1871	q
1872	r
1873	s
1874	t
1875	u
1876	A
1877	B

Year	Letter
1878	C
1879	D
1880	E
1881	F
1882	G
1883	H
1884	I
1885	K
1886	L
1887	M
1888	N
1889	O
1890	P
1891	Q
1892	R
1893	S
1894	T
1895	U
1896	a
1897	b
1898	c
1899	d
1900	e
1901	f
1902	g
1903	h

Year	Letter
1904	i
1905	k
1906	l
1907	m
1908	n
1909	o
1910	p
1911	q
1912	r
1913	s
1914	t
1915	u
1916	a
1917	b
1918	c
1919	d
1920	e
1921	f
1922	g
1923	h
1924	i
1925	k
1926	l
1927	m
1928	n
1929	o

Birmingham

Year	Letter
1773	A
1774	B
1775	C
1776	D
1777	E
1778	F
1779	G
1780	H
1781	I
1782	K
1783	L
1784	M
1785	N
1786	O
1787	P

Sterling silver
Marked in England

Marked in Scotland

gold

silver

gold

silver

Birmingham

Year	Letter	Year	Letter	Year	Letter	Year	Letter
1788	Q	1823	Z	1857	I	1893	t
1789	R	1824	A	1858	J	1894	u
1790	S	1825	B	1859	K	1895	v
1791	T	1826	C	1860	L	1896	w
1792	U	1827	D	1861	M	1897	x
1793	V	1828	E	1862	N	1898	y
1794	W	1829	F	1863	O	1899	z
1795	X	1830	G	1864	P	1900	a
1796	Y	1831	H	1865	Q	1901	b
1797	Z	1832	I	1866	R	1902	c
1798	a	1833	K	1867	S	1903	d
1799	b	1834	L	1868	T	1904	e
1800	c	1835	M	1869	U	1905	f
1801	d	1836	N	1870	V	1906	g
1802	e	1837	O	1871	W	1907	h
1803	f	1838	P	1872	X	1908	i
1804	g	1839	Q	1873	Y	1909	k
1805	h	1840	R	1874	Z	1910	l
1806	i	1841	S	1875	a	1911	m
1807	j	1842	T	1876	b	1912	n
1808	k	1843	U	1877	c	1913	o
1809	l	1844	V	1878	d	1914	p
1810	m	1845	W	1879	e	1915	q
1811	n	1846	X	1880	f	1916	r
1812	o	1847	Y	1881	g	1917	s
1813	p	1848	Z	1882	h	1918	t
1814	q	1849	A	1883	i	1919	u
1815	r	1850	B	1884	k	1920	v
1816	s	1851	C	1885	l	1921	w
1817	t	1852	D	1886	m	1922	x
1818	u	1853	E	1887	n	1923	y
1819	v	1854	F	1888	o	1924	z
1820	w	1855	G	1889	p	1925	A
1821	x	1856	H	1890	q	1926	B
1822	y			1891	r	1927	C
				1892	s	1928	D
						1929	E

Sheffield

Year	Letter	Year	Letter	Year	Letter	Year	Letter
1773	E	1807	S	1841	V	1877	K
1774	F	1808	P	1842	X	1878	L
1775	N	1809	K	1843	Z	1879	M
1776	R	1810	L	1844	A	1880	N
1777	H	1811	C	1845	B	1881	O
1778	S	1812	D	1846	C	1882	P
1779	A	1813	R	1847	D	1883	Q
1780	T	1814	W	1848	E	1884	R
1781	D	1815	O	1849	F	1885	S
1782	G	1816	T	1850	G	1886	T
1783	B	1817	X	1851	H	1887	U
1784	I	1818	I	1852	I	1888	V
1785	Y	1819	V	1853	K	1889	W
1786	k	1820	Q	1854	L	1890	X
1787	T	1821	Y	1855	M	1891	Y
1788	W	1822	Z	1856	N	1892	Z
1789	A	1823	U	1857	O	1893	a
1790	L	1824	a	1858	P	1894	b
1791	P	1825	b	1859	R	1895	c
1792	u	1826	c	1860	S	1896	d
1793	O	1827	d	1861	T	1897	e
1794	m	1828	e	1862	U	1898	f
1795	q	1829	f	1863	V	1899	g
1796	Z	1830	g	1864	W	1900	h
1797	X	1831	h	1865	X	1901	i
1798	V	1832	k	1866	Y	1902	k
1799	E	1833	l	1867	Z	1903	l
1800	N	1834	m	1868	A	1904	m
1801	H	1835	p	1869	B	1905	n
1802	M	1836	q	1870	C	1906	o
1803	F	1837	r	1871	D	1907	p
1804	G	1838	s	1872	E	1908	q
1805	B	1839	t	1873	F	1909	r
1806	A	1840	u	1874	G	1910	s
				1875	H	1911	t
				1876	J	1912	u

Duty Marks. Between 1784 and 1890 an excise duty on gold and silver articles was collected by the Assay Offices and a mark depicting the Sovereign's head was struck to show that it had been paid. These are two examples.

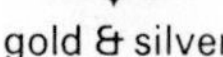

gold & silver

George III

Victoria

Edinburgh

Year	Letter
1705	A
1706	B
1707	C
1708	D
1709	E
1710	F
1711	G
1712	H
1713	I
1714	K
1715	L
1716	M
1717	N
1718	O
1719	P
1720	Q
1721	R
1722	S
1723	T
1724	U
1725	V
1726	W
1727	X
1728	Y
1729	Z
1730	A
1731	B
1732	C
1733	D
1734	E
1735	F
1736	G
1737	H
1738	I
1739	K
1740	L
1741	M
1742	N
1743	O
1744	P
1745	Q
1746	R
1747	S
1748	T
1749	U
1750	V
1751	W
1752	X
1753	Y
1754	Z
1755	A
1756	B
1757	C
1758	D
1759	E
1760	F
1761	G
1762	H
1763	I
1764	K
1765	L
1766	M
1767	N
1768	O
1769	P
1770	Q
1771	R
1772	S
1773	T
1774	U
1775	V
1776	X
1777	Y
1778	Z
1779	[illegible]
1780	A
1781	B
1782	C
1783	D
1784	E
1785	F
1786	G
1787	G
1788	H
1789	I J
1790	K
1791	L
1792	M
1793	N
1794	O
1795	P
1796	Q
1797	R
1798	S
1799	T
1800	U
1801	V
1802	W
1803	X
1804	Y
1805	Z
1806	a
1807	b
1808	c
1809	d
1810	e
1811	f
1812	g
1813	h
1814	i
1815	j
1816	k
1817	l
1818	m
1819	n
1820	o
1821	p
1822	q
1823	r
1824	s
1825	t
1826	u
1827	v
1828	w
1829	x
1830	y
1831	z
1832	A
1833	B
1834	C
1835	D
1836	E
1837	F
1838	G
1839	H
1840	I
1841	K
1842	L
1843	M
1844	N
1845	O
1846	P
1847	Q
1848	R
1849	S
1850	T
1851	U
1852	V
1853	W
1854	X
1855	Y
1856	Z
1857	A
1858	B
1859	C
1860	D
1861	E
1862	F
1863	G
1864	H
1865	I
1866	K
1867	L
1868	M
1869	N
1870	O
1871	P
1872	Q
1873	R
1874	S
1875	T
1876	U
1877	V
1878	W
1879	X
1880	Y
1881	Z
1882	a
1883	b
1884	c
1885	d
1886	e
1887	f
1888	g
1889	h
1890	i
1891	k
1892	l
1893	m
1894	n
1895	o
1896	p
1897	q
1898	r
1899	s
1900	t
1901	u
1902	w
1903	x
1904	y
1905	z
1906	A
1907	B
1908	C
1909	D
1910	E
1911	F
1912	G
1913	H
1914	I
1915	K
1916	L
1917	M
1918	N
1919	O

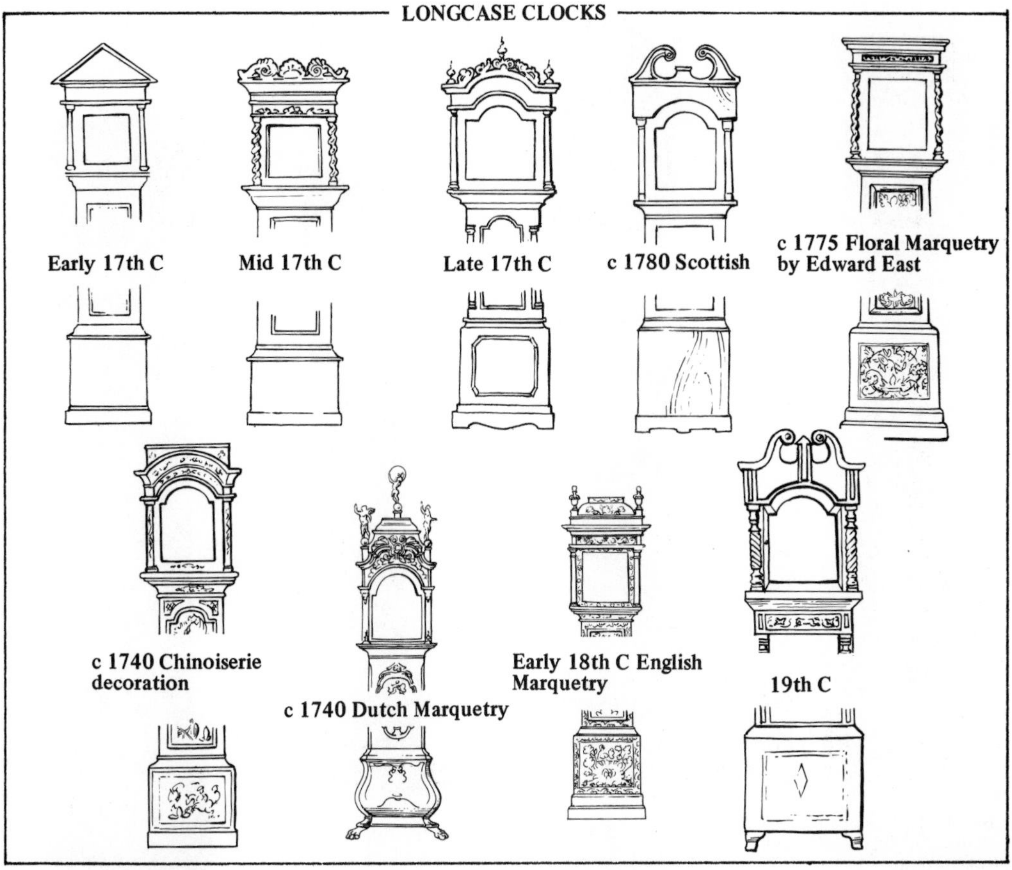

LONGCASE CLOCKS

Early 17th C | Mid 17th C | Late 17th C | c 1780 Scottish | c 1775 Floral Marquetry by Edward East

c 1740 Chinoiserie decoration | c 1740 Dutch Marquetry | Early 18th C English Marquetry | 19th C

A Mahogany Long Case Clock, the eight day movement rack striking, signed Tuton, Bristol, the polished case with shortened panelled plinth, 6 ft. 6 in. **£750-850** L

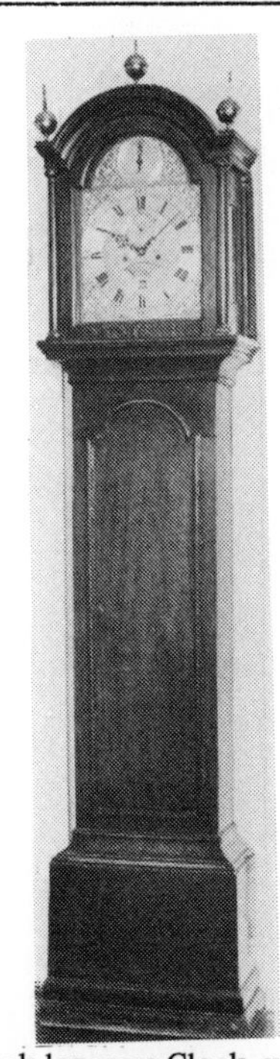

An oak longcase Clock, with 8-day strike movement, the dial inscribed Jaspr. Taylor, Holborn, London, c1720-35. **£850-950** NF

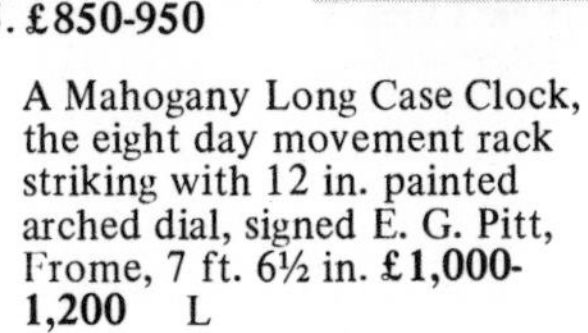

A Mahogany Long Case Clock, the eight day movement rack striking with 12 in. painted arched dial, signed E. G. Pitt, Frome, 7 ft. 6½ in. **£1,000-1,200** L

A Walnut Long Case Clock, the eight day movement rack striking, signed John Elliot, Plymouth, 7 ft. 2 in. (shortened moulded plinth). **£1,600-1,800** L

A late 17th C longcase clock of month duration, 6'4½" high. **£4,400-4,700** Bon.

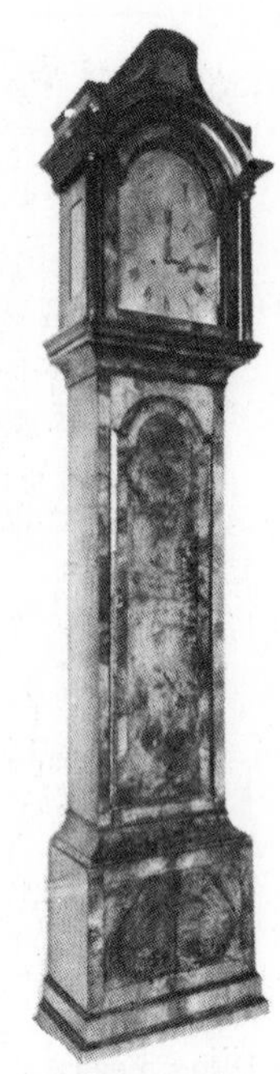

A Georgian walnut longcase Clock, the 8-day striking movement with brass dial inscribed Chalklin, Canterbury, 7'8½" high, c1760. **£1,400-1,600** GC

A Very Fine Marquetry Inlaid Late 17th C Longcase Clock in Walnut, the eight-day movement with count-wheel striking on a bell, and an anchor escapement, signed 'Robert Clements, London' 202cms high. **£4,940-5,100** SKC

A Marquetry Long Case Clock, the eight day movement with inside count wheel, signed Peter Walker, London, the case with shortened moulded plinth, the flat topped hood with plain pillars, c. 1685, 6 ft. 9¼ in. **£1,800-2,000** L

A late 17th/early 18th C walnut and marquetry longcase clock, with brass dial, seconds ring and an oval plaque inscribed Alexandre Giroust, London, 6'11" high. **£2,800-3,000** PWC

A Brass Inlaid Mahogany Long Case Clock with Rosewood Crossbandings, the eight day movement rack striking, 7 ft. 10 in. **£580- 750** L

An Oak Long Case Clock, the eight day movement rack striking, signed R. Hampson. Warrington. 7 ft. 4¾ in. **£600-800** L

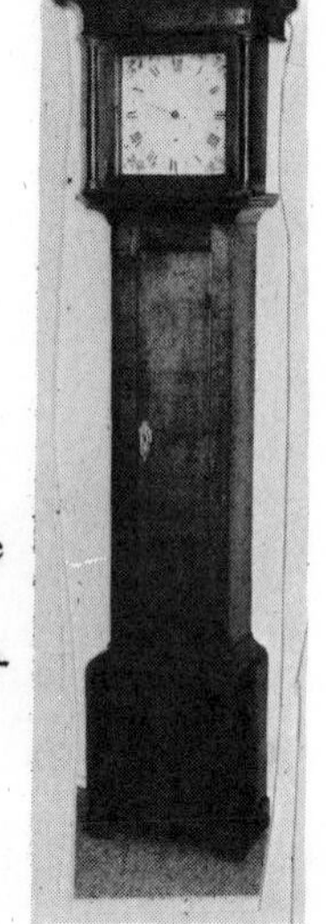

Small Oak Country Longcase clock with painted dial and single hand 18th C. 74 in. high. **£500-550** TT

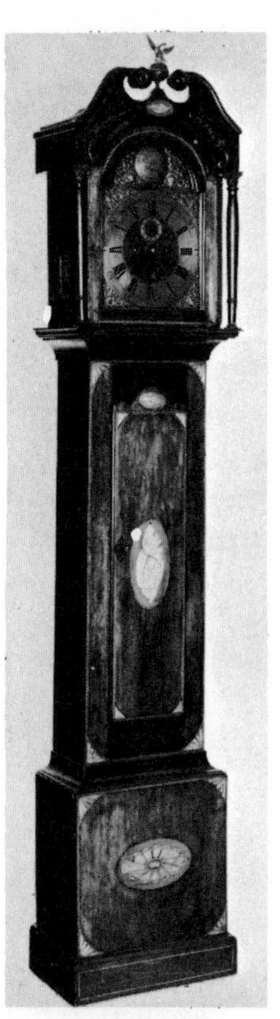

An Inlaid Mahogany Long Case Clock, the eight day movement with rack strike, the back plate inscribed Decembre 23 eme. 1746, No. 68, signed Nicolas Blondel a Guernesey. 7 ft. 3 in. **£1,200-1,400** L

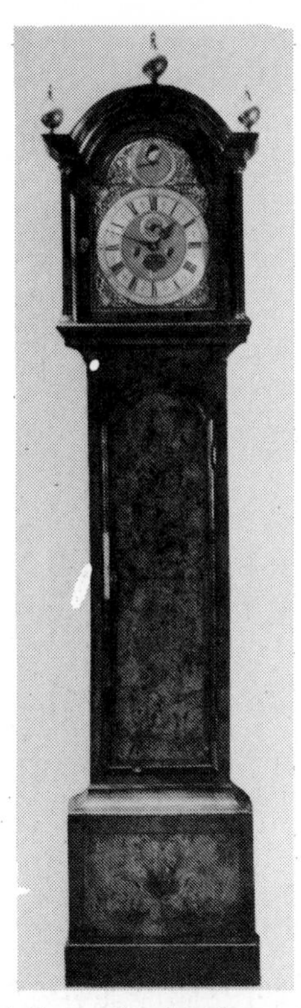

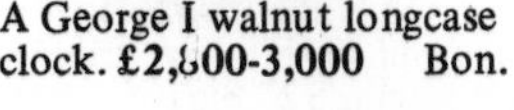

A George I walnut longcase clock. **£2,800-3,000** Bon.

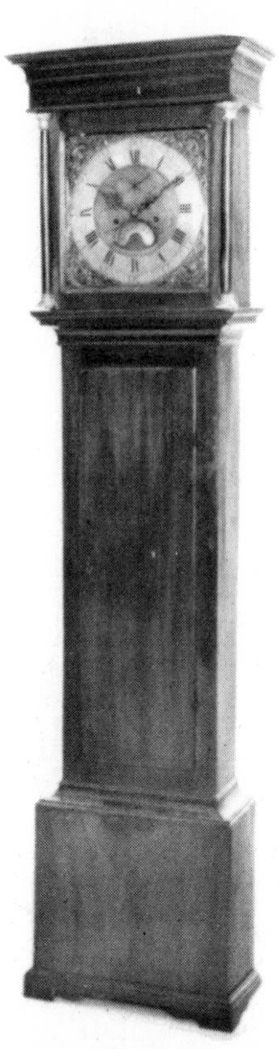

A Mahogany Long Case Clock, the eight day movement rack striking, signed Adam Cleak, Bridport, 7'1". **£880-1,000** L

An 18th C Eight-Day Longcase Clock by John Ewer, London, in oak case with later carved decoration, height 86" (218cms). **£400-450** SBe

An Early 18th C. Oak Longcase Clock with crossbanded and inlaid case, not original movement. **£1,450-1,550** RD

A 18th C mahogany longcase Clock inscribed Saml. Farquharson, London bell, striking, eight day movement, 7'5" high. **£2,000-3,000** P.W.C.

An 18th C 8-day mahogany longcase Clock by Joseph Marshall, Leicester. **£1,200-1,400** BW

right
A George III Mahogany Longcase Clock brass dial signed Jno. Catton, Gibraltar, the movement with four ringed pillars, anchor escapement and rack striking on a bell, 96 in., late 18th C. **£1,600-1,800** SBA

A Good Late George II Blue Japanned Longcase Clock the brass dial with chapter rings, signed Wm. Morgan, London, with strike silent dial in the arch, the movement with anchor escapement and rack striking on a bell, painted and gilt throughout with chinoiserie, 96½ in., mid 18th C. **£2,800-3,100** SBA

A Late 18th C Oak Longcase Clock, signed Jn. Fordham, Braintree, 8-day movement striking on a bell, 206cms high. **£530-600** SKC

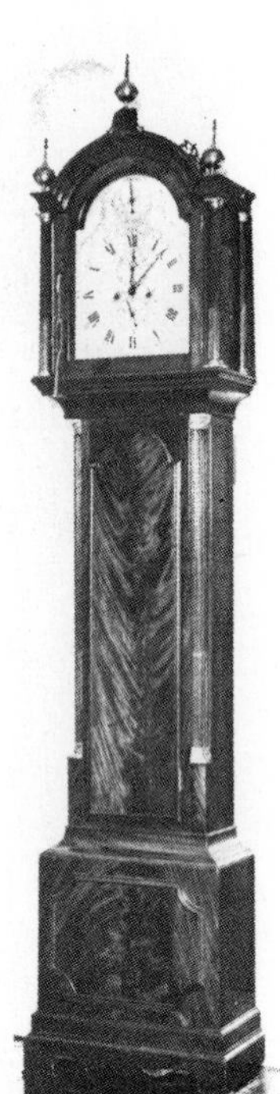

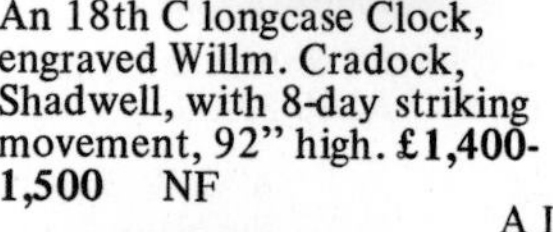

An 18th C longcase Clock, engraved Willm. Cradock, Shadwell, with 8-day striking movement, 92" high. **£1,400-1,500** NF

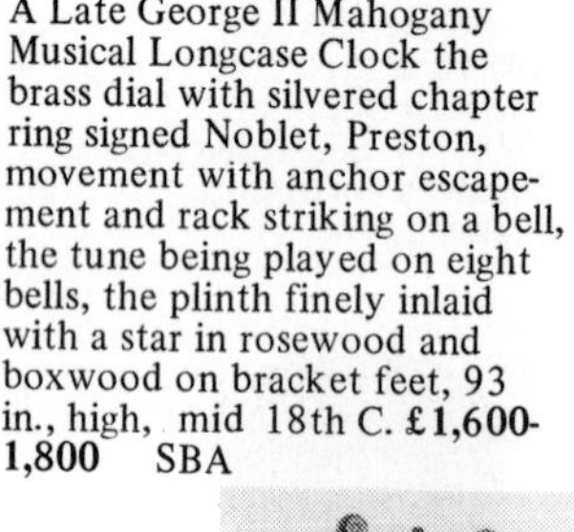

A Late George II Mahogany Musical Longcase Clock the brass dial with silvered chapter ring signed Noblet, Preston, movement with anchor escapement and rack striking on a bell, the tune being played on eight bells, the plinth finely inlaid with a star in rosewood and boxwood on bracket feet, 93 in., high, mid 18th C. **£1,600-1,800** SBA

A George II Long Cased Clock in a carved oak case dated 1736, with brass face and 30-hour movement with strike. **£850-950** M

A Good George III Eight-Day Long-case Clock by Major Scholfield, Rochdale, dial inscribed 'Time Flies', the movement with anchor escapement, striking on a bell and in plain oak case, height 92 in., 234 cm. **£1,000-1,200** SBe

A rare year duration longcase Clock with brass dial, with the Newcastle Coat of Arms signed Math. Featherstonhaugh, Esqre. Mayor, and Francis Rudston, Esqre, Sherriffe, 8'8" high. **£3,600-3,800** AG

A George III Longcase Clock by Joseph Batty, Halifax, with 8-day movement, 89" high. **£600-700** DH

A Mahogany-Cased 18th C Longcase Clock with inlay, signed 'Philip Burchett, London', the eight-day movement with count-wheel striking on a bell, 226cms high. **£860-920** SKC

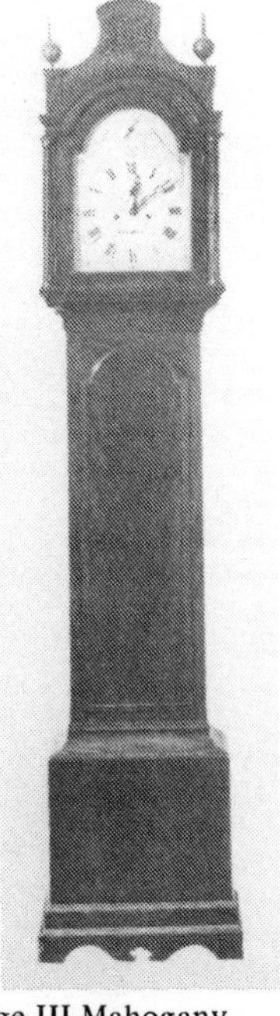

A George III Mahogany Longcase Clock, by Thomas Pace of London, 8-day striking movement, 7'9" high. **£1,220-1,300** SKC

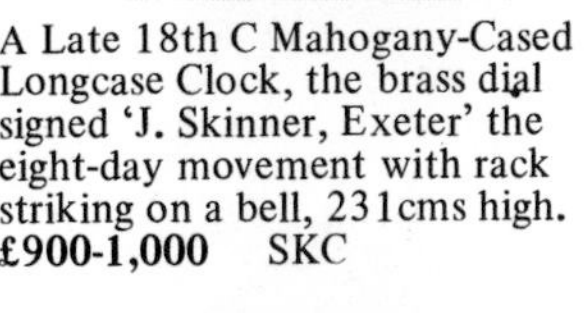

A Late 18th C Mahogany-Cased Longcase Clock, the brass dial signed 'J. Skinner, Exeter' the eight-day movement with rack striking on a bell, 231cms high. **£900-1,000** SKC

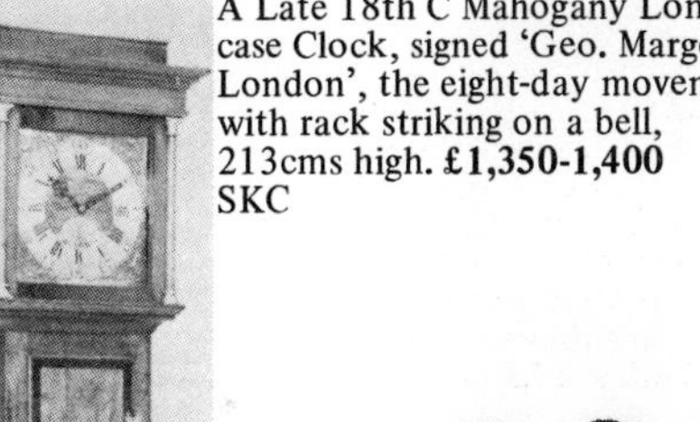

A Late 18th C Mahogany Longcase Clock, signed 'Geo. Margetts, London', the eight-day movement with rack striking on a bell, 213cms high. **£1,350-1,400** SKC

An Oak Long Case Clock, signed William Charles, Chepstow, now with three train, quarter 'rod' chiming movement, 6'4". **£700-800** L

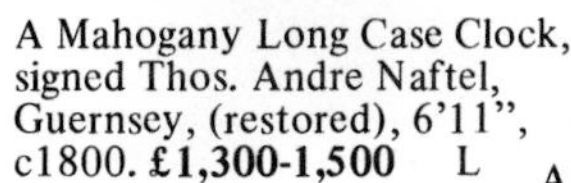

A Mahogany Long Case Clock, signed Thos. Andre Naftel, Guernsey, (restored), 6'11", c1800. **£1,300-1,500** L

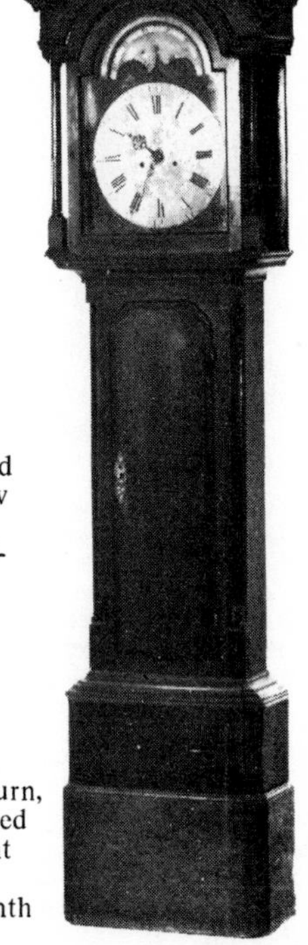

A Late George III Oak and Mahogany Longcase Clock, the brass dial signed E. Butler, Tutbury, the four ringed pillar movement with anchor escapement and rack striking on a bell, 86 in., early 19th C. **£950-1,100** SBA

A George III Oak Longcase Clock with brass arched dial, signed Samuel Ashton, Ashburn, the movement with four ringed pillars and anchor escapement with rack striking on a bell, 88 in., high, late 18th C., plinth restored. **£700-800** SBA

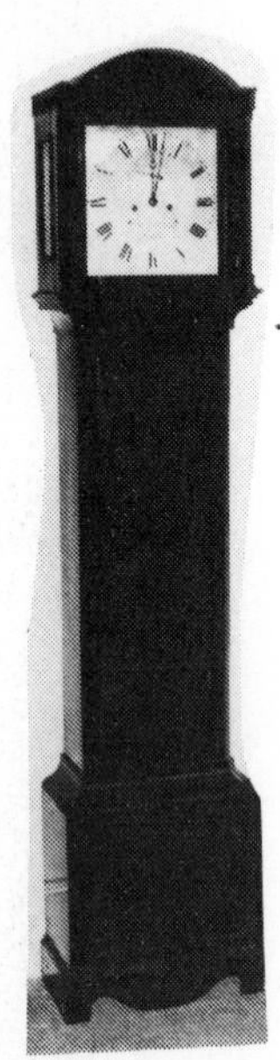

A Regency Regulator-Type Clock, London made, perfect condition, mahogany, 80 in. high, c. 1830. **£1,550-1,750** SHA

A George III mahogany longcase clock, signed Thomas Simson, Hertford, 7'11" (241cms) high. **£1,200-1,400** Bon.

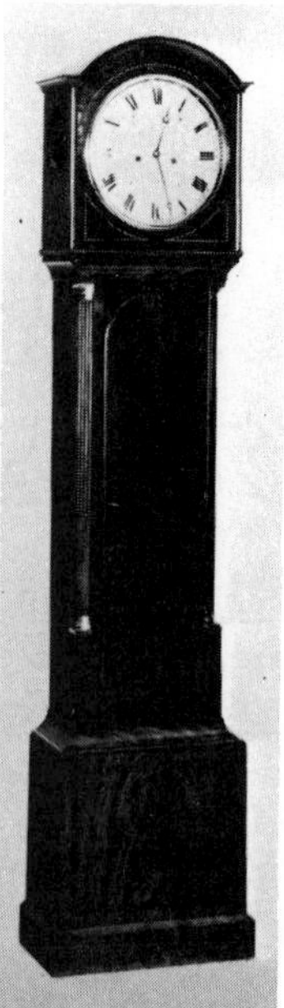

A Fine Figured Mahogany Long Case Clock, the five pillar eight day movement rack striking, signed French, Royal Exchange, London. 6 ft. 3½ in., c. 1810. **£1,450-1,650** L

A George III Mahogany Long-case Clock the brass dial signed J. J. Howard, Aldersgate Street, London, with anchor escapement and rack striking on a bell, inlaid with boxwood stringing throughout, 91 in., late 18th C. **£1,100-1,250** SBA

A 19th C chiming walnut longcase Clock, signed Murray, Chronometer Maker To The Admiralty, Royal Exchange, London, the three train movement quarter chiming on four gongs with dead-beat escapement, 9'2" high. **£2,100-2,300** AG

A Georgian Oak and Mahogany Longcase Clock, c. 1810. **£475-525** CSG

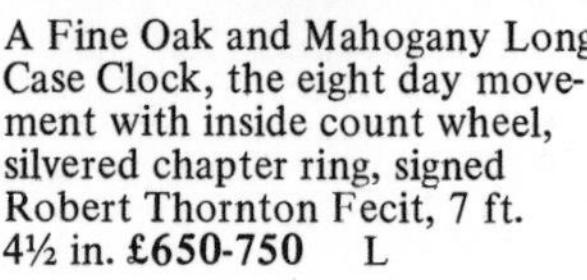

A Fine Oak and Mahogany Long Case Clock, the eight day movement with inside count wheel, silvered chapter ring, signed Robert Thornton Fecit, 7 ft. 4½ in. **£650-750** L

Inlaid mahogany and oak Long-case clock with eight day movement, 93 in. high. **£650-700** TT

A good walnut polyphon clock, the wire gong striking movement with wood rod and brass pendulum, brass weights, the polyphon with nine 10" metal discs. **£2,450-2,500** PWC

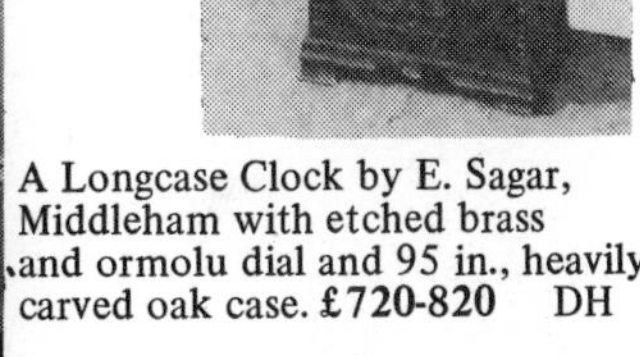

A Longcase Clock by E. Sagar, Middleham with etched brass and ormolu dial and 95 in., heavily carved oak case. **£720-820** DH

A fine quality carved mahogany longcase clock, three train movements with eight bells and a wire gong, striking on four or eight bells, 8'6" high. **£1,700-1,800** PWC

A fine quality mahogany and marquetry longcase clock, with three train movement with Whittington and Westminster chimes on nine tubular gongs, 8'7" high. **£2,300-2,400** PWC

A 19th C Longcase Clock by Thos. Fletcher, Barnsley, with 8-day movement, 88" high. **£380-450** DH

An 18th C. Provincial Red Lacquer Longcase Clock by Edward Stevens of Boston, case with panels in gilt of chinoiserie decoration, 80 in., 203 cm. high. **£800-1,000** B

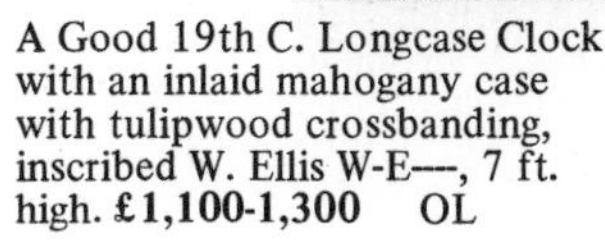

A Good 19th C. Longcase Clock with an inlaid mahogany case with tulipwood crossbanding, inscribed W. Ellis W-E—, 7 ft. high. **£1,100-1,300** OL

An Antique Oak, Mahogany, Ebony, Boxwood Strung and Crossbanded Long Case Clock with 8-day striking movement and 14 in. shaped painted face, by Barwise, London, 93 in. high. **£620-720** V

SOME IMPORTANT BRITISH CLOCKMAKERS (1600-1830) London.

- Arnold, John 1707-1723
- Bradley, Langley 1697-1738
- Colston, Richard 1682-1709
- Delander, Daniel 1702-1733
- Emery, Josiah 1750-1797
- Fromanteel (London) Various members 1625-1725
- Gould, Christopher 1682-1718
- Hindley, Henry (York) 1726-1771
- Knifton, Thomas 1640-1662
- Margetts, George 1779-1810
- Pinchbeck, Christopher 1695-1732
- Recordon, Louis 1778-1824
- Selwood, William 1633-1652
- Tompian, Thomas 1671-1713
- Vulliamy, Benjamin Lewis 1809-1854
- Windmills, Joseph 1671-1725

A late 19th C Longcase Clock, with 3-train movement and Westminster and Whittington chimes. **£1,900-2,100** A

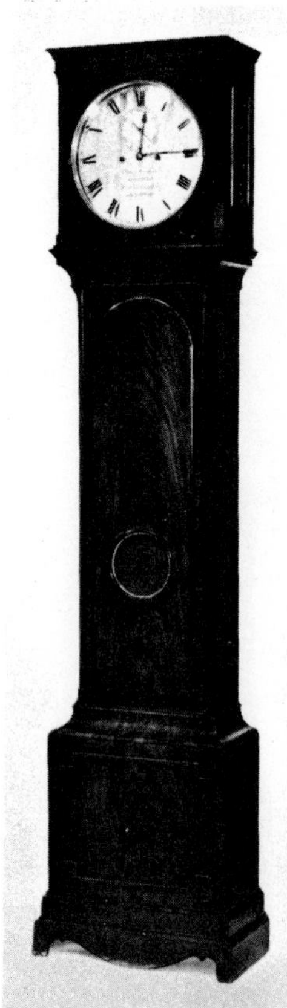

A Good Early 19th C. Eight-Day Longcase Clock by James Gorham, Kensington, the two train movement with dead beat escapement, in plain mahogany case, height 79 in., 201 cm. **£1,200-1,400** SBe

A Georgian black lacquered Longcase Clock, signed William Barrow, London, with rack-striking movement (now on gong) with anchor escapement, 8ft 6in (259cm) high, **£1,500-1,750** C

A Fine Edwardian Striking and Chiming Longcase Clock, Longcase Clock, inscribed "Pleasance and Harper. Bristol', with strike/silent, Whittington/Westminster dials in the arch, chiming on eight tubular gongs, height 105 in., 267 cm. **£2,700-2,950** SBe

A William & Mary marquetry Longcase Clock by Benj. Merriman, London, movement with five ringed pillars, outside countwheel strike and anchor escapement, c. 1700, 7ft 11in (242cm) high **£6,000-7,000** C

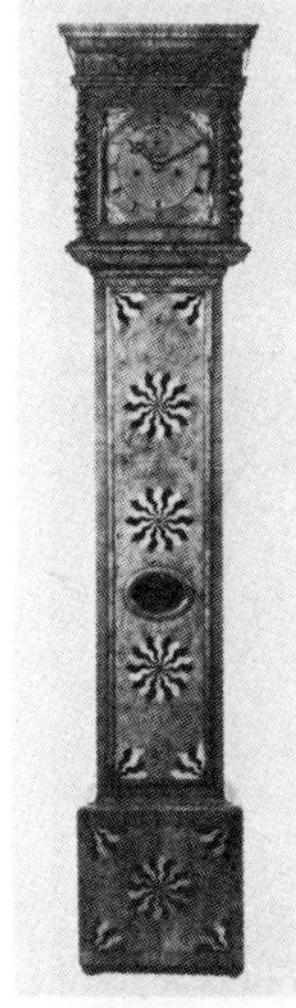

A Charles II walnut and parquetry Longcase Clock, signed William Clement, Londini fecit; with outside-countwheel strike and anchor escapement, the maintaining power work removed (with restorations), 6ft 7in (201cm) high, **£3,500-3,700** C

An early 18th C Bracket Clock by Henry Clarkson of Wolverhampton, in ebonised pearwood case, 8-day striking movement and verge movement, 19" high. **£2,320-2,500** SKC

POINTERS FOR BRACKET CLOCKS

- Earliest example 1670 severe in form with flat top.
- Domed top from 1675.
- Basket top 1680.
- Double basket top and inverted bell top and square dial 1700.
- Inverted bell top, arched dial 1720.
- Square brass dial pre 1720.
- Arched brass dial post 1720.
- Painted dials after 1750.
- Silvered dial after 1760.
- Round Dial after 1785.
- Broken arch to dial after 1795.

A Good early 18th C Bracket Clock, with quarter chime repeat, inscribed 'Pannel, Fecit', in simulated red tortoiseshell and lacquered case, height 19" (48cms). **£2,000-2,200** SBe

A Good 18th C. Bracket Timepiece inscribed 'Andrew Merchant, London', the single train fusee movement with anchor escapement, in ebonised case, height 21½ in., 54 cm. **£850-950** SBe

A late 18th C Bracket Clock with mahogany case, signed Fran. Zagnani, London, with 8-day dead-beat movement, double fusee with pump quarter repeat on two bells, 24". **£1,880-1,925** SKC

left

Birch & Gaydon, London. An ebonised Bracket Clock of small size, with three train fusee movement with an anchor escapement, quarter striking on gongs, 42cms high. **£1,000-1,200** P

A George III mahogany striking bracket clock, signed E. Evargluoh London with calendar aperture, scroll spandrels and strike/silent in the arch, movement with knife-edge verge escapement 20½ in., 52 cm. high. **£1,030-1,150** C

A good 18th C Walnut cased Bracket Clock, with bell striking movement with verge escapement, Calendar drive missing, 21" high. **£875-925** P.W.C.

A George III bracket clock, the 8-day movement striking on eight bells, pull repeat not working, the backplate engraved J. C. Jennens, London, 40 cm., 15¾ in. high. **£1,600-1,800** O

A walnut Bracket Clock, the brass dial signed Thos. Morland, Chester, the eight day movement with rack strike on bell and anchor escapement, 16" high, c1830. **£1,300-1,600** AG

A Regency Bracket Clock, the two train fusee movement with anchor escapement, having bell strike, in arched ebonised case, having inlaid brass stylized floral decoration, height 22 in., 56 cm. **£600-680** SBe

A Regency Mahogany, Brass Inlaid Striking Bracket Clock, double fusee movement, 15½" high. **£800-900** SQE

A good William IV mahogany Bracket Clock, the silvered dial inscribed Taylor & Son Bristol, with bell striking movement, 1' high. **£475-525** P.W.C.

An English Single Fusee Bracket Clock with ormolu mounts, c1840, 14" high. **£320-350** CCL

A George III ebonised striking Bracket Clock, signed Thos. Crofts Newbury, movement with lightly engraved backplate, now converted to anchor escapement, 18in (46cm) high, **£790-870** C

A George III Bracket Clock by James Warne of London, in mahogany case, 8-day striking movement, anchor escapement, 1'8" high. **£3,000-3,250** SKC

A George III ebonised striking Bracket Clock, signed John Dark Barnstaple, with verge escapement, 17½in (44cm) high, **£1,200-1,300** C

A 19th C. Mahogany Bracket Clock. **£150-175** SV

An Early 19th C 'Lancet' top rosewood veneered Bracket Clock, the treble fusee chiming striking and pull repeating movement on 13 bells, signed Udali, London, 60cms high. **£1,450-1,550** SKC

A mid-Georgian ebonised striking Bracket Clock, signed Wm. Allam London, movement with scroll engraved backplate and renewed verge escapement, 16in (40.5cm) high, **£2,000-2,150** C

English Bracket Clock by Charles Frodsham, c1901, 15" high. **£280-300** CCI

A George III mahogany striking Bracket Clock signed Chater, London, movement with lightly engraved backplate, now converted to anchor escapement, 16in (41cm) high, **£990-1,050** C

A late Georgian ebonised chiming Bracket Clock, the movement with anchor escapement chain fusees chiming on 8 bells, with the signature Samuel Toulmin Strand, 16¼in (41 cm) high, **£1,050-1,150** C

A Mid-19th C. Striking Bracket Clock in a walnut case, signed Green, Clifton, with anchor escapement and a double fusee with the strike on a bell, 42cms high. **£310-350** SKC

An Ormolu Mounted Quarter Chiming Ebonised Bracket Clock, the two train chain fusee movement with anchor escapement, chiming the quarters on eight bells, 18" (46.7cms). **£800-900** L

A Chinese wood-cased Bracket Clock, the chain fusee movement with verge escapement, 11¾in (30cm) high, **£1,300-1,450** C

A German 'Ting-Tang' Quarter-Striking Miniature Bracket Clock, c1900, 8¾" high. **£180-200** CCL

A Fine Victorian Striking and Chiming Bracket Clock with slow/fast, Westminster/chiming on eight bells, height 30 in., 76 cm. **£1,000-1,150** SBe

A Good Bracket Clock by George Graham, London, one supporting bracket scratch marked Law & Sons, December, 1879, in ebonized case, with later finials added, 17" (43cms). **£950-1050** SBe

A Louis XV ormolu-mounted Boulle Bracket Clock, signed Allioux a Paris, 58in (149cm) high, **£1,650-1,750** C

A Regency mahogany chiming Bracket Clock by Parkinson & Frodsham Change Alley London, movement with shaped plates, chiming on 8 bells, anchor escapement and pendulum with micrometer adjustment, 25½in (65cm) high, **£1,400-1,550** C

A Bracket Clock in the French style, with Vernis-Martin type painted decoration, 17½" high. **£320-360** NF

A Good Bracket Clock by Recordon London, with two train fusee movement, with anchor escapement, in mahogany case, height 13¼" (36cms). **£460-500** SBe

A Regence ormolu-mounted boulle bracket clock, signed J. B. Duchesne A Paris 21½ in., 54.5 cm. high. **£920-1,000** C

A rosewood and satinwood quarter striking Bracket Clock. **£750-950** Bon.

A Mahogany Bracket Clock, the two train wire fusee movement with verge escapement, short bob pendulum, bell striking, signed Patrick Russell, London, contained in a broken arched case with brass fish scale side frets, 12½ in., 31.7 cm. **£1,250-1,450** L

A Regence boulle bracket clock, signed Gosselin a Paris, with striking movement 27½ in., 70 cm. high. **£1,100-1,250** C

A Mahogany Bracket Clock, the wire fusee movement with shouldered plates, anchor escapement, bell striking and pull repeat, signed T. Cundliffe, Liverpool. 19¼ in., 49 cm. **£400-500** L

A George III ebonised striking Bracket Clock, movement with lightly engraved backplate, now converted to anchor escapement, 16in (41cm) high, **£660-750** C

A large 19th C Bracket Clock, with strike movement and back plate engraved Josh. Johnstone, Liverpool, 21" high. **£500-560** NF

An Eight-Day Mid-18th C pull quarter repeating Bracket Clock on 6 bells in an ebonised case, the movement has a verge escapement, with double fusee and engraved back-plate, 42cms high, and signed John Ellicott, London. **£4,200-4,500** SKC

POINTERS FOR FRENCH CARRIAGE CLOCKS

- Appeared approx. 1850.
- The mechanism in unfinished state made in various French towns and assembled by makers in Paris.
- Simple timepieces with various complications e.g. striking, repeating, quarter strike, alarm.
- English Carriage clocks made in French style but superior in quality with less complex mechanisms.
- The name on the dial is that of the vendor not the maker or assembler.
- Best examples produced in the 1870's.

A rare brass striking musical Carriage Clock with lever platform repeating/alarm on a gong, 7¼in (18.5cm) high **£2,400-2,900** C

A gilt-metal porcelain-mounted striking Carriage Clock, the movement stamped B encircled with lever platform, repeat/alarm on a gong, 6in (15cm) high, **£1,100-1,300** C

A Very Rare Brass Paul Garnier French Carriage Clock with a Grande Sonnerie repeating movement, signed 'No. 1103', c1835, with a shaft cutter escapement, (17cms) high. **£2,250-3,000** SKC

A gilt-metal small Petite-Sonnerie Striking Carriage Clock by Leroy with patent base wind, original travelling case, 4½in (10.8cm) high, **£1,000-1,500** C

An early French gilt-metal Pendule de Voyage, with strike/repeat, alarm and calendar, signed Dubos, Paris, c. 1780. 7½in (19cm) high, **£4,500-5,500** C

A Very Fine English Carriage Clock, the double fusee movement striking on a gong is signed 'French, Royal Exchange, London', with jewelled English lever escapement, 22cms high. **£1,780-1,850** SKC

A French brass Calendar Carriage Clock, with a lever movement and push repeat, 14.5cms high. **£1,550-£1,550-1,700** P

A Late 19th C Brass French Carriage Clock with Grande Sonnerie' 8-day movement striking and repeating, with an English lever platform escapement, 26cms high. **£2,450-2,500** SKC

A 19th C French Carriage Clock with repeater movement, 7" high. **£440-480** A

A Bronze Cased Double Fusee Striking Clock by Wilson of Stamford, c1790, 15½" high. **£950-1,100** SQE

A Fine Gorge-Cased Carriage Clock, signed 'Breguet, No. 3194', the French movement with petite sonnerie and alarm, with fully jewelled Swiss lever escapement, 13cms high. **£1,000-1,150** SKC

A French lacquered brass repeating Carriage Clock with alarm, signed Chas. Frodsham & Co. No. 19934, Paris, with eight day lever platform movement, 5¼" high. **£725-800** AG

A Very Fine Mid 19th C. French Alarum Carriage Clock, No. 1593, the lever escapement with repeat and striking on a bell, with inscription dated 1868, in leather carrying case, 7½ in., 19 cm. **£1,000-1,200** SBe

A fine late 19th C French Repeating Carriage Clock No. 61, the dial inscribed 'Goldsmiths Company, London, with presentation inscription dated June 13th, 1885, height 7½" (19cms) together with key. **£350-380** SBe

A French Carriage Clock, with visible escapement and compass and thermometer on the top, c1880. **£220-250** CCL

A Silver Case Miniature Carriage Clock by Liberty & Co., the French lever movement with the maker's mark of Duverdry & Bloquet, Birmingham 1908. **£330-360** L

A Grande Sonnerie carriage clock with calender work in an engraved oval case. **£1,700-1,900** Bon.

A French brass Carriage Clock, having a lever movement and push repeat, 18.5cms high. **£690-800** P

A Fine French Carriage Clock, on original stand in brass, Regency period. **£750-830** SA

A Small French Brass Carriage Clock, the two train movement with lever escapement, compensated balance and blued steel spiral spring, numbered 2087 and stamped E. M., faintly signed Edward & Sons., 5¼ in., 13.3 cm. **£420-500** L

A French Gilt Brass Carriage Clock, the two train movement with cylinder escapement, bell striking, numbered 3895, and signed R. Holdt et Cie, a Paris. (enamelled dial cracked) 7½ in., 18.7 cm. **£240-320** L

A gilt metal carriage clock, signed Shreve Crump & Low, Boston, subsidiary alarm dial, 6" high and leather case. **£350-400** SH

A Gilt Brass Carriage Clock, the two train movement with lever escapement and compensated balance, 7½" (18.6cms). **£470-570** L

A 19th C. French Repeating Carriage Clock No. 30019, having repeat striking on a gong, lever escapement and in brass case, 7 in., 18.5 cm. **£500-590** SBe

A French Brass Carriage Clock, the two train movement with lever escapement, compensated balance and blued steel spiral spring, numbered 2523, and stamped E. M. & Co., 6¾ in., 17.5 cm. **£250-350** L

A French Brass Carriage Clock, the movement with lever escapement, compensated balance, gong striking and repeating at will, inscribed Cromey & Son, Bristol, 6¾ in., 17.2 cm. **£360-400** L

A Silver Cased Miniature carriage clock, the French lever movement with the maker's stamp of Duverdry & Bloquet, 1920, 3¾ in., 9.6 cm. high. **£200-230** L

A Tortoiseshell Cased Miniature Carriage Clock the lever movement French. The mounts 1911 by William Comyns, and in original leather case., 4½ in., 11.5 cm. overall. **£240-270**

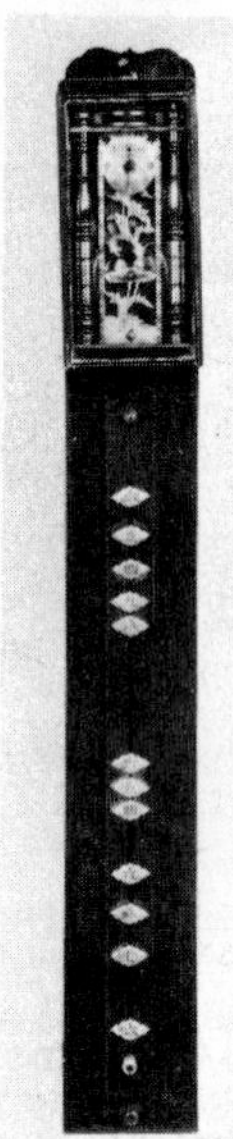

A Japanese Lacquer Fire Clock, 27½in (70cm) long, **£360-400** C

A 'Pendule d'Officeur' Striking Clock in green horn and ormolu, c1850, 7½" high. **£280-320** CCL

A Regency Mantel Clock by Gardener of Paris, in inlaid rosewood case. **£275-300** SAL

An unusual Japanese Stick Clock, the movement with pendulum verge escapement, 19½in (49.5cm) high, **£720-810** C

An American Cottage Clock in cast iron with visible pendulum, 30-hour, c1840, 13" high. **£45-65** CCL

A Biedermeier Stutzuhr signed J. Straub Bin Wein, movement quarter-striking on gongs, 22in (56cm) high, **£800-900** C

An Early 19th C. Repeating Mantel Clock, having verge escapement, inscribed Perigal and Duterrau, London, No. 1781, height 4½ in., 11.5 cm. **£440-500** SBe

c. 1850 galleried German mantel clock in walnut and ebony with metal dial, 24 in. high. **£180-190** TT

An American 8-day Mantel Clock, by Seth Thomas, with bugler alarm striking on bell and gong, c1860. **£50-65** CCL

French mid 19th C. mantel clock with brass and boulle inlay with silk suspension, 11 in. high. **£300-340** TT

A French Four-Glass Clock with brocot escapement and mercury pendulum, dial signed by J.W. Benson, 1860, 14" high. **£320-350** CCL

An Ansonia Striking Mantel Clock in mahogany case, c1890, 11" high. **£80-100** CCL

A late Louis XIV Mantel Clock by Gilles Martinot a Paris, movement disassembled and substantially missing, 13in (33cm) high, **£1,800-1,900** C

Mantel clock with malachite and brass on black marble with French movement, c. 1880. **£90-100** TT

A marquetry inlaid Mantel Clock, 10" high. **£85-95** CE

A 19th C. Inlaid Mantel Clock. **£70-80** SV

Inlaid Mahogany mantel clock with French movement 11 in. high. **£90-100** TT

Mantel clock with inlaid case and metal dial. Barrel movement. **£50-60** TT

French inlaid Balloon Clock with brass-filigree hands, 10" high. **£90-110** CCL

Fine quality French inlaid balloon mantel clock with silver dial 15½ in. high. **£200-230** TT

A French 8-Day Inlaid Lancet-Top Clock, c1900. **£50-65** CCL

A French balloon Clock, c1890, 11½" high. **£90-100** CCL

Walnut inlaid balloon mantel clock with enamel dial and French movement, 9 in. high. **£100-120** TT

A Regency mahogany mantel timepiece, signed Thomas Harlow, London, 15" high. **£390-430** SH

American clock with Rosewood veneer, 21 in. high. **£90-100** TT

Electric Clock, inlaid with birds-eye maple, c1926. **£20-30** CCL

A Regency Mahogany Mantel Clock, signed Jameson, London, height 17" (43cms). **£500-550** SH

A 20th C.French Regulator Mantel Clock, the 8-day movement with rack striking on a bell, with visible Brocot escapement, 31cms high. **£265-300** SKC

Balloon mantel clock with German movement and enamel dial, 11 in. high. **£80-90** TT

Inlaid Mahogany mantel clock with enamel dial and German movement. **£75-95** TT

Inlaid mahogany mantel clock with metal dial and German movement, 14 in. high. **£90-100** TT

Mantel clock with inlaid Oak case – and enamel dial – French movement, 11 in. high. **£90-100** TT

Small French mahogany mantel clock with enamel dial and original brass fittings. Eight day movement 10 in. high. **£150-170** TT

Art Nouveau mantel clock with copper inlay in oak. Enamel dial. **£120-140** TT

Inlaid Mahogany mantel clock with English movement, 11 in. high. **£90-100** TT

A 19th C. French 'Four-Glass' Mantel Clock No. 20181, gong strike, compensation mercury pendulum, in cast brass case, height 12 in., 31 cm. **£330-390** SBe

A French Rosewood Marquetry Mantel Clock, the two train movement with anchor escapement, outside locking plate, half hour bell striking by Japy Freres and inscribed Wm. Mott, Patent. London. Paris. 12 & 36 Cheapside, & P. Merle Paris. 19¼ in., 48.5 cm. **£180-250** L

A Miniature French Red Marble Four-Glass Clock with mercury pendulum, 9¼" high. **£260-280** CCL

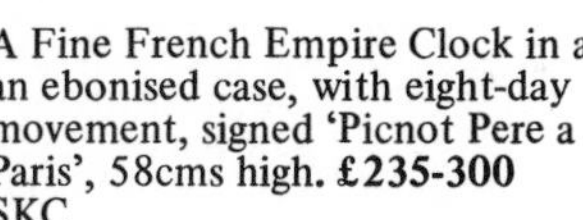

A Fine French Empire Clock in a an ebonised case, with eight-day movement, signed 'Picnot Pere a Paris', 58cms high. **£235-300** SKC

A Mantel Clock, signed JW Beason, Old Bond St., London, the movement with a mercury pendulum, 11¾" high. **£290-330** SH

A Very Fine French 'Regulator' style Mantel Clock, with an eight-day movement, signed 'Japy Frere', 30cms high. **£1,150-1,250** SKC

A 19th C French Mantel Clock, the 8-day movement with rack striking on a bell and glass cover at back. **£245-300** SKC

A Mid 19th C. French Mantel Clock, the movement inscribed M.O.Y. Freres, Btes, Paris, signed J. Pradier and inscribed Suisse Freres, height 16½ in., 42 cm. **£400-500** SBe

A French Gilt Bronze and Bronze Mantel Clock, the two train movement with silk suspension, outside locking plate, bell striking and signed Bienayme a Dieppe, 16½ in., 42 cm. **£240-300** L

A French ormolu four-glass Mantel Clock with a mercury pendulum, 41cms high. **£1,150-1,350** P

A 19th C French bronze and ormolu Mantel Clock, 57cms high. **£670-760** P

A French gilt metal clock of Louis XVI design, 11½" high. **£290-330** SH

A Regency Bronze and Ormolu Mantel Clock, with paw feet, 14 in., 37 cm. wide. **£1,050-1,100** C

A directoire ormolu, bronze and white marble portico mantel clock, signed Piolaine a Paris, 13¼ in., 33.5 cm. wide. **£500-550** C

A Mid 19th C. French Mantel Clock No. 56744, the back plate inscribed Japy Freres et Cie, and dated 1855, under glass dome, with plinth, height 16½ in., 42 cm. **£400-500** SBe

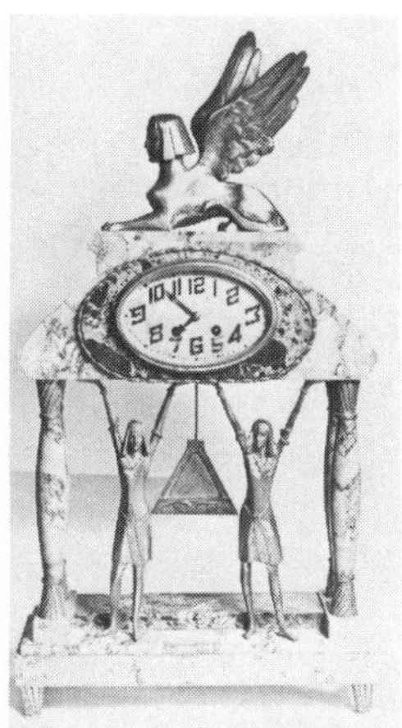

An Art Deco French Marble Clock, in Egyptian style, with bronze figures, 1930's, 26" **£350-400**

A Mid 19th C. Swiss Mantel Clock by Aubert and Klaftenberger, Geneve, height 18 in., 46 cm. **£550-650** SBe

A Louis XVI ormolu mantel clock, signed J. B. Lenoir A Paris, with later striking movement 15 in., 38 cm. high. **£500-600** C

A large ormolu Mantel Clock of Louis XVI design, signed Marquis a Paris, 19th C, 27in (68.5cm) high, **£1,400-1,550** C

A French Gilt Spelter Sculptural Mantel Clock, the two train movement with outside locking plate, bell striking and bearing the trade stamp of Japy Freres, 15¼ in., 39 cm. **£130-160** L

A French Porcelain Mounted Gilt Spelter Mantel Clock, the two train movement with Brocot suspension, outside locking plate, bell striking, bearing the trade stamp of Japy Freres numbered 43554 and signed Henry Marc, Paris, 14¾ in., 37.5 cm. **£140-180** L

A French Boulle Mantel Clock, the movement with Brocot suspension and bell striking., 16 in., 40.6 cm. **£360-420** L

A 19th C French Empire Clock, signed Guyerdet Aine Paris, with 8-day movement and locking plate, with an imitation gridiron pendulum, 53cms high. **£310-350** SKC

A 19th C. Mantel Clock, the movement inscribed "The British United Clock Co.Ltd., Birmingham'., 23 in., 58 cm. **£350-450** SBe

A Miniature French Green Boulle Striking Mantel Clock, c1870, 12" high. **£350-380** CCL

THURET – A rare Louis XIV boulle mantel clock. **£2,000-2,300** Bon.

A Mid 19th C. French Mantel Clock by Raingo Freres, striking on a bell and in gilt brass case (bell missing) height 16 in., 41 cm. **£310-360** SBe

A 19th C. French Gilt Mantel Clock. **£270-315** SV

An Ormolu Mounted French Mahogany Mantel Clock, the movement with outside locking plate and bell striking, 12½ in. 31.8 cm. **£130-190** L

A French ormolu Mantel Clock, striking on a bell, c1850, 10½" high. **£200-230** CCL

A Louis XIV Polychrome Boulle Clock, signed Raingo Freres a Paris with later striking movement, restorations, 15½in (39.5cm) high, **£620-680** C

A Good French Gilt Bronze Mantel Clock, the two train movement with outside locking plate, half hourly striking on a gong, bearing the trade stamp of Raingo Freres, Paris, 19¼" (49cms). **£500-600** L

An Empire bronze and ormolu Mantel Clock, 57cms high. **£420-520** P

A Late 19th C French Striking Buhl Clock, with tortoiseshell veneer and marquetry, signed Chomas and Co., Paris, 27cms high. **£280-380** SKC

A French Swinging Cherub Clock in alabaster case, c1870, 9½" high. **£150-170** CCL

A Fine 'Louis XVI' Style Lyre Clock No. 425, inscribed Causard, Bger du Roy. Paris, in pink marble lyre-shaped case with ormolu mounts, height 18½ in., 47 cm. **£1,800-1,950** SBe

A Liberty & Co. 'Cymric' silver Timepiece with the words 'Festina Lente' (make haste slowly) forming the hours, 14cms high, stamped L. & Co. 'Cymric' and hallmarks for Birmingham, 1903. **£650-700** P

A Bronze French Mantel Clock, the two train movement with Brocot suspension, bell striking, numbered 6707, signed Tiffany & Co. New York, 15¼" (38.7cms). **£300-400** L

A Liberty & Co. 'Tudric' pewter case Clock, reg. mark 740347, c1905, 6" high. **£60-70** SQE

A Victorian China 30-hour Mantel Clock, c1880, 7" high. **£20-30** CCL

A Mid 19th C French Mantel Clock by Raingo Freres, Pairs, in gilt brass case and with painted porcelain panels, height 16" (41cms), (bell missing). **£290-320** SBe

A Pewter rectangular Timepiece, attributed to Liberty & Co., 12.25cms high, the base stamped 0721. **£260-300** P

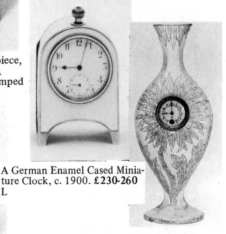

A German Enamel Cased Miniature Clock, c. 1900. **£230-260** L

An unusual Clock Vase, 34.5cms, c1900. **£100-130** SBe

A Good Large Meissen Mantle Clock, on oval base supported by bold scrolls and encrusted with flowers, 23 in. high. **£890-990** N

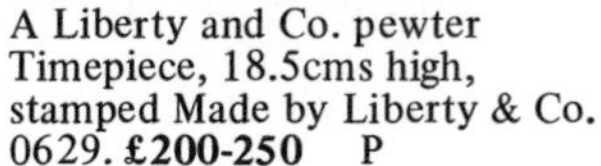

A Liberty and Co. pewter Timepiece, 18.5cms high, stamped Made by Liberty & Co. 0629. **£200-250** P

A Meissen Table Clock, height 44 cm., mark in underglaze blue, incised No. 2172, mid 19th C, some damage. **£1,550-1,700** S Be

A German gilt-metal Hexagona Table Clock, unsigned, with pierced screwed balance cock, verge escapement, 4½in (11.5cm) diam., **£1,700-1,850** C

A Continental Mantel Clock in bisque porcelain, with monogrammed mark in oval cartouche. The detachable figure group with small crack, late 19th C, by Henry Marc. **£500-550** SAL

A Jacob Petit Style French China Mantel Clock with apricot, green and gold scroll moulded case, 44.4 cm., mid 19th C., the clock movement by Leroy of Paris. **£330-400** S Be

A Travelling Clock in square 9 ct. gold engine turned case, with Swiss movement, 1938 maker's mark SJR., 7.7 mm. **£230-250** L

A Lalique opalescent glass Clock, moulded mark 'R. Lalique', 1920's, 11cms. **£320-360** SBe

An English gilt-metal striking Strut Clock in the style of Thomas Cole, signed Hunt & Roskell, London; movement with lever escapement and hour striking on a gong; fitted case 5½in (14cm) high, **£1,050-1,200** C

An Art Deco Marble Clock, 1920's **£24-28** AP

A Viennese giltwood Cartel Clock with verge striking on two bells movement, late 18th C, 40in (102cm) high, **£1,000-1,100** C

An English Dial Wall Clock, with an eight-day movement, having single fusee, 43cms diam. **£105-135** SKC

Ships clock 4 in. dial with top platform and cast brass case. **£80-90** TT

A 19th C. Dial Clock (8 day), 15 in. diam. **£140-170** OB

An English Single Fusee Clock with 8" dial, mahogany case, c1890. **£120-140** CCL

A German Miniature Brass Inlaid Black Forest Postman's Clock and alarm, 6" dial. **£90-100** CCL

An Art Deco Silver Clock, hallmarked 1932. **£65-70** AP

A Mahogany Veneered English Drop Dial Wall Clock with single fusee 8-day anchor movement, 53cms high. **£135-165** SKC

A George III, 8 Day Tavern Clock, 33 in. high, by John Jackson, c. 1778. **£875-925** OB

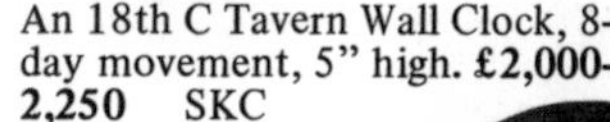

An 18th C Tavern Wall Clock, 8-day movement, 5" high. **£2,000-2,250** SKC

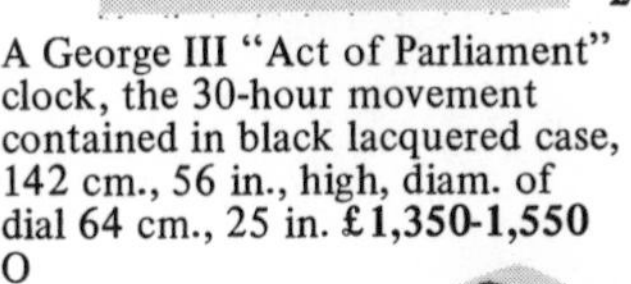

A George III "Act of Parliament" clock, the 30-hour movement contained in black lacquered case, 142 cm., 56 in., high, diam. of dial 64 cm., 25 in. **£1,350-1,550** O

Ansonia Regulator Clock with second hand, c. 1890. **£120-140** TT

An English Double Fusee Drop Dial Clock by Ebeneezer Fisher, Ellesmere, with convex dial and glass, c1820. **£500-600** CCL

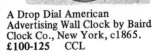

A Drop Dial American Advertising Wall Clock by Baird Clock Co., New York, c1865. **£100-125** CCL

Small double weight Vienna Regulator, 50 in. high. **£275-295.** TT

A Convex Fusee Dial Clock, by Roberts, Downham, c1830. **£160-180** CCL

An 18th C Ebonised hooded wall clock, the 10" brass dial inscribed Ratcliff W. Pool 274, bell striking 30 hour movement. **£400-450** PWC

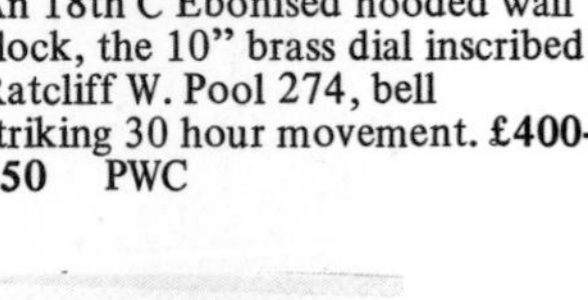

An 18th C Dutch Friesland Wall Clock, with 30-hour striking movement, anchor escapement, brass weight, 3'8" high. **£1,550-1,600** SKC

A German Vienna Double-Spring Clock, with steel and brass compensating pendulum, c1880. **£150-170** CCL

American inlaid Wall clock with original fittings. **£220-260** TT

A Converted Lantern Wall Clock, signed Cha's Edmonds of London, 30-hour movement with verge escapement, alarm dial, brass weight, 16" high (bell missing), dial signed Tho. Gullven, Horsmunden. **£1,120-1,320** SKC

A 19th C brass skeleton Clock, with dead-beat escapement, inscribed Willm. Grace, Clerkenwell, 21¾" high, c1860. **£550-620** GC

Art Nouveau repousse brass wall Clock. **£420-470** A.D.H.

A 19th C. Brass Skeleton Timepiece, the single chain drive with anchor escapement, under glass dome, height 14 in., 36 cm. **£350-400** SBe

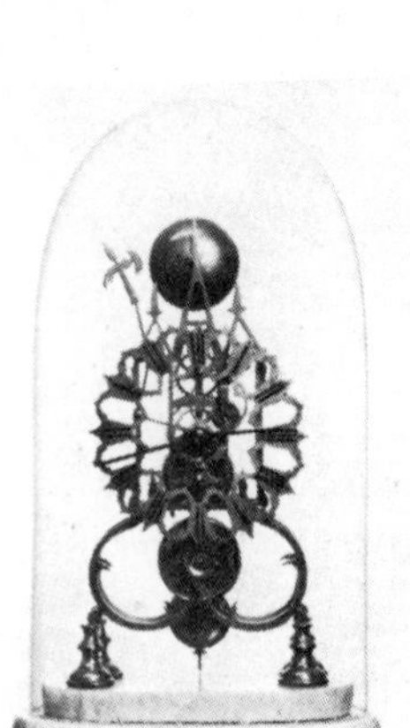

A 19th C Brass 'One at the Hour' Skeleton Clock, total height 19" (48.5cms). **£270-290** SBe

A Brass Lantern Clock, the engraved dial inscribed "Lac Mountfort at St. Albans' having single hand, the weight driven movement with anchor escapement, height 13 in., 33 cm. **£900-1,000** SBe

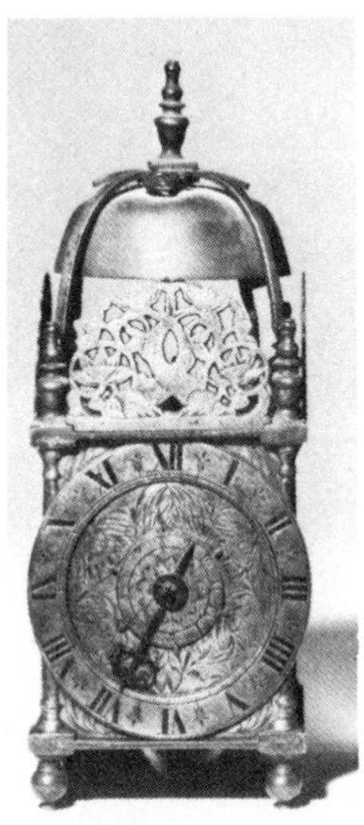

An English brass miniature Lantern Clock, unsigned, the movement with anchor escapement, countwheel strike and alarm on the bell, 9¾in (24.5cm) high, **£3,100-3,250** C

An English brass miniature Lantern Clock signed Windmills London, later canopied wall bracket with presentation inscription, 8¾in (22cm) height of clock, **£1,350-1,450** C

An early English Brass Lantern Clock, the movement with verge escapement and short bob pendulum, and early conversion from balance wheel escapement, signed John Pennock in Lothbury Londini Fecit., 15¼" (38.8cms), mid 17th C. **£2,600-2,900** L

A German Mantel Clock with striking movement, c1880, 15" high. **£230-250** CCL

An English Brass Alarum Lantern Clock, the movement with verge escapement, outside count wheel, stirrup and short bob pendulum. Signed Thomas Knight, London, (wall spikes, side panels, weights and rope missing), some restorations, particularly to alarum work. 15½ in., 38 cm. **£950-1,100** L

An 18th C brass Lantern Clock, with anchor escapement, 40cms high. **£950-1,050** P

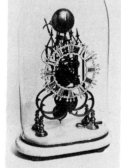

18th C Brass Lantern clock by John Draper dated 1705. **£1,500-1,800** A.D.H.

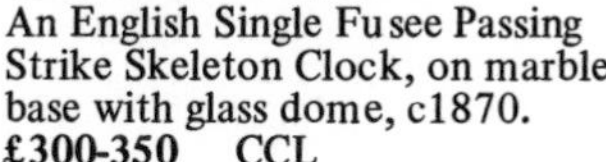

An English Single Fusee Passing Strike Skeleton Clock, on marble base with glass dome, c1870. **£300-350** CCL

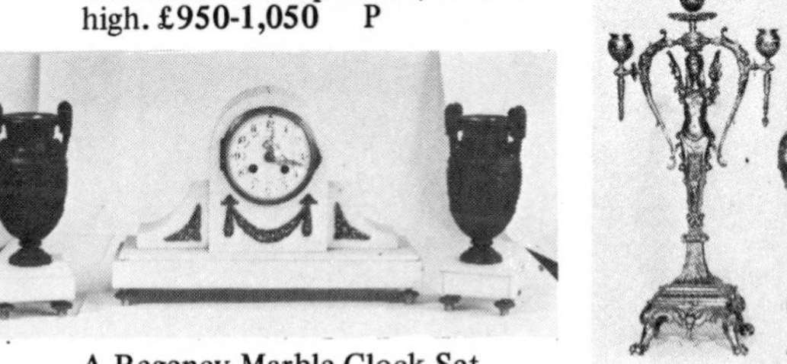

A Regency Marble Clock Set. **£395-440** SAL

A silvered bronze Timepiece Garniture, 16½in (42cm), flanked by a pair of Candelabra 18¼in (46.5cm), c. 1870, **£300-400** C

A 19th C French ormolu and Sevres porcelain Clock set. **£675-775** SAL

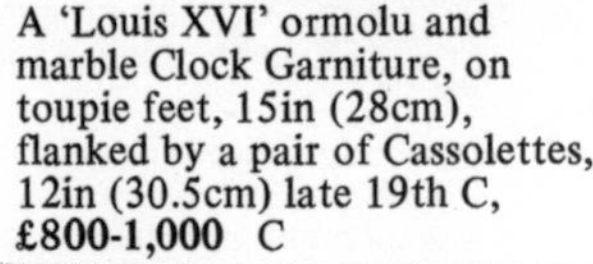

A 'Louis XVI' ormolu and marble Clock Garniture, on toupie feet, 15in (28cm), flanked by a pair of Cassolettes, 12in (30.5cm) late 19th C, **£800-1,000** C

A Good 19th C French China Clock Garniture, the clock inscribed 'Stevenard Boulogne' height 20½" (52cms), with a pair of cornucopia vases, height 13" (33cms). **£860-940** SBe

A Garniture du Chiminee with a 24" high Clock and a pair of matching 6 branch Candelabra. **£380-460** Lan

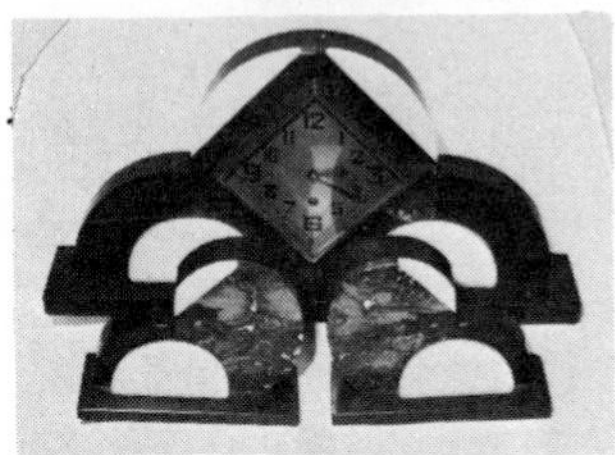

An Art Deco Marble Clock Set, 1920's. **£125-150** AP

right

A Good Mid 19th C. French Clock Garniture No. 549, inscribed Japy Freres et Cie, and a matching pair of two-light candelabra on similar bases, height 16 in., 41 cm. candelabra height 18 in., 46 cm. **£1,000-1,150** SBe

An Early Buhl 800 Day Battery Clock, mahogany base, with glass dome, 1920, 10" high. **£65-70** CCL

A Maple Wood Bracket 'Regulator' Timepiece, the chain fusee movement with dead beat escapement and power maintaining, signed E.W. Streeter, 8 New Bond St., 15⅝" (39.8cms), c1880. **£500-600** L

A Junghaus Brass Calendar Clock, c1880. **£40-45** CCL

A German 'Water Lion' Clock, c1880, 18" high. **£120-150** CCL

A 9ct gold Natham Hunter Pocket Watch, 1¾" dial. **£100-120** CCL

A Gold and Enamel Open Faced Keyless Fob Watch, stamped 18K, together with gilt bow brooch, 27mm. **£300-340** L

A French Inlaid Miniature Grandfather Clock, c1890, 15½" high. **£120-150** CCL

A Fine Quality 18ct. Gold Keyless Hunter Pocket Watch, with three-quarter plate jewelled fusee lever movement, signed 'J. Hargreaves and Co., Liverpool, No. 48583'. **£320-380** SKC

A Fine 18ct. Gold Hunter Pocket Watch, the keyless movement having a jewelled English lever escapement, signed 'J. Benson, Liverpool'. **£390-440** SKC

A Fine 18ct. Gold Pocket Watch, with a jewelled three quarter plate fusee lever movement, signed 'Dyson and Sons, Leeds and Wakefield'. **£310-380** SKC

A Keyless 18ct. Gold Half-Hunter Pocket Watch, with jewelled lever bar movement, with a micro-regulator on balance cock, with gold Albert chain. **£300-350** SKC

An early 18th C gold pair cased Pocket Watch with verge movement, inscribed S. Bouquet, London, n. 336. **£850-900** GC

An 18-carat gold open-faced lever Watch by J.W. Benson, London, full-plate movement with chain fusee and gold balance, hallmarked 1885, 49mm, and a key, **£250-350** SB

A silver hunting-cased crab-tooth duplex Watch, 49mm, **£200-250** SB

A Fine 18ct. Gold Full Hunter Minute Repeater Pocket Watch with 30-minute chronograph, probably made by E. Dent of London. **£1,270-1,300** SKC

A Fine Keyless 18ct. Gold Hunter Pocket Watch, with fully jewelled lever escapement, signed Thos. Russell and Son, Liverpool. **£750-800** SKC

An 18-carat gold open-faced lever Watch by Henry Frodsham, Liverpool, full-plate movement with chain fusee, hallmarked 1836, 44mm, with a floral key, **£300-400** SB

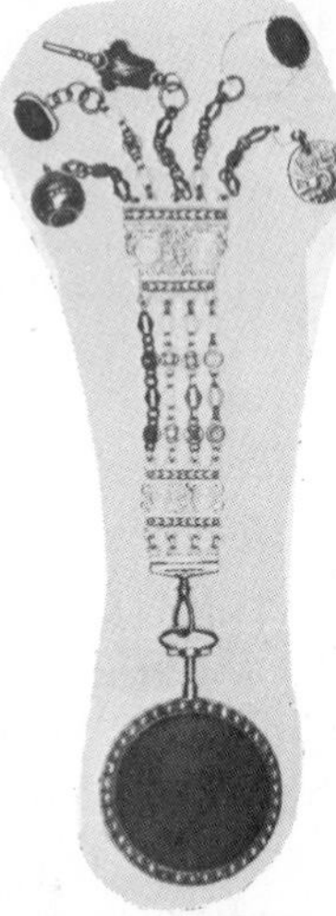

A French gold and enamel dumb quarter-repeating cylinder Watch, bridge-cock movement, with vari-coloured gold chatelaine, 49mm diam., **£2,750-3,500** C

An 18-carat gold hunting-cased lever Watch by Thomas Russell & Son, Liverpool, full-plate movement with compensation balance and chain fusee, hallmarked 1855, 53mm, with a key, **£400-500** SB

An 18-carat gold half-hunting cased keyless lever Watch by Waltham Watch Co, hallmarked 1908, 49mm, **£300-400** SB

A Swiss hunter-cased gold enamel and diamond-set keyless lever Watch, signed Omega, 48mm diam., **£2,000-2,750** C

A French gold and enamel dual-time Cylinder Watch, signed Le Roy a Paris, 42mm diam., **£420-475** C

A Continental gold and enamel hunter-cased Verge Watch with bridge-clock movement, 30mm. diam., **£600-700** C

An 18 Carat Gold Open Faced English Lever Key Wind Watch, the full plate fusee movement with footed cock, numbered V246, signed A. Meyers, Greenwich, hallmarked 1827, 51mm. **£320-370** L

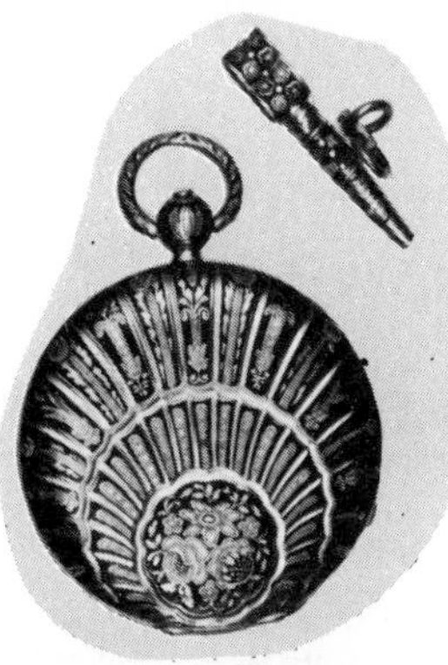

A Swiss gold and enamel cylinder Watch, Lepine-calibre movement, silvered engine-turned dial, 35mm diam., **£630-680** C

A Fine 18 Carat Gold Open Faced English Lever Watch, the full plate movement with plain footed cock, numbered 1651 and signed Robert Bryson, Edinburgh, hallmarked 1832, 44mm. **£400-550** L

A Triple Cased Turkish Market Verge Watch by Benjamin Barber, London, No. 6033, hallmarked 1786, tortoiseshell outer case with inlaid silver decoration. **£370-430** SBe

A Fine George III Gold Pair Cased Quarter Repeating Verge Watch by Windmills, London, No. 9001, hallmarked 1781. **£1,450-1,650** SBe

A George III Gold Keywound Cylinder Watch by Andrew Rich, Bridgwater, No. 7900, having fusee chain, hallmarked 1817. **£360-420** SBe

A Gold Key-Wound Lever Centre Seconds Watch No. 43825, the ¾ plate movement inscribed George Bradley, Sheffield, in 18 ct. gold case with a 15 ct. gold watch chain and fob. **£260-320** SBe

A Gold Hunter Cased Key-wound Lever Watch inscribed Hawley's, London, No. 1153, having compensation balance, chain fusee, with plain 18 ct. case. **£460-560** SBe

A Gold Quarter Repeating Ruby Cylinder Watch, the movement with plain three arm balance, blued steel spiral spring and Breguet compensation curb, the gilt cuvette numbered 8865, and signed Recordon a Paris, 56 mm. **£1,050-1,150** L

A fine late 18th C Quarter Repeating Musical Pocket Watch signed 'Le Roy, a Paris No. 8648', the cylinder movement playing a tune each hour. **£1,220-1,300** SKC

A good lever dress watch, with cut compensated balance in a plain 18ct. gold bassine case, 43mm x 4mm thick, also a gold and platinum dress Guard. **£250-300** P

A Gentleman's Slim 18ct. Gold Half Hunter Pocket Watch, with fully jewelled keyless Swiss lever bar movement and presentation case. **£175-200** SKC

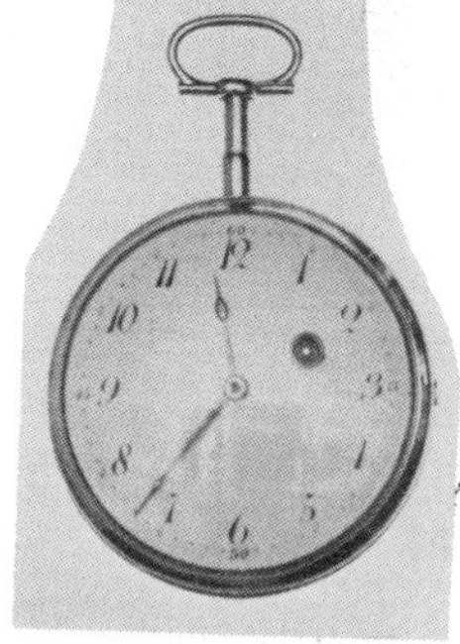

A French Gold Open Faced Quarter Repeating Key Wind Watch, 53mm. **£600-700** L

A Swiss 8-Day Pocket Watch, with enamel dial and visible escapement, in silver case. **£40-45** CCL

An 18-carat gold, hunting-cased, keyless lever centre-seconds Watch, no. 157536, by J. Harris and Sons, London and Manchester, with three-quarter plate movement, hallmarked 1890, 52mm. **£300-400** C

A Very Fine 19th C Decorative Gold-cased Continental Open Faced Pocket Watch, the jewelled lever bar movement signed Julien-Geneve. **£340-400** SKC

A Swiss Hunting Cased Minute Repeating Keyless Lever Centre Seconds Flying Calendar Chronograph, 55 mm. **£1,700-1,800** L

A Swiss Quarter repeating verge watch,unsigned, with full plate movement in silver case with gilt cuvette, c1800, 55mm. **£700-900** P

An 18 Carat Gold Half Hunting Cased keyless Lever Centre Seconds Minute Recording Swiss Chronograph, hallmarked 1911, with nine carat gold albert approx. ½oz. in weight, 49mm. **£340-400** L

An early 19th C mahogany banjo wheel barometer with hygrometer dial, mercury thermometer, inscribed C.A. Canti & Son, 16 Brook Street, Holborn, 38" high. **£250-300** PWC

A good early 19th C mahogany banjo wheel barometer with hygrometer dial, inscribed F. Armadio & Son, 118 St. John Street, London, spirit level dial, 42" high. **£300-350** PWC

19th C Mercury Banjo Barometer in rosewood case, with temperature bulb, level and hygrometer, 36½", c1850. **£180-220** STR

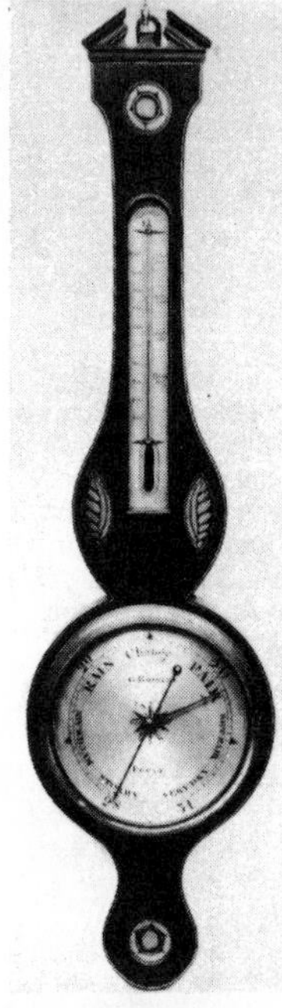

A Mahogany Veneered Early 19th C Banjo Wheel Barometer, the 8in silvered dial signed G. Broggi, 99cms high. **£235-250** SKC

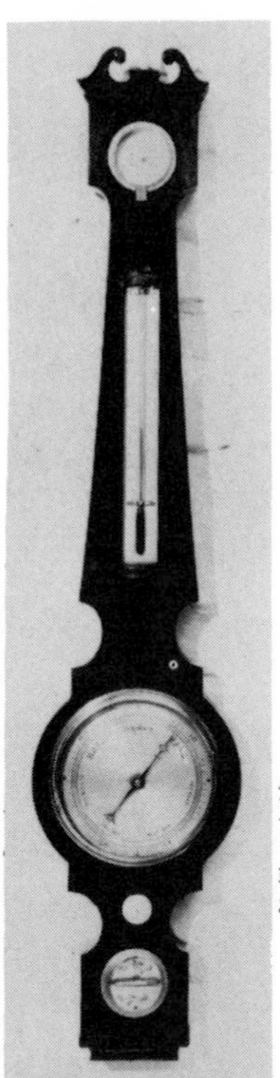

A George III Banjo Barometer by Lioni Somalvico and Company of 125 Holb'n Hill, London, in mahogany case, 3'3" high. **£465-500** SKC

A Walnut Veneered Mid-19th C Banjo Wheel Barometer, signed Stopani, Aberdeen, 95cms high. **£290-320** SKC

A 19th C mahogany banjo wheel barometer, with hygrometer dial, alcohol thermometer, inscribed F. Amadio, 118 St. Johns Street Road, London, 38" high. **£250-300** PWC

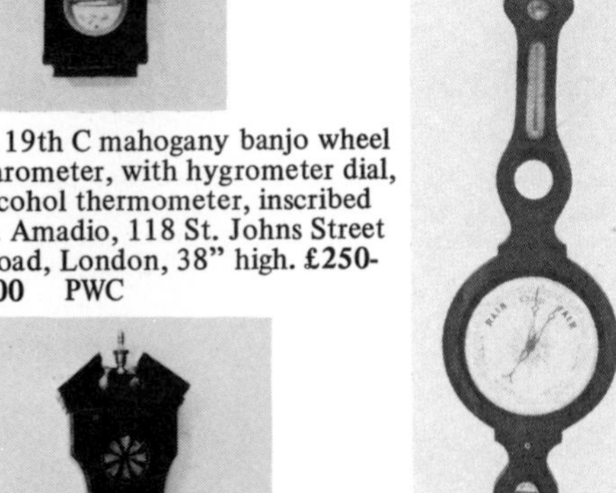

A Good George III Banjo – shaped Barometer, having thermometer, hygrometer and spirit level, in mahogany case with boxwood and ebony stringing and kingwood cross-banding. 44½ in., 113 cm. **£350-395** SBe

A Rosewood Banjo Barometer, 40 in., 102 cm., c. 1850. **£210-260** SB

A Sheraton period inlaid mahogany banjo wheel barometer, with alcohol thermometer, inscribed M. Salamon, Oxford, 38" high. **£250-300** PWC

A 19th C mahogany banjo Barometer. **£260-290** SAL

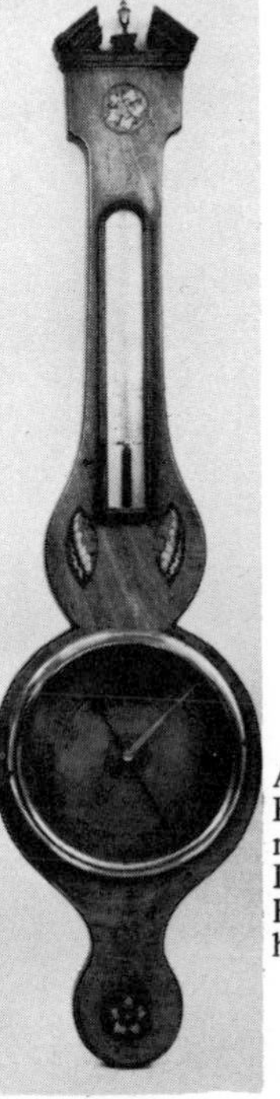

A Mahogany Wheel Barometer, dial signed A. Rivolta, Chester, (tube defective) the throat with alcohol thermometer, 38½ in. 97.8 cm. **£210-250** L

A 19th C Mahogany Banjo Wheel Barometer, with watch fusee movement signed John Roberts of London, with spirit level signed H. Marks, Bloomsburh, 112cms high. **£530-580** SKC

19th C Aneroid Barometer in mahogany case, with temperature bulb, 34". **£100-120** STR

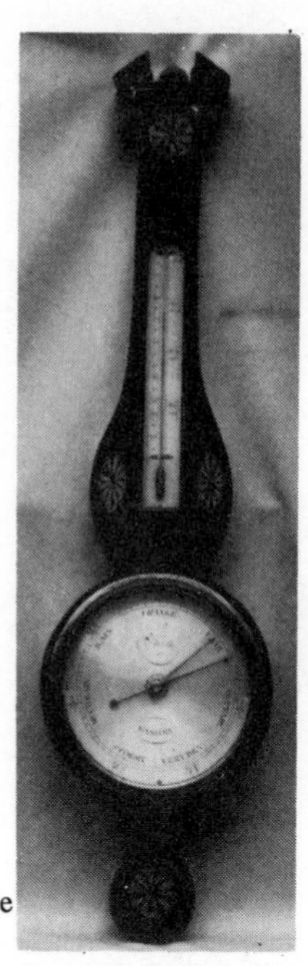

A Banjo Barometer, with Thermometer, with a mahogany case inlaid with paterae, maker C. Tarelli, 3 ft. 2 in. high. **£480-560** OL

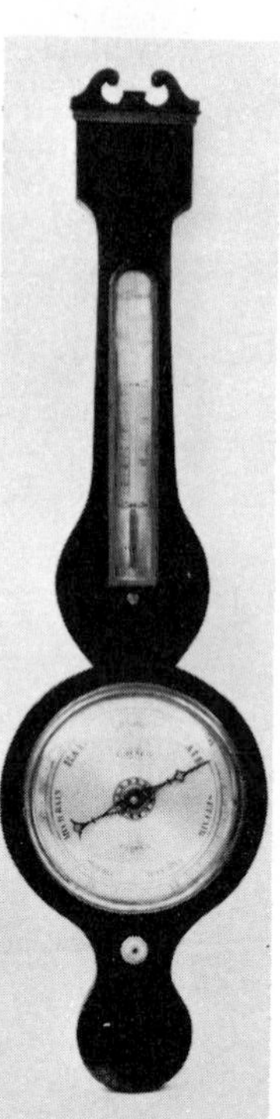

A Mahogany Wheel Barometer, the dial signed Hunt, Cork, the throat inset with an alcohol thermometer, 38 in. 96.5 cm. **£130-170** L

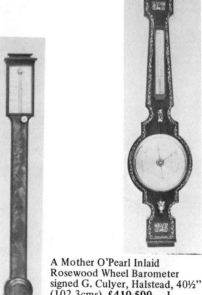

A Rosewood Wheel Barometer inset with hygrometer, alcohol thermometer, convex mirror and spirit level, 40½ in., 103 cm. **£130-170** L

Aneroid Barometer in carved oak case, with temperature bulb, 12" diam. **£70-100** STR

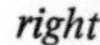

right

A Mahogany Stick Barometer, inscribed Robert Sharp, Longfor Macus, 1774, 37" (94cms). **£270-350** L

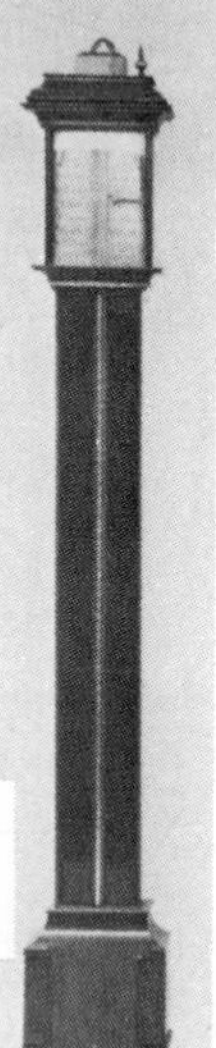

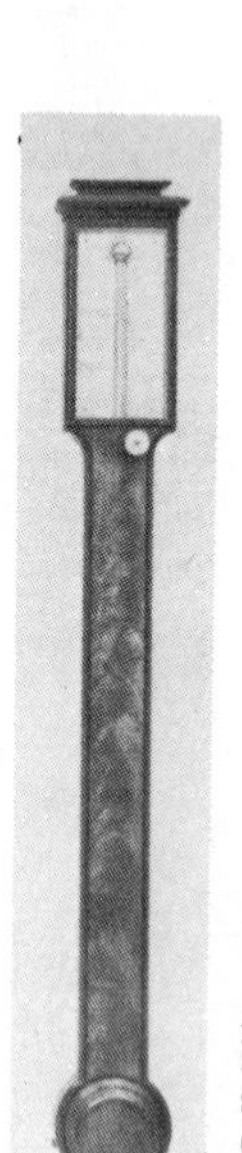

A Figured Mahogany Stick Barometer, signed Cary, London, 38½" (97.8cms). **£490-580** L

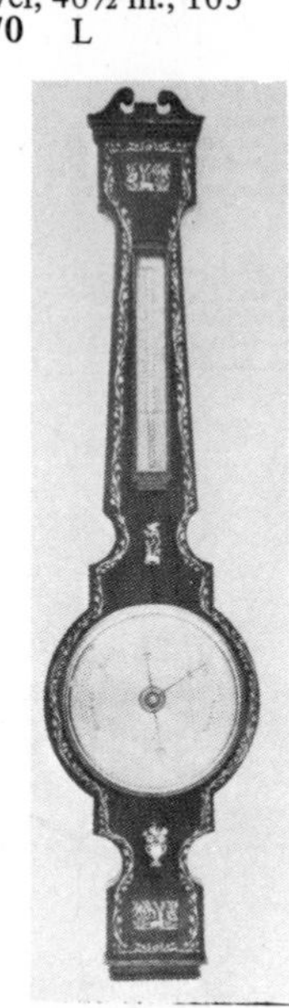

A Mother O'Pearl Inlaid Rosewood Wheel Barometer signed G. Culyer, Halstead, 40½" (102.3cms). **£410-500** L

A Brass Clock-Barometer Set in the shape of a bicycle, with 30-hour movement, c1890, 4½" high. **£45-60** CCL

Clock and Barometer set with French movement in a carved oak case, 11 in. high. **£110-130** TT

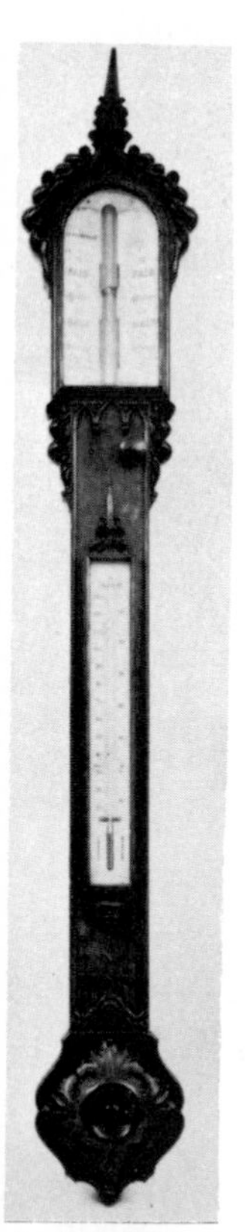

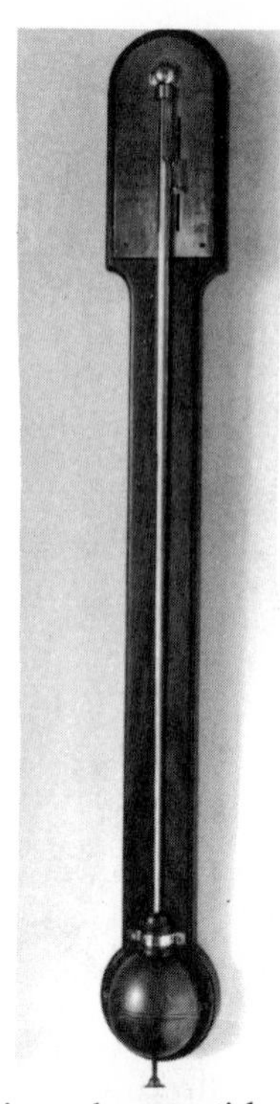

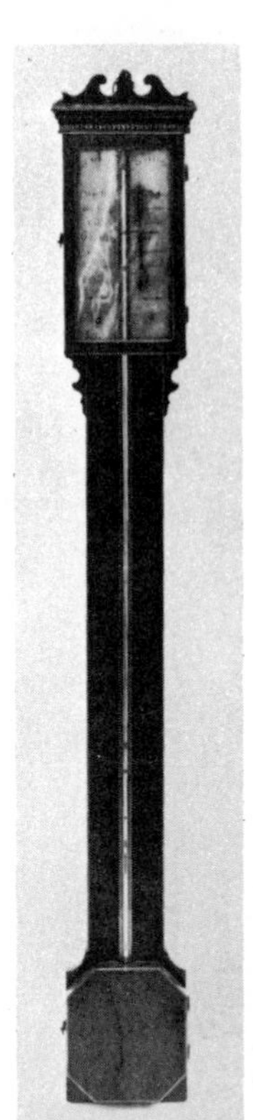

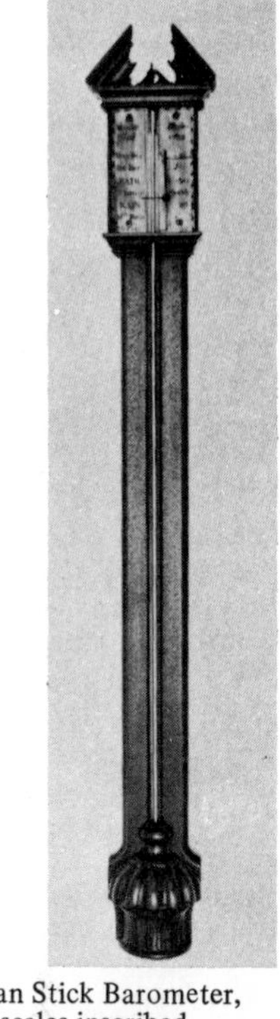

A Georgian mahogany stick barometer, with engraved brass plate inscribed Adams, Fleet Street, London, 3'1½" overall length. **£440-500** G & C

A Georgian Stick Barometer, the brass scales inscribed Meredith Hughes, Fecit 1763, 38 in., 97 cm. **£240-280** SBe

An Oak Stick Barometer, the ivory register plate with vernier scale, signed R. H. C. Wilson, Wilston St., Gray's Inn, London, with applied mercury thermometer, 43¾ in., 111 cm. **£240-280** L

A Good George III Stick Barometer, by John Kemp, Wakefield, having brass scales with pointer and in mahogany case, 38 in., 96.5 cm. **£350-395** SBe

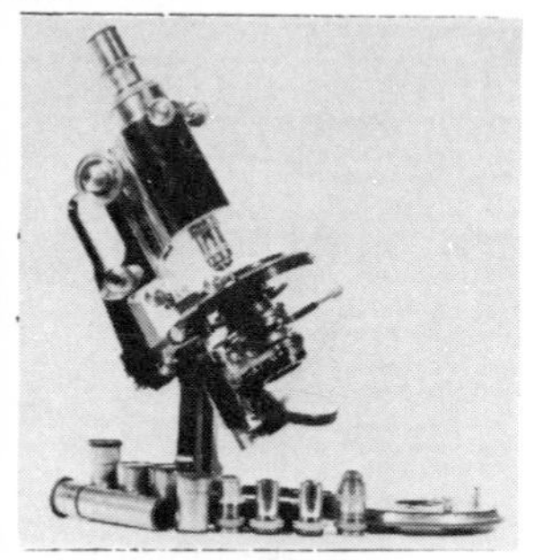

A Black Enamelled Microscope by Zeiss, No. 60509, with lacquered brass fittings, in mahogany case. **£200-230** CSK

A Brass Microscope of Culpeper type, signed T. Harris & Son, London, 10½" high, in mahogany case. **£440-500** CSK

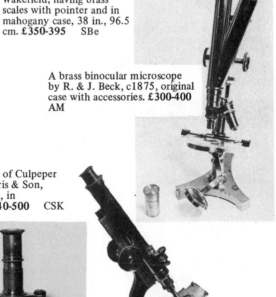

A brass binocular microscope by R. & J. Beck, c1875, original case with accessories. **£300-400** AM

A fine petrological microscope by J. Swift & Son with five objectives, five oculars, polarisor and analyser, condenser and stand bullseye, in case. **£210-250** CSK

A Victorian miniature Microscope, 6½" high, in mahogany case. **£60-75** SQE

A brass microscope by Horne & Thornthwaite, New Gate Street, London. **£185-250** AM

A microscope by T. Cooke, York with accessories. **£260-290** CSK

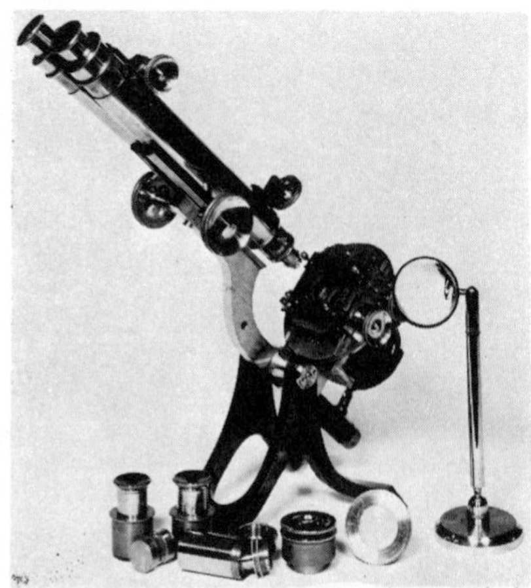

A Brass Binocular Microscope, the Lister-limb construction with dual adjustment to the eye-pieces, English, c. 1880 with accessories. **£350-390** SB

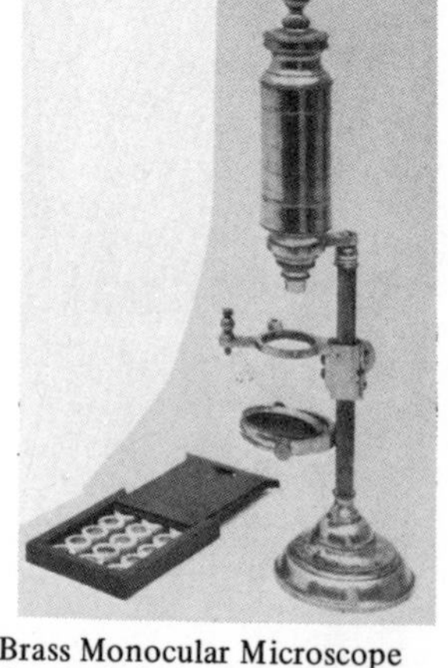

A Brass Monocular Microscope (mirror missing), contained in a mahogany case with spare numbered objectives, (late 18th C, most probably Dutch), 12½" (31.5cms). **£700-800** L

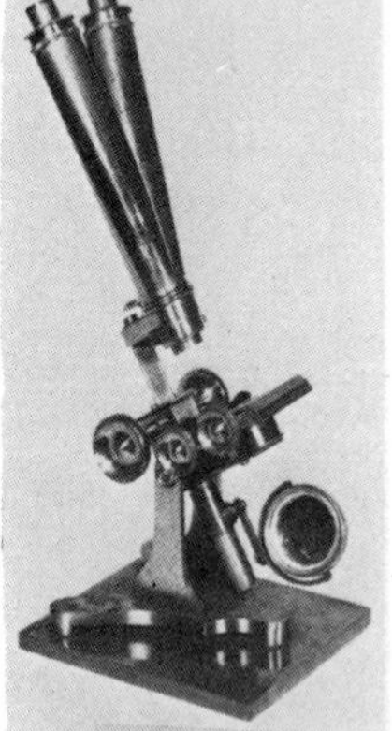

A Brass Binocular Microscope, the bar-limb construction with sliding tube adjustment to the eye-pieces, rack and pinion focusing, English, c. 1880. **£240-280** SB

Three botanist's microscopes:
l With box. **£75-125** AM
m With wooden handle. **£75-125** AM
r With ivory handle. **£75-130** AM

POINTERS FOR TELESCOPES

- First telescopes developed from 1605 to 1608.
- 17th C. refracting models made of vellum with horn binding.
- 1758 Dolland developed lens for day and night vision.
- 18th C. has greatest appeal for collectors as everything was hand made.
- 18th C. barrels made of mahogany, brass for metal parts.
- 19th C. plainer style, machine produced.
- Instruments still widely available. Currently excellent investment potential for 18th C. and good 19th C. examples.

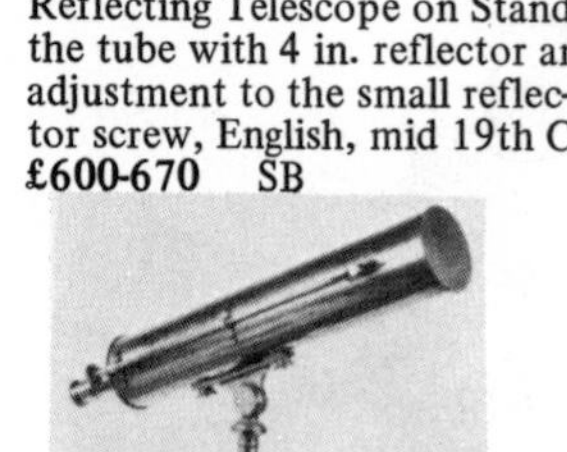

A William Struthers Gregorian Reflecting Telescope on Stand, the tube with 4 in. reflector and adjustment to the small reflector screw, English, mid 19th C. **£600-670** SB

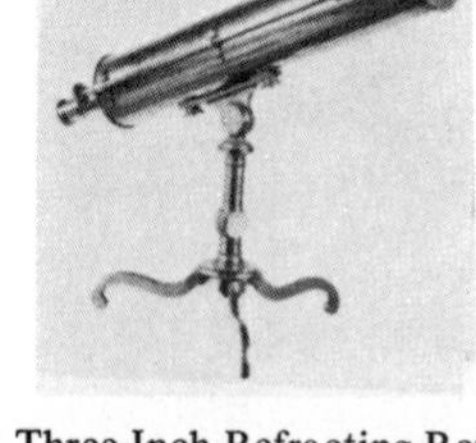

A Three-Inch Refracting Reflecting Telescope by Henry Pyefinch, Cornhill, London, of lacquered brass, tube length 17¾ in., 18th C. **£700-800** CSK

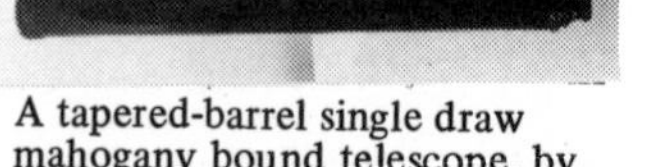

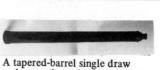

A tapered-barrel single draw mahogany bound telescope, by Spencer, Browning & Rust. **£95-150** AM

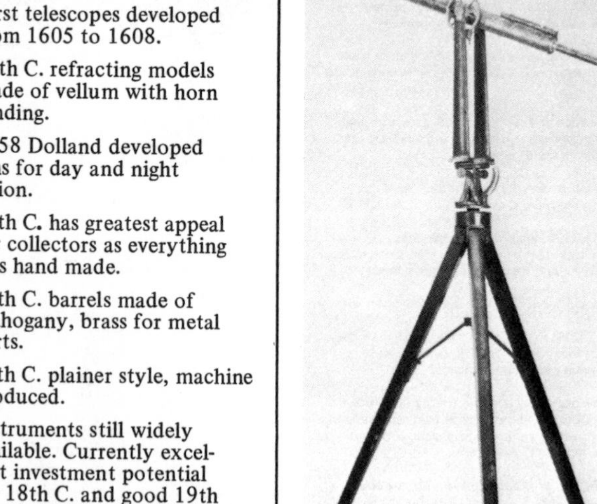

A Refracting Telescope by Dollond with one eyepiece, sighting telescope, tube length 42 in., height from ground 79 in., with fitted mahogany case. **£700-800** CSK

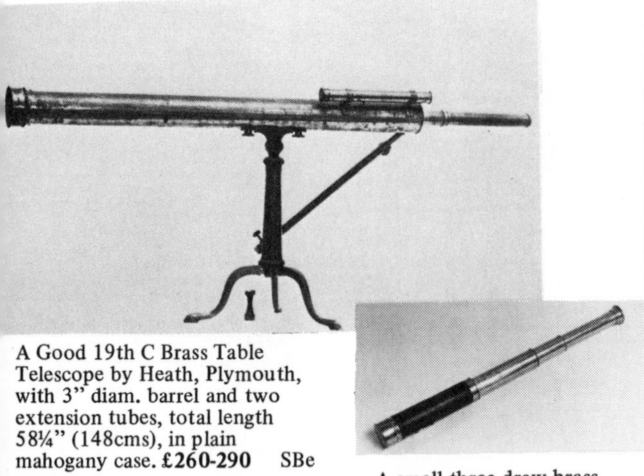

A Good 19th C Brass Table Telescope by Heath, Plymouth, with 3" diam. barrel and two extension tubes, total length 58¼" (148cms), in plain mahogany case. **£260-290** SBe

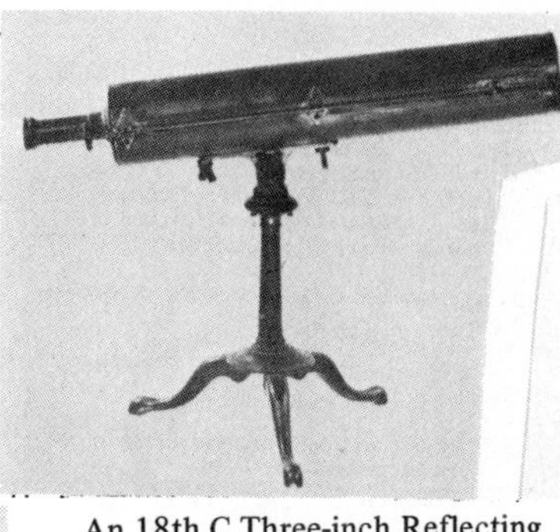

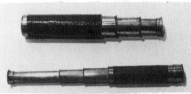

An 18th C Three-inch Reflecting Telescope by Nairne, London, tube length 19". **£500-750** CSK

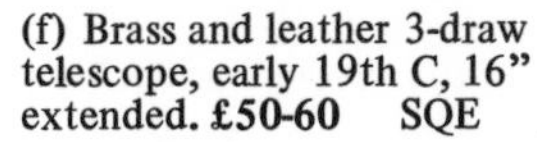

A small three draw brass telescope, leather bound, with lens cap, c1890-1920. **£30-60** AM

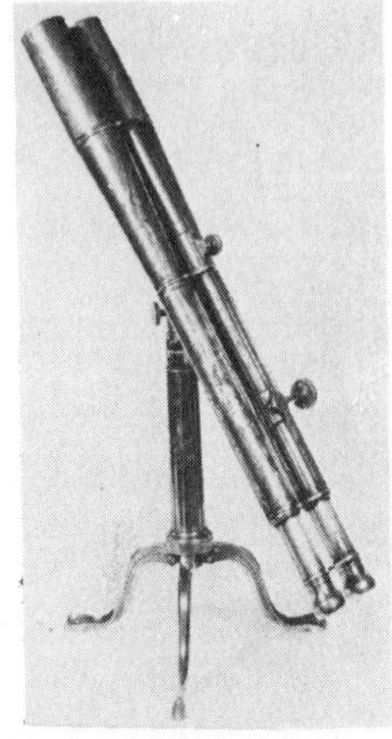

(b) Brass and leather 3-draw telescope, 19th C, 18½" extended. **£45-50** SQE

(f) Brass and leather 3-draw telescope, early 19th C, 16" extended. **£50-60** SQE

An Exotic and Unusual Silvered Brass Binocular Telescope on Stand, 2 ft. 10 in., 86 cm. probably Indian, late 19th C. **£1,100-1,200** SB

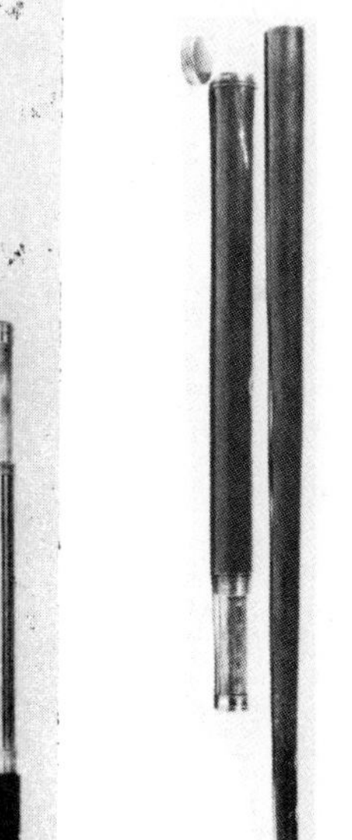

A Walking Stick Single-Draw Telescope by Thos. Harris & Son, No. 52, main tube length 12 in., overall length 36 in. **£160-180** CSK

A Rosewood Covered Walking Stick Telescope with detachable single-draw telescope section and ornamental gilt bands, 34 in. overall. **£260-300** CSK

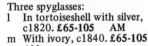

Three spyglasses:
l In tortoiseshell with silver, c1820. **£65-105** AM
m With ivory, c1840. **£65-105** AM
r With case, c1790. **£60-100** AM

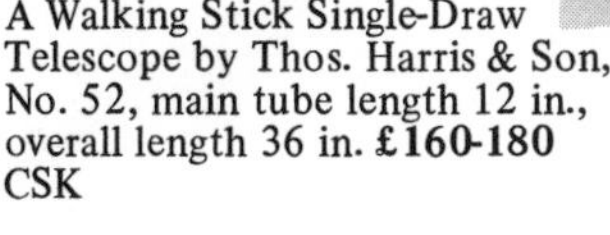

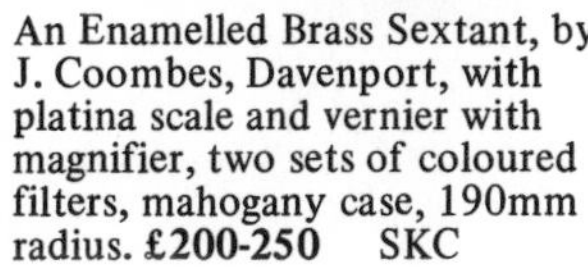

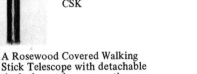

An Enamelled Brass Sextant, by J. Coombes, Davenport, with platina scale and vernier with magnifier, two sets of coloured filters, mahogany case, 190mm radius. **£200-250** SKC

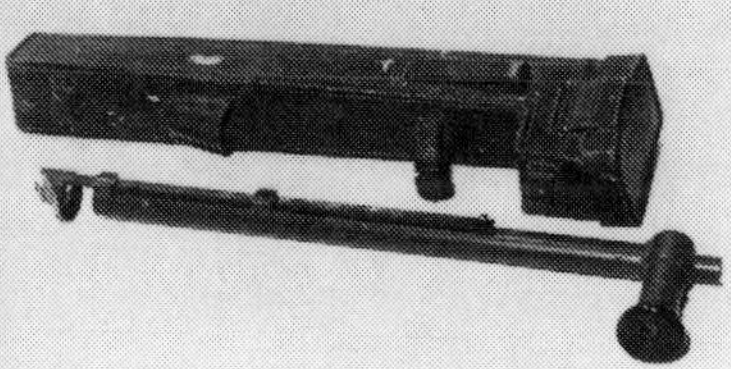

R. & J. Beck Ltd. telescopic Periscope No. 25, magnifying X6, dated 1918, extending from 17" to 25½", with shaped leather case. **£40-55** SQE

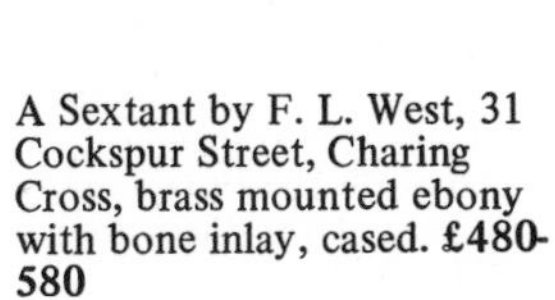

A Sextant by F. L. West, 31 Cockspur Street, Charing Cross, brass mounted ebony with bone inlay, cased. **£480-580**

A. D. McGregor and Co. Brass Sextant with silvered scale and vernier, lacking magnifier, 6 in., 15 cm., radius, in mahogany case with two telescopes, English, late 19th C. **£180-220** SB

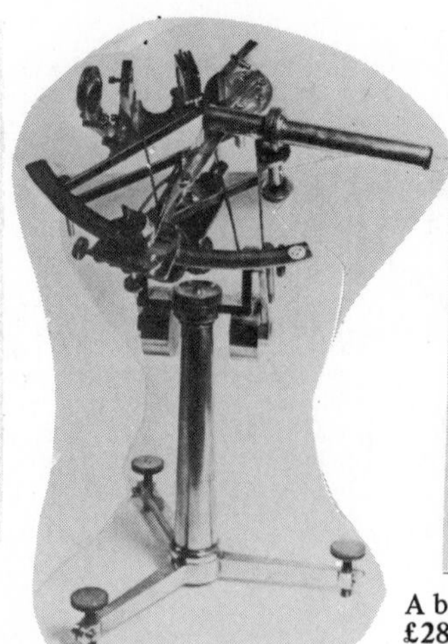

A brass sextant on stand with mahogany boxes, c1870, by H.G. Blair & Co. of Cardiff and Barry. **£800-950** AM

A brass sextant in mahogany case. **£280-400** AM

SEXTANTS

- Invented by Hadley in 1731.
- Double frame Sextant introduced c1780.
- Early examples of wood and metals.
- After 1800, generally of all brass construction.
- Addition of fine decoration, ivory and silver adds value.
- Makers of note: Cary, Troughton, Berge, Bardon.

A Troughton & Simms Brass Box Sextant with silvered scale and vernier with magnifier, English c. 1870 2¾ in., 7 cm. diam. **£120-140** SB

An ebony octant in oak box by Gray & Keen. **£350-450** AM

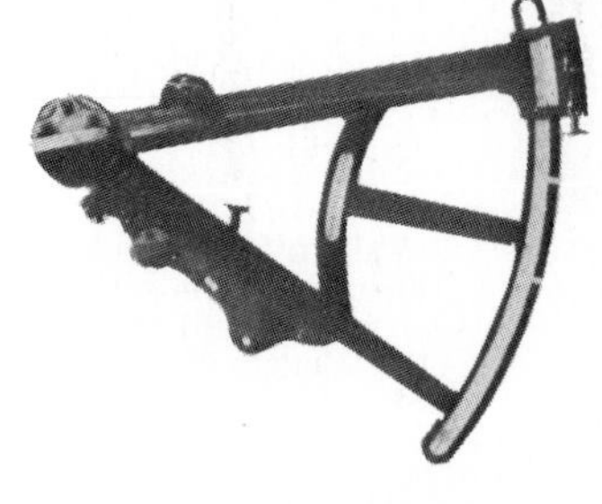

An Ebony and Brass Octant by Harris & Son, London, radius 11½", in oak case. **£400-450** CSK

An Ebony Octant, lacking maker's plaque, with brass vane and index arm with bone vernier scale, English, c. 1830 8¾ in., 22.2 cm. radius. **£240-280** SB

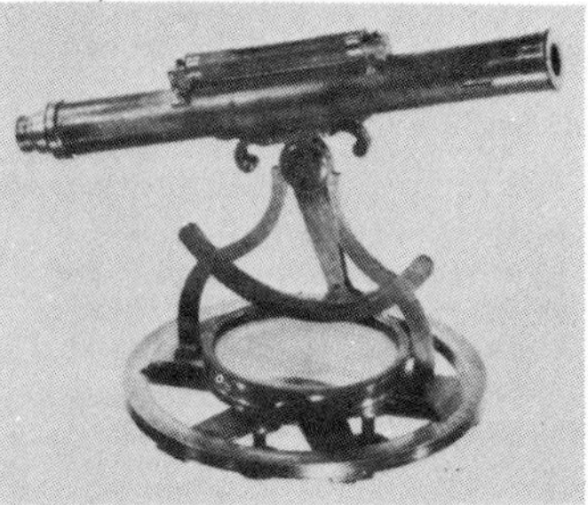

A Brass Theodolite signed Simons, London, with spirit level, 30 degree arc and three levelling screws – tube length 11". **£350-400** CSK

A Troughton & Simms Brass Transit Theodolite, also with magnifiers and vernier scales, 12 in., 30.5 cm. high, in mahogany case, English, late 19th C. **£400-450** SB

A Theodolite by J. White, Glasgow, c1870. **£375-500**

A Brass Theodolite, signed Berge, London late Ramsden, in mahogany case and with folding wood tripod (optics and other parts restored). **£340-390** CKS

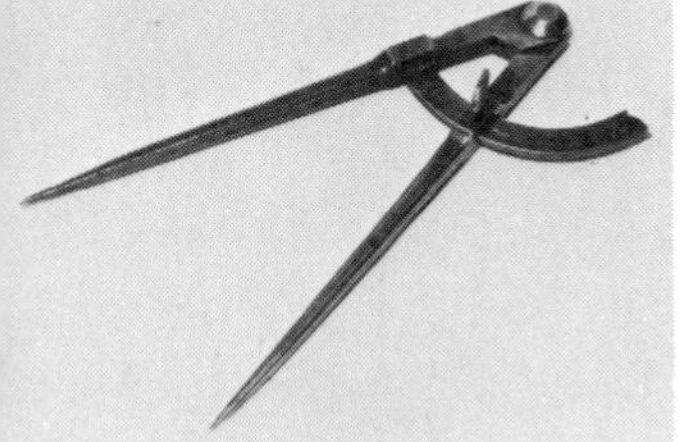

A Pair of Steel Dividers, early 19th C. **£35-40** RB

A Brass Dipleidoscope (meridian instrument) by E.I. Dent, London, in original mahogany case, c1840. **£350-380** GE

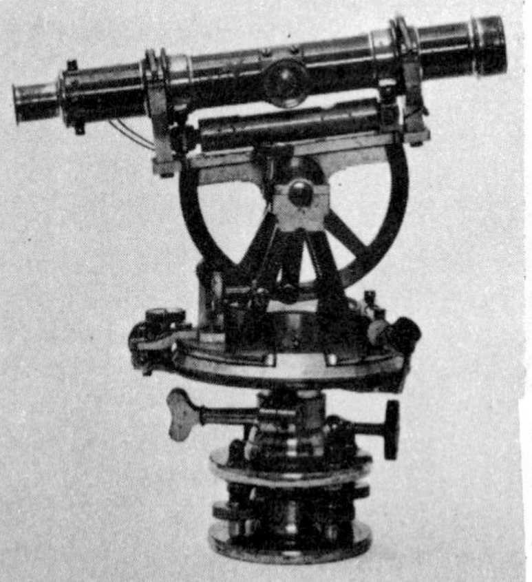

A 19th C. Brass Half Transit Theodolite having telescope supported by two brackets, the circular revolving table mounted with a compass inscribed on the dial 'Baker', 244, Holborn, London, with two spirit levels, thumb screw adjusting, in fitted mahogany case, 10¾ in., 27.5 cm. **£310-380** SBe

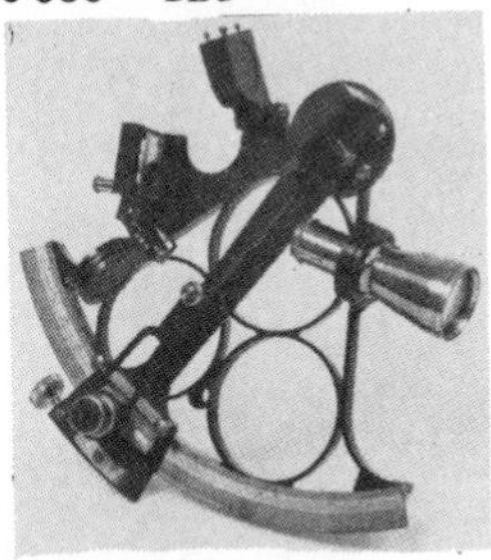

A 19th C Brass Douglas Reflecting Protractor No. 1760, by Cary of London, 14.7cms long, leather case. **£120-150** SKC

An Adams Two-Day Marine Chronometer, No. 3064, inscribed 'Adams, maker to H.R.H. Prince Albert, 36 Lombard St. London', in rosewood deck case with Victorian silver coin inserted in the lid, height 7" (18cms) width 6½" (16.5cms). **£770-870** SBe

A Douglas's Patent Reflecting Protractor by Cary, London, of lacquered brass construction, 5¾ in. wide, in fitted case signed J. H. Steward. **£520-600** CSK

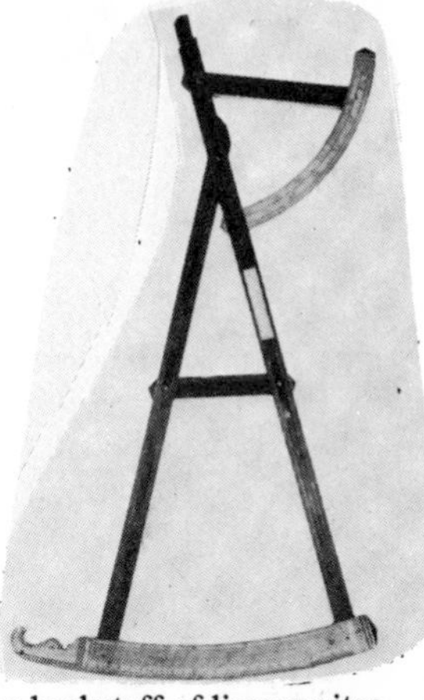

A fine backstaff of lignum vitae with pearwood arcs, diagonal scale and inlaid plaque inscribed Thos. Greenough Fecit 1749, 25 in. long. (lacks index). **£2,600-2,900** CSK

A Shoe Measure, c. 1800. **£96-106** HD

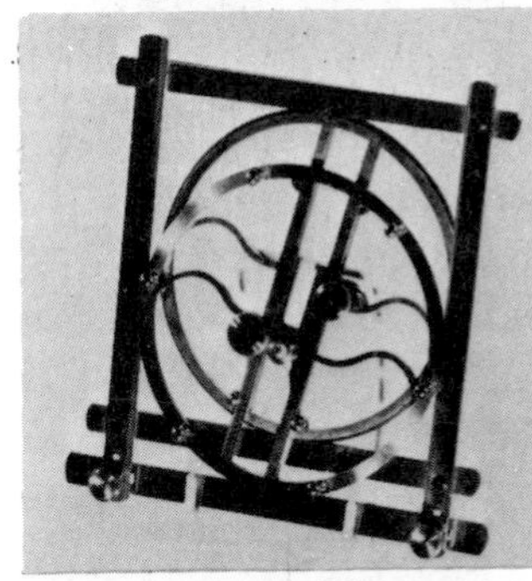

A Lacquered brass Elipsograph by W & S Jones, Holborn, in fitted mahogany case, £350-400 **CSK**

A Set of Parallel Rulers, 18 in. long, c. 1800. **£30-40** CP

Daniel Desbois. A two-day Marine Chronometer, No. 1632, contained in a mahogany case, 18cms. **£820-920** P

A two-day marine chronometer by William Farquhar, Tower Hill, 1850, in coromandel case with brass mounts. **£850-1,050** AM

A Ship's Chronometer with gimbal mountings in cases, No. 2864, maker Frodsham & Keen, 17 South Castle Street, Liverpool 56 hours, with Key. **£1,100-1,300** OL

A brass abney level. **£35-75** AM

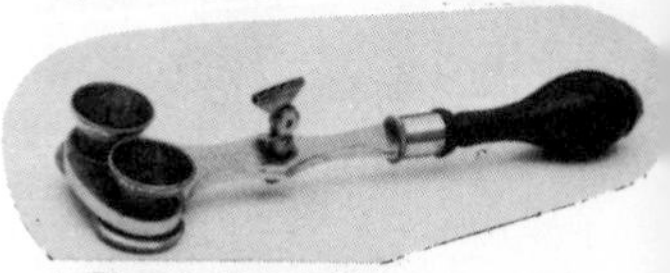

Early 19th C Boxed Compass with card face. **£18-25** IN

A Simple Brass Compass Microscope and tilting holder for the forceps (missing) 18th C or possibly earlier, 5 3/8" (14.3cms). **£390-450** L

A Late 18th C Dry Card Compass, 3" diam. in brass case. **£75-85** GE

A Brass Anenometer late 19th C, in original leather case. **£120-140** GE

A Nautical Liquid Compass, 3" diam., in case, c1860. **£65-75** GE

A brass green card compass with lid. **£65-125** AM

A brass miner's dial, with silvered dial by Zanetti, Manchester, c1870. **£150-200** AM

A Polished Oak Case Barograph, with seven-day movement, 35cms long, signed Turnbull, Edinburgh. **£225-280** SKC

A hydrometer with accessories, in a box, c1880. **£35-75** AM

A 19th C 8-Day Barograph with thermometer, by Barber & Son. **£120-150** CCL

A Portuguese Sundial Oblique Compass, 2" diam., in brass case, early 18th C. **£150-170** GE

A barograph, in oak case, c1900. **£150-220** AM

A Brass Pocket Sundial with lid, c1850, by Spear, in good condition. **£250-350** AM

A Turned Wood Pocket Sundial with lid, c1825, by Essex. **£75-125** AM

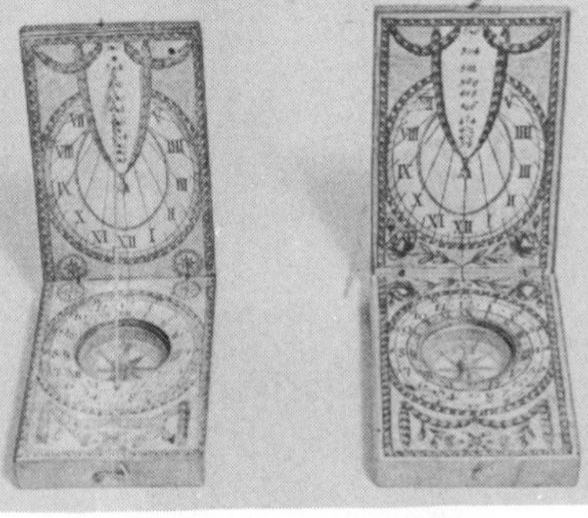
Two South German Dyptych Sundials, c1780, by S. Kleininger. **£175-250** each AM

A Good Universal Equinoctial Sundial made in England and sold in India by Herbert & Co. of Bombay, c1820-40. **£600-700** AM

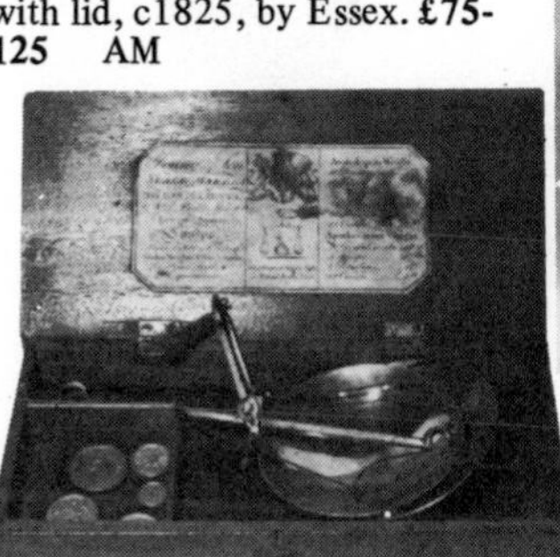
A Boxed Set of Coin Scales, late 18th C., box 8 in. wide. **£50-58** RB

A Universal Equinoctial Sundial by Cary, The Strand, London, with original case. **£650-750** AM

A 19th C French Universal Equinoctial Sundial for the northern hemisphere, c1840. **£450-550** AM

W. & T. Avery Beam Scales, 22½" long, with original case. **£60-85** SQE

A Set of 19th C. Brass Scale & Weights, with damage. **£120-150** SV

A Boxed Set of Weights, 20th C. **£38-40** VA

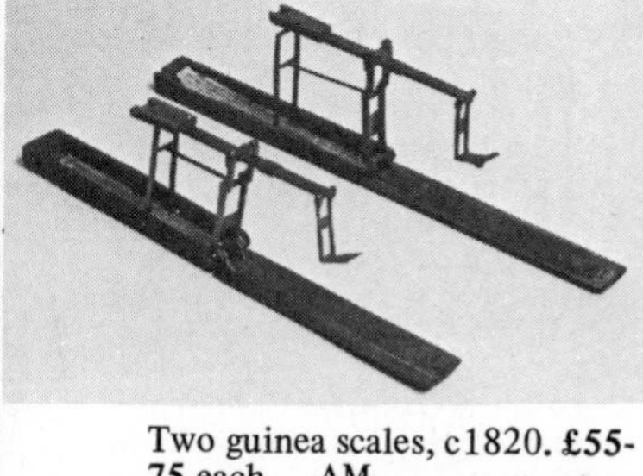

Two guinea scales, c1820. **£55-75** each AM

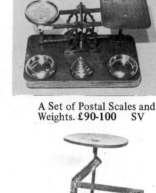

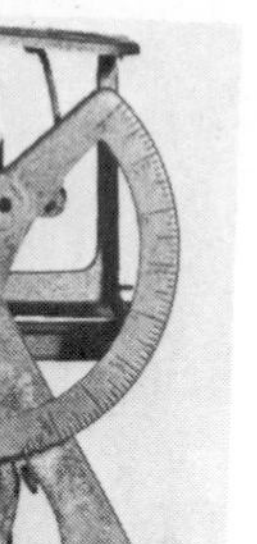

A 19th C. metal Letter Scale. **£16-19** SV

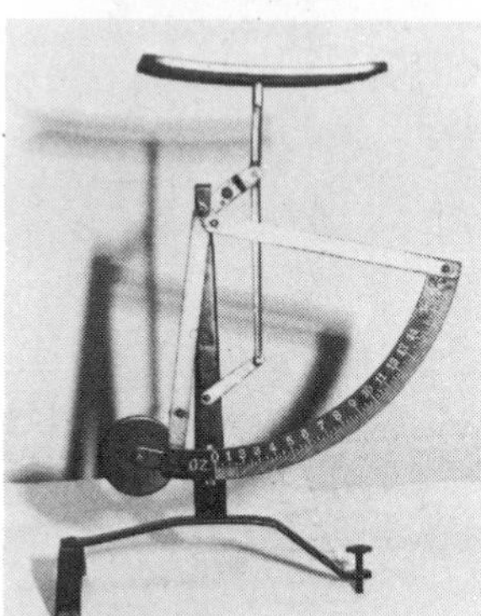

A 19th C. Letter Weight. **£8-10** SV

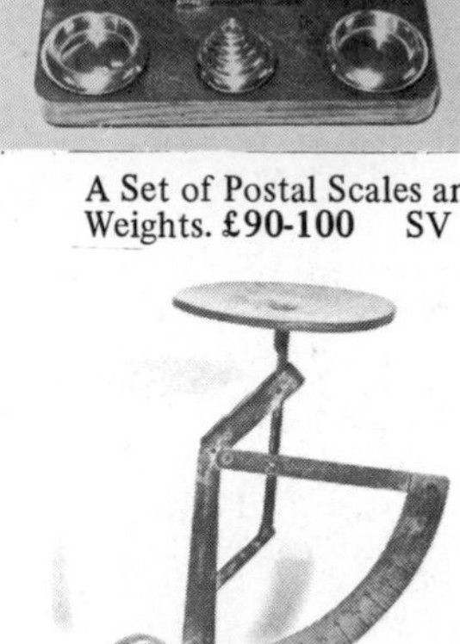

A Set of Postal Scales and Weights. **£90-100** SV

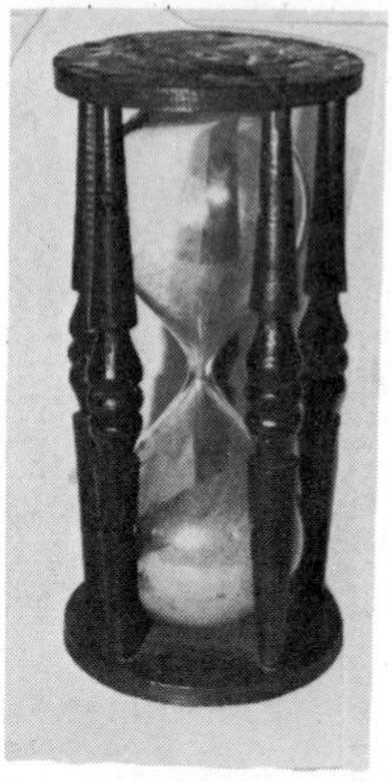

An 18th C. Sand Glass, 9¼ in. high. **£185-205** RB

A Painted Sand Glass 6½ in. high. **£325-400** CC

19th C French Postal Scales, made for export, 7¼" high. **£25-29** SQE

An Early 19th C three-inch Pocket Globe, inscribed 'A Correct Globe with the new discoveries', in a wooden outer case covered in fishskin, marked 'Dr Halley and Co.' **£255-300** SKC

A Late 19th C. Lacquered Sand Glass, 6 in. high. **£55-65** RB

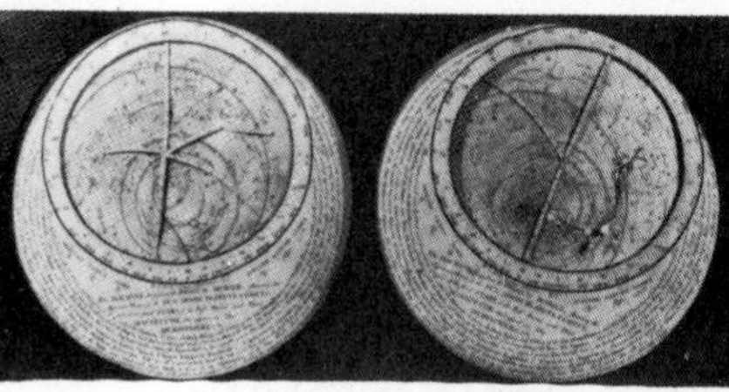

A Mahogany and Paper Planisphere with separate dials for northern and southern hemispheres, by W. Lacey, 1777, 6½ in., wide. **£360-390** CSK

A Celestial Pocket Globe by Newton, dated 1815. **£420-550** AM

A Pair of 'Malbys' Table Globes, each bearing a label, dated Dublin 1857, height 14½ in., 36 cm., some restoration. **£200-280** SBe

A Pocket Globe by Blueler, London, dated 1815, in fishskin case. **£565-675** AM

A French table globe 'par Robert de Vangardy, Paris, 1814', papier mache with wood stand. **£550-650** AM

A Revolving Terrestrial Globe, c1920, 14" high. **£40-50** SQE

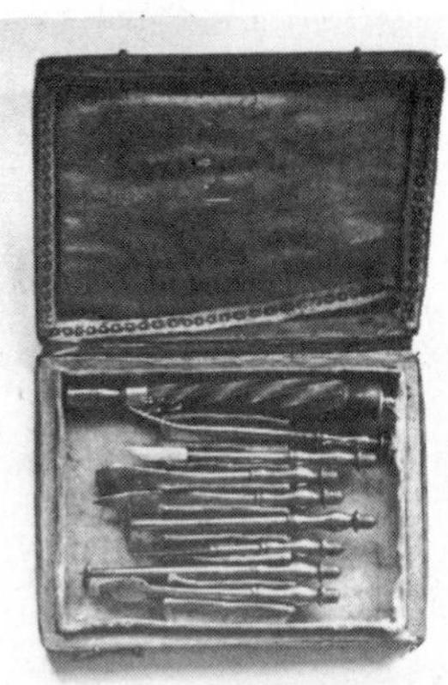

An 18th C. Dentist's Set in Steel and Leather, original case. **£195-220** SA

A post mortem set, c1860. **£150-225** AM

A. J. Weiss Army Surgeon's Instrument Case, the brass-bound mahogany case opening to three trays of instruments, English, 1917 1 ft. 6 in., 46 cm. wide. **£400-460** SB

A Fine Trepanning Set, with two trephirres, lenticular, elevator, raspatory, bone-handled brush, in case. **£550-600** CSK

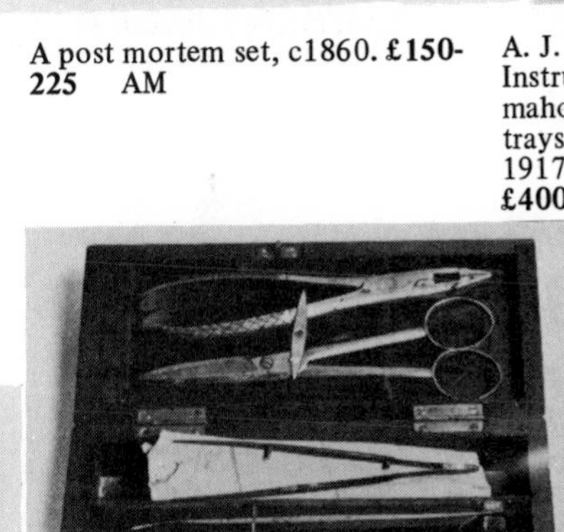

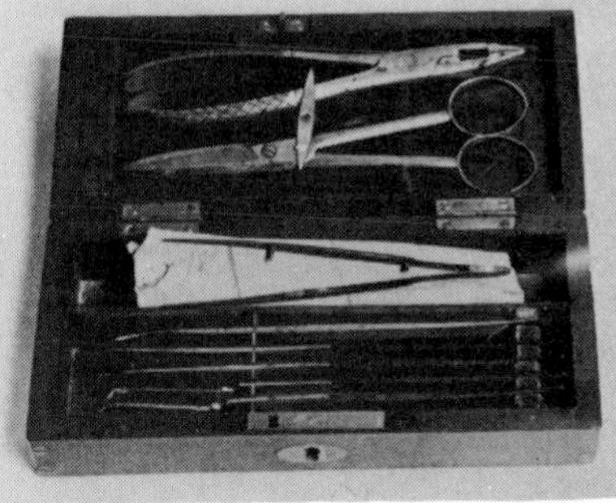

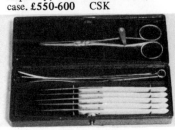

A set of operating scalpels, in leatherette case, c1860. **£55-100** AM

A set of small operating instruments with ebony handles in a wooden case, c1880. **£45-75** AM

A Late 18th C. Apothecary Cabinet, not totally complete 12 in. long x 9 in. high **£300-350** complete **£350-400** RB

An Asprey's Brass Watch-Maker's Lathe with a set of accessories, English, early 20th C. 10 in., 25.5 cm. wide. **£230-280** SB

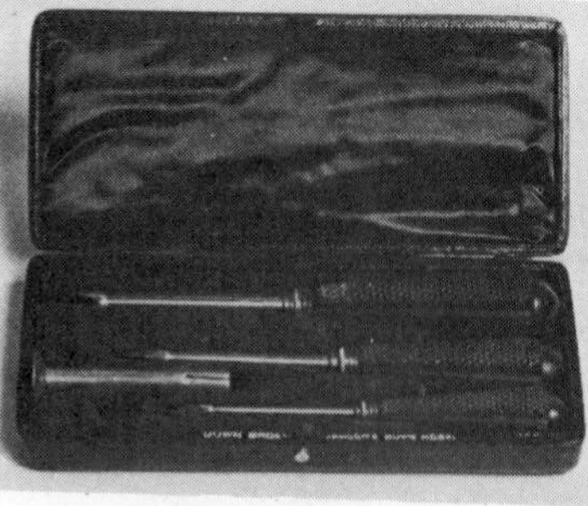

A tracheotomy set, c1850. **£40-75** AM

A French watchmaker's topping tool, c1860. **£200-300** AM

A watchmaker's lathe, brass and steel, on stand, probably Swiss, c1850. **£220-350** AM

An unusual early 19th C. Patent Portable Copying Machine by James Watt & Company, with built-in brass press rollers, drawer and ink powders, etc. 17½ in. **£100-120** O

An 18th C. French Brass Sector. **£150-175** RB

A Stick Telephone, 1926, 13" high. **£75-90** SQE

A brass scarifier, c1860. **£30-60** AM

A SCARIFIER

A small instrument containing a number of spring-mounted blades which, released by a trigger, lacerate the skin for medical purposes.

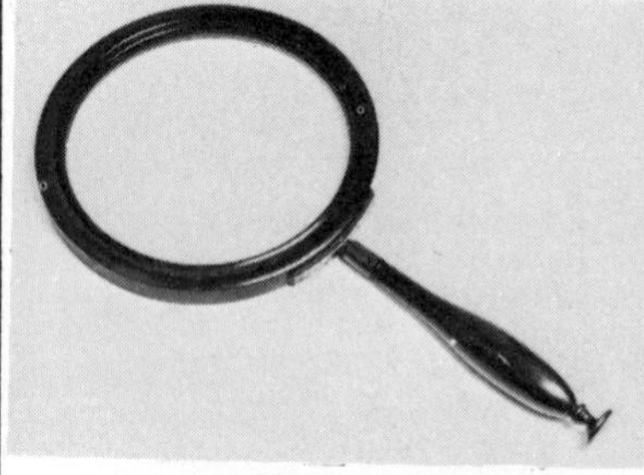

An English Rosewood Gallery Lens, c1820. **£140-150** GE

A 19th C Brass 8-Day 'Pigeon Clock', by Scente, Brussels. **£80-100** CCL

A Perman Brass Ship's Telegraph, English, early 20th C. 3 ft. 4 in., 102 cm. **£130-150** SB.

An Intercom Telephone, c1900. **£130-150** SQE

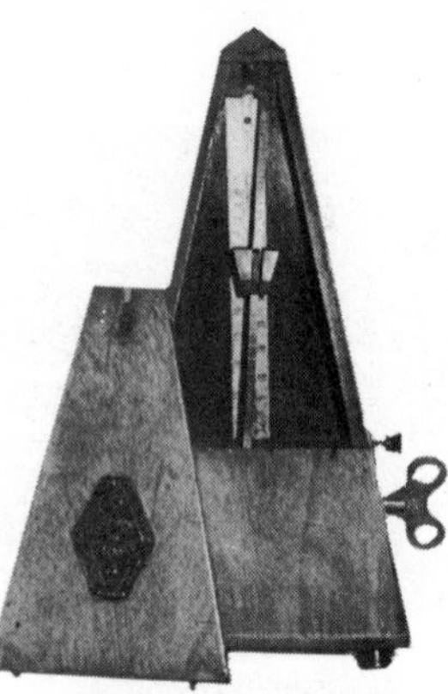

A Metronome with bell, by de Maelzel, 9" high. **£38-45** SQE

A Large Wind-Up Gramophone in Oak Case. **£80-90** VA

A Rare Gramophone & Typewriter Ltd. Gramophone with Clark-Johnson-type soundbox numbered J7534, c. 1900 (lacks leather elbow). **£600-650** CSK

A Magnum Horn Gramophone with mahogany case inlaid with crossbanding, 12 in. turntable, Thorens Caesar soundbox, 21 in. diam. **£270-340** CSK

A Phonograph with replaced trumpet. **£260-280** VA

GRAMOPHONES

- 1887-1888 - earliest period of Edison phonographs
- 1888-1900 - 'New Duplex' or 'Concert' phonographs by Edison
- 1887-1897 - earliest gramophones patented by Emile Berliner using circular discs
- 1900-1905 - gramophones provided with clockwork motors
- 1900-1910 - circumference of wax cylinders increased from 6 7/8" to 15" Amplifier horns mounted directly over the pick-up head
- 1925-1940 - earliest electric horns
- 1935 - automatic changers were introduced

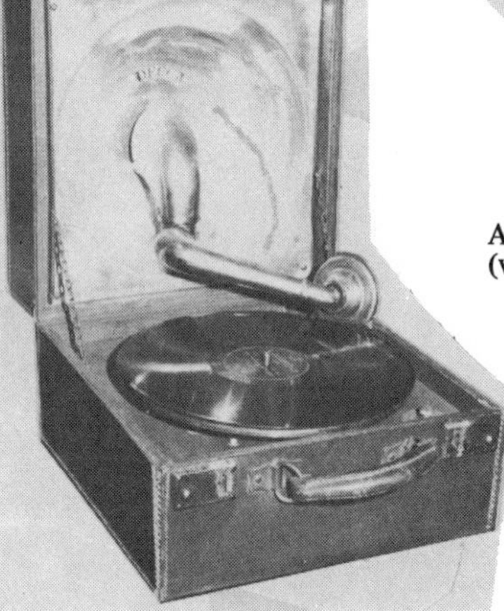

A Small Wind-Up Decca Gramophone with Leather Case. **£40-50** VA

A Gramophone & Typewriter Senior Monarch Gramophone with twelve-inch turntable, English, c. 1908. **£340-390** SB

An H.M.V. Table Model Wind-Up Gramophone with laminated wood horn, on oak base with transfer trade marks, 16¾" (42.5cms). **£300-330** SBe

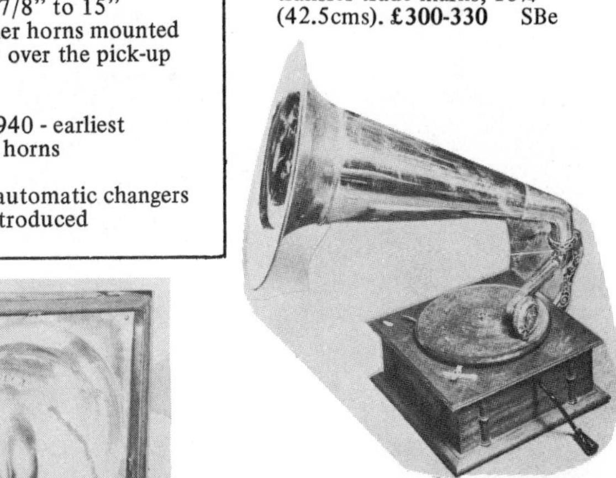

An Ansonia Record Player, c1920 (with later horn). **£120-140** CCL

A Style No. 2 Hand-Turned Gramophone by the Gramophone Company Ltd. with Gramophone & Typewriter Concert soundbox, 22 in. wide, c. 1900. **£800-890** CSK

A Good Gramophone & Typewriter Junior Monarch Gramophone with Exhibition Soundbox, with one tin of needles and a small record brush, English, c. 1908. **£360-400** SB

A Late 19th C. Amorette Disc Organ playing 12 in., 30.5 cm. discs, with hand cranked movement and on turned feet (case affected by woodworm), with fifteen discs, width 17½ in., 44.5 cm. **£250-350** SBe

A 7½ in., Monopol Disc, the periphery-drive movement with top-wind motor, with nine metal discs, German, c. 1905. **£320-380** SB

An 8¼ in. Polyphon Disc Musical Box, the centre-drive movement with single comb, 10½ in., 27 cm. wide, the comb with two broken teeth, with eighteen metal discs, German, early 20th C. **£340-400** SB

A Horn Gramophone with 10 in. turntable, modified eight-petalled painted tin horn, 1 ft., 30.5 cm., square and 9½ in., 24 cm. high, with a container of needles and two records. **£140-170** SB

A Good Pathe Democratic (Zero) Phonograph, with ten two-minute cylinders in cartons. **£180-220** SB

A Good Miniature Gramophone, English, c. 1920. **£140-170** SB

An 11¾ in. Britannia Table Disc Musical Box, 22 in. wide, and twenty-five discs. **£480-530** CSK

A 19th C. Polyphone with 12 discs, 15 in. wide. **£600-675** SV

A 15½ in., Polyphon Disc Musical Box, the periphery-drive movement playing on two combs, 1 ft. 9 in., 53 cm. wide, together with an unoriginal disc storage cabinet with nineteen metal discs, German, c. 1904. **£1,400-1,600** SB

A 19th C. Polyphon with 7 discs, in inlaid case, 20 in. wide. **£700-750** SV

A Good 'Hidden Drum and Bells' Cylinder Musical Box No. 10357, the 41 cm. cylinder playing six tunes accompanied at will by drum with ten strikers and seven graduating bells, on a rosewood stand., 25½ in., 65 cm. **£900-1,000** L

A 13½ in. Kalliope table disc musical box with two combs, long bedplate cast with Art Nouveau ornament and ten discs. **£600-700** CSK

A late 19th C. German 15¾ in., Polyphon disc musical box contained in walnut case with burr-wood panels with Schutz trade label. 54.5 cm., 21½ in. wide, together with 32 metal discs. **£700-900** O

A Key-Wind Forte-Piano musical box by Nicole Freres, No. 27510, playing eight airs (two per turn), 17¼ in. wide, the cylinder 9¼ in. by 2¾ in. diam. **£750-850** CSK

A Paillard's Amobean Interchangeable Cylinder Musical Box with six cylinders playing six airs each, 19½ in., the cylinders 5¾ in. **£950-1,050** CSK

A Polyphon Table Model Disc Musical Box No. 72088 playing 15½ in., 39.5 cm. discs, tempo regulator, side winding and stop/start button, on mahogany stand, together with five discs. 39½ in., 100.5 cm. total height. **£600-800** SBe

A Regina 15 Table Disc Musical Box with long bedplate No. 64192 22 in. wide; one Polyphon disc; and seven Porter discs. **£850-940** CSK

An Edison Diamond Disc Phonograph, Official Laboratory Model, with Diamond reproducer, double-spring motor, 50¾ in. high. **£280-360** CSK

A Monopol 8½ in. Musical Box with top-wind motor, 11½ in. wide, with twenty-three discs. **£240-350** CSK

A late 19th C. German 15½ in., polyphon disc musical box, in a walnut parquetry case with winding handle at side and Schutz trade label 54 cm., 21¼ in. wide, with eleven metal discs, No. 121047. **£800-950** O

A Musical Box playing eight airs accompanied by six bells, 22 in. wide, the cylinder 13 in. **£800-890** CSK

A Good Upright Coin-Operated Polyphon Disc Musical Box playing 19¾ in., 50 cm. discs, side winding handle, with walnut cabinet, with ten discs, width 24½ in., 62.5 cm. **£1,050-1,150** SBe

A 19th C. 3-bell Music Box, 17½ in. long. **£400-430** SV

A 19th C. Music Box in well inlaid case, 20 in. wide. **£400-440** SV

A Lever-Wind Mandoline Musical Box playing eight mainly operatic airs, 25½ in. wide, the cylinder 17 in. **£700-850** CSK

A Nicole Freres Cylinder Musical Box, No. 38025, the 33 cm. cylinder playing eight tunes by Verdi, Meyerbeer and Donizetti, 20 in., 51 cm. wide, Swiss, 1861-1863. **£900-1,000** SB

A 'Bells And Drum In Sight' Cylinder Musical Box, the 27.5 cm. cylinder playing eight airs, 2 ft., 61 cm. wide. Swiss, c. 1880. **£900-1,000** SB

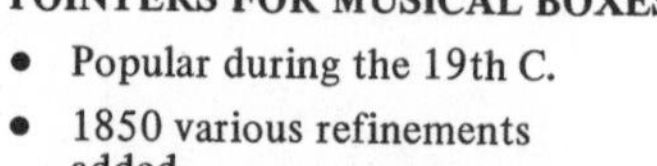

POINTERS FOR MUSICAL BOXES

- Popular during the 19th C.
- 1850 various refinements added.
- Nicole Freres of Geneva was one of the best makers.
- Rotating cylinder introduced towards the end of 18th C.
- 1885 new type of box introduced, utilizing a cardboard disc developed in Leipzig. This was called a Symphonion which later developed into the Polyphone, the card disc being replaced by metal.

A Gloria Interchangeable Cylinder Musical Box, the 23.5 cm. cylinder playing six airs, 1 ft. 9½ in., 55 cm. wide, Swiss c. 1900. **£670-750** SB

A 'Bells And Drum In Sight' Cylinder Musical Box, the 33.5 cm. cylinder playing twelve airs, 1 ft. 11½ in., 59.5 cm. wide, Swiss c. 1880. **£670-750** SB

A Lecoultre Key-Wound Musical Box, No. 10360, the 33 cm. cylinder playing eight airs, 1 ft. 8 in., 51 cm. wide, the governor mechanism lacking ruby, Swiss, mid 19th C. **£390-460** SB

A Gramophone and Typewriter Ltd. oak gramophone stand, 39¾ in. high, c. 1906. **£320-350** CSK

A Concert Roller Organ, 1 ft. 5 in., 43 cm. wide, American, late 19th C., with sixteen rolls. **£470-520** SB

A Melodia Paper-Roll Organette, 1 ft. ¼ in., 31 cm. wide, English, c. 1880-1890. **£120-160** SB

A Kirkman Rosewood framed boudoir grand piano. **£750-875** EBB

A Good Pathe 'Le Gaulois' Phonograph with original aluminium horn, reproducer and recorder (distressed) with thirty-three two-minute cylinders, French, c. 1905. **£500-580** SB

A mid-Georgian mahogany spinet fitted with rosewood and fruitwood keyboard. 66 in., 167 cm. wide. **£2,000-2,200** C

A Lambert Typewriter by the Gramophone and Typewriter Ltd. **£170-220** CSK

A Flashwriter wood-framed typing practice keyboard. **£65-75** CSK

The Globe Typewriter, No. 11309G, by the American Typewriter Co., the swinging sector design (rubber disintegrated), c. 1895. **£220-250** SB

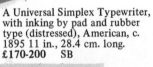

left
A Universal Simplex typewriter with rubber typeface, brass wheel and slide, in mahogany case with ink bottle. **£220-260** CSK

A Universal Simplex Typewriter, with inking by pad and rubber type (distressed), American, c. 1895 11 in., 28.4 cm. long. **£170-200** SB

A Lambert Typewriter No. 902, with oak case with accessories compartment. **£300-360** CSK

A World Typewriter, in maker's wood case (lacks type sector). **£440-480** CSK

A Star (Sun) Typewriter with piveted inking pad with reservoir pad, in bentwood case. **£150-190** CSK

TYPEWRITERS

- Patents taken out in U.S. from 1828
- First commercially successful machines marketed in 1873, made by Remington.
- Early manufacturers include Fitch, Yost, New Century, Williams, Empire Fay-Sho, Oliver, Crandall Blick.
- Post 1914 machines generally hold little interest for collectors.
- Condition of even earliest machines is most important.
- Date of manufacture usually within three years of date of latest patent found on back-plate.

A Fine Stereocycle Leroy Stereoscopic Camera by L. Leroy, and Bazin, Paris with Lacour Berthiot Eurygraphe lenses in guillotine shutter. **£350-390** CSK

A Contax 11 35mm Coupled-Rangefinder Camera No. 73593 with Tessar 5cm lens in maker's carton. **£120-160** CSK

A Nanna 45 mm., X 107 mm., Slim-Line Folding Stereoscopic Camera by A. Boreux, Basel with Goerz Dogmar 7.5 cm., lenses in coupled Compur shutters, **£320-380** CSK

A Fine Zeiss Contaflex 35 mm., Twin-Lens Reflex Camera No. A46128, in case. **£550-600** CSK

A Rare Richard's Homeos 35 mm. Stereoscopic Camera with Krauss 28 mm. lenses. **£900-1,000** CSK

An Ansco Memo 35 mm., Miniature Box-Form Camera with Cinemat lens in Ilex shutter, in carrying case. **£90-110** CSK

A Brownie Folding Camera, early 20th C. **£4-£6** VA

A Kodak Ektra 35 mm Coupled-Rangefinder Camera with Ektar: 35 mm., 50 mm., 90 mm., 135 mm., 153 mm., lenses, three film backs, one focusing back, clip-on range-finder, polariser, eight filters, four filter mounts, two lens hoods, flash unit and eight flash bulbs, in case. **£800-880** CSK

A Dallmeyer 120 Camera, Compur shutter, Pentac F2.9 lens, with cable release and original case. **£40-45** SQE

A Rare Dallmeyer Miniature Wet Plate Camera, 1½ by 2¾ in., stamped 1186, with Petzval-type Dallmeyer lens, focusing by rack and pinion, English, c. 1860. **£2,000-2,200** SB

A Tropical Sanderson Hand-And-Stand Camera, 3¼ by 4¼ in., with Dallmeyer Adon variable focal length telephoto lens, English c. 1910. **£220-260** SB

An Early Dry-Plate Tailboard Camera, 5 by 8 in., English, c. 1870's. **£240-280** SB

A Fine Adams Challenge Half-Plate Mahogany Tail Board Camera. **£210-240** CSK

A 15 in. by 15 in. Studio Camera on Stand, the lens with focusing by rack and pinion, English, c. 1880 5 ft. 1 in., 155 cm. high. **£190-220** SB

An Unusual Rouch's Patent Folding Stand Camera, 6½ in. by 8½ in., with Ross Rapid Symmetrical f8 lens, Taylor Hobson Cooke Anastigmat 7½ in., f6.5 lens, English c. 1895. **£130-160** SB

A Lizars Challenge Half-Plate Tropical Hand-and-Stand Camera, Medio-Anistigmat lens in Koilos shutter, in carrying case and tripod. **£220-300** CSK

A Fine 9 cm. x 12 cm. Monorail Camera by A. Stegemann, Berlin, with accessories. **£250-290** CSK

A Quarter-Plate Tropical Sanderson Hand-and-Stand Camera with Tessar 13.5 cm., lens in Compur shutter, leather carrying case. **£300-340** CSK

A Rothwell Plate Camera, c. 1890. **£90-100** VA

An Iron and Brass Folding Magic Lantern folding into tin case, 6¾" x 6¾" x 7". **£160-190** CSK

A W. C. Hughes 'Pamphengos' Bi-Unial Magic Lantern, spirit-fired, with brass lens unit mounted before, English c. 1890 1 ft. 6 in., 47.5 cm. wide. **£180-210** SB

A Quarter-Plate Tropical Hand-and-Stand Camera. **£230-270** CSK

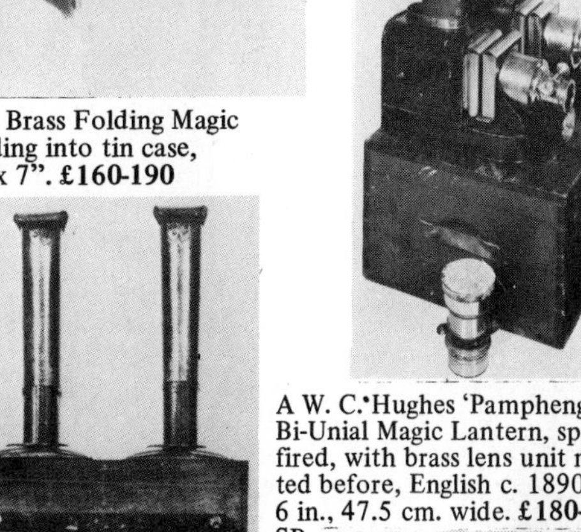

A Hughes Pamphengos Mahogany and Iron Double-Lens Magic Lantern, in fitted wood carrying-case. **£320-360** CSK

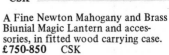

A Fine Newton Mahogany and Brass Biunial Magic Lantern and accessories, in fitted wood carrying case. **£750-850** CSK

A Praxinoscope-Theatre with candle holder, twenty-one coloured animated picture strips, in wood box. **£560-640** CSK

An Ives Stereoscopic Kromskop Viewer, and eleven Kromograms, English, c. 1900. **£600-700** SB

Victorian Stereoscopic Viewer with collection of 40 World War I 3-Dimensional pictures, in original box. **£40-45** SQE

A Magnum Glass Decanter presented by Queen Victoria, c1860's, 16". **£500-600**

A Zoomorphosis Optical Device with six coloured engravings, in fitted mahogany box. **£1,600-1,700** CSK

An Ale-Carafe, c. 1770, 25.5 cm. high. **£280-340** C

A Pair of 19th C red Bohemian Decanters. **£85-95** SAL

A Venetian purple glass Decanter, 1890-1900, 11½". **£75-100**

A Pair of shouldered Decanters and Stoppers, 9½" (24cms), late 18th C. **£190-220** SKC

An early lime glass Decanter and Stopper, mid-Georgian, 9". **£75-85**

A Pair of shouldered Decanters and Stoppers, 11" (28cms), late 18th C. **£235-250** SKC

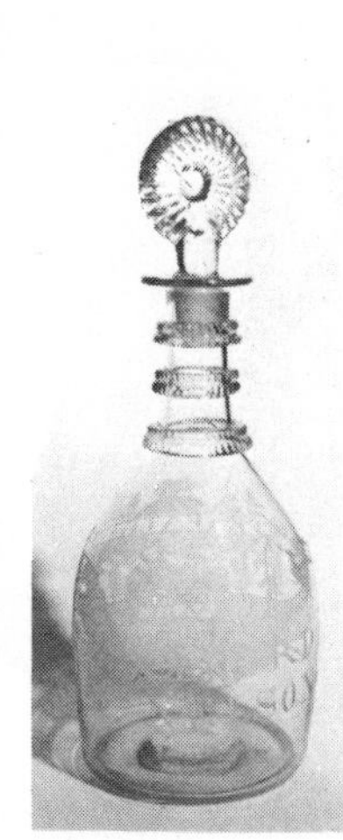

A Very Rare Commemoration Decanter, engraved with the Death Coach of Lord Nelson, engraved with 'Nile, Victory & Trafalgar', c. 1815. **£750-800** SA

A Rare Georgian Butler's Decanter (minus four tiny glass stoppers) in four sections, inside, facet and diamond cut, three cut rings, 9 in. **£60-65**
with stoppers **£150-170** CA

A Set of Three Bristol Blue Glass Decanters, with stoppers, 8 in. high, c. 1790-1820. **£230-250** CA

A Pair of Cork Glass Co. Engraved Decanters and Stoppers with a band of hatched foliate and star decoration above moulded flutes, marks to base, c. 1800, 28 cm. high. **£260-290** C

A Decanter, 42cms, late 19th/early 20th C, **£125-175** SBe

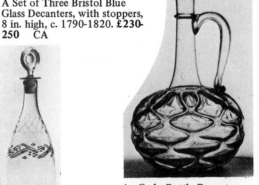

A Fine Pair of late 18th C Decanters and Stoppers of paper-beater form, 11½" (29cms) c1780-90. **£290-320** SKC

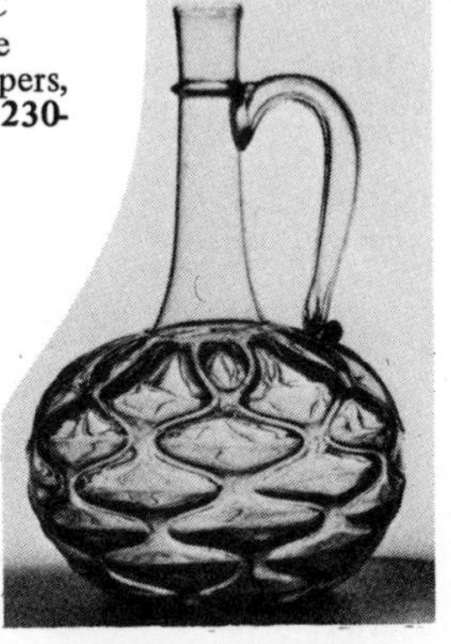

An Early Bottle Decanter, with kick-in base, English or Netherlands, c. 1680, 24.5cm high, **£380-420** C

A Shouldered Wine Bottle with high kick-in base, tapering neck and string-rim. c. 1735-1740., 7½ in., 19 cm. **£45-55** L

A Rare Early Sealed and Dated Wine-Bottle of green tint, the seal with the date 1699 and initials W.R.E. with portrait of King William (collar chipped), 13 cm. high. **£1,100-1,300** C

left
A Sealed and Dated Wine-Bottle of dark olive-green tint (slight rim chips), 1737, 19 cm. high. **£190-210** C

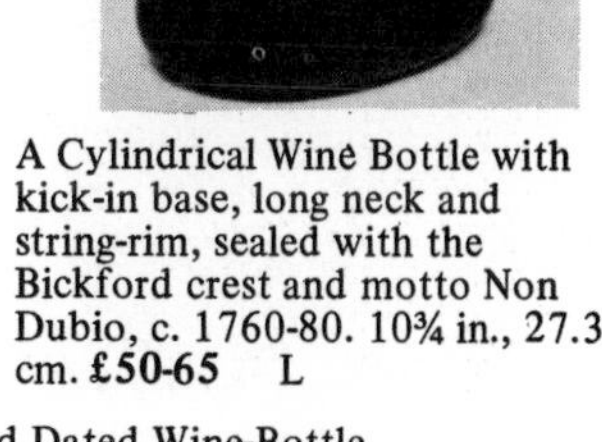

A Cylindrical Wine Bottle with kick-in base, long neck and string-rim, sealed with the Bickford crest and motto Non Dubio, c. 1760-80. 10¾ in., 27.3 cm. **£50-65** L

An English Wine Bottle, c. 1750 8½ in. high. **£85-95** SA

A Wine Bottle with kick-in base, short neck and string-rim, sealed with a crest and initials G.B., c. 1740-1750. 8½ in., 21.5 cm. **£65-75** L

An English Wine Bottle, c. 1770-80, 7½ in. high. **£85-95** SA

A Sealed Wine-Bottle of dark olive-green metal, with kick-in base, c. 1765, 24 cm. high. **£170-190** C

A Nailsea Spirit Flask, 5 in. high. **£58-68** SA

A Galle Enamelled Glass Bottle, in clear blue tinted glass decorated with dragonflies in green and brown enamel, a similar bottle decorated with a coat of arms on a tinted brown ground, each signed 'Emile, Galle a Nancy' and 'Emile Galle depose', French, c. 1890, with faults, 11.5 cm. **£320-380** SBe

A Staffordshire Opaque Scent-Bottle, stopper and gold screw cover, the base gilt with paterae (cover damaged), c. 1770, 7.5 cm. high. **£90-100** C

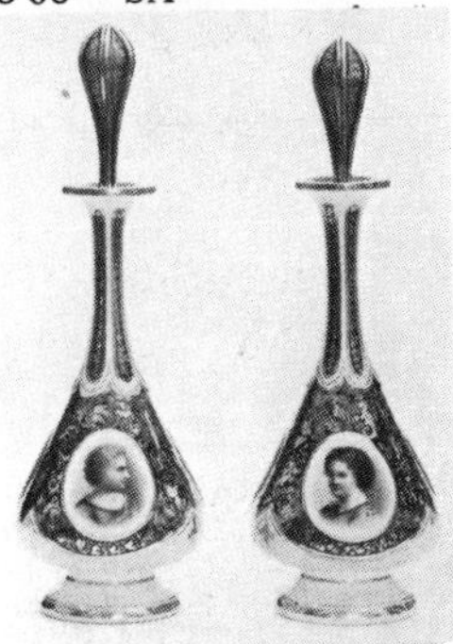

'Lunaria' A Lalique Perfume Bottle with floret stopper. Signe on the base Lalique, 7.50cms. **£250-290** P

A Pair of Bohemian Ruby Glass Bottles and Stoppers with white overlay 26.8cm, c.1850, **£280-320** SBe

A Bohemian Lithyalin Scent Bottle and Stopper of black glass with brown thread-like striations, c. 1835, 12.5cm, **£400-440** C

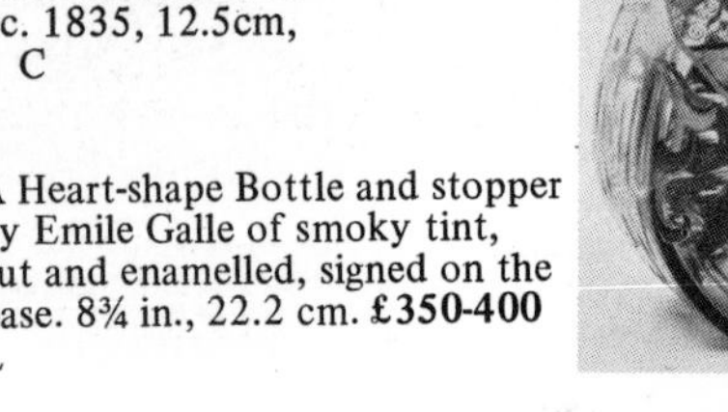

A Glass Rounded Snuff Bottle, painted from the inside and decorated in colours, with stalk and stopper, signed. **£130-160** L

A Heart-shape Bottle and stopper by Emile Galle of smoky tint, cut and enamelled, signed on the base. 8¾ in., 22.2 cm. **£350-400** L

'Salamandres' A Lalique Perfume Bottle and Stopper, heightened with green stain. Marked in script R. Lalique, 9.50cms high. **£220-250** P

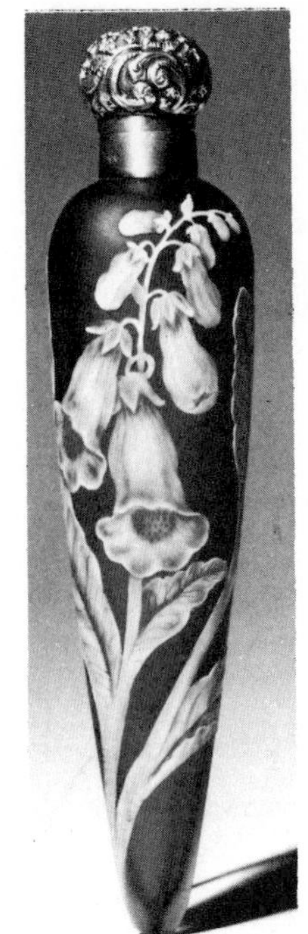

A Webb Cameo Silver-Mounted Scent Flask, c. 1885, the Silver London 1886, 18cm long, **£500-600** C

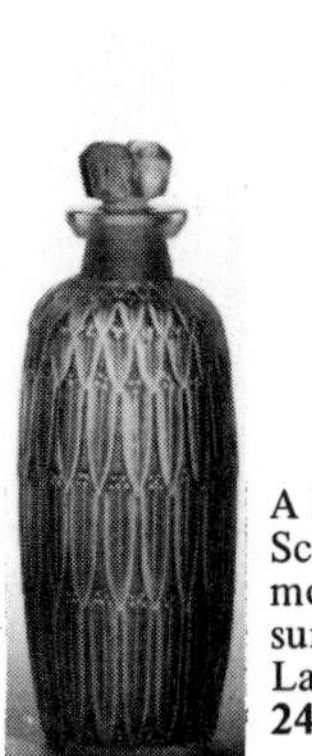

'Petites Feuilles' A Lalique Perfume Flask and stopper. Signed R. Lalique, France No. 478, 11cms. **£170-190** P

A Pair of Lalique clear glass Scent Bottles and Stoppers, moulded with flowerheads with sunken centres. Moulded R. Lalique, France, 8.50cms. **£190-240** P

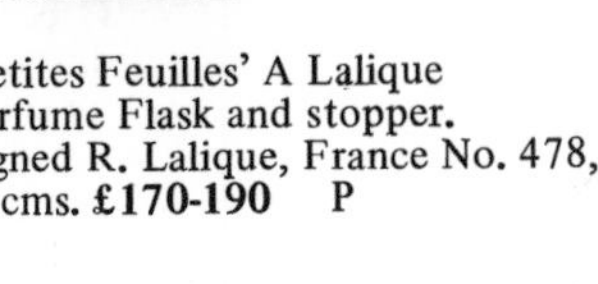

A Lalique Scent Bottle and Stopper, the stopper moulded with moths. Moulded Brevete R.L., 10cms. **£190-240** P

A Pair of French blue Opaline Glass Scent Bottles, c1850. **£75-85**

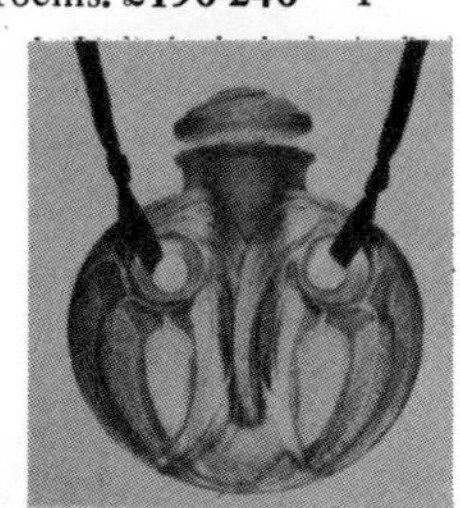

An unusual Lalique Scent Bottle Pendant, heightened with blue staining, 4.50cms, moulded Lalique and numbered 454. **£280-340** P

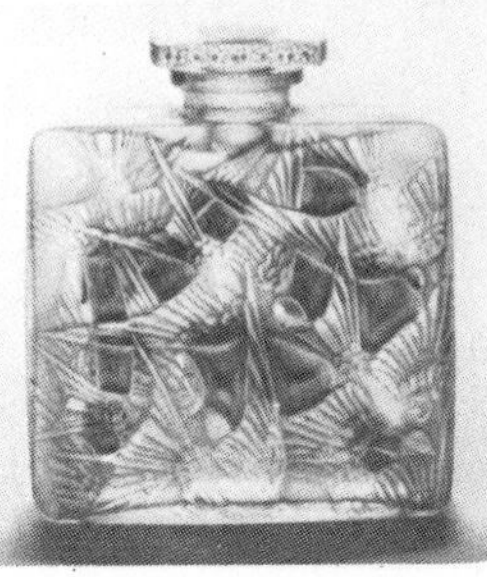

'Carre Hirondelles'. A Lalique square Scent Bottle and Stopper, 9cms high, moulded and engraved R. Lalique, France. **£500-580** P

A Bohemian Ruby-Glass Scent Bottle, with silver-gilt mounts, c1830, 4¼" long. **£170-190**

A Pair of Bohemian Overlay Scent Bottles and Stoppers, c1860, 11.5cms. **£140-180** S.B.

A Pair of Bohemian blue overlay Table Scent Bottles, c1870's, 10". **£300-350**

A Bohemian Overlay Scent Bottle, Victorian with silver-gilt top, 4 in., slight imperfections. **£35-40** CA

An antique green tinted faceted glass Scent Bottle, having enamelled motto 'Gage de ma fidelite. **£380-420** GC

POINTERS

FOR PERFUME - BOTTLES

- Made since the 18th C.
- Many good examples made in flashed and cased glass, particularly in Bohemia.
- Bottles of blue glass with bird decorations made in 18th C.
- Bottles of crystal cut-glass made in 1820's.
- Blue glass reappeared in the 19th C.
- Towards the end of the 19th C. bottles with glass base and atomizer appeared.
- 19th C. porcelain bottles fairly plain unlike 18th C. bottles which were often in figure or flower-bouquet forms.
- Gold, silver and enamel bottles are fairly unusual.

A 'Malachite' glass Scent Spray, with moulded bluebell decoration, possibly by Baccarat, c1920's. **£75-85**

An Art Nouveau amber glass Scent Bottle, probably Bohemian, c1920's, 7". **£75-85**

An Art Deco cut-glass Scent Bottle, with chrome fittings, 1930's. **£70-80**

An unusual Art Deco Perfume Bottle, 8cms high. **£170-200** P

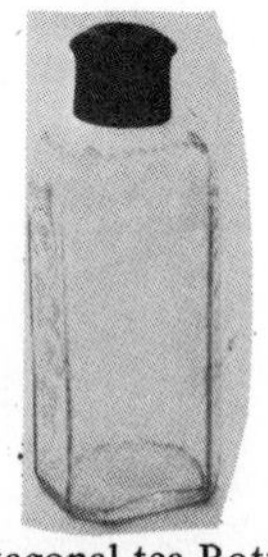

A 'Bonzo' Dog Scent Bottle, in frosted glass, c1930's, 3". **£30-40**

An hexagonal tea Bottle, engraved with baskets of flowers and scrolls, with turned lignum screw top. 6¾ in., 17.2 cm. **£65-75** L

A 19th C opaque white glass Perfume Bottle, encased in chased gilt brass mounts. **£35-45** WHL

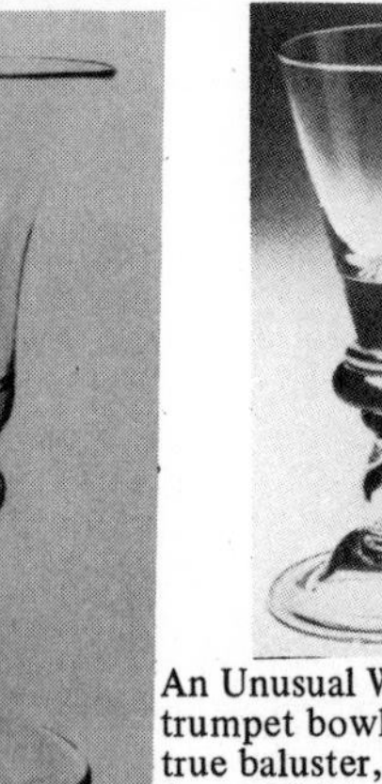

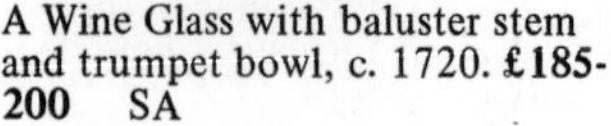

A Wine Glass with baluster stem and trumpet bowl, c. 1720. **£185-200** SA

An Unusual Wine Glass with trumpet bowl above a teared true baluster, supported on a domed folded foot, 5½ in., c. 1725. **£300-400** S

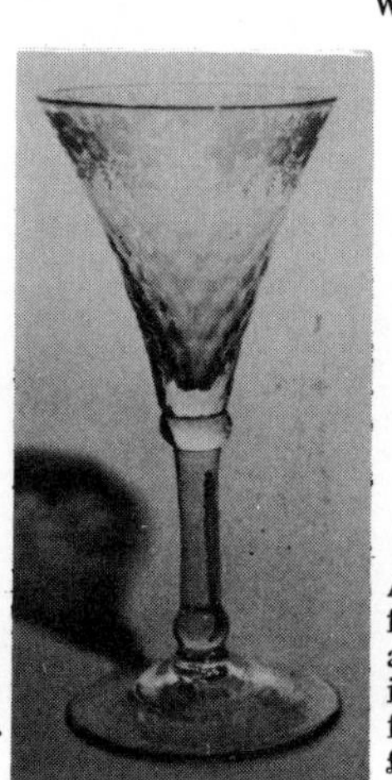

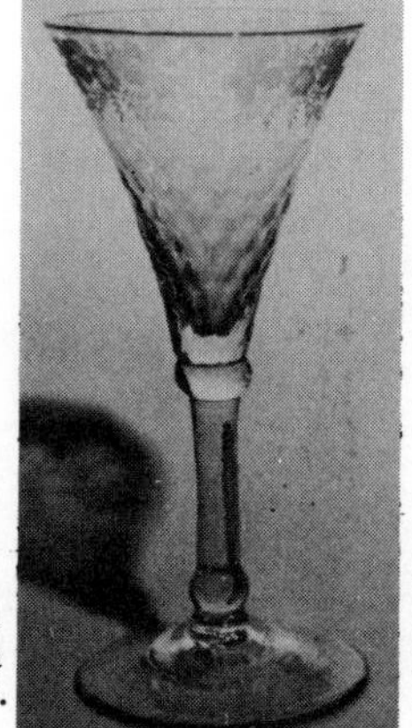

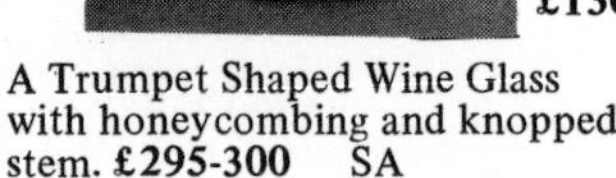

A Trumpet Shaped Wine Glass with honeycombing and knopped stem. **£295-300** SA

A Baluster Wine Glass, the flared bowl over a proto-annulated knop and teared inverted baluster, base knop and folded conical foot, c1720, 6". **£130-170** S

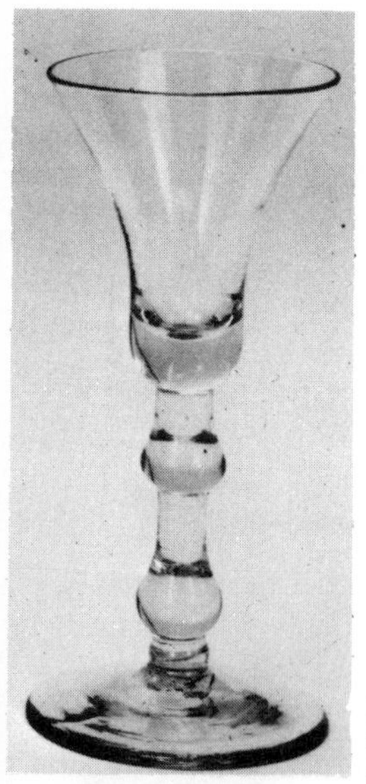

A Light Baluster Wine Goblet, with waisted bowl, c1730, 7¼"
£160-200 S

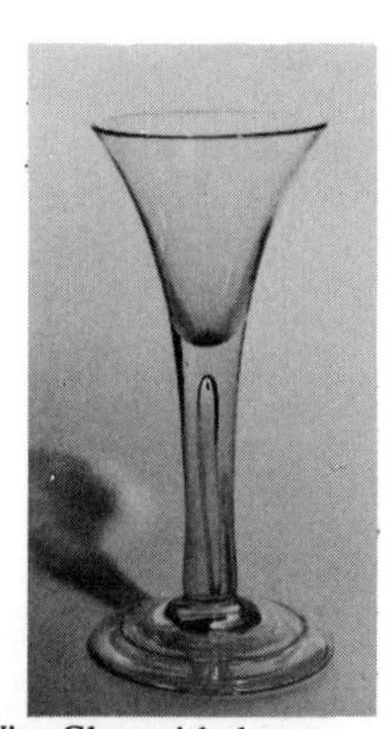

A Wine Glass with drawn trumpet bowl, plain stem, elongated tear and folded foot, c. 1730.
£85-95 SA

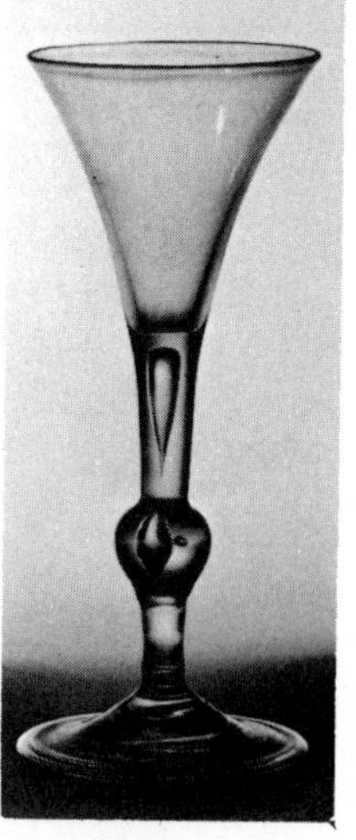

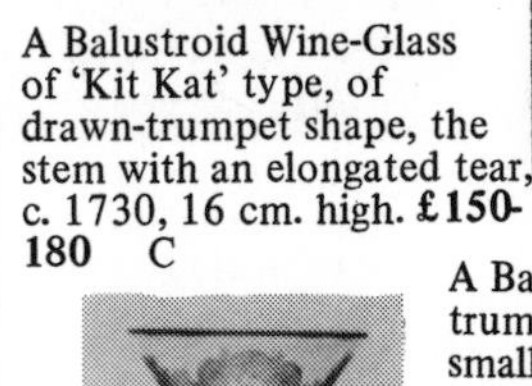

A Balustroid Wine-Glass of 'Kit Kat' type, of drawn-trumpet shape, the stem with an elongated tear, c. 1730, 16 cm. high. **£150-180** C

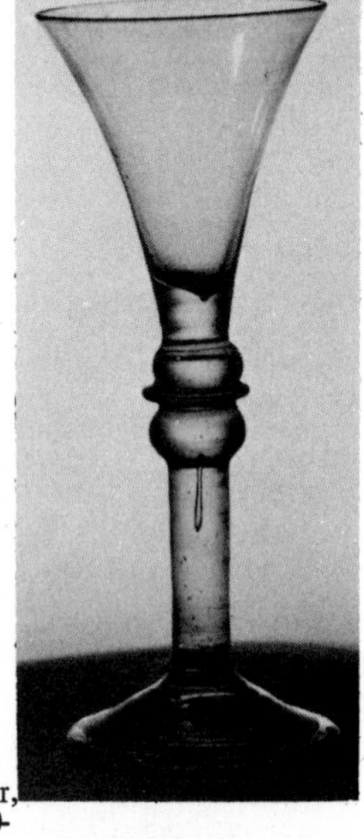

A Balustroid Wine-Glass, with trumpet-shaped bowl, with a small elongated tear (two chips to underside of foot), c. 1730, 17 cm. high. **£80-120** C

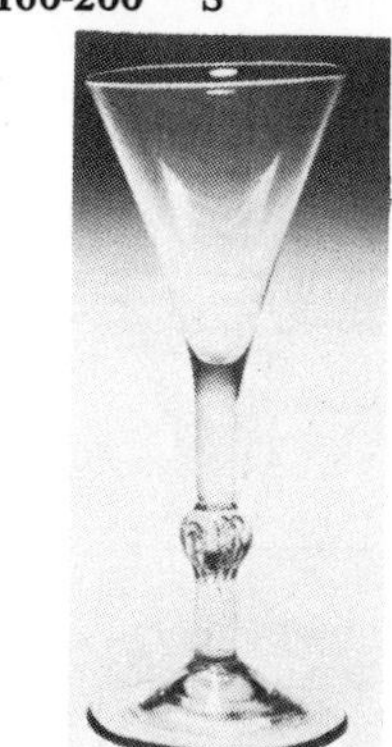

Light Baluster Wine Glass, ith trumpet bowl, c1740, 7¼"
130-160 S

A Jacobite Wine-Glass of drawn-trumpet shape, c. 1740, 14 cm. high. **£330-360** C

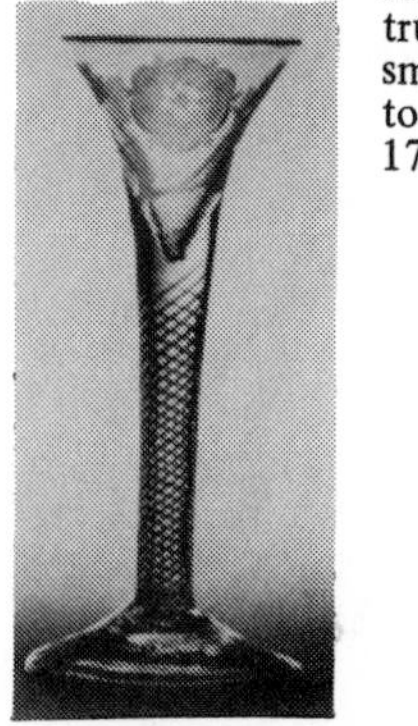

A Jacobite Airtwist Wine-Glass of drawn-trumpet shape, the stem filled with spirals and the foot with the motto 'Redi' (chip to foot rim) c. 1750, 15 cm. high. **£240-300** C

A Newcastle Plain-Stemmed Wine-Glass of slender drawn-trumpet shape, c. 1750, 18.5 cm. high. **£70-90** C

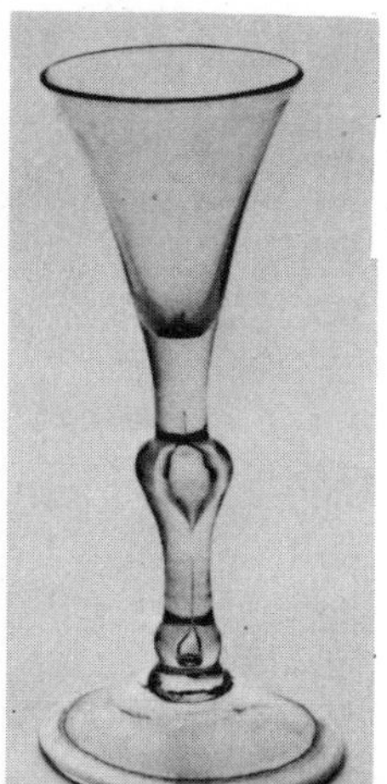

A Light Drawn Wine Glass with arge tear drop, on conical foot with folded rim. 6 in., 15.8 cm.
:60-70 L

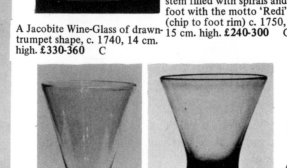

A Plain Drawn Stem Wine Glass, c. 1755. **£165-185** SA

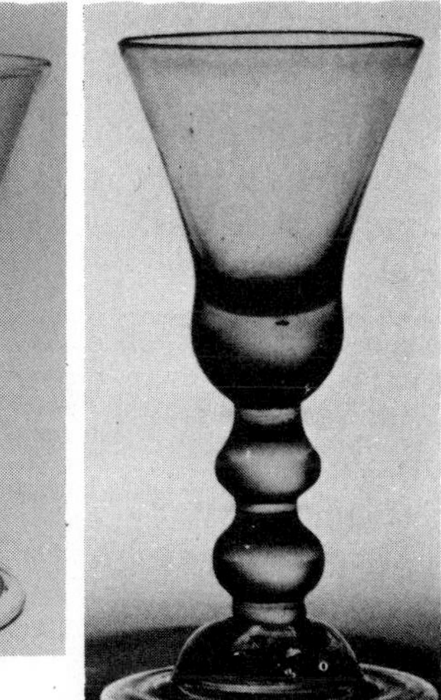

left

A Baluster Wine-Glass with bell bowl on a drop knop above a cushion knop (very slight rim chip), c. 1710 12.5 cm. high.
£135-165 C

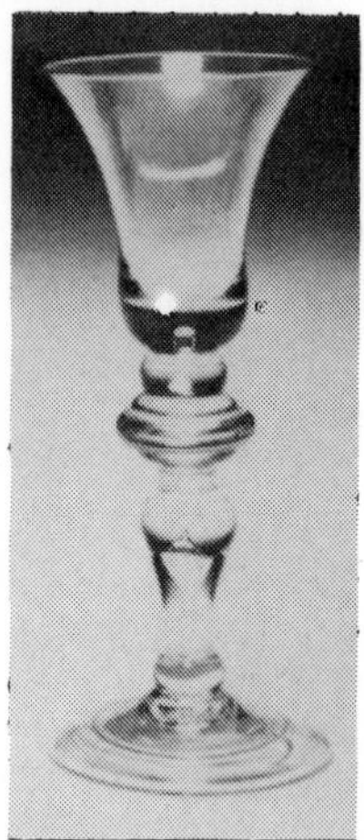

A Baluster Wine Glass, with teared bell bowl, c1720, 6¾". **£300-400** S

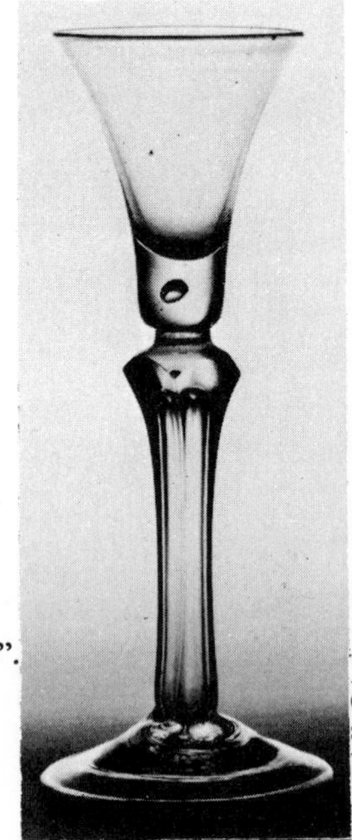

An Unusual Pedestal-Stemmed Wine-Glass with a bell bowl, stem with an elongated tear, c. 1730, 18.5 cm. high. **£300-340** C

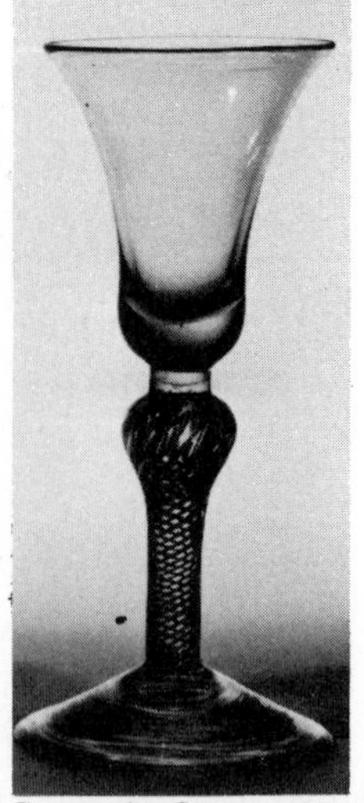

A Composite-Stemmed Wine-Glass with bell bowl with shoulder-knopped stem filled with airtwist spirals, c. 1750, 16 cm. high. **£100-140** C

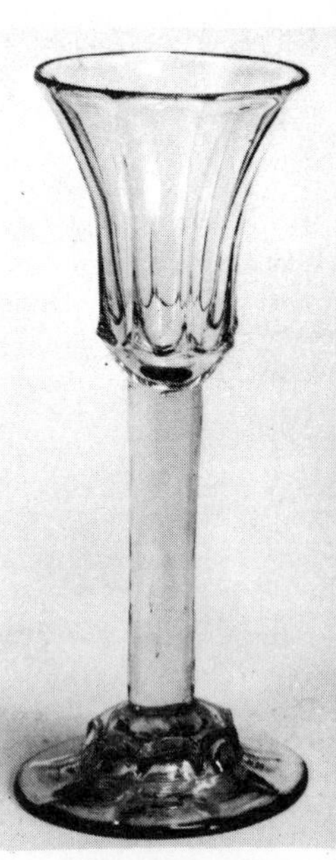

An unusual Wine Glass, the bell bowl decorated with vertical ribs, the matching domed foot, c1740, 6". **£135-155** S

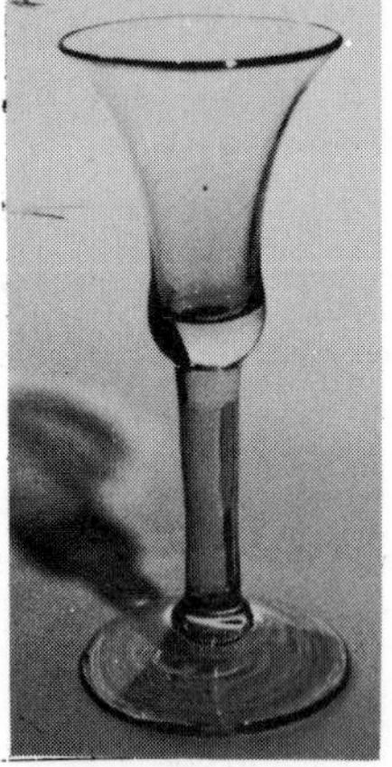

A Bell Shaped Wine Glass. **£138-165** SA

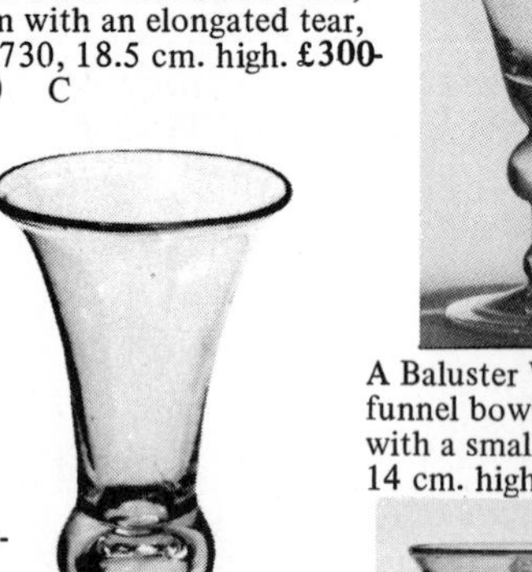

A Georgian three-piece wine glass 16 cm. high, c. 1750-60. **£50-60** SKC

A Baluster Wine-Glass with funnel bowl on a ball knop with a small tear, c. 1710, 14 cm. high. **£300-340** C

A Baluster Wine-Glass, the flared funnel bowl with an acorn knop with a small tear above a base knob, c. 1700, 14.5 cm. high. **£580-640**

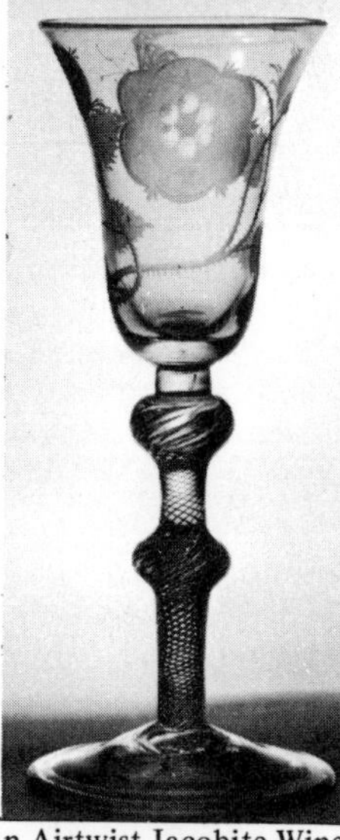

An Airtwist Jacobite Wine-Glass with bell bowl on a double-knopped stem filled with spirals (three slight chips to foot rim), c. 1750, 18 cm. high. **£170-200** C

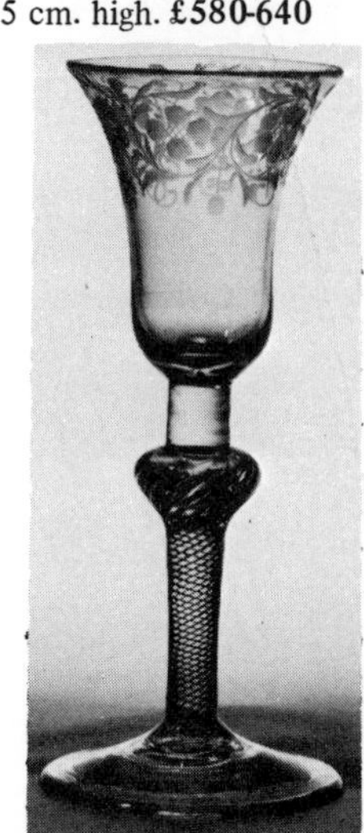

An Engraved Composite-Stemmed Wine-Glass with a bell bowl, shoulder-knopped stem filled with airtwist spirals, c. 1760, 16.5 cm. high. **£240-280** C

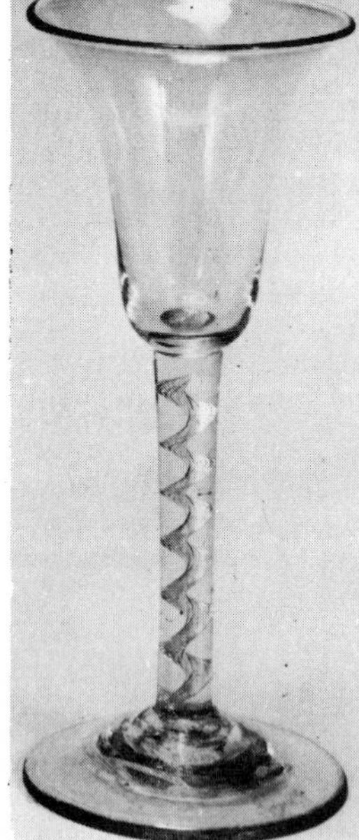

A Wine Glass, the wide bell bowl set on a stem with single mercury cockscrew, concial foot, c1750, 7". **£75-95** S

An Early 18th C. Wine Glass with a domed and folded foot, c. 1700-30, 5½ in. high. **£145-165** SA

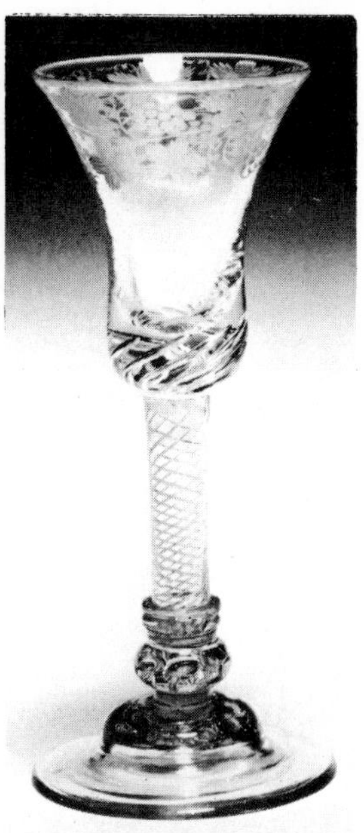

An Engraved Composite Stem Wine Glass with bell bowl on a multi-spiral air-twist stem, c1750, 6¾". **£190-240** S

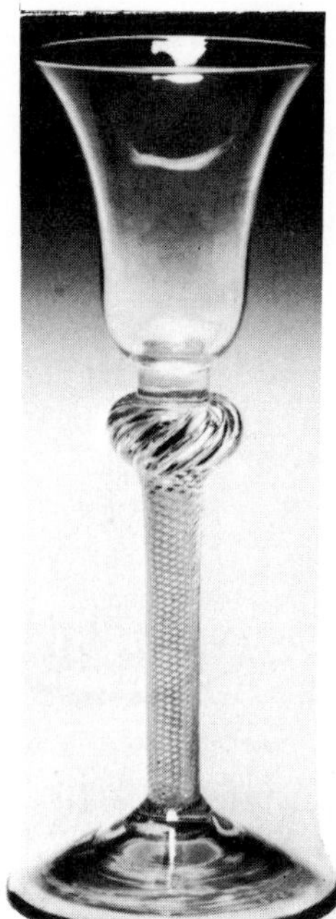

A Wine Glass with bell bowl, a multi-spiral air-twist stem with shoulder swelling, conical foot, c1750, 6¾". **£90-140** S

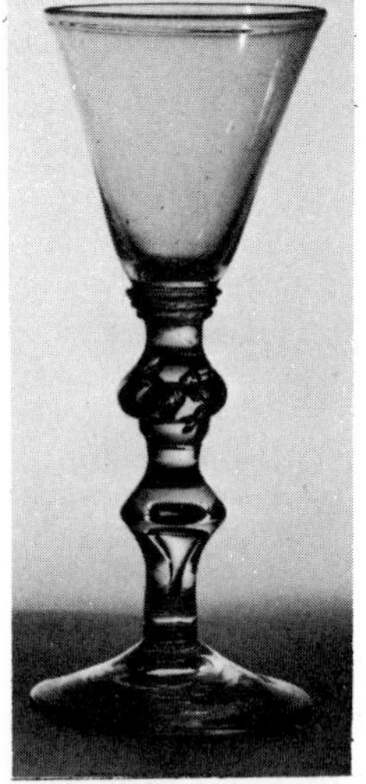

A Light Baluster Wine-Glass with flared funnel bowl, with an angular knop and a small tear, c. 1740, 16 cm. high. **£90-120** C

A Baluster Wine Glass, with flared bucket bowl, c1735, 5¾". **£145-185** S

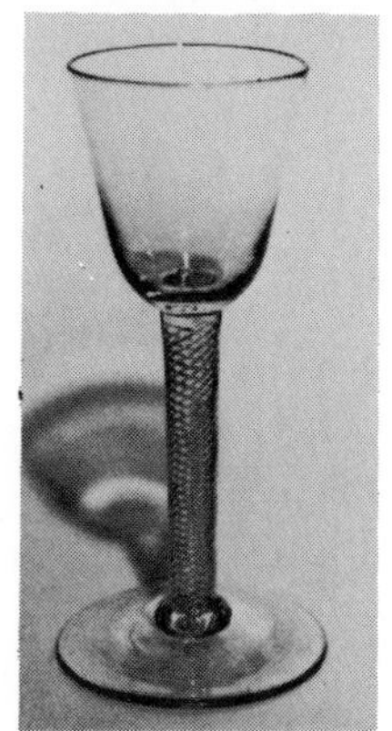

A Multi Air-Twist Stem Wine Glass, c. 1740. **£115-130** SA

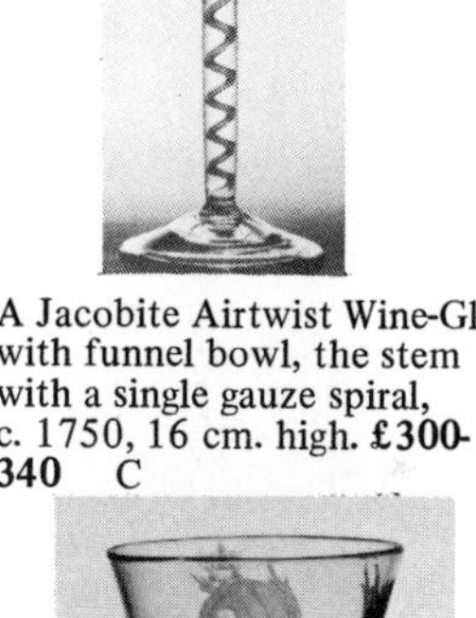

A Jacobite Airtwist Wine-Glass with funnel bowl, the stem with a single gauze spiral, c. 1750, 16 cm. high. **£300-340** C

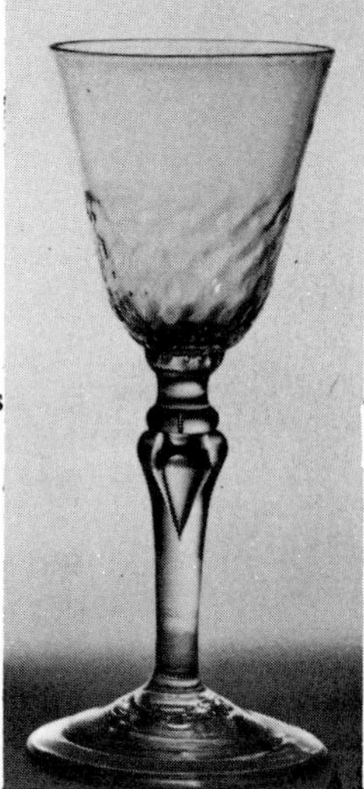

A Light Baluster Wine-Glass of Newcastle type, the funnel bowl with honeycomb-moulded lower part, with a tear, c. 1750, 16.5 cm. high. **£110-140** C

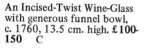

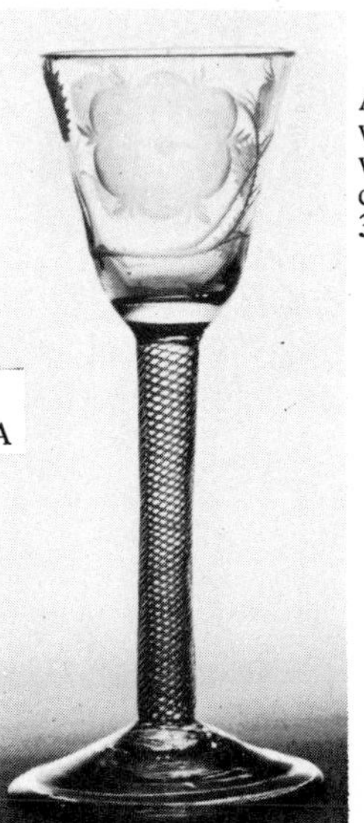

A Jacobite Airtwist Wine-Glass with funnel bowl and stem filled with airtwist spirals, c. 1750, 15.5 cm. high. **£200-230** C

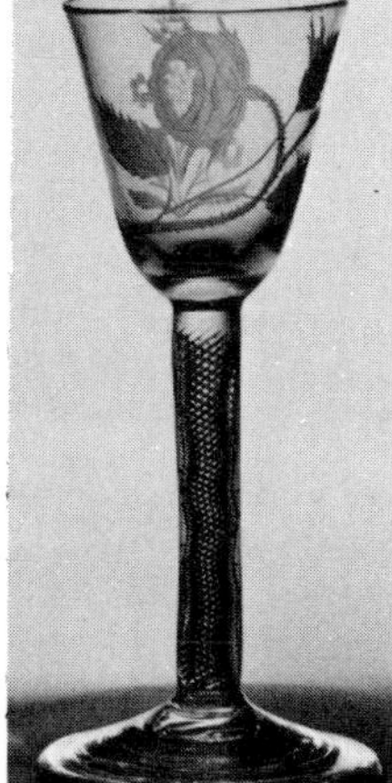

An Airtwist Jacobite Wine-Glass with funnel bowl, the stem filled with spirals, c. 1750, 15 cm. high. **£230-280** C

An Incised-Twist Wine-Glass with generous funnel bowl, c. 1760, 13.5 cm. high. **£100-150** C

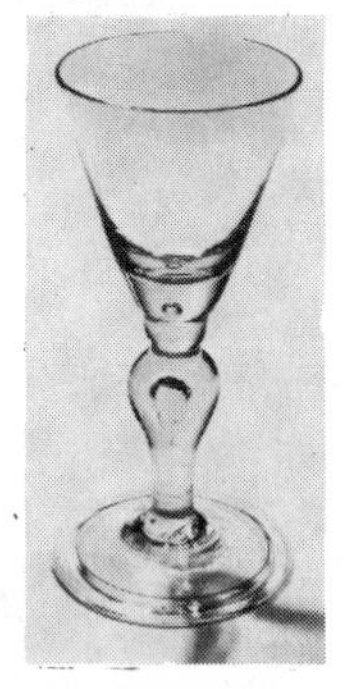

A Fine Baluster Stem Wine Glass of good metal, the stem with an inverted baluster incorporating an onion-shaped tear, 6¾" (17cms), c1700-10. **£640-680** SKC

A Small Baluster Wine-Glass with flared funnel bowl, the stem with an angular knop, base knob and elongated tear, on folded foot (slight chip to bowl), c. 1710, 13 cm. high. **£120-160** C

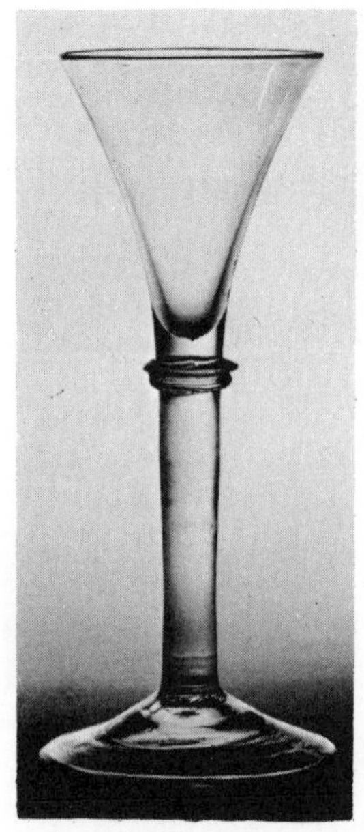

A Balustroid Wine-Glass with flared funnel bowl set on a collar, c. 1750, 17 cm. high. **£120-150** C

A Georgian air twist wine glass, 13.5 cm. c. 1750-60. **£30-40** SKC

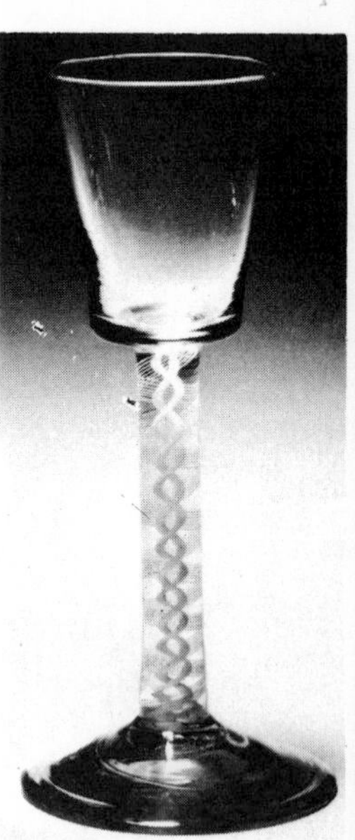

A Wine Glass with flared bucke bowl, c1760, 5¾". **£110-130**

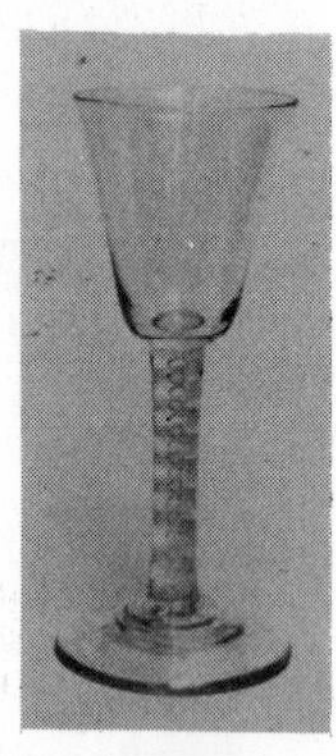

A Wine Glass with round funnel bowl and opaque stem, c. 1760. **£135-165** SA

A Wine Glass with opaque stem, c. 1760. **£115-135** SA

An Opaque Knopped Stem Wine Glass, c. 1760. **£285-300** SA

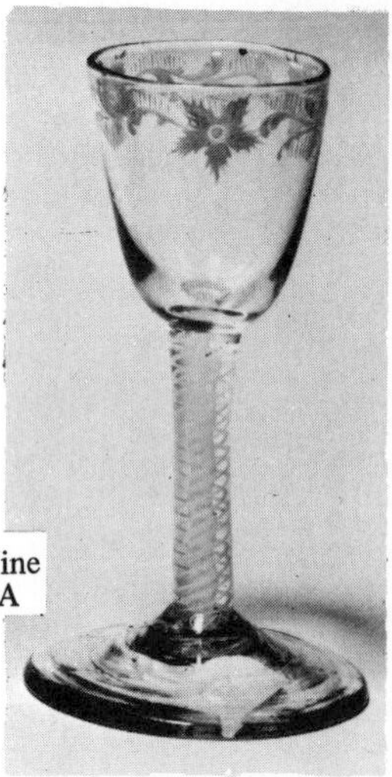

A Beilby Enamelled Wine Glass, possibly by Mary Beilby, c1765, 4½". **£500-600** S

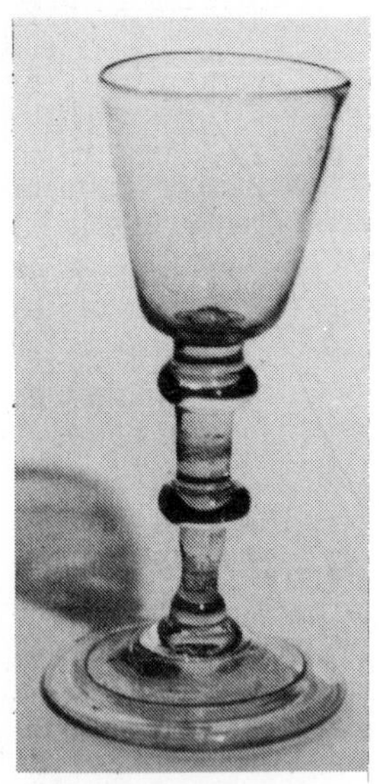

A Baluster Wine Glass with double knop stem, quite flimsy, (not a very good example) **£95-105** SA

A Pair of Wine Glasses with round funnel bowl set on a plain stem containing central opaque gauze with two red and two white spiral threads, 14.5 cm. mid/late 18th C. chip. **£60-70** S Be

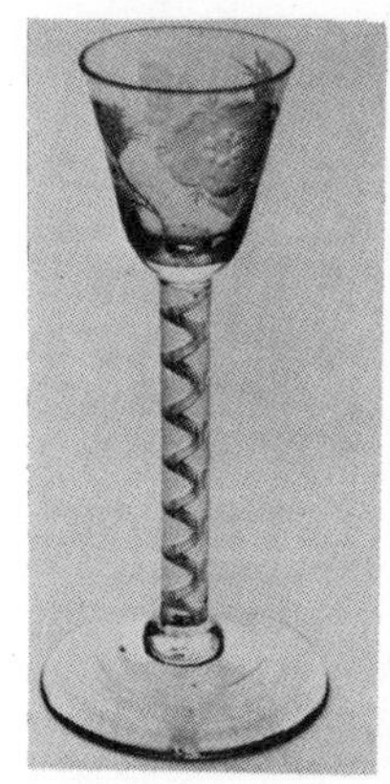

A Jacobite Wine Glass, with round engraved funnel bowl, on mercurial twist corkscrew stem and conical foot. 5¾ in., 14.5 cm. **£190-230** L

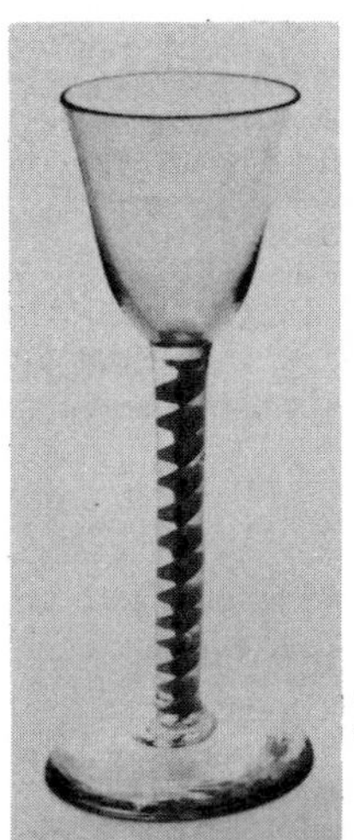

Two Wine Glasses with round funnel bowls, the opaque white stems consisting of corkscrew tapes. 6 in., 15.2 cm. **£85-95** L

An 18th C. Wine Glass with shoulder knob. **£140-160** SA

An Engraved Colour-Twist Wine-Glass in the Jacobite taste, with ogee bowl the stem with entwined red, green and white threads, c. 1770, 14.5 cm. high. **£300-340** C

A Good Old English Wine Glass with opaque or cotton twist stem. **£110-130** SA

A Green Wine-Glass of dark colour with double-ogee bowl, on plain stem, c. 1760, 15 cm. high. **£350-390** C

A Baluster Wine Glass of light green metal, with large double-ogee bowl, c1720, 6". **£190-250** S

A Facet-Stemmed Engraved Wine-Glass with ogee bowl on hexagonal facet-cut stem, c. 1780, 15.5 cm. high. **£180-210** C

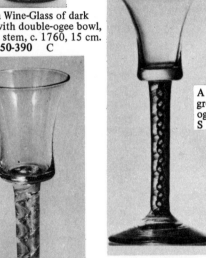

A Wine Glass with waisted bucket bowl and stem containing a double series opaque white twist, 16.2 cm., mid 18th C. **£50-70** S Be

A Wine Glass, the waisted bucket bowl set on a double-series air-twist stem and conical foot, c1750, 6½" high. **£100-130** S

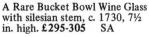

A Rare Bucket Bowl Wine Glass with silesian stem, c. 1730, 7½ in. high. **£295-305** SA

A Mixed-Twist Wine-Glass with waisted bucket bowl, the stem with entwined spiral gauze airtwist and a single opaque thread, c. 1760, 17 cm. high. **£210-240** C

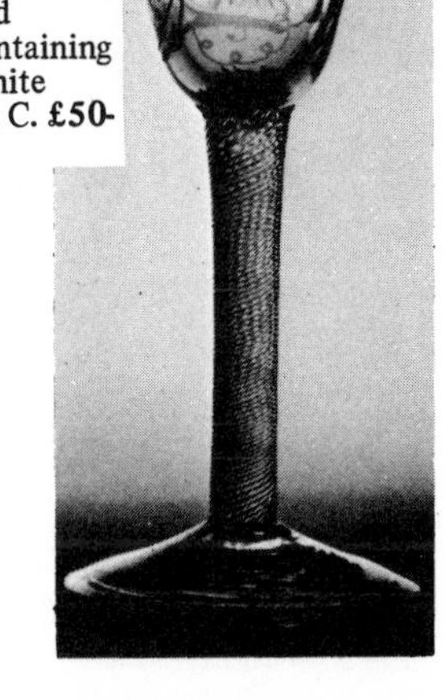

An Engraved Incised-Twist Wine-Glass, c. 1760, 15 cm. high. **£180-210** C

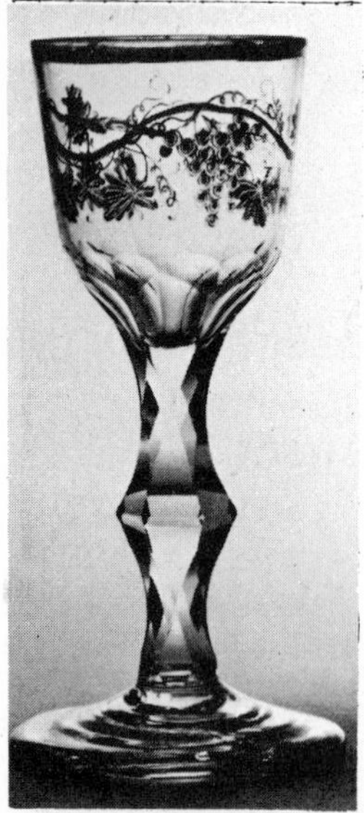

A Facet-Stemmed Wine-Glass, the ogee bowl with cut lower part gilt in the manner of James Giles, c. 1780, 15 cm. high. **£130-160** C

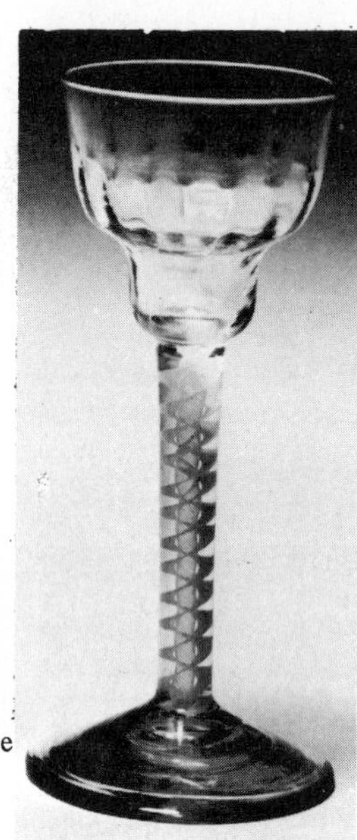

A Wine Glass, the unusual double-ogee bowl with moulded vertical ribs, c1760, 5¾". **£150-190** S

A Baluster Wine Glass, thistle bowl, teared solid base, annulated knop, teared baluster, conical folded foot, 6¾ in., c. 1720. **£200-250** S

An Attractive Wine Glass of dark metal, with an almost thistle-shaped bowl, 7½" (19cms), c171
£830-880 SKC

A Wine Glass with a bucket shaped bowl on a double cotton twist stem, 7 in. high. **£175-200** SA

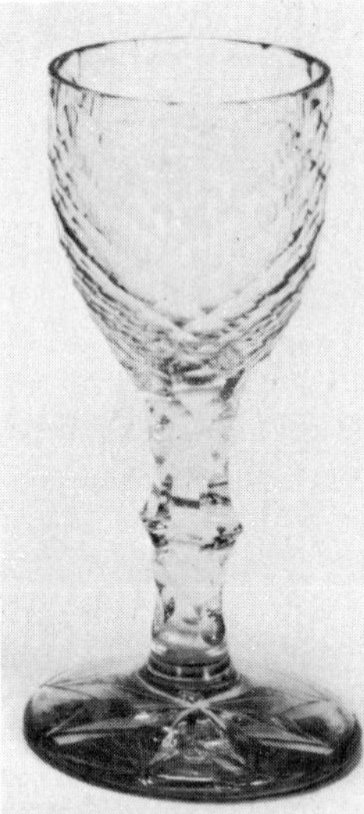

A Faceted Wine Glass, with ovoid bowl, c1770, 4¾". **£90-120** S

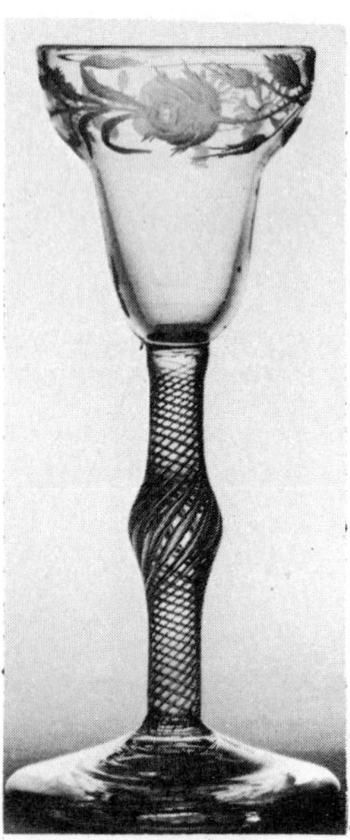

A Jacobite Airtwist Wine-Glass with pan-topped bowl, the stem with swelling waist knop filled with spirals, c. 1750, 15.5 cm. high. **£300-340** C

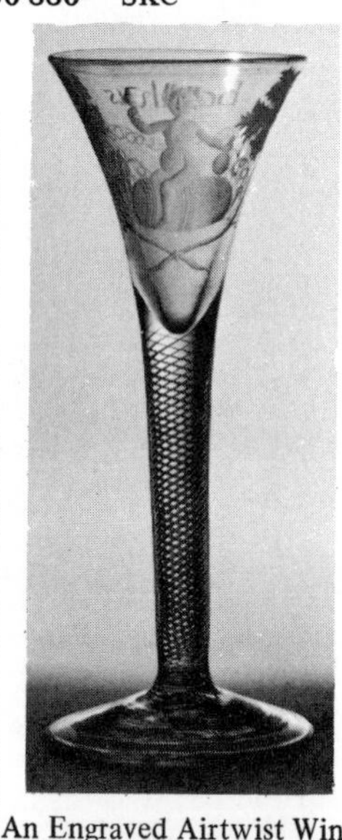

An Engraved Airtwist Wine-Glass of drawn-trumpet shape the stem filled with spirals, c. 1750, 17 cm. high. **£360-400** C

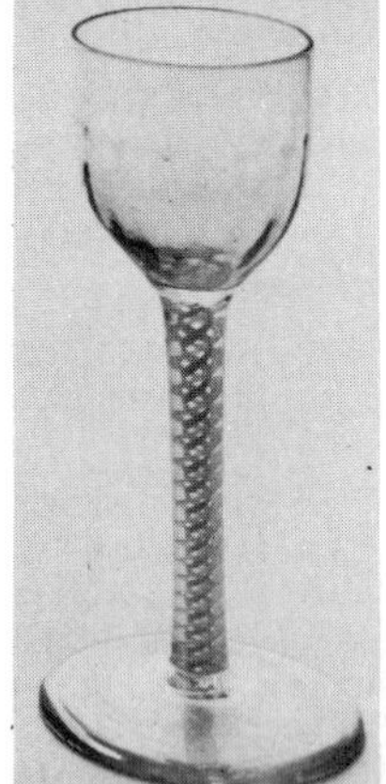

A Pair of Wine Glasses, the ovoid bowls partly moulded with flutes, on opaque white twist stems with a double tape in the centre surrounded by gauze corkscrews. 5 in., 13.3 cm. **£100-130** pr. L

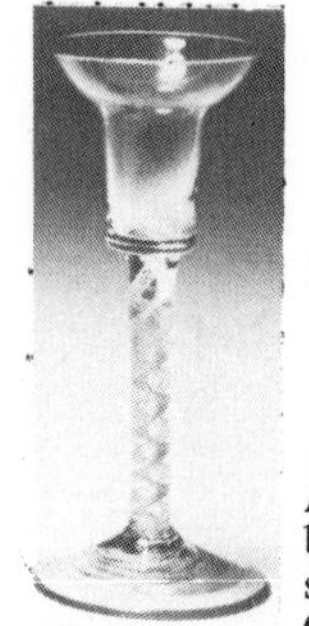

right

A Rare Baluster Ale Glass, c1690, 7½". **£400-700** S

left

A Wine Glass with pan-topped bucket bowl set on a double series opaque-twist stem, c1760, 6". **£90-130** S

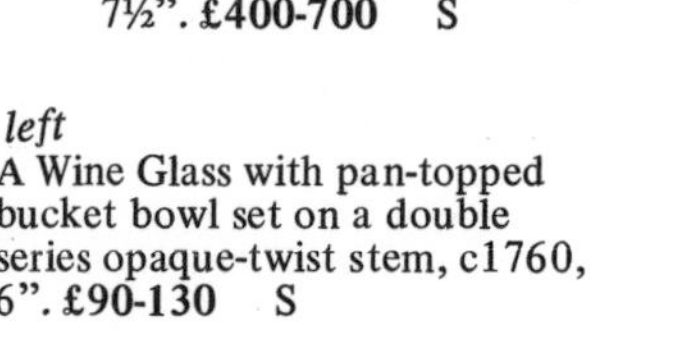

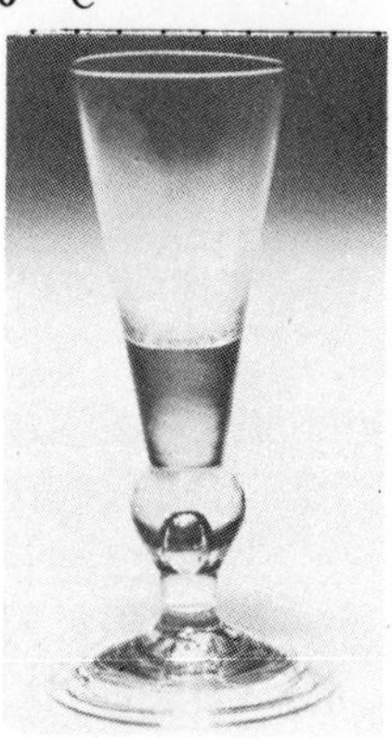

A Late 18th C. Bristol Wine Glass, 'rhomer' type, c. 1770, 4¾ in. high. **£44-55** SA

A Set of 6 Victorian cranberry Wine Glasses, 5" high. **£55-70** set SQE

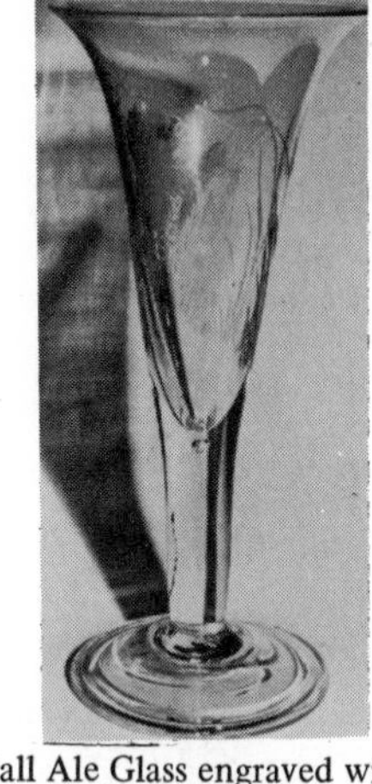

A Tall Ale Glass engraved with hops and barley, c. 1740, 10 in. high. **£165-185** SA

An Engraved Wine Glass, of possible Jacobite signficance, with pan topped bowl, set on a multi-spiral air-twist stem with central swelling, c1750, 6". **£140-180** S

A Light Baluster Ale Glass, the waisted bowl set on a knopped and bladed stem with conical foot, c1730, 8", small chip to foot rim. **£160-200** S

A Short Ale with conical bowl with moulded wrythen ribs, conical folded foot, 5½ in., c. 1720. **£240-300** S

A Set of Six Georgian Wine Glasses. **£125-150** for 6 CSG

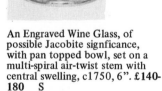

A Balustroid Engraved Ale-Glass with slender funnel bowl, the stem with a small tear, c. 1740, 18 cm. high. **£190-250** C

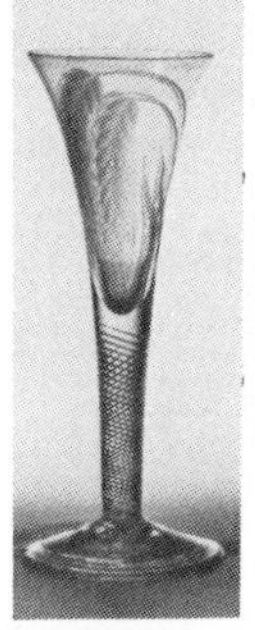

An Engraved airtwist Ale-Glass of drawn-trumpet shape (chip to foot rim) c. 1750, 18.5 cm. high. **£100-140** C

An Ale Glass with extended bell bowl on a multi-spiral air-twist stem, c1750, 7¼" high. **£110-150** S

left
An Ale Glass, the round funnel bowl with vertical fluting, plain stem containing a double series opaque twist, 18.6 cm., mid 18th C. **£50-60** S Be

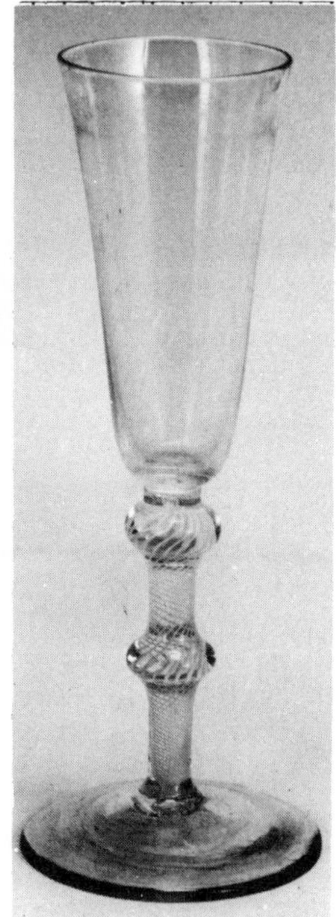

An Ale Glass, the tall round funnel bowl set on a multi-spiral opaque-twist stem, conical foot, c1760, 7¾". **£125-145** S

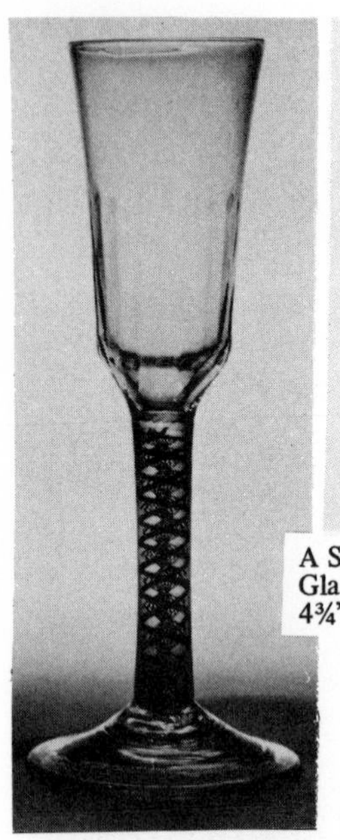

A Set of Seven Bristol Ale Glasses of emerald green metal, 4¾" (12cms). **£190-220** SKC

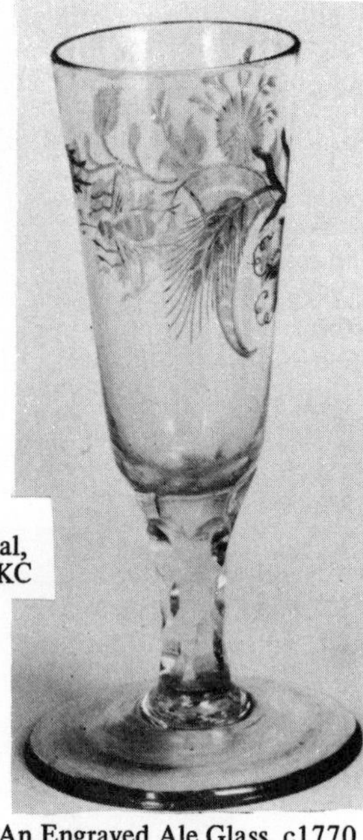

An Opaque-Twist Ale-Glass, with ogee bowl the stem with gauze corkscrew core within two spiral threads (slight chip to underside of foot) c. 1770, 19.5 cm. high. **£90-120** C

An Engraved Ale Glass, c1770, 6". **£90-140** S

An Ale Glass with conical bowl, c1780, 6¾". **£80-100** S

An Old English Glass with a teared stem. **£130-160** SA

An Anglo-Venetian Armorial Goblet of soda metal, with flared funnel bowl, on a hollow quatrefoil knop between mereses, English or Netherlands, late 17th C., 16 cm. high. **£900-1,000** C

A Tall Ale Glass with drawn stem, 18th C. 19 in. high. **£110-130** SA

One of a set of 4 Victorian Ale Glasses, 7" high. **£120-138** set SQE

A Baluster Goblet with funnel bowl on a wide angular knop and base knob enclosing two small tears, c. 1705, 16 cm. high. **£490-560** C

left
An Unusual Baluster Goblet of blue tint, with funnel bowl, a large bun knop and cushion knops with an elongated tear, early 18th C., 26 cm. high. **£600-650** C

A Bohemian Goblet and Cover, 32 cm., c. 1720. **£900-1,100** S

A Netherlandish Engraved Goblet with flared funnel bowl, the stem with hollow knop between two mereses, c. 1700, 16 cm. high. **£420-480** C

An Engraved Transitional Goblet on a domed and folded foot, 7¼ in., c. 1735. **£500-600** S

A Bohemian engraved Goblet, 21 cm., c. 1740. **£240-280** S

A Jacobite Balustroid Goblet, with thistle-shaped bowl, c. 1740, 17 cm. high. **£360-400** C

A Rare Electioneering Goblet, the bucket bowl inscribed 'Success To Sir Francis Knollys' (slight rim chip), c. 1745, 19 cm. high. **£440-480** C

A Dutch-Engraved Newcastle Goblet, inscribed 'PAX INTRANTIBUS' and 'SALUS EXEUNTIBUS', c. 1745, 18 cm. high. **£400-460** C

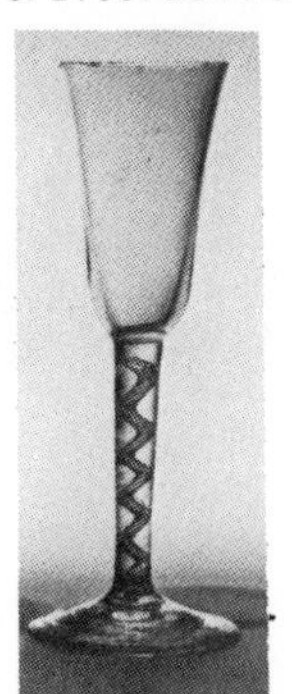

An Airtwist Ale-Glass with slender funnel bowl, the stem with spiral gauze core (rim slightly trimmed), c. 1750, 20.5 cm. high. **£110-140** C

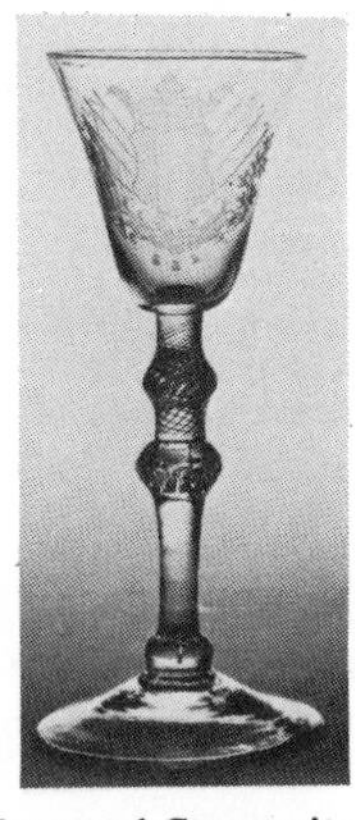

A Dutch-Engraved Composite-Stemmed Armorial Goblet, the funnel bowl engraved with the arms of Delft with swelling waist knop filled with airtwist spirals above a beaded inverted baluster stem with base knob (very slight chip to foot rim), c. 1750, 19.5 cm. high. **£1,000-1,200** C

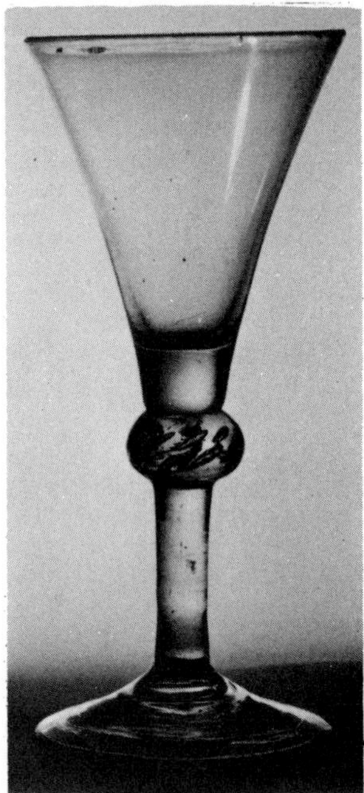

A Composite-Stemmed Goblet with flared straight-sided bowl, c. 1750, 19.5 cm. high. **£80-100** C

A Green Goblet of bright emerald colour, on plain stem and spirally moulded foot, c. 1760, 13.5 cm. high. **£140-180** C

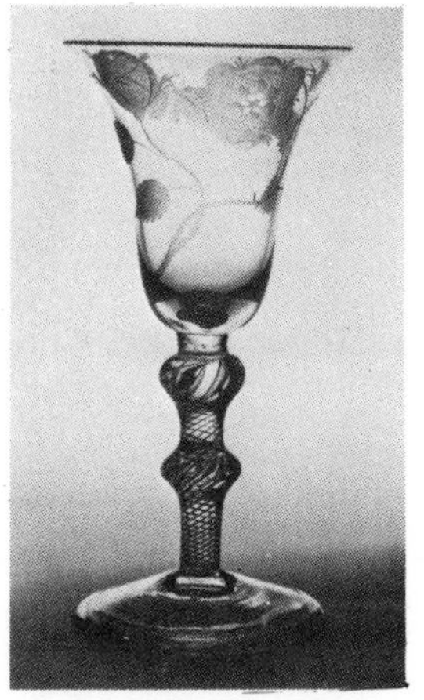

A Massive Jacobite Airtwist Goblet with bell bowl on double-knopped stem filled with spirals, c. 1750, 26.5 cm. high. **£500-560** C

A set of six Georgian green goblets, 13.5 cm., c. 1750. **£210-250** SKC

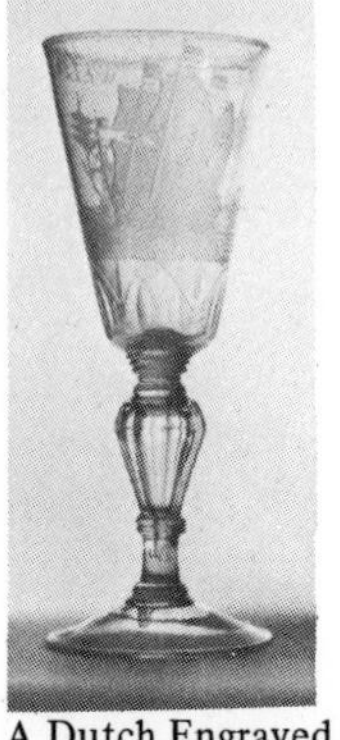

A Dutch Engraved Goblet and a Cover inscribed 'HET LANS WELL VAREN', on an inverted fluted baluster knop (tip to finial restored), c. 1765 the goblet 23 cm. high. **£330-360** C

A Saxon Armorial Goblet engraved with the arms of William, Duke of Cumberland, (plated repair to stem), c. 1760, 22.5 cm. high. **£180-220** C

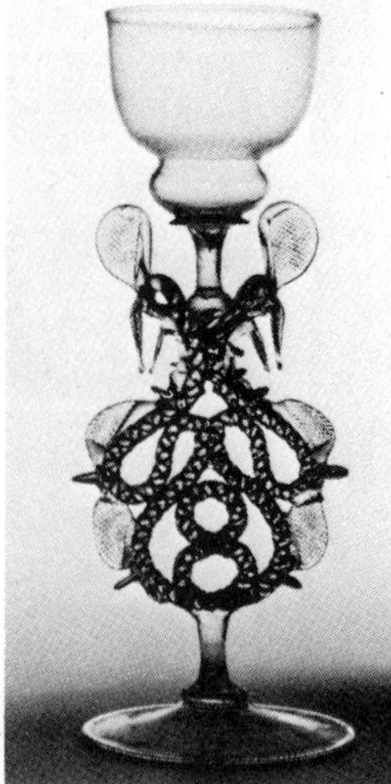

A Facon-de-Venise Serpent-Stemmed Goblet (Flugelglas), with double-ogee bowl, the elaborately coiled stem enclosing opaque-white, brick-red and green threads, Netherlands, 17th C, 26.5cm high, **£2,000-2,150** C

A Large Goblet, the cup-shaped bowl set on a plain stem and foot and engraved with a sailing ship, 1855, 17cm, **£80-100** SBe

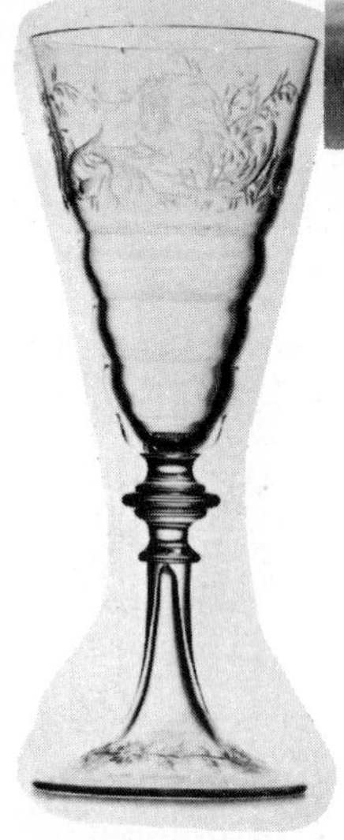

A Set of Six Large Continental Goblets with funnel shaped bowls, each with a double knopped stem and hollow engraved foot, 29 cm., some chipping, late 19th C. **£40-55** S Be

A Green Goblet, the cup-shaped bowl on an oviform-knopped stem moulded with vertical flutes, on domed foot, late 18th C., 16.5 cm. high. **£200-250** C

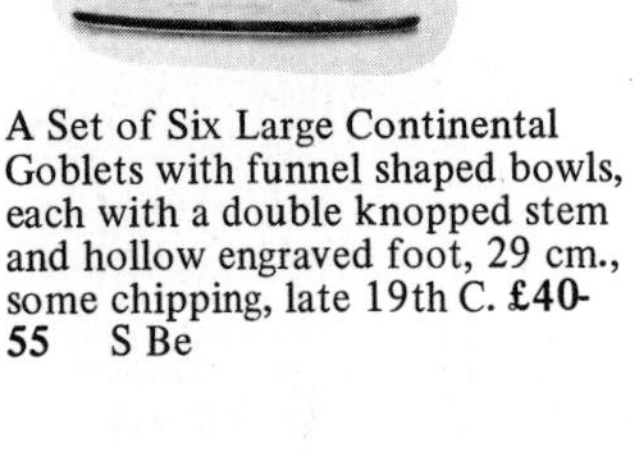

A Massive Dutch Engraved Goblet and Cover, inscribed 'STRINS WELVAREN W. V VLIET', (slight chip to finial) c. 1765, 47 cm. high. **£950-1,050** C

A Bohemian Ruby-flashed Goblet and cover, with double ogee bowl on hollow knopped stem and conical foot, c1840, 34.5cms. **£350-400** S.B.

A Mammoth Green-tinted Goblet, 11¾ in., 18th/19th C. **£150-250** S

A Rare Blue Goblet, the cup-shaped bowl with lightly hammered flutes on plain stem and conical foot, c. 1760 16.5 cm. high. **£1,000-1,600** C

A Bohemian Enamelled Goblet in semi-opaque white glass, 21 cm., c. 1840. **£130-160** SB

A Very Fine Nailsea Goblet, c. 1830, 9¼ in. high. **£345-400** SA

A Bohemian Amber-stained Goblet, c. 1850, 15.2 cm. **£140-180** SB

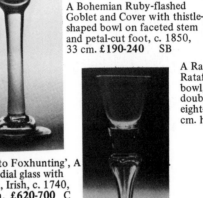

A Bohemian Ruby-flashed Goblet and Cover with thistle-shaped bowl on faceted stem and petal-cut foot, c. 1850, 33 cm. **£190-240** SB

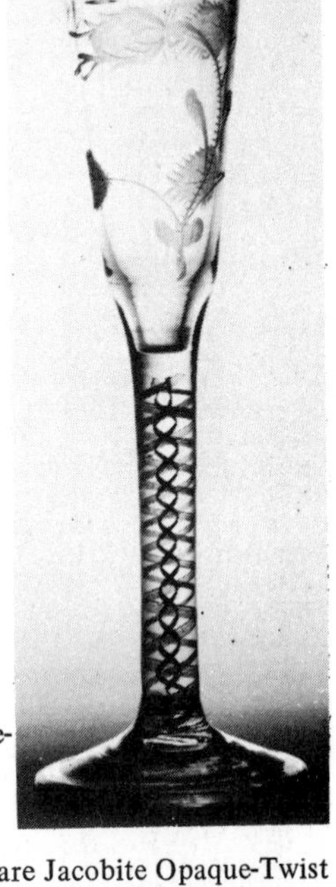

A Rare Jacobite Opaque-Twist Ratafia-Glass with slender ogee bowl, the stem with entwined double-thread core within an eight-ply spiral, c. 1765, 18 cm. high. **£280-340** C

A Deceptive Cordial with thick flared bowl, conical folded foot, 4¾ in., c. 1720. **£250-300** S

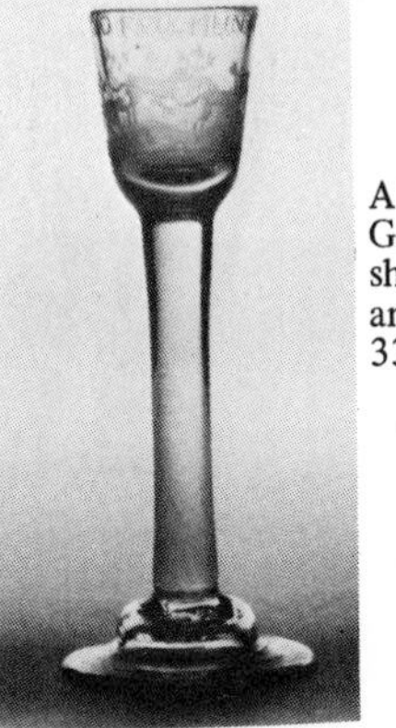
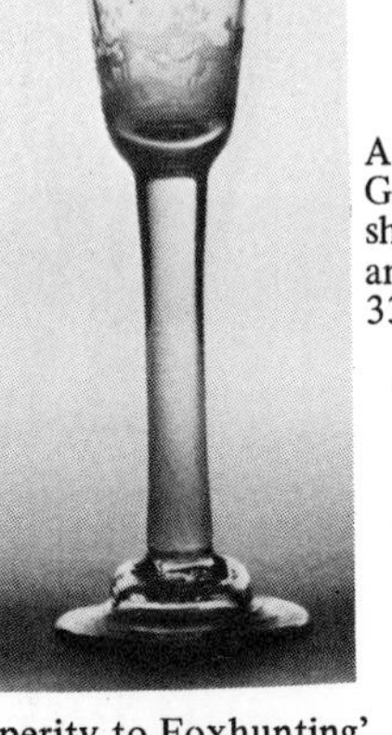

'Prosperity to Foxhunting', A sporting cordial glass with funnel bowl, Irish, c. 1740, 17.5cm high, **£620-700** C

A Cordial Glass with conical bowl, moulded pedestal stem, enclosing an extended air tear, conical folded foot, 5½ in., c. 1730. **£60-80** S

A Bohemian Amber-stained Goblet of thistle shape on cut foot, c. 1850, 14.5 cm. **£120-140** SB

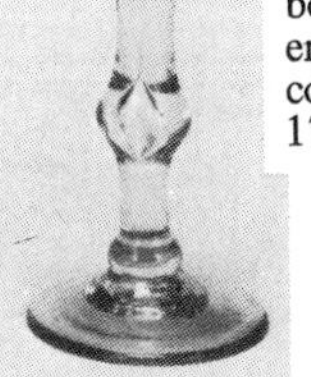

An early Cordial Glass, with small bell bowl, c1720, 6". **£155-200** S

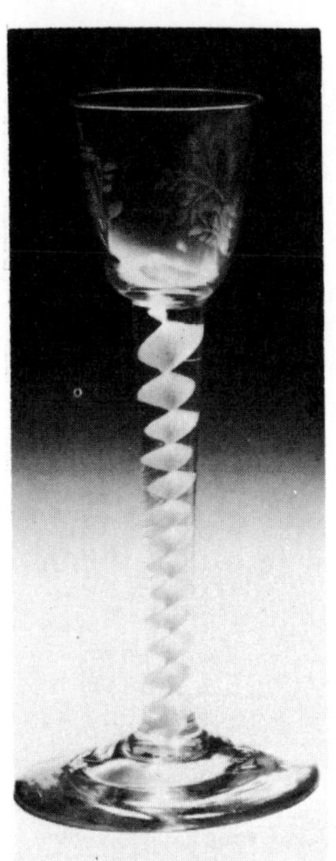

An Engraved Cordial, c1750, 6¾". **£100-140** S

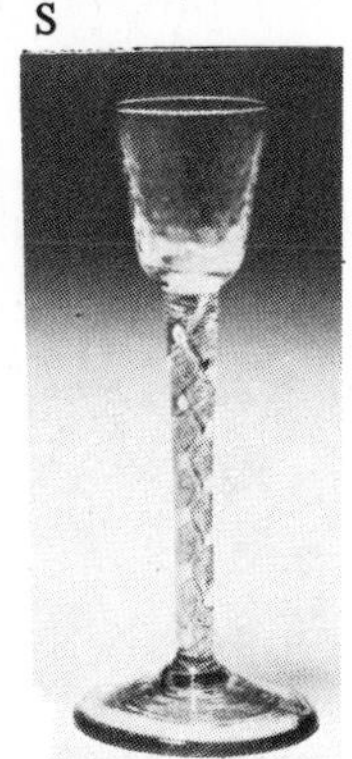

A Cordial, with round funnel bowl on a double-series air-twist stem, c1750, 7¼". **£80-100** S

A Coaching Rummer, 8¼ in., 1825. **£500-600** S

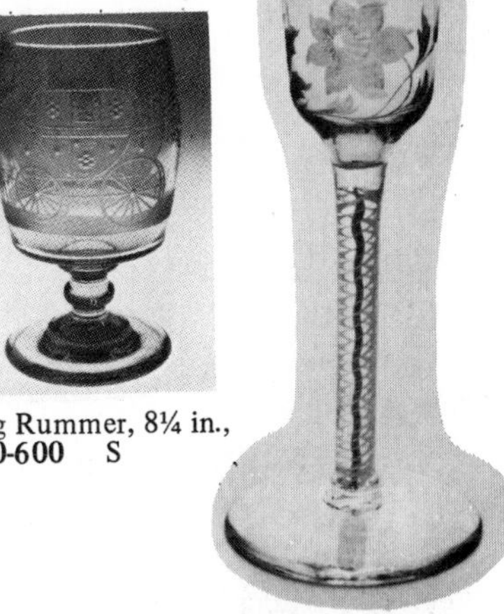

A Cordial Glass, the ogee bowl engraved, the opaque twist stem consisting of a spiral cable encircled by a pair of spiral tapes. 5¾ in., 14.6 cm. **£125-165** L

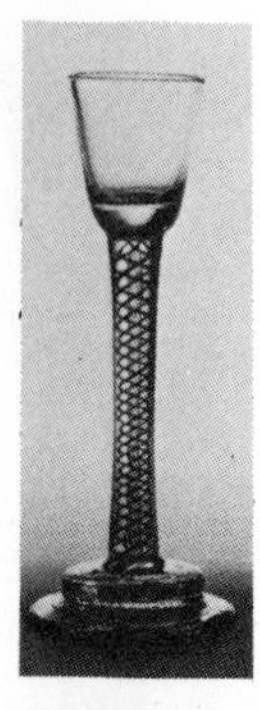

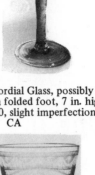

An Opaque-Twist Cordial-Glass with funnel bowl, the stem with gauze core within four spiral threads, c. 1765, 17 cm. high. **£300-340** C

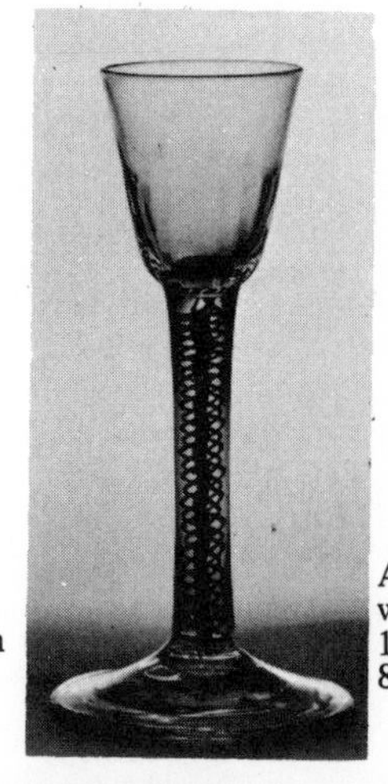

An Opaque-Twist Cordial Glass, with funnel bowl the stem with gauze-core within four spiral threads, c. 1765, 14.5 cm. high. **£80-110** C

A Cordial Glass, possibly Dutch, with folded foot, 7 in. high, c. 1790, slight imperfections. **£75-85** CA

A Roemer of light green tint with cup-shaped bowl on high trailed conical foot, Rhenish, 17th C. 14 cm., high. **£280-310** C

A Sunderland Bridge Rummer with flared bucket bowl on capstan stem, c. 1830, 13.5cm high, **£120-140** C

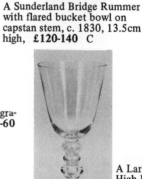

A Rare Deep Emerald Goblet, the large cup-shape bowl is set on a collar above a hollow vertically ribbed 'sausage' stem, 6½ in., c. 1760-70. **£425-500** SA

A Regency Rummer with engraved shield and cut stem. **£55-60** CA

A Large Rummer, engraved with High Level Bridge, Newcastle-on-Tyne, dated 1852. **£550-600** SA

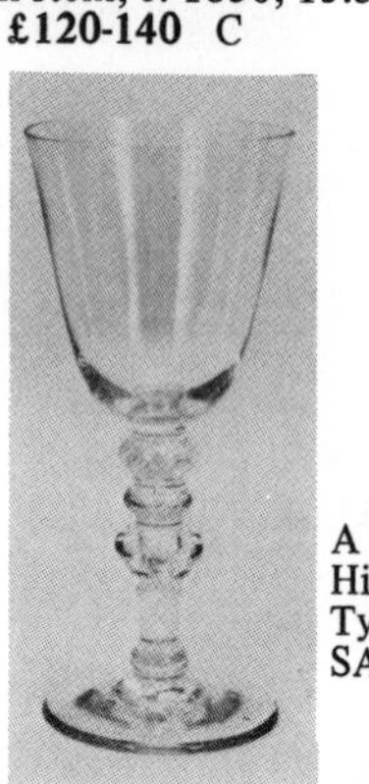

A Newcastle Goblet, with large round funnel bowl, on a conical foot, c1750, 9", foot slightly trimmed. **£210-260** S

An Old English Rummer with a capstan stem. **£35-40** SA

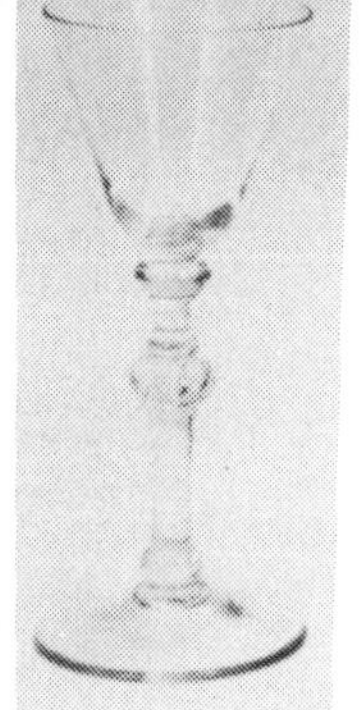

A Newcastle Glass with pointed round funnel bowl, c1750, 7¼". **£150-180** S

A mixed-twist stem flute Glass, the trumpet bowl on a stem with an opaque enamel gauze core within mercury spirals, conical foot, c1750, 7½". **£120-150** S

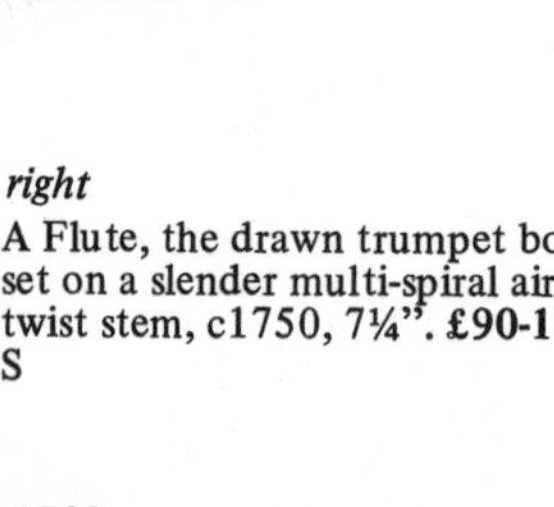

right

A Flute, the drawn trumpet bowl set on a slender multi-spiral air-twist stem, c1750, 7¼". **£90-110** S

A Double Bowled Glass, c1720, 4¾". **£70-90** S

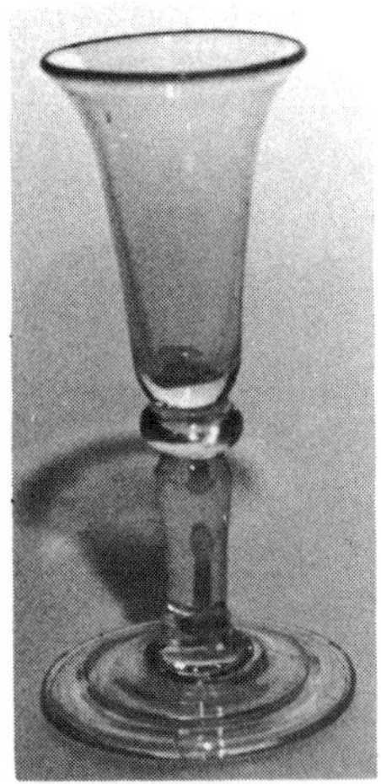

A Rare Bell-Shaped Gin Glass, c. 1720. **£78-88** SA

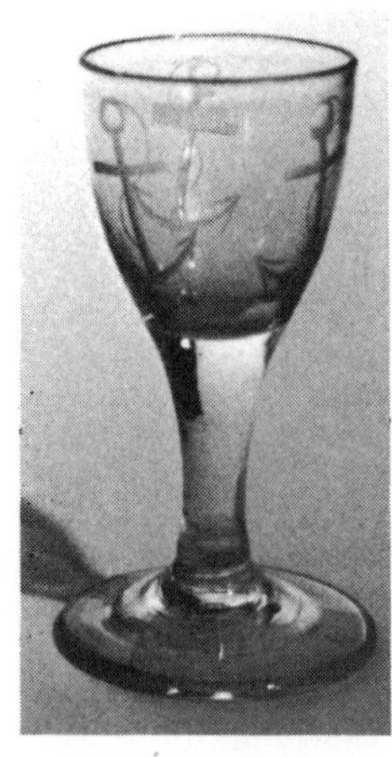

A Late 18th C. Port Glass. **£60-70** SA

A Set of 6 Sherry Glasses, on dolphin stems, c1920's. **£75-100**

An Engraved Composite-Stemmed Water-Glass with double-ogee bowl, the stem with beaded knop on a terraced foot c. 1745, 14 cm. high. **£110-140** C

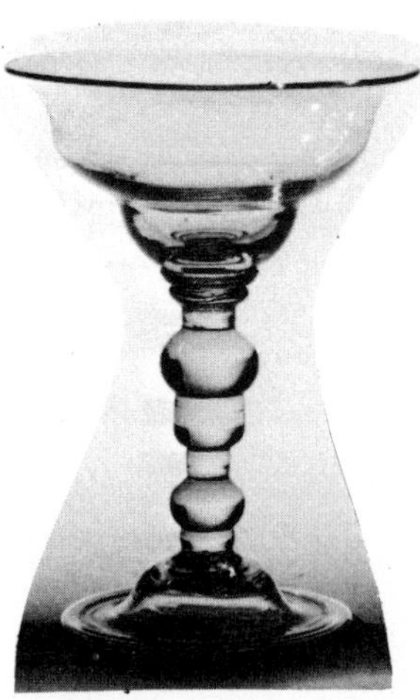

A Rare Baluster Champagne Glass with double-ogee bowl, c. 1725, 14cm high, **£440-500** C

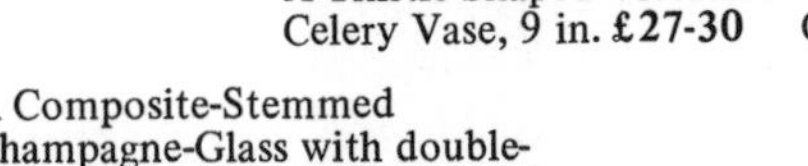

A Composite-Stemmed Champagne-Glass with double-ogee bowl on moulded pedestal stem, c. 1740, 15 cm. high. **£100-130** C

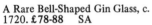

A Thistle-Shaped Victorian Celery Vase, 9 in. **£27-30** CA

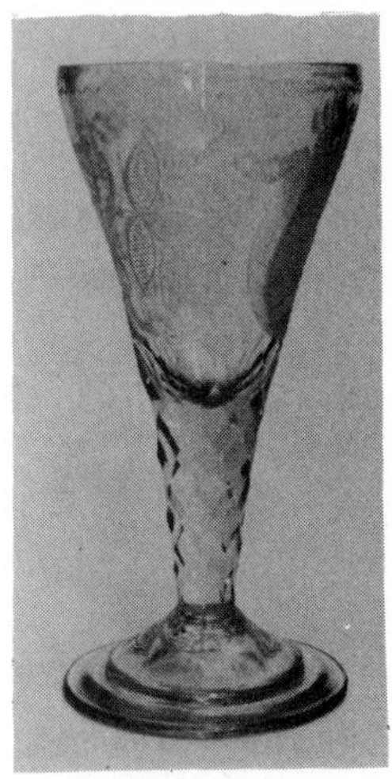

A Fine Dutch Glass on Faceted Stem with bowl engraved with Armorials, c. 1730. **£435-520** SA

A drawn Toasting Glass with trumpet bowl and slender stem, on conical foot. 7¾ in., 19.7 cm. **£100-120** L

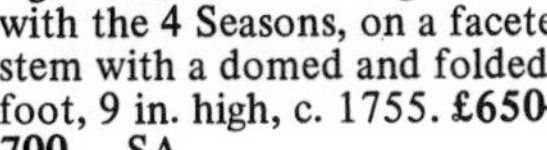

A Very Fine Dutch Glass with a gilt rim, the bowl engraved with the 4 Seasons, on a faceted stem with a domed and folded foot, 9 in. high, c. 1755. **£650-700** SA

A Silesian Engraved Sweetmeat Glass with oval ogee bowl, c. 1740, 15.5cm high, **£430-500** C

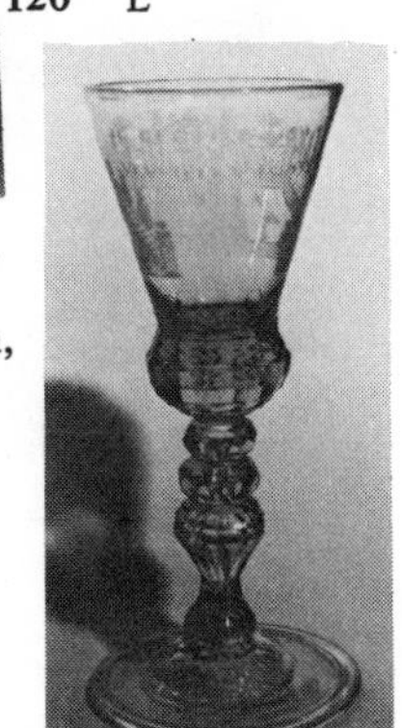

A Pedestal-Stemmed Sweetmeat Glass with double-ogee bowl, c. 1745, 16.5cm high, **£95-105** C

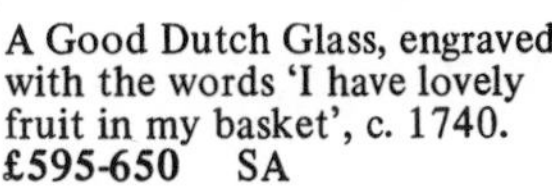

A Good Dutch Glass, engraved with the words 'I have lovely fruit in my basket', c. 1740. **£595-650** SA

A Pedestal-Stemmed Champagne-Glass with double-ogee bowl, c. 1745, 14.5 cm. high. **£85-100** C

A Good Pair of 18th C. Syllabub Glasses, 4½ in. high. **£65-75** pr. SA

A Very Early Sweetmeat Glass of small size, c. 1740. **£85-95** SA

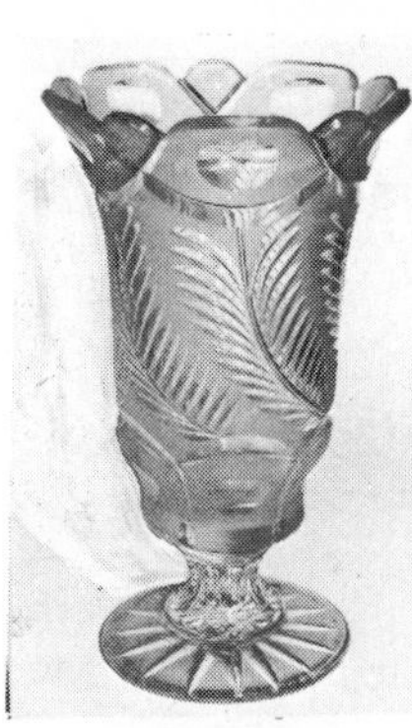

A Victorian Celery Vase with acid etched engraving 10 in. high, c. 1880. **£20-25** CA

A Very Early Firing Glass with sewn foot, c. 1740. **£95-105** SA

A Sweetmeat, applied turned-over handle and three splayed feet, 6.5 cm., 18th C. **£100-130** S

An Engraved Cylindrical Water Glass, 18th C, 9.5cm diam, **£85-100** C

An 18th C. Jelly Stand with moulded gallery, on a Silesian stem and domed and folded foot. 14 in., 36.2 cm. diam. **£55-65** L

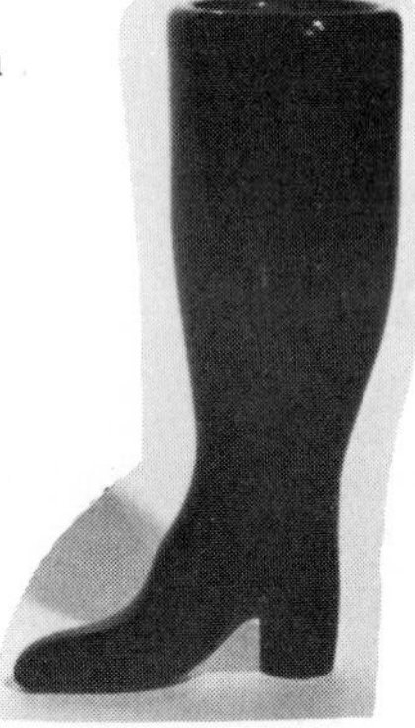

An Early 19th C. Boot Glass, 4 in. high. **£75-85** SA

A Jacobite Water Glass, c. 1750, 9cm diam, **£140-160** C

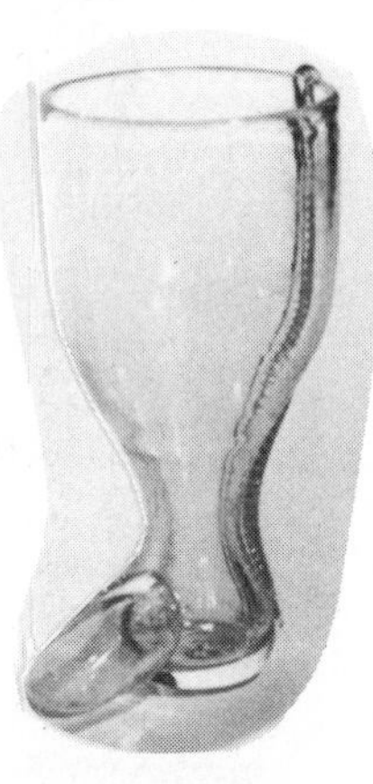

An Old English Stirrup Cup in the shape of a boot. **£95-105** SA

An early miniature Sweetmeat, c1710, 2". **£110-150** S

A Patch Stand, c1725, 3¼". **£90-110** S

A Rare Glass Stand with Folded Foot, 10 in diam., c. 1790 **£50-60** CA

A Fine and Rare Patch Stand with honeycombed, beaded, knopped stem, domed, 1730, 3 in. high. **£235-265** SA

A Frosted and Clear Glass Comport, John Ford, Holyrood Glass-works, Edinburgh, c. 1870. 28.5 cm. **£100-140** SB

An 18th C Irish Cut-glass Bowl with a waved rim, on a square lemon squeezer pedestal, 10" (26cms) high. **£80-100** SKC

A Pedestal-Stemmed Stand, on a slender moulded four-sided stem and folded conical foot, c. 1745, 12.5 cm. high. **£70-90** C

A Bristol Blue Boat-Shaped Salt with moulded lemon squeezer base c. 1820 **£70-78** CA

An Austrian Armorial Cut-Glass Cylindrical Tumbler, c. 1835, 9 cm. high. **£450-550** C

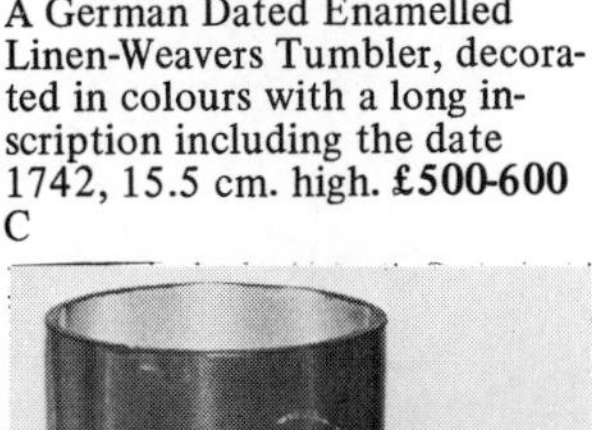

A German Dated Enamelled Linen-Weavers Tumbler, decorated in colours with a long inscription including the date 1742, 15.5 cm. high. **£500-600** C

A Bohemian Enamelled Beaker in semi opaque pink glass, the exterior enamelled in white, and gilt, c. 1850. 10.6 cm. **£90-120** SB

A Bohemian Mary Gregory Mug, 4 in., c. 1880 **£22-30** CA

A German Marriage Humpen, the reverse with trite motto, dated 1692, 19th C, 23,5cms. **£140-160** S.B.

An "Order of Oddfellows Beaker" inscribed, "Independent Order of Odd Fellows", 11 cm., early 19th C. **£40-50** SKC

An Enamelled 'Milchglas' Jug, 19.3 cm., Spanish or Bohemian, c. 1780. **£75-100** S

An enamelled 'Milchglas' Tankard, 13.2 cm., Spanish or Bohemian, c. 1780. **£100-140** S

A Rare Milk-Glass, probably Dutch, 6½ in., c. 1790 (damaged) **£70-75** undamaged **£450-500** CA

A Venetian Claret Jug, rose-pink ground with white looping **£65-70** CA

A Pair of late Georgian Claret Jugs and Stoppers, 13¾" (35cms). **£265-300** SKC

A Mappin & Webb Silver-mounted cut-glass Claret Jug, maker's mark, London, 1902. 28.3 cm. high. **£350-400** SB

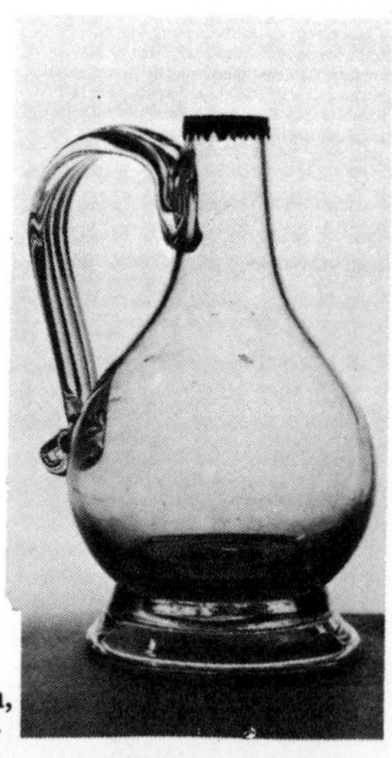

A Silver-Mounted Baluster Wine Jug, with contemporary silver mount, c. 1710, the mount probably Dutch, 18cm high, **£320-400** C

A Victorian Claret Jug, engraved with formal scroll foliage and hippocampi, 1865 by Messrs. Barnard, 11in (28cm) high **£390-420** L

A Very Heavy George III Cut Glass Water Jug, 6½ in. high. **£65-75** SA

A Large Cut Ewer in Neo-Classical style, 10½ in., c. 1830. **£200-300** S

A French blue Opaline Glass Cream Jug, c1850, 4", chipped **£20-30** perfect **£75-100**

A 'Mary Gregory' Green Glass Jug. **£22-25** AP

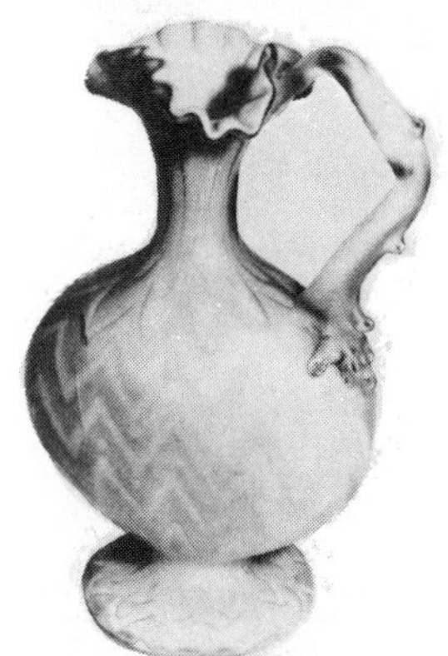

A Blue Quilted Satin Jug, 6 in. high, c. 1880. **£100-120** CA

A small pale green, jewelled opaline glass Cream Jug, with gilding, c1880, 3". **£60-75**

left
A Nailsea Baluster Cream-Jug with opaque white pulled decoration, with applied blue band to the rim, c. 1820, 9 cm. high. **£130-160** C

A Bohemian Mary Gregory Jug, 6½ in high, c. 1880. **£40-45** CA

A Small Nailsea Mug of dark brown metal, the lower part with a band of opaque-white loop decoration (minute chip to rim) c. 1780, 6 cm. high. **£80-100** C

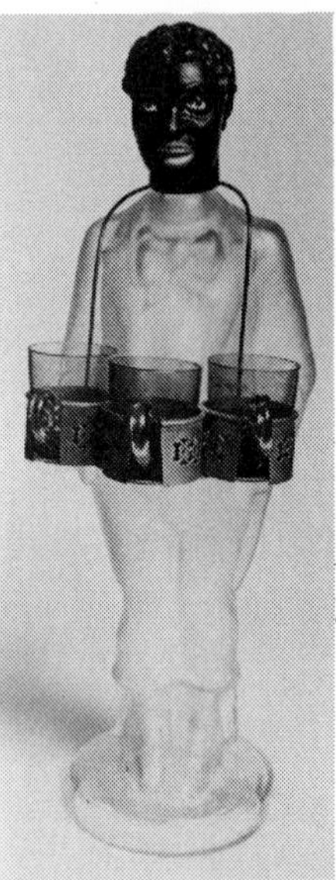

A Large Ale-Tankard with bell bowl, with trailed decoration to the rim, c. 1760, 20 cm. high. **£300-350** C

French frosted glass Liqueur Bottle and Glasses with 'black man' face, c1910-1915, 15". **£60-75**

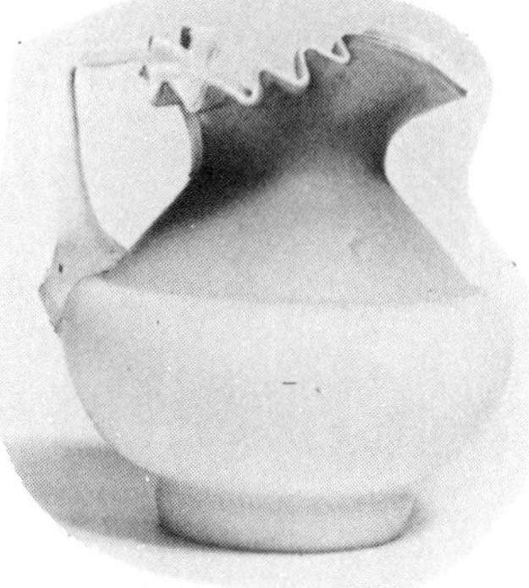

A Stourbridge Satin Glass Ewer, pale amber shading to darker, c1870, 5¼". **£60-70**

A Pair of Early 19th C Irish Floral Cut-glass Dishes, Covers and Stands, 8" (20cms) wide. **£240-280** SKC

A Large Cut Ewer in Neo-Classical style, c1830, 10¼". **£160-190** S

A Liqueur Set, comprising a decanter and six glasses, 1930's, with faults, 26 cm. **£60-70** SBe

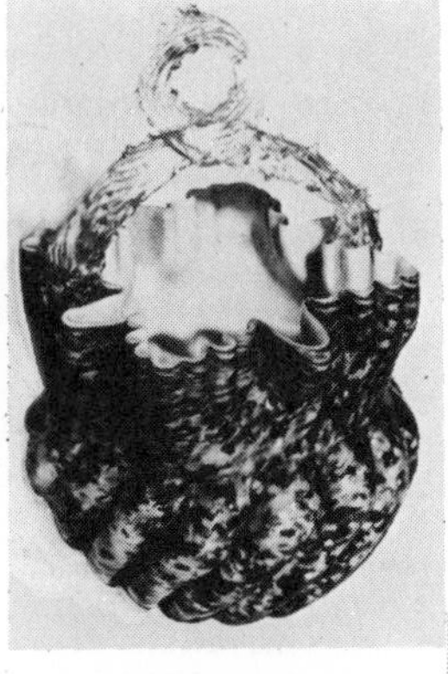

A Victorian 'End-of-Day' Glass Basket, 8 in. high, c. 1880. **£40-45** CA

A 19th C. Bohemian Glass Set, jug with 7 glasses. **£100-115** set. SV

A good Double-handled Jar and Cover, with reeded strap handles, 9½" (24cms), probably Irish. **£185-200** SKC

A Bohemian ruby tinted Tazza with white overlay and gilt painted ornamentation, 6¾" high. **£260-290** AG

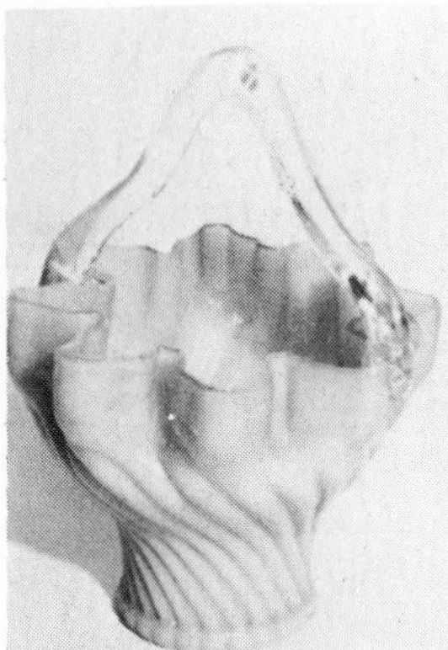

Victorian opaline glass basket **£15-18** AP

A Whitefriars Ink Bottle with matching stopper, 5½ in., 13.3 cm. high. **£120-150** L

A Pair of Bowls and Covers, cut with strawberry diamonds and having fan-cut everted rim, set on knopped and faceted stem and scalloped spreading foot, 23 cm. early 19th C. **£180-210** S Be

POINTERS FOR GLASS
(some different types)

- Cased Glass - glass of one colour covered with one or more layers of different coloured glass. Decoration is engraved through the upper layer. First made in Bohemia in the early 19th C.
- Cut-glass - Fashionable during late 18th C. Decorated with facets in the form of geometric patterns.
- Engraved Glass - Ancient type of decoration done with the aid of a diamond point.
- Etched Glass - Hydrofluoric acid was used to decorate glass during 19th C.
- Frosted Glass - Glass with a matt, opaque outer surface.
- Fruit Glass - First made in Venice during the 18th C. Revived in the 19th C. at Stourbridge. Usually arranged in a basket with glass leaves.
- Lacy Glass - Pressed glass with a stippled background. Manufactured in America by the Boston and Sandwich Glass Co., whose cupplates are especially sought.
- Lime Glass - Substitute for lead glass discovered in 1864 by William Leighton.
- Lutz Glass - Thin, transparent glass striped with coloured twists. Sometimes called 'candy stripe' glass. Introduced by Nicholas Lutz, a French glassworker.
- 'Mary Gregory' Glass - Glass printed with figures of children c. 1870.
- Vaseline Glass - Decorative glass often known as yellow opaline. Best qualities are greenish-yellow. Produced later end of 19th C.

A Bohemian Blue Cameo Glass Biscuit Barrel, with Egyptian scene, 7½ in., c. 1890. **£175-195** CA

An Irish Glass Oval Tea Caddy and Cover, silver-mounted, cut with two bands of large diamonds between flat flutes. 4¾ in., 12 cm. c. 1780-90. **£250-300** L

Degas, a Lalique circular bowl and cover of matt glass. R. Lalique, France, No. 66 mark. 8 cm. diam. **£250-280** C

Cheveux De Venus: a Lalique small bowl and cover, script R. Lalique, France, No. 63 marks. 7 cm. diam. **£250-280** C

A Baccarat 'Malachite' Glass Box, signed with a butterfly, c1920's, 6¾" x 3½", damaged **£10-15** perfect **£90-100**

A French 1920's Green Cameo Narrow Bowl, 4 in. wide, 9 in. long, with gilt floral cameo. **£75-85** CA

A Galle Box with lid, decorated with dragonflies and waterlilies, signed, c1890-1900, 4", small chip **£75-95** perfect **£300-400**

A Galle orange Powder Bowl, with dragonflies, c1890, lid badly damaged; as a bowl **£180-210** with perfect lid,**£300-400**

An Opaque-Blue Bowl and Stand, gilt and enamelled with white flowers, 27.5cms. **£140-160** S.B.

A Delacce Nancy Cameo Landscape Bowl, signed, c1920. **£200-250**

A Small 'Loetz' Green Bowl, not signed, 1920's, 5½" diam. **£60-75**

A Venetian Bowl, ht. 13.5 cm., diam., 43 cm., 17th C. **£800-1,000** S

A Large Cut Glass Fruit Bowl on detachable raised stand, 24cms, mid 19th C, slight chipping, **£110-150** SBe

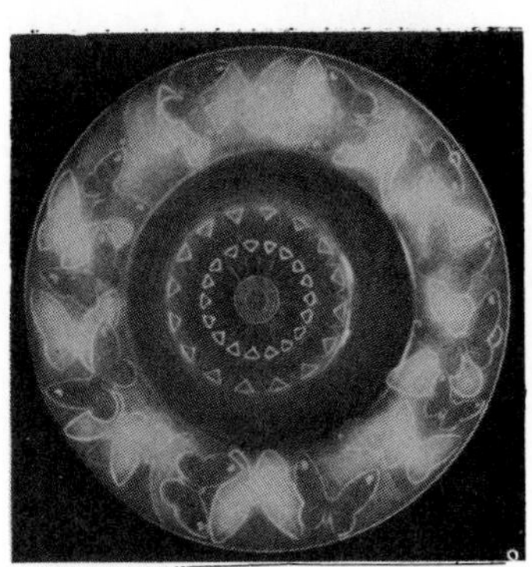

A Lalique Opalescent Glass Bowl, the rim with butterflies, engraved 'R. Lalique, France' 1920's, with faults, diam. 39 cm. **£230-280** SBe

A Spanish Latticinio Shallow Bowl decorated with swirling bands of opaque-white herring-bone, probably Catalonia, 18th C., 18 cm. diam. **£180-200** C

A Pair of Continental Glass Covered Bowls and Stands, 17cms high, late 18th/early 19th C, **£70-100** SBe

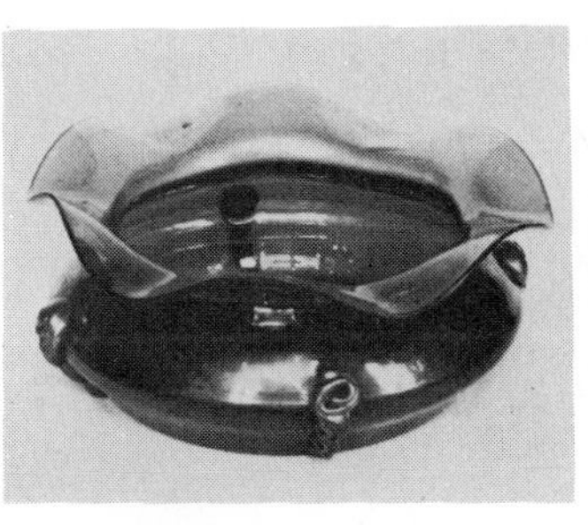

An Art Nouveau Lustre Bowl, c. 1910. **£44-48** AP

An Art Nouveau Lustre Bowl. **£44-48** AP

A Victorian Milk Glass Dish.
£19-22 AP

A Loetz cobalt blue glass papillon Vase, 7" high. **£325-375** SAL

A Pair of Loetz iridescent Vases with peacock blue iridescent splashes with a chased silver overlay of orchids, 18cms high.
£300-350 P

A Loetz iridescent glass Vase with a chased silver design, 31cms high. **£380-450** P

A Loetz type squat-shape vase of iridescent glass, with metal border of trellis lappets. 5 in., 12.7 cm.
£25-35 L

A Pair of Victorian Cranberry Glass Vases, 10½ in. **£65-75** pr. CSG

A French Pink Opaline Glass Vase, c1880, 6¾". **£30-50**

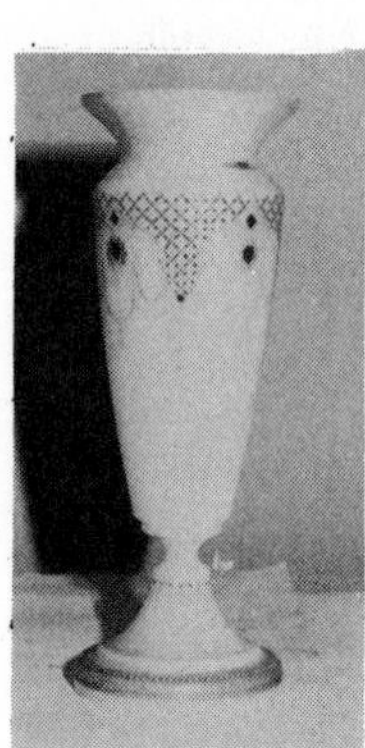

A French blue Opaline Glass Vase, c1880, 10". **£60-75** in France **£150-175**

An Art Nouveau Vase in the style of Loetz, blue with silvery and pink iridescence, splashed and marbled. 10¾ in., 27.3 cm. **£150-230** L

One of a pair of 19th C Opaline Vases, 12½in high. **£40-45 pr.**
SV

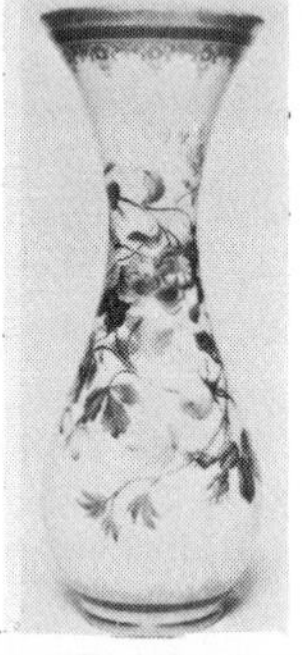

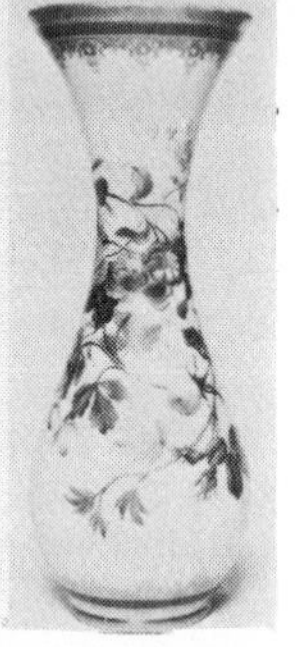

An Enamelled Opaline Vase, the foot and mouth rims with gilt and turquoise borders, c. 1850, 40.1 cm. **£170-200**
SB

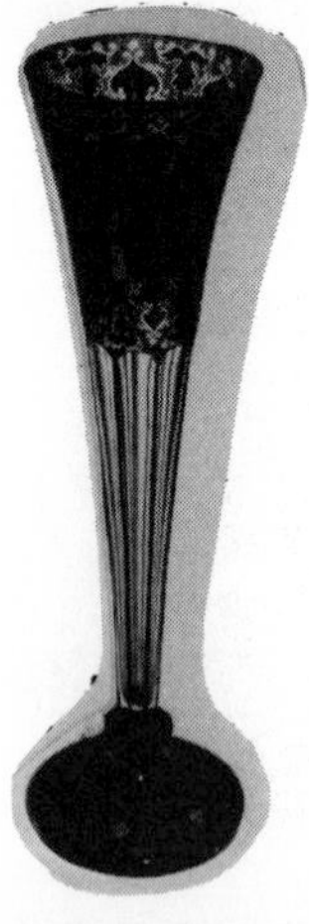

A Stourbridge Vase, jewelled, with small glass beads, c1870's, 5". **£45-50**

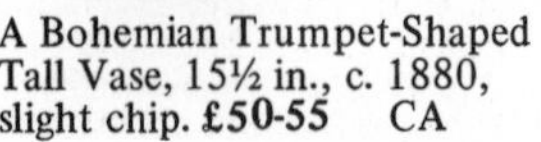

A Bohemian Trumpet-Shaped Tall Vase, 15½ in., c. 1880, slight chip. **£50-55** CA

A Pair of French Opaline Glass Vases with pink and blue flowers and green leaves, the stems outlined in gold, mid-19th C. 12¾ in., 32.4 cm. **£190-250** L

A Victorian Stourbridge Glass Vase. **£19-23** AP

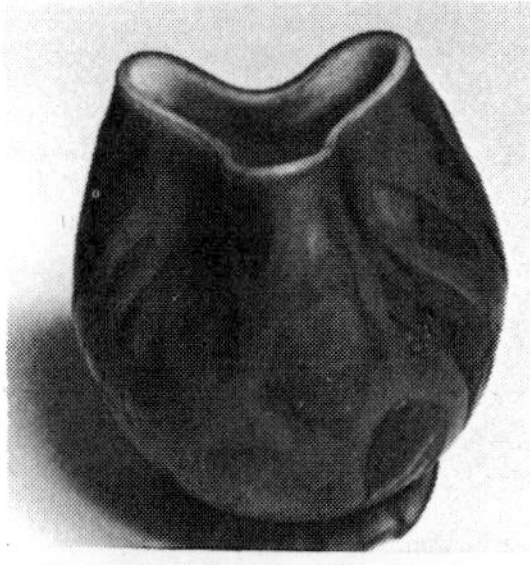
A Stourbridge small specimen Vase, with amber tiger's stripes, c1870, 3¼" high, with some blisters **£20-30** perfect **£75-95**

A Pair of lime/pale green Satin Glass decorated Vases, c1870, 8½". **£75-95**

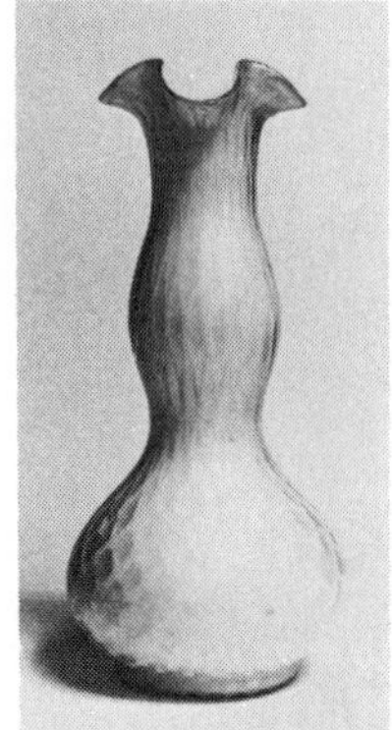
A Quilted Satin Glass Vase, pale blue shading to darker blue, c1870, 9½". **£50-60**

A Pair of blue quilted Satin Glass Vases, 8". **£75-95**

One of a Pair of Pink Quilted Satin Glass Vases with stripes, c1870, 9½". **£200-250 pr.**

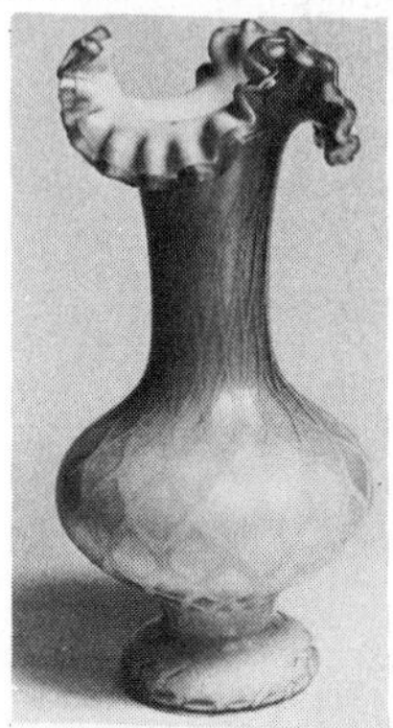
A Pink Quilted Satin Glass Vase, with frilly top, c1870, 9" high, perfect **£90-100** chip **£20-25**

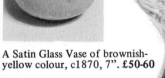

A Satin Glass Vase of brownish-yellow colour, c1870, 7". **£50-60**

A Satin Glass Vase, with 'frilly' top and blue decoration, c1870, 9½". **£75-95**

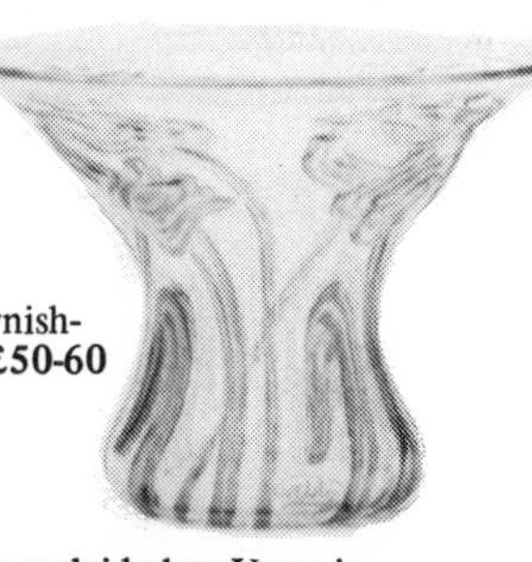
A Webb overlaid glass Vase, in pink overlay, cameo mark 'Webb', late 19th C, 17cms high. **£120-140** SBe

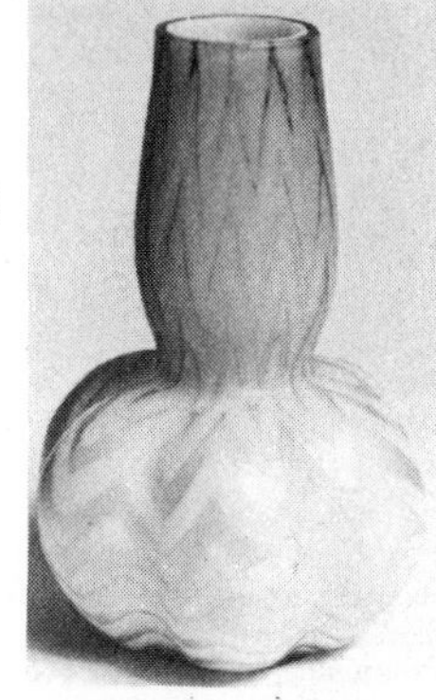
A Pale Blue Quilted Candy-Stripe Satin Glass Vase, c1870, 5¼". **£45-50**

A Very Rare Burmese Polished Decorated Vase, c. 1880, 4 in. high (only made for a few years), made from uranium and gold. **£200-230.** signed **£500-560** damaged **£50-60** CA

A Webb Green Glass Vase, the body overlaid in red and white, marked Thomas Webb & Sons, 1880's, 7.2cms. **£400-450** SBe

A Spanish Four-Handled Vase of bluish opalescence, with trailed decoration above a band of loops, early 18th C., 19 cm. high. **£200-220** C

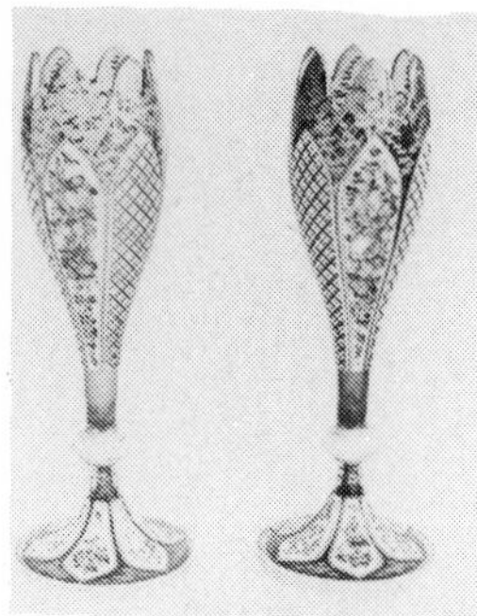

A Pair of 19th C cranberry glass overlay Vases, probably English, 11" high. **£238-300** SAL

A 19th C. painted glass Vase. **£25-28** SV

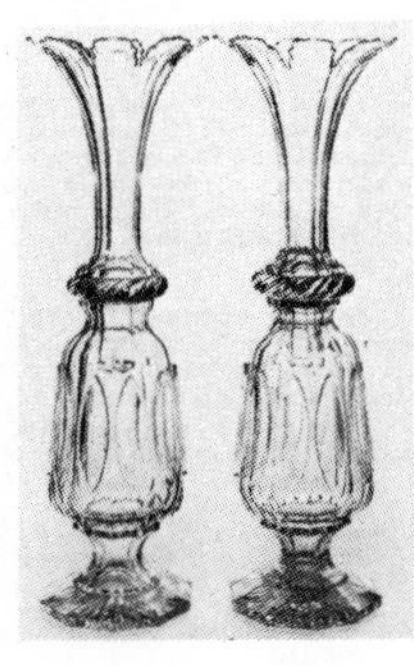

A Pair of Cut Glass Vases c1850, 59.2cms. **£180-200** S.B.

A Portrait Overlay Vase, in ruby glass, c1850, 42.5cms. **£280-320** S.B.

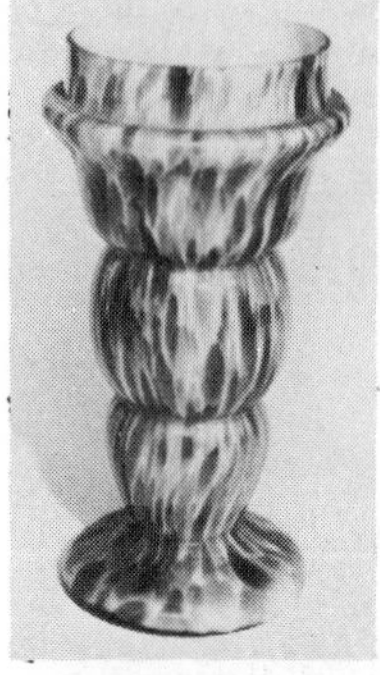

A Victorian 'End-of-the-Day' Glass Vase. **£9-12** AP

A Vase with elongated bell bowl on flattened knop and circular foot, marked E. Varnish & Co., Patent, London, c. 1850, 23 cm. **£320-380** SB

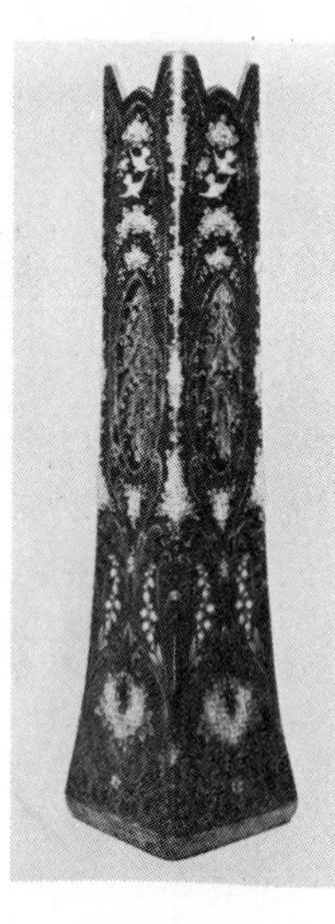

A Large Flower Encrusted Vase in amethyst glass, c. 1900 74.4 cm. **£150-190** SB

A Peking "marbled" glass vase with olive-brown and greenish yellow striations in the opaque grey body 18th C., wood stand 5½ in., 14 cm. high. **£80-100** C

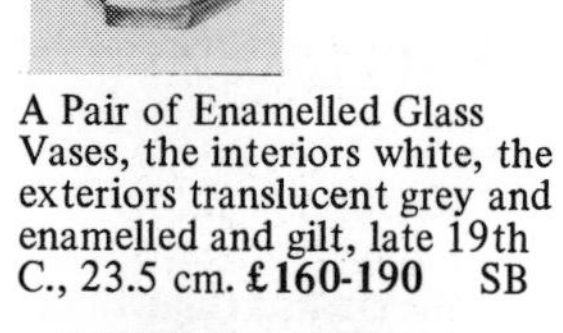

A Pair of Enamelled Glass Vases, the interiors white, the exteriors translucent grey and enamelled and gilt, late 19th C., 23.5 cm. **£160-190** SB

An unusually large pair of 'Mary Gregory' Ruby Glass Vases enamelled in white, c. 1850, 51.5 cm. **£270-310** SB

A Nailsea Vase, chipped, 4½ins high **£15-20** SQE

A fine small Galle cameo glass vase overlaid in lilac and green on a cloudy pink ground, 9 cm. cameo mark Galle. **£225-250** SKC

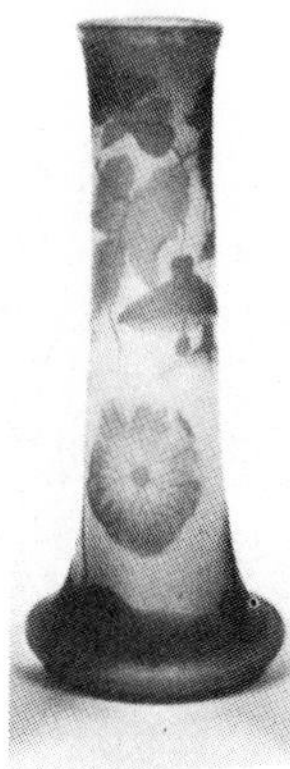

A Galle Cameo Glass Vase, the greyish body overlaid with two tones of orange glass acid-etched, signed with pseudo Oriental signature, 36cms high. **£380-480** P

An Escalier De Cristal Ormolu-Mounted Cameo Vase, the opalescent ground overlaid in pale pink and dark olive-green, signed on both the glass and ormolu, the glass probably by Galle, 16.5 cm. high. **£800-900** C

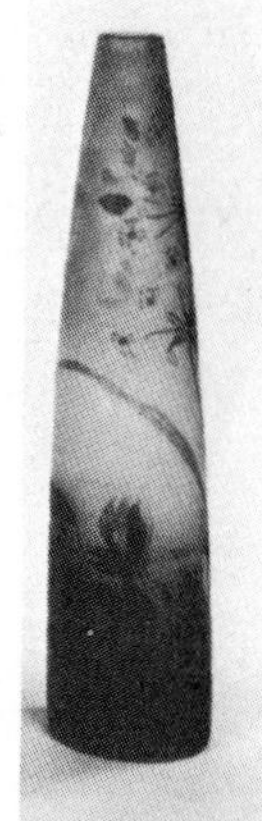

A Galle Cameo Vase, the grey body tinted pale green at the top and overlaid in brown and pale blue, 37.50cms high, signed in cameo Galle. **£530-580** P

A Galle Cameo globular Vase, overlaid with ruby glass, 9cms high, signed in cameo Galle. **£300-350** P

A Galle Cameo Slender Oviform Vase the matt green ground overlaid in lime-green, pink and brown, signed. 56.5 cm. high. **£920-1,000** C

POINTERS FOR ART GLASS

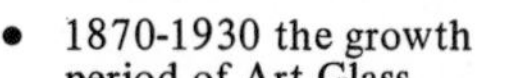

- 1870-1930 the growth period of Art Glass.

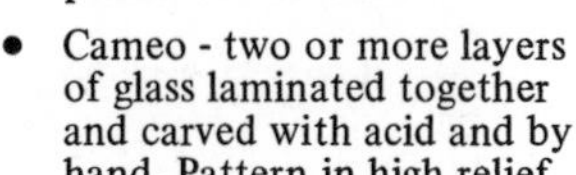

- Cameo - two or more layers of glass laminated together and carved with acid and by hand. Pattern in high relief.

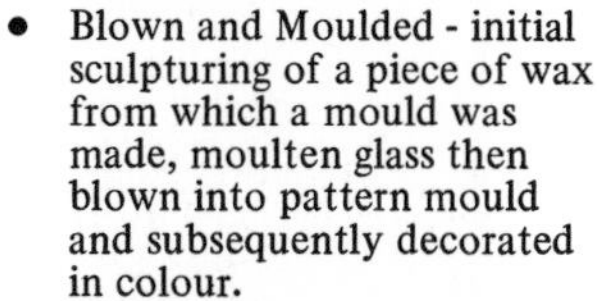

- Blown and Moulded - initial sculpturing of a piece of wax from which a mould was made, moulten glass then blown into pattern mould and subsequently decorated in colour.
- Metallic - decorated, silver, gold and other coloured metal trapped under the outer layer of glass.
- Intaglio - carved out work of the kind used in seals and signet rings.
- Enamelled - the addition of tin oxide to glass to produce an opaque white substance.
- Marquetry - the art of inlaying glass in glass.
- Moss Agate - used as fine decoration between glass layers.

A Galle cameo glass vase, the frosted ground overlaid in mauve and claret glass, 12 cm., Galle signature in cameo. **£350-400** SKC

A Galle Cameo Tapering Oviform Vase, the mottled peach ground overlaid in lime-green and olive-green, signed. 35 cm. high. **£1,000-1,200** C

A Galle Enamelled Three-handled vase in the Persian style, the bowl etched and flashed in amber enamelled with red, white and blue dots, handles enriched with gilding, engraved signature to base, 15 cm. high. **£700-800** C

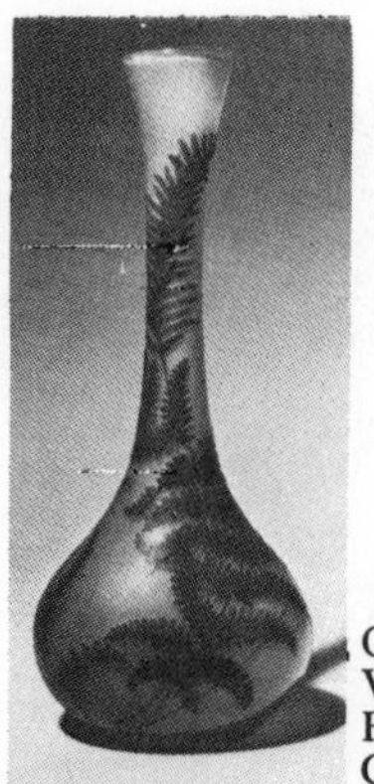

A Galle Cameo Soli-Fleur Vase, the mottled green and matt ground overlaid in green and carved and fire-polished, early signature. 39.5 cm., high. **£1,100-1,300** C

Ormeaux, a Lalique Globular Vase, script signature R. Lalique France, 6½" high. **£230-280** CSK

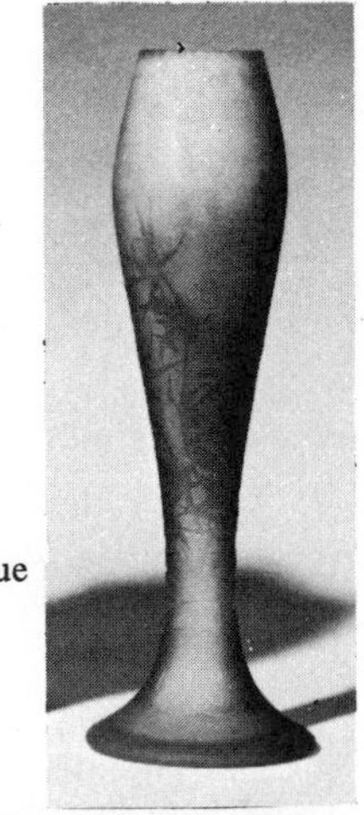

A Galle Cameo Vase the matt greenish-pink ground overlaid in lime-green, signed. 34 cm. high. **£400-450** C

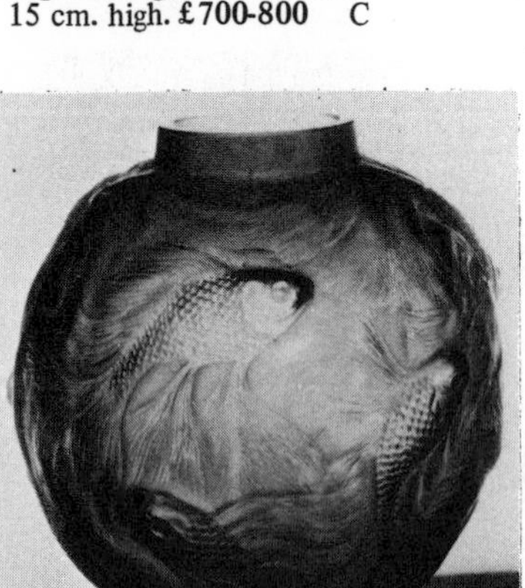

Formose: A Lalique globular vase script R. Lalique, France No. 934 marks. 16.5 cm. high. **£240-280** C

Prunes, a Lalique Vase of inverted bell form, signed R. Lalique France, 7" high. **£320-380** CSK

A Pale Blue Frosted Glass Vase by Lalique, signed in block R. Lalique France, 7" high. **£340-380** CSK

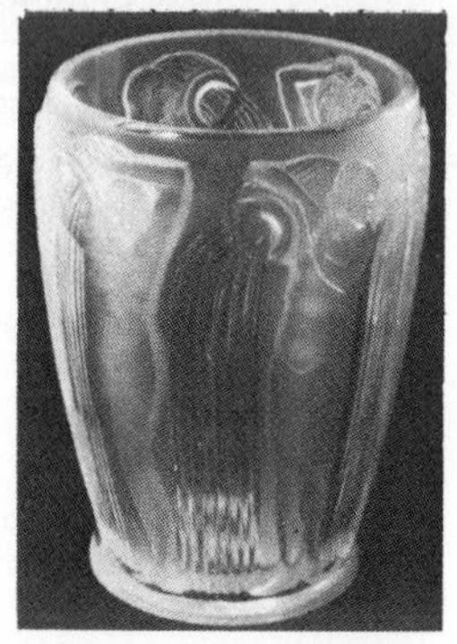

"La Source", a Lalique opalescent glass vase, 18 cm., moulded mark R. Lalique, engraved France. **£360-400** SKC

A Muller Freres Cameo Globular Vase the matt ground with yellow and blue mottling towards the base overlaid in red, signed. 15 cm. high. **£620-700** C

A Lalique glass vase, of bluish opalescent tone, marked R. Lalique. France. 7 in., 18.4 cm. **£370-470** L

A Large Lalique Oviform Vase (two small chips to foot rim). R. Lalique, France mark 21.5 cm. high. **£520-570** C

A Tiffany-Favrile Turquoise Iridescent Vase engraved L. C. Tiffany-Favrile, No. 8166 H mark. 13.5 cm. diam. **£450-500** C

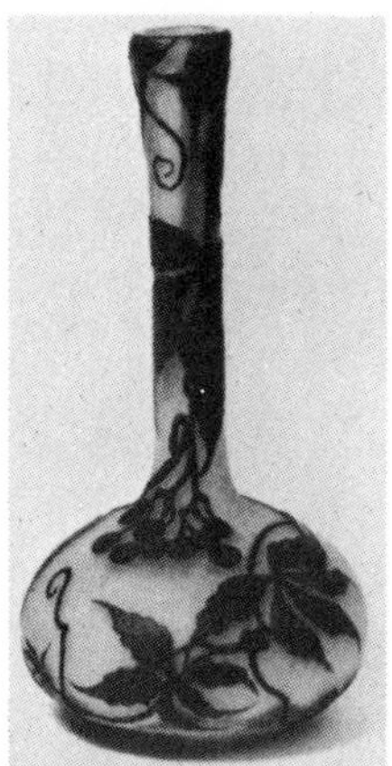

A Muller Freres Cameo glass Vase, the yellow body overlaid with reddish brown glass, 16.75cms high, Muller Fres Luneville. **£225-250** P

A Daum cameo Vase, the honey-tinted body overlaid with pale brown glass, 15cms high, signed Daum, Nancy. **£470-500** P

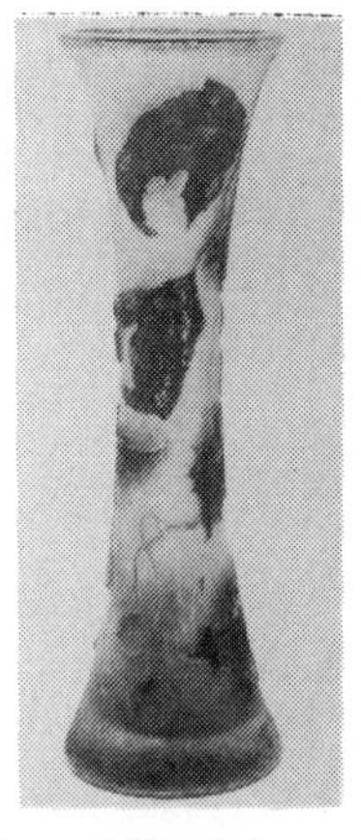

A Vase of Opalescent Frosted Glass by Daum, Nancy, decorated in relief in gold, 13½ in., 34.3 cm., signed Daum Nancy in gold. **£220-280** L

A Cameo Vase, the pale amber ground overlaid in opaque white (very slight chip to foot rim) impressed Stevens & Williams, Stourbridge Art Glass marks to base, c. 1890, 11.5 cm. high. **£220-260** C

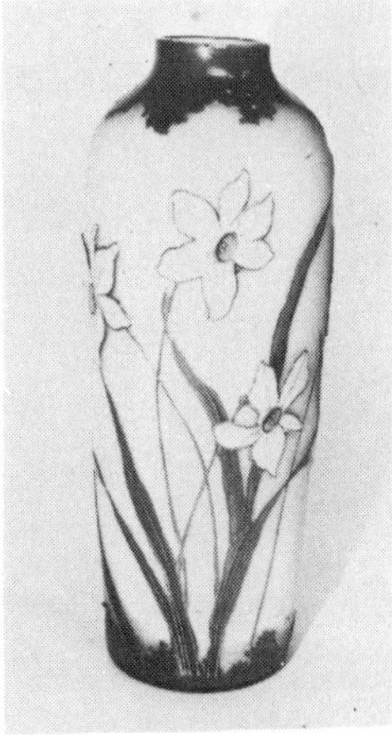

An Art Nouveau French Nancy Glass Vase. **£95-105** AP

A grey moulded glass Vase, with ormolu-type mounts, by G. de Feure, c1930's. **£90-100**

A J. F. Christy (Lambeth) Oviform Vase designed by Richard Redgrave for the Summerly Art Manufactures, printed R. Redgrave ARA, initial and monogram marks, 1847, 15 cm. high. **£450-500** C

A Pair of Ruby Overlaid Glass Lustres, 37 cm. 19th C. **£350-420** SBe

A Victorian Lustre with cherry red glass, 10 in. high. **£45-55** VA

A Victorian Lustre, with cherry red glass and ten lustres, 13 in. high. **£50-60** VA

One of a pair of 19th C. painted glass Lustres. **£200-245** pr. SV

A Le Verre Francais cameo glass vase, the dappled yellow body overlaid in orange and purplish-blue, glass acid-etched, 26 cm., engraved mark 1920's. **£290-320** SKC

An 18th C. Glass Candlestick, 7¼ in. high. **£385-400** SA

A Pair of French green and white Opaline Glass Candlesticks, c1880, 6". **£100-150**

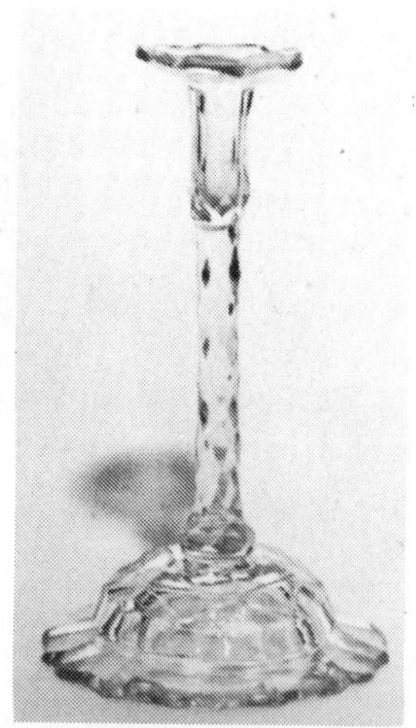

A Fine Late 18th C. Facet-Cut Taperstick, English, c. 1780, 5½ in. high. **£285-310** SA

A Moulded Glass Red Ashay Figure, 5¾ in., 14.5 cm. high, on chromium-plated Red Ashay base fitted for illumination. **£85-95** CSK

A Burmese Glass Epergne, the mounts marked 'Clarkes', 29cms. **£400-450** SBe

A Rare Pair of Opaque-White Tapersticks and Enamel Drip-Pans, (both nozzles and one foot restored) South Staffordshire, c. 1760, 18.5 cm. high. **£450-500** C

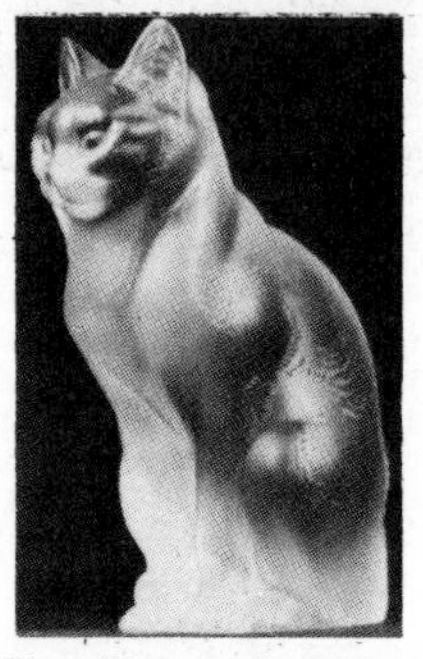

A Glass Figure of a Seated Cat, bearing indistinct Lalique France, signature, 8¼" high. **£440-500** CSK

A Sabino Carp, c1920's, 13" long. **£300-350** cracks in base **£50-60**

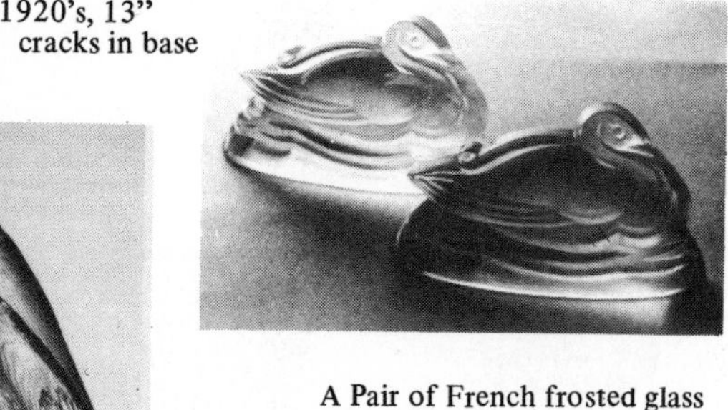

A Pair of French frosted glass swan Menu Holders, signed by Sabino, Paris, c1920's. **£45-55**

Faucon, a Lalique Glass Standing Figure, 6¼ in., 16 cm. high, moulded R. Lalique. **£520-580** CSK

A Pair of French frosted glass Squirrels, signed by M. Model, c1920's, 3½". **£75-85** pr.

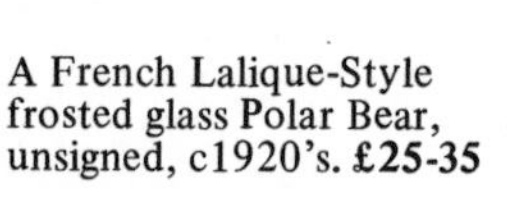

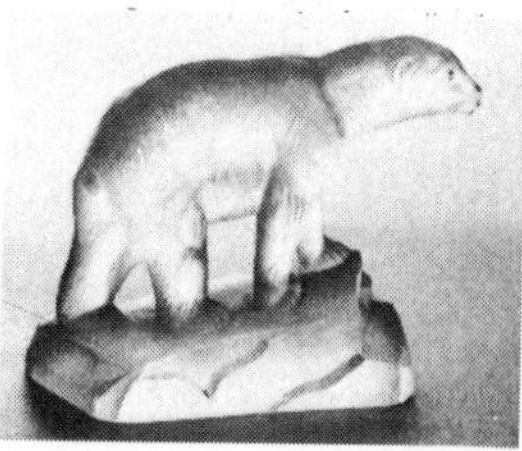

A French Lalique-Style frosted glass Polar Bear, unsigned, c1920's. **£25-35**

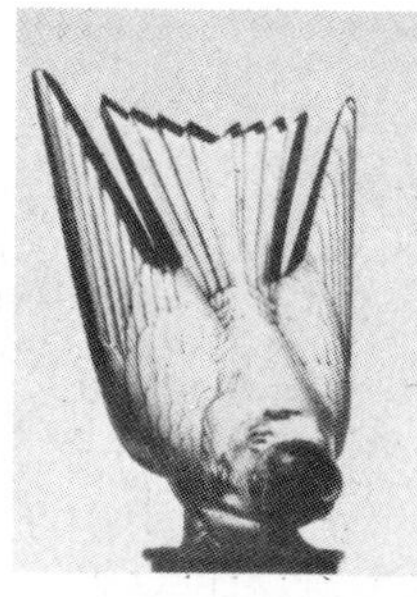

Hirondelle, a Lalique Glass Figure, 5½ in., 14 cm. high, mounted on nickel-plated brass Breves gallery mount. **£580-640** CSK

A Lalique Frosted Glass Figure of a Bison, marked Lalique France. 3½ in., 8.9 cm. **£120-170** L

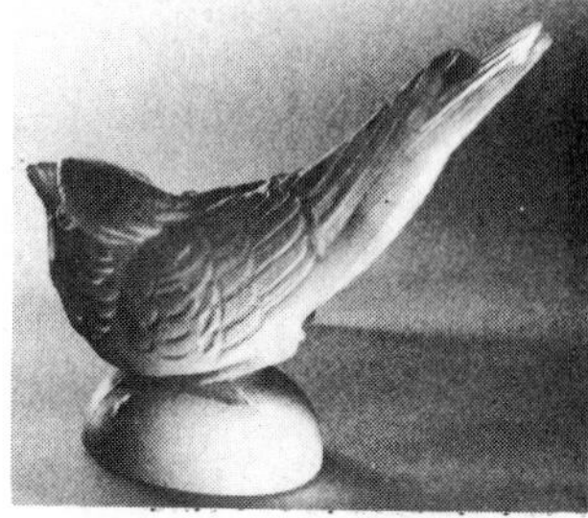

A French Lalique-Style frosted glass Bird, unsigned, c1920's. **£25-35**

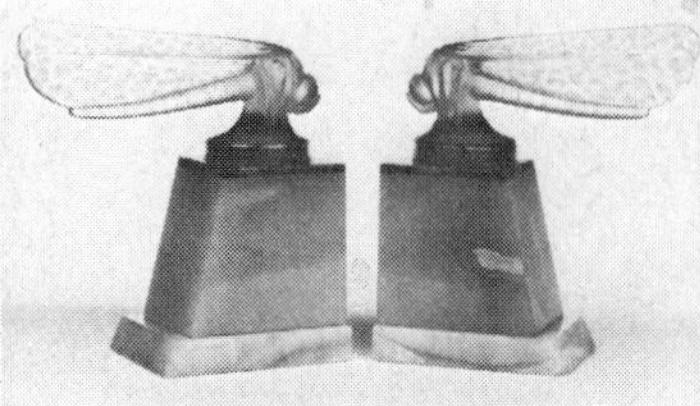

Petites Libellules: a pair of Lalique dragonfly car-mascots mounted as bookends, traces of moulded R. Lalique marks, 16.5cm wide, **£1000-1300** C

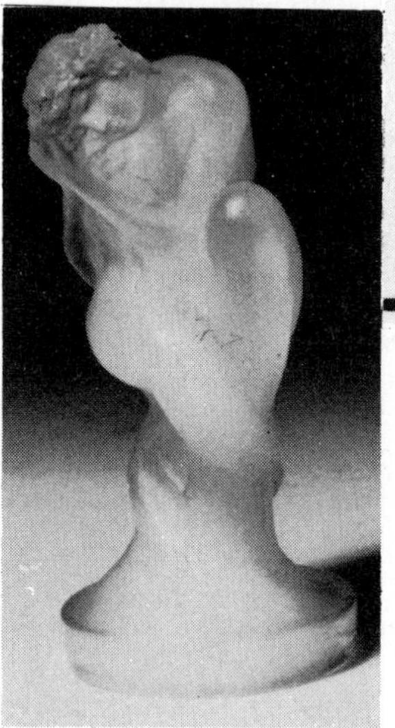

'Sirene'. A Lalique opalescent glass Figure, 10.5cms high, moulded R. Lalique. **£360-400** P

Cinq Chevaux, a Lalique Glass Stylised Figure of Five Rearing Horses 6 in., 15.5 cm. long. **£780-880** CSK

A Baccarat patterned mille-fiori weight, 8 cm. **£170-200** SKC

POINTERS FOR PAPERWEIGHTS

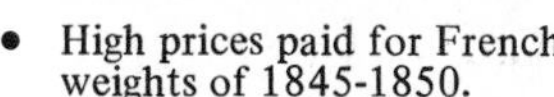
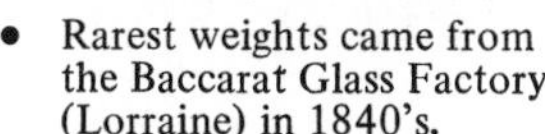

- High prices paid for French weights of 1845-1850.
- Rarest weights came from the Baccarat Glass Factory (Lorraine) in 1840's.
- Decorative glass weights introduced in 19th C.
- Most sought after are 'millefiori' and 'latticinio' types.
- Excellent weights made in Birmingham during 1840's.
- Fine weights came from Saint-Louis in 1840's.

A good St. Louis camomile weight 7.5 cm. (some damage). **£170-200** SKC

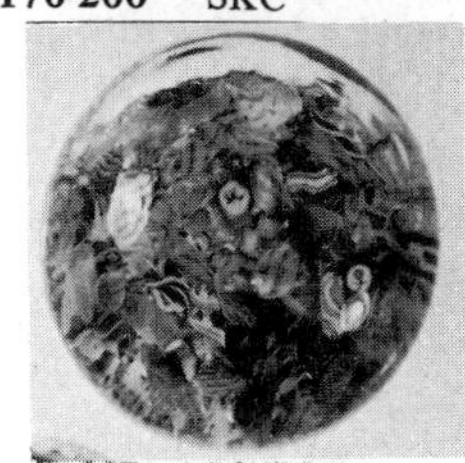

A St. Louis Macedoine Paperweight, magnum size. 4 in., 10.2 cm. **£185-210** L

A Whitefriars Paperweight with portrait of Queen Victoria, 2¾ in., 7 cm. **£85-105** L

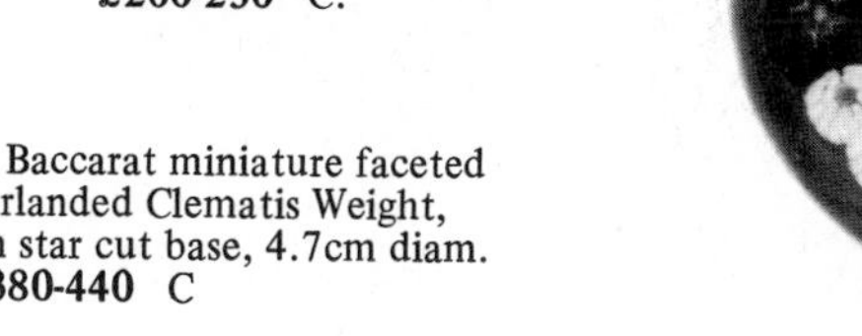

A Clichy blue-ground patterned Millefiori Weight, 5.3cm. diam. **£200-230** C.

A Baccarat miniature faceted garlanded Clematis Weight, on star cut base, 4.7cm diam. **£380-440** C

A Clichy swirl Weight, 6cm. diam. **£380-410** C.

A Baccarat dated concentric Millefiori Weight, dated 1849, 6.4cm. diam. **£540-600** C.

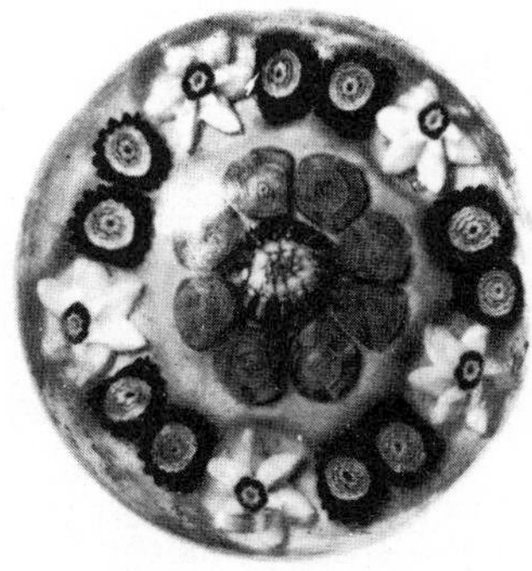

A Clichy miniature turquoise-ground concentric Millefiori Weight, 4.8cm. diam. **£600-680** C

A Baccarat spray Weight, with two dark blue flowers, on star cut base, 6cm. **£680-760** C.

A Baccarat white Clematis Weight, on star cut base, 5.5cm. diam. **£210-240** C.

A St. Louis Fruit Weight, 6cm. diam. **£410-460** C.

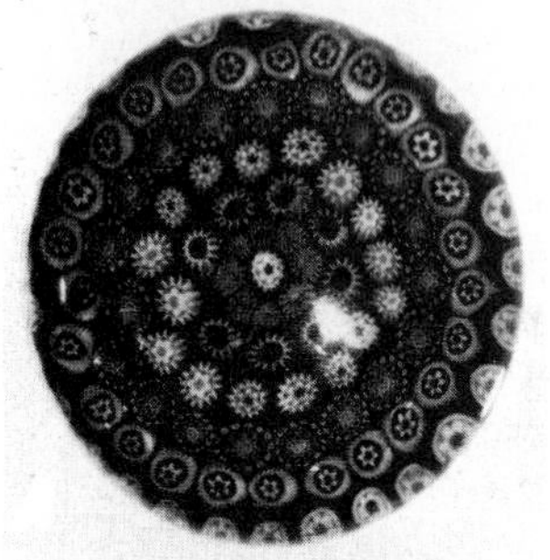

A St. Louis small close concentric Millefiori Weight, in shades of pink, turquoise, lime-green, blue, white and green. 5.5cm. diam. **£280-310** C.

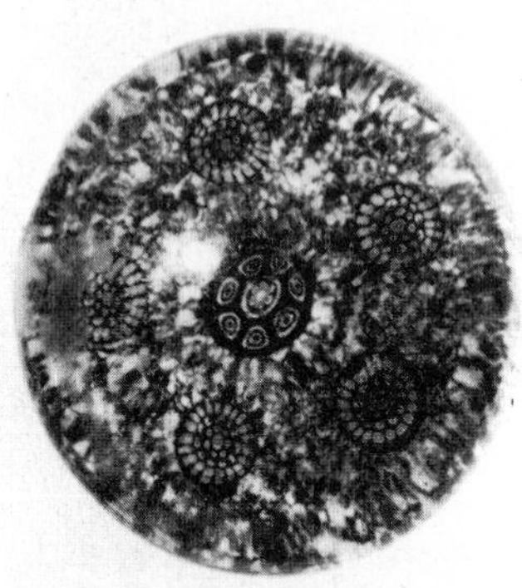

A St. Louis miniature pink jasper-ground concentric Millefiori Weight, 4.8cm. diam. **£180-240** C.

A St. Louis white Camomile Weight, set on a ground of alternate translucent pink and white swirling spirals, 5.7cm. diam. **£610-690** C.

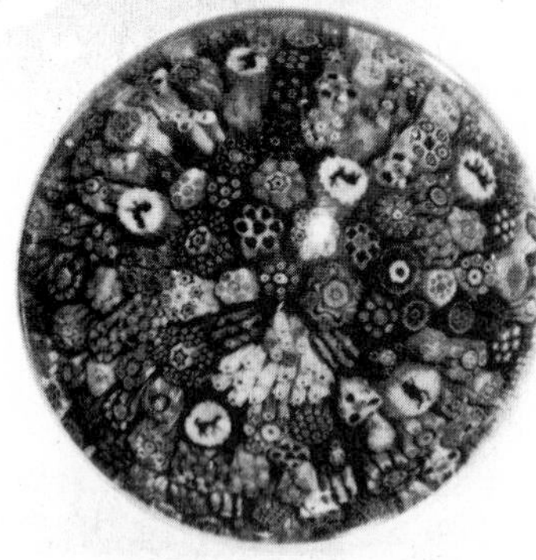

A Baccarat dated close Millefiori Weight, dated 1848, 6.cm. diam. **£350-390** C.

A Clichy miniature red-ground concentric Millefiori Weight, 4.7cm. diam. **£410-450** C.

A New England faceted yellow Poinsettia Weight, 6.3cm. diam. **£500-560** C.

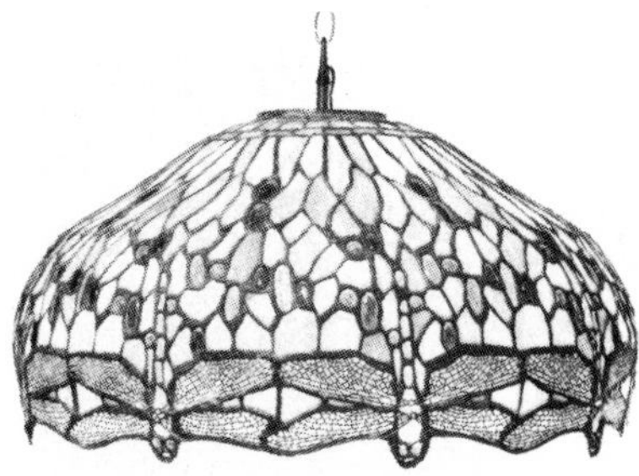

A Large Tiffany Style 'Hanging-Head' Dragonfly Shade, with Metal ceiling fittings and bulb holders, 61cms diam. **£560-680** P

A French Cameo Ceiling Shade, with cherries, c1920's, small crack **£75-85** perfect **£150-175**

A small Glass Oil Lamp and shade, marked 'Webb Queen's Burmese Ware Patented', 1880's, 21.5cms. **£250-280** SBe

A 'Le Verre Francais' Chandelier, the pink tinted glass overlaid with amethyst and acid-etched with crysanthemums, 40cms diam., signed 'Le Verre Francais'. **£420-480** P

A set of four George III cut-glass wall lights with giltmetal semi-circular central bracket supports, 26 in., 66 cm. **£2,000-2,200** C

A Pair of Regency cut-glass candelabra hung with pendant pear-shaped drops flanking Prince of Wales plumes, fitted for electricity, 16 in., 42 cm. high. **£550-600** C

A Late Victorian Silver-Mounted Glass Brandy Barrel, scroll supports and plated tap, 8½ in., 21.5 cm. long, by Hukin & Heath, Birmingham, 1896. **£280-310** SBe

A Candy-Stripe Satin Glass Night Light with pressed glass base, c1870, 4¼". **£60-80**

A French Lace-Maker's Lamp, the bowl with bulbous upper part, supported on a hollow shoulder-knopped stem with everted drip-pan, mid-18th C. 25.5 cm. high. **£160-190** C

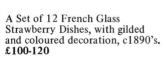

A Set of 12 French Glass Strawberry Dishes, with gilded and coloured decoration, c1890's. **£100-120**

A Daum cameo Table Lamp of greyish tone overlaid with mottled tones of yellow, orange and green, 34cms high, signed in cameo Daum, Nancy and with monogram. **£900-1,000** P

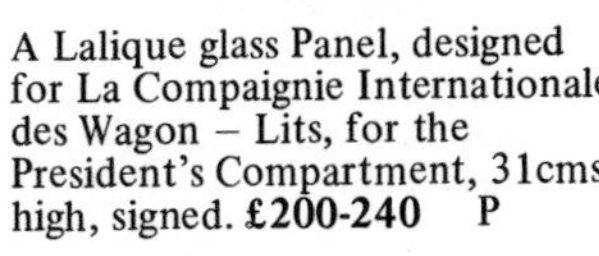

A Lalique glass Panel, designed for La Compaignie Internationale des Wagon – Lits, for the President's Compartment, 31cms high, signed. **£200-240** P

An English Stained Glass Panel in sepia and yellow, 11 in. x 8½ in., 28 cm. x 21 cm. early 16th C. releaded, set within later glass. **£450-500** S

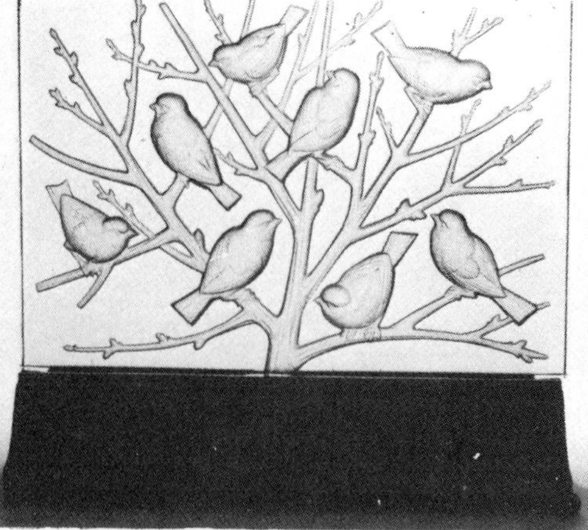

A Lalique Rectangular Glass Panel, the glass engraved in block R. Lalique, France, 34.50cms. **£1,800-2,000** P

A Leaded Glass Panel of Sir Galahad, 33 by 16¼ in., 84 by 41 cm., c. 1910. **£210-230** SB

A Georgian copper kettle classic shape, good condition 11 in. high. **£120-140** BA

A Georgian copper kettle brass handle and knob 10 in. high. **£120-140** BA

A Good Copper Kettle, of conventional form with high brass scroll handle, late 18th C., 13½ in., 34 cm. high. **£90-100** L

An early Victorian copper kettle with Georgian seam –
7 in. diam. **£85-95**
6½ in. diam. **£75-85**
6 in. diam. **£65-75**
5 in. diam. **£55-65** BA

A Small Victorian copper kettle 6 in. diam. **£30-40** BA

An early Victorian copper kettle, porcelain handle 8 in. high 5 in. diam. c. 1840. **£95-105** BA

A Copper Kettle, 11¾ in. high, c. 1860. **£59-65** CL

A large Victorian copper kettle, with brass knob 8½ in. replaced knob. **£63-73** BA

A Georgian Copper Bachelors' kettle 7 in. high. **£75-85** BA

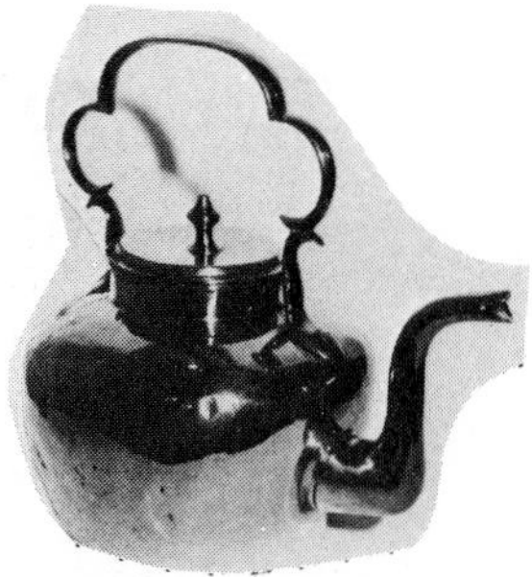

A Copper kettle Dutch style c. 1810 10 in. high 5½ in. diam. **£95-105** BA

Copper Kettle, mid 19th C., 9 in. high. **£50-55** TT

A Large Georgian copper kettle, unusual shape. **£140-160** 10 in. high 9½ in. diam. BA

A very early Victorian copper kettle 8½ in. high 6 in. diam. c. 1830. **£65-75** BA

COPPER

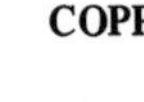

- Pre-18th C objects are rare and invariably highly priced.
- Folded, machine-made seams, if slightly uneven, indicate handmade, and usually pre-1850, manufacture.
- Old copper is always pitted to some extent and is generally heavier than modern reproductions equivalents.

A small Copper chocolate pot c. 1800 8¾ in. replaced handle. **£85-95** original handle **£100-120** BA

A Copper chocolate pot 10 in. c. 1820. **£80-100** BA

A 19th C Copper Saucepan, 5" high. **£35-38** A.L.

A copper chocolate pot, lovely simple lines 8½ in. c. 1820. **£80-120** BA

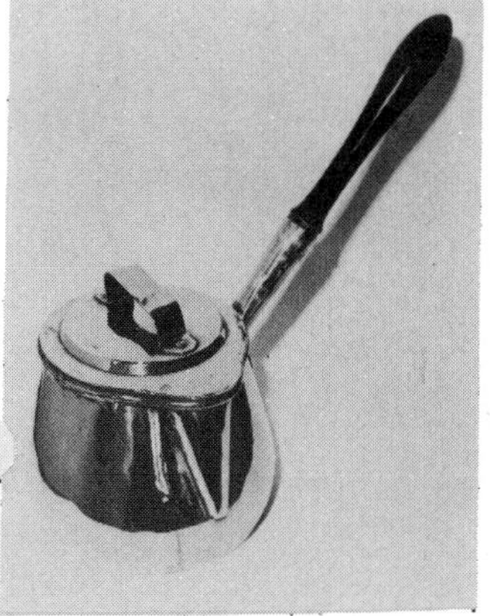

A Copper sauce saucepan Georgian 6 in. diam. **£105-120** BA

A Copper chocolate pot, early 19th C. **£44-55** BA

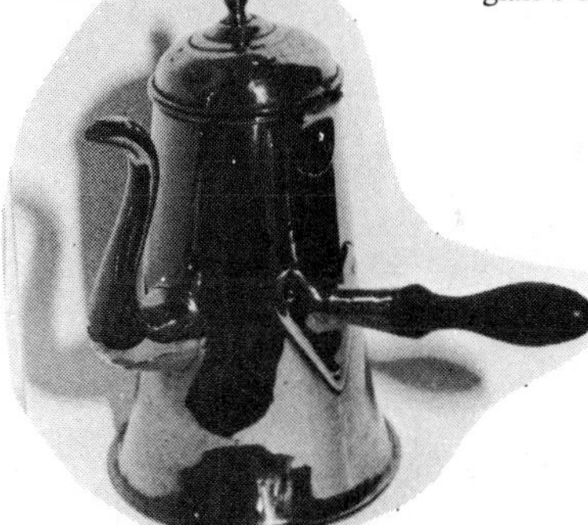

A Copper chocolate pot c. 1820 11 in. high. **£130-160** BA

A pair of Copper saucepans, 19th C, 5" diam., 6" diam. **£60-65** A.L.

A Copper Tea Urn c. 1840, 17 in. high Victorian brass tap, bronze handles. **£250-300** BA

19th C. Copper Pans, 6 in. diam. – **£35,** 7½ in. diam. – **£40-45** CSG

Georgian Copper ladle with wooden handle (Replaced) 2pt. **£47-54** BA

A Good Late Regency Copper Urn, the brass top with ivory grip, 16 in., 41 cm. high. **£100-180** L

An Early Victorian Copper Urn with opaque white glass handles and brass tap., 17 in., 43 cm. high. **£100-150** L

A Copper Urn with brass tap (tap fixture missing) 13 in. high, Georgian. **£125-150** BA

A Copper vegetable dish c. 1860 ceramic interior 10 in. wide. **£60-70** BA

A Lidded insulated copper jug, late Victorian 11 in. **£36-40** BA

A 19th C. Copper Measure, 7 in. high. **£25-30** CSG

A Copper Jug, late Victorian 11 in. high. **£30-40** BA

A Copper bucket c. 1900, 12 in. high. **£55-65** BA

A Copper Saucepan of almost pear shape with cylindrical iron handle, the removable cover with strap handle, 7 in., 18 cm. **£38-46** L

Five Copper Measures of haystack form, graduating in sizes from ½ pint to 1 gallon. **£180-250** L

A Dutch Copper and Brass Peat or Ash Bin, 15 in. high, c. 1810. **£150-170** CL

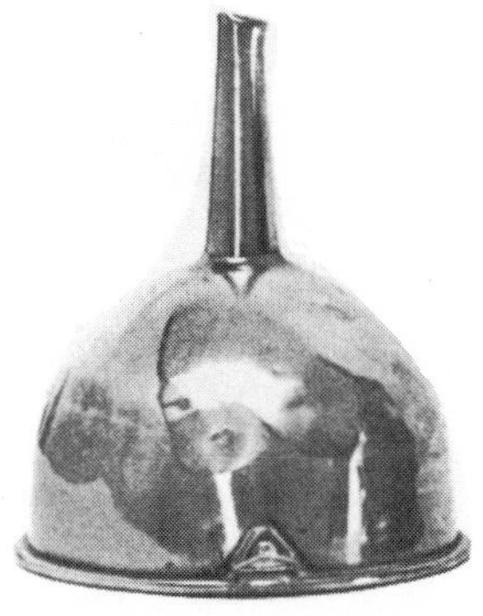

A copper funnel, 19th C. **£8-10** A.L.

A 19th C. Scottish Copper Whisky Measure, for one gallon. **£200-220** SA

A Victorian copper frying pan, with tinned interior. 7in diam. **£44-55** BA

A Copper Jam Pan 15 in. diam. Victorian. **£95-105** BA

A Victorian copper skimmer spoon with steel handle 22 in. long. **£35-45** BA

A Victorian Copper skimmer spoon with holes on one side, with steel handle 22 in. long **£35-45** BA

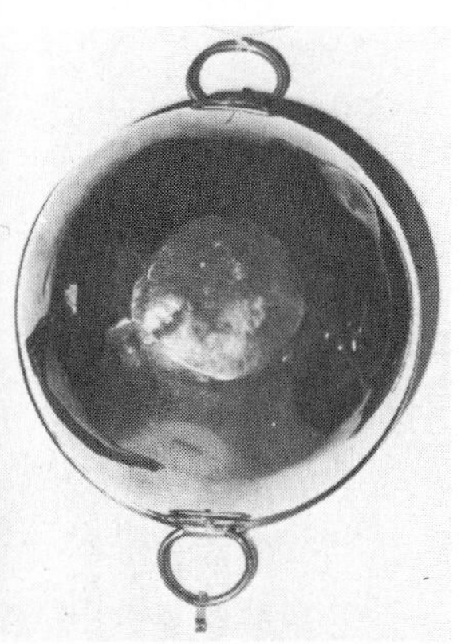

A Copper Bowl, 10¾ in. diam., c. 1875. **£45-50** CL

Two 19th C. Copper Jelly Moulds. **£46-50** CSG

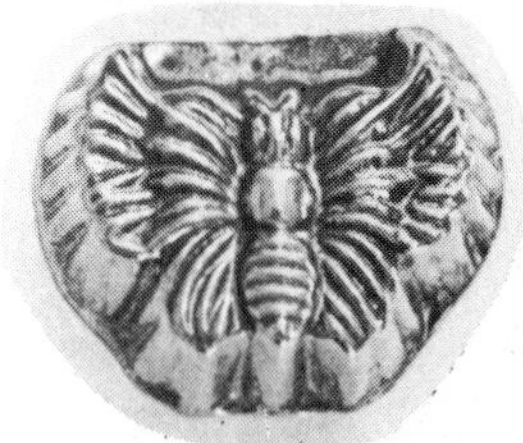

A pair of copper butterfly moulds, 3" diam. **£16-18** pair. A.L.

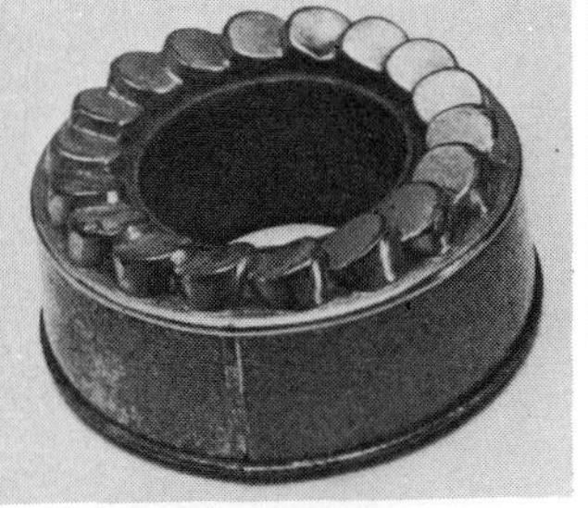

Copper and tin ring mould, 6" diam. **£25-30** A.L.

A Copper boar's head jelly mould c. 1900 6 in. wide. **£40-50** BA

A Victorian Copper Coal helmet scuttle. **£75-85** BA

Copper and tin mould. **£30-32** A.L.

A Georgian copper helmet scuttle c. 1820, very good condition. **£95-105** BA

A Copper hot-water bottle, Edwardian 9 in. diam. **£25-30** BA

A matched Graduated set of four Copper Beer Jugs, height 11½" – 7½" (29–19cms). **£420-480** SH

A 19th C. Copper Warming Pan. **£78-88** CSG

A Copper paraffin oil-can/ measure 3 in. high late 19th C. **£18-20** BA

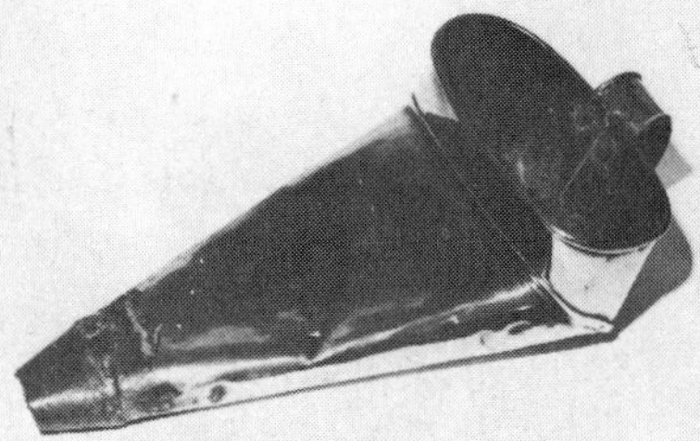

A Copper slipper wine muller, Victorian. **£45-55** BA

A Victorian Copper hot water can, **£30-40** BA

Copper candlesticks, c. 1820, were plated. **£65-75** BA

A Copper Art Deco electric fire, with brass feet. **£55-65** BA

A 19th C. copper figure of The Dancing Faun 81 cm., 32 in. high, **£210-250** O

A 19th C Oriental Coppered Dragon on stand, 7" long. **£80-95** SQE

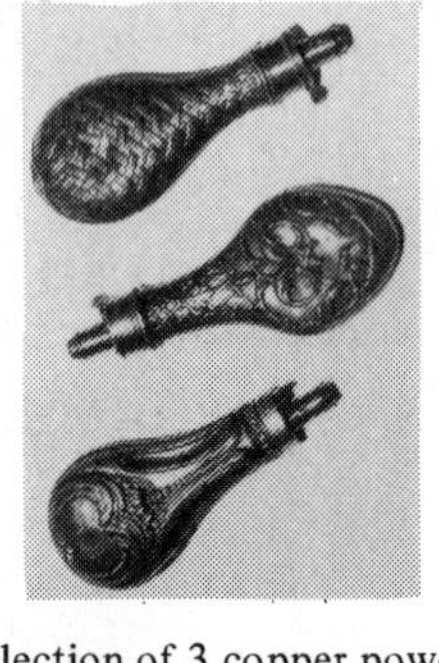

A selection of 3 copper powder flasks. **£45-65** BA

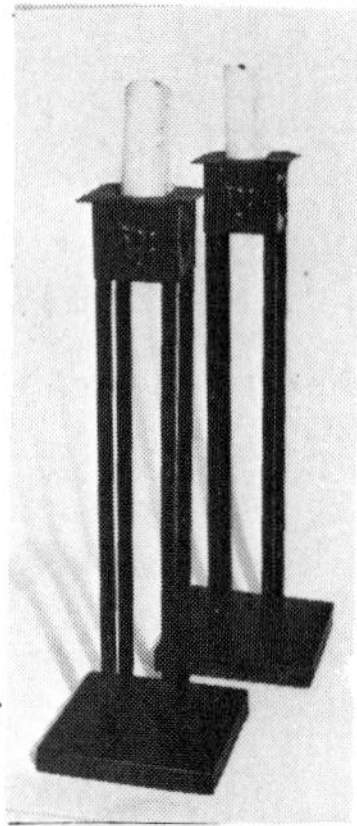

Art Nouveau Copper Candlesticks, c. 1914. **£45-50** pr. AP

An Art Nouveau Copper Mirror, 21½ in. high. **£65-75** SV

A Copper Coach foot warmer Victorian. **£45-55** BA

A Fine and unusual pair of copper and gilt-mounted ebony rounded rectangular small vases, signed on two gilt metal tablets Tsukahara Katao, late 19th C., 14.4 cm. high. **£900-1,000** C

An Art Nouveau hammered copper shop sign 'Antiques and Curios'. **£90-100** WHL

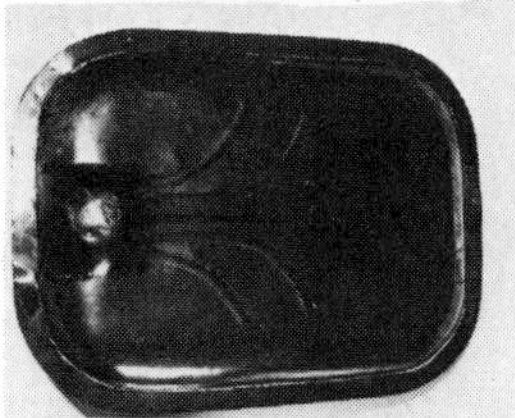

A Copper Turkey Dish 21 in. high, Victorian. **£35-45** BA

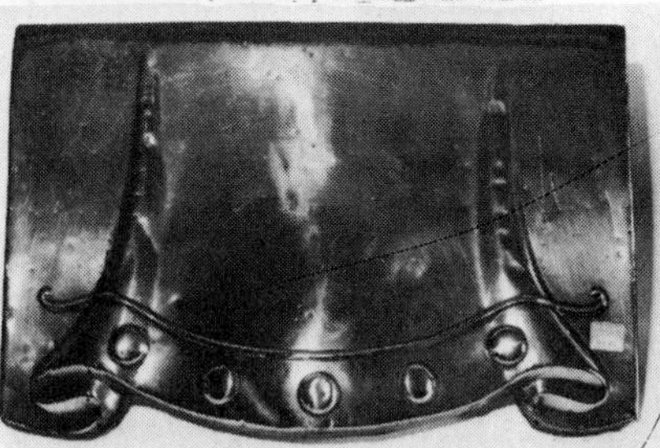

A Copper fire hood Art Nouveau, 20 in. wide. **£15-20** BA

A Brass Chamber Candlestick, c. 1840-50. **£36-46** CL

An 18th C Brass Chamber Candlestick, 6¾" (17cms) diam. **£20-30** SKC

A pair of brass chamber candlesticks, the knopped stems with slide pushers, early 19th C., 5 in., 12.5 cm. **£220-250** pr. L

A Brass Chamber Candlestick, c. 1860. **£32-42** CL

A George III Brass Oval Chamber Candlestick, 7½" (18cms) diam. **£45-65** SKC

A Brass Chamber Candlestick with push ejector, c. 1800. **£52-62** CL

A Pair of Early 19th C. Brass Candlesticks, 8 in. high. **£48-58** SA

A Pair of Brass Candlesticks, 9½ in. high, c. 1830. **£54-64** CL

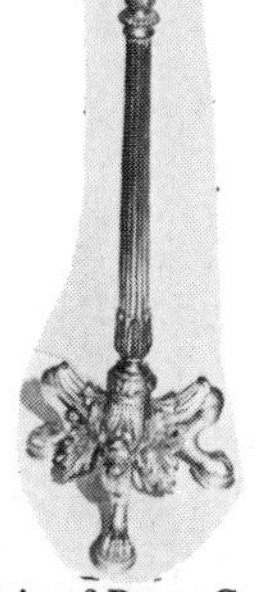

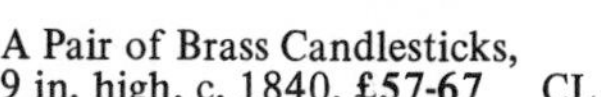

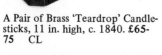

A Pair of Brass Candlesticks, 1870. **£75-85** CP

A Pair of Brass Candlesticks, 9 in. high, c. 1840. **£57-67** CL

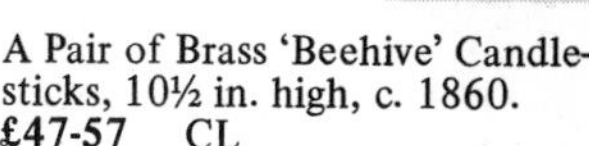

A Pair of Brass 'Beehive' Candlesticks, 10½ in. high, c. 1860. **£47-57** CL

A Pair of Brass 'Teardrop' Candlesticks, 11 in. high, c. 1840. **£65-75** CL

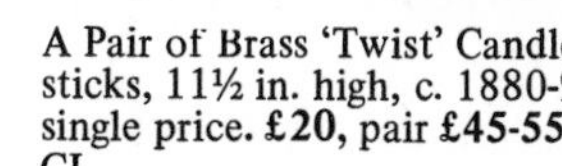

A Pair of Brass 'Twist' Candlesticks, 11½ in. high, c. 1880-90 single price. **£20**, pair **£45-55** CL

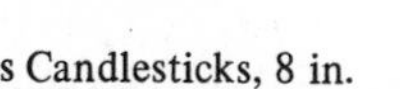

A Pair of Brass Candlesticks, 8 in. high, c. 1840. **£50-60** CP

A Pair of 19th C. Dutch Repouse Brass Candlesticks 9 in. high.
£320-360 CC

BRASS

- **Various alloys composed of copper and zinc**
- **c 1781 James Emerson patented golden tone brass**
- **Until Late 17th C most English work in imported brass**
- **Late 17th C small solid castings**
- **c.1730's machine rolled sheets for hand-hammered vessels**
- **c.1770's machine stamped shape and ornament**
- **c.1790's spun holloware**
- **c.1860's complex castings**

A Pair of brass and copper art nouveau candle sticks c. 1915.
£35-45 pr. BA

A Pair of Flemish Brass pricket Candlesticks, iron pricket, 13½ in., 34.5 cm., late 16th C. lacquered. **£1,000-1,500** S

A Good Pair of Brass Candlesticks, late 18th C. English, c. 1790, 10 in. high. **£130-150** SA

A Pair of Georgian Brass Candlesticks, 8½ in., 21.5 cm. Mid 18th C. **£260-320** L

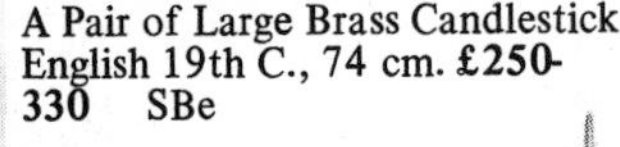

A Pair of Large Brass Candlesticks English 19th C., 74 cm. **£250-330** SBe

A Rare Pair of Mid 19th C. Brass Candlesticks of unusual size 6 in. high. **£68-78** SA

Pair of brass candlesticks 6 in. high, c. 1820. **£65-75** BA

Early Victorian brass candlesticks 11 in. high. **£85-95** pr

A Fine Pair of Flemish Brass pricket Candlesticks, 19 in., 48.5 cm. high, mid 17th C., drilled for electrical fittings.
£1,500-2,000 S

A Pair of brass candlesticks 10 in. early Georgian. **£140-160** BA

A Rare 17th C Dutch brass Candlestick, 8" high, c1675.
£125-150 SAL

right
A pair of brass trumpet-shaped Candlesticks, mid 17th C., slight variations, 5½ in. (14 cm.).
£1,100-1,210 C

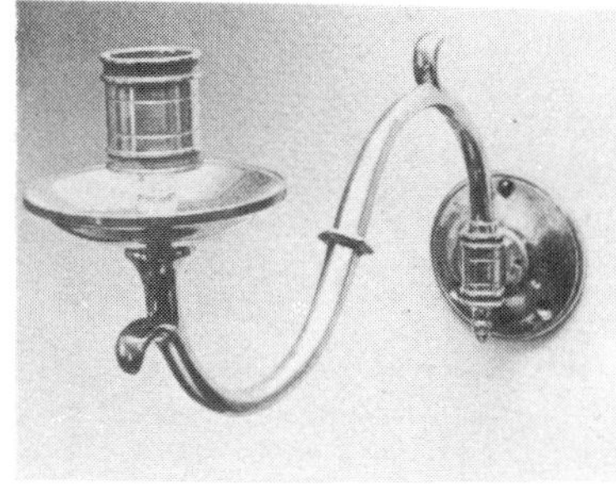

A Pair of early 19th C. brass wall sconces. **£399-450** CC

An 18th C. Brass bed warmer, possibly Dutch, with pierced lid and chased steel handle. **£340-380** BA

A Pair of Brass Tavern Table Candlesticks, height 13" (33cms). **£260-300** SH

An early Victorian Brass fan-shape skimmer. **£45-55** BA

A Dutch Repouse Brass Candlestick c. 1700 9 in. high. **£145-165.** CC

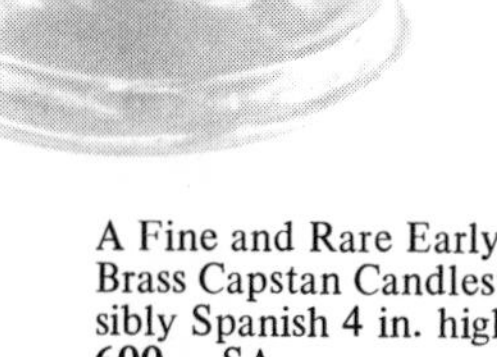

A Fine and Rare Early 17th C. Brass Capstan Candlestick, possibly Spanish 4 in. high. **£550-600** SA

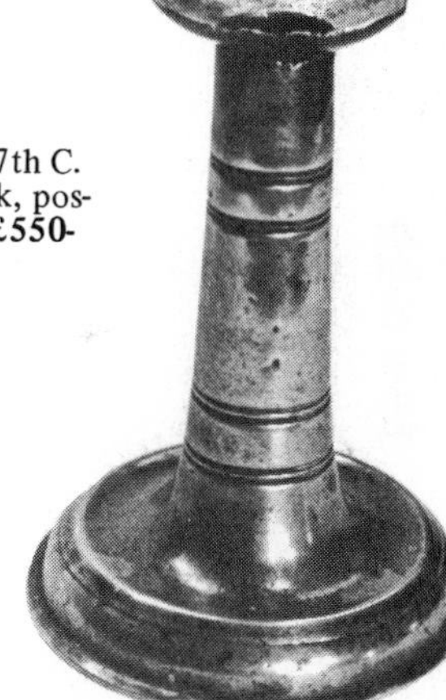

A 17th C. Brass Trumpet Candlestick 4½ in. high. **£220-240** CC

A French Brass Candlestick with Engraved Glass Base, 7 in. high. **£23-28** CA

A pair of 19th C Gilt Brass Candelabra, the stems with set turquoise ground 'Sevres' plaques, 21¼". **£265-300** WHL

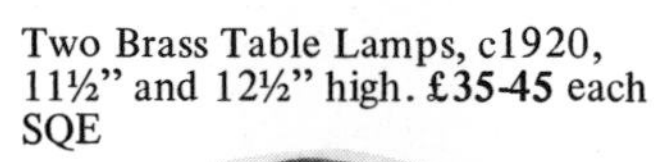

Two Brass Table Lamps, c1920, 11½" and 12½" high. **£35-45** each SQE

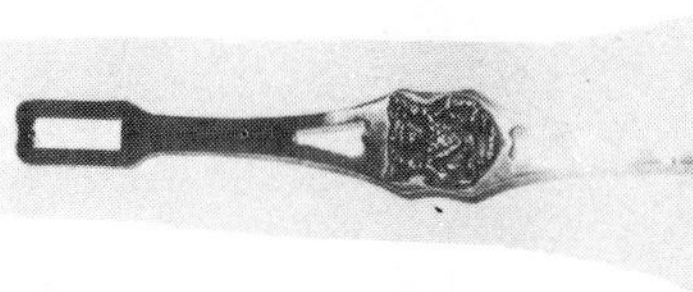

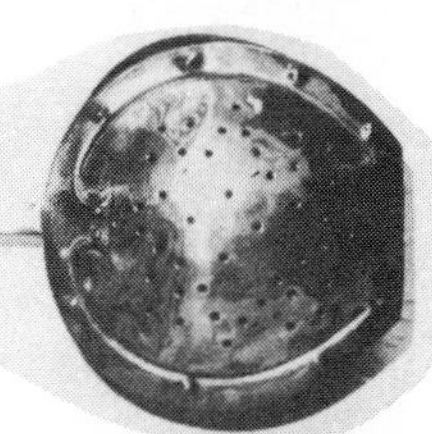

A brass chestnut roaster c. 1910. **£45-55** BA

Art Nouveau Brass 'Arts & Crafts' Candlesticks. **£18-22** pr. AP

A Brass oil lamp c. 1920's. **£35-40** BA

A Victorian Oval Brass Chestnut Roaster. **£65-75** CL

A Victorian Brass Chestnut Roaster, **£62-70** CL

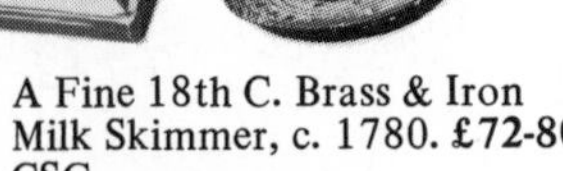

A Fine 18th C. Brass & Iron Milk Skimmer, c. 1780. **£72-80** CSG

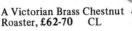

A Brass oil table lamp, mid-Victorian, with cranberry glass top. **£125-150** BA

A Victorian Brass Chestnut Roaster. **£65-72** CL

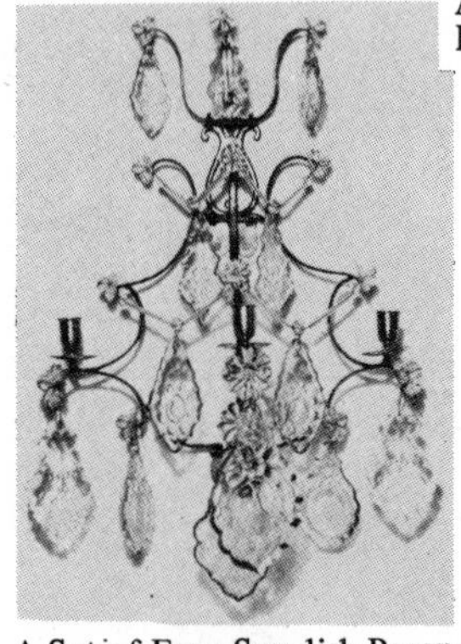

A Set of Four Swedish Brass and Glass Wall Lights, 23 in., 58 cm. high, mid 18th C. **£1,200-1,400** S

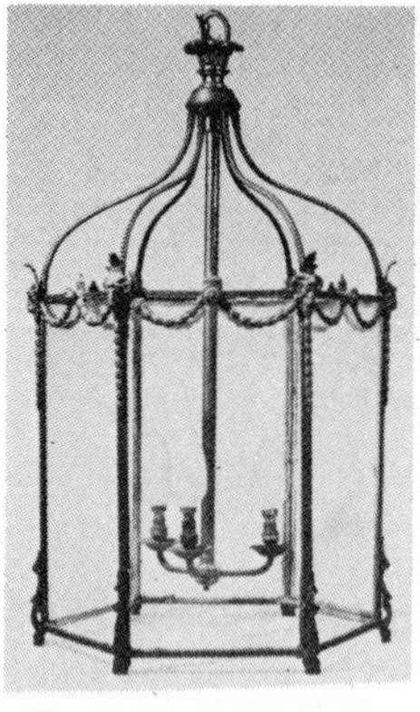

A George III Giltmetal Hall Lantern, fitted for electricity, 30½ in., 77 cm. high. **£1,550-1,650** C

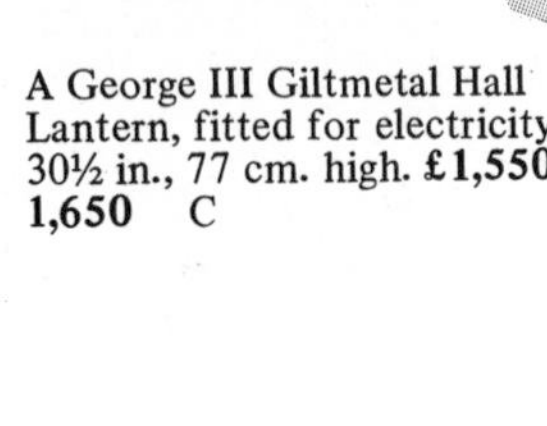

A Pair of Good Quality Brass 2-Light Wall Sconces, 15 in. high, c. 1875. **£120-140** CL

One of a pair of 19th C. brass and glass Wall Ornaments, 12 in. high. **£78-88** pr. SV

A Pair of brass Eastern candle holders and stands 9½ in. high c. 1920's. **£38-45** pr. BA

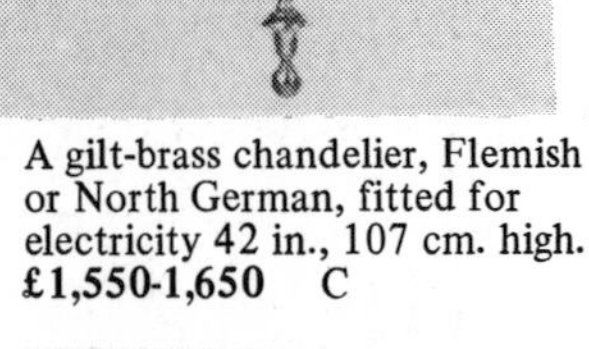

A gilt-brass chandelier, Flemish or North German, fitted for electricity 42 in., 107 cm. high. **£1,550-1,650** C

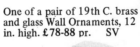

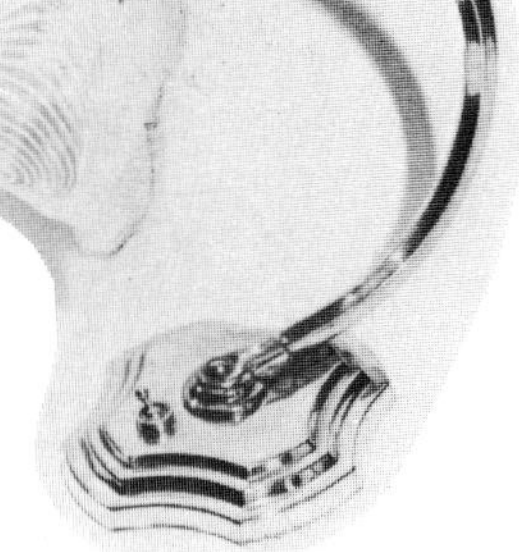

Brass Table Lamp, c. 1920. **£35-40** TT

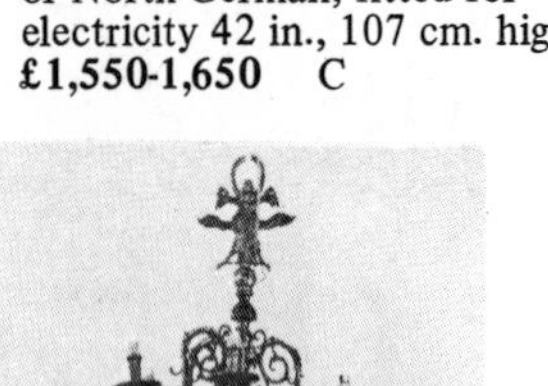

A Flemish Brass Chandelier, with seventeen branches, height 109cms (one branch missing). **£1,125-1,200** SH

Heavily engraved brass light fitting with cranberry shade. **£60-65** TT

A Dutch Miniature Chandelier, 4½ in., 11.7 cm. by Jan Bonket, Amsterdam, apparently 1761. **£550-600** S

Pair of late 19th C. Carriage Lamps. **£300-320** pair.

Gas Light fittings in cut glass and brass. **£90-100** pair. TT

A Very Rare Georgian Brass Table Trivet, 9 in. long. **£55-65** SA

A Pierced Brass Trivet, c. 1800. **£15-20** OB

A Pierced Brass Round Trivet, c. 1850. **£32-35** CL

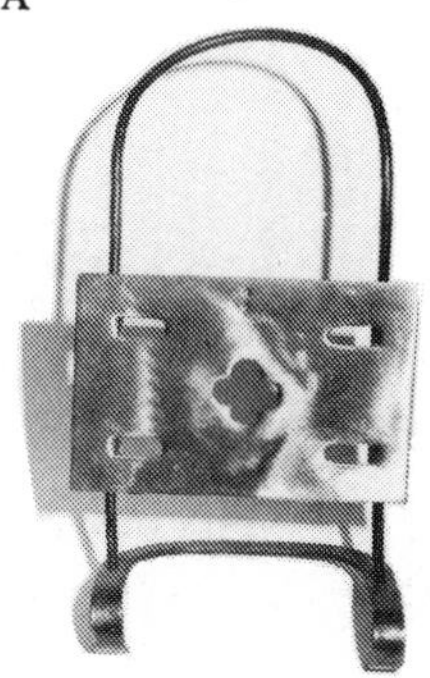

A Brass Fender Trivet, c. 1820-30. **£15-18** CL

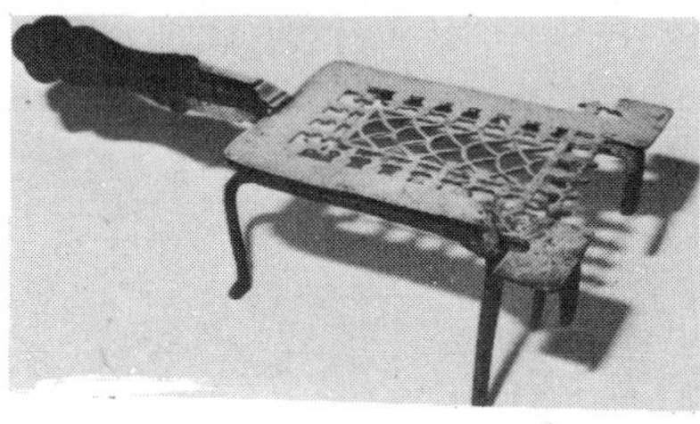

A 19th C. Brass Trivet. **£38-42** CSG

A Pierced Brass Rectangular Trivet, c. 1865. **£27-31** CL

A Small brass trivet, late Victorian 5 in. wide. **£10-12** BA

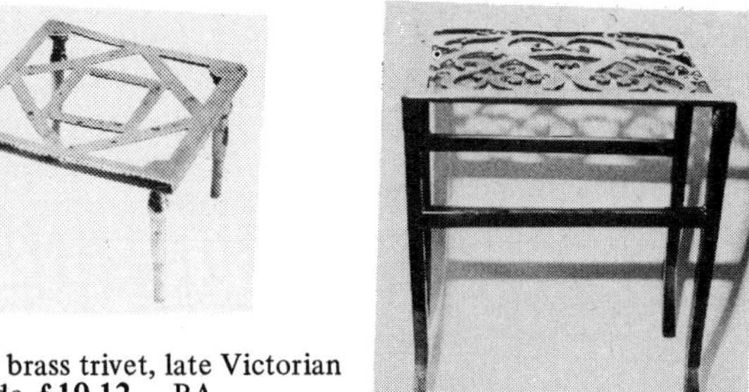

A Victorian Brass high trivet. **£46-52** BA

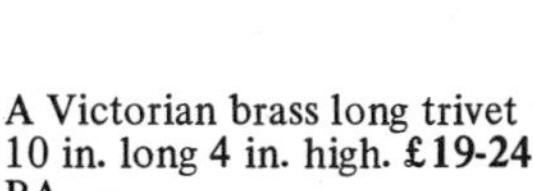

A Victorian brass long trivet 10 in. long 4 in. high. **£19-24** BA

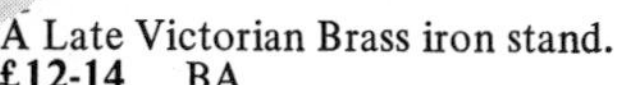

A Late Victorian Brass iron stand. **£12-14** BA

A late Victorian brass round trivet 7 in. diam. **£23-30** BA

A Brass Victorian fender trivet. **£25-30** BA

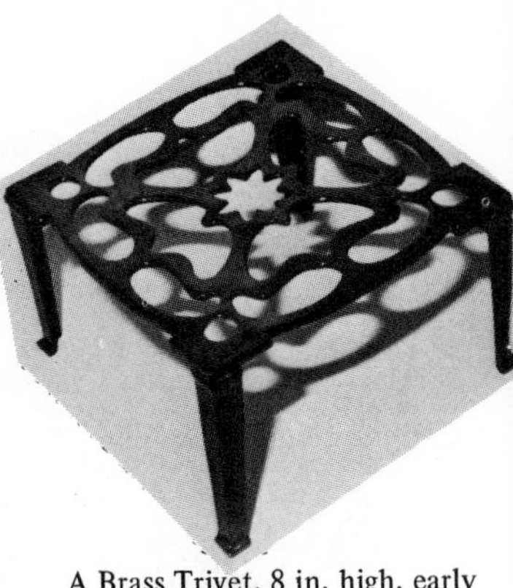

A Brass Trivet, 8 in. high, early 20th C. **£28-35** VA

A Set of Four Brass Weights, c. 1860. **£15.50-18** CL

A Set of Victorian Brass Letter Scales, c1880. **£45-50** CCL

One of a Pair of Second French Empire Brass Fire Dogs, c. 1860. **£125-155** AP

Victorian Mordan & Co. Brass Scales and Weights. **£85-95** SAL

A Brass Victorian folding guard. **£65-75** BA

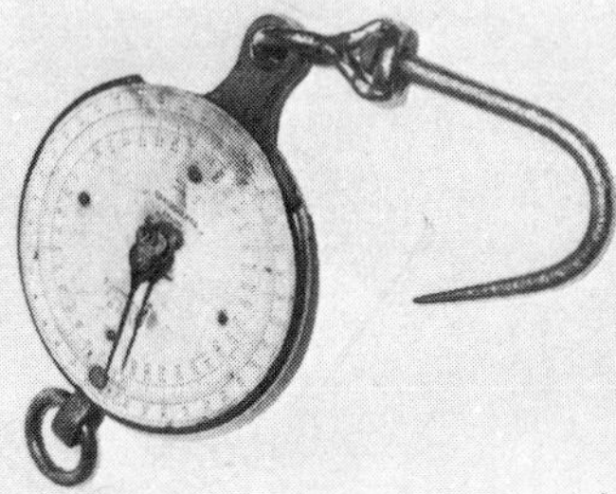

A set of brass Salters Wall scales. **£35-40** A.L.

A Brass Apothecary's Beam Balance with 11 Piece Weights First ½ 19th C. **£82-92** CL

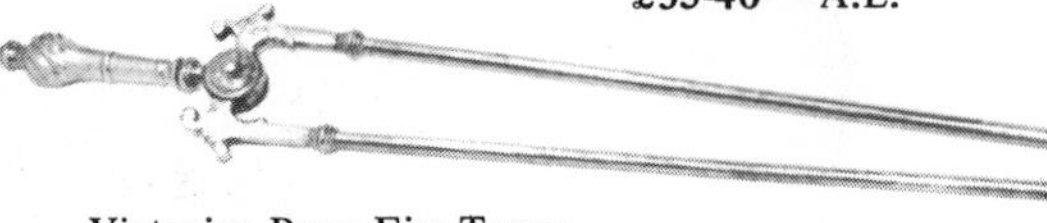

Victorian Brass Fire Tongs, 23" high. **£12-15** SQE

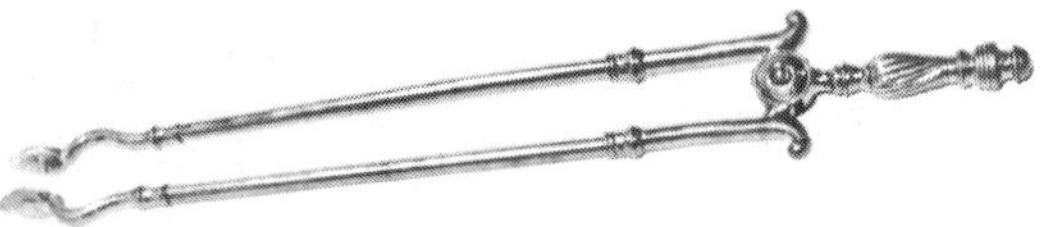

Victorian Brass Fire Tongs, 26" high. **£12-15** SQE

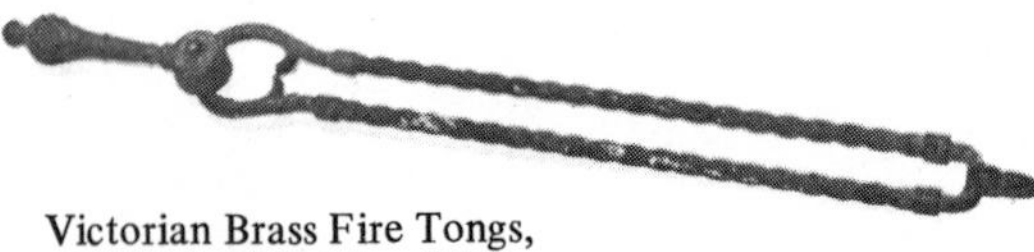

Victorian Brass Fire Tongs, 24" high. **£10-12** SQE

A Pair of 18th C. English Fire Dogs with fine brass terminals. **£300-330** pr. SA

Small brass hanging scales
6 in. diam., weigh up to 40 lbs.
£27-32 BA

A Brass toddy kettle with wooden handle c. 1830-1840, 8 in. high.
£95-105 BA

A Brass Coffee Pot, 11½ in. high, c. 1750-60. **£75-85** CL

A Copper & Brass Jug, c. 1920.
£30-35 CA

A Set of Victorian large brass scales and weights. **£170-190**
SAL

A Brass Georgian kettle c. 1820
10 in. high. **£85-95** BA

A Brass hot water can 11½ in. high, Victorian. **£50-60** BA

A Victorian Brass Hot Water Can, c. 1880. **£33-40** CL

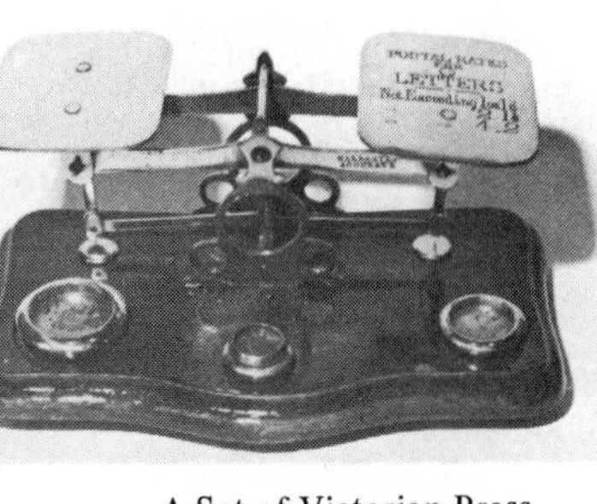

A Set of Victorian Brass Postal Scales with 4 Piece Weights. **£65-75** CL

A copper & brass kettle, with stand and lamp. 12¼in high, c.1870 **£70-80** CL

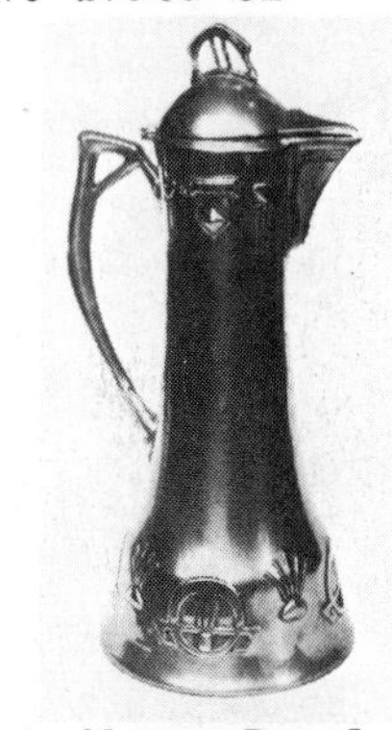

An Art Nouveau Brass Jug, German, c. 1910. **£90-100** AP

A Victorian Lidded brass jug 11½ in. high. **£28-38** BA

A Brass Mortar and Pestle, c. 1840. **£42-50** CL

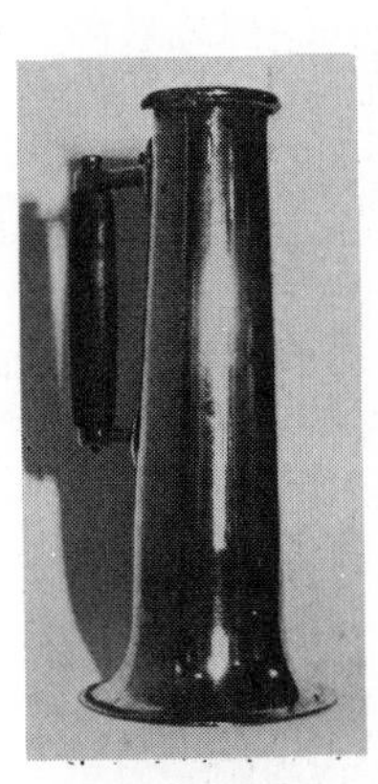

A brass naval measure 11½ in. Georgian. **£65-75**

A Brass Mortar and Pestle, c. 1780. **£59-69** CL

A Brass Mortar and Pestle, c. 1800. **£42-50** CL

An early 18th C. Brass Tankard, **£90-100** SKC

A Brass coffee Percolator 15 in. high, 1920's fitted for electricity. **£45-55** BA

A Brass Mortar and Pestle, c. 1760. **£54-65** CL

A Pair of Brass Milk Churns, marked H. White, London Road Dairy, made by W. J. Harrison, English, mid 19th C. 1 ft. 5 in., 43 cm. high. **£600-680** SB

A Brass sauce pan with steel handle 3 in. c. 1810, **£45-55** BA

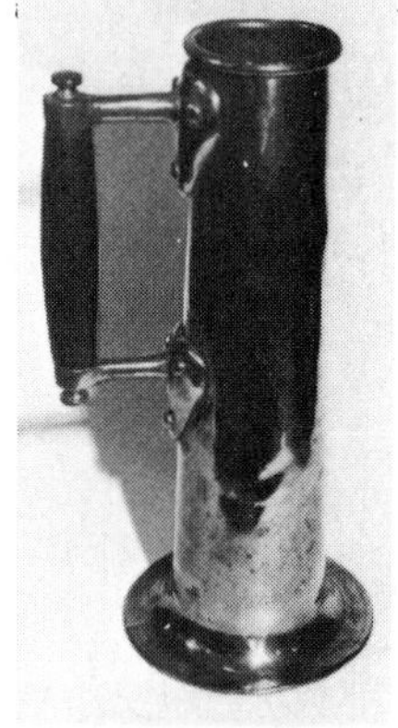

A Victorian/Edwardian Brass Hydrometer Measure. **£49-55** CL

A Brass and Wrought-Iron Skillet the handle with pierced heart-shaped top, 17th C. 23¼ in., 59 cm. wide. **£250-275** C

A Brass and iron saucepan, 7" diam. **£27-29** A.L.

A Small copper & brass sauce pan Georgian marked, made in Paris 3 in. **£45-55** BA

A Georgian brass bin with lions head ring handles and paw feet.
£240-280 BA

A Victorian Brass jam pan with copper handles 12 in. diam.
£75-80 BA

A Victorian Brass Pot on Stand.
£50-60 BA

A Brass ink-well 1920's. **£35-45** BA

A Brass public lavatory lock.
£28-34 BA

A Brass helmet scuttle, late Victorian. **£45-55** BA

A Deep Brass jam pan with Victorian copper handles 12 in. diam. **£95-105** BA

An 18th C. brass standish. **£290-310** CC

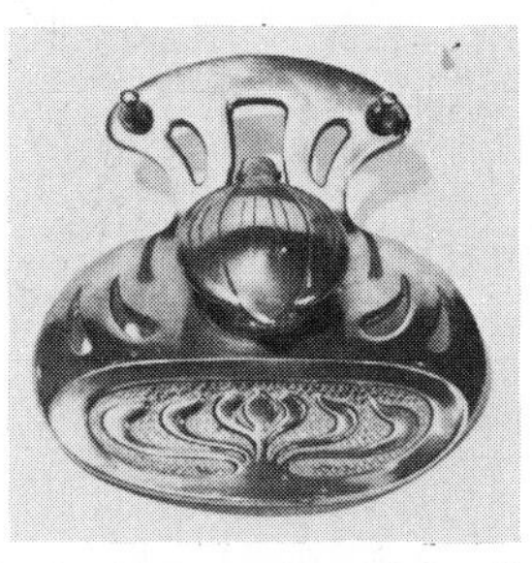

An Art Nouveau Brass Inkwell.
£28-32 AP

A Victorian Brass Door Fitting.
£25-30 CL

A Copper and Brass Coal Bucket, 14¾ in. high, Dutch, c. 1840.
£148-155 CL

A Brass coal box Edwardian.
£55-65 BA

Brass Inkstand, c. 1830. **£50-60** TT

18th C Brass flour sifter. **£60-65** A.L.

French Empire Brass Inkstand, c. 1830. **£50-60** TT

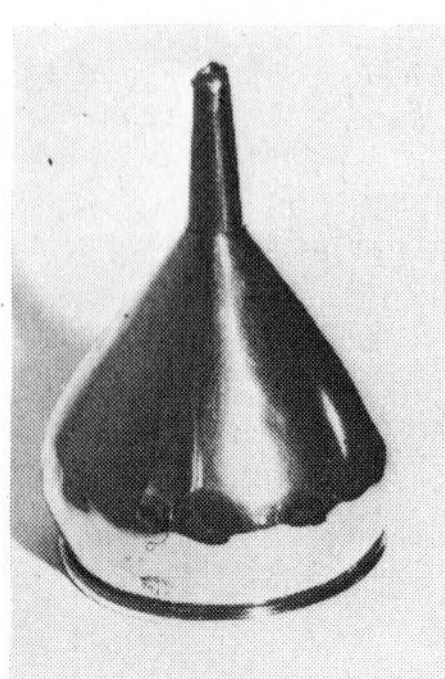

A brass funnel 3 in. diam. c. 1880. **£19-25** BA

17th C. Brass Nutcracker. **£140-160** RB

18th C. Brass Nutcracker. **£35-40** RB

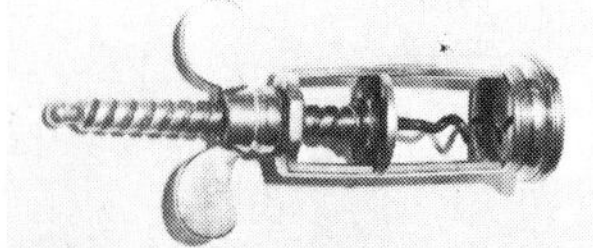

19th C. Brass Corkscrew. **£48-54** RB

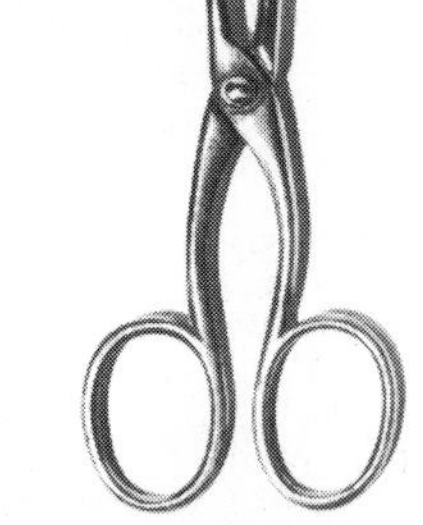

Early 19th C. Brass Ember Tongs. **£30-35** RB

Early 19th C. Brass Pastry Cutter. **£8-10** RB

A Victorian Copper and Brass Crumb Scoop. **£25-30** CSG

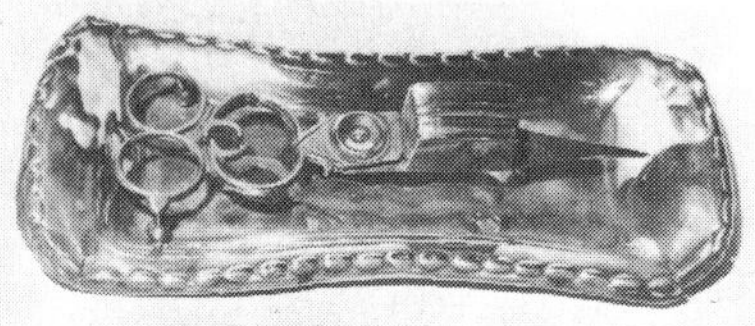

Early 19th C. Brass Candle Snuffers with Tray. **£35-40** RB

A Victorian Brass Stamping Machine. **£17.50-19** CL

Early 19th C. Brass Pastry Cutter. **£22-25** RB

A 16th C. Nuremburg Brass Plate 9 in. diam. **£420-440** CC

A 17th C German Brass Alms Dish, 14½" (37cms) diam. (defects). **£145-150** SKC

A small Victorian brass bible box 5½ in. long 3 in. deep 2½ in. high c. 1900. **£45-55** BA

A brass jewel casket 11½ in. long 3 in. high 3½ in. deep, late Victorian c. 1900. **£65-75** BA

A brass sewing casket, mid Victorian, with sewing accessories inside lid. **£85-95** BA

An Indonesian Brass Box, 8 in., c. 1800. **£70-75** RB

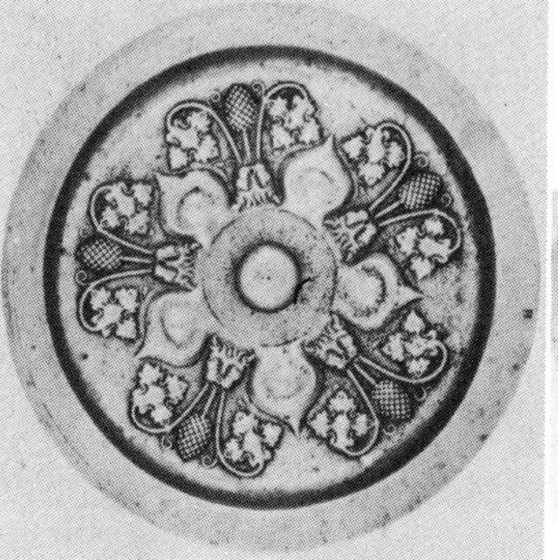

A German Brass Alms Dish, 15½ in., 39.5 cm. c. 1500. **£1,200-1,500** S

An 18th C. Dutch brass Tobacco box. **£370-400** CC

3 Brass tobacco boxes c. 1885
£40-55 BA

A brass Table Gong, c1840-60.
£115-135 SQE

A Victorian Brass table bell 6½ in.
£20-25 BA

A Victorian Bell-ringers' brass bell with leather handle 9½ in.
£27-35 BA

A Victorian brass school bell 9½ in. **£34-40** BA

A Fine 19th C. Brass Snuff Box.
£90-100 SA

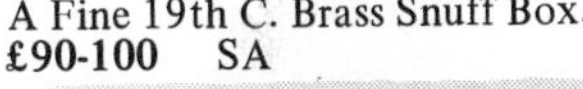

A Brass Taper/Spill Holder, c. 1840. **£29-35** CL

A brass Reading Lectern, c.1870
£40-45 CL

A Small brass gong c. 1915.
£15-20 BA

An 18th C. brass standing cup, 5 in. high. **£75-85** CC

An Old English Brass Bicycle Lamp. **£42-50** CL

A 18th C. brass plate stand 9 in. diam. **£95-105** CC

A French Miniature Display Cabinet, brass mountings and bevelled glass, c. 1880., 15 in. high. **£350-380** CA

A Brass Locomotive Engine Model of Antelope, 10 in. long, c. 1900. **£60-70** VA

Art Nouveau Brass Picture Frame, 9" high. **£20-25** SQE

A Victorian Brass Cribbage Score Board, c. 1870. **£22-28** CL

A Brass Bridge-Scoring Pencil Set, c1920, 5½" high. **£14-18** SQE

An Edwardian brass Stick-Stand, 23" high. **£70-90** SAL

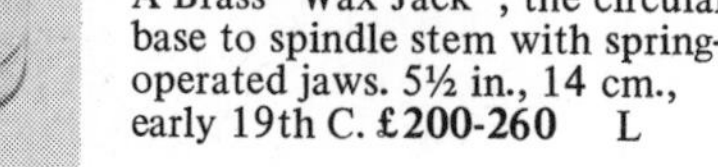

A Brass "Wax Jack", the circular base to spindle stem with spring-operated jaws. 5½ in., 14 cm., early 19th C. **£200-260** L

An Official Brass Imperial Half-Gallon Measure, engraved 'Imperial ½ gallon measure Calcutta mint F.70 No. 85' with maker's initials G.F. 6 in., 15 cm., high. c. 1820. **£240-290** L

A Brass Door Knocker/Letter Slot, c1870-90, 9½" long. **£24-27** SQE

A French Brass Tooth-pick Holder, signed, with Napoleon outside his tent. c. 1880 **£55-60** CA

A Pair of heavy brass cast church vases, 6 in. high c. 1900. **£32-40** pr. BA

Southern Railway, the Pair of Brass Cast Name Plates, Sir Launcelot, King Arthur Class No. 455. **£1,700-1,800**

A Brass double 'gophering' iron on iron base, mid Victorian. **£65-75** BA

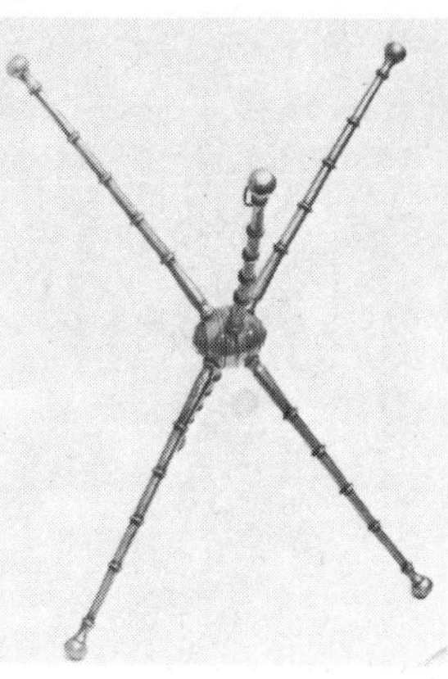

A Brass cat trivet, Victorian. **£55-65** BA

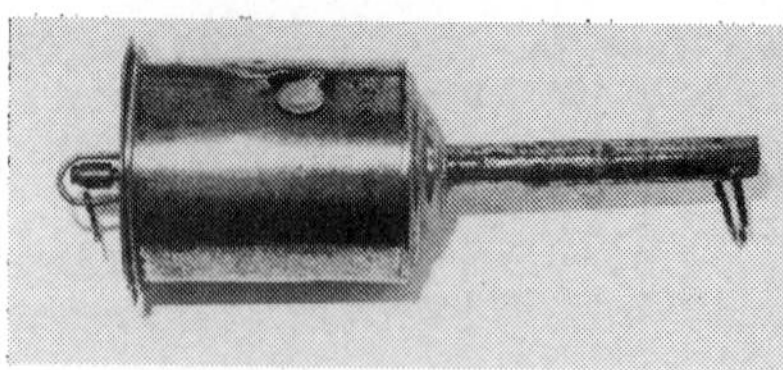

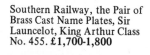

A tin and brass spit jack. **£23-25** A.L.

An Early 18th C. Brass Wine Cooler 25 in. wide. **£520-600** CC

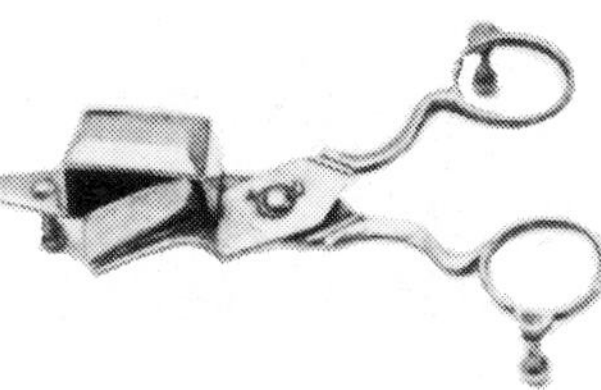

A brass candlesnuffer, 5½" long. **£20-25** A.L.

A Pewter Footed Wine Cup, c. 1800. **£35-45** CL

A Large English Pewter Standing Cup of 18th C. form; crowned rose touchmark, probably by member of the Townsend family, 10 in. high, c. 1760-1800. **£105-140** CL

A Pewter Beaker, engraved 'Prince of Wales', Sussex verification seal and touchmark of Harton & Sons, London, c. 1850. **£37-57** CL

A Pewter Imperial Pint Tavern Tankard inscribed under base The Hope, Beaver Lane, Hammersmith, c. 1850. **£36-42** CL

A Scottish Pewter Imperial Quart Tankard, Victorian excise seal and mark of Wood & Sons, Glasgow at rim, c. 1850. **£50-60** CL

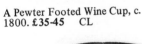

A Pewter ½ Pint Tankard bearing 'Hallmark', touches of Joseph Morgan of Bristol, c. 1820-30. **£32-40** CL

A Pewter Quart Tavern Tankard inscribed 'Duke of Edinburgh' and bearing verification seals of George IV, William IV and Victoria, maker James Yates, c. 1820-30. **£54-65** CL

A Half-Pint Pewter Bellied Measure. **£48-52** CL

A Guernsey Pewter Flagon of one pt. capacity, cover missing, c. 1750. **£220-240** in good condition and with cover **£450-500** CL

A Pewter Imperial ½ Pint Tavern Wine Cup, c. 1830. **£39-45** CL

A Pewter Beaker with 1826 verification and hallmarks at rim, and touchmark in base of C. Bentley of Woodstock St. London, c. 1830. **£39-49** CL

A Fine Set of Irish Pewter Haystack Measures. **£1,200+** SA

A Rare Antique Pewter Rimmed Imperial Pint Tavern Measure, c. 1850. **£85-95** CL

A Quart Pewter Measure, c. 1830. **£90-100** CL

A Swiss Stegkanne, probably 19th C., Bern, touch Abraham Ganting, 12½ in. (32 cm.). **£500-550** C

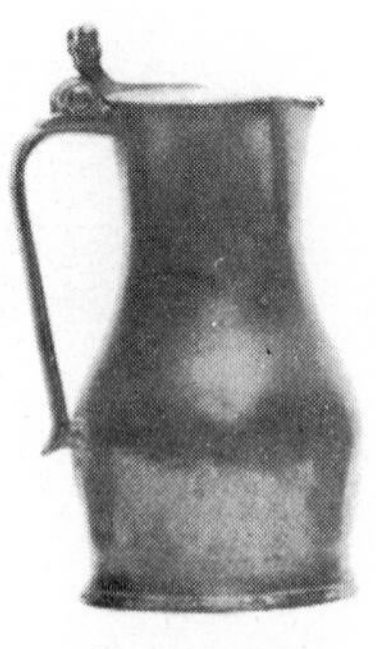

A lidded Jersey pewter measure by John St. Croix, 8½" high. **£300-340** Lan

A 18th/19th C Jersey Pewter measure, made by the maker IN, 11¼" high. **£370-400** PWC

A Continental Pewter Flagon of type known as Kelchkanne, of typical form with twin 'fig' thumbpiece, Swiss, c. 1770. **£430-470** CL

A Pewter Ale Jug with double-domed cover, open chair-back thumbpiece and covered spout, c. 1830. **£325-400** CL

An Antique Pewter Imperial Quart Lipped Tavern Measure, inscribed 'G. Parrish', white hart, c. 1840. **£57-67** CL

A Rare Dutch Pewter Flagon, good clear 'Hallmarks' on base, 10 in. high, c. 1750-60. **£425-500** CL

A Queen Anne flat-lidded Pewter Tankard by Thomas Ingles with 'S' scroll handle, 7" high. **£380-460** Lan

A Scottish Pewter Pear-Shaped Measure of 4 Gill (1 Pint) Capacity, domed cover with relief cast imperial seal, Glasgow, c. 1840. **£188-210** CL

A Dutch Flagon of bulbous form with cylindrical neck, domed cover, probably 18th C. **£340-380** CL

A Pewter Normandy Flagon of typical form, cover initialled A.J. 9 in. high, c. 1790. **£360-390** CL

A Pewter Brass Rimmed Tavern Measure of imperial pint, c. 1860. **£78-88** CL

A Continental Pewter Barrel Tankard, marked inside S.W., probably Carlsbad area, c. 1850. **£155-175** CL

A Rare Pewter Jersey Quart Flagon by Pierre du Rousseau, now restored, c. 1700. **£365-400** CL

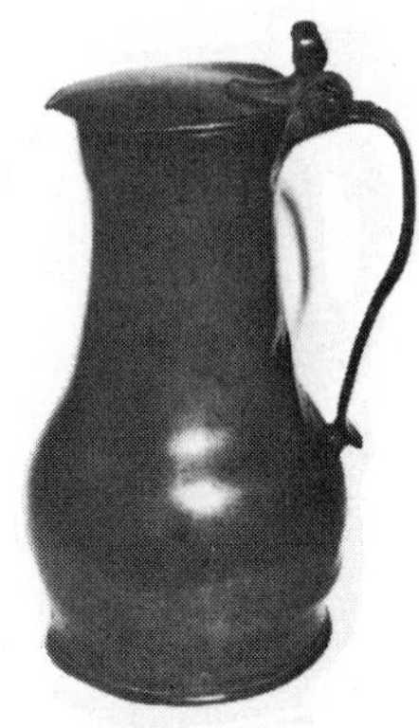

A Jersey Pewter Flagon of Pot size, with makers touchmark of Jean de St. Croix inside cover, 11 in. high, c. 1740. **£375-425** CL

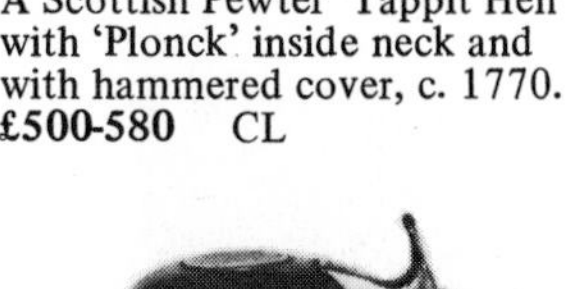

A Scottish Pewter 'Tappit Hen' with 'Plonck' inside neck and with hammered cover, c. 1770. **£500-580** CL

A Pewter 'Bierkrug' or Flagon of tall cylindrical form with stepped cover, dished top, ball knop and erect thumbpiece, North German, c. 1800. **£290-320** CL

A Continental Pewter Wine Can with 'pot' belly, incurved neck and domed cover, c. 1760-80. **£295-325** CL

PEWTER

- **An alloy, principal component is tin with minor additions of brass lead and antimony**
- **1666 Great Fire of London destroyed pewterers' Hall and all touch plates**
- **1668 Touch mark system revived**
- **In many cases dates appear in touches, these dates represent year of registration not of manufacture.**

A Continental Pewter Demi-Litre Lidded Wine Measure, 'Rudot a Lille' touchmark under base, c. 1840, slight damage to base **£93-100** perfect **£120-140** CL

A Continental possibly German, Pewter Lidded Jug, 13 in., c. 1920 **£140-160** CA

An Antique American Pewter Teapot with incurved neck and foot and domed cover, c. 1820-40 **£78-88** CL

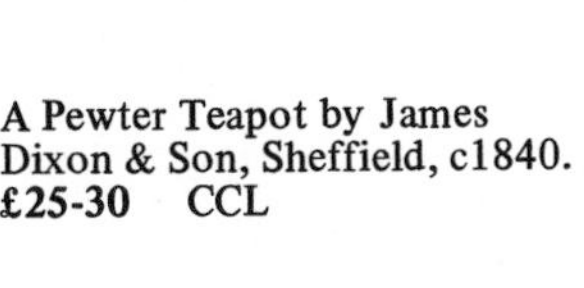

A Pewter Teapot by James Dixon & Son, Sheffield, c1840. **£25-30** CCL

A Good Coffee Pot in Empire style with relief cast decoration on body and cover, 10 in., dated 1850. **£155-175** CL

A Pewter Teapot with cast foot and handle, c. 1830-40. **£40-50** CL

A Continental Pewter Coffee Pot with fine clear touchmarks (inside base) of Johann Carl Breitfeld III, c. 1800. **£135-150** CL

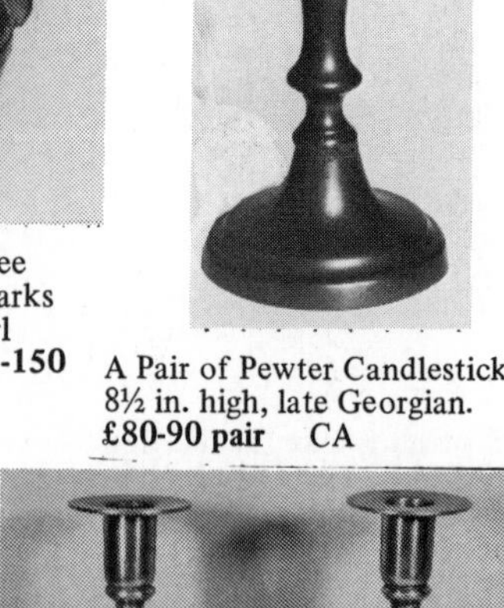

A Pair of Pewter Candlesticks, 8½ in. high, late Georgian. **£80-90 pair** CA

An Art Nouveau Pewter Teapot by L. Tyler, Sheffield. **£45-50** CCL

A Rare William & Mary Pewter Candlestick with ball knopped stem, c. 1690. **£600-660** SA

A Pair of 18th C. Pewter Candlesticks, English, c. 1720. **£350-400** pr. SA

A Pair of Antique Pewter Candlesticks, c. 1800-1820. **£125-150** CL

A Pair of Pewter Candlesticks with push ejectors, c. 1780-1800. **£135-155** pr. CL

A Pair of Norwegian Pewter Candlesticks by Nicholaus Justelius, Eksjo, one nozzle a replacement, c. 1800 each, 9½ in., 24 cm. **£95-110** L

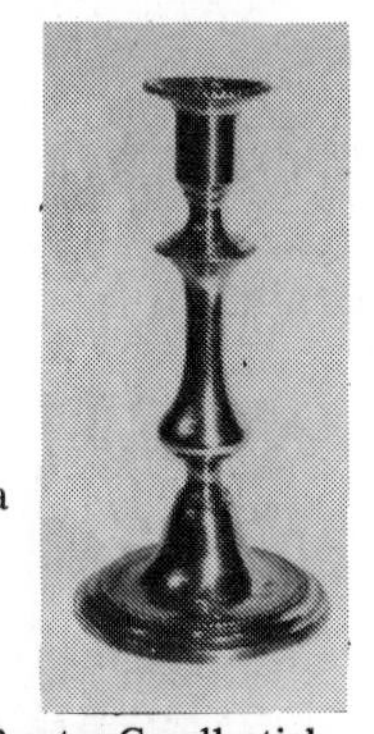

A Pair of Pewter Candlesticks with push ejectors, c. 1780-1800. **£130-140** pr. CL

A Pair of Pewter Candlesticks with push ejectors c. 1780-1800. **£135-155** CL

A Pair of Pewter Candlesticks, c. 1800-20. **£105-125** pr. CL

A Pewter Chamber Candlestick, c. 1840. **£39-48** CL

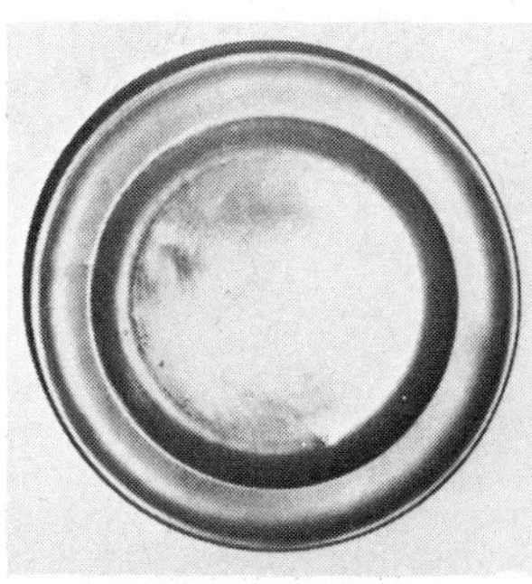

A Pewter Plate, 9½ in. diam. c. 1730-40. **£38-49** Multiple Reeded Plates, pre Fire of London, 1645+ **£120-140** CL

A Large Pewter 'Capstan' Inkwell with glass liner, c. 1840. **£45-55** CL

A Continental Pewter Sugar Bowl with Cover, bearing 'Schlagenwald' Fein Zinn touchmark inside base, c. 1800. **£35-40** CL

An Engraved Pewter Mounted Spirit Flask, c. 1850. **£13.50-20** CL

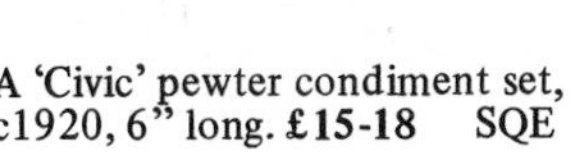

A 'Civic' pewter condiment set, c1920, 6" long. **£15-18** SQE

A Continental Pewter Dish or Bowl, makers touchmark under base, 8½ in. diam. c. 1820-40. **£42-50** CL

A Set of 24 Pewter Dinner Plates, 18th C. **£1,200+** SA

A Fine 19th C. Pewter ("Standish") Inkstand. **£78-88** CL

A Pewter 'Treasury' Inkstand, c. 1780. **£78-88** CL

A Pewter Ladle with wood handle, 18th C. **£22.50-25** CL

A 3-Piece Set of Antique Continental Pewter Baptism and Extreme Unction Cruets, c. 1800. **£92-100** CL

A Pewter 'Capstan' Inkstand with glass liner, c. 1820. **£36-40** CL

A Pewter Wine Tundish (funnel) c. 1800. **£27-35** CL

A Fine and Rare Pewter Soup Tureen with Cover, despite Continental form, possibly English due to quality, c. 1780-1800. **£345-385** CL

A Pewter Porringer or Wine Taster, the pierced ears with touchmark and initials, possibly German, probably Low Countries, c. 1760. **£145-165** CL

A Pewter Porringer with reversible lid, gadrooned border, traces of touches, early 18th C. 8½ in. (21 cm.). **£310-340** C

One of a Pair of Art Nouveau Pewter Dishes. **£48-54** pr. AP

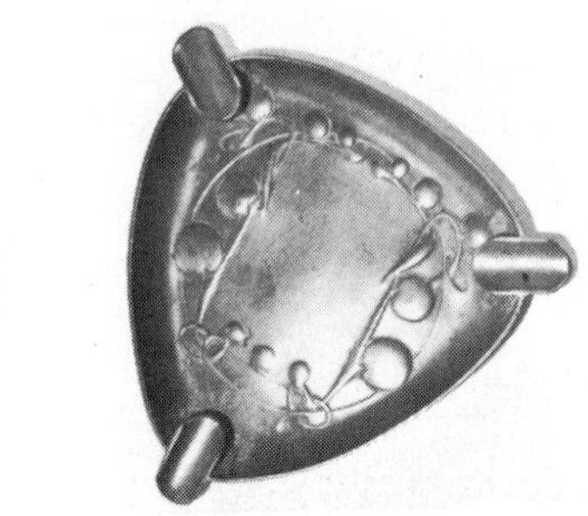

An Art Nouveau Pewter Ashtray, c. 1900. **£33-37** AP

A Liberty & Co. Art Deco pewter rosebowl, 10¼" diam. **£195-230** SQE

Art Nouveau W.M.F. Pewter Table lamp. **£140-160** A.D.H.

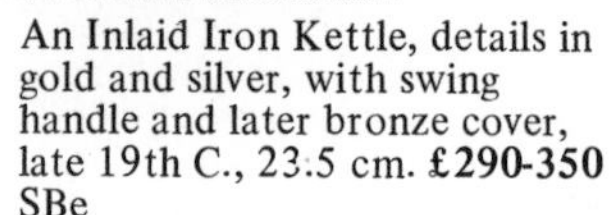

An Art Nouveau Pewter Dish, c. 1900. **£29-34** AP

An Iron candlesnuffer, 6½" long. **£15-18** A.L.

An Inlaid Iron Kettle, details in gold and silver, with swing handle and later bronze cover, late 19th C., 23.5 cm. **£290-350** SBe

A Selection of Keys:

1	18th C. Steel	**£16-18**
2	Roman 1st C. Bronze	**£75-85**
3	Early 19th C. Steel	**£6-8**
4	Early 19th C. Steel	**£6-8**
5	Early 19th C. Steel	**£5-7**

RB

'Deville Et Cie' Cast-Iron Stove, Lent Moyen Vif No. 451, in mid-green vitreous enamel with nickel-plated fittings, French, c. 1910 2 ft. 3 in., 68.5 cm. high. **£175-235** SB

A Cast-Iron and Ceramic Decorative Cooking Range, finished overall with blue and white ceramic tiles, French, c. 1900 2 ft. 6 in. by 3 ft. 2 in. by 2 ft. 1 in., 76 by 96 by 64.5 cm. **£500-600** SB

'La Non Pareil' Cast-Iron Stove, Deville et Cie. in blue-grey vitreous enamel with nickel plated fittings, French, c. 1920 1 ft. 10 in., 56 cm. high. **£250-300** SB

A Cast-Iron Stove, in black and marbled grey vitreous enamel, French c. 1910 2 ft. 3 in., 68.5 cm. high. **£250-300** SB

A 'Lux' Cast-Iron Stove, in azure vitreous enamel with nickel-plated details, French, c. 1915 1 ft. 1 in. sq. by 2 ft. 8 in., 33 by 81 cm. **£250-350** SB

A 'Monopole' Cast-Iron Free-Standing Stove, marked Deville et Cie., No. 115 Charleville, fuel loading at the top, eight-paned mica-glazed door at front opening to reveal combustion pot with sliding under-draught attachment, finished overall in maroon vitreous enamel with nickel plated fittings and decorated with Art Nouveau birds, French, c. 1910 2 ft. 10 in. by 1 ft. 1½ in., 86.5 by 34 cms. **£550-600** SB

A Chinese Silver-coloured-metal Tea Set: Tea Pot and hinged cover, Milk Jug and Sucrier, teapot: 19 cm., stamped marks, early 20th C., 914 gm. **£225-250** SB

A Victorian iron Trivet **£9-11** AC

A Bell metal jam pan with steel handle 9 in. diam. **£47-52** BA

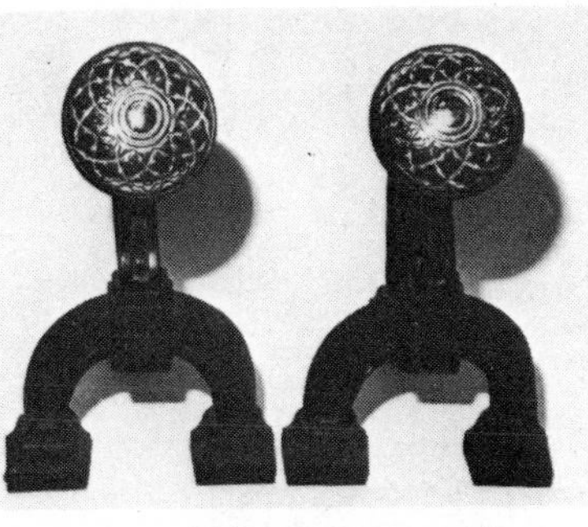

A Pair of 19th C. Brass and Iron Firedogs. **£75-85** pr. CSG

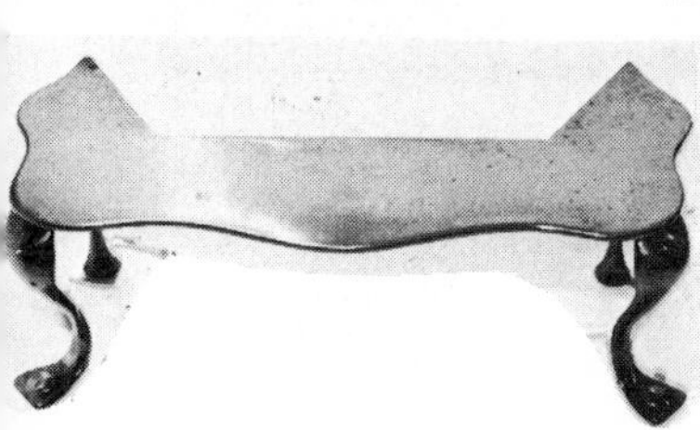

An Art Nouveau Steel Trivet. **£25-35** SQE

Bell metal skillet 8 in. diam. c. 1820 marked Warner. **£120-140** BA

A 19th C Iron Trivet 6" diam. **£8-11** A.L.

A Bell metal skillet c. 1780 6 in. diam. **£80-120** BA

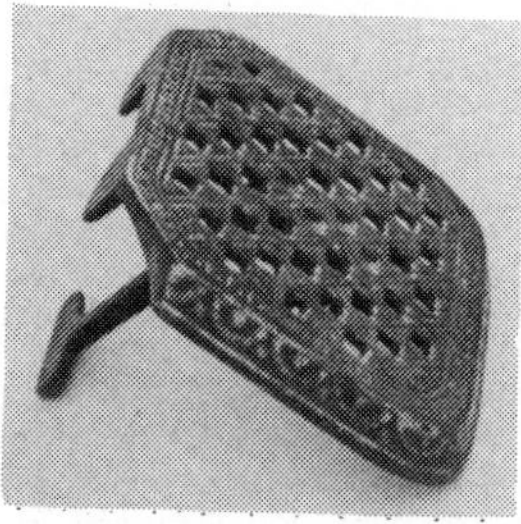

A 19th C square Trivet, 5in x 5in **£6-8** AL

A late 17th/early 18th C. bell metal bowl, 26 cm. wide. **£180-200** SKC

A Bell metal mortar and pestle c. 1810 4 in. high. **£65-75** BA

A Bronzed bell metal bowl 14 in. diam. c. 1790. **£65-75** BA

A Mackintosh Toffee Tin, 3" wide, 4" high. **£4-6** A.L.

A Late 18th C. Bell Metal Cup and Cover 8 in. high. **£245-265** CC

A White Metal Koro and cover, inlaid with gold and enamel, late 19th C., with faults, 12 cm. **£130-160** SBe

A Fine Rectangular Cherry-wood ship's chest (funadansu) mounted in iron with a Shochikubai decoration, 19th C., 47.7 cm. x 42.2 cm. x 39 cm. **£880-980** C

A set of five bell-metal Grain-measures, inscribed for the Manor of Winslow, County of Bucks, 1847, in fitted wooden case. 19 in. (48 cm.). **£480-530** C

A Rare 17th C. Tobacco Box, engraved with arms of England, incorporating Cannon and Royalist emblems, c. 1660. **£300-330** SA

A 17th C. Iron Casket 5 in. wide. **£320-360** CC

An Iron Armada Chest, Spanish, early 17th C, 16½" x 31" (42cms x 79cms). **£450-550** SBA

A 19th C Simulated Pietredure and Gilt-metal Casket, 6" (15cms) wide. **£45-55** SKC

A Dutch Iron Strong Box bound with iron strapwork, the cover plate pierced with grotesque birds, late 17th/early 18th C., the locking mechanism not working. 26¾ in., 68 cm. x 15 in., 38 cm. x 14 in., 36 cm. high. **£480-560** L

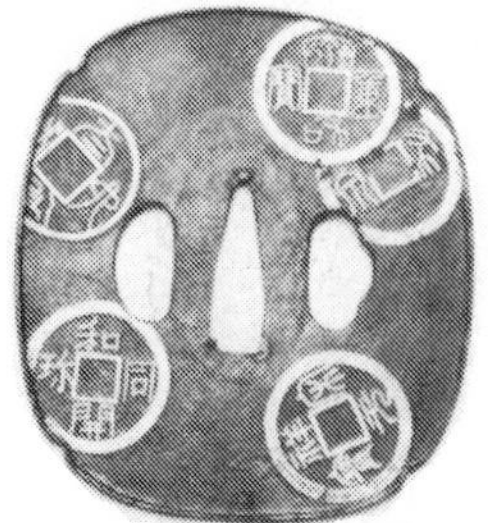

An iron tsuba of mokko form, decorated in gold and silver nunome, unsigned. **£235-250** SKC

An Art Nouveau Writing Set. **£38-45** AP

A Good Pair of Shakudo Tsuba for A Daisho, the katana tsuba signed Yasuchika, the other one with kakihan, 3¼ in., 82 cm. and 2¾ in., 72 cm. **£225-250** L

2 Welsh Miner's Lamps, in steel and brass, early 20th C. **£30-40** CCL

A Good Pair of Copper Tsuba for a Daisho, mounted with gold and other soft metals with minogame in landscapes, each signed, within frames of shakudo, the hitsu-ana of the katana tsuba and one of the other plugged with shakudo. 3 in., 75 cm. and 2¾ in., 72 cm. **£530-590** L

A Good Circular Iron Tsuba 2½ in., 6.5 cm. **£25-30** L

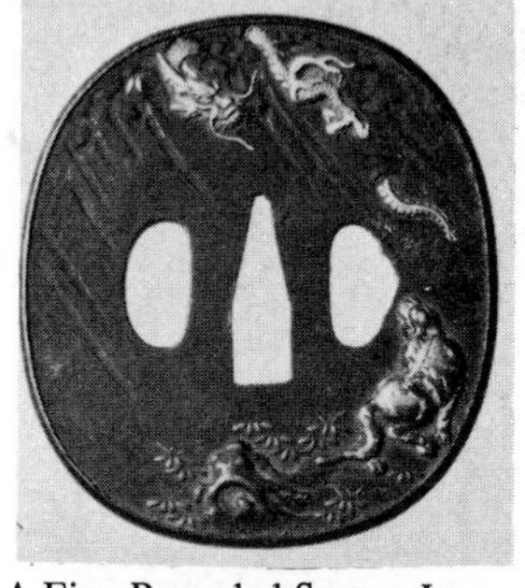

A Fine Rounded Square Iron Tsuba, decorated in relief with a shi-shi. 3 in., 7.5 cm. **£40-50** L

A Pair of George III Bell Metal Candlesticks, 9¾ in., c. 1775. **£115-135** pr. CSG

A Pair of Early 18th C. Bell-Metal Candlesticks, 5½ in. high. **£185-200** RB

A Lucas 'Silver King' Bicycle Oil Lamp, chrome plated, c1910. **£25-30** CCL

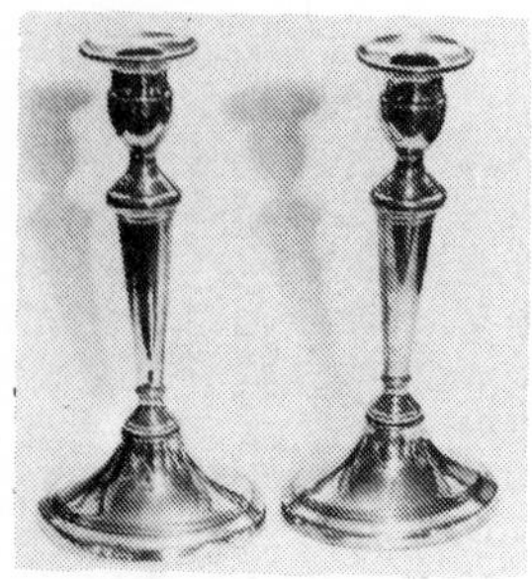

A Pair of early 19th C. Oval Bell Metal Candlesticks 10½ in. high. **£185-200** CC

A Small Art Nouveau Mirror. **£18-22** AP

An Art Nouveau Inkwell. **£28-34** AP

A Pair of Early 19th C. Bell Metal Candlesticks. **£60-65** RB

Art Nouveau Metal Picture Frame, 8" high. **£20-25** SQE

A Pair of Heavy Ormolu Putti Figures, 17 in., 43 cm. **£170-200** pr. L

An Art Nouveau Plated 'Amusing' Bird Box, c. 1909. **£25-28** AP

A pair of George III Ormolu Cassolettes by Matthew Boulton, with reversible gadrooned nozzles and urn-shaped bodies with turned socles. 8 in., 20 cm. high. **£680-750** C

An Art Nouveau signed French Spelter Bust, c. 1900. **£250-275** AP

A Pair of Large Spelter and Porcelain Ewers, 30 in., 76 cm., c. 1880. **£230-270** SB

A French Art Deco signed Spelter Figure of a Female and Gazelle 1920's. **£325-360** AP

A pair of Louis XV ormolu chenets with moulded supports and joined by a later fender 13½ in., 34 cm. high. **£390-430** C

A 'Little Joe' money bank, cast iron, late 19th C, 5¼" high. **£40-46** SQE

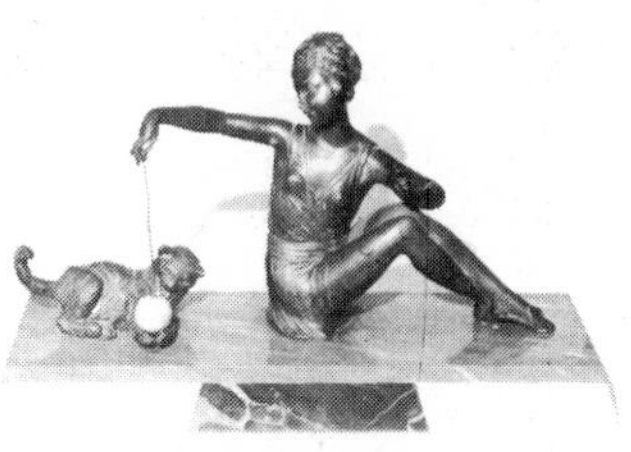

A Spelter & Marble Figure, 14 in. long, c. 1930's. **£90-100** CA

A Gilded Art Nouveau Figural Lamp, signed, Nelson, 26" high. **£270-320** CSK

An Art Nouveau Rectangular Jardiniere, 22" wide. **£570-650** CSK

A Nickel-Plated Female Figure, her hand upstretched holding a dove 11 in., 28 cm. high. **£65-70**

A Nickel-Plated Figure of a Jumping Horse and Jockey, the base inscribed C. H. Paillet and A. E. L. Copyright, 5½ in., 14 cm. high. **£70-80** CSK

A Nickel-Plated Figure of a Witch, mounted on a radiator cap 7½ in., 19 cm. high. **£120-130** CSK

A Russian cast-iron Group. **£135-150** SQE

A Pair of Spelter Mounted Figures, late Victorian, 14 in. high. **£140-160** pr. VA

Cast iron nutcrackers. **£13-15** A.L.

An Unusual finely cast model of a fish, probably a shachi, gold and shakudo eyes (damaged) signed Nihonkoku Maruki sei, late 19th C., 34.8 cm. long. **£820-920** C

A Chromium-Plated Stylised Figure of a Lincoln Greyhound, inscribed C. Brau and Depose, 9 in., 23 cm. long. **£140-160** CSK

A White-Metal Paper Weight and Inkwell modelled as L.N.E.R. locomotive, 10½ in., 27 cm. long. **£40-50** CSK

A Pair of Victorian Britannia metal tramp's boots, 4" long. **£30-35** pair SQE

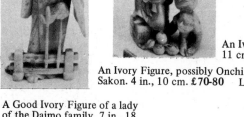

A Good Ivory Figure of a lady of the Daimo family. 7 in., 18 cm. **£80-90** L

An Ivory Figure, possibly Onchi Sakon. 4 in., 10 cm. **£70-80** L

An Ivory Group signed. 4¼ in., 11 cm. **£55-65** L

An Ivory figure of a man, the details stained, signed, late 19th C., 20 cm. **£360-400** SBe

left

A Tamahide Marine Ivory Group of a Fisherman, sepia stain, engraved 'tamahide' c. 1900, 22 cm. **£120-160** SBe

A Dieppe Carved Ivory Figure of a Palace Guard, French late 19th C. with faults, height 21 cm. **£350-430** SBe

A Fine Japanese Ivory Group of a Mushroom Farmer, signed on a red tablet. 3¾ in., 9.4 cm. high. **£310-390** L

An Ivory Group of a Warrior on horseback, sepia stain, signed, c. 1900, 26.5 cm. **£100-120** SBe

A Gyokuzan Marine Ivory Group of a Fisherman, sepia stain, engraved 'Gyokuzan' c. 1900, 27.5 cm. **£70-90** SBe

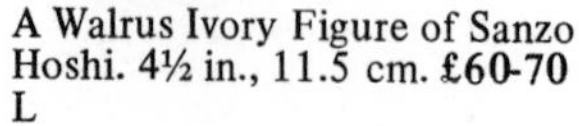

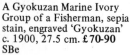

A Walrus Ivory Figure of Sanzo Hoshi. 4½ in., 11.5 cm. **£60-70** L

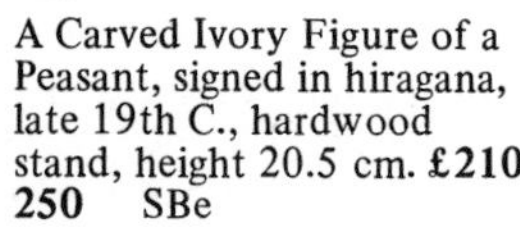

right

A Carved Ivory Figure of a Peasant, signed in hiragana, late 19th C., hardwood stand, height 20.5 cm. **£210-250** SBe

An Ivory Group of a Hunter, late 19th C., with faults., 16.5 cm. **£120-150** SBe

A carved ivory group 13.5 cm., incised square seal, late 19th C. **£350-400** SKC

A well-detailed stained ivory carving, (two small chips) rectangular red seal, Meiji/Taisho period, wood box, 14.2 cm. high. **£375-425** C

A very finely carved ivory group (base repaired) signed Dorakusai, Tokyo school, late Meiji period, 37.9 cm. high. **£2,400-2,500** C

A fine stained ivory carving, signed on a rectangular tablet . . . zan, Meiji/Taisho period, wood box. **£410-450** C

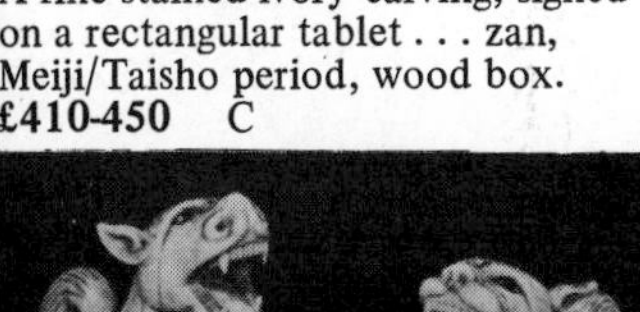

An Ivory figure of a Samurai Warrior, signed, late 19th C., with faults, 20.5 cm. **£180-220** SBe

An Ivory Okimono of Daruma. **£70-80** L

An Ivory Netsuke signed. **£70-80** L

A 19th C carved ivory Buddha. **£75-85** SAL

A pair of carved ivory temple dogs, 19th C. **£48-54** SAL

A Fine Bone Netsuke of Hotei **£35-40** L

A Shibayama Ivory Elephant, with beads in mother of pearl and hard-stone, late 19th C., 9 cm. **£260-300** SBe

A Fine Japanese Ivory and Wood Figure of an Armour Maker, signed on a red tablet. 4¼ in. high. **£580-680** L

An Ivory Netsuke of Jurojin. **£75-85** L

A Carved Ivory Okimono of a seated peasant, signed Mitsugioku, 2½ in., 58 cm. across. **£230-270** L

A Chinese ivory carving of an emperor, (small piece missing) silk brocade stand 19.4 cm. high. **£450-500** C

An Ivory Okimono of Kinko, sepia stain, late 19th C., 10.5 cm. **£190-220** SBe

A fine stained ivory carving of a Chinese sage, rectangular red seal, Meiji/Taisho period, wood box, 12 cm. high. **£420-470** C

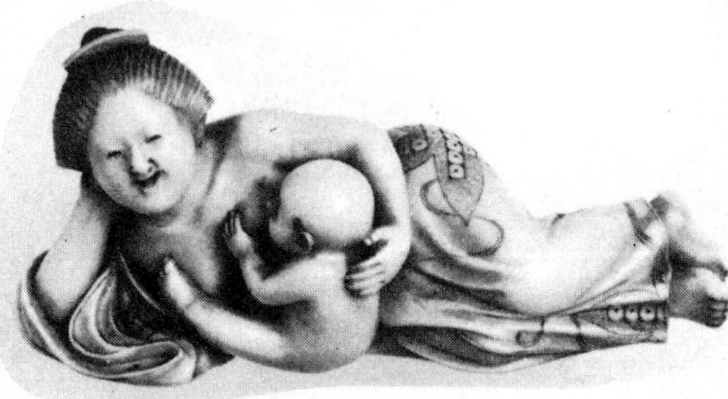

A well-carved ivory okimono-style netsuke, signed on a rectangular red tablet Seiko, late 19th C. **£420-450** C

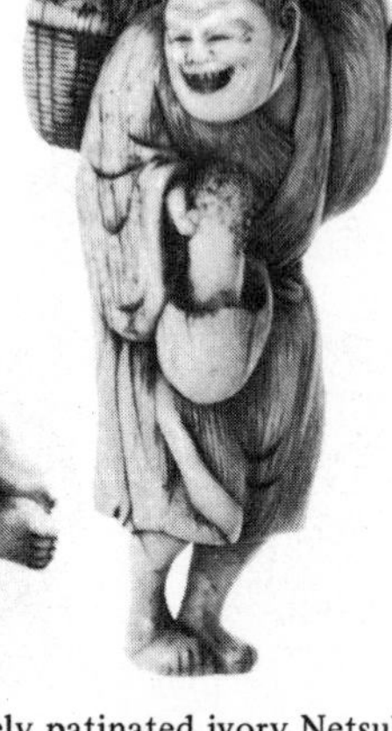

A finely patinated ivory Netsuke of a farmer, the details engraved (age cracks) unsigned, 18th C. **£350-375** C

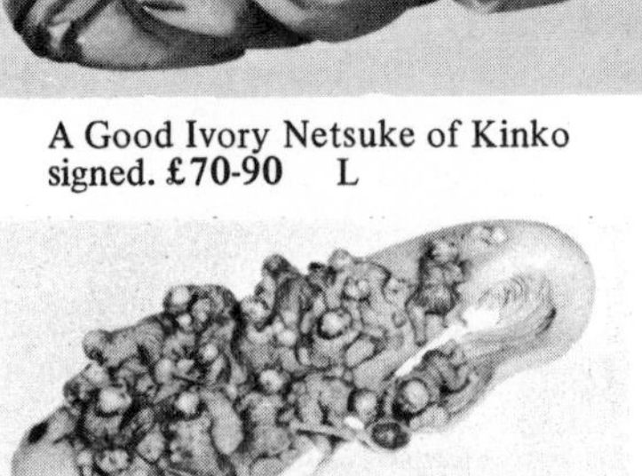

A Good Ivory Netsuke of Kinko signed. **£70-90** L

An Ivory Netsuke. **£45-55** L

An ivory Netsuke of Kan Yu, finely worn and patinated, unsigned, 18th C. **£375-400** C

An Ivory Okimono of a Cat Fish, signed, late 19th C., 12 cm. **£260-300** SBe

A Miyachika Carved Wood and Ivory Falconer, details picked out in mother of pearl, fixed lacquered wood stand, late 19th C., with faults, 33 cm. **£790-890** SBe

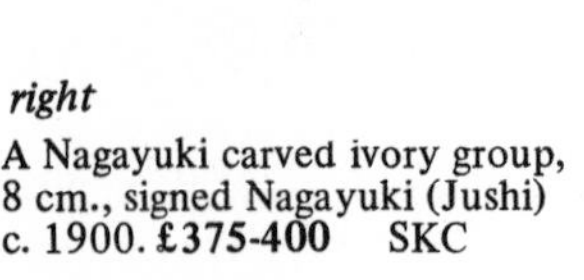

right
A Nagayuki carved ivory group, 8 cm., signed Nagayuki (Jushi) c. 1900. **£375-400** SKC

A 19th C Japanese carved ivory figure of a seated girl, signed, 6¼" high, with faults. **£325-380** GC

A carved ivory netsuke of a recumbent karashishi (slightly chipped) unsigned, late 18th C. **£440-480** C

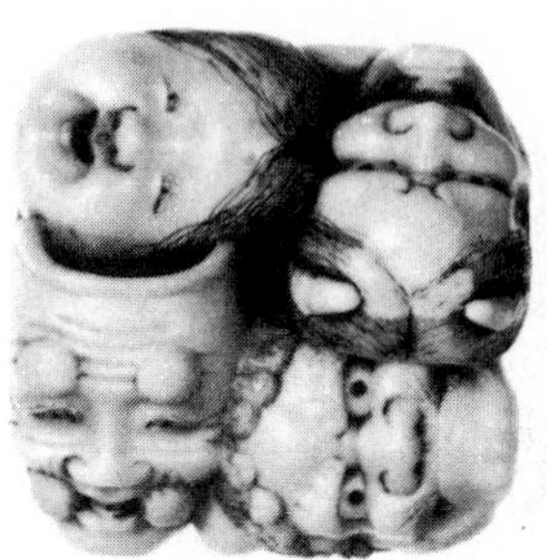

A finely carved ivory Netsuke of Seven Masks signed Tadachika, Tokyo (Edo) school, late 19th C. **£260-300** C

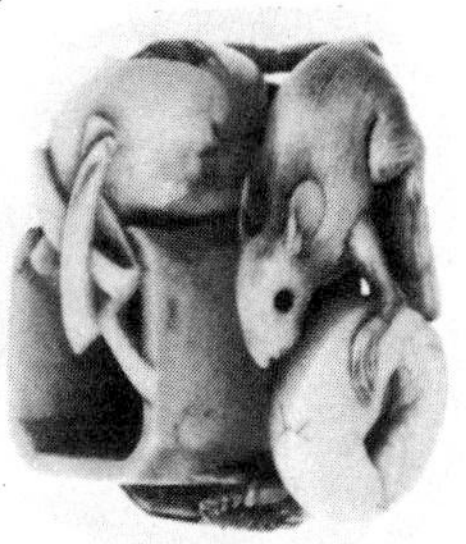

A lightly stained ivory Netsuke of a mouse, signed Gyokushinsai, 19th C. **£260-300** C

An ivory Netsuke of a Sennin seated on the back of a ho-o, unsigned, probably early 19th C. **£350-375** C

A well-carved ivory Manju Netsuke, decorated in shishiai-bori, signed Shunkosai (Chogetsu, Seisetsu, 1826-1892) 19th C. **£300-320** C

An ivory Netsuke of a monkey, signed Hompu, early 19th C. **£500-525** C

Japanese ivory netsuke, 2" high. **£35-40** STR

An ivory Manju, signed Homin wuth kakihan, mid-19th C. **£350-400** SKC

19th C Japanese ivory netsuke, 1¾" high. **£90-100** STR

A well painted ivory Netsuke of a seated Karashishi, engraved detail (age crack) signed Gyokushosai, early 19th C. **£275-300** C

Japanese ivory netsuke, 2" high. **£45-50** STR

left
A finely carved ivory Manju Netsuke, decorated in shishiai-bori with Seiobo holding a fan, signed Kogetsu, 19th C. **£675-700** C

A finely carved ivory Netsuke of a Sarumawashi, signed Yoshiyuki, and kao, late 19th C. **£300-350** C

A carved ivory netsuke, 19th C. **£58-65** SAL

A well-painted ivory Netsuke of a group of mice, unsigned, school of Masamitsu, late 19th C. **£375-400** C

A Pair of Ivory Brush Vases, each curved body inlaid with mother-of-pearl, tortòiseshell and hard-stone, fixed hardwood stand, late 19th C., some inlay missing, height 26.5 cm. overall. **£420-500** SBe

A Carved Ivory Lidded Bowl or Pot, c. 1870, Chinese. damaged **£20-25**, perfect **£150-170** CA

A Pair of Lacquered and Shibayama Ivory Brush Vases, the details in gold, red and black lacquer, mother of pearl and stained ivory, fixed lacquered stands, height 22 cm . **£310-360** pr. SBe

A Fine Ivory and Shibayama Tusk Vase inlaid in tinted mother o'pearl 6¾ in., 17.2 cm. **£530-610** L

An Early 19th C Chinese Ivory Jewel Casket, with gold hinges and escutcheons, 3½" high, 5½" wide. **£300-400** CA

A carved ivory Box and Cover of oval section, Japanese, late 19th C, 12cms. **£290-340** SBe

A Cantonese Ivory Work Box, the fitted interior including lace-making fitments, mid 19th C., glass dome and plinth, 30 cm. **£390-460** SBe

Japanese ivory scent bottle, in shape of a gourd, 3" long. **£32-36** STR

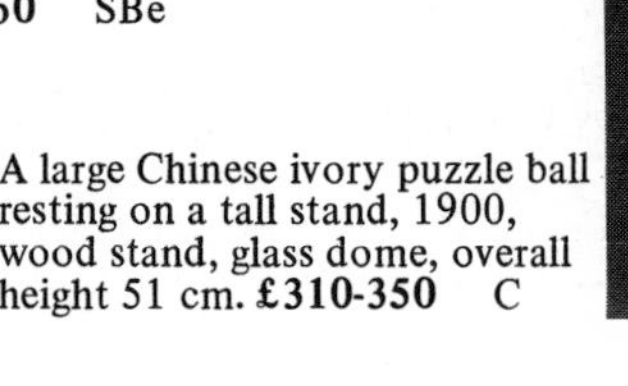

A large Chinese ivory puzzle ball resting on a tall stand, 1900, wood stand, glass dome, overall height 51 cm. **£310-350** C

A fine Chinese ivory tusk carving of a dragon-headed boat, carved wood stand 42.5 cm. long. **£750-800** C

A lightly stained ivory Netsuke of a chick, (age cracks) unsigned, 19th C. **£285-320** C

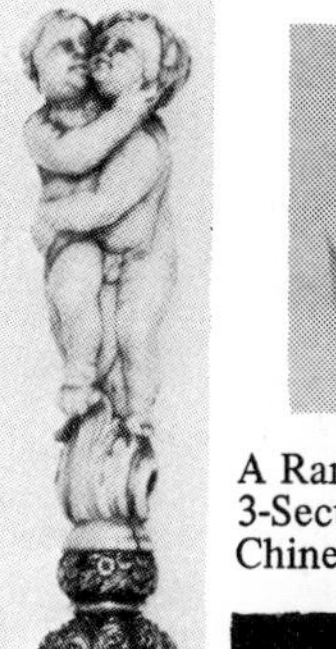

A gold-mounted ivory table seal with oblong white agate seal, the handle Flemish, late 17th C., the mount early 19th C., 3 in., 85 mm. high. **£420-450** C

A Rare Ivory Doctor's Tubular 3-Section Sash-Box, c. 19th C., Chinese. **£185-200** TA

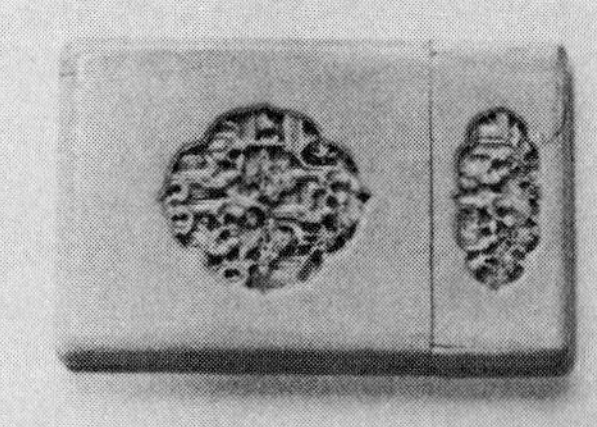

An Ivory Card Case, with finely carved insets. **£50-65** SQE

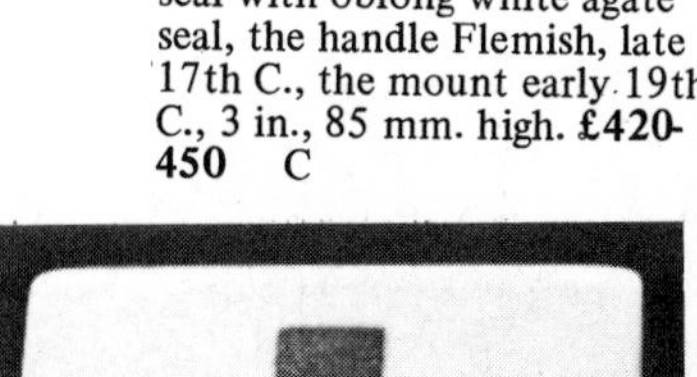

An 18th C ivory patch box with gold mounts. **£70-80** SAL

A Carved Ivory Figure by F. Preiss of a seated nude girl (hair cracks) 9 cm. high. **£445-490** C

An onyx and ivory Ash Tray, not signed, possibly by Preiss, c1920's, 4". **£150-175**

A Good Pair of carved wood and ivory beggars. German late 19th C. with faults, height 28 cm. **£890-990** pr. SBe

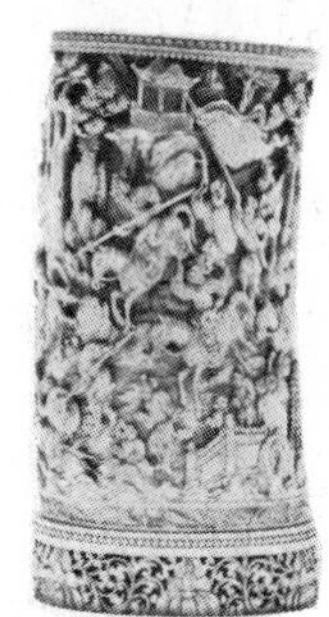

An Ivory Vase, late 19th C., with faults, 25.5 cm. **£300-380** SBe

"The Altar of Love" painting 'en camaieu' Ivory and Tortoiseshell Snuff Box, c. 1800, 3 in. diam. **£260-290** HD

A Fan, the leaf painted, the ivory sticks carved, pierced and painted, 10¾ in., English, c. 1750. **£220-260** CSK

A Fan, the leaf painted with the Triumph of Venus, the shaped ivory sticks carved, pierced and pique in silver, 10¾ in., Italian early 18th C. **£190-250** CSK

right

A Fan, the silk leaf painted, embroidered with gold and pink spangles, the ivory sticks carved, pierced, gilt and silvered, 11¼ in. French, c. 1780. **£240-300** CSK

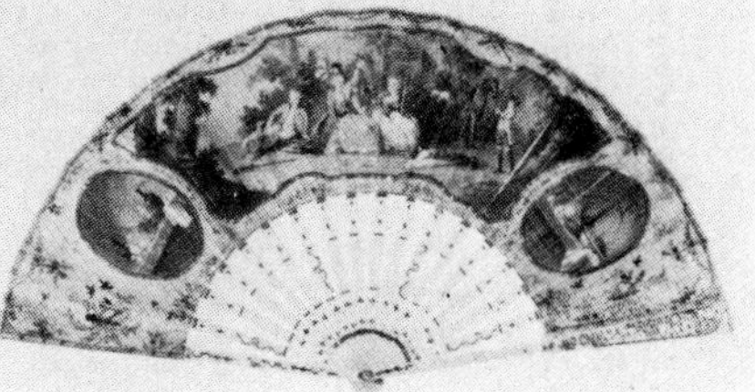

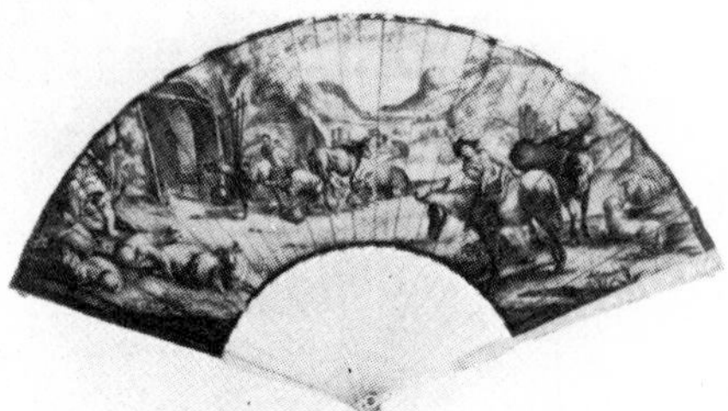

A Fan, the leaf painted, the ivory sticks carved with dancing figures, 10½ in., Italian, c. 1720, in fan case. **£280-340** CSK

A Fan, the leaf painted, the ivory sticks carved, pierced, silvered and gilt with Chinoiserie figures and trophies of Love, 10¾ in., French c. 1760. **£80-110** CSK

POINTERS FOR FANS

- Both rigid and folding fans originated in Japan and their quality has never been surpassed.
- The Portuguese introduced the fan to Europe.
- France was the centre of the European fanmaking industry.
- 18th C. was the height of the fan industry.
- 19th C. quality began to deteriorate.
- The change of life style during the 1st World War heralded the end of the fan.

An Amusing Fan, the mount composed of lily-leaf-shaped painted panels, with mother-of-pearl sticks, 10 in., late 19th C. **£45-55** CSK

A Fan, the ivory sticks carved with the vintage, silvered and gilt, 10in, English, c. 1750, **£160-200** CSK

A Fan, with leaf painted in the style of J.B. Pillement, 10½in, possibly Swiss, c. 1780, **£230-300** CSK

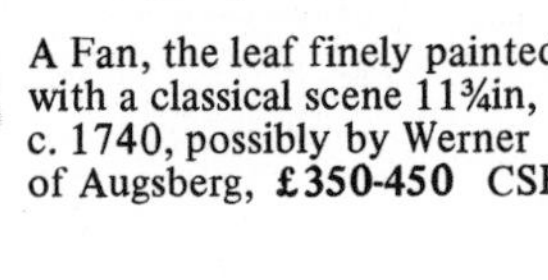

A Fan, the leaf finely painted with a classical scene 11¾in, c. 1740, possibly by Werner of Augsberg, **£350-450** CSK

A Mourning Fan, the leaf a tinted and silvered trompe l'oeil, the bone sticks silvered with straight and wavy lines, 10½in, English, c. 1750, **£100-130** CSK

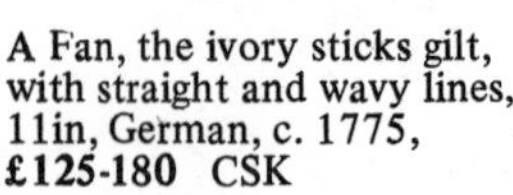

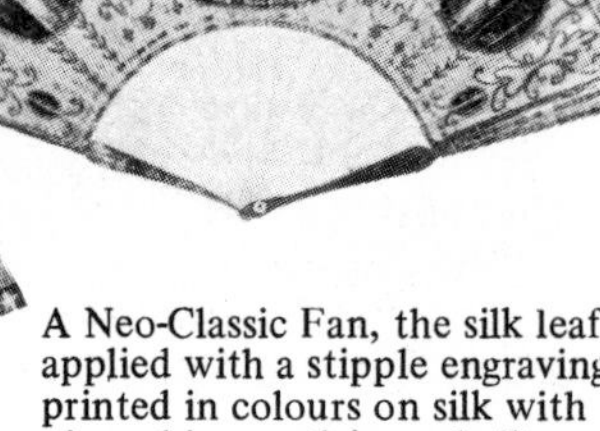

A Fan, the ivory sticks gilt, with straight and wavy lines, 11in, German, c. 1775, **£125-180** CSK

A Fan, with vellum leaf, with tortoiseshell sticks pique with silver, 11½in, Italian, c. 1730, **£350-400** CSK

A Neo-Classic Fan, the silk leaf applied with a stipple engraving printed in colours on silk with pierced ivory sticks and gilt metal guards set with paste, 9¾ in., c. 1790. **£150-180** CSK

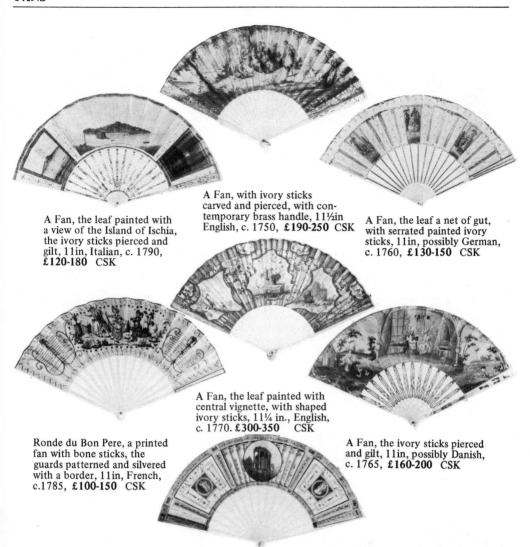

A Fan, the leaf painted with a view of the Island of Ischia, the ivory sticks pierced and gilt, 11in, Italian, c. 1790, **£120-180** CSK

A Fan, with ivory sticks carved and pierced, with contemporary brass handle, 11½in English, c. 1750, **£190-250** CSK

A Fan, the leaf a net of gut, with serrated painted ivory sticks, 11in, possibly German, c. 1760, **£130-150** CSK

Ronde du Bon Pere, a printed fan with bone sticks, the guards patterned and silvered with a border, 11in, French, c.1785, **£100-150** CSK

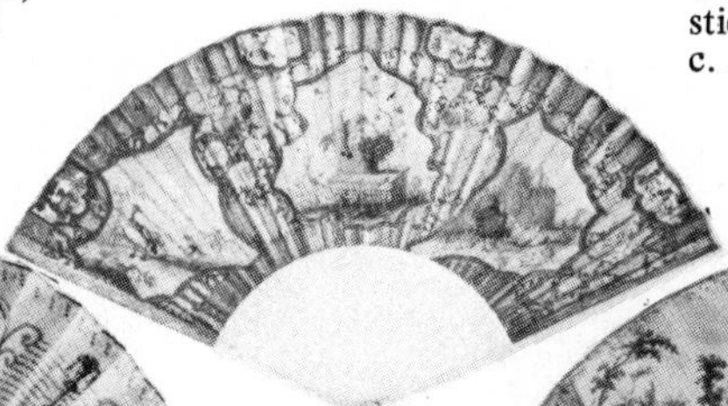

A Fan, the leaf painted with central vignette, with shaped ivory sticks, 11¼ in., English, c. 1770. **£300-350** CSK

A Fan, the ivory sticks pierced and gilt, 11in, possibly Danish, c. 1765, **£160-200** CSK

A Fan with chickenskin leaf, with plain ivory sticks, 11in, Italian, c. 1780, **£150-200** CSK

CHESS SETS

A Phillipine Set in horn, ivory and wood of abstract design, 18th C. height of kings 1½ in., 42 mm. **£700-800** C

An English Arcadian Porcelain Set, each piece painted with the coat-of-arms of Worthing, height of kings 3½ in., 90 mm. **£110-150** C

A Madras Polychrome Brass Set, the cast pieces fully armed and coloured red or green, 18th C., height of kings 3½ in., 90 mm. **£900-1,000** C

A Japanese Shogi Set with twenty pieces to each side length of board 14½ in., 37.3 cm. height of kings 2½ in., 67 mm. **£480-560** C

A Swiss Softwood 'Bears of Berne' Set, in light and darker hues, 19th C. height of kings 3¼ in., 84 mm. **£600-670** C

A Chinese Ivory Chess Set on Stand with Domed Glass Cover, 5½ and 2½ in. men, c. 1880. **£200-250** RD

An English Ivory Set of 'barley-corn' design, natural and red-stained, 19th C. height of kings 3¾ in., 95 mm. **£300-380** C

A Spanish Pulpit Set in Bone, one side stained brown, late 18th C. height of kings 5½ in., 140 mm. **£2,800-3,100** C

left

An English Ivory Set, natural and red-stained, (red king restored), 19th C. probably marketed by Messrs. Calvert of Fleet Street height of kings 3½ in., 90 mm. **£400-450** C

A French Ivory and Bone Set of Bust Type, Dieppe, c. 1800 height of kings 3¼ in., 85 mm. **£900-1,000** C

A French Bone and Ivory Set of Bust Type, one side natural, one tinted in dark green and black, Dieppe 18th C. height of kings 2¾ in., 70 mm. **£1,300-1,500** C

right

A Chinese Unusual Ivory Set, natural and red-stained, probably late 18th C. height of kings 3 in., 75 mm. **£950-1,050** C

An Indian Ivory Set, natural and brown-stained, c. 1800 probably Kashmir height of kings 3 in., 76 mm. **£500-580** C

A German Biscuit Porcelain Set, one side white, one blue, the kings and queens as 18th C. monarchs, height of kings 3¾ in., 95 mm. **£400-450** C

A Chinese Ivory Set Made For Export, natural and red-stained, 19th C. height of kings 4½ in., 118 mm. **£650-720** C

An English Ivory Set, natural and red-stained, 19th C. height of kings 4 in., 100 mm. **£260-290** C

A small Hinoki wood standing figure of Kichijoten (hands and toes missing), 16th/17th C, wood block base, 17.7cms high. **£175-200** C

A Chinese gilt-wood sculpture of a seated Bodhisattva (restored, left hand damaged), late Ming/ early Ch'ing dynasty, 24.2cms high. **£220-280** C

A finely carved Hinoki wood standing figure of Shaka Nyorai (hand and foot missing, other slight damage), 18th/19th C, wood block base, 24.3cms high. **£440-500** C

A Yosegizukuri wood sculpture of Kannon Bosatsu, lacquered red (left forearm missing, old damage and repairs), Edo period, 48cms high. **£285-325** C

A wood study of a Sarumawashi, unsigned, late 18th C. **£155-175** SKC

A Good Standing Carved Wood Figure of an Oni, late 18th/early 19th C. **£80-90** L

An Early 18th C. Tobacco Sign, 27 in. high. **£380-430** RB

An Interesting Carved Wood Figure of a Woman, probably American., 19 in., 48 cm. **£310-350** L

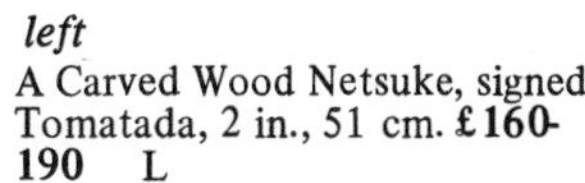

left
A Carved Wood Netsuke, signed Tomatada, 2 in., 51 cm. **£160-190** L

A Chinese ebony carved Elephant, with hardwood stand, signed. **£55-65** SAL

A Wood Group representing the legend of Kanshin, the Han Dynasty hero, unsigned, early 19th C. **£180-220** SKC

A Rare Pair of German Wood and Bone Figures, 18th C., 15½ in., 39 cm. **£650-730** L

A wood seated figure of Shotoku Taishi (slightly damaged), inscribed on the base Sukekichi kore o tsukuru, early Edo period, 21.7cms high. **£440-500** C

An 18th C. Carved Pair of Dogs-of-Fo, Chinese, 11½ in. **£240-260** pr. RB

An Oak Carving, 18th C. possibly German. **£200-230** RB

A Carved Wood Netsuke of mice, signed Tomokazu. 1¼ in., 34 cm. **£210-240** L

A Carved Wood Okimono of a snake, unsigned. 1¾ in., 46 cm. **£215-245** L

One of a pair of carved wood 19th C. Oriental Figures, 13 in. high. **£240-275** pr. SV

Early Victorian small travelling folding mirror. **£12-15** IN

19th C Shaving Mirror. **£45-55** IN

A Mahogany Hand Mirror, c. 1820, 13¾ in. long. **£65-75** HD

A 19th C. American Carved Figure, possibly part of a spinning wheel. **£75-80** RB

A small, late 18th C. carving of two Cherubim, probably from an Italian Frieze. 6 in. wide. **£30–50** SM

An Early 19th C. English Carved Wooden Figure. **£85-95** RB

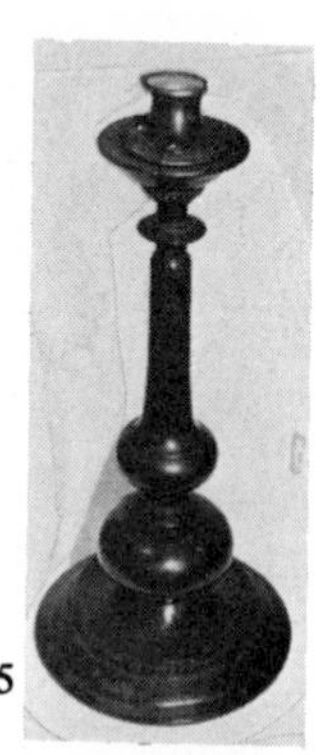

One of a Set of Four Kashmiri Late 19th C. Lacquered Wood Candlesticks, 17 in. high. **£140-160** set. RB

19th C. hardwood Hat Stretcher. **£15–18** MM

19th C decorative carved oak pieces, 11½" long. **£8-10** STR

A Pair of 19th C. Fruitwood Candlesticks, 8 in. high. **£48-58** pr. HD

A Pair of 18th C. Continental Wooden Candlesticks, 29 in. **£185-205** pr. RB

A Pair of 17th C. Oak Carvings. **£165-185** pr. CSG

One of a Pair of Early 19th C. Carved Wood Plaques, 16 in. x 20 in. **£175-200** pr. RB

An Early 19th C. Carving, 24 in. high. **£175-200** RB

A late 18th C. carved Angel's Head, probably originally part of a pine frieze. 12 in. wide. **£150–160** SM

Three Late 19th C. Wooden Nutcrackers, German or Austrian **£35-50** each. RB

A Well-Carved Indian Walnut Shrine, elaborately carved with deities and elephants, 114 cm. x 63.5 cm., late 19th C. **£250-300** SB

A Pair of 19th C. Walnut Brackets, with carved cherubs, 20 in. **£925-1,050** pr. CSG

An Early 19th Wooden Bowl. **£22-25** RB

An Old English Wooden Mixing Bowl, probably walnut, 9 in. diam. **£58-68** SA

Late 17th/Early 18th C Welsh Cream Bowl in sycamore, 19" diam. **£70-100** STR

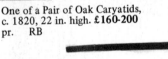

One of a Pair of Oak Caryatids, c. 1820, 22 in. high. **£160-200** pr. RB

An Olive Wood Tobacco Box, c. 1840, 7 in. high. **£110-130** HD

A Kava Bowl from Fiji, 19th C. 15½ in. diam. **£275-300** RB

A Stained Beech and Composition Corner Bracket, 30 in., 76 cm., 1880's. **£60-80** SB

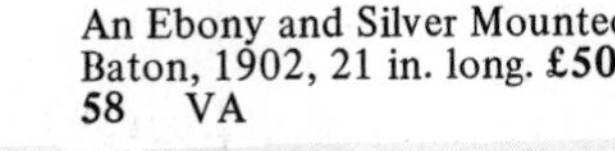

An Ebony and Silver Mounted Baton, 1902, 21 in. long. **£50-58** VA

Swiss Carved Wood Squirrel Nutcrackers, c. 1880. **£20-24** CA

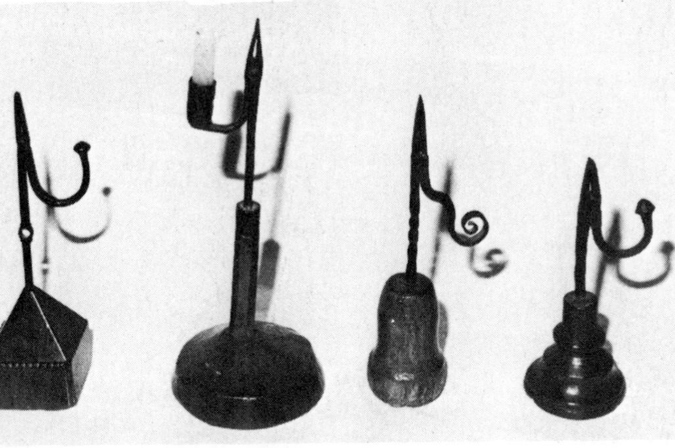

18th C. Rush Light Holders with fruitwood bases, 1-r **£75, £120, £65, £75** DB

An unusual pair of Queen Anne carved giltwood wall-lights fitted for electricity 24 in., 61 cm. high. **£2,530-2,600** C

Antique Group of carved wood Swiss chalet, figures and animals, under glass dome, 14" diam. **£105-120** SQE

A Polished Wood Walking Stick with silver band inscribed 'To John S. Clarke from his friend Harry Lauder, March 2nd 1938' 2 ft. 11½ in., 90 cm. long. **£80-120** SB

A Pair of 18th C. Mahogany wine carriers. **£1,250-1,300** CC

A Dutch Carved Oak Carriage Foot-Warmer the top pierced and carved with foliage and birds, early 19th C. 9¼ in., 23.5 cm. wide. **£340-375** C

An Inlaid Cribbage Board, c. 1860, 10 in. long open. **£46-50** HD

A Travelling Coat Hook, c. 1820, 22 in. open. **£75-85** HD

A shaped rectangular wood lectern decorated in gold, silver and red hiramakie and takamakie (rubbed), 19th C, 58.3cms high. **£310-350** C

An ebony Dressing Table Set: pair of candlesticks, 4" high, ring stand and pin holder, 19th C. **£15-20** SQE

A 19th C Swiss Carved Bear Umbrella Stand, 3' (92cms) high, c1850. **£355-400** SKC

An Old English Police Truncheon. **£55-65** SA

18th/19th C carved elm Yoke with hand forged chain. **£35-50** STR

A 19th C Boot Jack. **£45-55** SAL

A Painted Wood Model of a Shrine, the roof with copper tiles, 68.5 cm., c. 1900. **£175-220** SB

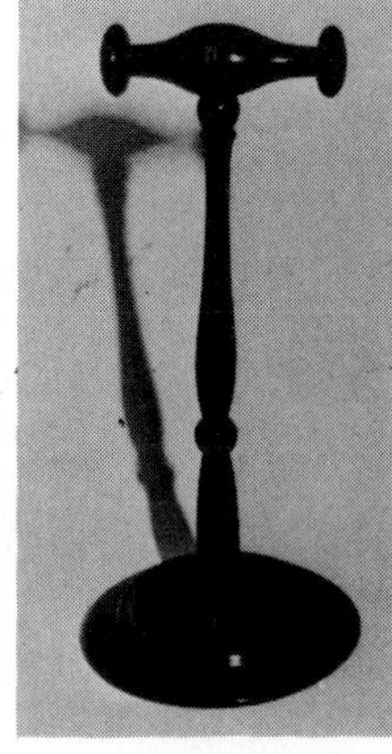

A Georgian Mahogany Wig Stand, c. 1810, 12 in. high. **£70-80** HD

A Regency Rosewood Turned Extending Candle Holder. **£165-185** HD

A Long-Handled Wooden Strainer, c. 1800, 17 in. long. **£50-55** RB

A Victorian brass bound wooden Tankard. **£25-30** A.L.

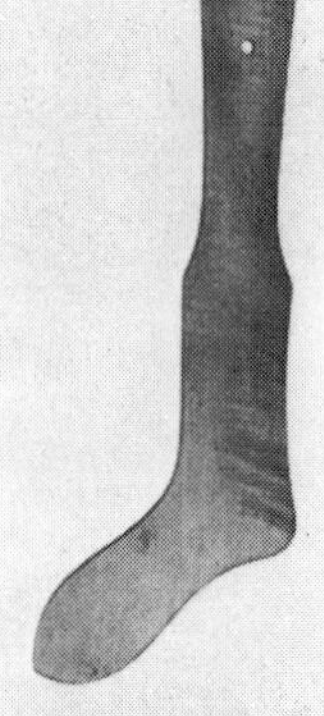

Wooden Stocking/Sock Display or Dryer. **£9-12** IN

An Early 19th C. Wooden Mortar and Pestle. **£65-70** RB

A prisoner of war pipe, carved 1902. **£30-35** SAL

19th C. Treen Nutcrackers 7 in. long. **£140-160** CC

TREEN

- Treen is a collective name for small wooden articles of domestic use - usually applied to turned objects.
- Unlikely to predate late 17th c.
- Early pieces usually rustic food containers and drinking utensils, made of alder walnut, poplar, fruitwoods, later boxwood and maple.
- After 1720, lignum vitae, ebony and teak used.
- Best period 1720-1790.
- Victorian treen generally clumsier than 18th c.
- Original fine carving adds value.

A Very Fine Quality Laburnum & Cherry Wood Bobbin Stand, early 19th C., 9 in. high. **£310-350** HD

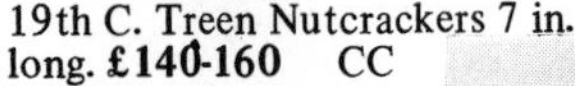

Early 19th C Treen candlestand with extending top. **£48-55** IN

Treen Letter Rack, Mauchline ware with 2 views of Canterbury Cathedral. **£7-10** STR

An Early 19th C. Scandinavian Tankard, 6 in. high. **£135-155** RB

(r) A Late Victorian Fern-ware spill holder. **£12-15** IN

An Old English Cotton Reel Stand, 7 in. high. **£95-105** SA

A Victorian Adjustable Candle Stand, 12½ in. high. **£65-75** SA

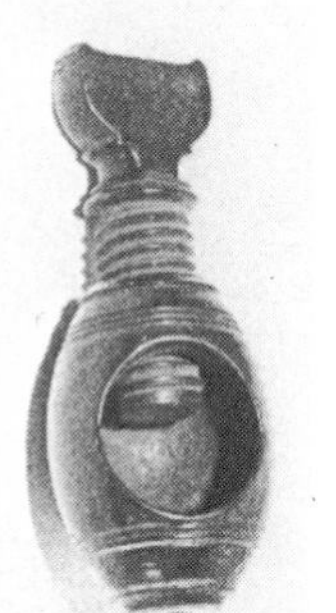

A wooden nutcracker, 3" long. **£15-17** A.L.

Treen thread holder. **£35-40** SAL

A Victorian wooden Tankard. **£25-30** A.L.

A Victorian Treen embroidery frame, 12" high. **£35-45** IN

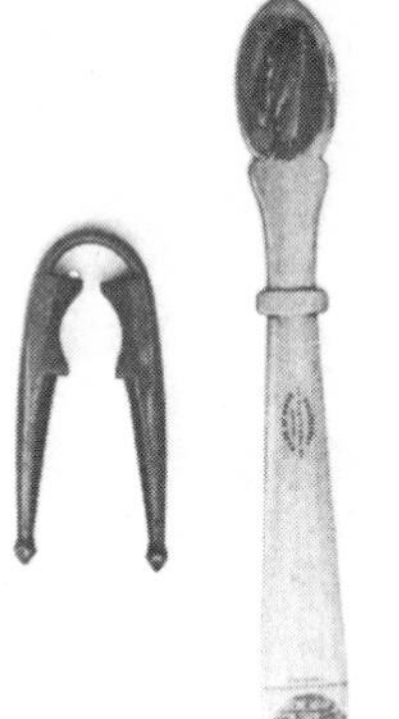

(l) 18th C Nutcrackers. **£20-25**

(r) A Treen paperknife. **£8-12** IN

A Victorian Adjustable Candle-stand, 13 in. high. **£55-65** SA

A Georgian Watch Stand, c. 1790, 7 in. high. **£110-120** HD

An 18th C. Scandinavian Peg Tankard 8 in. high. **£330-360** CC

A 19th C Scandinavian Treen Butter Carrier, 12" high x 12" diam. (30cms x 30cms). **£140-160** B

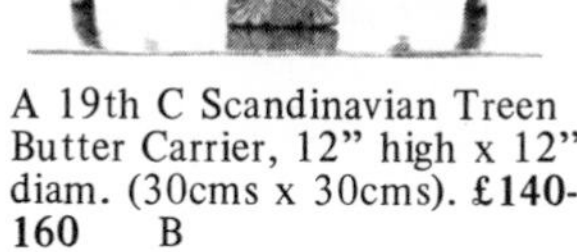

An Unusual Pair of Early 19th C. Treen Candlesticks with box-wood candles, 8½ in. **£320-350** SA

A 19th C. Treen Pot Pourri. **£15-18** AP

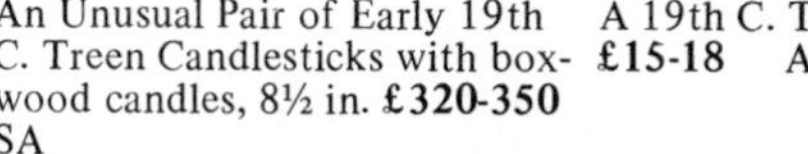

A Lignum Vitae String Barrel, c. 1840, 4½ in. high. **£70-90** HD

A Sycamore Pin Cushion, c1840-1880. **£10-15** IN

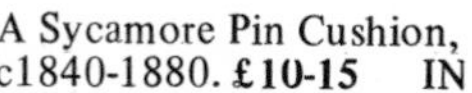

A Treen Looking Glass, 11½ in. long, c. 1800. **£115-130** HD

An Unusual Beehive String Box, c. 1840, 5 in. high. **£140-160** SA

19th C Ring Stand. **£8-12** IN

A Treen Goblet, 5" high. **£25-30** A.L.

A Treen Needlework Stand, early 19th C. **£95-105** HD

Wooden nutmeg grater in the shape of an acorn. **£35-40** A.L.

A Fine Mahogany 'Ring Tree', an unusual item in Treen, mid 19th C. **£15-20** TA

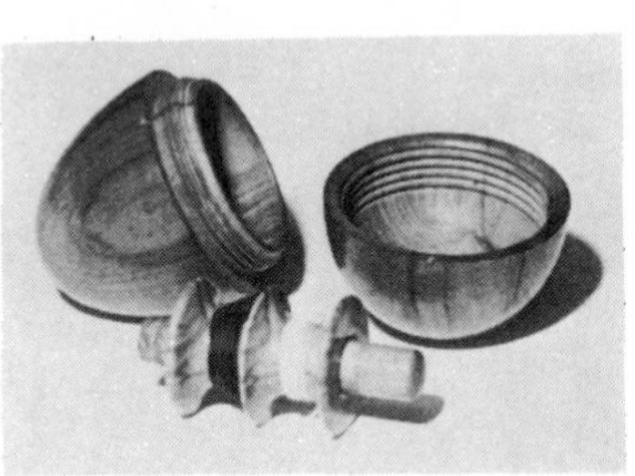
Treen Egg, containing bobbin and needleholder. **£20-25** STR

Treen chamberstick, 3" high. **£16-20** STR

A Treen Toothpick Holder. **£15-18** SV

A 19th C Treen perfume bottle holder, with original bottle, 5½" high. **£20-30**

A 19th C Treen glove powderer, 4¾" high. **£14-20** IN

Three George III Lignum Vitae Spice Grinders, divided in three unscrewing parts and with a screw-on lid, 11½ in., 29 cm. high, 10 in., 26 cm., high and 9¾ in., 25 cm. high. **£600-800** S

A Pair of Treen Pots, early 19th C. **£55-65** pair. RB

A Rosewood protected Match holder and Candle holder, 1810-25. **£35-45** IN

An Unusual Treen Chamberstick with snuffer stands and copperhandle, c. 1800, 5 in. high. **£235-255** HD

A Treen Powder Box, c. 1840, 3¾ in. **£25-30** HD

A Rare Pair of Treen Candlesticks 5 in. high. **£95-105** SA

A Lignum Vitae String Barrel, c. 1810, 3½ in. high. **£95-105** HD

A 19th C Treen set of chamber sticks, which collapse into a box. **£35-40** SAL

A Victorian Treen glove powderer, 6". **£18-20** IN

Treen ink sander, 4½" high. **£30-35** STR

A Rare Treen Penny-in-the-Slot Tobacco Box, early 19th C. This piece is unusual in wood and is more common in brass, wood **£400-460** brass **£200-250** SA

A 19th C. Treen Box. **£15-18** AP

A Treen Moores ointment box. **£4-6** A.L.

Treen Tambour Set with photographic scene possibly German. **£14-20** IN

Treen salve pot, 3½" high. **£20-25** STR

A Treen Shaving Soap Dish with lid, by Mornay of Regent Street, c1920, 4" diam. **£5-6** SQE

A Rosewood Needle Selector by Wheeler & Wilson, c1870. **£18-20** IN

A Treen powder Box with two views of Dawlish. **£4-6** A.L.

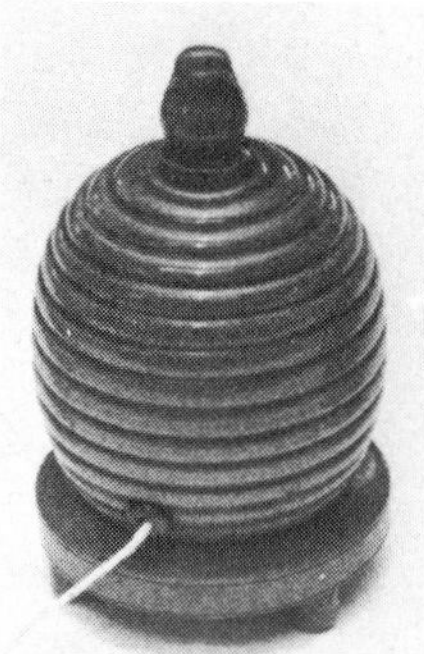

Treen beehive string dispenser with cutter, 4" high. **£60-70** STR

A Treen circular box. **£13-15** SV

A Treen spice turret, 8½" high **£40-45** A.L.

A Treen glass case with a printed picture of Weymouth. **£4-6** A.L.

A Treen Seed turret with four compartments reading Early Turnip, Fine Lettuce, Cabbage Lettuce and Carrot, 7" high. **£40-45** A.L.

Treen salve pot, 3½" diam. **£12-18** STR

A Spice turret for cloves and mace, 4½" high. **£25-30** A.L.

BRONZE

After Coustou: A Pair of French Bronze Marly Horses, 21 in., 53 cm., dark patination, late 19th C. **£350-400** L

A Seiya Bronze Animal Group, signed, late 19th C., wood stand, 17.5 cm. **£90-100** SBe

A Fine Massive Bronze model of a snarling tiger (tip of tail repaired) signed Dai Nippon Senryukei Seikoku zo, Meiji period. 122.5 cm. long. **£3,000-3,300** C

A gilt bronze figure of a recumbent horned mythical beast, probably Ming Dynasty, wood stand. 2¼ in., 6 cm. long. **£110-130** C

A Japanese Bronze, cast as a fan. 10½ in., 27.5 cm. **£200-250** L

A Bronze Group of Two Greyhounds, 8 in., 20.3 cm. late 19th C. **£310-350** SB

After A. Leonard, a gilt-bronze and ivory figure, signed 'A. Leonard', early 20th C., 29 cm. **£590-680** SBe

A French Bronze Figure of a Cow and Calf, unsigned, 19th C. **£250-280** SA

A Pair of bronze Rabbits by Edouard Marcel Sandoz, the rabbits 5cms high, inscribed Ed. M. Sandoz and Susse Fes. Ed. Paris. **£135-165** P

A Bronze Figure of Sheep by Rosa Bonheur, French, c. 1870's. **£300-330** SA

A Late 19th C. Bronze Lion, 9 in. long. **£125-135** VA

A bronze group of two horses by the Russian sculptor P. Tourguenoff, who was working in Paris, late 19th C. **£2,000-2,200** SAL

A pair of bronze taper holders cast as standing cranes (one holder and one stalk missing) 12¾ in., 32.5 cm. high. **£285-325** C

A Bronze Figure of an Eagle, wingspan 6¾ in., 17.5 cm. **£25-30** CSK

A Bronze Crane, Chinese, late 18th/early 19th C., 14 in., 36 cm. **£85-100** L

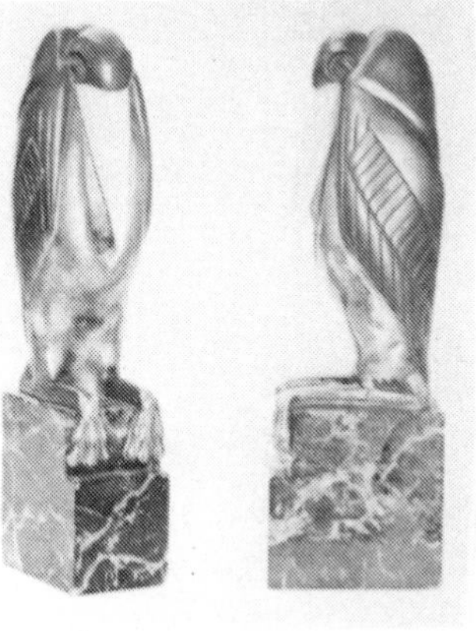
A Pair of Bouraine Silvered Bronze and Ivory Ravens, signed 'Bouraine', 1920's, 25cms high. **£220-250** SBe

A bronze model of a hawk, 45 cm., overall, Japanese, late 19th C. **£470-500** SKC

A gilt-bronze figure of a standing Buddhistic lion (tail damaged) Tang Dynasty 2¼ in., 5.5 cm. long. **£420-450** C

An inlaid bronze vessel, inset in silver and gold sheet (minor surface damage) Ming/Qing Dynasty 4 in., 10.5 cm. long **£500-550** C

A bronze vessel cast in the Warring States style, with patches of malachite encrustation, Song/Ming Dynasty 7¼ in., 20 cm. long. **£280-325** C

A pair of bronze censers cast as standing geese, their backs forming detachable covers, Qing Dynasty 9 in., 23 cm. long **£420-500** C

A pair of bronze figures of Caparisoned horses 5¼ in., 13 cm. high. **£240-280** C

A Bronze study of an Arab mare and foal, signed P. J. Mene, 12" (30.5cms), brown rubbed patination. **£790-840** SKC

A Fine bronze model of a tiger, signed Genryukei Seiya zo, Meiji period. 57.5 cm. long. **£740-840** C

A French 19th C. Bronze Figure of a Curlew by Delapierre. **£400-440** SA

After the antique, a bronze figure of Mercury, bearing founders mark Neapolitan, early 20th C., 55 cm. **£320-400** SBe

After A. Carrier Belleuse, a pair of bronze figures of medieval warriors and signed 'A. Carrier', French 1880, 63 cm. and 76 cm. **£1,700-1,900** SBe

After Bologna, a bronze figure of Mercury, signed 'Bologna' and a similar figure of Ceres signed 'Sobre' late 19th C. with faults, height 84 cm., height 80 cm. **£350-420** SBe

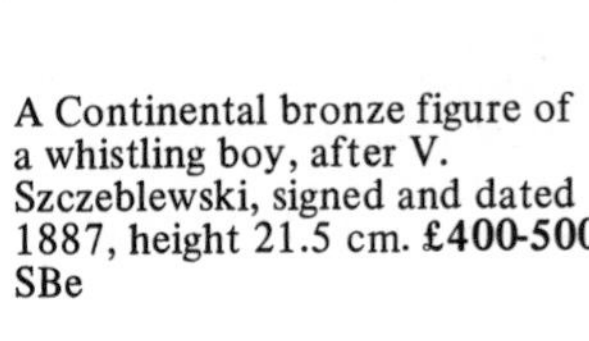

A Continental bronze figure of a whistling boy, after V. Szczeblewski, signed and dated 1887, height 21.5 cm. **£400-500** SBe

A Bronze figure of a girl, signed 'Albert Bruce Joy, SC' late 19th C., dark green patination, 89 cm. **£900-1,000** SBe

After Frederick Thrupp, a bronze figure of a young woman, inscribed "Mercy making garments for the poor", signed Fred Thrupp sculptor, c. 1870., 58 cm. **£410-500** SBe

After Giovanni Bologna a bronze group of 'The Rape of the Sabine Women' Italian c. 1900 total height 88 cm. **£450-520** SBe

A Bronze Figure of a Dancing Girl, dark brown patination late 19th C., 50 cm. **£320-390** SBe

A Pair of Elkington Bronze Figures of Entertainers, signed, dark brown patination, late 19th C., height 43 cm. **£660-760** SBe

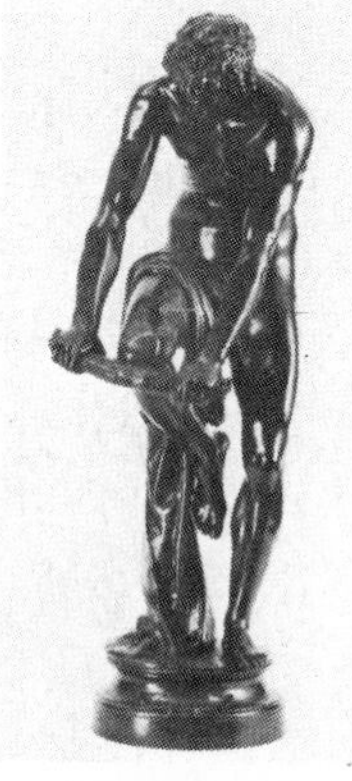

After Chambard, a bronze figure of Le Boucheron, signed 'Chambard' and entitled 'Boucheron Le Fable de la Fontaine' French 1880, 87 cm. **£550-620** SBe

A Norwegian bronze Group by Stephan Sinding, 21.5cms high, inscribed signature. **£350-400** P

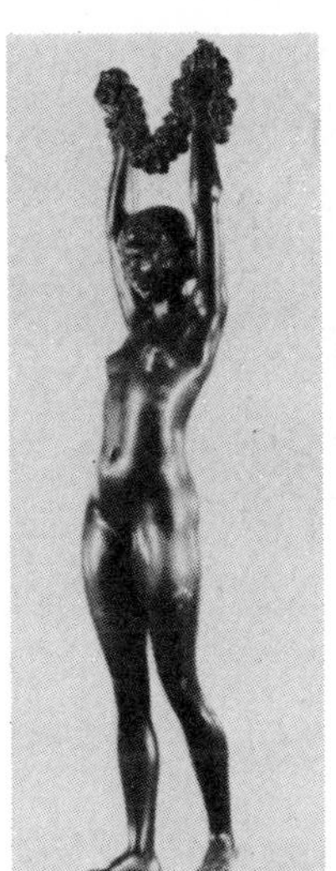

A Bronze Figure by Joe Descomps, base engraved Descomps, 16" high. **£210-240** CSK

A Fine Sino-Tibetan Gilt-Bronze Yama Group, 18th C., 7 in., 17.5 cm. **£425-470** L

A Carved Ivory and Bronze Figure of a Dancer by Fugere, the bronze signed 'Fugere' c. 1900, 43 cm. **£1,700-1,900** SBe

A Fine Bronze Statue in the form of a Greek Costumery Seller, possibly French or Italian, 27 in. high, 19th C. **£885-940** TA

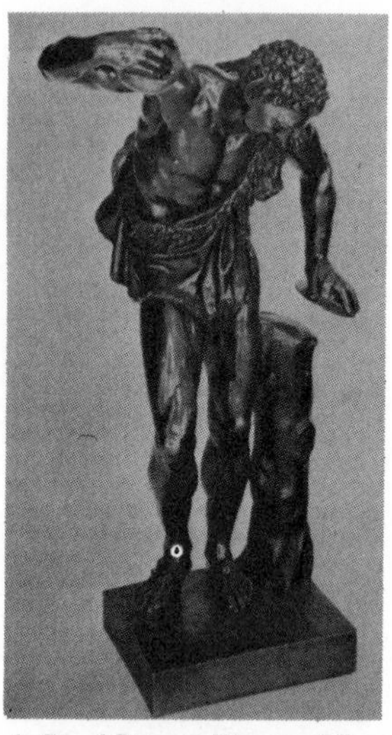

A Good Bronze Figure of Pan, base engraved Musee de Naples, 29 in., 74 cm., 19th C. **£630-720** L

A 19th C bronze figure of Diana, signed, 16" high. **£295-350** SAL

A 19th C Italian bronze figure of an Athlete, on marble plinth, 10". **£70-80** WHL

A Bronze figure of Hotei, late 19th C., 37 cm. **£150-190** SBe

A Bronze Figure of a Fisher-boy, signed De Martino, 15½ in., 39.3 cm., Italian, c. 1890. **£260-300** SB

A Barbedienne Bronze Figure of Penelope Waiting For Ulysses, stamped Barbedienne Fondeur J. Cavelier 584, 10¼ in., 26 cm. 1870's. **£120-180** SB

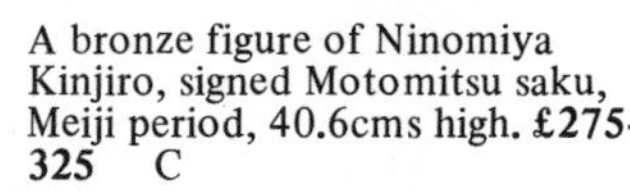

A bronze figure of Ninomiya Kinjiro, signed Motomitsu saku, Meiji period, 40.6cms high. **£275-325** C

A bronze Art Nouveau figure signed C. H. Korschann, Paris, 14½ in. **£650-750** PC

'Con Brio' a bronzed and ivory figure of a dancer by F. Preiss, signed, 12¼" high. **£1,800-2,000** CSK

left
A 19th C. bronze figure after the antique of Diana de Gabies, the base stamped S.B., beneath crown and with initials, 67 cm., 26½ in. high. **£420-480** O

Le Coup De Vent: a bronze and ivory figure of a girl by D. H. Chiparus, covered in a gilt bronze patina, signed 31.5 cm. high. **£1,500-1,700** C

'The Hoop Girl' A Preiss painted bronze and ivory Figure, green onyx stepped base, 23cms high, marked with PK founder's mark only. **£500-550** P

A Simard cold painted and silver-gilt bronze seated figure, signed M.L. Simard, Etling, Paris, 25" wide. **£1,200-1,400** CSK

Bronze Figure of a Woman signed F. Barbedienne Fondeur' stamped 'J. Cavelier 510' and with 'Collas Reduction Mecanique' stamp. French c. 1870, 36 cm. **£400-500** SBe

A Bruno Zach painted bronze Figure of a Girl, 42cms high, inscribed Zach. **£700-750** P

An Art Deco, Cold Painted Bronze Figure of a Dancer, signed B. Zack, Austrian 1930's, height 34 cm. **£230-300** SBe

"Lighter than Air, Ada May". A Preiss bronze and ivory figure of a young woman inscribed "Lighter than air, Ada May by F. Preiss' 1930's, 34 cm. **£900-1,000** SBe

A Bronze Figure of a Schoolgirl by D. H. Chiparus, signed on the bronze, 18.5 cm. high. **£440-500** C

After Rene Paul Marquet, a bronze and carved ivory figure of a musician, signed 'Marquet' 40 cm. overall. **£1,100-1,200** SBe

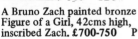

A Pair of 19th C. Bronze Figures, signed 'F. Lugerth', 11 in. high. **£400-435** pr. SV

left
A Gilt bronze and ivory Figure of a Dancer, green onyx base, 25cms high. **£650-750**

right
'Vanity' A good Preiss gilt bronze and ivory Figure, circular marble base, 21.5cms high, inscribed F. Preiss. **£900-1,000** P

A Descomps Bronze and Ivory Figure, 43 cm. the bronze inscribed Joe Descomps and dated 1920. **£450-500** SKC

An Art Deco bronze figure of a nymph, 35 cm. the tapered marble base incised Le Faguays. **£210-250** SKC

A French Gilt – Bronze and Ivory figure of a girl after Omerth, signed, numbered '7049', c. 1930, 26 cm. **£550-600** SBe

A bronze Ting, decorated with dragon and Pi disk, Hsuan Te period, 11" diam. **£230-300** Lan

After Frederick Thrupp, a bronze figure of a young woman, signed 'Fred K. Thrupp,' English, c. 1870, 74 cm. **£350-420** SBe

A Stylish Guiraud Riviere green-patinated bronze Figure, 59cms high, inscribed M. Guiraud Riviere, and Etling Paris. **£850-900** P

'Le Grand Ecart Respectueux' A Philippe bronze and ivory Figure, 21.5cms high, inscribed P. Philippe and with Ru.M monogram. **£800-900** P

A Good Preiss silvered bronze Figure on stepped black onyx base, 41.5cms high, marked F. Preiss on base. **£800-900** P

'Bat Dancer' A painted bronze and ivory figure on large circular green onyx dished base, 23cms high, inscribed F. Preiss. **£1,000-£1,100** P

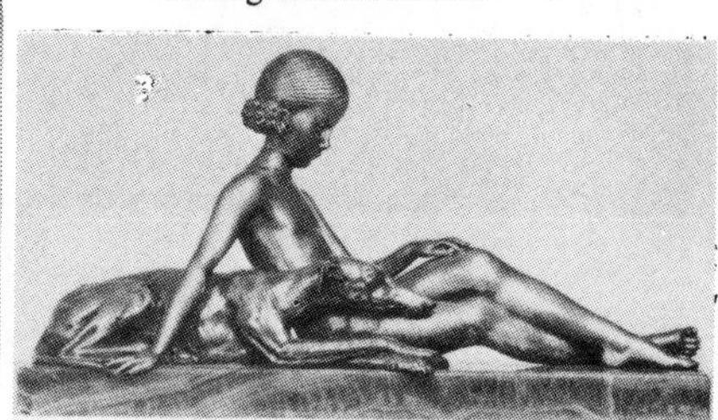

A silvered and gilded bronze Group by Richard Fath, signed, Etling, Paris, 24" wide. **£900-1,100** CSK

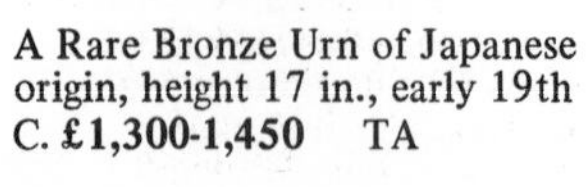

A Rare Bronze Urn of Japanese origin, height 17 in., early 19th C. **£1,300-1,450** TA

A Spanish Bronze Mortar, 4 in. 10 cm. high, late 16th C. **£250-350** S

A Yoshida Bronze Jardiniere, cast 'Kyoto, Yoshida, Tsukurn', c. 1900, 32 cm. **£110-130** SBe

An archaistic inlaid bronze tripod cauldron inset in gold-coloured sheet, malachite, turquoise and coral (with some damage to the inlay) Ming/Qing Dynasty 7¼ in., 18 cm. high. **£450-500** C

A Cherry-Bronze Incense Burner, probably Japanese, 9 in. high, early 19th C. **£145-165** TA

A pair of bronze rectangular pear-shaped vases, the bases with Hattori seal marks, late 19th C, wood stands, 19cms high. **£310-350** C

A Pair of Regency Bronze and Ormolu Urns with square plinths mounted with plaques emblematic of the seasons, 14 in., 36 cm. high. **£600-660** C

A bronze ritual vessel, Hsuan Te period, 5" long. **£360-400** Lan

A Pair of 19th C. bronze Vases. **£85-95** pr. SV

A Spanish Bronze Mortar, 3¾ in., 9.5 cm. high, early 17th C. **£200-300** S

A Bronze Figure of an Immortal, late 19th C. **£350-420** SBe

A Good Japanese Bronze Jardiniere with six deeply recessed panels decorated in high relief with two character mark. 19 in. 48 cm. **£260-290** L

A Bronze Storage Vessel on later stand with solid turned fruit-wood top, Pseudo-Ming marks, late 18th C. **£145-165** TA

A Bronze Centrepiece with Pseudo-Ming markings, surmounted by Chinese Dog-of-Fo, 10 in. wide, 8 in. deep, 16 in. high, c. 1800. **£425-475** TA

An Austrian bronzed and coppered Art Nouveau oval pen and ink stand, 14 in. wide. **£60-70** CSK

A Benin Bronze Head of an Oba, 19th C. 13 in., 34 cm. **£280-320** L

A Pair of Gilt-Bronze and Glass Candelabra, 15¼ in., 39 cm., c. 1850. **£370-410** SB

A Pair of Regency bronze lustre candlesticks 13 in. high. **£180-195** pr. CC

A 17th C. Dutch Bronze Candlestick 11½ in. high. **£390-430** CC

A Pair of Gilt-Bronze and Glass Vases, 11 in., 28 cm., c. 1880. **£170-200** SB

A Pair of Gilt-Bronze Candelabra, 18 in., 36 cm., c. 1870. **£100-130** SB

A Pair of 17th C. German bronze pricket candlesticks 17½ in. high. **£850-950** pr. CC

A bronze pricket lamp, the base cast with zoomorphic motifs (minor damage) Han Dynasty. 5¼ in., 13 cm. wide. **£110-150** C

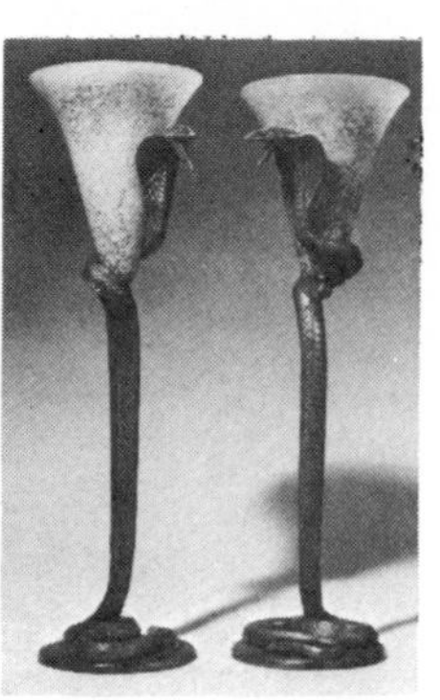

A Pair of Bronze Cobra Table-Lamps by Edgar Brandt with acid-etched opaque-glass shades (one tongue loose), marks. 51.5 cm. high. **£3,500-3,700** C

A Bronze Mortar and Pestle, c. 1740. **£89-99** CL

A Georgian bronze Mortar, 6½" diam. **£30-45** SQE

A Highly unusual bronze Table Lamp, 36cms high. **£1,250-1,300** P

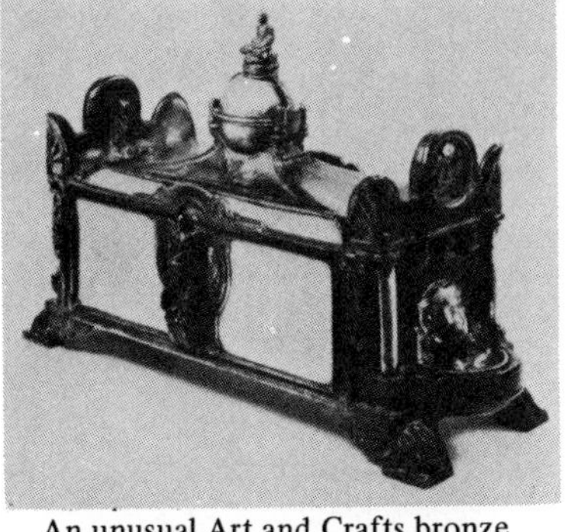

An unusual Art and Crafts bronze Smoker's Box, in the manner of Alexander Fisher, surmounted with a lighter and with removable elephant head ash-trays, 46cms long. **£325-375** P

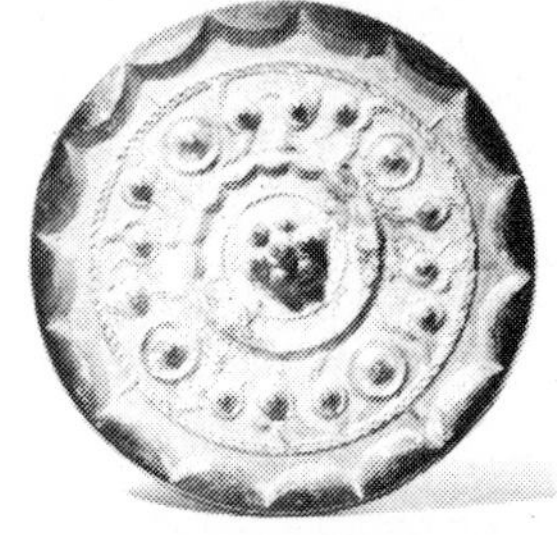

A bronze circular mirror, with areas of malachite encrustation (minor pitting) Han Dynasty, wood stand 4 in., 10.5 cm. diam. **£390-450** C

An Art Nouveau Bronze French Frame, signed. **£29-33** AP

A Late 18th C. Bronze Sundial, Cogger, Maidstone, 7 in. diam. **£75-85** RB

A Bronze Sundial, signed and dated 1784, 5 in. square. **£130-150** RB

Late 18th C Bilston enamel boxes. **£135-150** each MJ

ENAMELS

CLOISONNE

- **Enamel colours separated into compartments by vertical gold strip, edge-soldered to the gold base**

BAISSE TAILLE

- **Transparent enamel, covers metal which has been previously engraved or engine turned**

CHAMPLEVE

- **Pattern formed by scooping depression in metal surface to be decorated**

PLIQUE-A-JOUR

- **Rare technique using wires not premanently attached to background to confine transparent and translucent colours**

Two 18th C Bilston enamel boxes. **£275-300** each MJ

A Large Birmingham Snuff Box, c. 1760, 3 in. wide. **£635-700** HD

Two early 19th C Bilston enamel boxes. **£120-140** each MJ

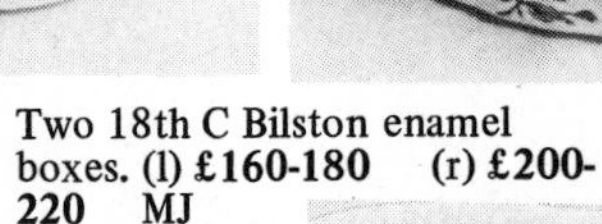

Two 18th C Bilston enamel boxes. (l) **£160-180** (r) **£200-220** MJ

A Large Birmingham Snuff Box, c. 1760, 2¾ in. long. **£455-500** HD

A Birmingham rectangular enamel snuff-box (chips and hair cracks) c. 1765, 3 in., 76 mm. long. **£265-300** C

A Large Rectangular Birmingham Snuff Box, c. 1755-60, 3¼ in. long. **£930-1,050** HD

A German Enamel Box, c. 1800, 4 in. long. **£280-300** HD

A Rectangular Staffordshire Snuff Box, the interior of the lid painted with the bust of a lady transcribing a book, wavy gilt-metal mounts, 6 cm. wide, c. 1760, chipped. **£340-380** S

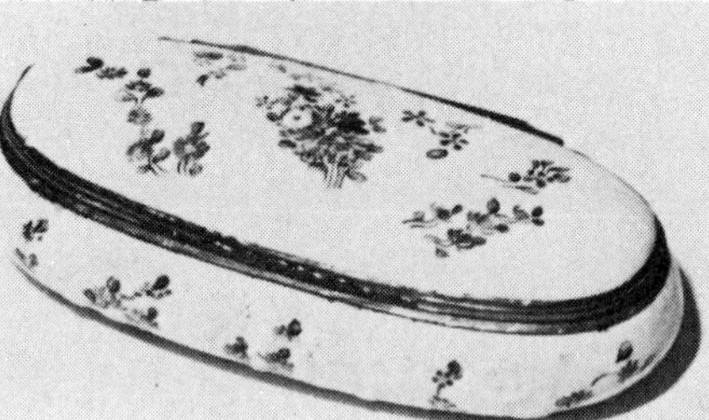

A German Oval Enamel Box, c. 1800, 5¼ in. long. **£415-435** HD

A Small Circular Box with painted enamel lid and straight gilt-copper sides, 3.7 cm. diam. c. 1750-1755. **£90-110** S

l A South Staffordshire Oval Enamel Box, c. 1770. **£460-480** HD

r A South Staffordshire Oval Enamel Box, c. 1770, 3 in. wide. **£325-375** HD

A Circular Snuff Box, the enamel lid painted, with silvered copper sides, 5.5 cm. diam. c. 1750-1755, some cracks. **£170-190** S

An Interesting Circular Snuff Box, the enamel lid painted, silvered copper sides, rose-turned composition base, 4 cm. diam., c. 1750-1755. **£150-170** S

An Unusual Rectangular Patch Box with gilt-metal sides, the base rose-turned, the enamel lid painted, mirror missing, 4.5 cm., wide, c. 1745-1750. **£90-110** S

A Small Patch Box, the enamel lid transfer-printed in black with silvered copper base, 3.2 cm., diam. c. 1755-1765, chipped **£55-75** S

ENAMEL

tc Bilston Enamel Box, c. 1790
£170-190 HD

l Bilston Enamel Box, c. 1800
£166-185 HD

bc South Staffordshire Enamel Box, c. 1790.
£190-210 HD

r A Rare Lozenge-Shaped Bilston Patch Box, c. 1806, with mirror
£530-550 HD

18th C Bilston enamel box. **£135-150** MJ

18th C Bilston enamel egg. **£120-150** MJ

A Bilston Enamel Box in the shape of a fruit, c. 1770. **£470-500** HD

A Bilston Bird Bonbonniere, 4.8 cm., high, c. 1775, beak chipped. **£300-340** S

Two 18th C Bilston enamel boxes. **£130-150** each MJ

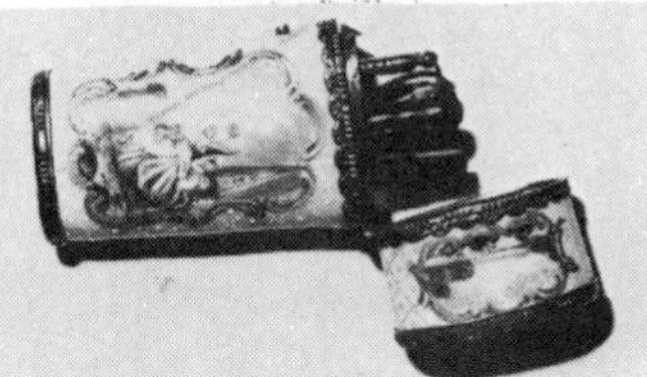

A South Staffordshire Enamel Etui, c. 1770. **£925-1,050** HD

A Pair of Bilston Pots, c. 1770. **£195-210** pr. HD

A Chelsea Bonbonniere, the enamel cover mounted in gilt-metal and painted with flowers, c. 1755, 5 cm. high. **£550-600** C

A Pair of English Enamel Table Candlesticks, 12" high, probably Staffordshire, c1700, damaged. **£225-275** SBA

An Enamelled Bonbonniere, with metal mounts, probably Bilston. **£230-280** SH

A Swiss enamel brooch, the oblong panel painted in colours, the gold frame stamped with shells and scrolls, 19th C. **£200-250** L

An 18th C. Bilston Plaque painted with pastoral scene. **£450-500** SA

Three English Enamel Etuis

l) Battersea Blue **£500+**

m) deep blue and gold **£800+**

r) pink classical **£500+** SA

A 19th C. Cloisonne Bowl, 5½ in. diam. **£25-28** SV

A Bilston Enamel Tray, c. 1780. **£145-165** HD

A Cloisonne Bowl, 31 cm., c. 1880, wood stand. **£600-650** SB

A 19th C. Cloisonne Bowl, 4¼ in. diam. **£15-18** SV

A Cloisonne Bowl, on black ground, beneath a 'Jui' border, late 19th C, 32.5cms diam. **£260-290** SBe

A 19th C. Oval Cloisonne Box, 1¾ in. high. **£70-76** SV

Selection of early 19th C enamel wine labels. **£65-75** MJ

A 19th C. Enamel Wine Label. **£55-60** HD

A 19th C. Enamel Wine Label. **£10-15** HD

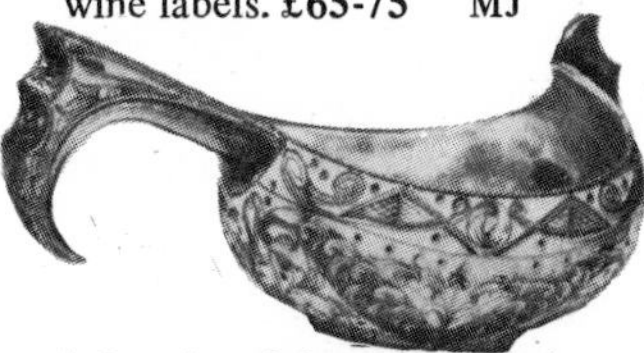

A Russian cloisonne enamel kovsh decorated in pale pinks, blues and greens Moscow, 1908-1917, maker's initials EA 5¼ in., 133 mm. long. **£1,200-1,300** C

A 19th C. Cloisonne Box, 4 in. long, with faults. **£40-45** SV

A 19th C. Cloisonne Lidded Box, chipped, 3 in. high. **£12-15** SV

A 19th C. Cloisonne Box, 5 in., long. **£100-115** SV

A Fine Pair of Cloisonne Vases with polychrome colouring and depicting a Chinese 'Horrific' Dragon, slight damage, 10½ in. high, 19th C. **£130-160** pr. TA

A Cloisonne box and cover, 8" Ch'ien Lung. **£230-270** SH

A Pair of Cloisonne Vases of predominantly pale blue and T-fret ground. Chinese. 13½ in., 34.4 cm. **£170-220** L

A Pair of Gin Bari Cloisonne Vases, in brightly coloured translucent colours on a stamped foil ground, c. 1900, with faults, 31 cm. **£140-180** SBe

A Pair of Cloisonne Vases, late 19th C., 25 cm. **£300-340** SBe

A Pair of Cloisonne Vases, pale cream ground, with appleblossom c. 1930. **£150-170** pr. CA

A Large Cloisonne Enamel Slender Baluster Vase decorated in colours on a grey ground, sentoku rim (star cracks) Meiji period, 62.8 cm. high. **£500-600** C

A Pair of 19th C. Cloisonne Vases, 3¾ in. high. **£65-70** pr SV

One of a pair of 19th C. Cloisonne Vases, 12 in. high. **£120-145** SV

A Cloisonne Vase, red ochre ground, 59.8 cm., late 19th C., **£475-525** SB

A Pair of midnight blue ground Cloisonne Vases, Japanese, late 19th C, 37cms high. **£270-300** SBe

A small Inaba Nanaho midnight-blue ground cloisonne enamel Vase 12 cm., signed, Japanese c. 1900. **£840-880** SKC

A large Hayashi cloisonne enamel Vase on midnight-blue ground, 42 cm., square seal, Japanese, late 19th C. **£1,150-1,200** SKC

A large pair of cloisonne enamel vases decorated in a late Ming Chinese style 76.5 cm. wood stands, Japanese. **£2,450-2,500** SKC

A 19th C Cloissonne Vase, 7¼" high. **£90-100** SAL

1 A 19th C. Enamel Pin Tray, 4 in. long. **£10-12** SV

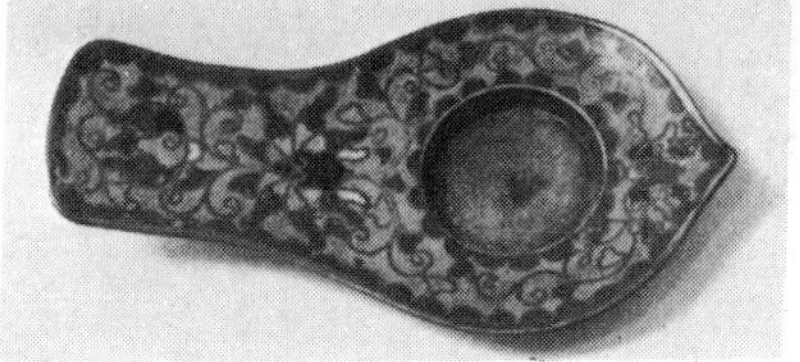
1 A 19th C. Cloisonne Inkstand. **£70-75** SV

A Cloisonne Spill Vase, with multi-coloured patchwork, Chinese, c1890, 10". **£150-200**

One of a pair of 19th C. Cloisonne Plates, 9½ in., diam. **£350-375** pr. SV

A 19th C. Cloisonne Dish, 5 in. long. **£13-15** SV

A Cloisonne Pilgrim Bottle, 30.5 cm., late 19th C. **£275-325** SB

A Pair of Cloisonne Rams, each animal 21 cm., 19th C. **£550-600** SB SBe

A Cloisonne Spill Vase, c1890, 3¾". **£90-110**

A pair of Cloisonne enamel censers modelled as birds, their wings forming detachable covers (minor pitting) 5 in., 13 cm. long. **£420-460** C

A pair of Cloisonne enamel figures of standing cranes (minor pitting) late 18th/19th C., 7½ in., 19 cm. high. **£275-325** C

A Pair of 19th C. Cloisonne Pepper Pots, 1¼ in. high. **£24-27** pr. SV

A Cloisonne enamel square room warmer (minor pitting) 18th/19th C., 10 in., 25.5 cm. square. **£385-420** C

A Cloisonne Vase, ruby red, with prunus blossoms and finch, Chinese, c1880's, 8½". **£90-110**

A Cloisonne enamel pomegranate, in red, yellow, green and blue, with gilded bronze figure, Ch'ien Lung, 9" high. **£4,800-5,400** Lan

A 19th C. Cloisonne Napkin Ring. **£10-12** SV

A Pair of Cloisonne Cranes, 28.5 cm., 19th C. **£825-850** SB SBe

A Pair of Cloisonne Lidded Cups, 10 in. high, c. 1930's (A.F.) **£35-45** pr. CA

A Cloisonne Enamel Ash Tray, c1920's. **£40-60**

A Rare Cloissonne Vase, embossed on silver paper, and decorated with a carp, 1920's, 5". **£130-150**

gold and silver pique and tortoiseshell box. **£75-85** SAL

£48-58 SAL

George III box. **£85-95** SAL

£75-85 SAL

A Very Fine Blonde Tortoiseshell Snuff Box, well inlaid with gold pique, English, c. 1720. **£1,500+** SA

A Late 18th C. Tortoiseshell Snuff Box, 1790. **£200-240** SA

A Fine Quality Scent Bottle Case, c. 1790. **£130-160** SA

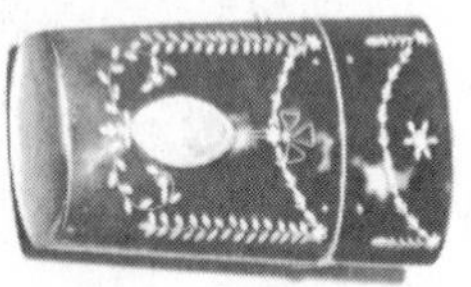

A Tortoiseshell and Silver Etui, c. 1790. **£340-370** HD

A Fine 19th C. Continental Silver Mounted Tortoiseshell Toilet Box decorated with silver and mother-of-pearl pique. **£970-1,050** HD

An English Papier Mache fitted box with accessories, not quite complete, mid 19th C. **£85-95** SAL

A Fine Hand-Painted Papier Mache Snuff Box, c. 1800, 4½ in. diam. **£180-200** HD

A 19th C. Papier Mache Box, Jenners & Betteridge. **£43-49** SV

A Papier Mache Box, c. 1850, 3½ in. diam. **£110-130** HD

Papier mache lacquered box, 7" wide, 5¾" deep, 2¼" high. **£6-10** STR

An early Victorian papier-mache tea-caddy decorated with sprays of summer flowers, 12 in., 31 cm. wide. **£75-85** C

An English Papier Mache Letter Rack, c. 1830. **£40-50** HD

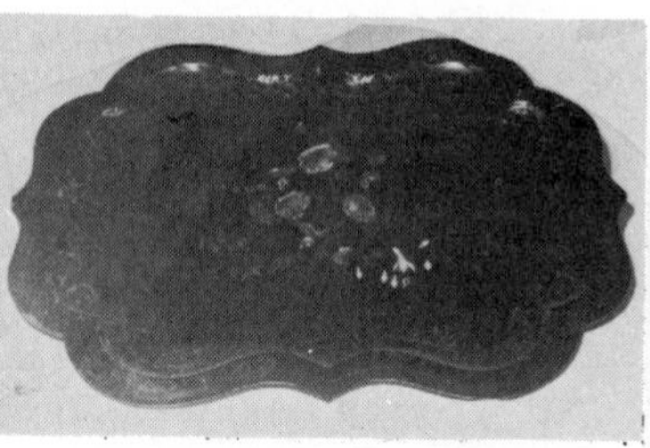

Papier Mache Tray with mother-of-pearl inlay and gilding (rubbed), 31" x 24". **£110-140** STR

A Penwork Letter Rack, c. 1810, 8 in. high. **£100-120** HD

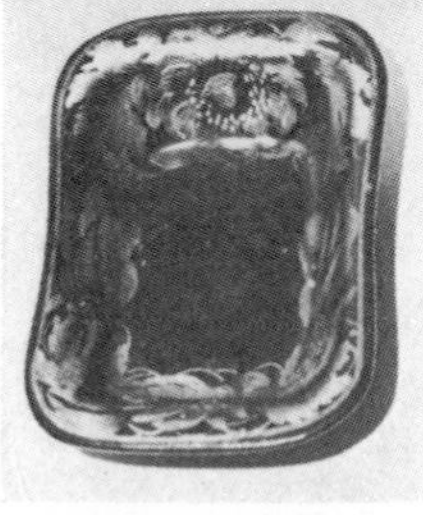

A 19th C. Papier Mache Pin Tray. **£26-30** SV

A Papier Mache Bread Basket, c. 1840, 14 in. long. **£90-100** HD

One of a Pair of Papier Mache Counter Trays, c. 1800, 4 in. long. **£180** pr. HD

A Pair of Fine Regency Pen-work Bellows, 14 in. long. **£80-100** HD

A Pen-Work Tea-Caddy, c1800. **£200-250** MJ

A Gold Lacquer Box and Cover, Japanese, late 19th C., with faults, 9.5 cm. **£150-180** SBe

A Penwork Sewing Box, with picture of Brighton Pavilion, c. 1820, 8 in. long. **£190-220**

A Rolled Paperwork Cribbage Board, c. 1800, 7½ in. wide. **£230-250** HD

An 18th C. Lacquer Box in original condition, 14 in. long. **£200-230** CP

A red Lacquer tall octagonal box and cover, (with some damage) Hongwu six-character mark, late Ming Dynasty 9 in., 23 cm. wide. **£120-175** C

A double fan-shaped box decorated in iroe hiramakie, togidashi and nashiji and inalid in Shibayama style with silver rims (small piece of inlay missing), late 19th C, 18.7cms wide. **£1,150-1,250** C

A 19th C. Lacquer Snuff Box. **£13-15** SV

A 19th C. Japanese Red Lacquer Box, 10 in. wide. **£68-78** HD

A Gold Lacquer Box and Cover, Japanese, late 19th C, 9.5cms, with faults. **£60-80** SBe

A rounded rectangular Fubako decorated in gold, silver red and black hiramakie, takamakie, okibirame and heidtsu on a nashiji ground engraved hoshi mon (chipped), 19th C, 29cms long. **£550-600** C

A 19th C. Oriental Lacquer Pen Box. **£30-36** SV

A Pair of Chinese Export Black and Gold Lacquer Caddies decorated with shaped panels of buildings and the monograms J.M. early 19th C. 8 in., 20 cm. wide. **£220-250** C

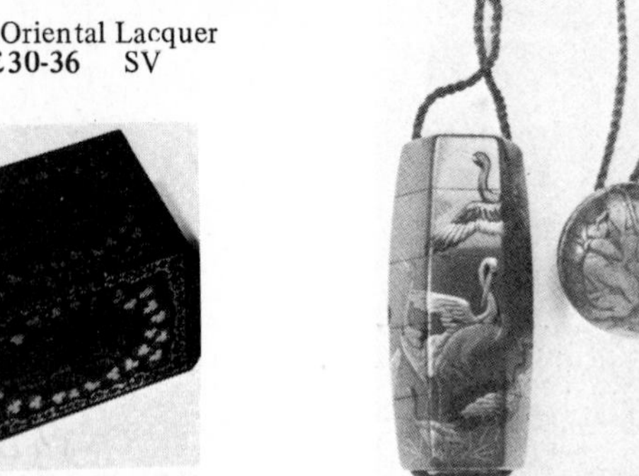

A four-case lacquer inro on red lacquer ground decorated in gold and black takamakie and kirikane with gilded metal ojime; pronounced wear, unsigned (wood box). **£480-520** SKC

An 18th C. Vernis Martin Snuff Box, 3½ in. diam. **£190-210** HD

A Chinese Lacquer Tea Caddy, c. 1850, 8 in. long. **£270-300** HD

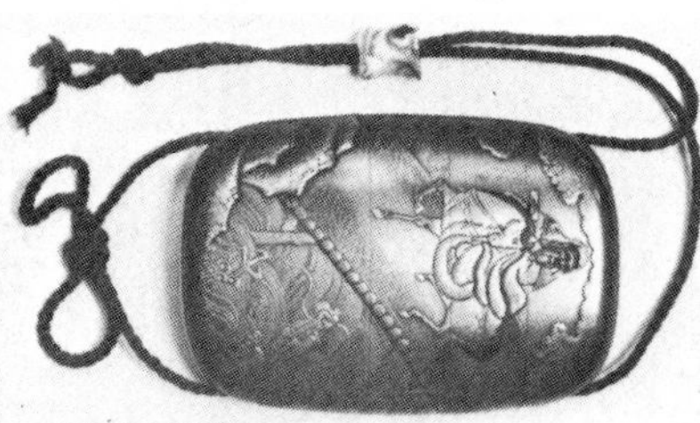

A four-case inro, the interior nashiji, signed Shibayama and Kyokasai in gold takamakie; together with a small carved ivory ojime in the form of a seated hare. **£1,000-1,150** SKC

A one-case iron inro, decorated in takabori, gold and silver takazogan together with a pierced iron Manju decorated in Usunikubori, unsigned. **£500-550** SKC

A Fine Three-Case Inro decorated in gold takamakie, the interior in red and gold hiramakie, with an ivory netsuke of Gama Sennin crouching with a toad. 2 in., 5 cm. long. **£80-100** L

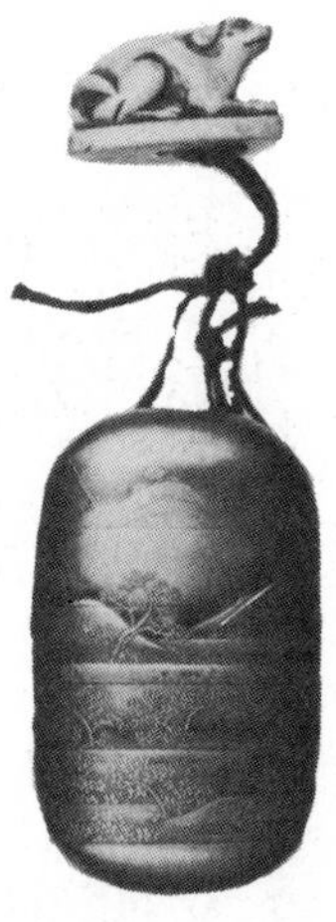

A four-case Inro decorated in gold hiramakie, takamakie and okibirame, nashiji interior (rubbed) unsigned, late 18th/19th C., with glass ojime and ivory netsuke, unsigned, late 18th/early 19th C. wood box. **£400-425** C

A one-case inlaid wood inro, decorated in carved and inlaid mother-of-pearl and ivory inlaid red stained oval raden reserve, signed Seisho in seal form. **£380-420** SKC

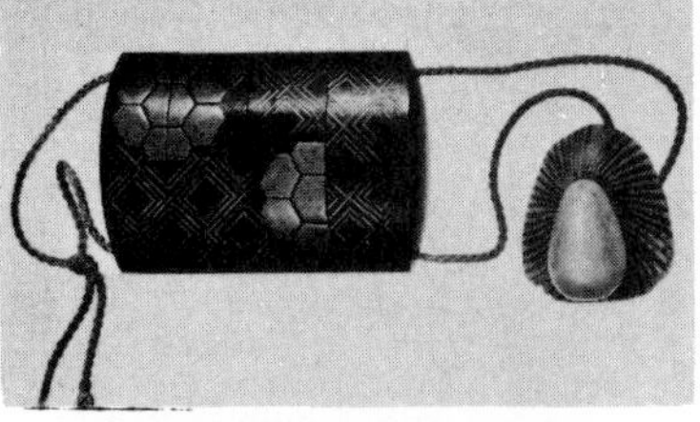

A Three Case Wood Inro decorated with gold lacquer flower mon designs, and an ivory netsuke formed as a mushroom. 2½ in., 6.4 cm. long. **£100-130** L

A one-case staghorn inro in the form of a Buddhist Mokugyo gong, and a pierced Ryusu ivory Manju inset with a hardstone at each end, unsigned. **£350-400** SKC

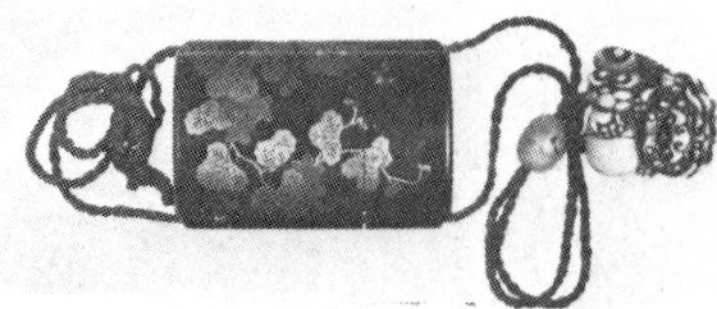

A five-case inro decorated in gold and silver togidashi and heidatsu on a roironuri ground, signed Kajikawa saku above a red tsubo seal, with attached coral bead ojime and ivory netsuke, unsigned, all 19th C. **£350-375** C

Tsunekawa: a five-case inro and matching two-part manju, the inro bearing a nashiji ground and decorated in gold and shibuichi takamakie, signed, together with silvered metal ojime. **£1,100-1,250** SKC

A Three-Case Lacquer Inro with a gold takamakie design, the interior of red and gold hiramakie ground. 2 in., 5 cm. long. **£100-140** L

A four-case inro decorated in gold hiramakie, takamakie nashiji, gold and silver takazogan, interior (slightly rubbed and chipped) unsigned, 18th/19th C. with attached faceted amber glass bead ojime. **£500-560** C

A four-case Inro finely decorated in gold, silver and red togidashi, signed Shoso 18th/19th C. with attached cornelian bead ojime and small ivory manju netsuke. **£550-600** C

A six-case inro finely decorated in gold and silver hiramakie, takamakie, okibirame and heidatsu on a fundame ground (rubbed, small restorations) signed Hasegawa Kyosensai Shigeyoshi saku, and red tsubo seal, late 18th/early 19th C. **£490-550** C

A red lacquer globular vase (damaged) 23 in., 58.5 cm. high. **£200-230** C

A four-case inro decorated in gold hiramakie, okibirame and togidashi on a fundame ground, interior (rubbed and slightly chipped), unsigned, late 18th/early 19th C. **£240-270** C

Tunbridge ware Box, 3½" sq. **£40-50** STR

An Oval Lacquer and Straw-work Bread Basket, c. 1800. **£170-190** HD

A 19th C. Japanese Red Lacquer Tray 12 in. long x 7½ in. wide. **£195-210** CC

A Bronze and Red Lacquer Lined Stirrup, Japanese 19th C., with faults, 29 cm. **£220-280** SBe

A Lacquered Smoker's Set (some damage to ashtray). **£33-38** SQE

TUNBRIDGE WARE

A small Victorian Tunbridge-Ware Box. **£48-58** CSG

- **Associated with Tonbridge and Tunbridge Wells**
- **Souvenir wood-wares from the Late 17th C**
- **Earliest form in geometric patterns similar to parquetry**
- **Developed into scenic views, landscapes etc.**
- **Made from thin strips of wood glued together, then fret cut into thin layers and veneered onto a variety of small objects e.g. boxes, table tops**

Tunbridge ware Box, 6½" x 4". **£60-70** STR

A Treen Tunbridge ware box. **£19-22** A.L.

A Tunbridge Ware Box with Modern Lining, 9 in. long. **£98-108** HD

Tunbridge ware dome-topped glove box, with key, Berlin-work decoration by T. Barton, T.Wells, 9½" long. **£175-225** STR

Tunbridge ware domed Glove Box, with key, 10½" wide, 4" high. **£220-270** STR

A 19th C. Tunbridge ware Box, 6 in. square. **£50-55** SV

Tunbridge ware waisted Box with view of Pantiles, Tunbridge Wells, on lid, 9½" wide, 4" long. **£220-260** STR

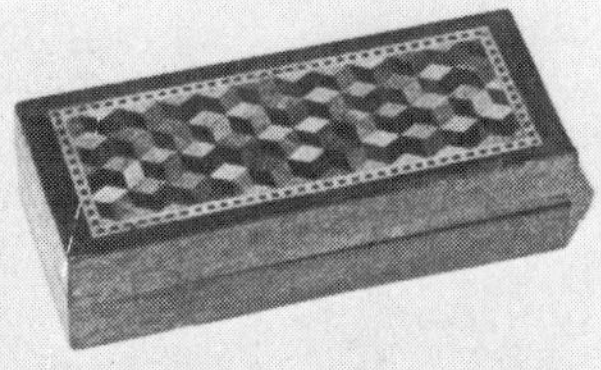
Tunbridge ware Box, with cube design, 4" wide. **£30-35** STR

Tunbridge ware Box with view of Tonbridge School on lid, 9¼" wide, 6" deep, 2¼" high. **£140-180** STR

Tunbridge ware Jewel Box, interior not original, 13" wide, 10" deep, 6" high. **£120-150** STR

Early 19th C Tunbridge ware Stationery Box, with cube design, sloping lid and inkwell, 11" wide, 9" deep, 3¼" high. **£100-120** STR

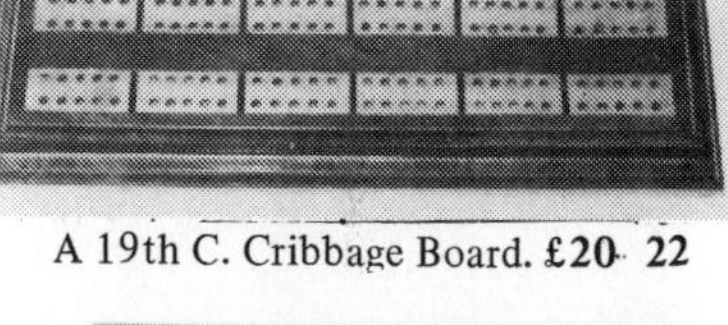
A 19th C. Cribbage Board. **£20-22**

Tunbridge ware stamp box, with Queen's head. **£50-70** STR

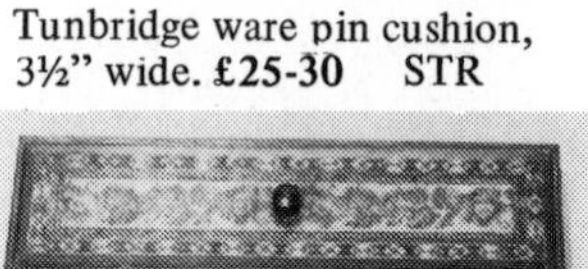
Tunbridge ware pin cushion, 3½" wide. **£25-30** STR

A 19th C. Tunbridge ware Box, 8½ in., long. **£50-55** SV

Tunbridge ware Tea Caddy, Berlin-work on maple, 9¾" wide, 4¾" deep, 5¾" high. **£200-250** STR

Tunbridge ware Soverign holder, 1". **£30-35** STR

Tunbridge ware patchbox, 1¾" diam. **£22-28** STR

Tunbridge ware needle cushion and thread waxer. **£34-38** STR

Tunbridge ware Soverign holder, 1". **£30-35** STR

A 19th C. Tunbridge ware Sewing Box Accessory. **£8-10** SV

A Tunbridge ware Pin Cushion. **£10-12** SV

Tunbridge ware cotton spool, 1". **£25-28** STR

Tunbridge ware Tea Caddy, with view of Dover Castle on lid, 10" wide, 6" high. **£220-260** STR

Tunbridge ware Inkstand, 11" wide. **£220-280** STR

Regency painted Tunbridge pin cushion. **£28-35** IN

Tunbridge ware miniature Chamber stick, 2" high. **£40-50** STR

Tunbridge ware Overmantle, inlaid with flowers, butterflies and setter dogs, c1850, 41" wide, 42" high. **£250-300** STR

Tunbridge ware Inkwell, 6" sq. **£80-100** STR

A Very Rare Tunbridge ware Necklace. **£250-300** STR

A 19th C. Tunbridge Ware Writing Slope, in excellent condition. **£200-245** SV

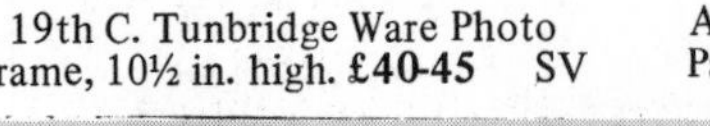

A 19th C. Tunbridge Ware Photo Frame, 10½ in. high. **£40-45** SV

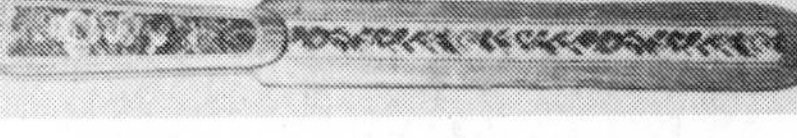

A 19th C. Tunbridge ware Paper Knife. **£20-22** SV

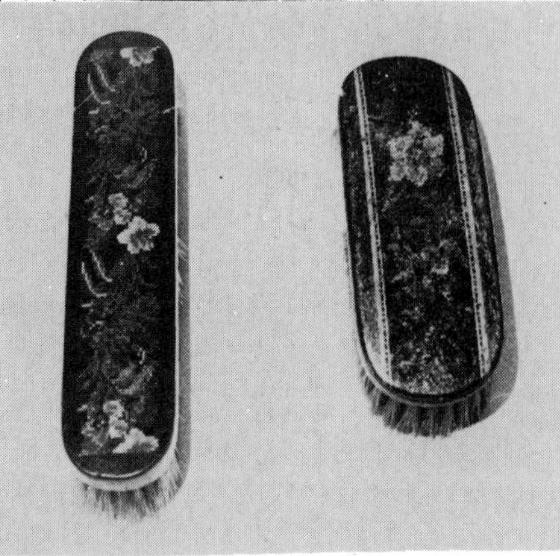

l A 19th C. Tunbridge ware Brush **£10-13** SV

r A 19th C. Tunbridge ware Brush. **£10-13** SV

Tunbridge Ware Book Ends, c. 1840. **£180-200** HD

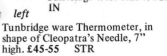

Tunbridge Ware Ruler. **£12-15** IN

left

Tunbridge ware Thermometer, in shape of Cleopatra's Needle, 7" high. **£45-55** STR

Pin Cushion. **£6-10** IN

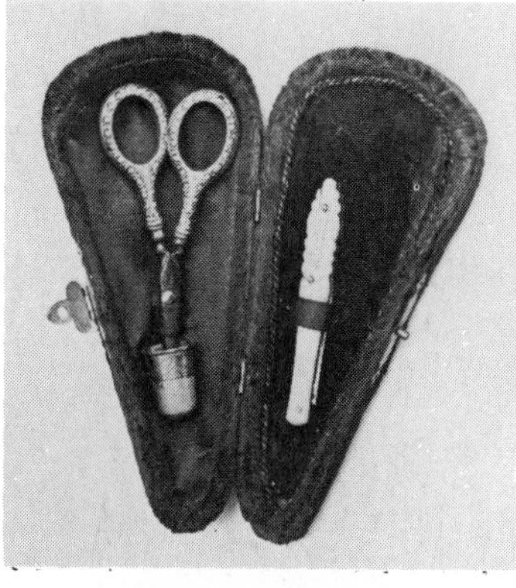

A Late Victorian Sewing Set with silver scissors and thimble. **£38-45** IN

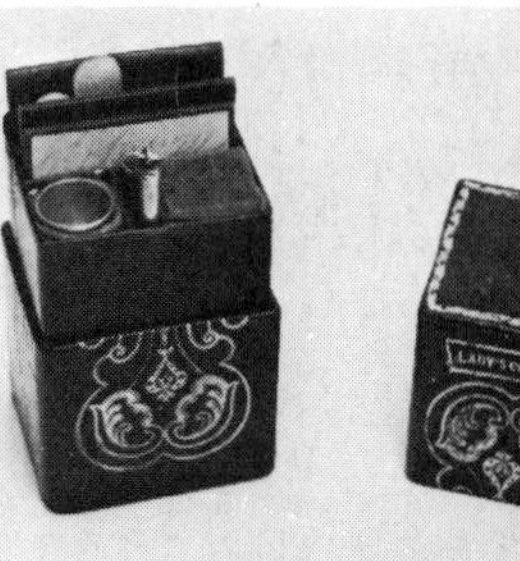

A Ladies' Companion, mid Victorian. **£42-50** IN

Needle Case. **£6-10** IN

A pair of implements to separate threads. **£10-12** IN

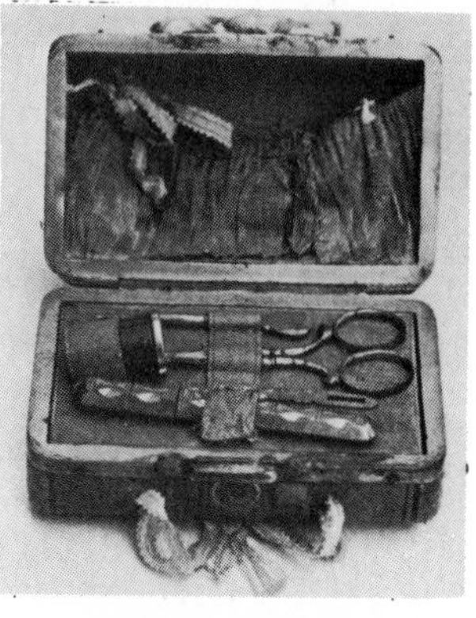

A mid-Victorian Sewing Set. **£32-38** IN

Victorian pin cushion **£6-10** IN

Silver Thimble in 1897 Jubilee Drum Case, Reg. No. 186097. **£25-35** IN

Three bone Thimbles. **£20-25** IN

Two mid-Victorian vegetable ivory Thimble Holders, including silver thimbles. **£25-35** IN

Aluminium Advertising Thimbles, 1920's-1930's. **£5-10**

Three silver Thimbles:
(l) **£9-12** IN
(c) **£18-22** IN
(r) Birmingham 1912, **£22-25**

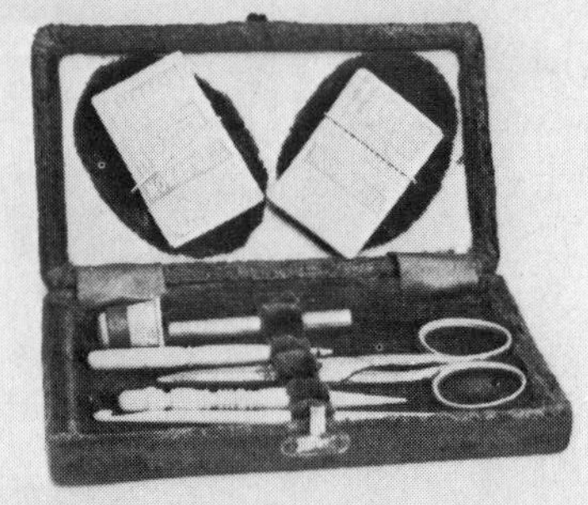

A Sewing Set, c1880. **£12-18** IN

A Carved Wood Continental Cotton Reel Holder/Pin Cushion, 3½". **£20-25** SQE

A Needlecase. **£5-8** IN

Lucet, used in making a cord. **£18-22** IN

3 mother-of-pearl bobbins, 1-1½". **£8-12** each STR

A Weaving Tool. **£5-8** IN

19th C French Shuttle for silk loom. **£18-25** IN

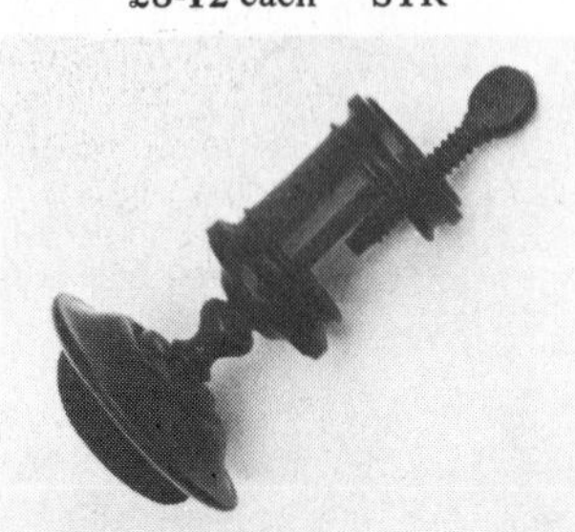

Early 19th C Sewing Clamp. **£42-50** IN

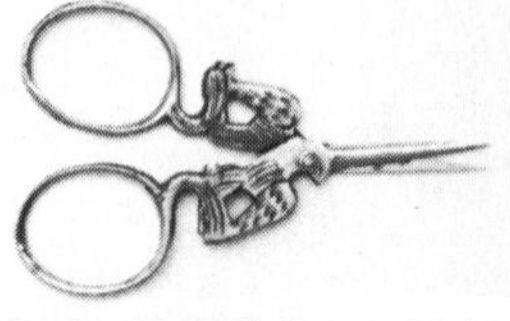

Embroidery Scissors. **£9-12** IN

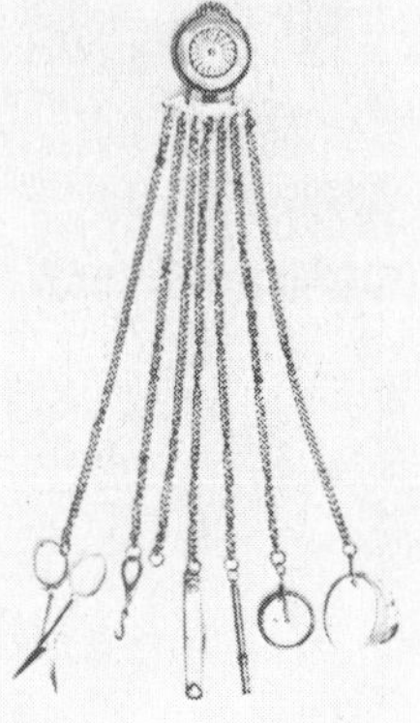

Cut Steel Chatelaine (note early scissors), mid-Victorian. **£98-120** IN

Weaving Tool to separate threads. **£3-5** IN

Selection on Knitting Sheaths. **£14-18** IN

A Mulberry Sewing Clamp with drawer and pin-cushion, c. 1810. **£185-200** HD

left
A Late Victorian wool-winder, 23" high. **£38-45** IN

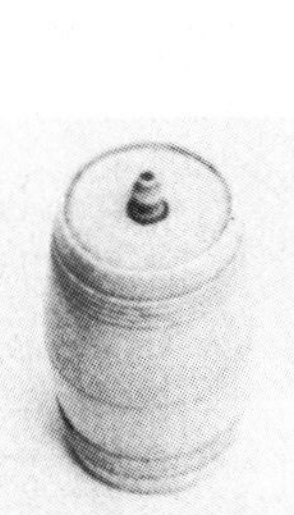

First ½ 19th C bone cotton barrels (used before cotton reels). **£12-16** IN

A mid-Victorian wool-winder with clamp, 12" high. **£12-15** IN

Victorian bone pin cushion. **£14-20** IN

Three Victorian pin cushions; 2 at **£8-12** 'From a Friend' **£4-8** IN

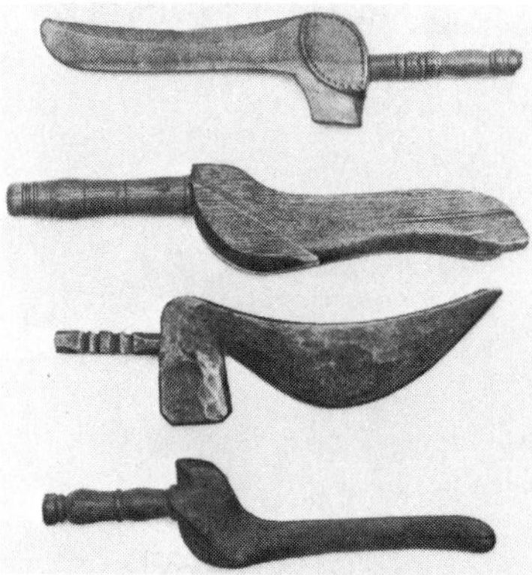

Selection of Knitting Sheaths. **£14-16** IN

Bone Tatting Shuttle. **£3-7** IN

A Guhl & Harbeck Sewing Machine, c1860-70. **£100-140** IN

A Clover Leaf Britannia Sewing Machine Cabinet. **£110-130** HG

Continental Lace Maker's Pillow, with bobbins. **£45-55** IN

A Weir 'Ladies' chainstitch sewing machine. **£180-210** CSK

A Weir hand chain-stitch sewing machine, marked W5812. **£120-150** CSK

An Improved Gresham lockstitch sewing machine with C frame and enclosed gearing. **£65-85** CSK

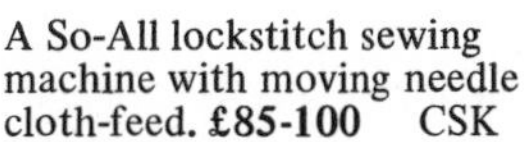

A So-All lockstitch sewing machine with moving needle cloth-feed. **£85-100** CSK

An Atlas B lockstitch sewing machine, No. 200342, made in Brunswick. **£70-80** CSK

An Arm and Platform sewing machine. **£260-290** CSK

A Gresham lockstitch sewing machine, No. 28386. **£100-120** CSK

A Wanzer Time Utiliser sewing machine, in wood box. **£50-60** CSK

A roller feed horizontal needle machine of early design. **£220-250** CSK

A Little Howe lockstitch sewing machine, No. 23397. **£170-200** CSK

An Agenoria sewing machine by the Franklin Sewing Machine Co. **£110-130** CSK

Late 19th C lock-stitch Sewing Machine, with case. **£18-25** IN

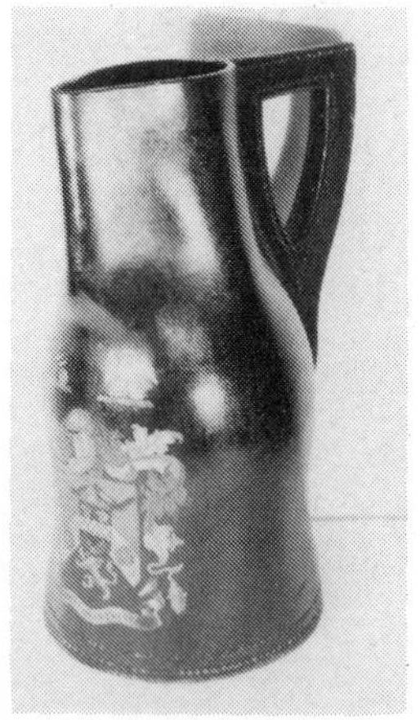

An Early 18th C. Black Jack, painted with fine armorial. **£600-650** SA

A pair of Georgian painted leather fire-buckets 11 in., 28 cm. diam. 12½ in., 32 cm. high. **£850-1,000** C

A Leather Stationery Cabinet, mid 19th C., 10 in. high. **£90-105** RB

A Leather Document Case with hinged lid embossed with dragons and birds, probably English, second half of 17th C. 16½ in., 42 cm. wide. **£600-660** C

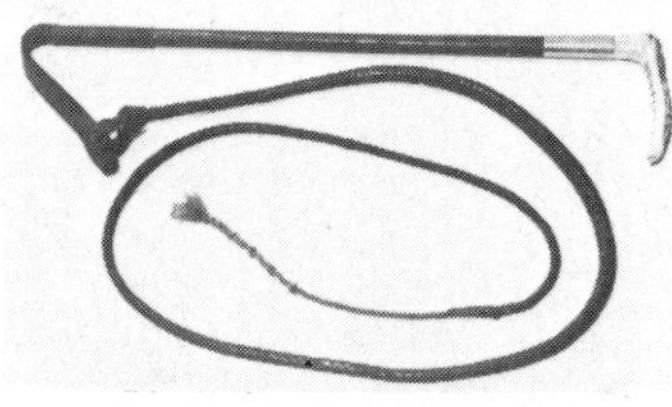

A Leather bone-handled Riding Crop with Whip, 85" in all. **£15-20** SQE

A Brass and Horn Vase, c. 1900. **£30-35** AP

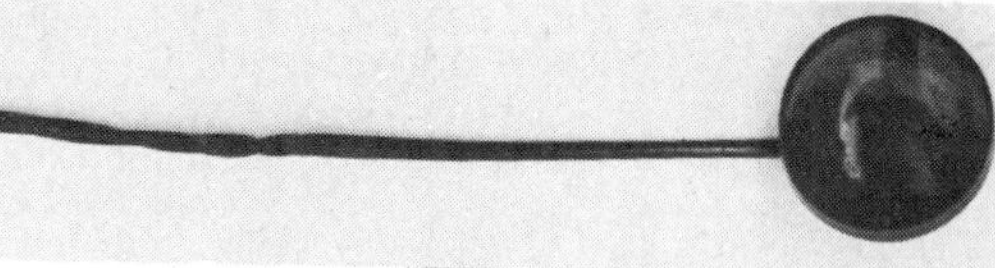

Mid 19th C horn ladle. **£20-30** IN

A 19th C. Horn Beaker. **£5-7**

An 18th C. Horn Beaker. **£40-45** RB

A Small Horn Beaker with Silver Plate Mounts, late 19th C. **£12-15** RB

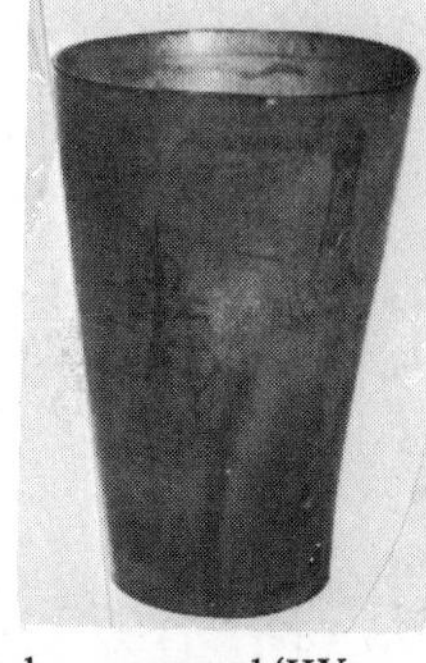

A Horn Beaker, engraved 'HY ARNOLD', 18th C, 5" high. **£75-85** SOE

Mid 19th C horn spoon. **£5-10** IN

A Horn and brass powder horn c. 1830. **£65-70** BA

An Early 19th C. Horn and Brass Flask. **£68-75** RB

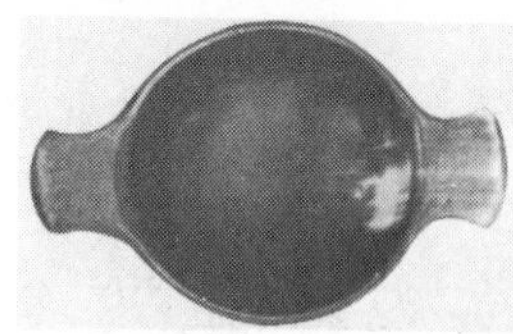

A mid 19th C horn quaich (Scottish drinking vessel). **£2-5** IN

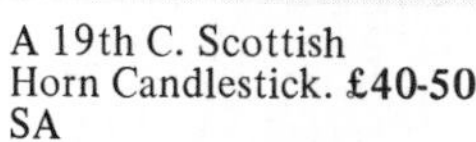

A 19th C. Scottish Horn Candlestick. **£40-50** SA

A Scottish Snuff Mull, mid 19th C. **£35-45** SA

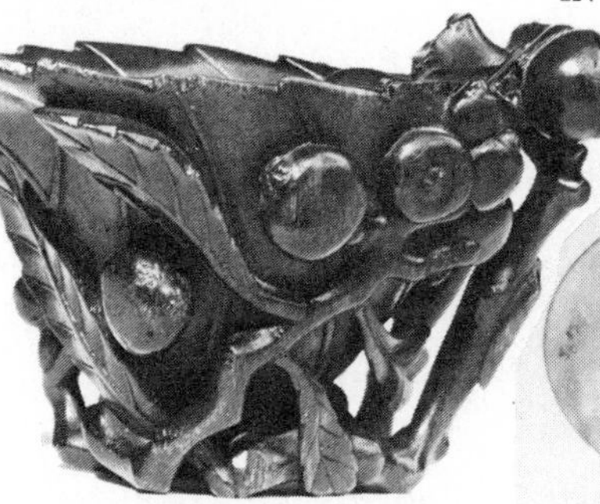

A rhinoceros horn libation cup (with some damage) 17th/18th C. 6 in., 15 cm. wide. **£440-480** C

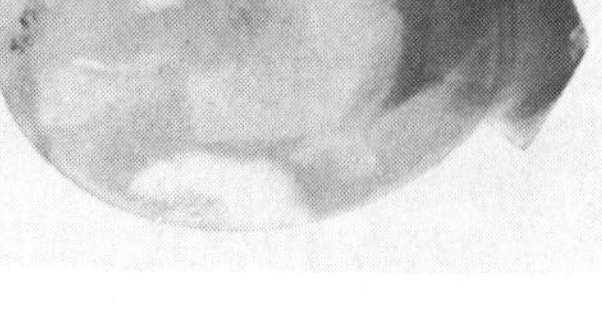

A mid 19th C horn scoop. **£5-10** IN

A South West Iran, probably Qashqai, rug. Colours: red, two blues, white, yellow, brown, green and pink. c1900. 8' (243cms) x 4'8" (142cms) Condition: good. **£1,450-1600** L

A Daghestan Rug, 4 ft. 4 in. x 3 ft. 6 in., 132 cm. x 76 cm., c. 1920, condition: fair, slight wear. **£400-470** S

A Fine Isfahan part silk rug with ivory field, a red-rust scalloped circular medallion and pendants enclosing leafy vine, 7 ft. 3 in. x 4 ft. 11 in., 220 cm. x 150 cm. **£2,800-3,080** C

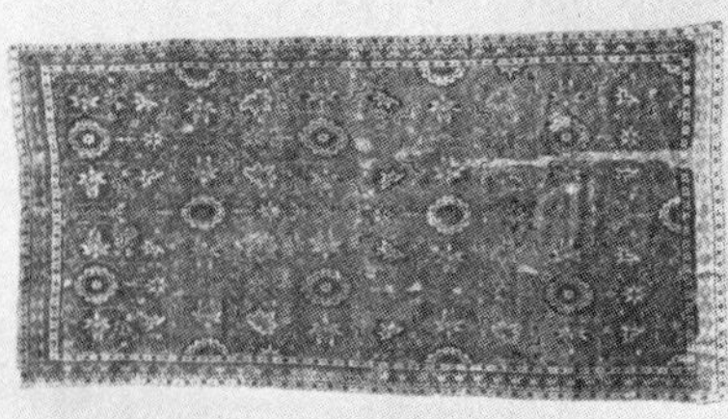

A 17th C Caucasian Carpet. Colours: blue, red, yellow, white, mauve, green and brown-black. 14'11" (455cms) x 7' (213.5cms) Condition: fair to worn. **£520-640** L

POINTERS FOR CARPETS

- Afghan - fairly course in texture and design.
- Chinese Turkestan - Influence of Chinese Art clearly defined in these rugs. Varied and unusual colouring, yellows, lacquer red and blue.
- Ghiordes (Turkish) - Finest of the Turkish type, colours are varied, borders usually consist of bold floral designs.
- Hamadan (Persian) - Heavy, long, durable pile. Well coloured, designs often embellished with animal figures.
- Herat (Persian) - Recurring leaf or 'fish' motif, ground shade is usually dark blue.
- Ispahan (Persian) - Medallion and vase designs used, wide range of colours.
- Kashan (Persian) - Woven in silk or wool. Medallion and prayer designs to the fore. Favoured colours, rich tones of red and blue.
- Kilim (Yugoslavian) - Tapestry woven rugs, floral and tree motifs treated geometrically.
- Kurdish (Persian) - Nomadic tribes wove these rugs. Virile designs, yarn is generally course.
- Shirvan (Caucasian) - Crude animal forms are often introduced, fairly course in quality.
- Turkoman - Generally dyed in deep reds with dark blue and black.

A Fine Isfahan Rug with flowering leafy vine border between dual floral stripes, an inscription cartouche at one end, 7 ft. 6 in. x 4 ft. 9 in., 229 cm. x 145 cm. **£1,800-1,980** C

A Gendje "Memling" rug. Colours: two blues, red, yellow, green, brown, white and corroded black. c1860. 7'3" (221cms) x 4'7" (140cms) Condition: fair. **£200-230** L

A Karabagh rug. Colours: red, black, two blues, yellow, green and some synthetic pink. c1880. 7'1" (216cms) x 4'9" (145cms) Condition: fair. **£180-230** L

A karabagh runner, the cherry-red field within a wide apple-green border. 11 ft. x 3 ft. 8 in., 335 cm. x 112 cm. **£620-650** SKC

A kazak rug, the black field surrounded by a wide madder border 7 ft. 11 in. x 4 ft., 241 cms. x 122 cm. **£450-500** SKC

A Kazak Rug with indigo and madder field, 6 ft. 7 in. x 4 ft. 1 in., 201 cm. x 124 cm., c. 1900, condition: worn. **£360-400** S

A good Kelim, with multi-coloured field, 9'10" x 4'8". **£500-550** PWC

A kazak runner, the saffron field within a wide ivory ground border 9 ft. 2 in., x 3 ft. 7 in. 280 cm. x 109 cm. **£210-250** SKC

A Pekin Rug, the ivory field with a lotus medallion, c1930, condition good, 83" x 48" (211cms x 122cms). **£120-200** SBA

A Kazak rug. Colours: brown-red, white, green, black, grey, purple-grey and an electric synthetic pink. c1880. 7'1" (216cms) x 5'7½" (170cms) Condition: generally good to fair. **£330-380** L

A Kerman Pictorial Rug, the ivory field with indigo border, 5 ft. 6 in. x 4 ft. 2 in., 168 cm. x 127 cm., c. 1900, condition: fair, slight wear. **£1,000-1,200** S

A Kuba, probably Seshour, rug. Colours: white, brown-red, two blues, pink, green, yellow and black, some synthetic. c1910. 4'7" (140cms) x 3'7" (109cms) Condition: good to fair. **£380-430** L

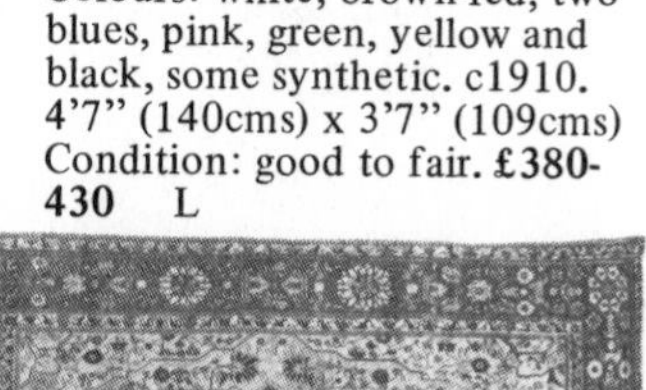

A Melas Prayer Rug, the ochre mehrab with stylized flowers, ivory spandrels, a beige border of guls, 5 ft. 9 in., x 5 ft. 2 in., 175 cm. x 157 cm., c. 1910., condition: fair. **£480-560** S

A Mohtashan Kashan Rug, the pale indigo field with a madder pole medallion and ivory spandrels, 6 ft. 11 in. x 4 ft. 5 in., 211 cm. x 135 cm., c. 1910., condition: slight wear. **£850-930** S

A Tekke Ensi with mihrab format. Colours: purple-red, red, two blues, white and dark brown. c1900. 4'8½" (143cms) x 3'10" (117cms) Condition: generally good, some areas of damage. **£280-340** L

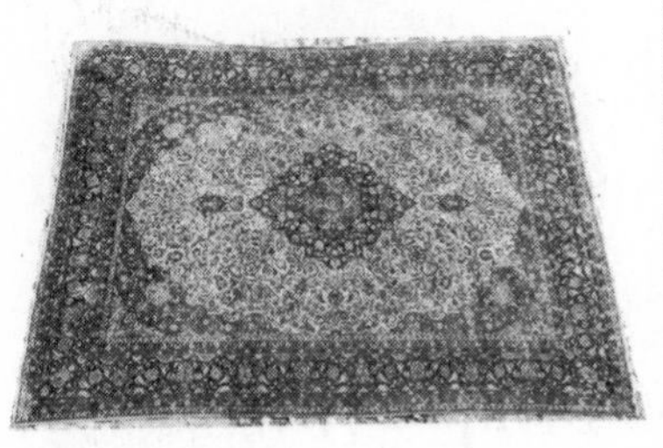

A Persian carpet on ivory ground with blue border, 11'5" x 8'11". **£2,500-3,000** P.W.C.

A Shirivan Rug woven with triple medallion on an indigo field and a pale blue main border filled with cruciform ornament, 49 by 41 in., late 19th C. **£270-300** SBA

An antique Yomut Dyrnak- Gol carpet. Colours: liver-red, brown-red, pink, white, two blues, dark brown and orange yellow. c1850. 9'5" (287cms) x 6'3" (191cms) Condition: fair. **£400-440** L

PIPES

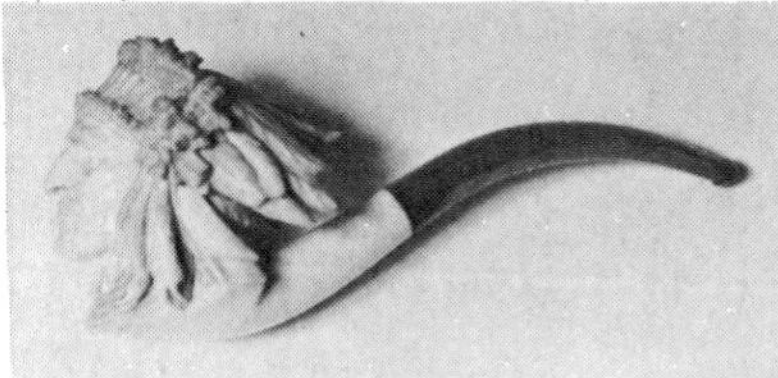

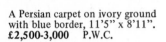

'Red Cloud', Chief of the Oglala Sioux, Meerschaum pipe with amber stem, c1870. **£900-1,000** As

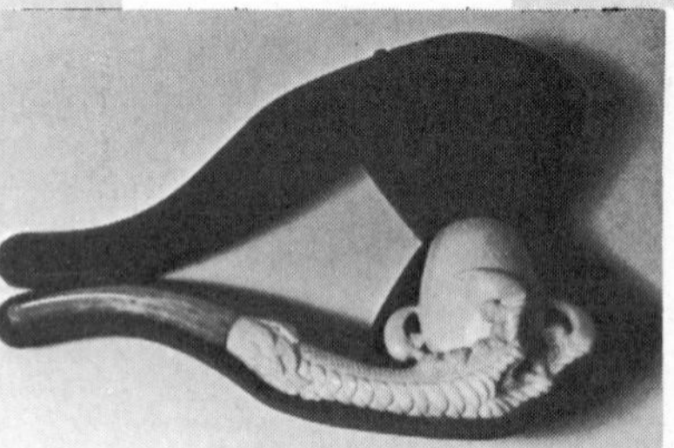

A 'Queen Victoria' carved Meerschaum pipe with amber stem, c1870. **£600-680** As

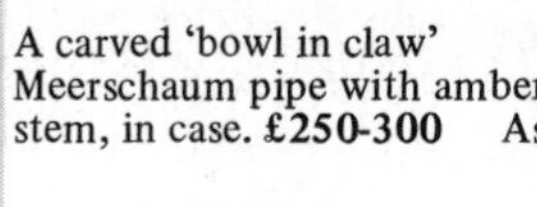

A carved 'bowl in claw' Meerschaum pipe with amber stem, in case. **£250-300** As

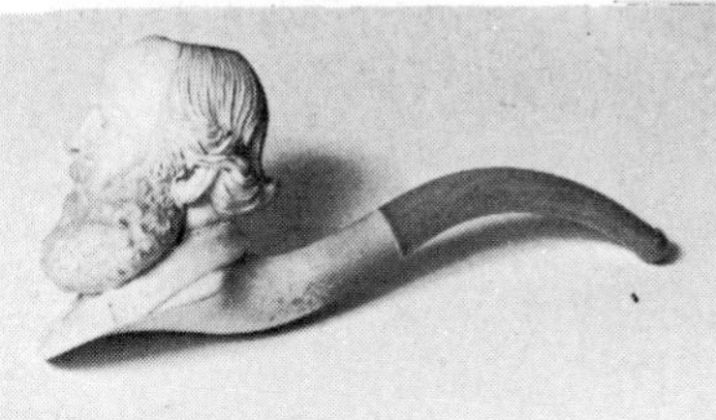

A 'Marquis of Salisbury' carved Meerschaum pipe with amber stem, c1870. **£600-680** As

A carved Meerschaum pipe with stem, 'head of Mephistopheles', c1870, in case. **£2,000-2,200** As

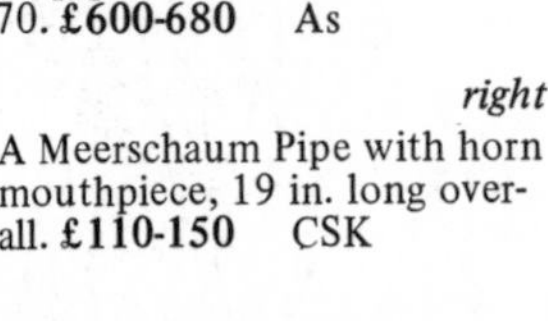

right
A Meerschaum Pipe with horn mouthpiece, 19 in. long overall. **£110-150** CSK

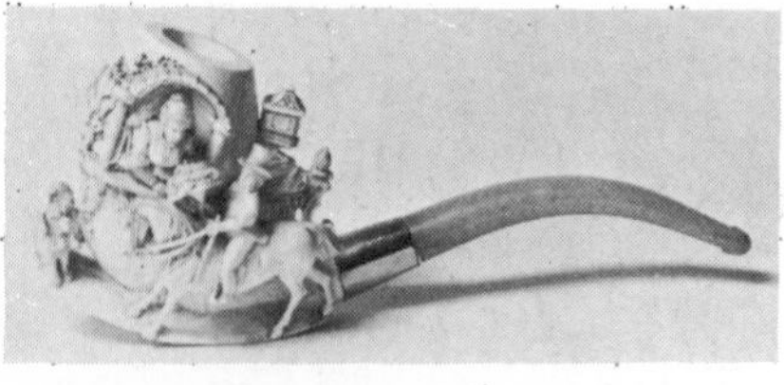

A carved Meerschaum pipe with amber stem of a man on a horse with a woman on a balcony, c1870. **£950-1,050** As

A Meerschaum Pipe and amber mouthpiece, 9 in. long overall, fitted case. **£140-170** CSK

A carved Meerschaum pipe of young woman and child with amber feet, in velvet-lined case, c1870. **£800-900** As

A Viennese carved Meerschaum pipe with amber stem, c1870. **£1,750-1,950** As

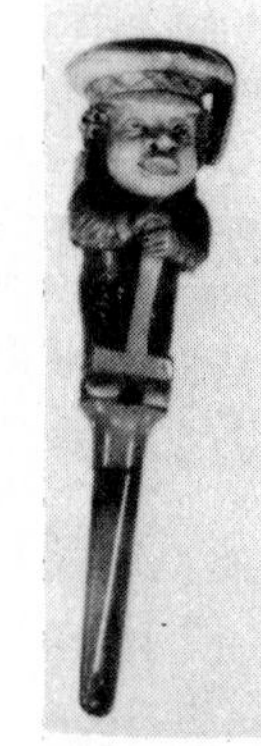

A Meerschaum Cheroot Holder with amber mouthpiece, 5 in. long overall, fitted case. **£130-160** CSK

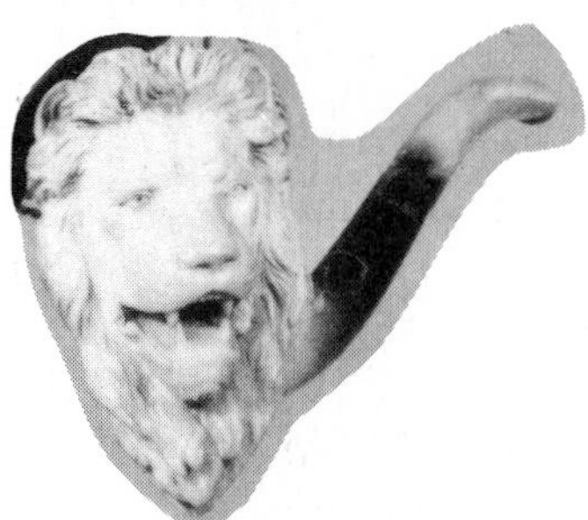

A Meerschaum Pipe with amber mouthpiece, 6 in. long overall, fitted case. **£260-290** CSK

A carved Meerschaum pipe of a seated cat-like wolf mythical creature with amber stand, head as a cover to the bowl, with pierced ears and mouth, c1870. **£950-1,050** As

A Fine Meerschaum Pipe Bowl, 5 in. long, and wood mouthpiece. **£320-360** CSK

A carved Meerschaum 'Rudyard Kipling' pipe with amber stand, in case, c1870. **£700-800** As

A carved Meerschaum cheroot holder with amber stem of 'St. George and the Dragon', c1870. **£1,500-1,600** As

MEERSCHAUM

- Meerschaum is a compound of Silicate of Magnesia, lime, water and carbonic acid
- Karl Kowates of Budapest made the first pipe over 100 years ago.
- 1850-1900 the finest carved Meerschaums produced; 80% by Viennese craftsmen
- Colouration - caused by smoking and selective application of wax
- Commonest carvings are 'claw and ball', negro and Arab heads with turbans
- Few carved pipes predate 1850 - but there are fakes purporting to do so.

A Meerschaum Water Pipe with hinged and pierced metal cover and mounts, 4¼ in. wide. **£30-40** CSK

A Meerschaum Pipe and Vulcanite Mouthpiece, 6 in. long overall, fitted case. **£35-45** CSK

A Meerschaum pipe, the bowl of an elephant, the stem in trunk with ivory tusks and detachable bowl. **£400-450** As

A Meerschaum Cheroot Holder with amber mouthpiece, carved with a nude girl, 6 in. long overall, fitted case. **£180-210** CSK

A Painted Tin Plate Figure with clockwork motor that causes her to advance on wheels, 8 in., **£300-340** CSK

H. Kienverger-Kico, The Great Billiard Champion, the mechanical tin plate toy with lithographed figure of a player, mint condition and complete with set of coloured balls in envelope and cardboard box, c. 1912, 6½ in., 16.5 cm. **£170-230** SBe

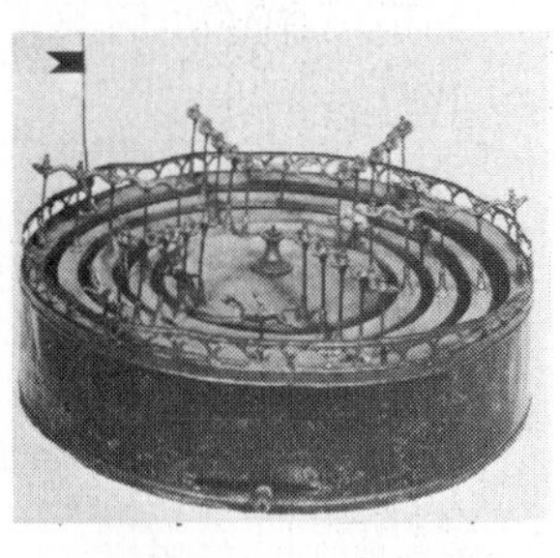

A Tinplate Jeu De Course, with four concentric rings holding two cast alloy horses on each, (some damage), 18 in., 46 cm., diam., probably French, c. 1900. **£110-135** SB

A German Tinplate Paddle Steamer, the paddles operated by clockwork motor, 10½ in., long, probably by Carette, c. 1910. **£200-230** CSK

A. J. Chein tinplate Popeye in barrel, stamped 1932 King Features Syndicate Inc., Copyright, 6½ in., 16.5 cm. high. American c. 1932. **£110-125** SB

POINTERS FOR TINPLATE TOYS

- Tin Toys produced late 19th C and beginning 20th C.
- The great continental toy firms include, Lehmann, Fischer, Schreyer of Germany and Ferdinand Martin of France.
- Tin Toys are fetching consistently good prices at auction.

A Kellerman tinplate frog, tries to catch a fly moving before him, driven by the clockwork mechanism, contained in original box 6 in., 15 cm. high. German c. 1930. **£185-225** SB

An F. Martin tinplate Chinaman toy, the clockwork mechanism causing both arms to wave menacingly. 7½ in., 19 cm., high French c. 1900. **£185-200** SB

Quack Quack, a printed tinplate mother duck pulling a wheeled basket of bobbing ducklings, 7½ in., long, by Lehmann, patented 12 May 1903. **£80-100** CSK

left
A Tinplate Photographer Toy, with lever operating the figure, moving the plate and bringing down his finger, German, c. 1920 5 in., 12.5 cm. long. **£110-130** SB

A Fernand Martin painted tinplate toy of a bell-puller, 7 in., high. **£130-150** CSK

A Bing tinplate limousine, (paint scratched and scuffed, wheel arches slightly bent) the clockwork mechanism driving rear wheels, side lamp and key, 27½ in., 10¾ in. German, late 1920's. **£250-300** SB

An early Victor Bonnet et cie tinplate musical clown, with five keys below which operate the relevant limb. 10¼ in., 26 cm. high. French c. 1916. **£625-675** SB

A Bing "United Motor Bus Company Limited" tinplate toy, the clockwork mechanism causing the twin rear wheels to revolve (together with key) 10 in., 25.5 cm., long. German c. 1920. **£950-1,000** SB

A Stock tinplate porter and trolley, marked W. St 195, the clockwork mechanism driving the spoked wheels and moving the legs of the porter, 7 in., 18 cm. long, German c. 1930. **£75-85** SB

A stock "Paddy's Pride" tinplate toy, the clockwork mechanism driving the axle and causing the butcher to wave his arms, contained in original box. 8½ in., 21.5 cm. long. German c. 1915. **£200-225** SB

A stock "Jim" the walking trolleyman tinplate toy, the clockwork mechanism driving the twin spoked wheels of the trolley, contained in original box. 6¾ in., 17 cm., wide. German c. 1915. **£215-235** SB

An Orobr tinplate fire engine, with clockwork mechanism driving the twin rear wheels. 6½ in., 16.5 cm., long. German c. 1920. **£145-175** SB

A German mechanised tin plate toy 'The Comical Clown', in original box. **£75-85** GC

A Tinplate and clockwork 'Busy Lizzie', 17cms high, German, c1915-20. **£145-155** SKC

A 2p tinplate Alfa Romeo, probably by CIF, with clockwork mechanism driving the rear axle, 21 in., 53 cm. long, French c. 1925-30 **£375-400** SB

A Lehmann 'Zikra' clockwork and tinplate bucking zebra cart with clown driver, with faults, 18cms long. **£85-95** SKC

An American Wooden-bodied Clockwork Man, walking on articulated wooden legs, on rollered feet, 9¾ in., by Ives & Co. **£150-180** CSK

A Carette Tinplate Renault Open Tourer Car with detachable driver and passenger, and clockwork mechanism driving the rear wheels. German c. 1907 (varnished overall) 10 in., 26 cm. long. **£90-100** L

An F. Martin violinist tinplate toy, clothes damaged , the clockwork mechanism causing the figure to appear to play the instrument. 8 in., 20.5 cm. high. French c. 1900. **£185-200** SB

Lehmann's Halloh, a printed tinplate clockwork pedal cyclist with a motor operating the rear wheel through a spring "chain", c1910, in original box, 9" long. **£470-500** CSK

A Lehmann 'Oh My' Dancing Negro Clockwork Tin Plate Toy, No. 690, with original box, height 10½" (26.5cms). **£130-145** SBe

Oh My, a printed tinplate dancing Negro, with clockwork mechanism. By Lehmann c1930, in original box, 10" high. **£210-250** CSK

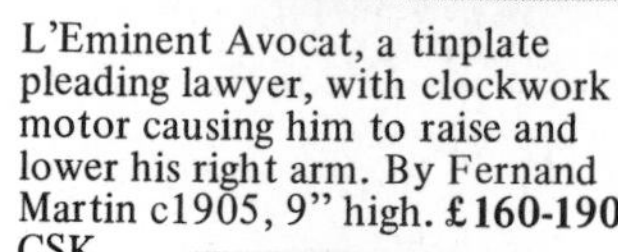

L'Eminent Avocat, a tinplate pleading lawyer, with clockwork motor causing him to raise and lower his right arm. By Fernand Martin c1905, 9" high. **£160-190** CSK

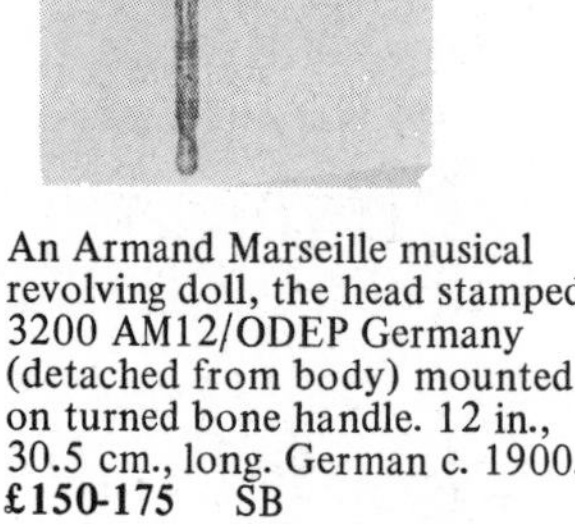

An Armand Marseille musical revolving doll, the head stamped 3200 AM12/ODEP Germany (detached from body) mounted on turned bone handle. 12 in., 30.5 cm., long. German c. 1900. **£150-175** SB

Nina, a Lehmann mouse-chasing cat, c1927, 10½" long. **£170-200** CSK

A "walking zouave" toy, the clockwork mechanism operating the legs, causing each to move backwards and forwards, 10 in., 25.5 cm. high, c. 1870. **£150-175** SB

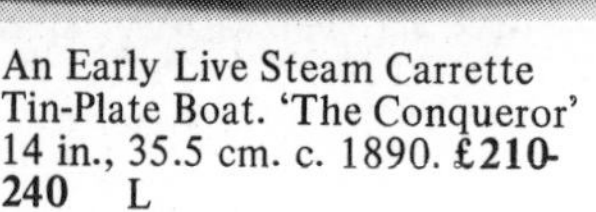

An Early Live Steam Carrette Tin-Plate Boat. 'The Conqueror' 14 in., 35.5 cm. c. 1890. **£210-240** L

A Gunthermann Crawling ladybird, with clockwork motor, 1911 patent 7¾". **£54-64** CSK

A Negro Minstrel Musical Automaton, with a papiermache turning head and moving eye lids and lips, height 30" (76.5cms), (wig lacking, considerable restoration). **£620-680** SBe

A Bisque-Headed Automaton Figure, as the music plays she raises the tub showing alternating objects beneath, 17" high, the head by Jumeau. **£880-980** CSK

A good nouveau jouet "tres tres presse" porter and trolley, with clockwork mechanism causing the wheels to revolve and the porter's legs to move backwards and forwards, 7½ in., 19 cm. long. French c. 1915. **£180-200** SB

A Musical Automaton Figure of a violinist, 10 in. high, with circular ebonised base and glass dome. **£220-320** CSK

A pierrot musical automaton (re-clothed) with single-air musical movement (the chair re-painted) with controlling lever and winding key on one side 24 in., 61 cm. high, probably French, c. 1900. **£1,250-1,500** SB

A Mickey Mouse Organ Grinder, probably by Distler, c1929, mechanism operated by musical accompaniment, (Minnie one arm missing, Mickey with restoration and repainting) 20cms high. **£245-280** SKC

An F. Martin piano player toy, with clockwork mechanism moving torso and arms. 5¾ in., 13 cm. wide (the clockwork motor and movement detached) French c. 1900. **£200-225** SB

A Printed Tinplate Mickey Mouse Mechanical Bank, the tongue retracts when his ear is lifted, printed with the verse: "If you only pull my ear, You will see my tongue appear. Place a coin upon my tongue, Save your money while you're young." 7 in., German. **£650-720** CSK

A monkey "pianist" automaton with movement to the right and left arms, the eyelids close and the mouth moves to the accompaniment of cylinder musical movement, the figure re-clothed, 19 in. by 15½ in., probably French c. 1900. **£440-480** SB

A cast-iron banjo-player clock, the movement connected to operate the eyes, on rectangular base, lacking hat, 15½ in., 39.5 cm. high. American c. 1880. **£250-300** SB

An Intermittent Singing Bird Automaton, English, late 19th C, 19¾" (50cms). **£700-800** L

An Imhof & Mukle singing-bird automaton, with musical and mechanical movement and start/stop control to one side, the bird turning his head from side to side and moving its beak and tail to the piping song (distressed) 11 in., 28 cm., c. 1900. **£175-200** SB

A Singing Bird Automaton with brightly feathered bird. French. 1920-30 9 in., 23 cm. **£130-160** L

A Singing Bird in Cage by Bontems, No. 990, the bird with moving head, tail and beak, 19½ in. high. **£580-680** CSK

A Phillip Vielmetter tinplate drawing clown, the base 5 in., 12.5 cm., square (rust and worn) complete with maker's mark, German, c. 1900. **£300-390** SB

A 1930's tinplate and clockwork Silver Bullet Record Car, by Gunthermann, (one applied flag missing), 56cms long. **£225-250** SKC

A clockwork "cat and kitten" automaton, the mechanism causing the head to nod whilst the eyes roll and mouth opens and shuts. 14 in., 35.5 cm. high probably French, early 20th C. **£250-300** SB

An Early 1920's 'Orobr' (Orowerke, Brandenburg) tinplate double garage, containing a clockwork limousine, 15cms long long and an open touring car, 16cms long. **£255-280** SKC

A Tipp Clockwork Tin Plate 'Old Bill' Type Bus, painted in traditional colours, 10" (25.5cms), (An interesting fault shows the adverts above the lower deck windows to be applied in reverse), c1937. **£140-155** SBe

A 1930's tinplate and clockwork 'Golden Arrow' Record Car, by Gunthermann, 54cms long. **£90-100** SKC

A Tin-Plate Clockwork Model of Grand Prix Alfa Romeo P II Racing Car, rust deterioration to body and paintwork, wheelbase 13¾ in., 35 cm. **£100-110** CSK

An early Marklin gauge "two" 2-2-0 clockwork locomotive and tender (retouched) 13 in., 33 cm. long overall. Gebruder Marklin & Co., German c. 1898. **£295-325** SB

A Good large model of the Clyde paddle steamer 'Duchess of Montrose', c1920, 245cms long. **£340-380** SKC

A Fine Scratch Built G. W. R. Coach, 17½ in., 44.5 cm. **£40-50** L

A Hornby O Gauge 'Lord Nelson' Electric 4-4-2 Locomotive and Tender, 16¾" (41.5cms), in original box. **£280-360** L

A tin scale clockwork model of The Golden Arrow Land Speed Record car wheelbase 10 in., 25 cm., **£180-210** CSK

A Carette gauge 1 clockwork 0-4-0 locomotive and tender, 39.5cms long, c1914, with a Carette gauge 1 guard's van, an open truck and a cattle wagon, (restored). **£155-170** SKC

A Hornby Gauge O Clockwork O-4-O Locomotive and Tender, painted in Great Western livery and numbered 2301., 12 in., 30.5 cm. overall. **£105-125** L

A Bing Clockwork Tug with trade label B.W. Germany, contained in original box. 8 in., 20 cm. **£75-85** L

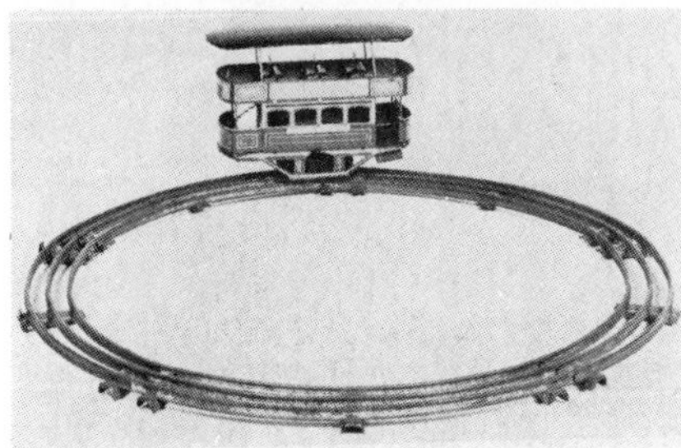

A Bing gauge "O" tinplate tram on four wheels operated by electric mechanism 6¼ in., 16 cm., long together with five sections of curved rail. German c. 1930. **£225-250** SB

A clock picture automaton, "Interieur de Ste Madeleine de Paris", with clock face and moving band of figures depicting a holy procession, 34 by 40 in., 86.5 by 110.5 cm., French, late 19th C. **£350-400** SB

An American Iron money box with revolving door, late 19th C. **£85-95** BA

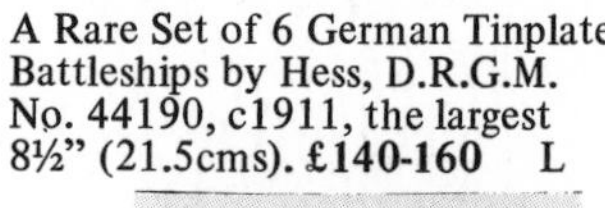

A Rare Set of 6 German Tinplate Battleships by Hess, D.R.G.M. No. 44190, c1911, the largest 8½" (21.5cms). **£140-160** L

A Novelty Merchantman Crane Amusement Machine, by Exhibit Supply Co., with stained oak casing, containing model of ships hull with grab crane, 6 ft., 183 cm., high, American, c. 1960. **£240-275** SB

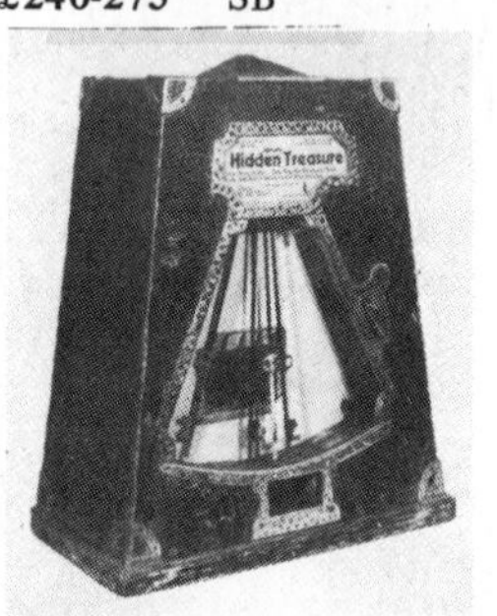

A Bryans 'Hidden Treasure' 'Penny-in-the-slot' amusement machine, 70cms high x 60cms wide. **£55-65** SKC

An American Money Bank in the form of the Bank of New York, c. 1840. **£80-90** CP

A Cast Metal Bank modelled as Mickey Mouse, 8½ in., **£50-60** CSK

A spirit-fired live steam yacht with small pot boiler, single oscillating cylinder 16 in., 40.6 cm. long. **£210-225** SB

A Painted Cast Iron, Mechanical Bank, 'I always did s'pise a mule', late 19th C., patent date April 22nd, 1879, 8½ in., 21 cm. **£130-170** SBe

A Bryans '12-Win Clock' 'Penny-in-the-slot' amusement machine, with instructions, 65cms high x 50cms wide. **£35-45** SKC

Magic Bank, a cast iron savings bank, patented 1873 and 1876 by H. W. Prouty manufactured by J & E Stevens Co., 4¾" long 5¼" high. **£100-130** CSK

A 'Pickfords' cab and trailer, 1930's. **£14-18** BB

An Extremely scarce Set of Hornby modelled miniature Motor Vehicles No. 22, some slight chips, some small pieces missing, original box. **£1,600-1,650** SKC

A Cast Metal Vintage Car, c1935, 8" long. **£45-60** SQE

A Bing Clockwork Tin Plate Taxi, 8½" (21.5cms), (repainted). **£80-90** SBe

A Bull Dog Money Bank early 20th C. 8 in. high. **£145-165** CC

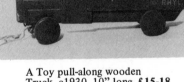

A Printed Tinplate Limousine, 11½ in., long, probably by Carette. **£400-450** CSK

A Dinky Toys pre-war 22 series Tractor. **£75-80** SKC

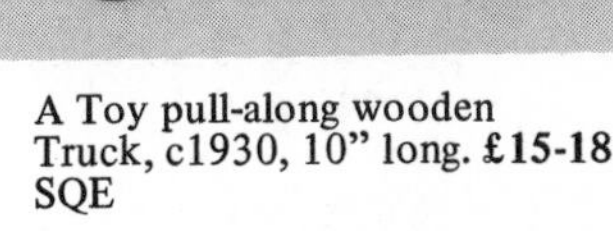

A Toy pull-along wooden Truck, c1930, 10" long. **£15-18** SQE

An Unusual American cast iron savings bank, the coin is introduced into the bank by placing it between the donkey's hind legs and depressing a lever, patented August 1880, 8½" long. **£170-200** CSK

Set of 16 Britains Mexican Infantry (14), with officers (2), (one officer's head damaged), contained in a Britains box. **£80-85** SB

A scarce Dinky Chrysler Air-flow Saloon. **£65-70** SKC

A Dinky Toys pre-war 25 series Lorry, with detachable canopy. **£35-40** SKC

A Victorian Dolls House, of wood construction, rooms on three floors, width 20½" (52cms) height 27½" (70cms), (some damage). **£105-125** SBe

A Painted Wooden Dolls House in chinoiserie style, 95 in. wide on wood stand, early 19th C. **£1,200-1,500** CSK

A scarce Pre-war Dinky 28 series 2nd type 'Dunlop Tyres' Delivery Van (displays slight metal fatigue, faults). **£65-70** SKC

Set of 11 Britains Cossacks, mounted in original Whisstock box no. 136. **£35-40** SB

A Printed Paper on wood Doll's House, 20" high, French 1890. **£340-390** CSK

A Victorian Doll's Purse. **£8-10** LM

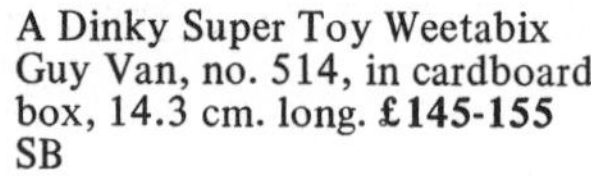

A Dinky Super Toy Weetabix Guy Van, no. 514, in cardboard box, 14.3 cm. long. **£145-155** SB

A Pull Along Toy of a Nurse Pushing a Three-Wheeled Pram, 15 in. long. **£280-340** CSK

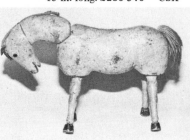

A Victorian Doll's Spectacle Case. **£10-12** LM

A Dinky Trojan Van 'Esso'. **£25-30** SKC

A carved wooden horse, c1900. **£10-15** BB

A Britains Set of South Australian Lancers, comprising five seated horsemen contained in original Christmas Box, one leg broken. **£150-170** L

A Straw-work Noah's Ark, the flat-bottomed vessel's superstructure removing to reveal wooden carved and painted animals within, 15 in., 38 cm. long, mid 19th C. **£200-250** SB

Miniature Sewing Machine, German with original box, c. 1930's. **£20-25** LM

A Very Interesting Pull-along Toy with animated doll figures, the bisque head doll impressed 'Classic, England', the operation is for the girl doll to move head and arms in a sideways direction and the standing figure to move its head and right arm (head of boy doll and article he should be holding, lacking). c. 1925, **£200-260** SBe

A Child's Tinplate Cooking Range with brass fittings, fired by spirit burners with bainmarie, kettle, coffee pot, two saucepans and a frying pan, the whole 18¼ in., 46.3 cm. wide, probably French, c. 1900. **£175-200** SB

An unusual child's galloper push chair, the horse with hair mane and tail and leather harness, 38 in., 96.5 cm. long. English, late 19th C. **£300-350** SB

A Child's Metal Toy Stove, 20 in. wide. **£190-220** CSK

A good straw-work Noah's ark and animals, holding one hundred and eighty-five animals, birds and figures, 21 in., 53 cm. long. (worn and some animals lacking legs) probably Bavarian, c. 1850. **£250-300** SB

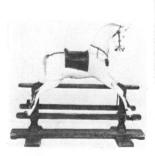

A Carved Wooden Rocking Horse, with horsehair mane and tail, 47 in., 119.5 cm. long. **£155-200** SB

A Good Victorian Carved Wood Horse and Cart. The tip-up cart with name Benetfink & Co., contractors, on two spoked wheels, 29 in., 73 cm. **£40-50** L

A Sixteen Piece Tea Set in original box, made in Germany by Gebruder Heubach in Lichte Porcelain Factory. **£30-34** LM

Two cardboard Easter eggs, with painted faces, 1920's. **£6-8** BB

Original Victorian Bentwood Dolls Furniture, 6 piece suite. **£25-28** LM

A Group of Painted Cloth Dolls representing Snow White and the Seven Dwarfs, Snow White 16 in., the Dwarfs 10 in. high, marked Chad Valley Hygenic Art Dolls. **£480-560** CSK

Votes for Women, painted composition and wood pair of figures, dressed in muslin, 6¾" high. **£60-70** CSK

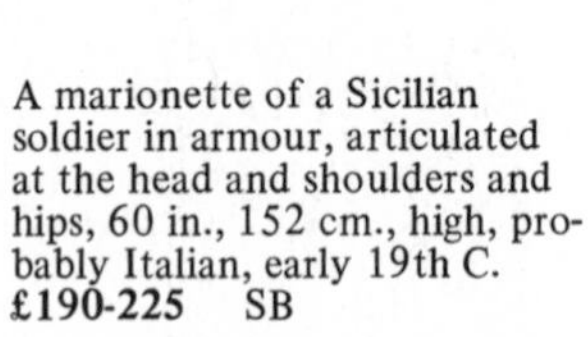

A marionette of a Sicilian soldier in armour, articulated at the head and shoulders and hips, 60 in., 152 cm., high, probably Italian, early 19th C. **£190-225** SB

A set of painted brass Beatrice Potter characters, 1¼" (3cms). **£155-175** SBe

Comical Metamorphoses, twelve disassembled, interchangeable sets of legs, torsos and heads, in original box c 1870. **£140-180** CSK

Sample from 150 piece set Britains Lead Toy Farm. **£180-200** A.D.H.

A Zeotrope, the painted tin drum with thirteen pierced slots, with twenty-one printed paper strips, English, c.1870, 1ft. (30.5cm) diam. **£130-160** SB

A German Game of 'Flipperty-Flop', slightly distressed. **£4-6** IN

A collection of Doll's clothes made by a child in the 1860's. **£410-460** CSK

A Small Spirit Stove, c. 1920 **£22-25** LM

A Barrel-shaped container for the Koawase game (slightly damaged) 19th C., 7.8 cm. high. **£490-600** C

A Set of Five Skittles with two felt-covered wooden balls, 7½"–10" high. **£90-110** CSK

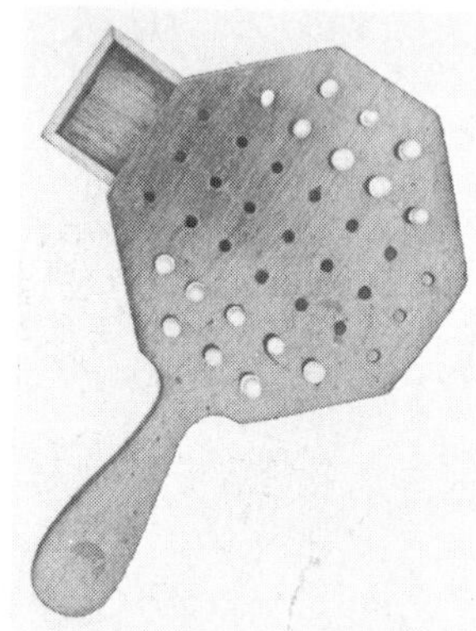

Mid 19th C Fox and Goose Game, (with drawer). **£25-30** IN

Childs wooden dolls sink with scrubbing brushes, sink 9½" long, brushes 3¼" long. **£15-17** A.L.

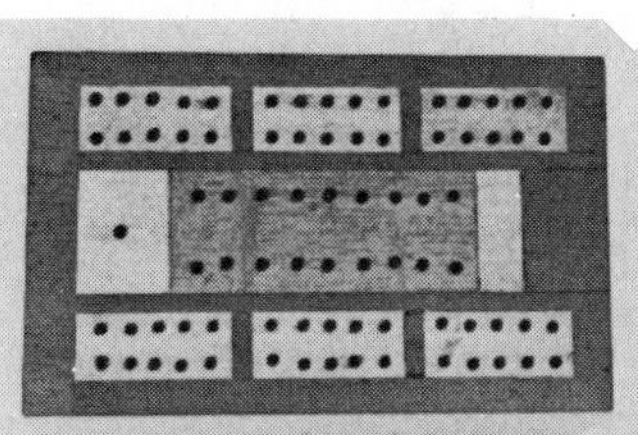

19th C Cribbage Set. **£12-15** IN

A Stuffed Toy Lion – well used! 1920's. **£15-20** LM

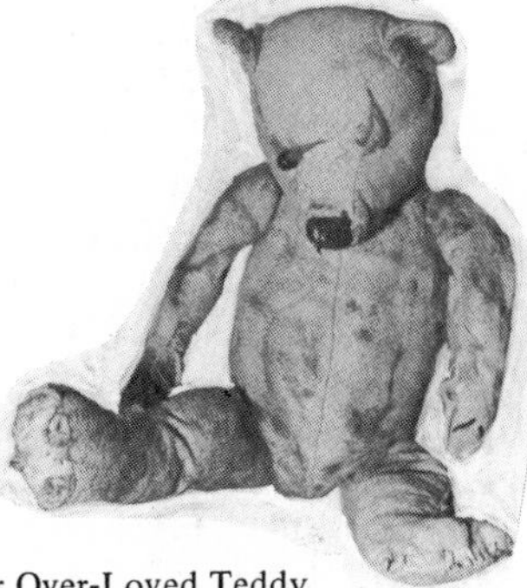

A Rather Over-Loved Teddy, with all faults, 1930's. **£15-18** LM

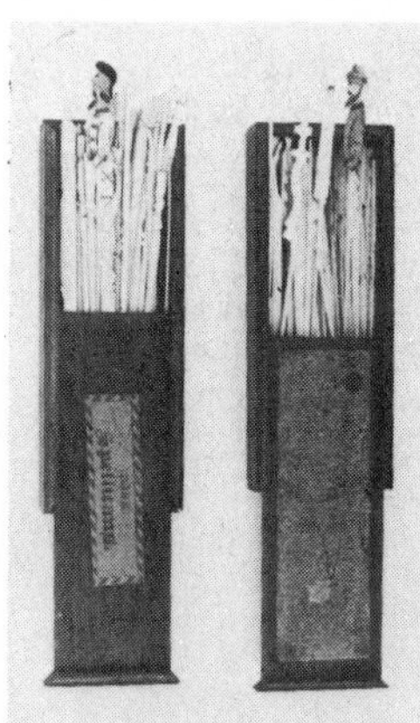

2 Sets of bone spellicans, with rules. **£14-17** set IN

A Child's Game 'Embossed Pictures', c1920's. **£8-12** IN

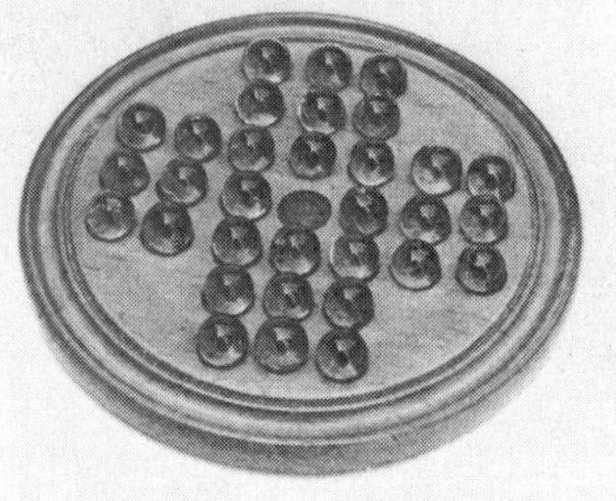

Mid 19th C Treen Solitaire, 5½" diam. **£25-30** IN

A Child's Game 'Happy Hours' Printing Box, c1920's. **£8-12** IN

A Promotional Stuffed Doll for Force wheat flakes, 15 in. 1928. **£18-28** LM

POINTERS FOR DOLLS

- Wax dolls date from the late 18th C.
- Slithead Wax Dolls from c. 1810.
- Poured Wax Dolls from c. 1855.
- Note any Dolls made by Charles Marsh.
- Papier mache dolls made between 1800-1850.
- Glazed porcelain heads made after 1840 mainly German.
- Bisque or Parian Heads made from 1855, most sought after are those with swivelling heads and glass eyes.
- The French Bebe dolls appeared from 1870 well known makers include Bru, Steiner of Paris, Robery & Delphieu, Jumeau.
- Note condition of dolls, do not get rid of clothes even if shabby, original clothes are desirable.
- There are many reproductions particularly of the bisque dolls.

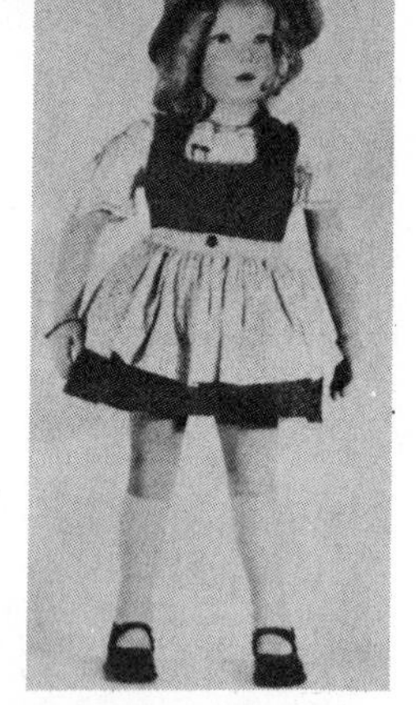

A Painted Cloth Shop Model of a Girl with stuffed stockinette body, 35 in., high, by Kathe Kru[illegible] **£350-380** CSK

A Bisque Head Doll, Hair Stuffed body, made in Germany by Armand Marseille, Mold '370', 1865-1925. **£165-185** LM

A Black Bisque Head 'Dream Baby' made in Germany by Armand Marseille in Kopplesdorf, closed mouth, 6 in. tall, 1865-1925. **£170-190** LM

A Pair of Mickey and Minnie Mouse stuffed dolls, with trademarks of Dean's Rag Book Co. Ltd., 31cms high (rubber tail to Mickey, missing). **£145-185** SKC

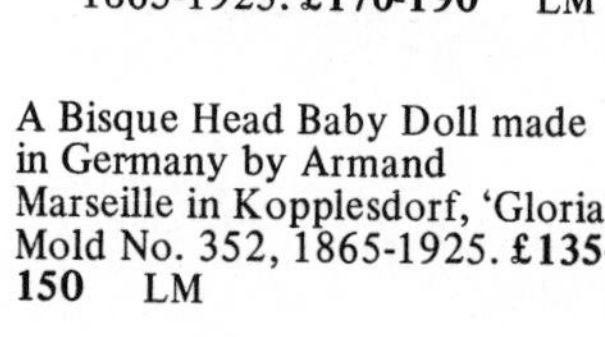

A Bisque Head Baby Doll made in Germany by Armand Marseille in Kopplesdorf, 'Gloria' Mold No. 352, 1865-1925. **£135-150** LM

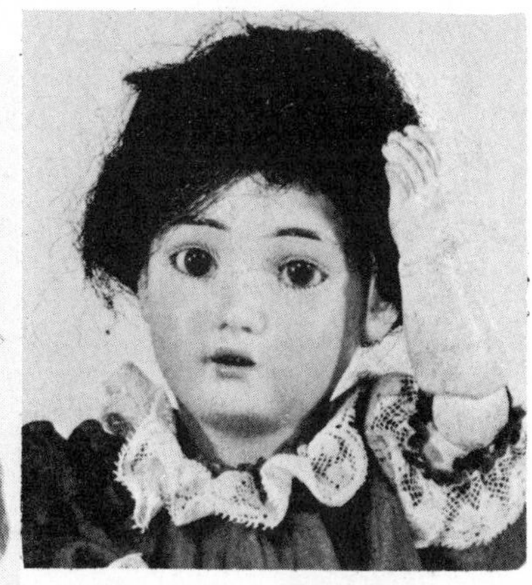

A Bisque-Headed Oriental Character Doll with jointed composition body, 10½ in., marked 1329 Simon & Halbig S & H 2. **£320-350** CSK

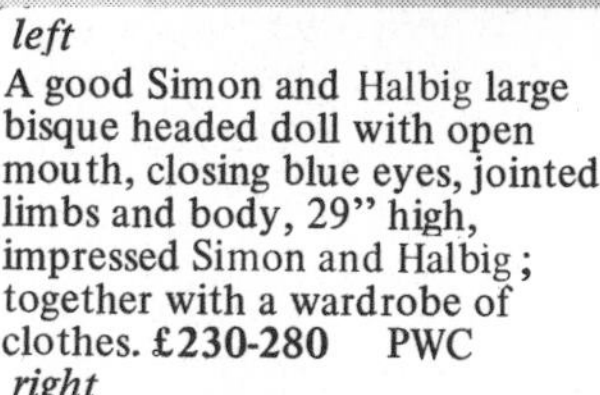

left
A good Simon and Halbig large bisque headed doll with open mouth, closing blue eyes, jointed limbs and body, 29" high, impressed Simon and Halbig; together with a wardrobe of clothes. **£230-280** PWC

right
A good wax head and shoulders doll, with fabric body and wax limbs, 26½" high; together with a wardrobe of clothes. **£190-230**

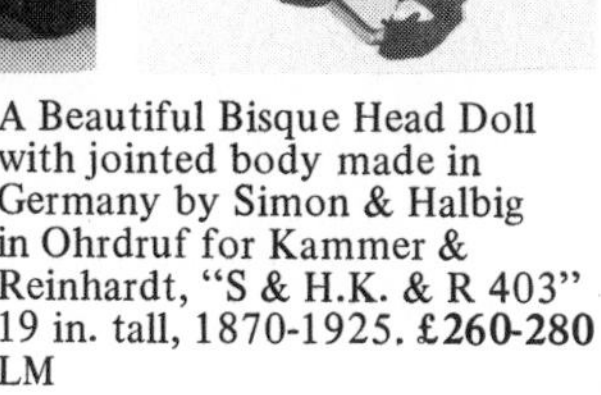

A Beautiful Bisque Head Doll with jointed body made in Germany by Simon & Halbig in Ohrdruf for Kammer & Reinhardt, "S & H.K. & R 403" 19 in. tall, 1870-1925. **£260-280** LM

right
A Bisque Shoulder Head Doll made by Armand Marseille in Germany, 'Floradora' (has slight crack under wig). **£145-155** LM

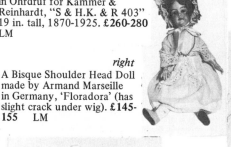

A Simon & Halbig Doll with bisque head and jointed composition body, 36 in. tall, c. 1910-14. **£295-395** LM

A French Bisque Doll, possibly by Huret, the socketed head with pale blue glass eyes, closed mouth, the gusseted kid body with china forearms, c. 1860, in contemporary clothing, **£1,050-1,200** SB

A Bisque Head Doll with jointed body made by Th. Recknagel in Germany, marked 'R.A.', 9 in. tall 1886-1925. **£112-120** LM

left
A Beautiful Bisque Head Doll made in Germany for Strobel & Wilken, Ohio, U.S.A., all original clothes, 1864-1925. **£195-215** LM

right
A Bisque Head Jointed Doll made in Germany by Armand Marseille in Kopplesdorf, 9 in. tall, mold '390' AM, 1865-1925. **£125-135** LM

A Bisque-Headed Baby Doll 17 in., marked Playstar R. Simon Halbig 12242. **£140-170** CSK

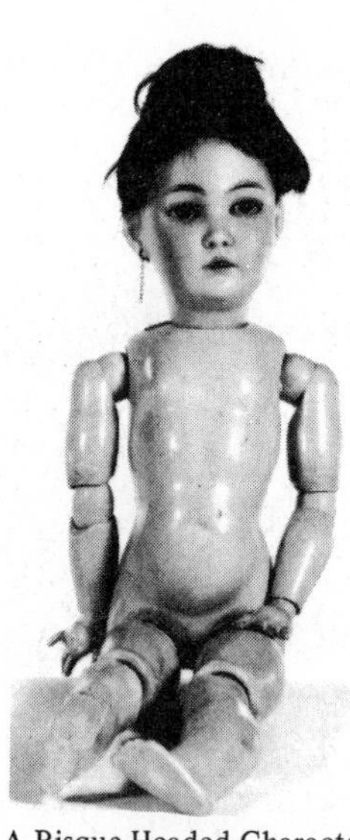

A Bisque-Headed Character Doll with jointed yellow composition body, 18 in. high, marked 1329 Halbig S & H6. **£550-610** CSK

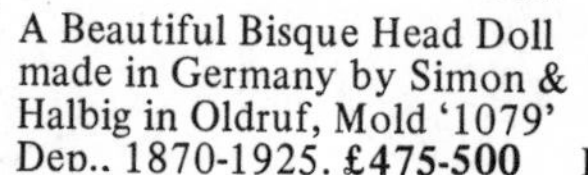

A Beautiful Bisque Head Doll made in Germany by Simon & Halbig in Oldruf, Mold '1079' Dep.. 1870-1925. **£475-500** LM

A Beautiful French Doll with bisque head and jointed body made by Jumeau in Paris, 26 in. tall, c. 1842-99. **£785-825** LM

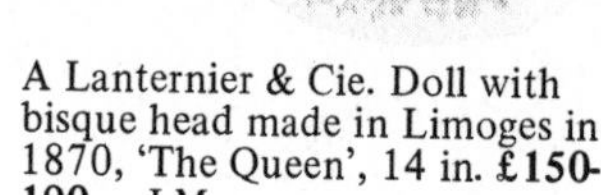

A Lanternier & Cie. Doll with bisque head made in Limoges in 1870, 'The Queen', 14 in. **£150-190** LM

A Bisque Head Jointed Doll made in Germany by Th. Recknagel in Alexandrinenthal, marked 'R.A.', 1886-1925. **£195-215** LM

A Jullien Doll with jointed composition body, wooden arms and legs, bisque head, made in Paris, c. 1875 (and trunk). **£1,100-1,300** LM

A Bisque Head Jointed Doll made in Germany by C. M. Bergmann in Walterhausen, 22 in. tall, 1877-1925 (Collectors Doll) **£230-250** LM

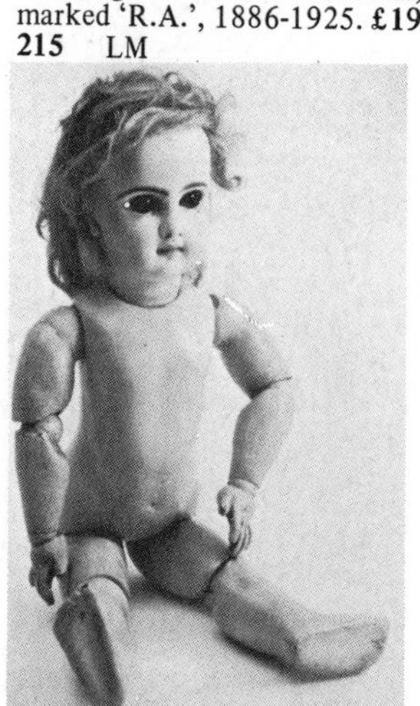

A Good Jumeau Bisque Headed Doll, stamped in red depose Tete Jumeau S.G.D.G.8 with fixed blue eyes, closed mouth, pierced ears, 19 in., 48 cm. **£825-925** L

A Bisque Head Bent Limbed Doll made by J. D. Kestner in Walterhausen, Germany with 'Mama' box – a character doll. **£215-225** LM

A Bisque Head Closed Mouth Doll on soft body, made by J.D. Kestner in Germany for Anchor Toy Co. in USA, c. 1870 **£210-230** LM

A Raybery and Delphieu Doll with bisque head on jointed composition body, 16 in. c. 1895. **£180-225** LM

"Twins" – A Pair of Bisque Head Toddlers made in Germany by Strobel & Wilkens for U.S. market, 1864-1925. **£280-310** pr. LM

A Beautiful French Jointed Doll, bisque head from Limoges by Lanternier & Co., 30 in. tall, 1855-1925. **£375-400** LM

A Beautiful Bisque Head Doll made in France by Jumeau in Paris, 24 in. tall, size 10, 1842-99 (specially designed clothes). **£875-925** LM

"Einco" A Bisque Head Bent Limb Boy Doll made by Eisenmann & Co. in Bavaria, 1905-25. **£295-315** LM

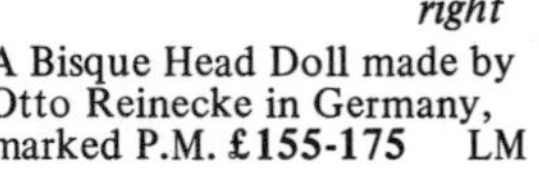

right
A Bisque Head Doll made by Otto Reinecke in Germany, marked P.M. **£155-175** LM

A Bisque Headed Bebe with sleeping eyes, pierced ears, brown wig and jointed body with pull strings for voice box, 16 in. high, marked 7 and stamped Bebe Jumeau. **£460-520** CSK

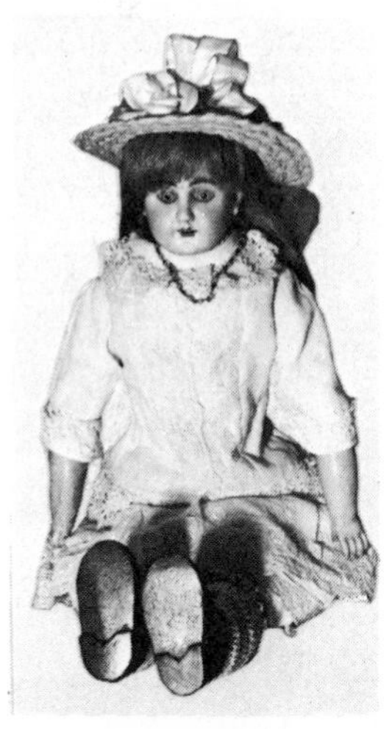

A Bisque Head Shoulder Plate Doll on kid leather body, made in Germany probably for Cuno & Otto Dressel in Sonnenburg, all original, 18 in. tall, 1880-85. **£245-265** LM

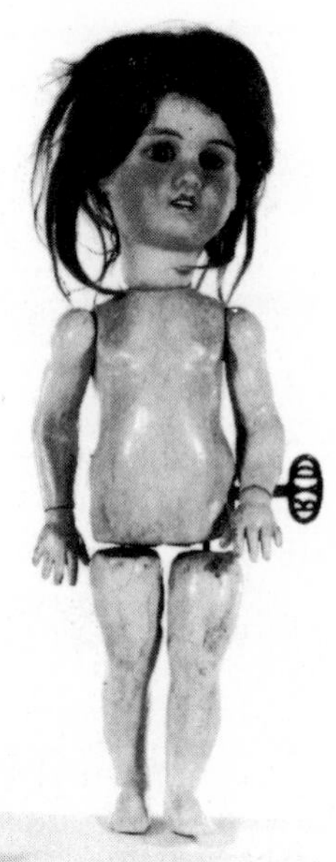

A Bisque-Headed Clockwork Walking Doll with jointed composition arms and rigid composition legs, the mechanism pulls in the feet to make walking movement, 14 in., French, probably by Roullet & Decamps. **£220-240** CSK

A Bisque Head Jointed Doll made in France by S.F.B.J., all original clothes, 1901-1925. **£150-170** LM

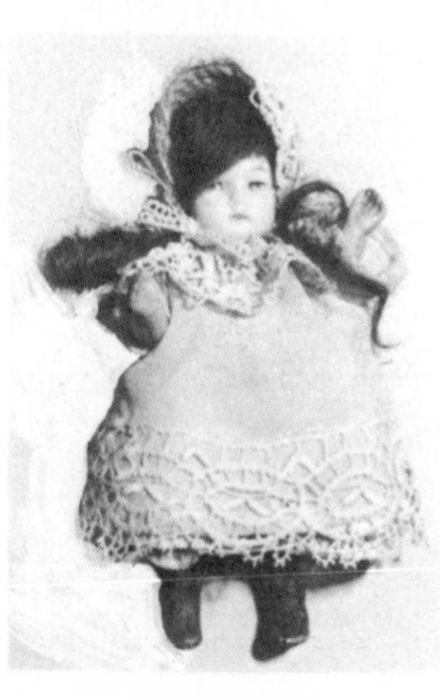

All Bisque Doll made in Germany, mark '612', 5½ in. tall. **£65-70** LM

A Beautiful Small German Bebe with bisque head and bent limb body, made by Hermann Steiner in Sonneburg, c. 1921-25. **£155-175** LM

Little Bru Doll with bisque head and wooden jointed body, 12½ in. c. 1890. **£600-700** LM

A German Parian Doll, white bisque with painted face and fabric body, unmarked, made for Victorian market, 25 in. tall, 1865-1885. **£120-180** LM

A Bisque-Headed Bebe with fixed blue eyes, closed mouth, pierced ears, 13 in. high, marked 3. **£600-700** CSK

A Rare German Shoulder-Bisque Doll's Head, with closed mouth, with blue glass eyes and pierced ears, 14 in., 10 cm. **£450-500** SB

A Bisque Head Doll with soft body made in England, all original, 1890-1900. **£52-60** LM

A Bisque-Headed Doll, jointed composition body, in contemporary embroidered wool dress, with assortment of clothes and a rattle, the doll 12 in. long. **£280-310** CSK

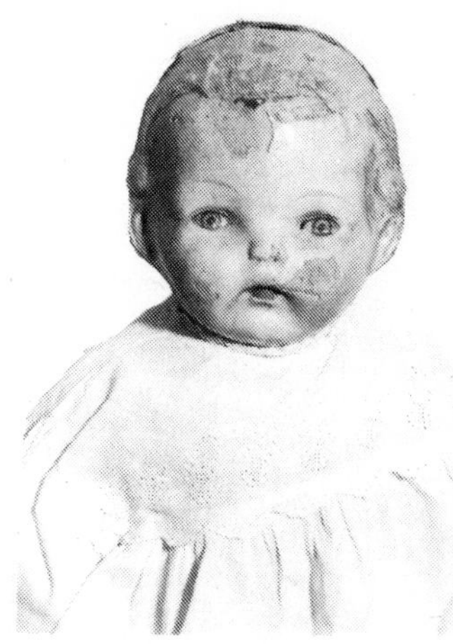

A Pressed Cardboard Doll, the fabric body in bad condition, 22 in. **£20-25** LM

A Bisque Shoulder-Headed Child Doll, wearing original contemporary blue wool dress, 17½ in. high. **£120-160** CSK

A Small Pierotti Doll with poured wax arms and legs and fabric body, 12 in. tall, c. 1875-80. **£150-220** LM

A Bisque Shoulder-Headed Sewing Doll with painted features and stuffed body with bisque limbs, 11 in. **£150-170** CSK

A Bisque Shoulder-Headed Doll with stuffed body with bisque limbs, 17 in., high. **£200-230** CSK

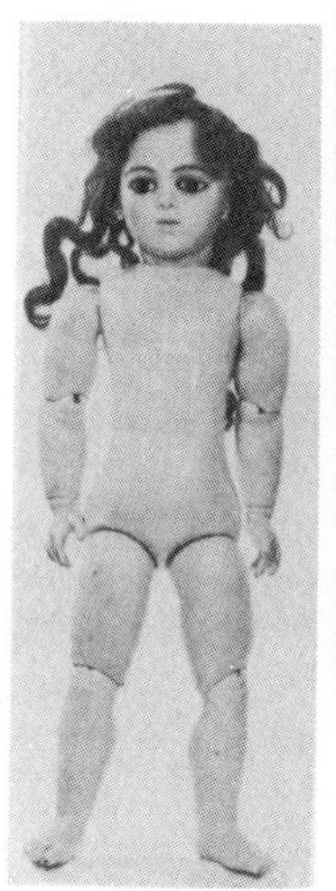

A Bisque Headed Bebe with open-closed mouth, jointed composition body with brown wig, 18 in. high, marked BRU JNE 8. **£2,500-2,800** CSK

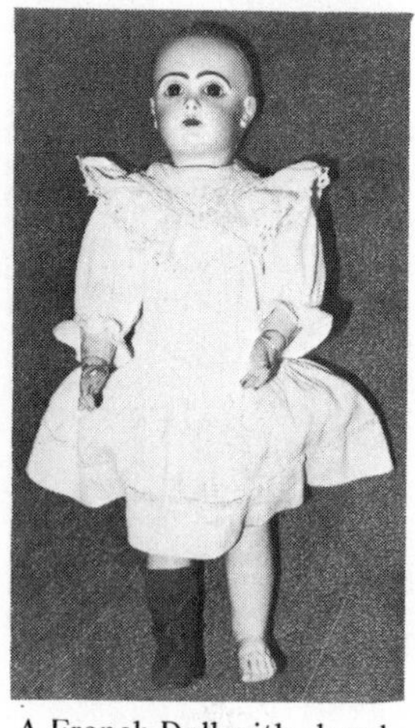

A French Doll with closed mouth by Jumeau, awaiting restoration, 23 in. long. **£1,200-1,400** LM

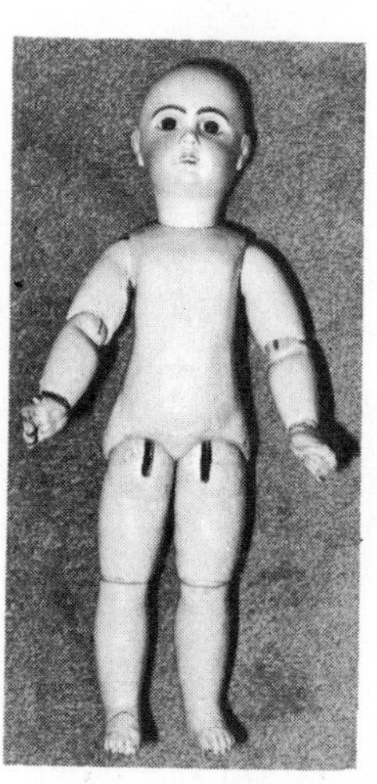

A Doll with open mouth by Jumeau. **£450-650** LM

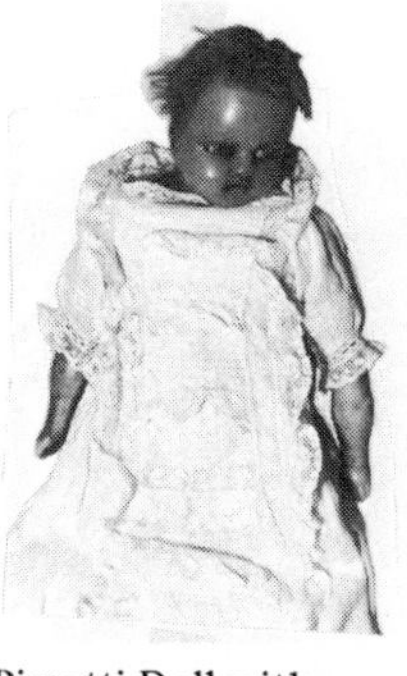

A Pierotti Doll with poured wax head, shoulders, arms and legs, fabric body, eyes open and head to one side. **£425-485** LM

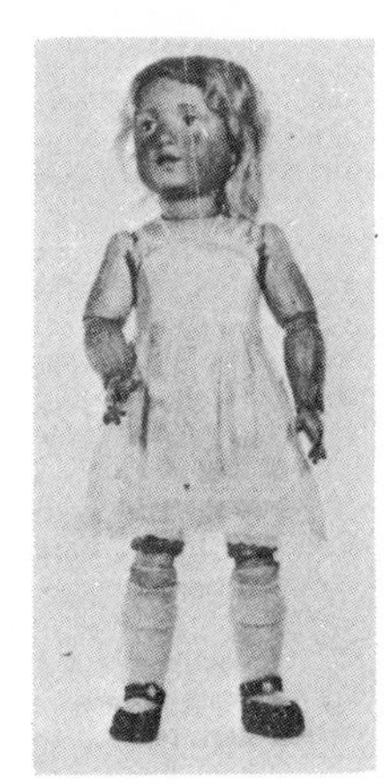

A Bisque-Headed Character Child Doll with closed mouth, 18 in. high, marked K*R 109 46. **£1,500-1,700** CSK

A Pierotti Doll with poured wax head and shoulders on fabric body, composition legs and arms, unusual sleeping eyes, 19 in. long. **£650-700** LM

A Good Wax Doll with fixed blue eyes, closed mouth and painted features, the stuffed cloth body with wax lower limbs, wearing contemporary costume, 22 in., 56 cm. **£200-230** L

A Good Wax Boy Doll with fixed blue eyes, closed mouth and painted features, the stuffed cloth body with wax lower limbs, wearing original costume., 15 in., 39 cm. **£90-110** L

A Poured Wax Child Doll with stuffed body and waxed limbs, in original frock 17½ in. high, c. 1880. **£260-290** CSK

A 19th C Poured Wax Head and shoulders Girl Doll, having blue glass eyes, stuffed body and dressed in original clothing, with green leather shoes, 29½", with faults. **£140-180** SH

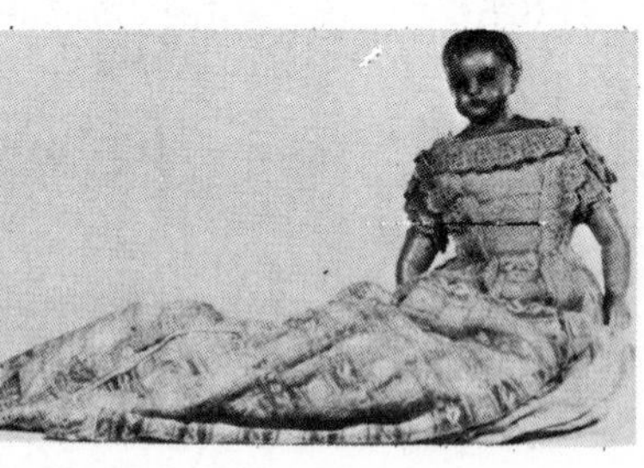

A Poured Wax Child Doll with stuffed body and poured wax limbs, 20 in. **£270-300** CSK

A Poured-Wax Child Doll, the stuffed body with wax limbs wearing original lawn frock, 23 in. high, in wooden box. **£320-360** CSK

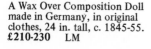

A Wax Over Composition Doll made in Germany, in original clothes, 24 in. tall, c. 1845-55. **£210-230** LM

An English Wax Over Composition Doll in original clothes, perfect condition, 14 in. tall, c. 1870-90. **£275-290** LM

An English Poured Wax Head and Shoulders Doll with soft body with wax limbs, (three fingers lacking) 33 in., 84 cm. **£275-325** SBe

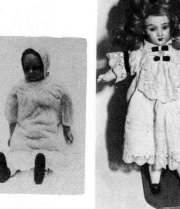

A Gebruder Krasse Doll made in Germany with composition arms and jointed body, c. 1905. **£150-195** LM

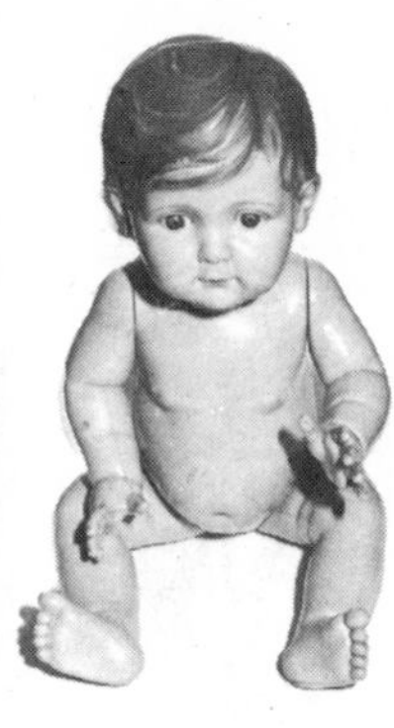

A Kestner Closed Mouth Character Doll with sleeping eyes, No. '212', 16 in. long, **£375-475** – with slight crack across eye **£200-280** LM

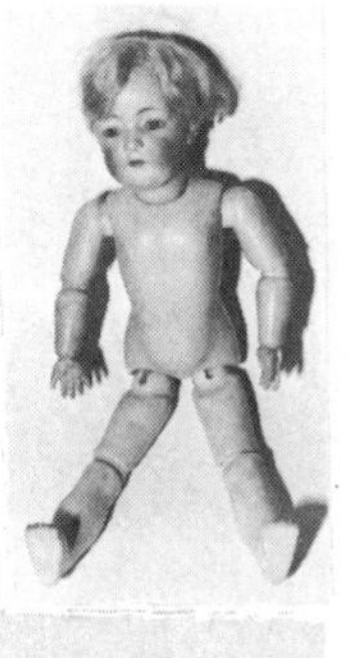

A Celluloid Boy Doll, made in Japan for European market, 23 in. long, c. 1928. **£45-50** LM

Queen Anne Doll of carved wood with jointed arms and legs, English made, c. 1730. **£1,500-2,500** LM

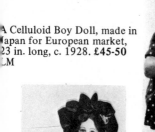

Two Rubber Character Dolls with painted faces, open-close mouth, in original clothes, one with knitting, 11 in. high, by M. J. Pimmel and manufactured by W. Gobel. **£40-60** CSK

A French Fashion Doll with closed mouth, all kid leather body, made in Paris by Lantenier & Co., c. 1890. (Made for fashion houses) 12 in. tall. **£425-475** LM

A fine late 19th C French 'Fashion' Doll with bisque socket head, the kid body bearing the label Spira Firs, 17 Bouley & Sebastopol, 18 Rue Saint Denis, height 17" (43cms), (clothing damaged). **£500-550** SBe

A French Rabery Delphieu Walking automaton, with bisque head and pierced ears, with key, in working order, 15 in. tall, 1885-90. **£475-575** LM

A good mid-19th C. pedlar doll with a paper and ink label with the name 'Molly Bushell licensed hawker 1780', 12 in., 31 cm., c. 1850 base and glass dome. **£365-400** SB

A French Wax Fashion Doll with fabric body and composition arms and legs, 12 in., c. 1880. **£150-200** LM

CIGARETTE CARDS

Taddy. Boer Leaders, a set of twenty. **£40-50** CSK

Murratti. Japanese Series, fifty one cards from a set of fifty two with one duplicate. **£50-80** CSK

Taddy. Russo-Japanese War, numbered 1-25, a set of twenty five. **£40-50** CSK

Player. Old England's Defenders, a set of fifty. **£180-230** CSK

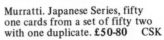

Wills. Advertisement Card "Westward Ho", c1893-4. **R25-35** CSK

Taddy. Royalty Series, a set of twenty five. **£40-50** CSK

Wills. Our Gallant Grenadiers, a set of twenty. **£60-80** CSK

Smith. Boer War Series, coloured, forty five cards from a set of fifty. **£100-150** CSK

A.Kuit, Manchester. 'British Beauties' cigarette cards, twenty-five cards from a series of thirty. **£170-190** CSK

Smith. Naval Dress and Badges, descriptive back, a set of fifty. **£50-70** CSK

POSTCARDS

G.E. Studdy, Bonzo Series postcards (30). **£35-45** CSK

Randolph Caldecott. A set of forty eight postcards, numbered A1–H6, published by F. Warne & Co. **£25-35** CSK

Twenty-Two political cartoon postcards, by A. Ludovici. **£50-60** CSK

Wills. Double Meaning with Playing Card inset, a set of fifty two. **£60-80** CSK

Railway Stations Postcards. Photographic interiors (17). **£65-75** CSK

Louis Wain, 'Tuck's Write Away' (3) and 'Humorous' (4). **£45-50** CSK

Louis Wain, a collection of seven early cards, including an unusual Easter greetings card. **£45-55** SB

'The Prince and the Showgirl' starring Marilyn Monroe and Laurence Olivier, a film poster, framed and glazed, 3 ft. 1 in., 94 cm. high. **£70-90** SB

A Collection of Huntley and Palmer's Trade Cards, "Travelling During the Nineteenth Century," set of twelve, backs printed in English; "Biscuits in Various Countries," nine from a set of twelve, backs printed in French. **£60-70** SB

Advertising. Great Western Railway Pictorial Poster Facsimile series, 'Land's End by Rail and Motor' and 'The Upper Thames'. **£70-80** CSK

1954 Calendar showing a coloured photograph of Marilyn Monroe entitled 'Golden Dreams'; in the photograph she wears no clothes, but a censoring sheet of cellophane covers her with a corselette; this sheet is removable, 39 by 24 cm. **£80-100** SB

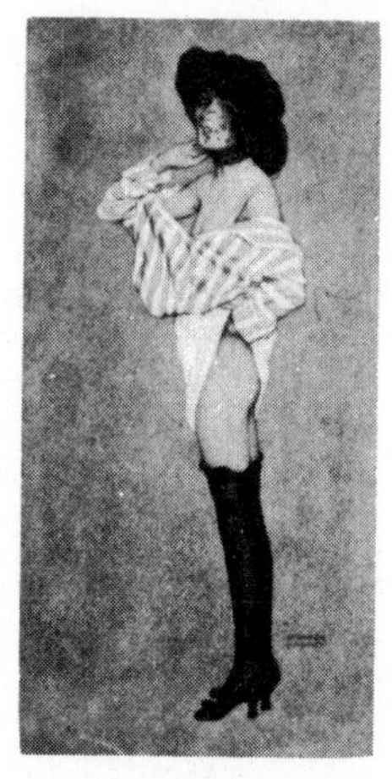

Glamour. Six cards by Raphael Kirchner c1916. **£35-40** CSK

A Tiffany Studios 'Peacock Feather' Leaded-glass and gilt-metal Table-Lamp, the domed shade with panels of mottled blue green glass (some panels cracked) impressed Tiffany Studios mark, 56 cm. high. **£1,300-1,500** C

A pale celadon and striated brown jade figure of a standing lady, wood stand, 2½ in., 6.5 cm. high. **£100-125** C

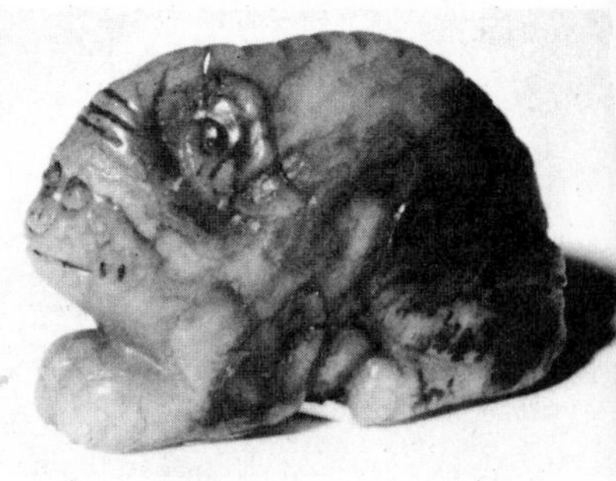

A pale celadon, brown and black jade figure of a crouching Buddhistic lion, wood stand. 1¾ in., 4.5 cm. long. **£100-125** C

A steatite figure of Budai 18th C. 2¾ in., 7.5 cm. wide. **£530-580** C

A pale buff and brown jade annulet (slightly chipped) 18th/19th C. 2 in., 5.5 cm. diam. **£150-200** C

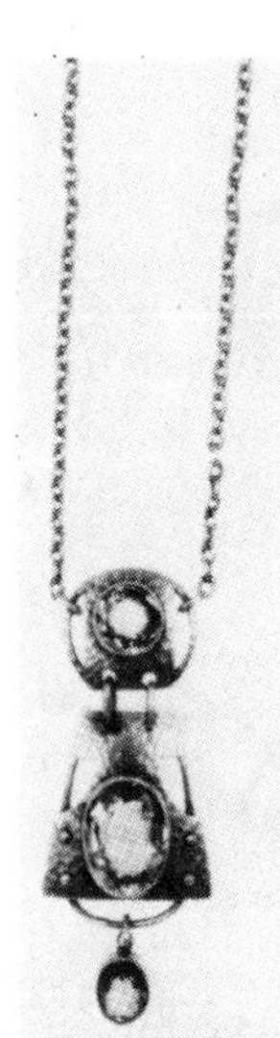

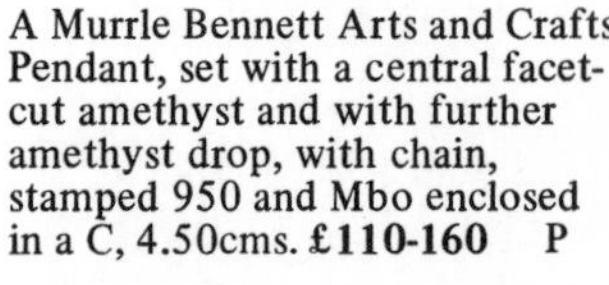

A Murrle Bennett Arts and Crafts Pendant, set with a central facet-cut amethyst and with further amethyst drop, with chain, stamped 950 and Mbo enclosed in a C, 4.50cms. **£110-160** P

A pale celadon jade tripod libation cup 18th/19th C., inlaid wood stand and pierced cover 5 in., 12.5 cm. wide. **£220-280** C

A Theodor Fahrner Plique-a-jour Pendant, picked out in pale blue translucent enamel, enclosing a turquoise cabochon drop, with chain stamped TF in monogram 950 and with Murrle Bennett mark as retailer, 3.50cms. **£300-380** P

A white jade annulet carved as a looped dragon, wood stand, 2 in., 5 cm., wide. **£360-420** C

A Pair of striking Sibyl Dunlop Art Deco Drop Earrings of facet-cut rock crystal, with amethyst, moonstone and rose quartz, 6.5cms, case. **£175-200** P

An Art Deco hexagonal sapphire and diamond cluster Ring, in a platinum mount. **£135-150,** SKC

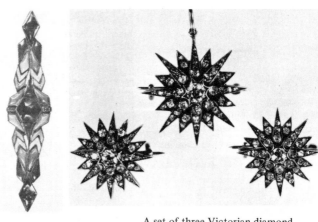

An Art Deco 'Bizarre' Brooch, perhaps by Geoffrey Hunt, **£170-200** L

A set of three Victorian diamond star brooches, with pins removable to facilitate their mounting on to a hair ornament, the frame of which is now missing. **£1,000-1,500** L

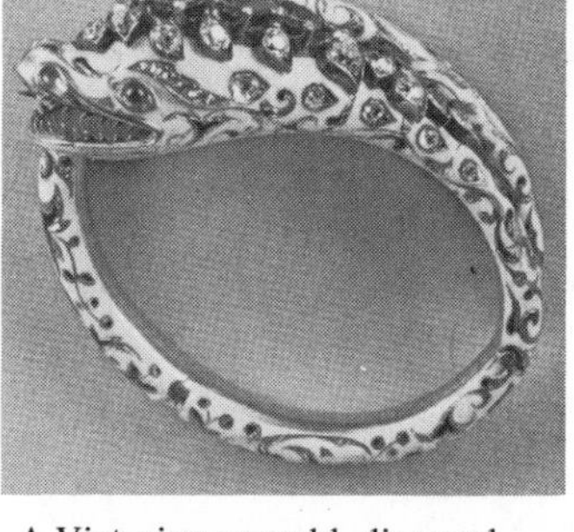

A Victorian emerald, diamond and enamel snake bangle, the body sprung hinged in three places and mounted with green and white enamel. **£2,000-2,500** L

An Art Nouveau gold and plique a jour Brooch, 3.5cms, stamped with Austrian Import marks on pin. **£350-400** P

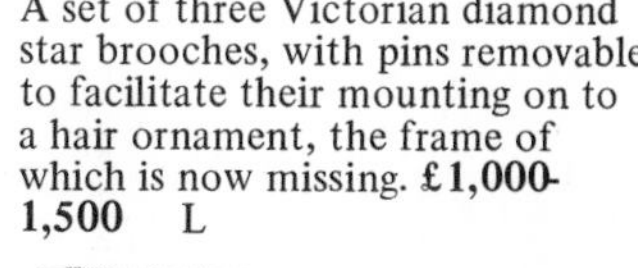

A Late Victorian diamond necklace, the chain a replacement and removable for use as a tiara, the frame defective, in a case from The Goldsmiths & Silversmiths Company Ltd. **£450-550** L

An Antique Sheraton Mahogany Church Warden's Clay Pipe Stand with 2 drawers, c. 1790, 24 in. high. **£400-500** SA

A Victorian pearl bangle of triple band hinged design, in leather case. **£200-300** L

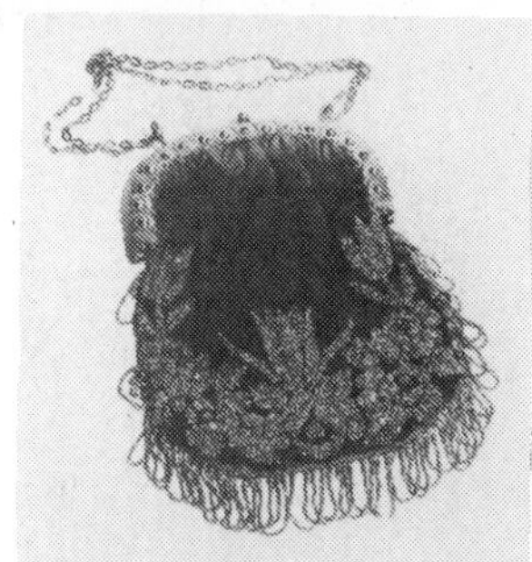

Beaded Velvet Evening Bag, with steel clasp, Edwardian. **£50-60** VA

A French Bead Bag, c. 1910. **£29-33** AP

Mid 19th C Handbag, in steel and silk. **£48-55** IN

A Carved bone Netsuke, unsigned. 1½ in., 40 cm. **£65-75** L

A Chromium-Plated and Enamelled Brooklands Aero Club Badge 3¾ in., 9.5 cm. high. **£200-220** CSK

An early black-painted Velocipede bone shaker 1868, 52" (132cms) high. **£400-600** CSK

A Chromium-Plated and enamelled Brooklands Automobile Racing Club Badge 4¾ in., 9.5 cm. high. **£100-120** CSK

Victorian Child's Pull-Along Cart, in elm, with iron wheels. **£50–55** AL

An orange yellow soapstone seated Sage, Chi'en Lung, 1736-1795, 8" high. **£1,600-1,800** Lan

A Chromium-Plated and Enamelled Road Racing Club Badge, inscribed 26 3 in., 7.5 cm. high. **£70-80** CSK

An Edwardian 'Flying Dutchman'. **£150-200** SAL

A white marble head of a Bodhisattva 15¾ in., 40 cm. high. **£275-325** C

A good pedal harp, with brass plate inscribed "I & I Erart Patent Harp, Manufacturers, 23 Berners Street, London no. 2185' and royal coat of arms, 67" high, with original box. **£575-625** PWC

A Red Painted Penny Farthing Ordinary Bicycle, with drop handle bars and sprung loaded saddle, some weld repair to steering, 58 in., 148 cm. high. **£700-780** CSK

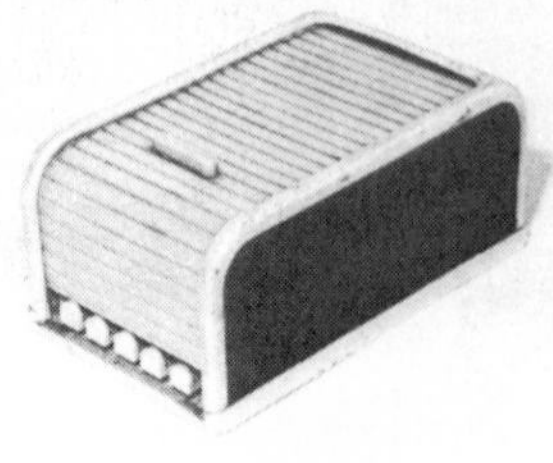

An Art Deco Plastic Cigarette Case, 1930's. **£18-20** AP

A 1937 Jaguar SS 2.5 litre Saloon Motor Car, black bodywork, recorded mileage 34,759. **£3,500-4,000** PWC

A Chinese dragon robe with a gauze-like weave. **£75-85** PWC

A Circular Patch Box, the lid of blue and aventurine glass, lined with a steel mirror, silver copper baluster sides, 3.4 cm., diam. c. 1760. **£90-110** S

A Roman White Marble Bust of The Virgin, 22½" (57cms) high. **£225-300** SKC

Early Georgian Coconut Cup with silver mounts, possibly German or Dutch, 4". **£200-300**

A George III Silver-Mounted coconut cup and Cover, 6½" (16.5cms) high, by John Langlands and John Robertson, probably Newcastle, 1798. **£200-230** SBe

A Chinese mandarin's robe with pale indigo ground, 19th C. **£75-85** PWC

A Straw-work Card Case, c. 1820, 3½ in. long. **£48-54** HD

Victorian Photograph Album Musical Box, 11" x 7". **£45-95** STR

A Prisioner of War type bone 'Spinning Jenny', handle activating spinning wheel, 12.5cms high. **£170-200** SKC

Four Chinese silk panels (badges) embroidered in coloured and gilt metal threads, now sewn together, 44" x 12" overall. **£300-350** PWC

A Fine 19th C. Sampler, dated 1848. **£125-150** CSG

A Victorian Wedding Album on Stand, 9 in. wide. **£50-60** BA

A Good Greek Icon, the top portion depicting The Deesis, with a further six images beneath, inc. the three hierarchs of the Orthodox Church, 31½ in. x 21 in., 80 cm. x 53 cm., dated 1838. **£340-380** L

A Box Scene Commemorating the Marriage of the Prince of Wales, with flag inscribed June 1863, 25 in. wide. **£220-260** CSK

A 19th C. Green Tea Tin 13 in. high. **£65-75**

A Stuffed Woodpecker in Box, very good condition, 15 in. high, c. 1880. **£40-50** SHA

An Art Deco 1930's Compact, Lipstick and Cigarette Holder. **£8-10** AP

A stuffed Canary in wood and glass box. **£15-18** A.L.

A stuffed baby alligator, 22" long. **£35-40** SQE

Irish Peat Bellows, c1800. **£180-200** SAL

An 18th C. Terapin Shell Punch Ladle, with lignum vitae turned handle. **£210-240** SA

A 19th C Royal Insurance Company Fire Bucket. **£95-105** SAL

A rare gents Etui Case by J. Rodgers of London, c. 1850. **£255-275**

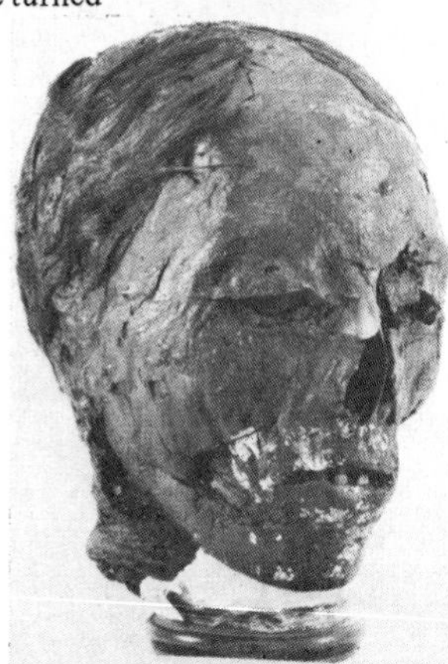

Egyptian Mummified Head in an excellent state of preservation, with hair still intact and extensive traces of gilding around the mouth and base of the neck, probably late period ca.5th/3rd century BC. 8½ in., 21 cm. high. **£210-240** L

An 'Auto Rotary Expressa' toothpaste tube squeezer, in original box, c1920. **£8-10** SQE

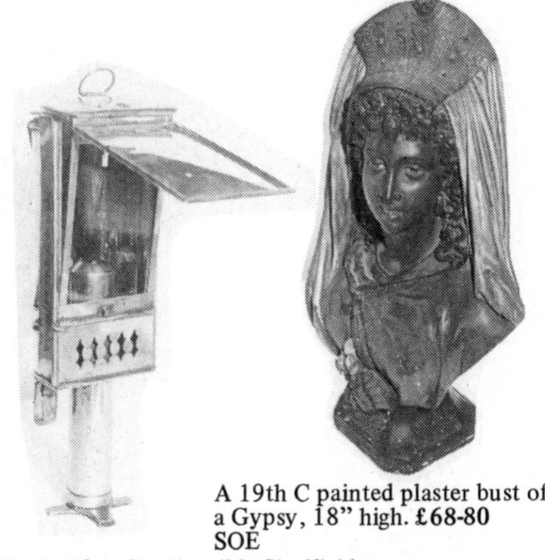

Early 19th C collapsible Sheffield Plate Coaching Lamp, with spring-loading candleholder and vesta. **£80-90** STR

A 19th C painted plaster bust of a Gypsy, 18" high. **£68-80** SOE

A set of 16 West Riding Bell-Metal Weights ranging in size from 56 lb. to 1 dr., inscribed West Riding County Council, Sowerby District, 1908, in fitted oak case, **£1,200-1,400** C

A 19th C. Shell-Work Sailor's Valentine. **£105-125** RB

A 19th C Australian Egg Group with two emu and two ostrich eggs carved with animals, 21" **£265-300** WHL

A Drew Motorist's Travelling kettle and spirit stove, 11 in., 28 cm., high in box. **£45-55** CSK

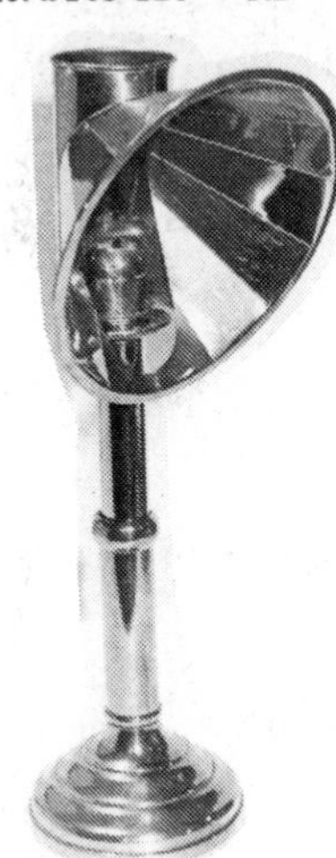

A 19th C telescopic 'nurses/ students' Candle Lamp, 15" high. **£75-87** SQE

Victorian Wig Powderer. **£16-20** IN

A stuffed and mounted ram's head Snuff Mull, 12" high. **£180-220** AG

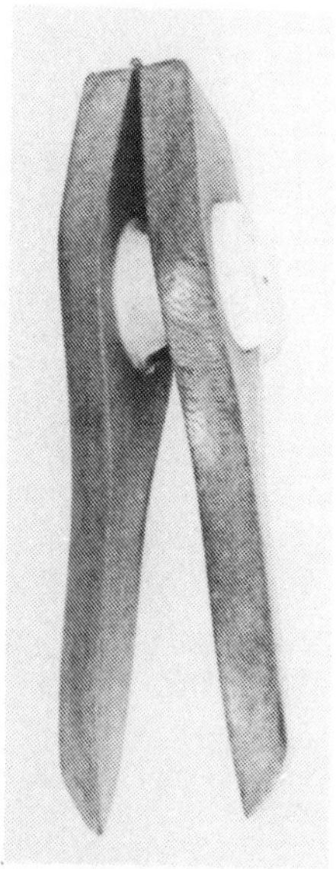

A wood and china Lemon Squeezer. **£17-19** A.L.

An 18th C Welsh spoon rack. **£130-140** A.L.

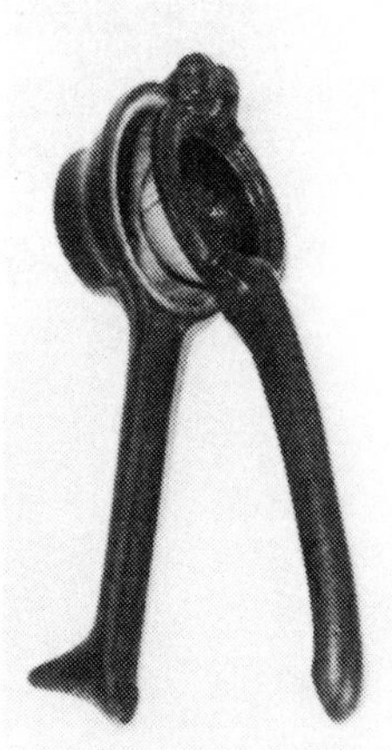

Iron Lemon Squeezer. **£16-18** A.L.

A 19th C Tin Strainer, 4" diam. **£3-5** A.L.

A marble and wood pestle and mortar, 4½" diam. **£15-17** A.L.

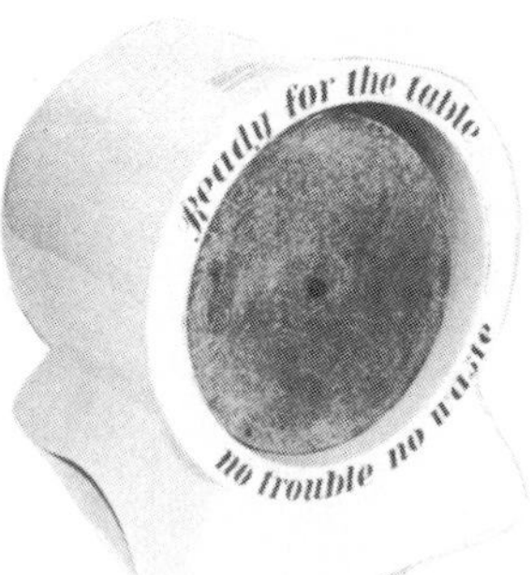

Ready for the table
no trouble no waste

A white china Ham slicer. **£23-25** A.L.

A 19th C chopper. **£6-8** A.L.

Adjustable Scales. **£13-15** A.L.

A Rum barrel from Rye Sussex. **£36-38** A.L.

A Curved chopper, 19th C. **£12-14** A.L.

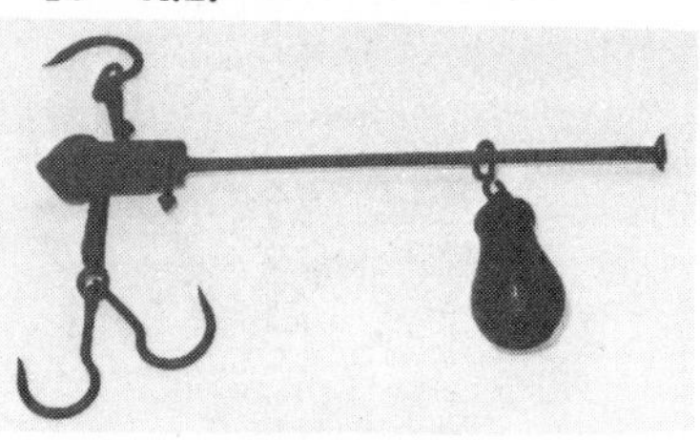

Small Steel Yard, 16" long. **£24-26** A.L.

A 19th C Tongue Dish. **£11-13** A.L.

A ½pt. Milk measure with brass handle. **£8-10** A.L.

Early slipware dish repaired. **£20-30** A.L.

A 'Q' Manufacturing Co. Waffle Iron in original cardboard box. **£7-9** A.L.

An Earthenware butter cooler with glass liner. **£3-5** A.L.

A white china rabbit mould, 6" diam. **£15-17** A.L.

An earthenware milk cover. **£3-5** A.L.

A white and green china Quick Cooker. **£24-28** A.L.

A white china Ham Stand, c1820. **£18-20** A.L.

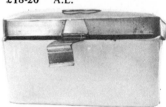

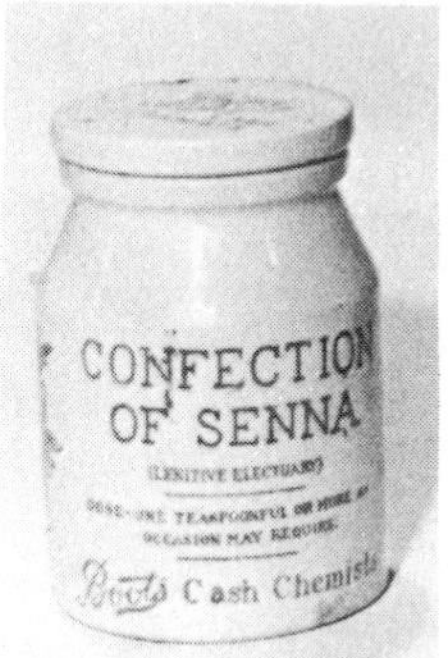

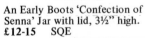

A Brown and Polson Blanc-mange bowl. **£15-17** A.L.

An Enamel Sandwich Tin. **£5-7** A.L.

An Early Boots 'Confection of Senna' Jar with lid, 3½" high. **£12-15** SQE

A Shelley swan mould in white china, 8" long. **£20-23** A.L.

(l) A Noritake Biscuit Barrel, 7" high. **£27-32** SQE

(r) A Victorian hand-painted, moulded floral Biscuit Barrel, 6½" high. **£16-20** SQE

Early Spode butter dish. **£35-40** A.L.

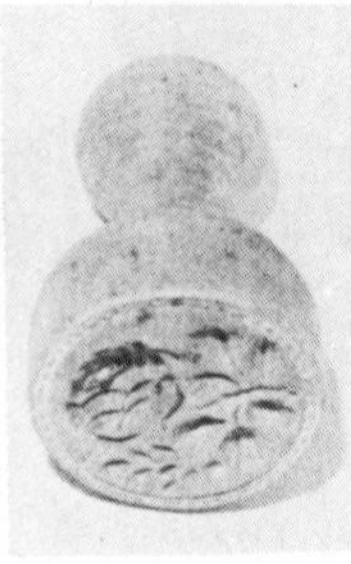

A Butter stamp with strawberry mark, 1¾" diam. **£15-17** A.L.

A Terracotta earthenware crock highly glazed, 11" wide. **£15-17** A.L.

A Wedgwood dry body Game Dish, 7½" long. **£75-85** A.L.

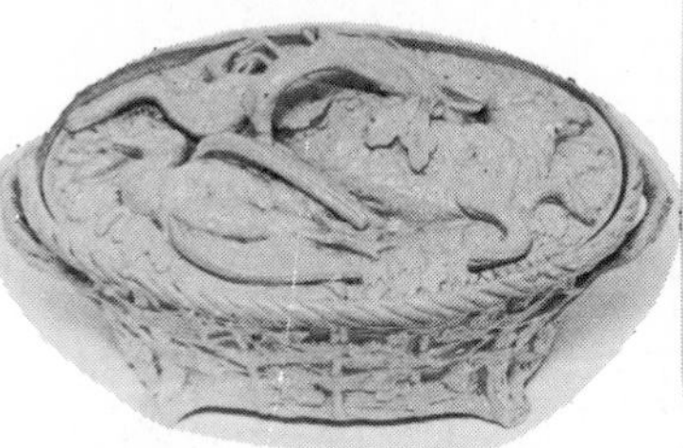

A glazed Minton Game Dish, 12" long. **£75-85** A.L.

A Wooden Welsh Butter worker. **£8-10** A.L.

Bryant & May Spice tin with graters; the tin embossed with flowers, 5" x 5". **£15-17** A.L.

A Wooden Meat Dish with gravy channel. **£15-17** A.L.

An unusual Brawn Press in white china, 19th C. **£24-28** A.L.

A butter stamp with rose mark, 1½" diam. **£15-17** A.L.

A glazed basket weave Game Dish, 8½" long. **£75-85** A.L.

An earthenware saucepan. **£6-8** A.L.

A wooden butter wheel, 7" long. **£15-17** A.L.

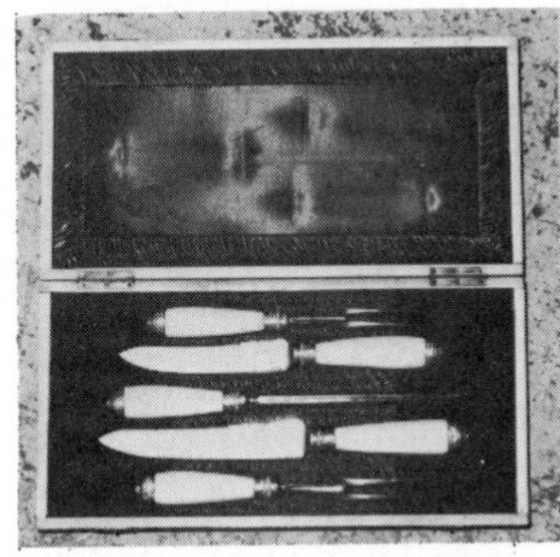

A Boxed Carving Set with Bone and Silver Plate Mounts, stainless steel blades, Edwardian. **£90-100** VA

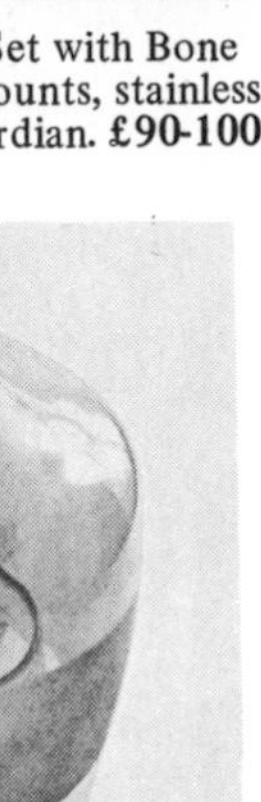

A Victorian Glass Wasp Catcher. **£15-18** A.L.

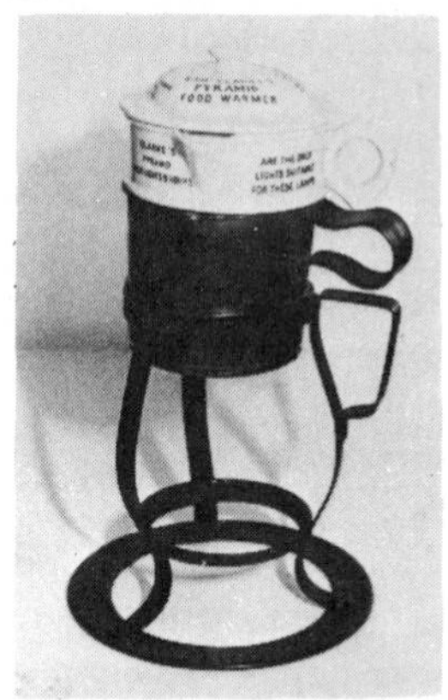

A Samuel Clarke Pyramid Food Warmer. **£30-35** A.L.

A 19th C Hob Kettle (repaired), 12" high, 9" diam. **£15-18** SQE

Dr. Nelsons Improved Inhaler with glass mouthpiece. **£6-8** A.L.

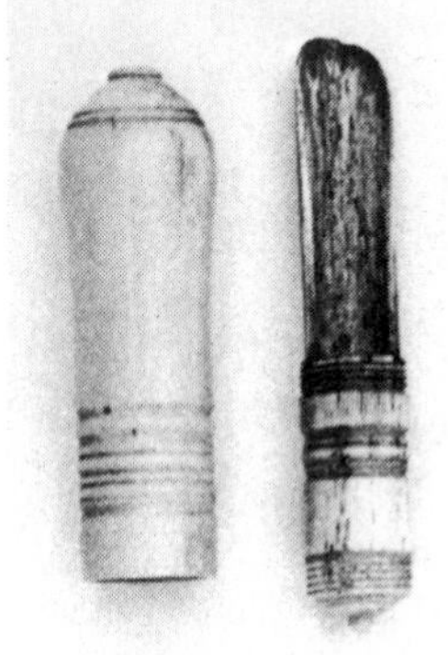

18th C bone cheese scoop. **£20-30** IN

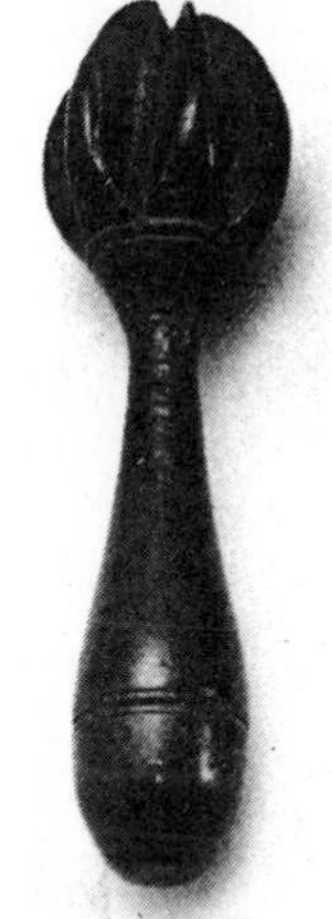

Wooden Lemon Squeezer, 19th C, 6" long. **£30-35** A.L.

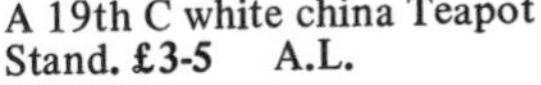

A 19th C white china Teapot Stand. **£3-5** A.L.

A brown glass Lime Squeezer. **£6-8** A.L.

A Set of three game pie moulds. **£15-20** IN

A 19th C hair sieve. **£4-6** A.L.

A Tin of pastry cutters, 19th C, 3" diam. **£7.50-9.50** A.L.

A Doulton Improved Stoneware Footwarmer. **£13-15** A.L.

A Mahogany Cheese Paster, 18th C., 10½ in. diam. **£145-165** SA

Early blue and white china Egg Stand. **£15-17** A.L.

A Victorian sardine tin opener, 5" long. **£8-10** A.L.

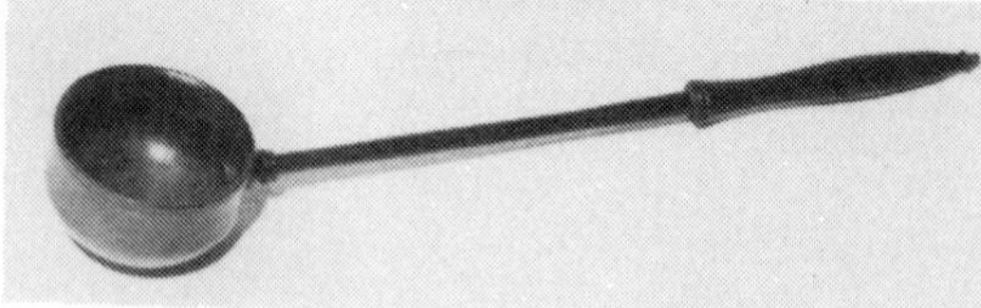

An Early 19th C. Wooden Ladle **£30-35** RB

A 19th C Mouse trap, 4½" long. **£4-5** A.L.

Set of Kitchen Cutters, c1900. **£9-15** IN

An Egg Rack. **£4-6** A.L.

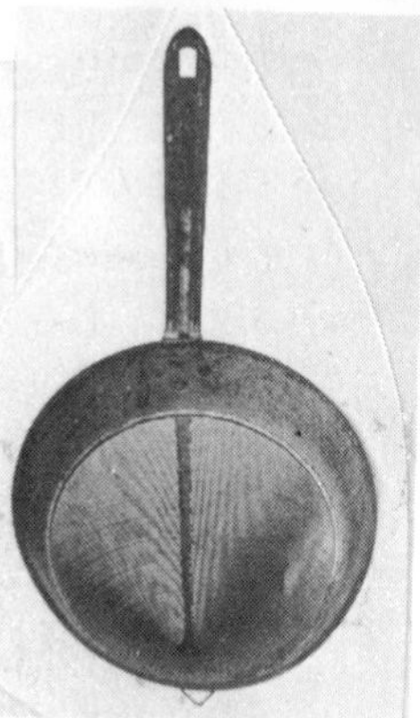

A 19th C Tin funnel sieve. **£3-6** A.L.

An Egg Rack. **£7.75-8.75** A.L.

A set of rare wooden butter scales, 18" high, 19" wide. **£120-130** A.L.

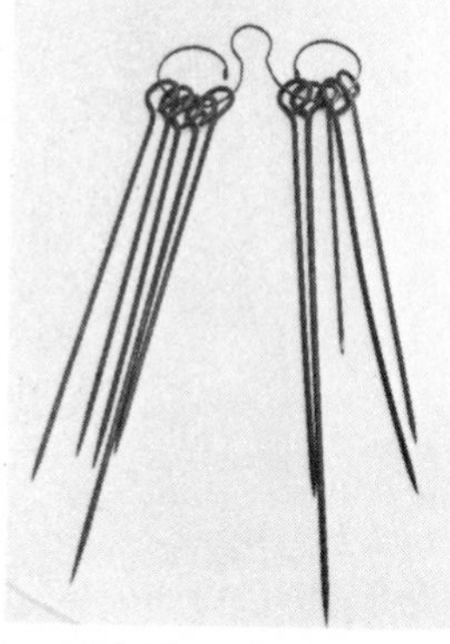

A Set of 10 Victorian skewers, 12" long. **£10-12** A.L.

A C.C. Clark and Co. of Wolverhampton cast iron Coffee Grinder. **£40-45** A.L.

A wood garlic press. **£8-10** A.L.

A wood and rubber Pioneer Window Dryer and Polisher. **£3-5** A.L.

A Victorian Toffee Hammer, 7½" long. **£3-5** A.L.

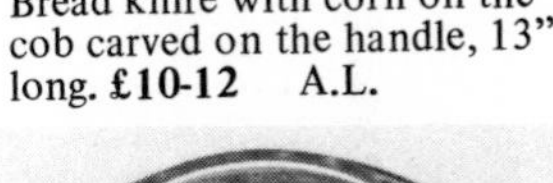

Bread knife with corn on the cob carved on the handle, 13" long. **£10-12** A.L.

A Butter dish with glass liner. **£6-8** A.L.

A pair of Georgian sugar nips, 10" long. **£15-17** A.L.

A Butter dish inscribed 'Manners Mayketh Man'. **£7-10** A.L.

An Egg Rack with double sliding tray. **£7-9** A.L.

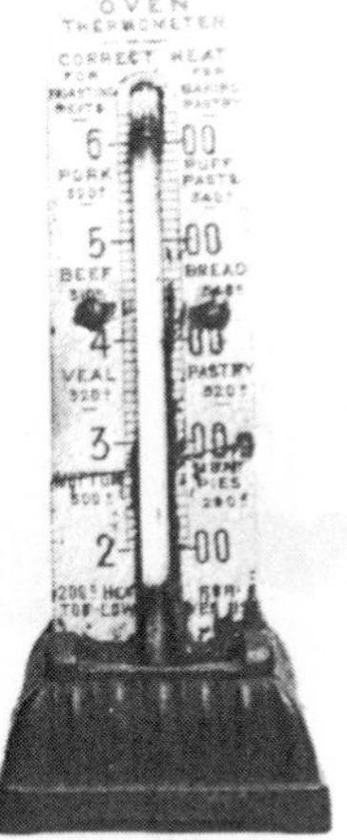

An Oven thermometer, 7" high. **£15-17** A.L.

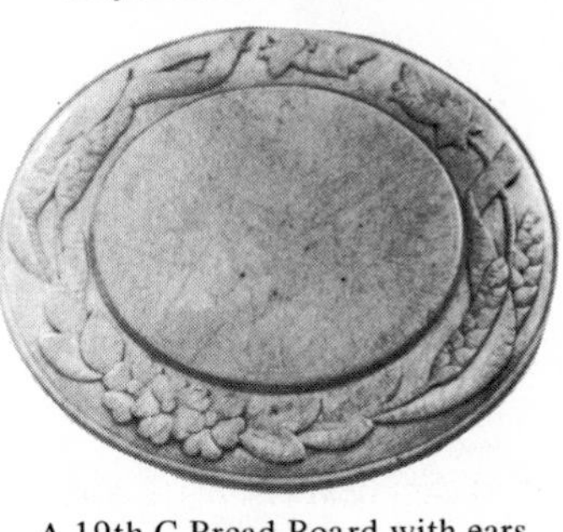

A 19th C Bread Board with ears of wheat carving. **£7-10** A.L.

A wooden cucumber slice, 19th C, 12" long. **£4-5** A.L.

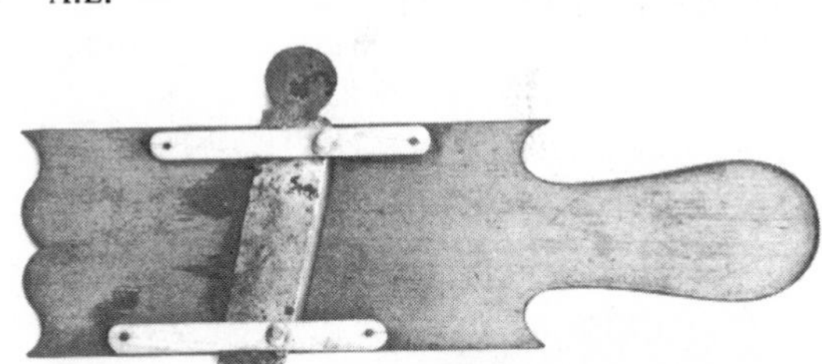

A cucumber slice. **£25-30** IN

A Wooden butter stamp. **£23-25** A.L.

Three miniature jelly moulds, 2" high. **£10-12** each A.L.

19th C wood pastry marker. **£4-8** IN

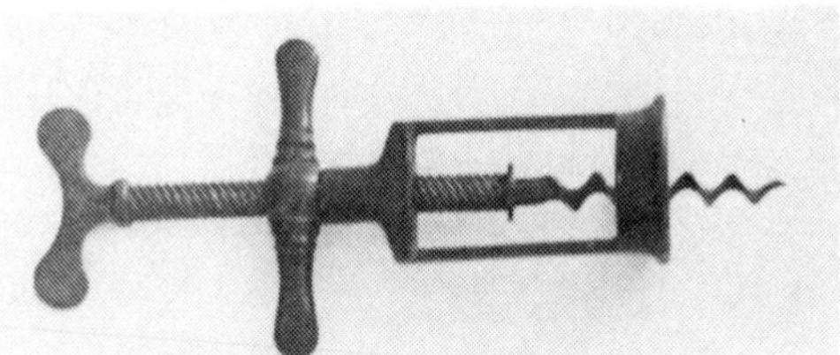

An Iron Corkscrew. **£9-10** A.L.

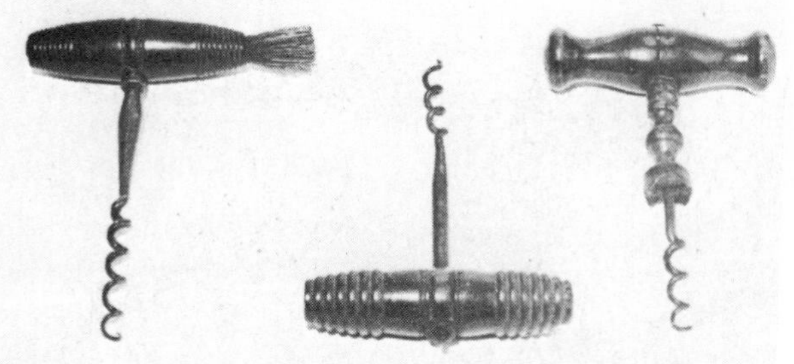

A Selection of 19th C. Corkscrews. **£17-24** SV

A Beldray Rapid Vacuum Ice Cream Freezer in tin. **£13-15** A.L.

The Gourmet Steriliser. **£14-16** A.L.

A Victorian enamel Bread Bin. **£6-8** A.L.

A pewter chocolate mould, 3" diam. **£7-9** A.L.

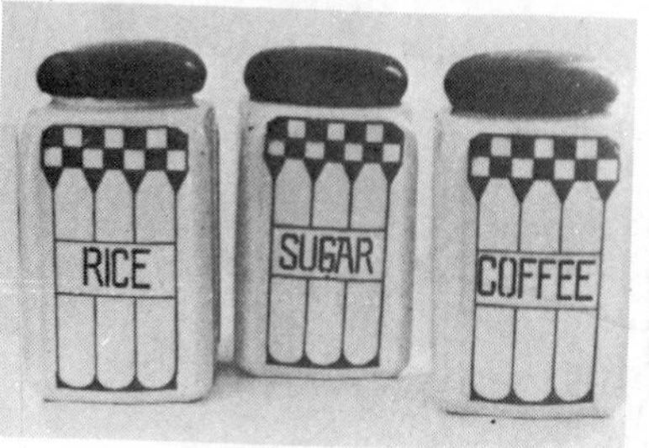

A set of 1920 Storage Jars with wooden lids. **£5.25-6.25** each A.L.

A Tin Peace Mug, c1919. **£16-18** A.L.

A pewter mould, 9" diam, 6" high. **£40-43** A.L.

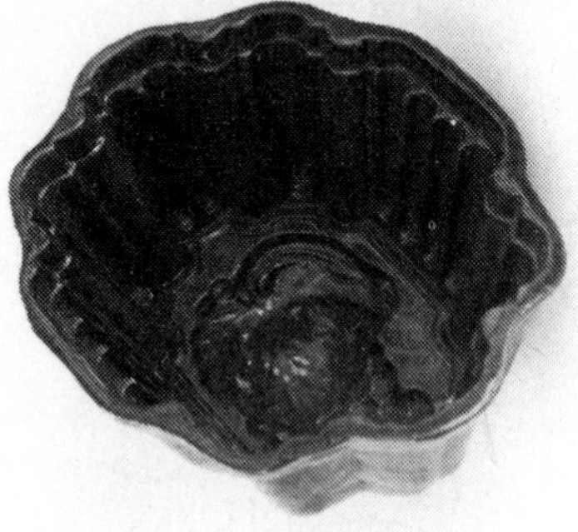

A highly glazed brown earthenware Jelly Mould. **£20-25** A.L.

An Early 19th C. Smoothing Iron. **£33-36** RB

A Bread knife, 13" long. **£8-10** A.L.

A 19th C Iron with slug. **£23-25** A.L.

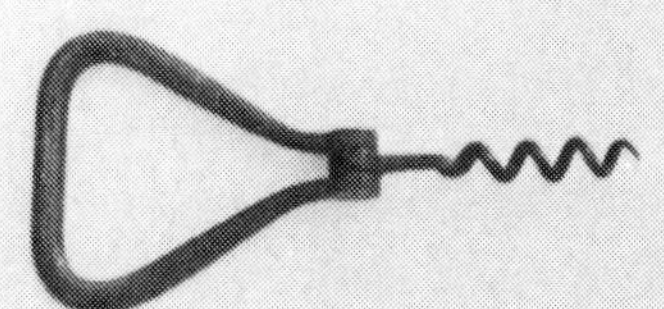
A Corkscrew. **£4-6** A.L.

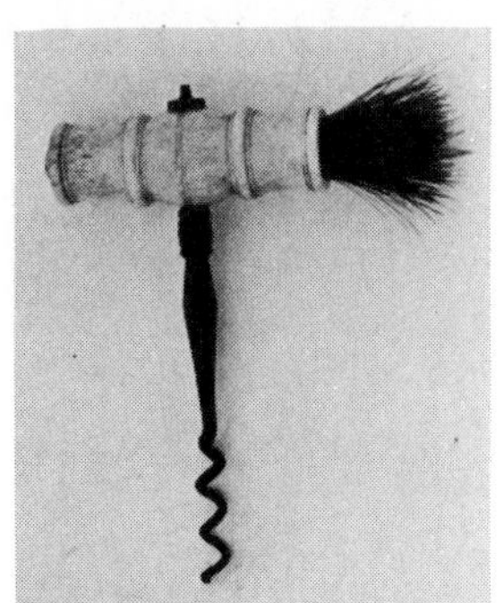
A Bone and iron corkscrew. **£25-28** A.L.

An Iron bound wooden tig, 19th C. **£30-35** A.L.

A Victorian Peek Frean biscuit tin. **£4-6** A.L.

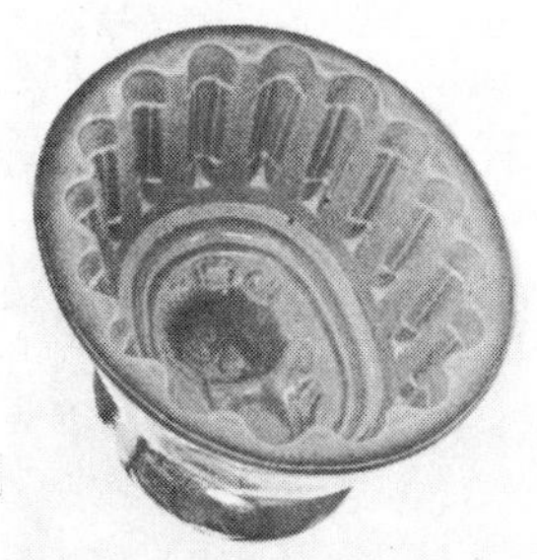
A 19th C Earthenware Jelly Mould with lion shaped base. **£12-14** A.L.

An Iron Knife Cleaner, 15 in. high, c. 1850. **£32-40** SHA

A Besway knife cleaner, 19th C, 9½" high. **£15-17** A.L.

A set of small Victorian wooden measures, ½pt., 1pt., 1 quart. **£25-30** A.L.

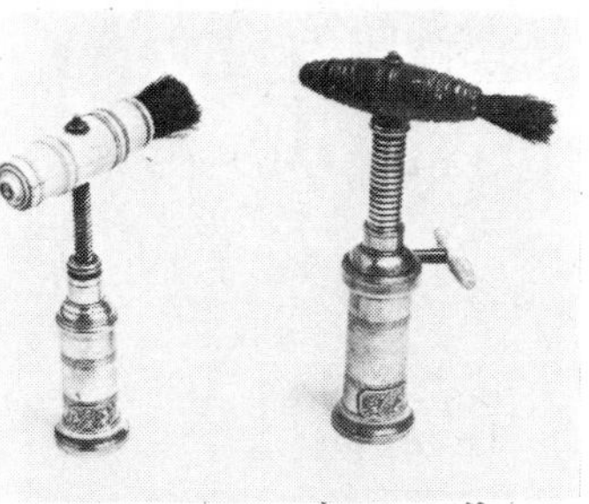
(l) A Brass Barrel Corkscrew with ivory handle and coat-of-arms, c1840. **£95-105** GE

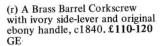

(r) A Brass Barrel Corkscrew with ivory side-lever and original ebony handle, c1840. **£110-120** GE

Iron Goffering Iron, 7" high. **£15-18** A.L.

A Tea Tin with Chinese design. **£2-4** A.L.

An earthenware flour bin, 19th C, 14" high. **£7-9** A.L.

A Victorian MacFarlane and Lang Biscuit tin. **£4-6** A.L.

A George III Mahogany Plate Bucket, 15 in., 38 cm. diam. x 16 in., 41 cm. high. **£450-520** L

A 1930 round tin for currants. **£5-7** A.L.

A 1930 green and gold Rice tin. **£4-6** A.L.

Victorian pine Flour Bin with lid and wooden hoop handle. **£25–30** MM

A 19th C pine Butter Churn, with Butter Pats. **£25–30** MM

A 19th C. bucket-shaped pine Ice Cream Maker, iron bound with carrying handle. **£40–50** AL

A Victorian pine Corn Measure 12 in. high. **£45–50** AL

A collection of 19th C. wooden Butter Stamps on white porcelain butter dish. **£30–40** GW

Late 19th C. pine Meat Safe with close wire mesh panels in sides and and single door. One internal shelf. 22 in. wide, 16 in. high, 16 in. deep. **£28-35** AL

An Edwardian pitch pine Flour Bin on bun feet. **£45–55** MS

Set of spice drawers 7 in. wide, 6 in. high, 4 in. deep. **£27-37** AL

Steel and brass extending toasting fork, 13" long. **£5-7** A.L.

A Good Georgian Candlebox, c. 1790. **£85-95** CP

A deep, 19th C., pine Knife Box of rude construction. **£4–5** MM

Late 19th C. pine Meat Safe. Close wire mesh panels in sides and doors and one internal shelf. 35 in. high, 37 in. wide, 25 in. deep.
£45-50 AL

A Victorian wall hanging Candle-box with match drawer above.
£15–20 MS

A 19th C. elm Nail Box with six compartments. 8 in. long, 14 in. wide. **£4–6** AL

A 19th C. wallhanging pine Candle-box with pierced trefoil decoration
£10–12 MS

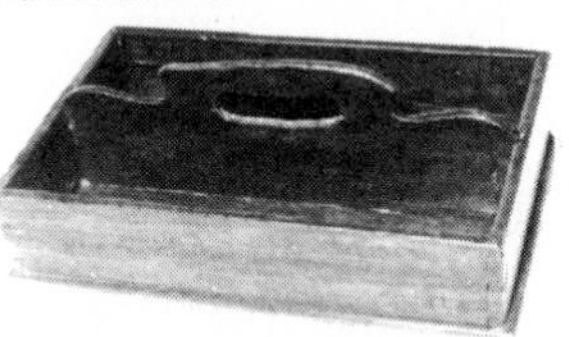

An early 19th C. dovetailed pine Knife Box with shaped carrying handle. **£14–16** MM

A horn handled carving fork. **£4-6** A.L.

A 19th C. painted pine Salt Box with double back plate. 12 in. wide. **£55–65** GW

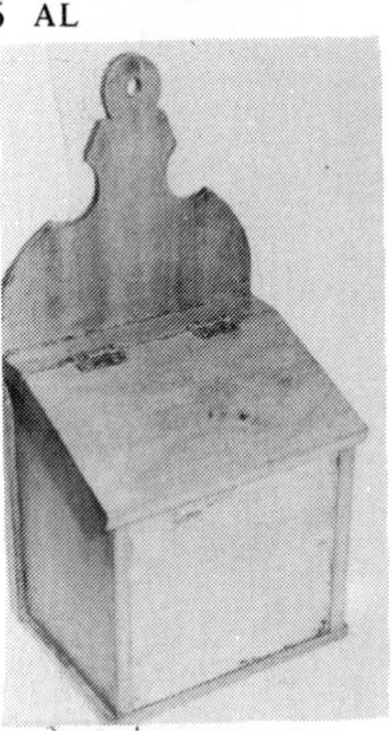

An antler handled carving knife, 13½" long. **£4-6** A.L.

19th C. pine Wall Hanging Salt Box with hinged lid and shaped back plate. **£18–25** MM

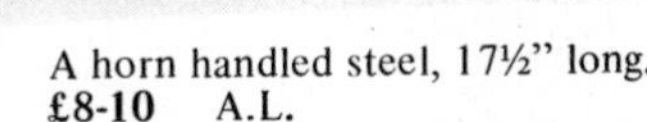

A horn handled steel, 17½" long.
£8-10 A.L.

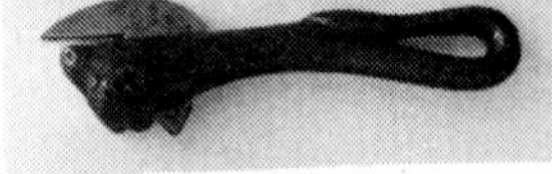

An iron Bulls Head Can Opener.
£4-6 A.L.

A horn handled carving knife, 16" long. **£4-6** A.L.

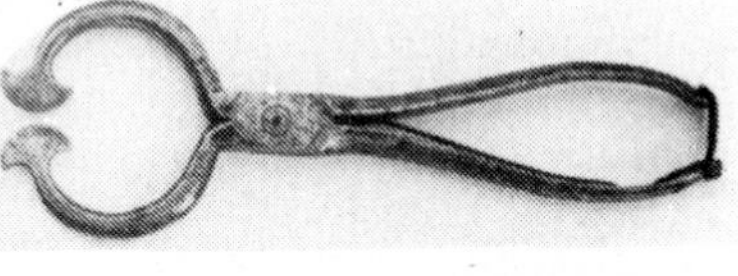

Fire tongs, 10" long. **£5-7** A.L.

A pair of 19th C Sugar Tongs.
£15-18 A.L.

An Ice Cream scoop. **£5-7** A.L.

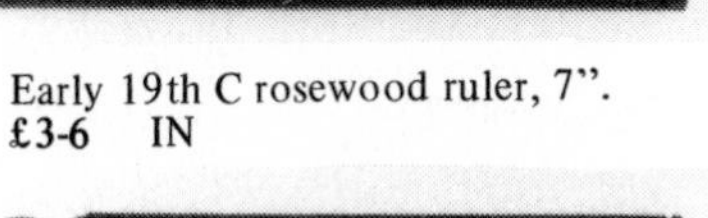

Early 19th C rosewood ruler, 7".
£3-6 IN

Rosewood ruler, seal and pencil, pre-1840. **£10-15** IN

An Earthenware Colander. **£11-13** A.L.

A 19th C iron Candle snuffer.
£5.50-7.50 A.L.

INDEX

INFORMATION BOXES